NINETEENTH-CENTURY DESIGN

NINETEENTH-CENTURY DESIGN

Edited by
Clive Edwards

Volume III

Production and Practices of Design

LONDON AND NEW YORK

First published 2021
by Routledge
2 Park Square, Milton Park, Abingdon, Oxon OX14 4RN

and by Routledge
52 Vanderbilt Avenue, New York, NY 10017

Routledge is an imprint of the Taylor & Francis Group, an informa business

© 2021 selection and editorial matter, Clive Edwards; individual owners retain copyright in their own material.

The right of Clive Edwards to be identified as the author of the editorial material, and of the authors for their individual chapters, has been asserted in accordance with sections 77 and 78 of the Copyright, Designs and Patents Act 1988.

All rights reserved. No part of this book may be reprinted or reproduced or utilised in any form or by any electronic, mechanical, or other means, now known or hereafter invented, including photocopying and recording, or in any information storage or retrieval system, without permission in writing from the publishers.

Trademark notice: Product or corporate names may be trademarks or registered trademarks, and are used only for identification and explanation without intent to infringe.

British Library Cataloguing-in-Publication Data
A catalogue record for this book is available from the British Library

Library of Congress Cataloging-in-Publication Data
A catalog record has been requested for this book

ISBN: 978-0-367-21142-4 (set)
eISBN: 978-0-429-26566-2 (set)
ISBN: 978-0-367-23356-3 (volume III)
eISBN: 978-0-429-27948-5 (volume III)

Typeset in Times New Roman
by Apex CoVantage, LLC

Publisher's Note
References within each chapter are as they appear in the original complete work

CONTENTS

VOLUME III – PRODUCTION AND PRACTICES OF DESIGN

Acknowledgements   xi

General Introduction   1

Volume III Introduction   18

PART 1
Art Industries and Manufactures   29

1. 'Further Remarks on the Report of the Committee on the Arts and Principles of Design', *Mechanics' Magazine*, 704, 4 February 1837, pp. 323–329   31

2. W. S. W., 'Art Applied to Manufactures', *The Art-Union*, 4, 37, February 1842, pp. 23–25   41

3. George Wallis, 'Recent Progress in Design as Applied to Manufactures', *Journal of the Society of Arts*, 173, 4, 14 March 1856, pp. 291–301   53

4. Denis O'Donovan, 'The Uses of Art & Design in Manufacture', In Frederick McCoy, *Lectures Delivered by Professor McCoy . . . [et al.] in the Lecture Room of the Museum, During the Second Session of 1871* (Melbourne: Samuel Mullen, 1872), Extract, pp. 79–83   73

5. Jacob Falke, 'The Vienna Exhibition in Connexion with Art-Industry. IX, Furniture', *The Workshop*, 7, 4, 1874, pp. 49–51   77

CONTENTS

6 Tom Taylor, 'The Study and Practice of Art', *The British Architect: A Journal of Architecture and the Accessory Arts*, 1, February 1874, pp. 133–135   84

PART 2
Decorative and Applied Arts   93

7 John Stewart, 'Art Decoration, an Employment Suitable for Women', *Art Journal*, 6, 1860, pp. 70–71   95

8 Prof. [J. H.] Chamberlain, 'The Progress of Design', *Birmingham Daily Post*, 28 May 1863   103

9 Christopher Dresser, 'Hindrances to the Progress of Applied Art', *Journal of the Society of Arts*, 20, 12 April 1872, pp. 435–440   110

10 Emma Lazarus, 'A Day in Surrey with William Morris', *Century Magazine*, 32, July 1886, pp. 388–394   126

11 Anon, 'A Studio of Design: An Interview with Mr. Arthur Silver', *Studio*, 3, 1894, pp.117–122   136

PART 3
Drawing   141

12 Jacques-Eugène Armengaud, *The Practical Draughtsman's Book of Industrial Design: Forming a Complete Course of Mechanical, Engineering, and Architectural Drawing Translated from the French of Armengaud Ainé and Armengaud, Jeune and Amouroux; Rewritten and Arranged with Additional Matter and Plate Selections from and Examples of the Most Useful and Generally Employed Mechanism of the Day by William Johnson* (London: Longman, Brown, Green, and Longmans, 1853), Preface, pp. III–V   143

13 William Dyce, *The Introduction to the Drawing-Book of the School of Design, Published in the Years 1842–3, Under the Direction of W. Dyce*, (London: Chapman & Hall, 1854), pp. V–XXIV   149

CONTENTS

14 Lewis Foreman Day, 'Of Designs and Working Drawings', *Arts and Crafts Exhibition Society, Catalogue of Second Exhibition*, 1889, pp. 93–109   157

PART 4
Design Principles   **163**

15 George Wallis, 'The Principles of Fine Art as Applied to Industrial Purposes', *The People's Journal*, 3, 1847, pp. 230–233   165

16 [Anon], 'Universal Infidelity in Principles of Design', *Journal of Design and Manufactures*, V, August 1851, pp. 158–161   173

17 'Examples of False Principles in Decoration', *A Catalogue of the Articles of Ornamental Art, in the Museum of the Department, for the Use of Students and Manufacturers, and the Consultation of the Public. With Appendices, Third Edition* (London: Printed by George E. Eyre and William Spottiswoode for Her Majesty's Stationary Office, 1852), Appendix C, pp. 22–32   181

18 [Anon], 'The Principles of Design Essential to the Construction of Artistic Furniture', *Furniture Gazette*, 3 May 1873, p. 51, 17 May 1873, pp. 84–6, 31 May 1873, pp. 115–6, 7 June 1873, pp. 132–3   198

19 Lucas Baker, *Theory of Design: A Treatise on the Theory and Practice of Design and the Methods of Instruction Suited to Teachers, Designers, and Art-Students, and a Text-Book for Schools* (New York: Ivison, Blakeman, Taylor, and Co, 1883), pp. 5–13   211

20 Walter Crane, 'Design in Relation to Use and Material', *The Claims of Decorative Art* (London: Lawrence and Bullen, 1892), pp. 90–105   218

21 Selwyn Image, 'Of Design and the Study of Nature' in A. H. Mackmurdo (Ed.), *Plain Handicrafts: Being Essays by Artists Setting Forth the Principles of Design and Established Methods of Workmanship; A Guide to Elementary Practice* (London: Percival & Co., 1893), pp. 1–6   230

PART 5
Elements of Design   235

5.1
Colour   237

22 John Gardner Wilkinson, *On Colour and on the Necessity for a General Diffusion of Taste Among All Classes, with Remarks on Laying Out Dressed Geometrical Gardens. Examples of Good and Bad Taste Illustrated by Woodcuts and Coloured Plates in Contrast* (London: J. Murray, 1858), pp. 1–4   239

23 Lucy Crane, 'Colour', *Art and the Formation of Taste* (London: Macmillan 1882), pp. 97–101   243

24 John D. Crace, 'The Decorative Use of Colour', *The Journal of the Society of Arts*, 36:1851, 1888, pp. 696–704   246

25 Roberts Beaumont, *Colour in Woven Design*, (London: Whittaker and Co., 1890), pp. 1–5   255

5.2
Form   259

26 Horatio Greenough, 'American Architecture', *The United States Magazine and Democratic Review*, New York, 13, August 1843, pp. 206–210   261

27 David R. Hay, *The Natural Principles and Analogy of the Harmony of Form*, 3rd Edition (London: W. Blackwood and Sons, 1842), pp. 1–6   270

28 Lucy Crane, *Art and the Formation of Taste* (London: Macmillan, 1882), pp. 61–68   274

29 Henri Mayeux, *A Manual of Decorative Composition for Designers, Decorators, Architects and Industrial Artists* (London: J.S. Virtue and Co, 1889), pp. 1–4   279

30 Hugh Stannus, 'Some Principles of Form-Design in Applied Art', *Journal of the Society of Arts,* 46, 14 October 1898, pp. 885–889   283

5.3
Materials 293

31 Emil Braun, 'Electrotyping Applied to Art Manufactures', *Art Journal*, 12, 1 July 1850, pp. 205–207   295

32 George Dodd, 'Papier Mâché', *Curiosities of Industry* (London: George Routledge and Co, 1858), pp. 17–22   306

33 [Anon], 'Design in Relation to Material', *Morning Post*, 2 January 1869, p. 3   314

5.4
Manufacturing Methods 323

34 Adam Smith and Dugald Stewart, *The Works of Adam Smith* (London: Printed for T. Cadell, 1811–12), pp. 15–19   325

35 William Cooke-Taylor, 'The Mutual Interests of Artists and Manufacturers', *Art-Union*, 10, 1 March 1848, pp. 69–70   329

36 James Ward, *The World in Its Workshops: A Practical Examination of British and Foreign Processes of Manufacture, with a Critical Comparison of the Fabrics, Machinery, and Works of Art Contained in the Great Exhibition* (London: Williams S. Orr and Co., 1851), pp. 1–16   339

37 Joseph Whitworth, and George Wallis, *The Industry of the United States in Machinery, Manufactures, and Useful and Ornamental Arts: Compiled from the Official Reports of Messrs. Whitworth and Wallis* (London: G. Routledge & Co., 1854), pp. III–XI   354

38 William Morris, 'The Revival of Handicraft', *Architecture, Industry & Wealth; Collected Papers* (London: Longmans Green, 1902), pp. 214–227   361

39 Frederick W. Taylor, *The Principles of Scientific Management* (New York: Harper & Bros., 1911), pp. 9–15   370

5.5
Craft Machine and Design   377

40 Charles R. Ashbee, 'Decorative Art from a Workshop Point of View', A Paper Read at the Edinburgh Art Congress, November 1889, pp. 1–11   379

41 John Dando Sedding, 'Design', *Arts and Crafts Essays* (London: Rivington Percival, 1893), pp. 405–413   389

42 Fred Miller, 'Design and Craftsmanship', *The Training of a Craftsman* (London: J.S. Virtue & Co Limited 1898), pp. 24–35   393

43 Thorstein Veblen, 'Pecuniary Canons of Taste', *The Theory of the Leisure Class: An Economic Study of Institutions* (New York: The Macmillan Company, 1899), pp. 157–165   400

44 Esther Wood, 'Home Arts and Industries Exhibition', *The Studio*, 17, 1899, pp. 99–109   407

45 Oscar Lovell Triggs, 'Rookwood: An Ideal Workshop', *Chapters in the History of the Arts and Crafts Movement* (Chicago: The Bohemia Guild of the Industrial Art League, 1902), pp. 157–162   413

46 J. Scarratt Rigby, 'Remarks on Morris' Work and Its Influence on British Decorative Arts Today', *The Art Workers' Quarterly: A Portfolio of Practical Designs for Decorative and Applied Art*, January and April 1902, pp. 2–5, 61–63   417

ACKNOWLEDGEMENTS

This project was initiated by Kimberley Smith at Routledge, and I am grateful to her for encouraging me to undertake the role of compiler and editor of this set of volumes.

A compilation work of this nature necessarily builds on the efforts of other scholars and researchers; therefore, my first acknowledgement of debt must go to the authors and compilers who have explored and are exploring the field of nineteenth-century design. In the compilation of the introductory sections, headnotes, and editorial notes, in particular, I have made great use of both general and specialised published and online resources. In particular, these resources have been of great assistance in matters relating to biographies, bibliographies, and historical details. I would therefore like to thank the compilers and contributors whose work has been immensely helpful in informing this project. In addition, the librarians and archivists at the British Library, the Royal Society of Arts, Heidelberg University Library, and the National Art Library (V&A) have offered valuable guidance and advice.

I should also like to thank Simon Alexander at Routledge, for his constant assistance and advice on editorial matters.

For her continuing support, advice, and help throughout this project, I should like to express my heartfelt gratitude and thanks to Lynne Edwards.

GENERAL INTRODUCTION

A four-volume edition of primary source materials that document the histories of design across the long nineteenth century (c.1789–1914) gathered together in a comprehensive and accessible format. The four-volume format has offered an opportunity to multiply the number of texts and their length, as opposed to short or edited excerpts, so much of this selection includes complete articles or book chapters. The texts are arranged thematically, then within the sub-themes, chronologically. The mix of well-known and lesser-known texts is intended to demonstrate a range of, sometimes competing, approaches to the themes.

It might be argued that the availability of online sources of published works has made anthologies redundant. However, the prodigious amount of information now available electronically actually increases the need for some form of direction and navigational assistance through an edited selection of texts. Therefore, anthologies remain essential as guides to a field that would otherwise be overwhelming. Anthologies also act as compact accounts of a larger story that stand as both a gateway and a guide. Inevitably, anthologies are about exclusions as inclusions, but the choices made in this selection are considered as one part of a set of helpful tools towards an understanding of the beliefs and practices, theories, actions, politics, and practices related to design in the nineteenth century.

The introductions to each volume prepare the reader for a greater understanding of the particular subject matter than would otherwise be possible if considering the sources without some context. The introductions then provide pointers on how to read the materials in relation to major issues, and offer an overview of the shifting patterns of many aspects of design. At a more drilled down level, the headnotes to each text offer details about the author, where known; details of the publication and its after-history if relevant; and any thematic and textual relationship to other works by the author, as well as to other contemporary works. The contemporary critical reception of the texts is also of interest because this offers further insights into the attitudes and debates of the time. In this regard, extensive reference and quotation from primary sources are made.

The volumes are intended to stand alone, but each one will inform the other in an overall picture of nineteenth-century design. Taken together, these annotated sources with their contextual introductions and headnotes present a valuable overview of a broadly defined field of design during the long nineteenth century.

This general introduction first considers the definitions of design as used in the period. It then considers some of the general themes and strands covered by the entire edition. It then briefly considers the publishing history of nineteenth-century design. Next, it moves to consider the major design issues of the century, which is followed by an overview of the individual volume content that delves into these matters. Finally, there is a brief note on the rationale and on the editorial processes used.

Definitions of Design[1]

During the nineteenth century, the term 'design' had several meanings, both as a verb and a noun. They are often related to each other and are usually dependent upon context for the precise sense of use. For example, Thomas Sopwith, a Newcastle cabinet-maker and architect explored the definitions in his work 'On the Principles of Design' (1836): 'Design in its most comprehensive sense, includes whatever is undertaken by man, as a reasoning creature; but, in its more restricted sense, it is applied to works of contrivance in mechanism, and in the fine and useful arts'.[2] This is fine as far as it goes, but there were more specific definitions used to understand the term during the period, which ranged from broad concepts to particular applications.

Jamieson's 1829 *Dictionary of Mechanical Science, Arts, Manufactures, and Miscellaneous Knowledge* explains the term in a little more detail:

> Design, in Painting, the first idea of a large work drawn roughly, and on a small scale, with the intention of being executed and finished in large. In Manufactures, design expresses the figures with which the workman enriches his stuff or silk, and which he copies after his own drawing or the sketches of some artist. In Building, the term ichnography may be used, when by design is only meant the plan of a building, or a flat figure drawn on paper; when some side or face of the building is raised from the ground, we may use the term orthography: and when both front and sides are seen in perspective, it may be scenography.[3]

The following subdivisions build on this definition.

Design as a Conceptual Process

For some, design referred to the first stage, a mental aim, scheme, or plan conceived in the mind, as a visualising process towards a goal. The American drawing teacher Charles Barry seems to sum up this idea: 'As it would be necessary in English composition to first have an idea to express, and then to clothe it in words; so, in design-composition, similar reflection and care are necessary'.[4]

This leads to the idea of invention as contriving and devising something. The American engineer and author C. L. Redfield linked design, invention, and skill: 'Design is the product of a knowledge of the laws and materials of nature joined to a sense of the fitness of things. Skill is an acquirement attained by practice upon one thing or class of things. Of these four elements relating to the progress of mechanics, invention, and design are most intimately associated with each other. Discovery is more closely connected with invention than with design; skill more closely with design than with invention'.[5]

Design as an Art or Skill

The 'art of design' was also a language or a set of practices, attitudes, and methods. Initially, it referred to preliminary drawings or sketches that played a major part in works such as painting, sculpture, or architecture. In an article discussing art and design education, *The Fine Arts Journal* (1847) developed the conceptual process by suggesting that design was an ability to translate the conceptual to the visual: 'The art of design is therefore not a distinct quality of art; but the result of a combined talent of acquiring power in the hand to put down correctly what the mind is capable of dictating clearly'.[6] The term was also widely used in relation to schools that systematically taught the 'art of design', as applied to decoration, and intended for manufacture, rather than fine art.

Design as Fine Art

In this usage, design often indicated a composition or a piece of finished artwork. Discussing the work of the artist Benjamin West, the *Library of Fine Arts* (1832) in an article titled 'The British School of Design' used the term specifically in relation to fine art.

> Looking to the design of his [West's] pictures, there are few which do not afford examples of the most perfect composition. His drawings and cartoons, preparatory to his finished pictures, are among the finest specimens of design, and are in many instances preferable to his larger and more finished works; but this must happen in all cases, where the mind pours itself out in the rapidity of its first impressions of the subject.[7]

In the same sense, the *Art Journal* defined design in this instance as 'sometimes used synonymously with Sketch or Study, to indicate the first composition for a picture'.[8]

At the other end of the century, in 1884, William Morris, in his evidence to the Royal Commission on Technical Instruction, noted the link between art and design: 'The really good artistic designer must, in order to be successful, be equally talented and just as highly trained as the artist painter, and it is a mistaken notion to believe that designers are as a rule failures in art'.[9]

Design as Referring to the General Form or Composition of an Object

The term in this case refers to the completed product or result of the design process. It may also refer to a shape, style, or model of objects. For example, J. C. Loudon mentioned in his 1835 work *An Encyclopaedia of Cottage, Farm, and Villa Architecture and Furniture* how 'The principal Styles of Design in Furniture, as at present executed in Britain may be reduced to four':[10] More explicitly a judge's report on prizes offered by the Royal Dublin Society, noted 'Among these, the designs for Porcelain, Muslins, and Wall Decoration, evince a degree of correct taste in form, composition, and colour, highly creditable to the Students'.[11]

Design as Decorative Patterns

The term design could also be understood as a template for production. Lewis Foreman Day suggested how this developed: 'we begin to see that, had there been no such thing as pattern design before, and no traditional forms of design for us to follow, those very forms must have been evolved as certainly out of the more complex conditions of modern manufacture as they were out of the simple contrivances of primitive handicraft'.[12] Walter Crane also discussed 'the structure of decorative pattern' in his explanation of design as pattern:

> The ornamental designer is not so absolutely bound by structural laws as the architect; but the fact that the structural laws which govern his art are more mental than physical does not make them less binding or less real. Designing is not mathematics or geometry, but there appears to be a certain logic of line and colour in design which, given certain fundamental forms and characters, demands certain necessary sequences.[13]

Design as an Architectural Drawing or Plan

Here, the word denotes an architectural drawing that suggests that a design is a plan to be carried out or followed. Many architectural pattern books of the period were titled 'A series of designs' or suchlike. A design in this sense may also be a preliminary drawing or sketch; a plan, outline, or model produced to show the look or function of a building, machine, or other object before it is made or built. In 1879, *The Hub*, a journal for carriage manufacturers, discussed the development of a design drawing:

> In considering how a [automobile] body should be proportioned as regards outline or style, the school in which the designer's taste has been cultivated forms a subject for consideration . . . the criticising process continues for days; and the drawing remains unfinished on the board, in many cases, from two to three weeks, until at last the design has reached the degree of perfection and beauty desired, when a working draft is made.[14]

Most of these various senses of the word will be found in this collection, where the usage is usually evident from the context. The definition of design is clearly multifaceted. Therefore, readers will find entries relating design to historical and practical topics, as well as entries concerning design and aesthetics, gender, politics, ideology, and so on.

General Themes and Strands Covered by the Entire Edition

The nineteenth century, often imprecisely described as the Victorian Age,[15] was particularly distinguished by immense and volatile changes and progress in most arenas of activity. Although there were numerous wars and conflicts, political upheavals, dynastic changes, and economic disruptions, great progress was made in the fields of science and technology, arts, literature and culture, and some progress on social changes. Alongside these issues were the continuing development of capitalism and business, the politics of colonialism and abolition, and an increasing interest in philosophy and religion. Britain's attitude to these changes was initially one of certainty and conviction built partly on economic success, but this was ultimately usurped by feelings of doubt about its role and position in the world.

The Industrial Revolution – Workshop of World

The Industrial Revolution is a blanket term that embraces the technological, scientific, and industrial innovations that were further developed during the century thus fuelling a massive increase in production and subsequent consumption. The French economist Adolphe Blanqui invoked the inventions of James Watt and Richard Arkwright in his *Histoire De L'Économie Politique en Europe* of 1837 as being the crucial moment of change:

> Just as the French revolution witnessed great social experiences of earth-shaking proportions, England began to undergo the same process on the terrain of industry. The end of the eighteenth century was signalled by admirable discoveries which were destined to change the face of the world and increase in an unforeseen manner the power of their inventors. The conditions of labour underwent the most profound alteration since the origin of societies. Two machines, henceforth immortal, the steam engine and the spinning machine, overthrew the old commercial system and gave birth, almost at the same moment, to material goods and social questions unknown to our fathers.[16]

Blanqui later mentions the works of Charles Babbage and Andrew Ure. He talks about Babbage's work on the division of labour and the use of machines; and Ure's work on the manufacturing system, but like later critics, bemoans the fact that the imperfections of these systems were not taken into account in terms of the operatives. Indeed, Ure's *Philosophy of Manufactures* (1835) defended the factory system whereby the factory itself was seen as a 'co-operative body' that linked workers, machines, and products together in harmony. This model was hotly debated throughout the century and had repercussions for design.

Babbage's *On the Economy of Machinery and Manufactures* (1832) takes a different view that suggested that machinery was the expression of abstract efficiency. In terms of design, this efficiency resulted in the production of objects that were more than commodities; they were signs of progress. In his Introduction, Baggage mentions the intellectual pleasure resulting from this contemplation:

> There exists, perhaps, no single circumstance which distinguishes our country more remarkably from all others, than the vast extent and perfection to which we have carried the contrivance of tools and machines for forming those conveniences of which so large a quantity is consumed by almost every class of the community. The amount of patient thought, of repeated experiment, of happy exertion of genius, by which our manufactures have been created and carried to their present excellence, is scarcely to be imagined.[17]

As the extracts will show, the topics of division of labour, novel products, new techniques, and materials feature in much of the nineteenth-century discourse on design and production.

In response to these enormous changes and the upheaval they brought with them, there were many who found the revolution highly disturbing and morally unsatisfactory. They challenged the conditions within the workplace, the use of child labour, and the development of cities with their associated pollution, poverty, and disease. These challenges were addressed directly by social reformers, but in terms of design, it was often the case that the opposition between industry and culture was expressed in nostalgic and romantic terms.

Social Reforms and the Growth of Democracy

Rapid and unregulated industrialisation not only brought about increases in wealth and economic success but also brought a host of social and economic problems. These were characterised in the population by poor health, unemployment, poverty, and rioting. This age saw the rise and growth of political movements, particularly socialism, liberalism and later, organised feminism. The Chartists organisation of workers helped create an atmosphere open to further reform, whereby religious belief in the infallibility of the Bible, and the nature of the human species in the universe, were increasingly called into question.

Although society was ostensibly ordered by rankings, there were some opportunities for social and geographical mobility. Entrepreneurs used their growing prosperity to buy into society, professionals developed their practices and a growing middle class developed. The impulse to emigrate, for hopes of self-improvement, was also a key feature of the century. However, by 1901, forty per cent of adult men were still ineligible to vote, and no women were enfranchised, so for many, democracy was an illusion.

Nevertheless, the social changes that included the growth of the concept of domesticity, a clear work ethic, the model of improvement, the developing roles for women, the increasing educational and employment opportunities, and the growth of leisure were particularly linked to the rise of the middle classes. In terms of design, these classes required differentiation in their consuming patterns but conversely were somewhat limited by the demands of social conformity.

Idealisation of the Family and Homely Domesticity

The ideal of a respectable family and the associated cult of the home developed through the century. The home was one of the opposites in a series of culturally separate spheres, which included 'the inside' and 'the outside', respectability and deviance, and industry and home. The introduction to the Census of Great Britain for 1851 confirms this ideal of home: 'The possession of an entire house is, it is true, strongly desired by every Englishman; for it throws a sharp, well-defined circle round his family and hearth — the shrine of his sorrows, joys, and meditations'.[18]

As the subtle graduations of goods developed ever more, the meanings they held, which were designed in part to deal with the nonverbal communications, became more complex. Knowledge and understanding of the narrative nature of selected objects intended to reinforce respectability were increasingly important. Furnishings became more domesticated and homely, although they initially related morals to comfort, and not directly to presentation. These considerations were achieved in great measure by the common use of a language of display that was both shared and individual, which was both purchased from a retailer and constructed at home.

Expansion of Empire and a World Power

The rise of competitive colonialism was linked to Britain's trading dominance, naval, and military strength, and the growth of other major nation states. In the latter part of the century i.e. from 1870, there were increasing threats to Britain's military and economic supremacy. Nevertheless, the jingoistic idea of Empire was a very powerful concept that was supported by British notions of free trade and Christian civilisation, which were buoyed by attitudes of racial superiority that made expansion seem almost inevitable. In terms of design, there was two-way traffic in both goods and cultural imagery that was seen as commercially successful in England, but at the same time was potentially debasing to indigenous cultures.

Design as an Issue in the Nineteenth Century

British taste and design were both favourable and influential in Europe at the end of the eighteenth century. The spread of Anglomania in Europe during the eighteenth century was initially part of the Enlightenment, partly as an intellectual experience, but also as a stylistic matter. For example, the first edition of the German style magazine *Journal de Luxus und Der Moden,* published in 1786, enthusiastically discussed English fashions, furniture, musical instruments, carriages, Wedgwood ceramics, and even Coade stone.[19] England was seen as a rival to France in its approach to design. English design appeared to encompass simplicity, usefulness, and ease, compared with the French taste that was seen as lavish, often impractical and rigid. This was rather ironic, as for much of the nineteenth-century French design was held to be the model of taste and quality to which British designers and manufacturers should aspire. Indeed, there was already a taste in Britain for French designed products in the early years of the century.

However, already by the 1790s, a plurality of design styles was developing that included versions of the classical, the exotic, and the gothic. These were all linked to aesthetic judgements that were often based around the picturesque, which stressed both the importance of the visual and the unity of the arts. This plurality was to grow into a major concern for nineteenth-century design reformers, not least in relation to the issue of a national taste or style.

The idea of the development of a national taste that would raise the aesthetic threshold and act as a guide to morality and propriety was therefore of great concern. The perceived problem of novelty and fashion which appeared subversive had to be countered by the development of 'good taste' and appropriate education. This was to be easier said than done. In fact, a major issue that was to confront the British design world was the rapid development of a design infrastructure in Europe, especially in France and Germany. By the beginning of the nineteenth-century, these countries had already developed design education, with specialist schools and technical institutes established. Both countries had also begun to develop exhibitions of manufactured goods, in France from 1798 and in Germany from 1812.

Apart for these two crucial endeavours, France and Germany produced fashion journals that included actual samples of the textiles being discussed. The *Journal de Luxus und Der Moden,* (1787–1812) and the *Journal Für Fabrik Manufaktur, Handlung und Mode* (c. 1791–1806) were two such examples, which must have influenced Rudolf Ackermann in his later British publication *The Repository of Arts, Literature, Commerce, Manufactures, Fashions, and Politics* (1809–1828). The French offered fashion journals, such as *Journal des Dames et des Modes* (1797 to 1829), the *Petit Courrier des Dames* (1821–1868), and *Le Follet* (1829–1892), as well as publications offering interior design schemes. Indeed, Henry Cole's famous *Journal of Design and Manufactures* was based on German formats. Other influences on British design came from European individuals, including Prince Albert and his collaborators, Ludwig Gruner and Gottfried Semper. In a different sphere, French designers were quite frequently employed in prestigious British factories.[20]

A more optimistic assessment of British prowess, by the painter and illustrator William Marshall Craig, in 1821 considered that

> Our great wealth is evidently the result of our flourishing commerce, the unexampled extent of that commerce is chiefly owing to the very great superiority of taste and design manifested in all our manufactures, and these qualities are ramifications of those notions in imitative art, diffused throughout the kingdom by our national school of painting and sculpture [Royal Academy].[21]

Despite this positive analysis, the nature of design was still a major topic of concern. The argument around the aesthetic hierarchy that put 'fine art' at its head was questioned. It was argued that the decorative arts (design) also had aesthetic significance, as well as functional and other meanings. This concern also reflected the tension between the commercial bourgeoisie and those who espoused high aesthetic doctrines.

In 1835, the Government commissioned an enquiry into the problem of art and design applied to manufactures.[22] The purpose of the committee was 'to inquire into the best means of extending a knowledge of the Arts, and of the Principles of Design among the People (especially the Manufacturing Population) of the Country; also to inquire into the Constitution, Management and Effects of Institutions connected with the Arts'. The resulting report published in 1836 was stinging in its criticism.

> In many despotic countries, far more development has been given to genius, and greater encouragement to industry, by a more liberal diffusion of the enlightening influence of the arts. Yet, to us, a peculiarly manufacturing nation, the connexion between art and manufactures is most important: and for this merely economical reason (were there no higher motive), it equally imports us to encourage art in its loftier attributes; since it is admitted that the cultivation of the more exalted branches of design tends to advance the humblest pursuits of industry, while the connexion of art with manufacture has often developed the genius of the greatest masters in design.

Nearly thirty years later, the designer Owen Jones could still comment about the apparent muddle and chaos in British art and design.

> We are amazed at the shortsightedness of the manufacturers, who do not see how much it would be in their interest to begin by having a real and proper design from the hands of an artist. The manufacturer answers, where are these artists? I admit they are few indeed, but it is for the manufacturer to help to make them. So long as they consider the design of such little importance, that they trust this important branch of their

business to mere work-men without art-education of any kind, they cannot hope for any improvement or find artists to help them.[23]

Despite this, the French were becoming concerned about the progress in design Britain since the 1851 exhibition. In 1852, a Central Committee of Artists and Industrial Artists requested the French state to develop a museum for industrial arts, a principal school of arts applied to industry, as well as exhibitions of designers' works. In 1863, this movement was formalised the *Union Central des Beaux Arts Appliqués à l'Industrie*. These changes were clearly a response to the British initiatives at South Kensington.

Gradual changes in approaches to design in Britain signified (a) a move away from concerns around design as a moral issue to one more related to aesthetics; (b) the clash between utility and ornament; (c) the notion of style; and (d) a change from ideas of the application of universal design principles to a recognition of the role of personal taste.

The relationships between beauty, ornament, morality, and utility or function were multifaceted and were addressed in many differing ways. Ruskin, in his lecture *The Two Paths* delivered in Bradford in 1859 touched on this issue:

> Design is not the offspring of idle fancy: it is the studied result of accumulative observation and delightful habit. Without observation and experience, no design— without peace and pleasurableness in occupation, no design—and all the lecturings, and teachings, and prizes, and principles of art, in the world, are of no use, so long as you don't surround your men with happy influences and beautiful things.

For many reformers, their concerns particularly centred on the role of utility and ornament. The *Art Union* pointed out that 'The problem to be solved, in all cases of the invention of new forms, or the adaptation of old ones to useful purposes, is this—given the precise kind of utensil, it is required to find the shape best suited to fulfil its uses, and at the same time to develop the utmost degree of appropriate beauty'.[24]

The idea of function as design, based on utility was best seen in engineering design with many examples that point to the form being derived from the functional requirements without additional ornament. When ornament was added, there was often some incongruity in the overall effect that was criticised by reformers but was often commercially successful. The examples of domestic appliances, such as sewing machines with printed decorative graphics, or coal scuttles with painted rustic scenes, come to mind. These alleged 'horrors' were partly derived from the ability to mechanise decoration cheaply and thus offer novelty.

Underscoring many of the concerns was the search for a national British style that was suitable for the time. In 1840, H.W. Arrowsmith in his *House Decorator and Painter's Guide* wrote somewhat apologetically: 'The present age is distinguished from all others in having no style which can properly be called its own'.[25]

This anxiety was more than just deciding on the appropriate fashionable taste; it was also a response to the Hegelian idea of *Geist der Zeiten* that art reflected the spirit and culture of the time in which it is created, as it was created by people living in that time.

The irony was that the more the search continued for this elusive style, the more varied became the choices on offer. This eclecticism was promoted by the publication of a wide range of ornament and pattern books such as Owen Jones's *Grammar of Ornament*. The range of available styles also often reflected political, social, or religious positions. Hence, many styles looked to the past. The Renaissance revival for example, seemed to be highly appropriate, as it met most of the principles of design as set out by reformers.

By contrast, the versions of the Gothic Revival, including the Reformed Gothic and the Geometric Gothic, looked to the church and issues of morality initially, but later took a less pious and more art-based approach. These seemed to offer a bulwark of historically based stability in a confusing period. The influence of William Morris and the Arts and Crafts movement was the epitome of the moral crusade that had often underpinned design reform for much of the century. Although these were also sometimes linked to 'Romantic Interiors' which were related to an interest in Antiquarianism, the growth of the collector and a regard for the vernacular in design were to be rooted in political agitation and reform.

A return to a different approach was found in the demand for the importance of naturalism in design, again supported by numerous books on drawing and design from nature. This had derived from the French or rococo revival of the early part of the century, where natural imagery was important to the style. This approach was often used in a narrative way initially but gave way to designs that tried to relate natural decoration to the object's function.

Yet another example is the interest in the exotic, arising from world-wide interactions from trading and exploration that resulted in the rise of styles such as the Egyptian revival, Japonisme, and the adoption of selected imagery from a wide variety of other cultures.

The Queen Anne Revival and the Aesthetic Movement were attempted to introduce an eclectic mix into design, drawn from a range of disparate sources, while the Art Nouveau and the Glasgow School were influencing the Continent, as well as creating a commercial fashion in both the high-end stores such as Liberty, and, often in a debased form, the lower-class emporia.

At the end of the century, there was a return to British influence in Europe. Hermann Muthesius's *The English House* was hugely influential in his native Germany in promoting Arts and Crafts ideals but also encouraging modern technology in the home. *The Studio* magazine was also prominent in its publication of modern designs from across Europe, with an emphasis on British works. Other examples include Siegfried Bing's fashionable Parisian shop which sold English goods, and the Vienna Museum of Art and Industry that collected examples of British wares for the use of their design scholars.

All the concerns around design as an aesthetic or moral issue, the clash between utility and ornament, the notion of style; and a change from ideas of the application of universal principles to personal taste are evident in the documents in these volumes.

Previous Publishing History on Nineteenth-Century Design

Early academic interest in the topic was demonstrated by the 'Victorian Exhibition' held in 1931, which took over 23a Bruton Street, London where its rooms were furnished in a mid-Victorian style. One-time director of the V&A (1909–1924) Sir Cecil Harcourt-Smith chaired the scheme. A contemporary review of the exhibition noted 'Leading from this landing was the Morris Room, excellent as showing the contrast between the truly Victorian taste and that of the first of the Moderns, though its vivid clashes of colour and insistence on pattern would make it a very trying room to live in to-day'.[26] In this vein, Nikolaus Pevsner's *Pioneers of the Modern Movement* (1936 and later editions) developed an argument for the links between twentieth-century modernism and the nineteenth-century design theories and practice, especially works by William Morris, John Ruskin, Owen Jones and the industrial architects of the period. In 1952, a seminal exhibition, titled *Victorian and Edwardian Decorative Arts,* was held at the V & A and was responsible for raising the level of Victorian designs studies far more widely.

Publications began to flow in response to the revisions around Victorian design and practice. In 1957, the Norwegian art historian Alf Bøe published *From Gothic Revival to Functional Form: a study in Victorian theories of design.* In 1970, Herwin Schaefer's *Nineteenth-Century Modern: the functional tradition in Victorian design* (1970) confirmed the Modernist ideal of form over ornament, through a historical analysis of 'functional' objects. In 1972, a private collection of objects was lent to the exhibition at the Royal Academy titled *Victorian and Edwardian Decorative Art: The Handley-Read collection,* which produced an important catalogue.

Subsequently, a whole industry around 'Victorian design' has grown up, with an enormous range of publications from decorator magazines to coffee table books, from journals to academic publications on many aspects of the period and its design in the broadest sense. These include period surveys, books on individual designers and critics, books on various product groups, all ranging across a wide field, from the popular to the collector/connoisseur, to academics of many various persuasions. Finally, a word should be said about published readers or anthologies that have addressed the topic more recently. One of the first was Bernard Denvir's *Documentary History of Taste in Britain.* The relevant volumes were *Art Design and Society – The Early Nineteenth-Century 1789–1852* (1984) and *The Late Victorians 1853–1910 (1986).* This was followed by Paul Greenhalgh's *Quotations and Sources on Design and the Decorative Arts* (1993), and then Isabelle Frank's more specialised *The Theory of Decorative Art: An Anthology* (2000). Subsequent art and design history 'readers' have included small extracted samples on nineteenth-century design.

Overview of the Contents of Each Volume

The first volume considers theories and discourses on design and thus looks at the ideas around aesthetics, beauty, and taste, that were to inform design over the century. To elaborate on these, the issues of ornament, design reform, exoticism, state interventions, economic imperatives, invention and copyright, and education are all considered as part of the wider context for design.

The matter of aesthetics and beauty, through the notion of associationism, was initially a major part of an understanding of the problems associated with design and its reform. However, it was the issue of utility and its relation to beauty that was a major practical concern. On the one hand, the French poet and critic Théophile Gautier proclaimed in 1835 that 'Nothing is truly beautiful except that which can serve for nothing; whatever is useful is ugly'.[27] On the other hand, William Morris, towards the end of the century, argued that 'nothing can be a work of art which is not useful'.[28] The issue of morality was closely connected with this, as well as the perceived distinctions between artists and artisans (designers).

Taste, its origins and tenets, the issue of bad taste, and the diffusion of good taste among all classes, were all linked to design principles. The concept of improvement of taste was not just an economic issue but a social one. For many, 'good taste' equated to a universal standard that enabled people to recognise beauty and if taught correctly would eliminate 'bad taste'.

The interest in ornament led to a growing awareness in the decorations of other cultures, as well as their histories. There had been a long-standing European interest in non-Western art, but the fascination for exotic styles was fuelled by significant displays of non-Western art at many of the international exhibitions from 1851 onward.

The well-known *Report of the Parliamentary Select Committee on Art and Manufactures* of 1836 set an agenda for design reform in relation to its application of art to industry. Design reformers worked towards a set of specific beliefs. Initially, they argued for the supremacy of form over ornament; secondly, they considered that form is closely related to function and the natures of materials; and thirdly, that designs should be drawn from a pool of historic, exotic, and natural examples that were refined into modified and abstracted forms.

To foster these agendas and encourage both production and consumption, Governments moved to promote the protection of invention and copyright against pirating of design; they developed education and teaching to develop artisans and designers and supported libraries and museums for others to educate their tastes. In addition, art and design education represented a realistic conduit for movement between social classes, particularly for certain groups of women, seeking a widening of career options beyond that of governess.

The second volume considers objects, images and spaces, or areas of design activity as visual and material culture. In this regard, examples of texts that discuss material goods including domestic design, industrial art, metalwork, jewellery, ceramics glass, furniture, textiles, graphic and visual design, wallpaper, dress and fashion, engineering, and urban design (inc. architecture) are included.

Domestic design played an important part of the nineteenth-century development of the notion of homes. Numerous pattern and advice books were published to try and educate and cajole the public in certain directions. The goods associated with the domestic interior were either the products of industrial art manufactures or individual domestic work. In the field of metalwork, for example, works in silver, gold, bronze, iron, and brass were created for numerous applications in the home. Metalwork also encompassed the ecclesiastical and architectural ironwork and other artefacts. Jewellery was a specific branch of this business that attracted particular attention. In contrast, the encouragement of home crafts allowed people to individualise their spaces to a degree.

Ceramics and glass included a wide range of artefacts, such as architectural ceramics, tableware, art pottery, majolica studio pottery, and stained glass, all of which catered for varied markets and tastes. Furniture followed a similar path, being designed as either functional objects or display pieces, but following a stylistic trend dependent on the fashions. These types of products were also displayed in exhibitions, usually as examples of high-quality design and craftsmanship, thus reflecting national pride and status.

Graphic design, as the art of selecting and arranging visual elements to convey a message to an audience, had developed rapidly during the century. Like other advances, the evolution of graphic design as a practice and profession was closely bound to technological innovations, changes in society, and the influence of various art and design movements. Wallpaper was another product that benefited from the industrial revolution just as did textiles. Up until 1840, all wallpapers were produced by hand by means of the block-printing process. By adopting the methods used in the printing of calico, wallpaper printing machines were developed, and the market grew rapidly.

Various decorative and visual arts movements, as well as changing perceptions of the traditional gender roles, also influenced fashion. Technology also played its part in the development of the fashion industry, when sewing machines were introduced in the 1850s, along with the employment of new synthetic dyes for textiles. The expansion of the media encouraged participation in the fashions, which was linked to associated developments in retailing and promotion.

The matter of the role and status of the designer, architect, and engineer also caused many arguments. This volume allows some exploration of the issues arising from, for example, the role of ornament in engineering, and the concept of utility over decoration. In terms of nineteenth-century architecture, two principal features are evident; the use of a variety of historical styles and the development and application of new materials and construction systems.

The third volume investigates the nature of production and the practices of design and manufactures. The texts considered here are associated with topics such as the art industries, decorative and applied arts, drawing and design principles, the elements of design (e.g. colour, form, materials) and manufacturing methods. The conflicts around the craft, machine, and design are also represented.

The application of art to industry, in the form of design, was at the top of many of the mediators' agendas. For many, drawing was the key; whether this was technical drawing, sketching, or indeed, the argument about the role of life drawing, its role in education and any subsequent applications, was considered crucial.

The elements of design, whether conceptual, visual, relational, or practical, were discussed in great detail in terms of both theory and practice. In particular, disputes about form, the role of colour, the use of materials, and the imitation issue were fervently debated in these texts. The concomitant issues of the role and nature of craft and its connection to design, as well as the 'hand versus machine' debate, were also significant themes.

The fourth volume offers documents related to the actors, intermediaries, and mediators associated with the design domain; firstly as individuals including artists, architects, designers, artist-designers, pattern drawers, and engineers; secondly, as mediators as organisations and businesses, and thirdly, looking at other mediating systems, including critics and style debates, advice books and journals, exhibitions, and museums, all of which influenced aspects of design theory and practice. Often, the communication of information by mediators, actors, or agents affected the message of the meanings of things, via a variety of channels. These mediated communications also shaped the individual, the institutional, and the societal, and in the reverse order as well, when meanings are reworked and appropriated. The mediating channels themselves are designed artefacts, and are therefore of interest.

The topic of design and the discourses around it had been well established in the eighteenth century, but it was to develop into a major issue for nineteenth-century critics, philosophers, and design reformers, who mediated the discussion around the role and nature of the design. At the heart of the debates was the issue of a style that reflected the century and all its changes, not least the impact of technology. This search for a style that had unified a culture in the past was seen to be missing. The concepts of erudition, accumulation, and copies of the past were seen as poor substitutes.

The problem was that design movements are based on a style or prevailing inclination in art or design that upholds a specific philosophy or ideal and is followed and promoted by a group of individuals for a defined period. Therefore, their influence may be limited or widespread.

Texts and images are the overarching form of communication media. These included advice books directed to homemakers, fashion followers, collectors and art lovers, and journals (specialist art journals, trade and special interest journals, magazines specifically directed at men or women, and journals attached to societies and groups). Finally, museums and exhibitions are yet other channels of mediation that were embraced during the century, particularly for their apparent didactic qualities. Taken together, all these mediating categories form a network of involvements that closely engaged with the theory and practice of design during the nineteenth century.

GENERAL INTRODUCTION

A Note on the Selection and Presentation of the Texts, and the Editorial Principles

The aim is to offer an overview of aspects and attitudes to design during the long nineteenth century: It is not a history of design in the period, rather it is a collection of selected texts that explore and explain a range of aspects of design in the period from philosophical aesthetics to practical engineering. All the texts are ultimately about design. Some of the texts are well-known, and others less so. In many cases, we have tried to reproduce the full text of an article or chapter. In some cases, missing text is indicated by [. . .]. Original spellings and ellipses are kept in texts. Any footnotes that occur in the original are reproduced as footnotes.

It is also important to note that different editions, and even individual copies of the texts transcribed here, can have variations.

In some cases, extracts are used that make a particular point. It is worth noting that several of the selected texts cross over the topic divisions or themes in which they are located and could easily fit elsewhere. The texts are mainly by English authors, though there are occasional examples of other nationalities introduced, when relevant.

Each volume is arranged in appropriate sub-themes, then chronologically within each section. Each volume has an introduction that focuses on the themes therein. The thematic structure attempts to offer appropriate texts that are then sorted chronologically and can thus offer connections and contradictions within a theme. Each text has an introductory headnote, which includes brief details of the author, the publication history and its critical reception, and, where relevant, its connection to other authors and events. Wide and extensive use of contemporary reviews, analysis and criticism have given context to the editorial headnote texts. Editorial endnotes have also been included with many of the documents, to inform or explain where necessary.

Finally, it is recommended that these readings are combined or connected with viewings of actual objects in relevant collections, in order to relate to them more closely and therefore understand something of the nature and dilemmas of nineteenth-century design and designers.

Notes

1 The Oxford English Dictionary was helpful in clarifying some aspects of the word and its uses.
2 T. Sopwith, 'On the Principles of Design', *Architectural Magazine*, 3, 31, September 1836, p. 393.
3 A. Jamieson, *A Dictionary of Mechanical Science, Arts, Manufactures, and Miscellaneous Knowledge* (London: Henry Fisher, 1829). Entry on Design.
4 C. A. Barry, *Primer of Design* (Boston: Lee and Shepherd, 1878), p. 29.
5 C. L. Redfield, 'The Relation of Invention and Design to Mechanical Progress', *Factory and Industrial Management*, Vol. 12 (New York: McGraw-Shaw Company, 1896–97), p. 286.
6 'The Art of Design', *Fine Arts Journal*, 1, 18, 6 March 1847, pp. 278–279.

7 'The British School of Design', in *Library of Fine Art* (London: M. Arnold, 1832), 3, 13, February 1832, pp. 89–95.
8 'Terms in Art', *Art Journal*, 12, 1850, p. 288.
9 Evidence to *Second Report of the Royal Commissioners on Technical Instruction* (London: Printed by Eyre and Spottiswoode, 1884), pp. 150–161.
10 J. C. Loudon, *An Encyclopaedia of Cottage, Farm, and Villa Architecture and Furniture* (London: Longman, 1835), p 1039.
11 *The Journal of the Royal Dublin Society*, 5, 1870, p. 529.
12 L. F. Day, *Ornamental Design: Embracing the Anatomy of Pattern, the Planning of Ornament, the Application of Ornament* (London: B.T. Batsford, 1890), p. 22.
13 W. Crane, *The Claims of Decorative Art* (London: Lawrence and Bullen, 1892), p. 40.
14 *The Hub*, 21, 9, December 1879, p. 390.
15 George III reigned up to 1820, George IV from 1820–1830, and William IV between 1830–37.
16 A. Blanqui, *Histoire de L'Économie Politique en Europe* 2 (Paris: Guillaumin, 1837), pp. 207–8.
17 C. Babbage, *On the Economy of Machinery and Manufactures* (London: R. Clay, 1832) p. 3.
18 *The Census of Great Britain in 1851* (London: Longman, Brown, Green, and Longmans, 1854), p. 8.
19 Coade Stone: An imitation stone product devised by Eleanor Coade (1733–1821) made from a mix of clay, terracotta, silicates, and glass fired together for four days in extremely hot kilns.
20 Well-known names include Antoine Vechet, Léonard Morel-Ladeuil, Léon Arnoux, and Albert-Ernest Carrier-Belleuse.
21 W. M. Craig, *A Course of Lectures on Drawing, Painting, and Engraving, Considered as Branches of Elegant Education. Delivered in the Saloon of the Royal Institution, in Successive Seasons, and Read Subsequently at the Russell Institution* (London: Longman, Hurst, Rees, Orme, & Brown, 1821), p. 444.
22 [Interim] *Report from Select Committee on Arts and Manufactures*. London: September 1835; and *Report from the Select Committee on Arts and Their Connexion with Manufactures*, August 1836.
23 O. Jones, *On the True and the False in the Decorative Arts: Lectures Delivered at Marlborough House, June 1852* (London: Strangeways and Walden, 1863), p. 3.
24 'Art Applied to Manufacturers', *Art Union*, 1 February 1842, p. 24.
25 H. W. Arrowsmith, *The House Decorator and Painter's Guide, Containing a Series of Designs for Decorating Apartments, Suited to the Various Styles of Architecture* (London: Thomas Kelly, 1840), p. 111.
26 B. B., 'Ghosts at the Victorian Exhibition', *Connoisseur*, 88, July 1931, p. 58.
27 T. Gautier, preface to the 1835 edition of *Mademoiselle de Maupin* (Paris: Renduel, 1835), (*Il n'y a de vraiment beau que ce qui ne peut servir à rien; tout ce qui est utile est laid . . .*').
28 W. Morris, *The Decorative Arts: Their Relation to Modern Life and Progress; an Address Delivered Before the Trades' Guild of Learning* (London: Ellis and White, 1878), p. 27.

INTRODUCTION TO VOLUME III
Production and Practices of Design

The texts in this volume investigate the nature of production and the practices of design and manufactures. They deal with both general issues and specific aspects relating to art industries, decorative and applied arts, drawing and design principles. The elements of design (colour, form, materials), as well as manufacturing methods and the conflicts around craft, machine, and design, are also included.

The application of art to industry in the form of design was at the top of many of the mediators' agendas. The major concerns were (a) to encourage economic activity especially in competition with France; (b) to establish a set of principles that applied across the designed world including not only the formal principles but also the relation between construction and ornament; (c) the distinction between artist and designer; and (d) between hand and machine work. For many, drawing was the key to solving many of these issues. Whether this was technical drawing, sketching, or indeed the argument about the role of life drawing, its role in education was considered crucial.

The elements of design, whether conceptual, visual, relational, or practical, were addressed in great detail in terms of both theory and practice. In particular, disputes about form, the role of colour, the use of materials, and the issues around imitation were fervently debated in these texts. The concomitant concerns of the role and nature of craft and its connection to design were linked to this.

The texts are arranged by issue and concerns, starting with the perennial question which was how to successfully link art and manufactures. This is followed by discussion of the role and definition of decorative and applied art; the key role of drawing; the actual design principles engaged with, and the specific elements of design; and finally consideration of manufacturing methods, including the hand versus machine debate.

Art, Design, and Manufacturers

Although the issue of art applied to manufactures had already been examined by the Select Committee of 1836, the topic was still very much alive ten years later. In 1846, the address to Council of the Society of Arts explained the connexion and their potential role:

The application of the Fine Arts to our Manufactures. The manufactures of this country have, [Prince Albert] observed, attained an eminence for solid execution, for perfect finish, for mechanical accuracy, and for cheap production, which distinguished them in these respects beyond those of any other country. But there are some countries that excel ours in the beauty of design, in the perfection of colouring, in symmetry of form, in elegance of pattern: it is the application of the arts of design to the mechanical manufactures of this country that is alone requisite to enable her to stand without a rival. Of high art in this country there is abundance of mechanical industry and invention—an unparalleled profusion; the thing still remaining to be done, is to effect the combination of the two, to wed high art with mechanical skill. The union of the artist with the workman, the improvement of the general taste of our artificers, and of the workmen in general—this is a task worthy of the Society of Arts, and directly in the path of its duty'.[1]

A similar approach was taken by the Scottish Art Manufacture Association, but included the general public. In the preface to the 1856 *Catalogue for the First Art Manufactures Exhibition held at National Gallery, Edinburgh*, it was stated:

The object of the Art Manufacture Association is to offer opportunities for elevating the imperfectly cultivated taste of the public, by making them familiar with the best Ancient and Modern specimens of Art Manufacture, and at the same time to encourage Manufacturers and Designers to leave the beaten track, and produce Works worthy of the place which the nation occupies in every other department of intellectual exertion.[2]

The collection of documents begins with 'Further Remarks on the Report of the Committee on the Arts and Principles of Design', in the *Mechanics' Magazine* (1837), which provided a harsh critique of the Committee's report which, they argue, appears to damn every aspect of English work and design, in favour of foreign examples. The article considers that much British work was of better design than French, and the evidence of important persons in the art and design world supported that.

The second document, W. S. W.'s article on 'Art Applied to Manufactures'(1842), raised many familiar matters including the need to teach first principles based on beauty and utility, and the distinctions between training for an artist or designer.

George Wallis, in his 'Recent Progress in Design as applied to Manufactures'(1856), discussed the role of manufacturers and retailers in design and identified the conflict between artistic design and commercial ideas, although he saw an improvement since 1851 in art manufactures generally. Denis O'Donovan's 'The Uses of Art & Design in Manufacture', 1871, took this further and explored some of the fundamental issues of Art industry: the distinction between constructive or ornamental; the importance of utility and fitness; and truth to purpose and the avoidance of imitation.

Jacob Falke's discussion of the 'Vienna Exhibition in Connexion with Art-Industry' (1874) noticed the diversity of national styles in art manufactures based on historic precedent especially the Renaissance, Rococo, and Gothic, along with the relative decline of French influence.

One solution to the linking of art and industry was promoted by Tom Taylor, in his 'The Study and Practice of Art' (1874), where he argued that the nature of design was all-encompassing, whether it was fine or industrial art. For him, the human body was the basis of all design, and his discussion centres on the practice of teaching the basics of art/design as art industry.

Decorative and/or Applied Art

The terms decorative or applied art are apt to cause confusion, but essentially they both refer to the application of art to industry in a practical manner. One commentator made a distinction suggesting that 'applied art' referred to when raw materials were worked up and combined, in contrast to 'refined arts', where elements of beauty are added. He gives the example of carpentry and weaving as termed 'applied art', while upholstery and tailoring are considered 'refined arts'.[3]

The first text in this section reflects upon one particular aspect of decorative or applied art, noticed early on, which was the potential for women to work within its sphere. John Stewart's, 'art decoration, a suitable employment for women'(1860), initially argued that a woman's place was naturally in the home and family, but if women had to work, they would be useful as designers, wood-engravers, porcelain-painters, or employed in other similar occupations, particularly wallpaper designing.

Less specific was Christopher Dresser's, 'Hindrances to the Progress of Applied Art' (1872), that considered a range of issues relating to art manufactures including the palpable commercial value of art. He particularly noticed the hindrances to the progress of applied arts. These included matters of education, the role of manufacturers, the adverse effect of middle-men with no taste, and indeed the public's lack of appreciation, along with museums that simply venerate the old. All this led to his conclusion that there was a need for an Academy of Design.

A less polemic discussion of decorative arts from a craft point of view is seen in Emma Lazarus's paper titled 'A Day in Surrey with William Morris'(1886). This is a poetic description of a visit to one of the important players in the decorative arts of the later nineteenth century from an American viewpoint. It shows the other side of rampant commercialism and also points to the arguments about hand and machine work. This is followed by an interview with the freelance designer Arthur Silver, (1894) which shows the studio system at work in conjunction with manufacturers, thus linking decorative art workers with producers. It is interesting to see that Silver suggests that sometimes abandoning principles in favour of artistic freedom are sensible, as long as the ensuing design is fit for purpose.

Drawing

The crucial importance of drawing in terms of design but also to improve competitiveness was already an issue in the eighteenth century. In 1741, the Bishop of St. Asaph published a sermon upon the then unpopular subject of general education, that emphasised the importance of drawing, incidentally, raising the spectre of French superiority that went on to haunt many nineteenth-century commentators. Charles Babbage in *On the Economy of Machinery and Manufactures* (1832), linked drawing skills to machine design: 'It can never be too strongly impressed upon the minds of those who are devising new machines that to make the most perfect drawings of every part tends essentially both to the success of the trial, and to economy in arriving at the result'.[4]

This issue was addressed in the first document in the selection by Jacques-Eugène Armengaud, in *The Practical Draughtsman's Book of Industrial Design* (1853), where, in this context, industrial design refers to drawing. Armengaud's publication was highly influential in engineering and industrial design. A later and fascinating comment by the engineer James Nasmyth in his autobiography of 1883, explained the value of drawing: 'Without the alphabet of mechanical drawing, the workman is merely "a hand". With it, he indicates the possession of "a head"'.[5]

Within the debate around drawing one of the most controversial topics was the role of life drawing. Benjamin Haydon, writing in his journal for 1837, noted how important the figure was in designing:

> I made a clear statement to Poulett Thomson, proving that the figure was the basis; that the same principle regulated the milk-jug and the heroic limb; that the ellipsis was the basis of Greek Art, and the circle of the Roman; that if the figure was not the basis, the Government money would be thrown away, and the public disappointed.[6]

The alternative to life drawing was a so-called trade system of drawing based on a scientific and geometric approach that was supported and promoted by William Dyce and his Drawing Book of the Government School of Design of 1842–3. Dyce rejected studios, figure drawing, and the creation of artists in design schools. Haydon in a later lecture to mechanics made his point crystal clear:

> The Government is determined to prevent you from acquiring knowledge. You might become artists but you will be denied the power to advance yourselves . . . the method employed by Mr. Dyce, a flower of the dry, hard, Gothic German school is based on the German Gewerbeschule, whereas my proposals are based on the practice of the school at Lyons - and which do you think is best German design or French?'[7]

Whatever the case, Dyce's, *Introduction to the Drawing Book of the School of Design, Published in the Years 1842–3,* offered a complex theoretical discussion planned with ornamentists at the centre, sitting between the artist and the mechanic. For Dyce, artists draw imitations of nature, ornamentists represent abstractions of nature for manufacturing purposes. Dyce described incremental and guided steps for drawing students, and his publication was widely used.

Some while later, the argument was still raising passions. William Burges in his *Art Applied to Industry* (1865), discussing the value of drawing the human figure as a proper acquirement for students wrote: 'As to the designer for manufactures, he will do well to remember what no less a man than Haydon said upon this point, namely— that a man who could draw a head could draw a leaf, but it by no means followed that a man who could draw a leaf could draw a head'.[8]

The final text on drawing by Lewis Foreman Day considers distinctions between working drawings and exhibition or presentation drawings (1889), which pulls some thoughts together about the distinctive role and nature of drawing for both working and for selling purposes. The architect J.D. Sedding argued that the role of drawing should not be proscriptive:

> adequate working designs can be expressed on paper. Possibly so, yet to me the incidental in old art is its chief charm. To fasten an able craftsman down to strict adhesion to some feeble effusion from an architect's office is to degrade the man. Fancy the Heckington Sepulchre, or the Antwerp Well, or the Hampton Court gates, being evolved out of paper designs and work[9]

Design Principles

Principles of design (those that could be taught) were key to the thinking about design improvements. Again, the eighteenth century provided precedent for these thoughts. In 1769, Sir Joshua Reynolds strongly suggested that ' Every opportunity should be taken to discountenance that false and vulgar opinion, that rules are the fetters of genius: they are fetters only to men of no genius'.[10] The design principles or rules that relate to the concepts of topics, such as balance, graduation, repetition, harmony, dominance, unity, proportion, rhythm, pattern, movement, emphasis, and variation, were similarly crucial to nineteenth-century design pedagogy.

The 1836 Select Committee on Arts and their Connexion with Manufactures confirmed that '[T]he principles of design should form a portion of any permanent system of national education'.[11] Indeed, the schools of art were rigorous in developing this approach to education, with two important texts published: one by the Department of Science and Art titled *Principles of Decorative Art* (1853) and the other by Richard Redgrave, *On the Necessity of Principles in Teaching Design,* (1853).

The first text in this section considers 'The Principles of Fine Art as Applied to Industrial Purposes' (1847), where Wallis argues for a distinction between the reproductive embellishment of industry and the idealised imitation of fine art.

He suggests some principles are common to both but their application differs. His comments are of value in distinguishing concepts: 'With some, to *draw* is to *design*. With others, to *design* is to *invent*. With a third party, to *draw* means merely to copy, and to *design* means *dovetailing* together in congruous or incongruous mixture certain things already done by somebody else'.[12]

The next text titled 'Universal Infidelity in Principles of Design', published in the *Journal of Design and Manufactures* (1851), examines the principles, in relation to utility, by drawing comparisons between tasteless ornament which ignores utility, and working machinery which is the opposite. This is followed by 'Examples of False Principles in Decoration', published in an exhibition catalogue describing examples of bad taste that were in contravention of design principles. The analysis of each entry is followed by a justifying statement by an authority. The anonymous paper on the 'Principles of design essential to the construction of artistic furniture'(1873), especially considers the key issue of fitness.

One of the other major issues relating to principles was the concept of utility. Lucas Baker's text 'Utility and Beauty' (1883), analysed beauty, arguing that nature was the supreme example of beauty and utility linked into one. Fundamental laws and attributes that provide harmonic arrangements are found in nature, hence it is the best source for designers. Selwyn Image also argues for a similar approach in his 'Of Design and the Study of Nature' (1892), where he sees nature as a store of ideas, not for imitation necessarily, but for analysis of how to use nature to create a design.

Of course, the reformers were fighting against an apparent tide of 'bad design' that was represented as the enemy of good taste. Vulgarity was the main adjective for this sort of design. F. W. Fairholt in an article for the *Art Journal* in 1862,[13] posited a fear of uncontrolled design that was lacking in principles that went beyond amusement into the realm of the excess, somewhere between manmade design and nature and hence the grotesque. Nevertheless, the grotesque held a fascination for the Victorians. Just in design terms, the taste for Minton majolica realism, Martin Brother's ceramics, insect jewellery, bird hats, and copies of Palissy ware are some simple examples.

Elements of Design

The three major elements of design are the visual elements (especially colour, and ornament (See volume one); the conceptual elements (especially form), and the practical elements (especially materials and function). These are discussed in the next set of texts.

Colour

Although Isaac Newton's *Optiks* had intimated a study of colour and light, it was not really until Johann Wolfgang von Goethe's *Theory of Colour* (1801) and Abraham Gottlob Werner's *Nomenclature of Colours,* (1814) that colour was seriously considered in terms of design and manufactures. It was M.E. Chevreul's work in the law of colour contrasts that was also crucial.

In the first text by John Gardner Wilkinson, *On Colour and on the Necessity for a General Diffusion of Taste Among all Classes* (1858), he argued that colour theory and rules do not take the place of the perceptive faculty of a designer. Lucy Crane's text, 'Decorative Art—Color, Dress, and Needlework' (1882), contrasts with Wilkinson by suggesting guides to colour harmony should be made through rules of analogy, contrast, variety, delicacy, and repetition. John D. Crace's 'The Decorative use of Colour' (1888), considered colour from a practical point of view, pointing out how movement was linked to fashion, and solidity linked to surfaces, so colour should be used in relation to structures. As an interior designer, for him, colour as an expression of structure was the main issue. This practical aspect of colour is also found in Roberts Beaumont's text, *Colour in Woven Design*, (1890). Here he points out that an understanding of colour must be based on a knowledge of (in his case) weaving practice and techniques, as they will greatly influence the final effect.

Concerns about appropriate colour usage continued into the new century. Alexander Millar, in a paper to the International Art Congress (1908) argued for more education in colour language. He contended that popular taste in matters of colour was ruled by fashion, suggesting that there were 'distinct signs of decadence, and in the shop windows, which at one time were an unfailing delight to the cultivated eye, we now see chintzes and wall-papers of Early Victorian crudity'. In an effort to teach correct methods of colour use, he proposed a museum of colour for use by both the public and trade designers, in which might be found 'a revival of what once existed at South Kensington,—a small chamber of horrors in which bad colour combinations might be exhibited and their faults pointed out'.[14]

Form

For many reformers and critics, the issue of form was closely related to concepts of function, fitness, and utility. M. Digby Wyatt in his *An Attempt to Define the Principles Which Should Determine Form in the Decorative Arts* (1852) argues that nature was the model through its use of four principles: 'Variety—Fitness—Simplicity—Contrast'.[15] These ideas had been expressed earlier in a different way. A. W. N. Pugin's *The True Principles of Pointed or Christian Architecture*, (1841) argued that: 'The two great rules for design are these: first, that there should be no features about a building which are not necessary for convenience, construction, or propriety; second, that all ornaments should consist of enrichment of the essential construction of the building'.[16]

The first text from Horatio Greenough's 'American Architecture' (1843) expresses another way of considering form. The adaptation of forms to functions is discussed using the example of ship design, but he also refers to anatomy, skeletons, and organic approaches to form as developmental. The next text, David R. Hay's, *The Natural Principles and Analogy of the Harmony of Form* (1842) also considers principles of form founded upon nature. He argues that science helps to understand form, using examples of music and colour as a harmonic set of relations.

Lucy Crane's text on *Art and The Formation of Taste* (1882) considers the role of materials, place, and use in relation to form and returns to the concept of a 'normal' form for particular objects. While in Henri Mayeux's, 'Decorative Art Composition' (1889), he argues that composition as form is the basis of use, citing ancient Greek examples. The fourth text by Hugh Stannus, 'Some Principles of Form-Design in Applied Art' (1898), is an essay on the relation between fitness, variety, proportion, material, and construction, as well as form in relation to human bodies.

Material

For some, the idea that materials have a particular nature that meant that the way they were worked and how they would look was peculiar to them. This seemed to suggest that the form and decoration would follow naturally. Of course, these dogmatic assertions ignore the skills of makers, as well as some delight that was found in using material imaginatively. Indeed, there was much pleasure in using one material in imitation of another, either as a curiosity or as economic imperative.

The application of 'meaning' to an object by the imitation of particular materials was part of the process of signalling refinement in homes. The ability of the machine to print wallpaper, produce marbled linoleum and plated metal, and myriad other copies or imitations was of huge significance to the nineteenth century. These ideas of imitation connect with the idea that it was not the actual process of manufacture that was important to the consumer, but the ability of the object to 'stand for' a particular form of production, even though it may be derived from another completely different one.

One of the main ideas about materials was that their use in relation to design should somehow reflect the concept of 'truth to materials'. For Pugin for example, 'All plaster, cast-iron, and composition ornaments, painted like stone or oak, are mere impositions, and, although very suitable to a tea-garden, are utterly unworthy of a sacred edifice'.[17]

In 1852, Matthew Wyatt took this further and argued that using inappropriate materials was in contravention of the principles of good taste.

> In acknowledging, the correctness of the undeniable proposition, that every material, insomuch as it differs in organic constitution, should vary correspondingly in the form and proportion into which it should be wrought, an admission was made, that the ordinary system of copying in metal forms proper for stone, and in stone forms proper for metal, wood, etc., was as contrary to the true canons of good taste, as it was subversive of any prospect of consistent originality.[18]

John Ruskin took the ideas still further and associated moral values with Gothic styles, in particular, the maxims of 'truth to materials' and 'honesty of construction'. These ideals were highly influential on the later Arts and Crafts movement.

An interesting comparison can be made between these ideas and those of the German theorist Gottfried Semper. For Semper, it was not the properties inherent in the material and the technique but the human judgement and ingenuity that determine artistic forms. He introduces the idea of Stoffwechsel (material metamorphosis) to transgress material boundaries. He ignored the ordering of artefacts by their material but considers them in the light of his four proposed elements of architecture (design): (a) hearth = metallurgy, ceramics; (b) roof = carpentry; (c) enclosure = textile and weaving; and (d) the mound = earthworks.

The three selected texts refer directly to the issue of imitations in popular materials. The first is Emil Braun's 'Electrotyping Applied to Art Manufactures' (1850), that considers the practice of electrotyping and mechanical reproduction. The second, George Dodd's 'Papier mâché', in his *Curiosities of Industry* (1858), uses a very popular material as an example of new materials and their design pitfalls; while the third text, which is anonymous, considers 'Design in Relation to Material' (1869), through an analysis of stone, wood, metal and plaster, again making a plea for honesty in their use.

Manufacturing Methods

The great debate over the development of factories and the subsequent division of labour, the nature of handwork and the role of machines, ran through most of the century. For some, the changes reflected progress and development. Charles Babbage saw a progressive expansion in manufacturing technologies and methods. This evolutionary model links to other contemporary thoughts like Darwinism.

The first text in this section is from Adam Smith who proclaimed that the division of labour was an important development that helped to create wealth. The example given is of a simple workman's coat, that requires numerous contributors to complete the work. Alternatively, and in a differing vein, William Cooke-Taylor's 'The Mutual Interests of Artists and Manufacturers', (1848), analysed the important links between artist and manufacturer, which he saw as akin to the alliance between an author and publisher.

James Ward, in his *The World in Its Workshops* (1851), considers the Great Exhibition as a display of a metaphoric battle between nations and economies in which design plays an important part. The fourth text, Joseph Whitworth, and George Wallis's report on *The Industry of the United States in Machinery, Manufactures, and Useful and Ornamental Arts* (1854), offers a comparative analysis of the industries of the United States and Great Britain, with particular discussion around the division of labour, machinery usage, and the role of design patents.

In 1892, Walter Crane argued for different classes of art – industrial, decorative, applied and fine, but the hierarchy changed so that now useful objects were at the peak, with the machine developing work under the artistic designer. He explained in *Claims of Decorative Art*:

> We have "industrial," "decorative," or "applied" art, as we now call it, and "fine" art — fine art and "the arts not fine," as my friend Mr. Lewis Day has it. . . . Nor is this altogether wonderful, considering how, under our system of wholesale machine production, the appliances of common life have lost their individuality, interest, and meaning, together with their beauty.'[19]

Of course, linking with Crane's idea above were those of William Morris. In his text 'The Revival of Handicraft' (1902), the conflict between machinery versus handicraft was discussed within the context of a wider argument for dramatic changes in society.

However, division of labour never went away and was re-visited by Frederick W. Taylor, in his *Scientific Management* (1911). In this last text, Taylor argues that these ideas had the same goals of efficiency that would benefit all but were to be achieved in different ways.

Craft Machine and Design

In a long article titled the 'Philosophy of Architecture', *The Artizan* concluded their discussion by mentioning operative arts and their role: 'It is with the artizans that art has ever originated: it was born in the workshops of Athens, and resuscitated in the workshops of Italy; and if it be destined to experience another renovation, it will be in the workshop, we are confident, where the revival will take place'.[20] The texts in this section look at the issues arising from the nature of the interactions between crafts, designs, and machines.

The first text from Charles R. Ashbee's, 'Decorative Art from a Workshop Point of View' (1889), considers the social influence on art and design. It amusingly compared the role of workshop versus studio, arguing that the workshop is most important as the basis for a community of co-operation. John Dando Sedding's short article 'Design' in *Arts and Crafts Essays* (1893), takes the example of the craft of needlework and makes a comparison with historical work and the use of nature in contemporary work. In Fred Miller's chapter 'Design and Craftsmanship' in his *The Training of a Craftsman,* (1898), he revives a recurring theme that argues that the artist, designer, and craftsperson are all in one, but the nature of the material will reflect particular choices.

Discussing fine book printing and binding, Thorstein Veblen's text suggests that, as in the parallel case of the apparent superiority of hand-wrought articles over machine products, intrinsic excellence is imputed to costlier and more awkward articles. Veblen's argument is that machine-made products are often better in matters of utility than are the hand-made goods. He discusses the code of marks reflecting status and taste that certain crafts provide in terms of honorific value.

In a more practical manner Esther Woods's, article on the 'Home Arts and Industries Exhibition' (1899), discusses the exhibits and introduces the many small school craft classes, with critiques that remind us of the interest in arts, crafts, and design at a local and regional level.

The arts and crafts theme is continued by Oscar Lovell Triggs's *History of the Arts and Crafts Movement,* (1902) which is a eulogy of the values of the Arts and Crafts movement and the role of co-operation. Finally craft, and especially the work of William Morris is discussed in J. Scarratt Rigby's 'Remarks on Morris Work and its Influence on British Decorative Arts Today', (1902) which is supportive though not wholly hagiographic analysis of Morris work and contribution to the crafts.

Notes

1 'Transactions of the Society of Arts 1846–7' discussed in *The Artizan: A Monthly Journal of the Operative Arts*, 3, 1848, p. 64.
2 *Catalogue of the First Exhibition of the Art-Manufacture Association: In the National Galleries, Edinburgh* (Edinburgh: Printed by Thomas Constable, 1856), Preface.
3 J. Fergusson, *An Historical Inquiry into the True Principles of Beauty in Art, More Especially with Reference to Architecture* (London: Longmans, 1849), pp. 92–106.
4 C. Babbage, *On the Economy of Machinery and Manufactures* (London: Chas Knight, 1832), p. 208.
5 J. Nasmyth, and S. Smiles, *An Autobiography* (London: James Murray, 1883), p. 125.
6 B. R. Haydon, and T. Taylor, *Life of Benjamin Robert Haydon, Historical Painter, from His Autobiography and Journals*, Vol. 3 (London: Longman, Brown, Green, 1853), p. 66. Poulett Thompson was the Committee chair.
7 Cited in S. Macdonald, *The History and Philosophy of Art Education* (London: University of London Press, 1970), p. 84. See also F. W. Haydon. *Correspondence and Table-Talk* (Boston: Estes, 1877), p. 243.
8 Review of W. Burges, 'Art Applied to Industry', *Athenaeum*, July 1865, p. 88.
9 J. D. Sedding, "On the relation of Architecture and the Handicrafts" read at the General Conference of Architects 3 May 1887. Reprinted in *American Architect and Building News*, 21, 25 June 1887, p. 311.
10 Sir J. Reynolds, *First Discourse on Art*, Opening of the Royal Academy, January 1769.
11 *Report of the Select Committee on Arts*, 1836, p. 6.
12 *The People's Journal*, 3, 1847, p. 231.
13 F. W. Fairholt, 'Grotesque Design', *Art Journal*, March 1862, pp. 89–92.
14 'Colour-Training and Colour Museums', I. *Art Journal*, November 1908, pp. 328–331 and 357–360. The idea for a museum had the support of artists, including Edward Burne-Jones, G. F. Watts and Walter Crane.
15 M. D. Wyatt, *An Attempt to Define the Principles Which Should Determine Form in the Decorative Arts* (Lectures on the results of the Great Exhibition, second series, 19, London: D. Bogue, 1852), p. 417.
16 A. W. N. Pugin, *The True Principles of Pointed or Christian Architecture* (London: T. Weale, 1841), p. 1.
17 Pugin, p. 45.
18 M. D. Wyatt, *Metal-work and Its Artistic Design. Dedicated, by Express Permission, to the Right Hon. Henry Labouchere* (London: Day & Son, 1852), Preface.
19 W. Crane, *The Claims of Art* (London: Lawrence and Bullen, 1892), p. 109.
20 'Philosophy of Architecture', *The Artizan*, IV, 30 April 1844, p. 81.

Part 1

ART INDUSTRIES AND MANUFACTURES

1
'FURTHER REMARKS ON THE REPORT OF THE COMMITTEE ON THE ARTS AND PRINCIPLES OF DESIGN'

A Select Committee was appointed in 1835 to 'inquire into the best means of extending knowledge of the Arts and of the Principles of Design among the people (especially the Manufacturing Population) of the country; also to inquire into the Constitution, Management and Effects of Institutions connected with the Arts'. The Committee published their report in 1836, which had as a main conclusion 'that, from the highest branches of poetical design down to the lowest connexion between design and manufactures, the Arts have received little encouragement in this country'.[1] The Committee reported on several aspects of design, including the lack of instruction (and Schools of Design); the contrast with French practices; the role of museums, galleries and academies; the issues of copyright; and the commissioning of works. Many of these considerations were to affect the artisans and mechanics of the time.

This article was an excoriating critique of the 1836 Select Committee's report, particularly in relation to the apparent ignoring of British superiority and efficiency in many areas of art and design. The article sifts through the report and uses some of the evidence produced to try and counter many of the seemingly unfavourable comments about British workers and their efforts, especially when used in comparison to foreign work and workers.

There was probably an element of 'playing to the audience' of the journal. *The Mechanics Magazine* was a weekly periodical founded in 1823 and edited by Joseph Clinton Robertson, who also wrote under the pseudonym of Sholto Percy. Aimed at the working man, the object of the publication 'was one of entire novelty, and no inconsiderable importance'. It was aimed at that "numerous and valuable portion of the community, including all who are manually employed in our different trades and manufactures," who felt the want of 'a periodical work, which, at a price suited to their humble means, would diffuse among them a better acquaintance with the history and principles of the arts they practise, convey to them earlier information than they had hitherto been able to procure of new discoveries, inventions, and improvements, and attend generally to their peculiar interests as affected by passing events'.[2]

'Further Remarks on the Report of the Committee on the Arts and Principles of Design', *Mechanics' Magazine*, 704, 4 February 1837, pp. 323–329

Sir,- In a former communication (No. 696, p. 187),[3] I ventured the remark, in reference to the Parliamentary Report on the Arts in Connexion with Manufacture, that "the Committee seemed to have entirely lost their memory as to any fact creditable to the talents of their countrymen"—following up the observation with a few pretty striking proofs of the fact. On looking over the evidence on which the Report *ought*, at least, to have been founded, proofs of the same nature are to be found at every step "as plenty as blackberries"—so plentifully, indeed, that it becomes in some sort an amusement to detect the shifts to which the writer of the Report has been continually put, in contriving to omit all mention of British proficiency, and more especially of British superiority, and forcing forward every iota of testimony in favour of foreign pre-eminence, in order to justify the monstrous conclusion that the fine arts in England are in the lowest conceivable state of degradation, and particularly that the arts of design in connexion with manufacture, present, to use Milton's phrase, "in the lowest deep a lower deep." The leading members of this illustrious Committee were evidently "all agog" to convict the artisans of England of every possible species of bad taste; and several at least of the witnesses seconded, with might and main, their patriotic endeavours. And with all this note of preparation, what does their bill of indictment amount to at last? Why, truly, its counts, after all, are so miserably few, and, few as they are, so many of them will not "hold water," as the lawyers have it, that the defendants may well think it hardly worth while to plead to them at the bar of public opinion. In fact, when the matter comes to be investigated, the *evidence* on which the prosecutors rely either flies so directly in their faces, or with a little sifting breaks down so completely, as to put them out of court at once and for ever, with "not a leg to stand upon!"

"The want of instruction experienced by our workmen in the arts," observe the Committee, "is strongly adverted to by many witnesses. This deficiency is said to be particularly manifest in that branch of our industry which is commonly called the fancy trade; more especially in the silk trade; and most of all, probably, in the ribbon manufacture. Mr. Martin (the celebrated painter)[4] complains of the want of correct design in the china trade; Mr. Papworth (an eminent architect),[5] of its absence in the interior decorative architecture of our houses, and in furniture. *Hence* the adoption of the designs of the era of Louis XV. (commonly dignified with the name of Louis XIV.), a style inferior in taste, and easy of execution. To a similar want of enlightened information in art, Mr. Cockerell[6] attributes the prevailing fashion for what is called Elizabethan architecture; a style which (whatever may be the occasional excellencies of its execution) is undoubtedly of spurious origin."

And this is the sum and substance of the Committee's charges, a true copy of the whole bill of indictment! Well may we exclaim, "Is this the mighty ocean, is this *all?*" But it would be in vain to look for more, and, few and frivolous as these charges are, they lay a much greater weight on the shoulders of "our workmen" than they ought to bear. Passing by, for the present, that regarding the silk manufacture, let us look a little into the grounds of the rest.

"China-painting" may be soon disposed of by referring to the evidence. Mr. Martin *did* testify that the art was now in "a very low state;" but, at the same time, he gave a very good reason why it should be so—"when I first came to London, it was *just going out of fashion.*" This at once clears up the mystery; there was no want of "correct design" when correct design was well paid for—"it was their knowledge of drawing, &c. that made Mr. Moss[7] and Mr. Marsh[8] so superior to others; but owing to the decline of china-painting, they were compelled to leave it; and it has since entirely gone to the ground." So that it was no fault of "our work-men" that china-painting declined, but of their patrons; it "went out of fashion," and, being out, the inducement to attain excellence in its practice, or even for those who *had* attained it to continue in it, was gone. And "workmen" might as well be blamed for their want of skill in boring wooden water-pipes as in this insignificant branch of the fine arts—always supposing Mr. Martin's evidence to be undeniably correct. But Mr. Martin's evidence was by no means all that came before the Committee on the subject, although no other is alluded to in the Report. "Why? Because it was favourable to the British artisan! The Committee were so anxious to express their sorrow at the comparisons which the witnesses "too frequently, *if not uniformly*, felt themselves compelled to draw" to the advantage of "our foreign rivals," that they could not find room for the slightest notice of the evidence of Mr. Batt, of the bronze and porcelain department at Howell and James's[9] to the effect, that "in some branches of the porcelain manufacture the French are superior to us in design, in others *inferior*. In that description of porcelain which is of the same nature as the old Dresden china, ornamented with raised flowers, *we are vastly superior to them*, and a considerable quantity of such porcelain is, I believe, annually exported to Paris, and considered by the French *superior to their own.*" As a matter of course, also, while they devote a paragraph to the praise of the French, even for "their close study of the living flower," they are mute as to the evidence of Mr. Factory-Inspector Howell,[10] who found "our workmen" at Worcester painting flowers on china from nature. To suppose, for a moment, that they should deign to notice the same gentleman's testimony as to the attendance of the Worcester china-painters on the lectures of Mr. Constable, the R.A., would be ridiculous; and equally so to imagine that they should chronicle the unsavoury information (from the same quarter), that " there is an impression that the manufacture at Worcester is improving," and that he saw "a very beautiful service making for the Pacha of Egypt." Evidence of improvement is only admissible when it refers to our foreign rivals.

Now for Mr. Papworth, a gentleman of no great eminence in his profession at home, but who became a first-rater in Germany, when the King of Wirtemberg sent from the immediate neighbourhood of "the classic country of the arts" to find an architect capable of building him a palace, and could find none nearer than that abode of dullness, England! We need only turn to his evidence, to perceive at once that the Committee have grossly misrepresented its purport, and to find, that so far from attributing the prevalent defects in art to "our work-men," he lays the fault at the door of that Legislature of which the Committee formed an unworthy fraction. "I think," he observes, "the defects in art, as applied to manufactures, chiefly arise from the want of (not instruction, but) *protection*, because *there are a great number of clever artists in this country* who would occasionally (were their works protected) model a tablet, a frieze, or some other *work of art*, and would cast and sell the work in such numbers as would produce remuneration to the artist." Not a word have we here to bear out the charge of the Committee— but plenty to invalidate it, and that, too, be it remembered, from the mouth of one of the witnesses specially put forward to bolster up their cause. It is just the same with the next count:—"*Hence*," say the Committee (i. e. from the "want of instruction experienced by our work-men") "hence the adoption of the designs of the era of Louis XV." But what says the evidence of Mr. Papworth to which they refer? "The *absence of protection* has induced manufacturers to seek a style of ornament capable of being executed with facility by workmen unpossessed of theoretical knowledge, and without practical accuracy. This style has been fostered to a great extent, and erroneously termed that of Louis XIV." &c. &c. &c. Can anything be more conclusive than this? Is anything more wanting, after a comparison of the conclusions of the Committee, as in this instance, with the very evidence from which they profess to be drawn, to show in all its deformity the anti-national *animus* which must have actuated the getters-up of the concern ? That charge must, indeed, be a rotten one, the evidence in whose favour is quite sufficient to prove it without foundation; and desperate, indeed, must be the condition of those who are reduced to the barefaced juggle of adducing, in proof of their "want of instruction" theory, the testimony of a gentleman who, like Mr. Papworth, distinctly traces the evil to so thoroughly different a cause as the "want of protection," and who, moreover, far from joining in the hue and cry against native talent in the arts, repeatedly bears witness not only to its existence, but its excellence!

The next burden "our workmen" have to bear is a heavy one. "*To a similar want of enlightened information in art,* Mr. Cockerell attributes the prevailing fashion for what is called Elizabethan architecture." Indeed then the natural inference to draw would be, that Mr. Cockerell had made a very ridiculous assertion, and, even if he had made it, it argues a considerable capacity of swallow on the part of the Committee that they could entertain, for a moment, so preposterous an idea as that the prevalence of the Elizabethan, or any other style of architecture, is to be attributed to the "want of enlightened information upon art" among "our workmen" !!! Whether Mr. Cockerell or the Committee originated the notion is of no consequence—it was most probably the latter —and the worthy architect perhaps little thought, when he was aiming a side-blow at the "want of enlightened information in art" displayed by the Houses of Lords and Commons in adopting the Elizabethan style for the new Hall of Legislature, that it would be turned against a body which usually has so little occasion to dabble in architecture as the working mechanics of the country. Whoever has to answer for the absurdity, "our workmen" require little to be said to defend them from *this* charge. The Elizabethan style is for the moment popular, and, of course, most of the architects of the day, and their patrons, think it ought to be so. Mr. Cockerell thinks otherwise, and the Committee appear to adopt his conclusion.* But what has all this to do with the "want of information" among "our workmen?" The only persons in fault (if there be any) are clearly the patrons of architecture and its most eminent professors, with, at the head and front of all, Mr. Barry and the two Houses of Parliament. Let them look to it, and leave "our workmen" to answer for their own imputed offences against good taste as best they may, without being called upon to take upon them the sins of their superiors.

With regard to the "fancy-trade, and especially the silk manufacture," we are not referred by the Committee to the evidence of any particular witness, although this is undoubtedly their "great gun." It may be admitted, that our silk-weavers are not so forward in the race as many of our other manufacturers, but, at the same time, any Committee but such a one as this might have discovered plenty of indications in the facts which came before them, that the march of improvement has begun to be extremely rapid in this branch as well as others, and that "our workmen" in the silk line promise ere long to give their foreign rivals the go-by,—of which more anon. But why did this most candid of Committees omit to notice those branches of the fancy-trade in which British superiority is most decided,—why include all in one sweeping clause, without a particle of reservation, when scarcely a single witness was examined before them who did not make mention of some proof of British skill, aye, in those very "Arts of Design" most in connexion with manufacture? Why leave out the very name of iron-casting, in which we excel all our competitors so transcendently?—a line of art-manufacture far exceeding in extent and importance, as well, as mechanico-artistical ingenuity, ten thousand such petty trades as China painting. Nay, why, if they can find room to particularise the exertions of an individual Frenchman to bring to perfection the Cashmere shawl, can they not do as much to celebrate the efforts of Mr. Smith,[11] the very first witness they examined, to apply a higher order of fine art than usual to fenders and stove-fronts? Why could they not (always bearing in mind their

---

* The reasons advanced (according to the Committee) by Messrs. Papworth and Cockerell for their respective condemnations of the styles of Louis XIV. and Elizabeth are worthy of notice. The former, we are told, is not only "inferior in taste," but "easy of execution." Wherin consists the force of this latter objection? Would the Committee recommend the purchase for the National Gallery of the works of Cornelius Ketel, who painted, not with a pencil, but with his great toe? Surely, the usual method, that pursued by Raphael and Titian, must have been quite "easy" in comparison! Mr. Cockerell's objection to Elizabethan architecture is more formidable: it is, says he, of "spurious origin"—that is, we suppose, its parts have been invented at different periods. Mr. Cockerell is of that class of architects who would pull down St. Paul's. Why? Because it is not in the pure Grecian style; the Greeks were ignorant of the principle of the arch, and therefore (a very good reason) never introduced a dome!

anxiety to record instances of individual ingenuity *among the French*,) leave upon record that these productions were so beautiful as to call forth the admiration of Sir Francis Chantrey,[12] or the more important fact that, among the artisans of Sheffield (who share with their neighbours the stigma of knowing nothing of art) "there are several artists capable of producing such models as those," which excited the admiration of our great sculptor, and *which were produced* in proof of the skill of "our workmen' *before the Committee*? But it would be endless to enumerate all their omissions of this kind, although it may be worth while to note one of the most glaring. Among a Committee charged with such an investigation as theirs, it might certainly be expected that some persons would be found who had heard of the superior excellence of British pottery, both in its merely useful and in its artistical relations;—yet in no corner of the Report do we find a word about "Wedgwood ware," and this, notwithstanding Mr. Martin, whose testimony the Committee bring forth with so much parade when he condemns our productions in China-painting, had pronounced the articles of that ware to be "beautiful works of art," and notwithstanding another witness had duly informed the Committee that "Mr. Wedgwood improved the forms of pottery, and diffused them more than any other person." Had he and his work-people been Frenchmen, we should have heard enough of the obligations the world lay under to him and them for the wider diffusion of art. Wanting that requisite, they are treated with silent contempt; the most extraordinary instance on record of a manufacture rising up within the memory of man, and in the heart of England, and diffusing classic grace of form in every habitation of the land (and not only our land but others), from the palace to the cottage, is passed by without a syllable of notice by a Committee sitting for the special purpose of tracing *the progress of the arts of design in connexion with manufactures in this country*! Why?—because all this did not take place *abroad*. Mr. Cockerell could be quoted in proof of the charge that "our workmen" are guilty of bringing into vogue the Elizabethan style of building, but nothing is heard of his whereabout when he is so injudicious as to observe, "I have found Wedgwood's works esteemed in all parts of Europe, and placed in the most precious collections of this description of works." So inconvenient a fact must have gone horribly against the grain.

Instances of point-blank contradiction, in the evidence of the witnesses, to the *very incorrect* statement of the Committee (or their reporter), as to the "too frequent, *if not uniform*" occurrence of a comparison disadvantageous to native talent, in the matter of design, in said evidence, are "too numerous to mention." A few may suffice. Mr. Smith is asked, with reference to his branch (iron ornaments), "Do you think the foreign models are superior, or inferior to the English?" And he replies (with a small degree, indeed, of "uniformity"), "In this branch of manufacture I think they are *inferior*." Mr. James, the eminent mercer, testifies to a very considerable improvement in the colours and patterns of the silk manufacture, and that "the importation of French silks has almost ceased in consequence of this improvement." Mr. Harrison observes particularly, that "there is *no want of talent* (for design) in the country, because there are a great many persons *engaged* *exclusively in the production of designs* for printed cottons, challis, and bandanas,"—but who are not *yet* so conversant with the figuring of silk. The evidence of Mr. Batt, as to the superiority of British porcelain, at least in some departments, has been already adverted to: he concedes very freely to the French the superiority of design in metallic manufactures "with a few exceptions," which make sad havoc with the Committee's "uniformity," as they include no less than the whole of "the manufactures in silver, gold, jewellery, and castings in iron, in which," Mr. Batt thinks, "we *excel* them in design." Mr. C. H. Smith,[13] architectural sculptor, deposes that "the public demand for architectural ornaments increases and that the workmen have gradually improved,—that he has no *difficulty* in finding useful assistants, providing he can afford to give them a fair remuneration." Mr. Samuel Wiley,[14] of the firm of Jennings and Betteridge, of Birmingham, adduces facts so important, and so strictly bearing on the question, that the omission of any allusion to them in the Report, taken in conjunction with the sweeping condemnation of English talent in design, and the succeeding paragraph as to the exceeding abilities of the French workmen in that particular, is rather extraordinary even for our Committee. He says, that the firm to which he belongs "have made great improvements in the japan trade of late years. Being men of taste, and stimulating their apprentices and teaching them the art of drawing, our men have inserted works of art in the Birmingham exhibition* and other places. * * * * * Every workman designs his own pattern. A good designer is well encouraged—he is a most valuable man. *The French prefer our articles,* because they are much better in material, workmanship, and design, in character, beauty, and everything. They do not seem to raise the japan-trade to an art; they appear merely to daub it over, and call it japan; there is neither design nor beauty of execution in French work. * * * Our workmen generally come at twelve or fourteen years of age. We teach them first of all *drawing and designing*, and then manufacturing." A pretty specimen this, of that uniform testimony borne by the witnesses to the fact of English inferiority in the arts of design which the Committee so fervently lament! After this, to cite more instances would be an useless task:—anything more complete, more thoroughly condemnatory, more satisfying as to the Committee's *animus* could hardly be expected.

Another proof of the foreign bias of the Committee might be drawn, if it were required, from the simple fact, that the only witnesses who were subjected to what may be termed a cross-examination, were precisely those who had the temerity to express an opinion in favour of our native workmen, amongst whom the editor of the *Mechanics' Magazine* came in for the greatest share, although his cross-examiners certainly "took nothing by their motion." It is impossible to read without

---

* Mr. Wiley might have mentioned that the late eminent R. A., Mr. Bird, whose pictures of Chevy-Chace, and Illustrations of the Bible, elicited such high admiration, was originally a painter of tea-trays at Birmingham. It was mentioned to the Committee that Flaxman, the sculptor, and Mr. Wyon, of the Mint, were brought up at Soho.

amusement the answers returned by this witness to some of the *puzzling* questions propounded by the wiseacres of the Committee,—to observe without a smile the manner in which he makes his replies *tell* to the confusion of his pragmatical questioners. For instance, when some M.P. is determined to make it appear that the public call for none but the most classical of designs, while the workmen persist in thrusting inferior designs down their throats, sorely against their will, how completely is he put down by the quiet observation, "there is a pattern which was a long time in very general use for table-service, called 'the willow pattern '—*there is nothing very classical in that!*" Again, how pleasantly are the Committee rebuked for their disposition, to run down our home-bred taste to the exaltation of every nation "on the Continent," by the remark that "very much of the bad taste of this country has been owing to the circulation of wretched prints all over the country, and still more wretched stucco-images," and that "this inundation of execrable taste has not proceeded from native artists, *but from Italians!*" Oh! for a Cruikshank[15] to have sketched the elongated physiognomy of the Honourable Member at this truly home-blow! Shocking, indeed, it must have been to the feelings of the whole Committee to be reminded thus unceremoniously that the public taste is now too improved to put up with the trash these foreigners were guilty of perpetrating, but required something far superior, in the shape of casts from the works of Chantrey, an English professor of the "highest branches of poetical design," and of Thom,[16] one of the very class of mechanics whose inferiority in the arts of design is so deeply to be deplored!

A good sifting cross-examination might have been employed to better effect in a far different quarter. Mr. Donaldson,[17] the architect, gave a first-rate opening for any member of the Committee—had there been any, with a British feeling, to "show up" the true value of his evidence. This gentleman, by way of illustrating his position as to the cheapness of art in France, instanced his own work on doorways, the plates to which would have cost him four guineas each in England, whereas he "sent his drawings to Paris, and had estimates from four French engravers, put the work into the hands of the best of these,—*a man who is second to none in Europe in his art*,—paid the expense of the carriage of the plates to England, the duty of 30 per cent., and various incidental expenses, and the whole cost did not exceed two guineas! Now it appears that Mr. Donaldson had just before introduced to the Committee the "*Vorbilder fur Fabrikanter und Handwerker*,"[18] of which we hear so much in their Report. What, then, if our imaginary cross-examiner, after a due time spent in admiration of the most elaborate of all the plates, had begged of Mr. Donaldson to give him the name of the engraver. Would he not have felt a little embarrassed as he answered "WILSON LOWRY?"[19] Suppose the same process repeated with a second, a third, a fourth, the masterpieces of the whole work—would Mr. Donaldson have been able to suppress a blush as he stammered forth the names of TURRELL,[20] ROFFE,[21] and MOSES,[22] all well known as first-rate *English* engravers? Terribly would he have been perplexed as the annoying questions poured in upon him. How was it that Professor Benth[23] entrusted none of his elaborate embellishments to the

Frenchman, "who is second to none in Europe in his art?" How came he to pass him by, with all his cheapness, and send his work to the high-priced English engravers, paying to boot "the expense of the carriage of the plates to Germany, the duty, and the various incidental expenses connected with their being executed in London and transmitted to Germany?" Simply, of course, because Mr. Donaldson's Parisian engraver could not come nigh our countrymen in the practice of the highest branches of the art. Mr. Donaldson's doorway plates may have been done cheaply, but they can hardly have been done well,—as well as they would have been here. To suppose otherwise, is to suppose Professor Benth a natural-born fool and the Prussian government a sad waster of its cash. Nor can the Germans in general be much wiser than the Professor, for with them a book *"mit Englischen stablistichen"*[24] is considered a very superior affair. The Russians, too, must be a stupid set, when they send to "dear old England " if they want a first-rate embellishment, instead of putting in requisition the talents of the half-price Frenchman, "who is second to none in Europe in his art." But what are we to say to the French themselves, who, in spite of their possessing this cheap first-rate, –" second to none in Europe in his art," not only invite English second-rate engravers to Paris (who there suddenly find themselves promoted to the front rank of the profession), but actually encounter the higher charges of our artists, and all the expensive *etcetera*, whenever they wish to bring out a book or a print *in the very first style of art*. It is so notorious that even Mr. Donaldson must have allowed it, had it been put home to him, that any Parisian engraving of unusual excellence will be found, on examination, to have an English name in the corner.

This letter has already extended to so great a length, that, for fear of trespassing too long on your and your readers' patience, I hasten to conclude by subscribing myself,

Sir, yours most respectfully, H.
London, Jan. 17, 1837.

Notes

1 *Report from the Select Committee on Arts and their Connexion with Manufactures, with Minutes of Evidence, Appendix and Index*, House of Commons Papers, 1836, p. iii.
2 *Mechanics Magazine*, 1, 21, 1825, Preface.
3 "Remarks on the Report of the Committee on the Arts and principles of Design" *Mechanics' Magazine*, 696, December 1836, pp.187–9.
4 John Martin (1789–1854), an English Romantic painter.
5 John Buonarotti Papworth (1775–1847), architect.
6 Charles Robert Cockerell RA (1788–1863), Architect.
7 Mr Charles Muss (1779–1824), china painter- a friend of Martin.
8 William Marsh (1805- ?), china painter at Worcester.
9 Howell James & Company was a firm of jewellers and silversmiths located in Regent Street, London (1819–1911).
10 T. Jones Howell, barrister and factory inspector.
11 John Jobson Smith, (1809–1878), Sheffield ironmaster.
12 Sir Francis Chantrey RA (7 1781–1841), English sculptor.
13 C. H. Smith, architectural sculptor?

14 Samuel Wiley worked for the papier-mâché manufacturing firm Jennens and Bettridge of Wolverhampton.
15 George Cruikshank (1792–1878), a British caricaturist.
16 Robert Thom (1774–1847), a Scottish civil engineer.
17 Thomas Leverton Donaldson (1795–1885), an architect.
18 *Vorbilder fur Fabrikanter und Handwerker*, [Examples for Manufacturers and Craftsmen] Patterns and design books published in Berlin between 1821(?) and 1837. Predominantly historic shapes and patterns, the images were intended to support the trade schools and producers of Prussia.
19 Wilson Lowry FRS (1762–1824), an English engraver.
20 Edmund Turrell (1781–1835), English engraver.
21 John Roffe (1769–1850), English engraver.
22 Henry Moses (1781–1870), English engraver.
23 Professor Benth [actually Beuth]: Christian Peter Beuth (1781–1853), a Prussian statesman, responsible for the establishment of an Industrial Institute (Gewerbeinstitut) in Berlin, Compiler with K-F Schinkel of the *Vorbilder fur Fabrikanter und Handwerker*.
24 *mit Englischen stablistichen:* with English engravings.

2

W. S. W., 'ART APPLIED TO MANUFACTURES'

The *Art Union,* first published in 1839, initially intended 'to supply to artists accurate and useful information upon all subjects in which they are interested, and to the public the means of justly ascertaining and estimating the progress of art both at home and abroad'.[1] Although it did report on a few issues associated with design in the early years, by 1842 they were increasingly interested in the decorative, as well as the fine arts. The editor S. C. Hall rather self-importantly explained in his memoirs: 'It is my duty to give details of the circumstances under which, in the *Art Journal*, I brought art into association with art-manufacture. Such association was commenced in the year 1842'.[2]

In that year, they published a set of three articles on the topic of the arts applied to manufacture. They explained in the first article that 'in commencing this series of papers, a brief statement of their scope and plan may be desirable. Our aim is to awaken the attention of all who take an interest in the promotion of the Useful, as well as the Fine Arts, to the importance of studying the beautiful, both in form and colour; to exemplify the true principles of beauty in relation to common things, no less than to the rarest products of ingenuity; and to point out the right way of developing, by educational means, those perceptions of elegance and fitness which are known by the name of taste'.[3]

The first article in this series by W.S.W. was titled 'Connexion of Beauty and Utility – Use and Progress of Schools of Design' [this article]; the second was 'Education of The Artisan — Study of Form and Proportion-Methods of Teaching Drawing — Drawing Classes at Exeter Hall';[4] and the third was 'Instruction in The Art of Design — Study of The Human Figure—Dupuis' Models'.[5]

This article looks at the issues around beauty, utility, and principles of design, three matters that exercised numerous reformers during the period, as well as the role and operation of schools of design. The article ends with a copy of the Prospectus of the School of Design at Somerset House, along with a copy of a letter and a set of questions sent out to provincial cities with a view to ascribing grants for the establishment of branch schools at these locations.

Incidentally, the reply to this request from Dublin is of interest. The Secretary of the Royal Dublin Society replied saying 'I beg leave to state, that for fourscore years past and more, Public Schools of Design have been in constant and active operation in this city, under the auspices of our Society. 'The schools are four in number, each one being under its respective master: "1. For the study of the human figure". "2. For architecture and plan drawing". "3. For general ornaments, as applicable to decorations, carvings, stucco work, patterns for manufactures, &c. &c". "4. For modelling in clay."'[6] The instruction was free, and it was often the case that the apprentices' indentures stipulated a period of time for study at this institution.

W. S. W., 'Art Applied to Manufactures', *The Art-Union*, 4, 37, February 1842, pp. 23–25

NO. 1.—Connexion of Beauty and Utility—Uses and Progress of Schools of Design

In commencing this series of papers, a brief statement of their scope and plan may be desirable. Our aim is to awaken the attention of all who take an interest in the promotion of the Useful, as well as the Fine, Arts, to the importance of studying the beautiful, both in form and colour; to exemplify the true principles of beauty in relation to common things, no less than to the rarest products of ingenuity; and to point out the right way of developing, by educational means, those perceptions of elegance and fitness which are known by the name of taste. With a view to accomplish this end, we shall arrange the subject under two divisions: the first, and principal one, being devoted to an exposition of the general principles that govern the art of design, as applied to useful and ornamental purposes; the uses of Schools of Design, and the direction and nature of the instruction they should afford. In the second and subordinate division, we propose to record the proceedings of these Institutions; and especially to report the progress of the Central School of Design, recently established by Government at Somerset House, under the direction of Mr. W. Dyce. In this latter branch of the subject we shall be indebted for our information to the able and zealous director of the school; but the writer, in his capacity of reporter, will assume the privilege of commenting upon the plans and results of instruction, in the frank and kindly spirit of friendliness, as a fellow labourer in the field of popular education in Art.

The pleasure derived from the contemplation of beautiful objects is an inborn desire, the gratification of which is as much a want of our common nature as the grosser necessities of daily existence. It was implanted in us by the Divine Creator, for the beneficent purpose of gladdening and refining the exercise of our senses. Every object in nature ministers to it, and its enjoyment is as exquisite as it is blameless and beneficial: it is an appetite that knows neither surfeit nor vicious excess; and its indulgence, to use the expressive terms of the Latin poet, "softens the manners, and suffers not men to be brutal." In our pursuit of the means of delighting this fine sense, the most intellectual of all, we are apt to look too exclusively to the gifted sons of genius, the poets, artists, and musicians, as the sources whence ideal images of grace and loveliness are diffused around, overlooking the numberless beauties that exist in the wondrous realities of creation, and the humbler class of artificial objects where elegance is subservient to utility. The commonest jug, if it be of a pleasing shape, is gratifying to the cultivated taste; and to make it of a comely form costs no more than if it were ugly, while in that case it is not merely an indifferent but a disagreeable object: the cheapest cotton print may present an harmonious mixture of colours, that shall cause it to be preferred to the most costly satin of ill-assorted hues. We are all of us more or less sensible to such impressions, though often unconsciously; and if these sensations be slight and transient they are also frequent, and not the less real for being unrecognised. Indeed the character of the material objects by which we are surrounded, influences the mind and disposition through the outward senses; so that the beautiful exerts a moral as well as an intellectual sway over mankind: we need go no further than this general remark, that the most cheerful and happy people delight in ornament and gay colours, to prove the efficacy of ocular perceptions on human character. There is a numerous and active class of persons, who with objects of daily use, that are either agreeable to the eye, or the reverse: these are the artisans, or skilled craftsmen, the designers of the shapes and patterns of dresses, furniture, and utensils; they have the power of contributing extensively, if not materially, to our momentary enjoyments; and as purchasers mostly prefer a pretty thing to an ugly one, according to their degree of discrimination, it is the interest of this vast body of producers to please the public: they strive to do so to the best of their ability; but they are not taught how to accomplish their intention effectually. To give them this teaching is the object of Schools of Design; and in this view alone it is an important object. But in a commercial point of view, it is a question that concerns national wealth, the prosperity of our manufacturers, and the feeding and clothing of the working population. Let those who doubt this, ask the shop-keepers who deal in any description of "fancy goods," or the manufacturers who produces them. The want of a scientific knowledge of Art, of education for the eye, of cultivated taste in short, kept the people of this country, from the time when the gloom of Puritanism repressed the national vivacity until the present, in a state of insensibility to the beauties of form, proportion, and colour in common things, and generally speaking in rarer objects; and the plain, dogged, practical understanding of John Bull takes so strong a hold of the tangible idea of utility, that he was prone to regard beauty as a quality not only fanciful and superfluous, but inimical to use, and which at any rate added to the cost of a thing. John left the study of elegance to "foreigners;" and when ornament was wanted he supplied expensive finery; the consequence has been, that foreigners have taken some of John's best customers from him, and he is now forced by the loss of his trade to set up a taste: the breeches-pocket, that most sentient nerve in honest John's organization has been touched; and conviction has reached his brain through this influential channel. As the shortest way of laying in a stock of this (to him) strange article, taste, he has been borrowing from his neighbours; but in so bungling a way that he cannot rival them, and does but increase by his clumsy imitations the demand for the genuine originals: he cannot even copy a beautiful article correctly for want of a knowledge of first principles.

First principles: yes, these are what our countrymen want to know; for this knowledge is essential to enable them to "steal with judgment" from others, much more to invent for themselves. It is not enough to know that the shape of a Grecian vase is beautiful, that the colours of a Persian carpet or an Indian vase are rich and agreeable to the eye; an understanding of what constitutes their peculiar beauties is essential, in order to preserve the character of the original in the imitation: a still more scientific acquaintance with their characteristics is requisite to adapt their fine qualities to other purposes, or to vary the application of the main principles on which they are designed; for a very slight deviation may vitiate the reproduction. It is not uncommon to see the characteristic feature of a beautiful vase ignorantly exaggerated into deformity by way of improvement; and pattern specimens of handiwork, where the craftsman has lavished his utmost labour and ingenuity, are not unfrequently monstrosities in point of design. There is no greater fallacy than the vulgar notion, that "taste is arbitrary choice:" this error has been the prolific parent of ugliness; for if the fancy be not guided by right principles it wanders into all sorts of incongruities. Whoever admires a beautiful object ought to be able "to give a reason for the faith that is in him," that shall satisfy a rational questioner: how much more necessary is it for the manufacturer to know in what consists the beauty he aims at producing? Science is the rudder and compass of Art, by which the daring inventor is enabled to discover new worlds of beauty without running on the rock of deformity. Beauty and utility go hand in hand, and those who divorce them separate a pair joined by nature; whose union, cemented by "the eternal fitness of things," is the means of filling the world with shapes of loveliness strung with nerves of power. As in the man the easiest attitudes are also the most graceful, so with artificial objects the most serviceable may be rendered the most becoming: when a thing is essentially ugly, the chances are that it is not so handy for its purpose as it might be made; and as mechanical inventions are improved they become more shapely. Ugliness is an evil to be avoided whenever possible, which it is in most cases. Utility engrafted on simple beauty gives rise to endless varieties of form, that are pleasing because they are fitted for their purpose: as examples of this we may instance the commonest agricultural implements; the plough, the scythe, the sickle, and the basket with which

> The sower stalks, and lib'ral throws the seed
> Into the faithful bosom of the ground.[7]

So with dress; the Greek mantle or chlamys,[8] the Roman toga, the Turkish turban, the Arab bournous,[9] and the mat of the New Zealand savage, are each graceful after their kind.

"But what is meant by beauty" it may be asked. "Is it a positive quality to be defined?"' We reply, Yes. There is an abstract beauty of form and proportion as well as of colour, which always delights the eye; but the mind to be fully satisfied demands also expression of character or purpose; that is, the combination of fitness and utility with beauty. An object is beautiful, because of the ideas excited by it; these constitute its attractiveness, for they are the fruition of beauty: those persons who have most lively imaginations, therefore, derive the greatest amount of pleasure from the contemplation of beautiful objects. Hogarth's "Line of Beauty"[10] is a mere figment; for though undulating curves are pleasing to the eye, they convey no meaning to the mind, unless their contour expresses some intelligible form. Beauty has been well defined to be the combination of uniformity and variety: let us apply this definition to the simplest geometrical forms.

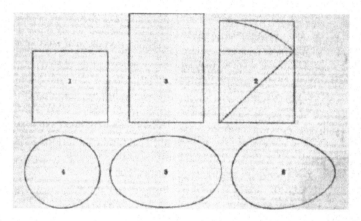

The square (figure 2.1) is a uniform figure, solid, compact, and conveying an idea of stability and strength: it is satisfactory from its symmetry, every one of its sides being alike, and each contributing in an equal degree to the integrity of the form: the square has only one element of beauty, uniformity. The oblong square, or parallelogram (figure 2.2), is also solid, compact, and uniform, and, equally with the square, conveys ideas of stability and strength; but it includes, in a degree, the element of variety, the just proportion of the height to the breadth of the figure, producing an additional pleasure the height of this, "the parallelogram of beauty," as it is called, is equal to the diagonal of the square of the base (vide figure 2.2); this graceful proportion blending the characteristics of altitude and squareness in one form. In the parallelogram (figure 2.3) the idea of altitude or length predominates; this figure is in a less degree suggestive of compactness and stability, and strikes the sense as not so justly proportioned as figure 2.2. Rectilinear figures, however, are far less agreeable to the eye than curvilinear; for besides that straight lines have no variety in themselves, the angles are harsh: regularity, strength, and stability are their leading characteristics. The sphere (figure 2.4) combines compactness, solidity, and strength with uniformity, rejecting the harshness of angular figures; the unbroken regularity of the form, which presents the same outline in whatever way it is viewed, is not only satisfactory but pleasing. But the eye quickly runs the round of the circular outline, and soon comprehends the beauty of the figure; hence the heightening grace of variety is wanting in the sphere, which is supplied by the ellipsis (figure 2.5); the regularity of this figure, however, in which the two ends and two sides precisely resemble each other, is soon apparent, and its variety quickly exhausted. It is in the oval or egg-shape (figure 2.6) that the two elements of beauty—uniformity and variety—are combined in perfection, without any diminution of the ideas of compactness and solidity: the devious contour of the oval presents a variety of curves in its flowing line; and graceful proportion is superadded, the relative width and length of the figure corresponding with that of figure 2.2. In this attempt to estimate the comparative beauty of these simple geometrical forms, and to demonstrate the surpassing elegance of the oval, while testing the definition of beauty, only some of the abstract ideas of form awakened by each have been adverted to; the qualities of surface, for instance, have been purposely overlooked, as unessential to the indication of the characteristics of form and proportion. The constructive fitness of the form of the egg, with its two domes or arches of unequal dimensions blended together, so as to support each other, develops the new ingredient of beauty, the principal of utility. This standard of beauty is equally applicable to complex forms, in enabling us to form a judgment of the proportions in the masses and of the shapes in the outline. The balance of rotund and tapering form, of solid bulk and projection, of curves and right lines in a vase, are equally determinable by this simple test: but the question of fitness enters so largely into the consideration, that abstract beauty of form and proportion is greatly modified, though its laws never can be directly contravened without detriment. The problem to be solved, in all cases of the invention of new forms, or the adaptation of old ones to useful purposes, is this—given the precise kind of utensil, it is required to find the shape best suited to fulfil its uses, and at the same time to develop the utmost degree of appropriate beauty.

The application of this standard of beauty to ornamental design is infinitely more complicated; and a new element, colour, here comes into operation. Ornamental art is unjustly, or rather ignorantly despised; the investigation of the principles of beauty in ornamental design requires more recondite research than in the instance of natural forms, where the forms are not arbitrary. In the conformation of natural objects there is a reason for everything, if we could but find it out; and in controlling the exercise of invention by a rational exercise of scientific knowledge, man is following, though at an immeasurable distance, the order of the universe. In painting and sculpture the artist imitates the perfection of nature; in ornamental design he is licensed to deviate from the natural ideal into the fantastic ideal; and his invention is only controlled by the laws of abstract beauty, and the conditions of his particular branch of decorative art. The knowledge of these laws and conditions, and of the natural characteristics of the divers objects which the decorative artist impresses into the service of ornament, ought to be acquired in Schools of Design.

The institution of Schools of Design has been regarded as only serviceable in teaching the artisan to draw, and making him familiar with what has been already done in the way of ornament, so as to be able to produce new modifications of known devices. This is taking a very superficial and imperfect view of the nature and scope of the course of education required to produce skilled inventors; and, without the scientific exercise of invention, ornamental design is of no worth, and will do little towards establishing or maintaining our national equality in ornamental manufactures. To be able to draw is obviously an essential, but the least part, of the education of the designer of ornament: in the science of form and colour, and their application to the purposes of decoration, the artisan ought to be proficient. He should not only know what has been done in ornament, and how it is done, but why it was done; that he may be able to do something new, and as good or better than his predecessors: for novelty in ornament is incessantly demanded, not only by the caprices of fashion, but by the competition of manufacturers; and the designer who supplies it in the greatest variety, and of the most beautiful kind, will be most prized. Study cannot teach the dull brain to invent, but it will restrain alike the plodding and the lively fancy from falling into errors of judgment, and vitiating the popular taste. So little has the subject of artisan education been considered, that we find writers, eminent for their love and knowledge of Art, not only at variance with each other as to the course of instruction, but entirely wrong in their notions on the subject. Mr. Haydon[11] advocates drawing the human figure as the one thing needful; on the principle that the greater includes the less, he contends that when an artisan can draw the figure, he can draw anything. Mr. Allan Cunningham,[12] on the contrary, ridicules the notion of making artists of artisans by teaching then to draw the human form; and humorously observes, that "we don't want to have the Greek warriors of the Elgin frieze galloping round the rims of plates and dishes." With deference to both these distinguished men, they are alike beside the point: it is not the being able to draw the human figure that makes an artist or an artisan; the human form is one of the objects that both have occasion to represent—the painter and sculptor principally, the designer of ornament incidentally. To a certain point, the education of both artist and artisan—to use the broad distinctive terms commonly recognised—proceeds in the same way: both require elementary instruction in the art of drawing, modelling, and painting; for the use of the pencil or modelling-tool is as necessary to both as it is for the bookkeeper and the author to be able to use the pen. When this power of imitating natural objects is acquired, the course of education of the painter and sculptor takes a totally different direction from that of the ornamental designer. The painter and sculptor study and imitate nature with a view to represent scenes and persons, whether real or ideal, in the aspect of life; their aim being not only to delight the sense by the imitation, but to influence the mind, by communicating their ideas through the exercise of their so potent art. The object of the ornamental designer is simply to gratify the eye, subordinately to some useful purpose which he serves by the means of appropriate embellishment; his invention has a wider latitude, but a more limited influence than that of the painter or sculptor. The treatment of the same object by the pictorial and ornamental designer, is essentially different: take the honeysuckle for example; the *studies* of the flower itself by the landscape painter and the decorator may be similar; but how different the use they make of it. The one gives to the entire plant the pensile lightness, the luxuriance, and movement of nature: the other detaches the flowers from their stems and sticks them flat and upright, side by side, or with some fanciful shape inter-mixed; giving to them rigidity, and regularity, and altering both shape and colour. The one presents the natural characteristics of the plant in the most picturesque aspect: the other takes the hint of a beautiful form, and applies it to an arbitrary use, according to a conventional necessity. The designers of ornament for architecture, for carpets, for damask hangings, for cotton prints, for vases, for arabesque scrolls, for lace work, for glass painting, for paper hanging, &c., would each treat the honeysuckle in a different way, according to the requirements of his peculiar branch of decoration: neither would imitate nature exactly, but each in his deviation should preserve the beautiful characteristics of the original, whether in form or colour; and in order to do this he must know in what these characteristics consist.

The most common and glaring mistake made by our designers, is that of introducing pictorial imitations of natural scenes and objects as ornaments: it is not only an infraction of the first principles of the art of decorative design, but a source of the most monstrous absurdities. Tigers crouched on hearth-rugs, lap-dogs on foot-stools, parrots perched on chair-seats, swans sailing on the floor of a drawing-room, snakes and lizards crawling into cups, flower stalks blossoming with wax-lights, Corinthian columns supporting tall candles, walls opened with myriad repetitions of the same view in every conceivable distortion of false perspective, grates like castles, gothic crosses doing duty as door-keepers, and Grecian urns stuck up for chimney-pots—these are among the most flagrant instances of that want of scientific acquaintance with the principles of decorative Art, which it is one great object of schools of design to supply.

These introductory remarks have extended to such a length, that our mention of Schools of Design must be very brief, and limited to the Metropolitan School at Somerset House, and its off-shoot in Spitalfields; and we must be content to give a mere sketch of these. The School of Design at Somerset House, was established by the Government on 1st May, 1837, in pursuance of a parliamentary grant of money for that purpose; under the direction of Mr. Papworth; Mr. Dyce was appointed Director in August 1838. The instruction given may best be described in the words of the Prospectus.

Branches of Instruction

Section I.—ELEMENTARY INSTRUCTION.—I. Drawing. 1. Outline Drawing, Geometrical Drawing, Freehand ditto; 2. Shadowing, the use of Chalks, &c.; 3. Drawing from the Round; 4. Drawing from Nature. II. Modelling. Modelling from the Antique, &c.; Ditto from Nature. III. Colouring. 1. Instruction in the use of Colours; 1. Water-Colours, including Water Body-Colours, and Fresco; 2. Oil Colours; 2. Copies of Coloured Drawings; 3. Colouring from Nature.

N.B. The Instructions in Colouring are given only in the Morning School.

Section II.—INSTRUCTION IN THE HISTORY, PRINCIPLES, AND PRACTICE OF ORNAMENTAL ART.—This Section will embrace, according to circumstances, the study of, 1. The Antique Styles; 2. Styles of the Middle Ages; 3. Modern Styles. In this department Lectures will occasionally be given to the students.

Section III.—INSTRUCTION IN DESIGN FOR MANUFACTURES.—1. Study of the various processes of manufacture, so far as may be requisite, including those of Silk and Carpet Weaving, Calico Printing, Paper Staining, &c., &c., &c.— N.B. The Class for Silk Manufacture is open every Tuesday and Thursday, from eleven to two.

2. The Practice of Design for Individual Branches of Industry—1. Subject considered generally; 2. With reference to the prevailing modes. Masters, under the general superintendence of Mr. Dyce, are engaged to afford instruction in the various branches above enumerated.

ADMISSION TO THE SCHOOL.—Such persons as are desirous of attending, must apply at the School between twelve and three. Candidates for admission will be reported to the Council, by whom the students are admitted. Mr. Dyce, however, is vested with a discretionary power of admitting, as probationers, such applicants as may be considered by him qualified, until the decision of the Council be ascertained.

FEES OF ADMISSION.—To the Morning School. per month, 4s.; to the Evening, 2s. Morning students have permission to attend the Evening School free of payment. The fees of admission are payable in advance from the 1st of each month; but students may be admitted in the course of the month on making the fractional payment.

HOURS OF ATTENDANCE. — The Morning School is open from ten till three every day, except on Saturday, when the School closes at two o'clock. The Evening School is open from six till nine every evening, except Saturday. The school is supplied with a variety of examples for study, consisting of prints and drawings, casts from antique sculptures of the human figure, animals, and architectural ornaments; specimens of paper and silk hangings. Of these a great variety has recently been brought from Paris by Mr. Dyce, who at the same time made arrangements for purchasing two valuable and extensive collections of casts from the antique, which are in course of transmission to this country. These are the collection of sculpture in the Louvre, which comprises the most celebrated statues, groups, bas-reliefs, busts, and fragments of Greek and Roman Art; and that at the *Ecole des Beaux Arts*, consisting of a prodigious quantity of ornamental work of all kinds, styles, and dates, from the Egyptian to the time of Louis XV. These collections, formed at great expense by the French Government, require a considerable annual outlay to keep the moulds from which casts are taken in proper order, by renewal or otherwise. When the casts arrive, which will be so soon as a suitable place has been prepared for their reception, it is intended to have moulds made from the finest and most useful, from which other casts can be taken for supplying branch Schools of Design, and other Institutions, at the cheapest possible rate; the original collection remaining at the central School for study and exhibition. The purchase of these two collections is £600, independently of the cost of package and carriage, and the expense of making moulds from them.

Mr. Dyce is also preparing an Elementary Drawing Book, for the use of the students; the two first parts of which, with directions for the teachers, may shortly be expected. Mr. Dyce's appointment of Professor of Fine Arts to King's College, will afford him the opportunity of giving the more advanced pupils of the Somerset House School admission to a course of lectures on Ornamental Design that he is preparing to deliver to the students of King's College.

The School of Design at Somerset House opened this year, with 150 pupils, of various ages, juvenile and adult, including those in the Normal School, who are candidates for six exhibitions to masterships in provincial Schools.

Preliminary to the formation of Branch Schools, the following circular, and string of queries have been addressed to the proper authorities of the following places: viz, Aberdeen, Belfast, Birmingham, Coventry, Derby, Dublin, Glasgow, Leeds, Liverpool, Macclesfield, Manchester, Newcastle, Norwich, the Potteries, Sheffield, and York.

Sir,—A Parliamentary grant has recently been made for the encouragement of Branch Schools in connexion with the School of Design already established in London, for the purpose of teaching Ornamental Design as applicable to manufactures, both to those employed as Pattern Designers and to Artisans generally, and also for the formations of collections of casts of works of Art, for the purpose of instruction in such Branch Schools: such collections to be gratuitously accessible under certain regulations to the inhabitants of towns in which they shall be placed.

The council of the School of Design with a view to obtaining the information necessary to guide them in disposing of the above-mentioned grant, request to be furnished with answers to the subjoined queries. The council also request, that if there be any School or Institution now existing in ____, in which Design is taught with a view to its application to manufactures, you will acquaint them with the fact at your earliest convenience, as in that case they would be desirous of procuring from you some additional, particulars of information in reference to such School.

By order of the Council, &c. &c. &c.

Queries

1. Are you of opinion that if a School of Design were established in ____, the Artisans engaged in any, and what particular kinds of manufacture, or the persons employed in the preparation of Patterns or designs for manufacture,

or any other class of persons, would be disposed to receive instruction in such School, in Ornamental Design as applicable to manufactures?
2. Are you of opinion that such Artisans, or other persons would be disposed to send their sons to such school for such instruction ?
3. Are you of opinion that the parties would be willing to make a moderate payment for such instruction ?
4. Can you give any opinion as to the probable average number of persons who would avail themselves of such instruction ?
5. Are there any public buildings in which such school could be established?
6. Are there any town funds already subscribed applicable to this purpose?
7. Are you of opinion that if aid were afforded for the establishment of a School of Design in _____, out of the funds provided by Parliament, upon condition of a proportionate subscription on the part of the inhabitants, such subscription, could be obtained?
8. Are you of opinion that a proper building would be provided at the expense of the town funds, or by a subscription of the inhabitants, for the reception of casts of works of Art for gratuitous popular exhibition under proper regulations, if a donation were made to the town of such a collection, or if aid were given towards its formation ?

Only six Schools will be established, in the first instance, at those towns which are most in want of the assistance to be afforded by the council.

Meanwhile the progress of the Spitalfields' Branch School gives earnest of the advantages that the country Artisans will soon share: the number of pupils is 110, and the average attendance is 85. The work of National Education for workmen is fairly begun, and will progress steadily; and it will be the constant endeavour of this journal to aid its advancement.

W.S.W.

Notes

1 *Art Union*, February 1839, p. 1.
2 S. C. Hall, *Retrospect of a Long Life, from 1815 to 1883* (New York: Appleton, 1883), p. 211.
3 W. S. W. 'Art Applied to Manufactures', *Art Union*, 4, 37, February 1842, p. 23.
4 Exeter Hall, a London venue situated in the Strand. It was here Mr. Butler Williams gave drawing classes based on Dupuis' model.
5 Dupius' models refer to a French system of design published as A. Dupuis, *De l'Enseignement du dessin sous le point de vue industriel, par Alexandre Dupuis* (Paris: Giroux, 1836). It was adapted by J. Butler Williams as *A Manual for Teaching Model-Drawing from Solid Forms: The Models Founded on Those of M. Dupuis; Combined with a Popular View of Perspective, and Adapted to the Elementary Instruction of Classes in Schools and Public Institutions* (London: John W. Parker, 1843).
6 *Minutes of Proceedings of the Royal Dublin Society*, 78, 1842, Appendix, p. iii.
7 Adapted from J. Thomson (1700–1748), *The Four Seasons*, 'Spring'.
8 chlamys: A short cloak, worn only by men, it was a draped around the upper shoulders, and pinned on the right shoulder with a brooch.

9 bournous: A hooded mantle or cloak extensively worn by Berbers and other Maghrebis.
10 Hogarth's line of beauty. Hogarth's *The Analysis of Beauty* (1753), defines, a "serpentine line" as the "line of beauty," in contrast to straight or curved lines.
11 Benjamin Robert Haydon (1786–1846), painter and author.
12 Allan Cunningham (1784–1842), author and biographer of artists.

3

GEORGE WALLIS, 'RECENT PROGRESS IN DESIGN AS APPLIED TO MANUFACTURES'

George Wallis was well qualified to discuss design progress, as he had been one of the commissioners of the Great Exhibition held in London in 1851 and also of the 1853 exhibition at New York's Crystal Palace. He was particularly interested in the American system of manufactures (see 3.37) and brought back to England a piece of American machine-made furniture as an example.[1] In 1857, Wallis became a keeper at the South Kensington Museum.

The Scottish engineer and author, Robert Scott Burn, in his *Ornamental Drawing, and Architectural Design* explained how 'Decorators or ornamentists are divided into two great classes, one of which advocates the strict following of "nature", in the adaptation of her own graceful and varying forms, to the purposes of decoration; while the other repudiates this strict adherence, and advocates the necessity of conventionalising them before applying them to decoration'.[2] Wallis was one of the latter. He was also keen to promote the application of art to industry and drew a distinction between those who would produce goods, as long as they sold, and those who thought that the application of art to industry was a vulgar misappropriation. He was also keen on using modern techniques and processes to improve design and production.

> it is fearlessly asserted, that he is a negligent worker in the present, and a betrayer of the interests of the future, who does not avail himself of every means which modern invention and discovery affords him to reproduce, in suitable form and material, such beautiful objects of art-manufacture as shall tend to the refinement and instruction of his fellow-men.[3]

This paper was identified by the author as a stock-taking exercise, taking the reader through the textile, fictile, vitreous, metallic, and miscellaneous manufactures to ascertain the rate and nature of progress in the respective industries. Wallis invited responses to the paper in the hope that it would add to the evaluation of the then current situation and offer ideas for future developments. Ruskin gave a response to one part of the paper that was a particular bugbear of some design reformers, stating that he could not, as Mr. Wallis did, blame the ladies for promoting a base manufacture of carpets, admitting the complete imitation of flowers, ... Nor could he see, since the first thing we usually did to make the ground fit to be walked upon by any festive procession, was always to strew flowers upon it, why we should refuse to have flowers on our carpets, lest we should stumble over them, any more than we should refuse to have pictures on our walls, lest we should knock our heads through them.[4]

Ruskin then went on to attack Wallis's pleas for more engagement with the machine: 'in no way, therefore, could good art ever become cheap in production. . . . The paper seemed to dwell wholly upon the advantage of art to the consumer, or only to the producer as a mercantile matter. He was sorry it did not show the effect of the production of art on the workman; surely the happiness of the workman was a thing which ought to be considered'.[5]

Wallis's responses to the written remarks about his paper were published in the journal a week after the lecture. One reply picked up on Wallis's comment on 'ugly' designs and argued that many were purchased for their usefulness and/or economy and not for the design itself. The 'willow pattern' ceramic was the example to which he referred. Wallis was uncompromising in his response:

I am afraid Mr. Joseph Lockett's[6] good-natured apology for the 'willow-pattern' plate, coming after his admirable remarks upon his own special industry, will not do now-a-days; since there is a little too much of the 'Oh, it don't matter,' and 'It is easy to be matched' style of argument in it. Now as good a covering pattern might be obtained by simple mosaic forms in a geometric arrangement, and one, too, which would print quite as easy, and come quite as cheap. Happily, a little more abuse of this monstrous piece of decorative inconsistency will effect its utter repudiation by all persons who think about what they buy and use.[7]

George Wallis, 'Recent Progress in Design as Applied to Manufactures', *Journal of the Society of Arts*, 173, 4, 14 March 1856, pp. 291–301

It cannot fail to be interesting, and may, certainly be useful, to note from time to time the progress or otherwise which, as a nation, we may be making in any special phase of art or science. Merchants and manufacturers have their periodical stock-taking, by which they ascertain the precise position of their affairs, consign out-of-date productions to the limbo of "job-lots," clear their wares rooms of goods which do not improve by keeping, and get rid of dead stock for the benefit of living capital. This is a wholesome process, which, judiciously applied, may have a healthy tendency on the action of other affairs beside those of commerce, and might be used much oftener than it is to test gain or loss in matters of education, alike national and individual.

For some years past efforts have been made to impress the manufacturers of this country, as producers, and the people as consumers, with the value of art as applied to trade; and although the former generally repudiate all interference between them and their customers, yet it so happened that some 20 years ago the utter neglect of almost everything which tended to give refinement to the forms in which articles of every-day use were furnished to the public, attracted the attention of a few artistic and scientific busy-bodies, who could not understand why ugliness should be so much more economical than beauty, and who even had the hardihood to declare that the latter was as cheap as the former, and *much better*! Strange to say, recent experience has confirmed these people in the conviction thus expressed, and has even carried them further, for they now declare that beauty is much cheaper than ugliness, when the principles of art are understood and judiciously applied. It is scarcely to be supposed, however, that everybody is as yet convinced even of the truth of the theory that beauty is as cheap as ugliness; but we certainly have progressed to the point at which art, as applied to manufactures, is really thought to be worth something, since in nearly all manufacturing pursuits into which decoration enters as an element, there has been an attempt, more or less successful, to improve upon past forms and embellishments. It has been found, too, that the markets have not stagnated became goods were a little prettier than formerly, and it has even been hinted at, though this is looked upon with suspicion as a dangerous commercial heresy, that public instruction in art, by means of lectures, schools of art, art publications, and the free access to galleries of works, has had something to do with this change, which it is now confessed has come over the spirit of the home market, in relation to the ornamentation of articles of every-day demand.

During the initiation of this change, those engaged in urging it forward have generally found two very opposite influences at work, each tending to counteract a really healthy development of the art-power of the country. One of these influences came out of the determined enunciation by the ultra-practical manufacturer, of the dogma, that all art, as applied to trade, was useless, unless it could be proved that it would "sell," whilst at the same time the proof by trial was refused. The other opposing influence was to be found in the apathy or antagonism of those who, looking upon art as little better than an elegant abstraction, intended only for the use of the wealthy and the wise, denounced all application of its principles to the utilities of life or to the purposes of trade and commerce as an unrighteous attempt to vulgarise it. By the manufacturer popular art was considered as an impertinence, by the connoisseur *par excellence*, it was regarded a profanation.

It was thus between these two horns of a dilemma that the advocates of art-education had to steer at the outset. It is all tolerably plain sailing now, since fashion has rendered the constant movement of the producer a necessary part of his existence; but it was not always so, and reminiscences of wrathful manufacturers, and still more angry shopkeepers, whose customer had dared to have an opinion of their own, even though obtained at secondhand, will, at times, present themselves. Thus one has sometimes been compelled to listen to a statement how two customers, who had attended a lecture on art the night before, had impudently dared to call the last new design for a chandelier, "a brass gooseberry bush turned upside down;" and worse still, one has been compelled to father and defend the principle of the criticism, and declare that the said chandelier *was* more like an inverted gooseberry bush than anything else in creation. Then the complaint that, "Really the women were getting so particular about the dress patterns," that in spite of the last new *de laine,* printed in 400 colours by the agency of an unlimited number of blocks or cylinders, they could not be induced to buy, since they had got a notion from some pragmatical art-critic, that a lady's dress looked none the better for reminding the beholder of fourteen yards of rainbow done in wool!

Happily these small miseries, arising out of the action of a spirit of innovation upon the established interests and vested rights of the British public in ugliness, are rapidly vanishing, and it would be at once ungenerous, as it would be unwise, to expect the manufacturer to make, or the shopkeeper to keep for sale, goods which the public are not sufficiently educated in art to appreciate. Our complaint rather refers to the pertinacity with which too many set themselves up as arbitrators for the public, and decide what it shall *buy,* inasmuch as they will not make or keep anything except what they consider good to *sell.* Their standard being frequently very much lower than that of their customers; hence the constant complaints of the latter. This is, in itself, some evidence that the consumers have a perception of an abstract excellence beyond the reality submitted to them, and this fact has had much to do with that recent progress in design which it is intended to specifically indicate under various industrial heads in this paper.

All are tolerably well agreed that some progress has been made, especially within the last three or four years, although there is no doubt a considerable difference of opinion as to the real character and value of that progress. Many persons, looking from the manufacturer's point of view, will ask, "Do the articles in which improvement is most manifest *sell* better?" Viewed as seen by the merchant and shopkeeper, the question will probably be as to increased profit, whilst from the ultra-artistic point of view, it is more than probable that it will be disputatiously declared that the movement made is no improvement, because it is not in precise conformity to some abstract principle in which the question of realization by an economic process is considered as altogether a secondary matter, or, it may be superciliously maintained that English design means absence of all true art, and that the less we trouble ourselves about the matter the better, since they manage these things more wisely in France!

Again, the lover of antiquity, who affects ancient types and methods, and believes that all the labour-saving inventions of modern times are so many mechanical abominations, to be repudiated by all earnest and true spirited art-workers, forgets altogether that the question of mechanical power is only one of degree, since the hammer, the file, and the chasing tool are mechanical contrivances for facilitating labour which could not be executed so well or so speedily by more primitive means.

The secret of all this horror of stamping, electro-depositing, printing, power-loom weaving, and so forth, lies, it is to be feared, in the fact that the almost exclusive possession of a work becomes impossible. Duplication spoils that flattering unction which your pure and legitimate connoisseur lays to his soul as to the uniqueness of his treasure. The beauty of a fine work may be a joy to others as well as himself, therefore he loaths the vile, short, cheap, and ready processes by which this is effected. But then it is argued there is such a sameness in these mechanical reproductions, the charm of variety is wanting, and a sensation of commonness takes the place of that of rarity, and this everlasting repetition of the same form is a traitorous use of art. As if, because green peas are so much alike, a love of *petit pois* is treason to good eating; or because the individual sheep of a flock so strongly resemble each other, there is to be an universal repudiation of mutton.

If modern art, whether applied to industry or the higher illustrations of the power of the beautiful, is ever to make a distinct place for itself in the coming time, it will be out of the wise and perfect use of those mechanical means and appliances with which an All-wise Providence has seen fit to furnish mankind for their use in this age; and it is fearlessly asserted, that he is a negligent worker in the present, and a betrayer of the interests of the future, who does not avail himself of every means which modern invention and discovery affords him to reproduce, in suitable form and material, such beautiful objects of art-manufacture as shall tend to the refinement and instruction of his fellow-men. Nay, more; if he loves the past and those earnest workers of the olden time whose examples he quotes, let him be told that had they had the means at their disposal for shortening their labour, extending its sphere of action, and enabling them to do the work of two, ten, perchance twenty lives in one, he pays but a poor compliment to their earnestness and their love of art, to tell us that they would not have availed themselves of them. They did their work in their way, and that, too, the best which their age and opportunities afforded them, and we certainly follow in their spirit much more by doing our work in and for our own time and wants, and consequently in our own way; thus doing as they did, using all the means afforded us, and not going back to obsolete methods, and tying ourselves down to processes which, though the best when they were used, are no longer *the* best.

All this has been said in order at once to repudiate all test of recent progress by methods rather than by results. It is the complete fact in the work itself with which we have to deal, not whether a man pottered for a month over a piece of work with a hammer and chisel, or struck it out at a blow with a die and press, cast it in a mould, or deposited by voltaic action. Nor, on the other hand, can the most beautiful scientific or mechanical process be admitted into the consideration of the merits of the result obtained thereby, certainly not as any excuse for defects.

It is proposed, for convenience and brevity, to divide the subject under consideration into four special sections, with a fifth, which may be termed supplementary. These may be stated under the heads of design as applied to Textile, Fictile,

Vitreous, Metallic, and Miscellaneous manufactures. This classification, if not scientifically correct, yet in such a summary as this paper is necessarily confined to, gives the advantage of breadth of view and ease of reference.

Commencing with

Textile Manufactures

the first point to consider is the recent tendency of public taste, indicative of the nature of the demand which the manufacturer has been called upon to supply. In dress goods, this tendency has been most decidedly towards plain-dyed or self-coloured goods, or such as presented comparatively little variation from the effects producible by shades of a single colour; and, although in the majority of instances it is feared that the character of the ornamentation has been generally such as could not be called either artistic in design or treatment, yet it is something to have arrived at a point at which great contrasts in colour are rather the exception than the rule. The best class of Yorkshire wool and mixed fabrics present features in design which contrast favourably with goods of a similar class manufactured five or six years ago.

In calico prints, except of the highest and best class, or of the very simplest and plainest madders,[8] the change appears rather for the worse than otherwise; yet good authorities in the Midland Counties, at least, say that the great mass of the people who usually buy these things prefer the smaller, neater, and more simply coloured designs, to the blotchy abominations which used formerly to be sought after, and which, in too many instances, are still presumed, by the less observant manufacturer and retailer, to constitute the taste of the working classes. Taking Birmingham as an example, it may be stated, without hesitation, that the neater and more elegant designs in cheap calicoes are most in demand. Taking the opinion of one of the best authorities on this subject in Europe, given the other day at Manchester, it would appear that whilst the printer and engraver are both anxious to do better things, they are persecuted into the production of uglinesses of such a character, that the workmen who have to engrave the cylinders look upon them with disgust, and often declare, in language more expressive than polite, on beginning a new pattern, that, "If the fools had tried to produce an uglier thing, they could not have done it." In short, design, as applied to a large portion of the British calico print trade, just now appears to be literally "a thing of shreds and patches"—mixtures from old pattern books, heterogeneously hurled together at hap-hazard, without regard to purpose, unity of effect, or any other constituent of an artistic design. As a matter of course, the houses with established reputations for the production of the better class of patterns, which come out in neat, simple, and perfectly textile effects, producible in madders-pink, lavender, and chocolate, or in half-mourning prints, keep their ground, and their customers, and "pooh pooh" artistic design as a useless thing to the nation, except so far as it cultivates the general taste of the people to the full appreciation of the simple ornamentation which they have the good sense to employ. To educate the consumer up to this point, is a laudable thing; but to urge the producer to aim beyond these is commercial treason; as if we, as a manufacturing nation, are not more employed in production than consumption; whilst in our home trade the producer of one article is the consumer of another, and it is more than probable that the exact standard of taste to which the producer manufactures is that to which he will appeal as a buyer.

In silks there is a decided progress in design, as applied to some classes of goods, and these, too, of the cheaper kind, and, consequently, most in demand. The Spitalfields productions exhibited at Paris gave evidence of this, and, although Macclesfield[9] was not adequately represented in the Universal Exposition of 1855, a recent visit to the manufactories of that town has proved in a most satisfactory manner that a quiet but steady progress has characterised the designs brought out at Macclesfield during the past three or four years. The ultra-imitation of natural objects is gradually giving way to more severe ornamental forms, which, if not always of the true textile type, are yet geometric in character and precise in form. Two or three specimens of the successful application of the most tasteful of these in neckerchiefs are now exhibited, and there is little doubt of their being highly successful in the market. It has been thought worthwhile, too, to select one as an example of the influence which the Macclesfield School of Art is exercising. The designer of this, in the employ of one of the largest houses, formerly dealt largely in peacocks, cottages, butterflies, and other equally absurd subjects, as decorations suited to the angles of a lady's neckerchief. They have given way under the teaching of the school, in this instance at least, to floral arrangements upon a geometric basis, of which the specimen produced will give a fair idea. Formerly the Macclesfield silks were more noticeable for the gaiety and contrast than for the taste or their colouring. Checks and stripes are, undoubtedly, a severe test of the power of the manufacturer to combine tints judiciously; and the mania for introducing these in great variety often led and still leads to strange effects. At present there is a decided preference for two, or at most three, tints; and even in the combination of more than these, failure seems to arise more from an uncertainty as to the proportional quantity of each, than in the tints or colours brought together. This is a great step, inasmuch as the question of quantity is simply a question of numbers when properly studied and rightly applied.

In furniture silks the designs of the last three or four years appear to have been based upon much sounder principles than formerly. Geometric forms, and the severer elements of the generic styles of ornament, have been introduced, not only with success, as regards the artistic result, but also as regards their sale. In fact, as a whole, there are few departments of industry into which design enters as an element in which there has been a greater change than in the various textile fabrics used by upholsterers without asserting that this change is universal, for it is not, it may be safely stated that successful efforts have been made to introduce a more suitable style of decoration; and designs which five or six years ago would have been pronounced too architectural and stiff, are now not only manufactured, but sold in great quantities. In curtains and table-covers, for instance, either plain surfaces, with borders of an elegant character, as compared with those in vogue eight or ten years ago, are preferred to the "all over" patterns, which were pronounced as the only things which would ever *sell* in the English market. Where it is not desirable to have blank surfaces of colour, powderings in geometric, or, at least, severely symmetrical forms are frequently introduced, either by embroidery or by weaving. Nor is this tendency to the use of more tasteful drapery in furniture confined entirely to the costly productions. An eminent Manchester house has, in connection with their productions in silk and embroidery, introduced, with great success, printed borders for curtains, the majority of the designs for which are of a severe type in form and colour, chiefly frets and gulloiches in one colour, or at most two. A few of these borderings have also been designed to meet the views of those who think that all severe ornament must be stiff in effect, and that no forms except flowers can be made satisfactory vehicles of a colour. This compromise between artistic principle and the supposed requirements of the market, is certainly not successful as regards the former, and it is to be hoped it will not be so as regards the latter, since manufacturers who really have the enterprise to introduce a good thing to the public, ought also to know that their best interest lies in keeping up the character of these productions alike in design and execution. In embroidery, the ultranaturalesque forms which prevailed some six or seven years ago, are giving way to a class of design more suited to production by the needle. Much of this is doubtlessly to be attributed to the severe character of the ecclesiastical embroideries, for which there has more recently been so large a demand. In gymps and edgings, too, the character of a trimming has been gradually taking the place of the wiry and unmeaning nonsense which used formerly to be so difficult to put upon a fabric in a satisfactory manner, but which it was still more difficult to keep upon it.

In connection with silks and the question of edgings and trimmings, a few words may be said at once about ribbons. The French have had the credit of producing the most tasteful things in a certain class of silks, and French ribbons have always held a good position. In fact, those of English manufacture have always been looked upon as inferior, alike in make, colour, and design. Now a ribbon, if it is anything, is simply an accessory to something else in dress. It comes in as a rosette, a border, and, in special cases, in the character of a festoon. Floral design, where suitably arranged, is, after all, not so much out of place as some hypercritics might suppose, since a wreath of flowers is not an unbecoming ornament to a lady's bonnet, cap, or hair. It is quite clear, however, that the best designed ribbon is that which carries out the idea of an ornamentally-arranged border, in which form and colour are so combined, as to give finish to that portion of the dress upon which it is used. Tested by this standard, what becomes of the supposed excellence in taste of French ribbons? And, however gay and often exquisite in point of colour, many of those exhibited at Paris in 1855 certainly were, a goodly number of those now produced at Coventry are superior articles in the principle of their ornamentation. There is one point, however, which must ever be borne in mind, with respect not only to French ribbons, but many other articles produced in France for foreign markets, especially English and American. That a certain standard of ugliness in forms, and violence of contrast in colour, producing vulgarity, is essential to suit the peculiar notions of the wholesale buyers, who act as the arbitrators of taste for the British public and that of the United States. Whoever saw Frenchwoman wearing the party-coloured trimmings? It is certainly no compliment to those who do wear them be told that the people who make them know better than to wear them, but consider them good enough, artistically, for the barbarous taste of their customers.

In the important articles of linen damasks, whilst a few excellent things have been produced from time to time, by the leading manufacturers, it is feared that no great progress has been made towards a purer style of ornamenting an otherwise beautiful fabric, and that designs in which much excellent drawing is thrown away upon unsuitable subjects, are still produced, and that, too, as specimens of progress. It is, however, something to have got rid of an immense amount of unmeaning ornamentation, whilst specimens of diaper-work for centres, and of symmetrical, if not absolutely geometrical, arrangements in borders, have occasionally made their appearance, which cannot fail to produce a good effect, since they commend themselves by contrast with their more ambitious predecessors.

In cotton quiltings, too, diapered effects are taking the place of costly and ineffective arrangements of form, in which the character of the fabric and its purpose were sacrificed to the whim of a manufacturer, who first gets himself into a difficulty by aiming at the production of some elaborate absurdity, which is generally supposed to be an impossibility, and then finds himself in a still greater difficulty after he has achieved his object, on discovering that he has thrown away time and money upon a work which, from its inconsistency, those who do not understand it are careless about, and those who do understand it condemn. This was illustrated in a few strange things—such as views of the building in Hyde-park—exhibited at the Great Exhibition of 1851; and again in certain attempts at the production of historical subjects in lace exhibited in the Universal Exposition of 1855. The absurdity of this latter attempt was the more glaring from the fact that abundant evidence was afforded that in the lace trade of England, especially in the machine-laces of Nottingham, great progress had been made in design since the International Exhibition in Hyde-park. This was decidedly proved in the cheap curtains exhibited at Paris, in which a fitness of ornamentation was shown which cannot fail to largely influence design as applied to other departments of the lace trade.

In Irish laces and sewed muslins the progress in this respect has been of a marked and healthy character. Setting out from a point at which all needle-work types would appear to have been repudiated, this industry has gradually but surely progressed, so as to stand in such a position at the present time as to fairly challenge criticism in all the higher class of work; and ii is probable that as much may be said of a considerable portion of the Honiton lace, as manufactured by and for the best houses, In short, in these, by no means unimportant departments of national industry, in which form in outline or in mass, or both in combination, is alone available, the three common-sense questions:—What is the material ? What are the means? What is the use? appear to have had fair-play, and an attempt, at least, at honest solution.

These three questions, if applied to carpets, which must form the last point for consideration under the head of textiles, would, it is feared, receive but a very imperfect and unsatisfactory response. Yet some progress has been made even in carpet designs, which, a few years ago, appeared to be hopelessly abandoned to an incessant ringing of the changes upon artistic pit-falls, man-traps, and floral stumbling-blocks in velvet pile and terry fabrics in wool. A few manufacturers, as also a few dealers, seem to have arrived at the point that, inasmuch as a carpet is a covering for a floor, it ought to look like a floor—that is, a surface to walk upon,—that a carpet is not the only article in a room, and that its lines and its colours ought rather to be subordinate to the more prominent pieces of furniture, than to challenge attention by the brilliancy of its hues in masses, or the tortuosity of its lines in the boundary of its forms. A conviction, too, has arisen that forms in projection are inconsistent with the position of the surface upon which they are represented; and that, even granting that flowers, tastefully, arranged and judiciously treated, are not unsuitable objects for the decoration of a carpet, yet there is no reason why the flower-basket should be represented too.

The statement that floral designs in carpets are still preferred by the consumers, and that the ladies especially, in spite of the best geometric designs, insist upon roses done in wool, is a fair argument enough in its commercial application, but in an artistic sense only proves that the people lack a knowledge of principles by which to test these things. The ladies still buy the Indian pine-pattern shawl, and will probably continue to do so, not from any conviction of its eminently textile character as a vehicle of colour, but simply from association of idea, just as the old willow-pattern plate was formerly, and still is, to a great extent, the only true and veritable representation of popular notions of fictile decoration. It will be thus seen that the admirers of floral design in carpets, and Indian pines in shawls, are at cross-purposes with themselves, so far as common sense is concerned. It is much easier, however, to say, "Out upon your common sense and art-tests too, so long as people buy!" than to prove that the advocates of the application of sound principles are wrong, even commercially, if care is taken to judiciously introduce a purer style of art, without a sudden repudiation of prevailing ideas.

Looking at the probabilities of future progress in textile design, the great stumbling-block appears to lie in the mania amongst large buyers, and even retailers, for concocting their own patterns—it would be a libel on all art to call it *designing*. But for this, the probabilities are strongly in favour of a more rapid improvement in the future, since manufacturers themselves are beginning to feel that a knowledge of drawing and the principles of design is of considerable use in the preparation of those patterns with which, it left uninfluenced, they would endeavour to supply the market. So long, however, as the mere agent between the manufacturer and the public is permitted to substitute the traditions of the market for the common-sense principles of art, and empirically dictate what the one shall *make* and the other shall *buy*, matters will go on much as they have done, except that it is just possible the taste of the dealer himself may improve, where it happens that he is not convinced that he is the embodiment of all-perfect wisdom in his own special trade.

Fictile Manufactures

In no department of British industry has the value of a gradual introduction of improved modes of decoration been more clearly proved than in that of porcelain and ordinary earthenware. To anyone who, like the writer of this paper, visited the Staffordshire Potteries nineteen years ago, and observed the state of things at that time, and has had the privilege of an occasional visit at stated intervals during the period which has intervened, it must be very obvious that a change, such as we frequently hear pronounced as impossible in other industries, has come over nearly the whole of the productions of that district. Far from resting satisfied, however, with even the present state of things, it is quite clear that every coming year will tend to still greater progress than that already realised, and that those who pertinaciously persist in the common fallacy that to do as they have done is all-sufficient, will be left behind in the race.

The illustration of the fictile manufactures of Staffordshire in the Paris Exhibition was of such a character as to prove most unmistakeably that a great improvement had taken place since 1851; and, without being prepared to approve, on artistic grounds, of all that had been done, yet, with the experience of the past upon our memory, it would be unjust not to award the credit due to intelligent effort and steady enterprise. To two houses, those of Messrs. Minton and Co. and Messrs. Copeland, the credit of the earlier movements is due; but others have followed who applying a better style of art to less exceptional articles than those produced by these two firms, have certainly aided in no slight degree the more recent improvements; and it is quite evident that at the present time, whatever fault may still be found with the subjects employed for the purpose of decorating the cheaper ware, yet that the character of the art employed is much higher than formerly. In the blue transfer ware, for in stance, there is a decided tendency to mosaic forms, less attempt at projection in light and shadow, and although the details are often more architectural than fictile, yet the result is felt to be more suited, alike to the use of the article, the surface decorated, and the method of ornamentation.

In these forms, too, one can trace the influence of the merest elementary outlines in use in our schools of art, of which that established in the Potteries eight years ago has been one of the most practically useful.

In the cheaper kinds of porcelain, neatness approaching severity is gradually taking the place of the blotchy floral designs which formerly disfigured forms which ought to have suggested more tasteful decorations. Nor have the forms themselves been neglected, since in many articles of every-day use, a purity of outline formerly unknown has taken the place of the eccentric convolutions which bid defiance to common sense and the ordinary rules of proportion.

Into the higher class of porcelain painting an artistic refinement has been introduced which contrasts in a remarkable manner with the hard, wiry, and laboured results of some twelve or fifteen years ago. One feels that the workman is more of an artist, and yet not the less of an artizan than formerly.

It may be reasonable asked, to what cause is this change to be attributed? and it may be replied that at one period matters were really so bad that a change was inevitable in order to retain the trade in the higher branches, and there can be no doubt that the efforts after improvement in this direction led to corresponding efforts in the production of less costly articles. The introduction of Parian,[10] however, would appear to have given the first impulse towards a higher style of art. The enterprise which prompted the employment of artistic talent in the production of statuettes, either original or as reductions from celebrated works, modern and antique, was soon engaged in the improvement of analogous branches of fictile art. The keynote was struck in Parian, but the theme has been carried out step by step in other materials and modes of application, such as tiles, vases, garden decorations, and domestic services.

Recently the efforts to emulate the productions of Palissy, and rival the Majolica of the best periods, have been attended with so much success, that he must be a hyper-critic indeed who would not join in a congratulatory compliment to the skill which had solved the problem of modern progress in British fictile art, so successfully.

In thus endeavouring to do justice to the progress made in the Staffordshire potteries, the productions of Worcester must not be forgotten. In 1846, a first visit to this city showed the writer how much in arrear its porcelain manufacture then stood, even as compared with that of Staffordshire. Since that period a marked improvement has taken place, and "the faithful city" bids fair to resume its old position, and even excel it, in the manufacture of the higher class of porcelain, Here, again, the influence of reproductions in imitation of past modes of decoration has had its influence, and the imitation of Etruscan methods in the manufactory of Messrs. Kerr and Binns,[11] followed as this has been by the successful production of admirable specimens, which go far towards rivalling the best class of Limoges ware, cannot fail to influence other departments, and stimulate to corresponding improvements. Good work of any kind always has this healthy influence, that it renders the mind impatient of that which is less perfect, and thus imperceptibly necessitates progress. In this fact lies the value of bringing fine works of art of every kind before the people. The mind once imbued with a true sense of the beautiful, detects at a glance any anachronism in form or colour, although the "why and wherefore" of the defect may not be so readily discovered. This can alone come of sound education and a knowledge of principles.

Let it not be supposed, however, that all recent progress in fictile art is confined to reproductions and imitations of antique types or methods. During a visit, the other day, to the Staffordshire potteries, two new modes of decoration presented themselves. Of one of these, specimens are forthcoming. This consists of an inlaid coloured body upon Parian, and seems admirably calculated, from its conditions, to necessitate severity in ornamentation. The process has been so far worked out by Messrs. Rickuss and Toft,[12] and is of an economical character. Of the other process, now in the course of development by Messrs. Pratt,[13] no specimen has, unfortunately, being forwarded, owing, as it would appear, from the proprietors not being at present prepared to bring it before the public. Some admirable things, however, are in progress, and, judging from a complete specimen, the results appear likely to be of a very satisfactory character. The process consists of enamelling upon terra-cotta, the outline of the ornament being printed by transfer, and the colours afterwards put in with a brush.

Having thus briefly sketched the progress of design as applied to fictile manufacture, the next and somewhat analogous section of our subject presents itself.

Vitreous Manufacture

It may, perhaps, be said that all progress in the manufacture of glass in England during the last 200 years has been recent, since our fiscal restrictions completely kept an important branch of industry aloof from any contact with modern science and art until within a comparatively short period. Good use, however, has been made of the interval, and except that in some departments there still exists an affection for weight of metal and deeply cut facets, rather than a desire to produce pure forms with appropriate ornamentation, the glass trade of Britain has made extraordinary progress in many points, and in none more than the production of a good character of cheap glass, in which, if there is no very remarkable development of beauty, there is certainly nothing very offensive as regards either form or decoration. There is one point, however, which nearly all modern glass manufacturers of every country appear to neglect, and this is the crystalline nature of the material, and the necessity for adapting the ornamentation so as to make the most of what may be termed its inherent beauty. This is frequently proved in the results obtained in "*pressed*" glass, in which the conditions of manufacture compel the manufacturer to study the material. The effects produced, though often crude, and, viewed from a merely mechanical point of view, unsatisfactory as regards finish, are yet so admirably adapted to the material as to commend themselves in spite of other drawbacks.

Perhaps the best illustration which could be given of the value of this adaptation of form and ornamentation to the character of the material, was to be found in the candelabrum exhibited by Messrs. Osler, of Birmingham,[14] in the Paris Exhibition, which contrasted so favourably with works of a similar class exhibited on that occasion. In this work a thoroughly crystal type was followed throughout, by means of an arrangement of prisms and cutting in facets. The contrast it thus presented to similar works contributed by the French was remarkable.

In these specimens, the usual compliment of scroll work, brackets, bosses, and imitations of acanthus foliage, were to be found; and their inconsistency became only the more apparent from comparison with the English candelabrum, in which these details were studiously avoided, whilst the result was far more brilliant and ornamental. In fact, the inappropriateness of architectural details, the value of which as ornaments consists in their outline, and the effects resulting from a play of light and shadow, being applied to; and in a material in which the effects are obtained mainly by light in transition, is at once obvious; if that very simple, but much neglected, question, as to the nature of the material to be used, is ever fairly asked and honestly answered.

In coloured glass there can be no doubt much improvement has been made of late years; and, without exactly maintaining that the Bohemian standard has been reached, it may safely be affirmed that where care has been taken not to attempt too much, some of the articles in coloured glass produced in Birmingham are of a very tasteful and pleasing character.

In stained glass for windows, the progress in England has been of a very remarkable kind. From an exceptional employment, the manufacture of decorated windows has become a general one; and although the best works yet produced have been either copies of old windows, or based upon ancient types, yet, as the beginning of a revived industry, there is more upon which to congratulate ourselves than to condemn. Those who are impatient of results, and see no reason why the oak cannot be grown as rapidly as the mushroom, will perhaps object to this. Let it be so. All really permanent results take time to develop themselves.

Metallic Manufactures

In the wide and constantly extending field of the fancy metal trades of Great Britain, the opportunity for progress in design is so great, that, with much to regret and find fault with, there is also much which cannot fail to satisfy and encourage all who take an interest in the application of art to industry, Perhaps the greatest revolution in the higher departments of design, especially as applied to gold and silver, has arisen out of the great modern discovery in science of the deposition of metals by galvanic action. A few specimens of high class productions in electro-metallurgy, by Mr. Edmund Heely,[15] of Birmingham, are now exhibited as illustrations of the value of this process in its applications to the reproduction of ancient and modern works in the precious metals and bronze. The opportunity thus afforded for copying or reproducing, at a comparatively reasonable cost, the fine works of past times, has tended to educate the taste of the people, and lift us to a higher plane of judgment in modern productions. Thus, the test by mere material value in bullion weight, which had usurped the place of the aesthetic value conferred by art, has been gradually giving way, and the importance of the latter is gradually becoming more and more recognised. This is seen in the character of the works now usually produced for testimonial services and for racing prizes. It is useless to say that these are not always appropriate,—often, indeed, exceedingly inappropriate,—but as an evidence that a desire for something more than a given number of ounces of gold and silver is giving way to some consideration of the form in which the metal comes, they are proofs of progress.

Again, let any person whose recollections of the displays made by our gold and silver plate manufacturers date back some fifteen or twenty years, compare the character of the productions then exhibited in showrooms with that of some of the leading houses now, and then consider the change. In the showrooms of Messrs. Elkington, Mason, and Co., of Birmingham, there are at the present time ten times more works, in which appropriateness and purity of design, in connection with excellence of art workmanship, is displayed, than could have been produced, twenty years ago, by all the houses in England put together.

The progress made in the manufacture of church plate and general metal work for ecclesiastical purposes, as indeed in all matters connected with church ornaments, is well known to all who take an interest in the progress of the arts of design. The manufactories of Messrs. Hardman, of Birmingham, Skidmore, of Coventry,[16] and others, have produced works from time to time, within the last few years, which would have done credit to any country and any age, if the fact is taken into account that the question of cost was a serious element in their manufacture. And here it may be permitted to say a word about the influence which one mind alone undoubtedly exercised, not only on the particular department of art to which he specially devoted his attention, but, indeed, upon all of a kindred character, in which other minds were engaged who could appreciate his arguments, and apply the principles he enunciated. For however much we may differ in many points from the late Mr. Pugin, as to his special views of the mission of art, and the application of modern scientific and mechanical means to the reproduction of works of excellence, his earnest and fearless denunciation of all "shams"— his exposure of false systems of ornamentation—his thoroughly zealous working out, "in season and out of season," of his own views in his own way, must ever command the respect of every true and earnest lover of art, since it is to the influence of his example, in one direction, that we owe so much of the progress to be recorded in other departments of art-manufacture. It is therefore but an act of justice to his memory, which all who differed from him on special points, can at least afford to perform—to fairly and honestly acknowledge how much he did, in his comparatively limited time, for the domestic and manufacturing arts of his country, both directly and indirectly.

That an enormous amount of work is still thrown away upon, comparatively, very indifferent designs in gold and silver is quite true, That the human figure and animals are pressed into service, rightly or wrongly, and that these are often wonderful examples of the ignorance of their producers, is also true. That ornamental types, originally designed for any material but metal, are introduced without the slightest consideration as to fitness, is a fact which is patent to all who interest themselves in this question; yet, with all these drawbacks, and many more not so easy to enumerate, it is affirmed that much has been done during the past few years for design as applied to gold and silver plate and its imitations.

In brass and bronze work the same may be said; for, notwithstanding the ultra-naturalesque character of many productions still in the market, and likely still to "sell," an approximation has been made towards a much purer style, and this, too, since the Great Exhibition of 1851. It must never be forgotten that much of the over-ornate tendency, so visible in the ornamental brass manufactures of Birmingham, arose from a slavish and unmeaning following of the French, especially after the Exposition of 1844. It is satisfactory to know, however, that the present tendency has not its origin in this direction, and that in the brass and bronze chandeliers, gas-brackets, and works of an analogous character, efforts are now being made, and some of them very successful ones too, to work out a more severe style of treatment as applied to those useful articles, and, whilst giving less weight of metal and more hand-work, to produce tasteful results by a little more brain work at the outset. In fact, manufacturers are beginning to acknowledge that artistic talent, carefully directed to practical ends, will *pay* when it secures simplicity and elegance in design. Nor is this applied so much to the costly articles as to those coming within the means of persons of moderate income. In short, the construction required by the use appears to be first considered in the specimens alluded to, and then the ornamentation is carefully adapted to the embellishment of the necessitated form. This, we apprehend, is sound practice, based upon sound principles. Under any circumstances the results are satisfactory, so far as manufacture goes; and that the articles will make their way in the market in due time, it would be as unreasonable to doubt as it would be to doubt the influence of light upon darkness.

In iron castings, especially those suited to the furnishing of entrance-halls and garden decorations, to quote the display of the Coalbrookdale Company in the Paris Exhibition, will be quite sufficient as an indication of progress in this direction; for without absolutely declaring that everything manufactured by this firm is perfection, one cannot hesitate to acknowledge that the improvement, even since 1851, must be visible to the most careless observer.

In connection with this part of our subject, the remarkable strides in design, as applied to the Sheffield manufacture of stoves, grate fronts, &c., must be noticed. It will be remembered how thoroughly well Sheffield maintained its position in the Great Exhibition of 1851. Since that time great progress has been made, and although this was not illustrated to its full extent at Paris, it is not the less a fact. It is not the less gratifying, too, to know that here, at least, the influence of the instruction given in the School of Art has been acknowledged, and that those who availed themselves of its teachings have sought to do it honour.

Before quitting the section of metallic manufactures, let us seek to do an act of justice to a much misunderstood and grossly abused branch of Birmingham industry—that of jewellery. It has been usual, almost from time immemorial, to describe any article of manufacture, especially in the precious metals, which appeared of doubtful quality or workmanship, under the generic term of "*Brummagem*." This epithet involves the very essence of the term "sham." Unfortunately, on the one side, there has been but too much foundation for the term being understood to represent something at once very pretentious and very unreal, but it is equally unfortunate that on the other side much excellence, alike in design and handicraft, has been misrepresented and misunderstood. It is desirable, therefore, to call attention to the fact, that whilst Birmingham jewellery has made a decided advance within the last three or four years, alike in design and excellence of workmanship, it is not the unreal thing some persons appear to imagine; nor does it follow that, because, as compared with the highest class of jewellery, there is not that weight of metal used which is in itself bullion value only, that the gold used is less pure than in the more *solid* article. And here it may be desirable to explain the technical use of this word "*solid.*" In the Birmingham sense it does not imply that the whole mass of form is filled up with metal, but that all the metal used in the manufacture is of the standard value it purports to be.

In order to illustrate, as far as circumstances would permit, the present state of design as applied to the manufacture of jewellery and ornaments for the person in Birmingham, a small but varied selection has been made from the productions of some sixteen manufacturers, and in order that no article should be specially prepared, all have been collected within the last three days, in some instances from stocks in which very little choice could be exercised, from the constant demand for the articles as fast as they can be manufactured. These will give a general idea of the style and character of the articles now in the course of production for the home market. Of course they are not sold retail as Birmingham make. They are indifferently recommended to the public as "Town made," "Paris made," or as the special productions of Pekin, or Timbuctoo, or any other place rather than of Birmingham! The change in the character of the designs of these productions must strike every person who has paid any attention to works of a similar class as manufactured some years ago. The vulgar contrast of coloured stones, the obtrusive and inappropriate details in the ornamentation, the loose character of the workmanship, have in a great measure vanished; and except that the Birmingham manufacturers have still the traditionary fear of shooting over the head of their customers, by making their articles too chaste and unobtrusive, it is quite clear, after a careful examination, that as beautiful work, alike in design and execution, can be, and often is, produced at Birmingham as at any other place where the jewellery in ordinary demand is manufactured.

It must, however, be carefully borne in mind that this industry is in a transition state of even more recent date than that of the other manufactures we have noticed, and that, from an intense and unreasoning vulgarity, it has had to make its way to something like fixity of principle and purity of style. In effecting this, the first step has been to make a brooch like a brooch in form; to try to get rid of the conceits so much in vogue, and to appeal to the eye of the purchaser rather by sparkling and brilliant effects in a concentrated form than in the outrageously diffusive contrasts of twisted gold and coloured stones. The revival of the use of the cameo, with its quiet tints and expressive forms, would appear to have had a tendency to produce a still further leaning towards quiet effects, in which thoughtful arrangement and skilful handicraft takes the place of careless redundancy and hurried construction. In some of the signet and ladies' rings, shirt studs and pins, now displayed, the character of the setting is as pure and unexceptionable as the most fastidious person could desire.

It is not, then, too much to assert that a great step has been made in the right direction as regards design as applied to the manufacture of Birmingham jewellery in all its leading branches. Of course in the speciality of imitative jewellery there is the same foundation for distrust as ever, and it is to the reproach of our Registration of Designs law,[17] that the manufacturer of the genuine article is the constant victim of imitators of his best designs in spurious metal: as of course these people do not find it to their advantage to make new designs, but to copy those of a genuine character which have been found most successful in the market.

Miscellaneous Manufactures

Having thus glanced at the progress of art-manufacture under the four great sections into which it has been thought most convenient to divide our national industry for the immediate object in view, it is now desirable to indicate, before concluding, some evidences of improvement in other manufactures which cannot be said to come within either category.

In the general style of furniture manufactured in England there does not appear to have been that improvement which might have been expected, except probably in the accessories of carved work. In this latter respect there is certainly considerable improvement in executive skill, but as regards the question of its application it is quite clear that we have much to learn on this head. On the production of high-class furniture, the Great Exhibition of 1851 has exercised a decided influence, and since that event works have been successfully carried out which a few years ago would not have been attempted. Still, in all that applies to the supply of the general wants of the people, little change appears to have been effected.

In the manufacture and decoration of Papier Mâché there appears to be a growing tendency towards a more severe style of ornamentation; but this, so far as Birmingham is concerned, has not manifested itself at present in a very palpable form. The facile power of hand displayed by our japanners is often very great, but this is too frequently directed by nothing more than the merest tradition of the workshop. The inventive power, too, of some of the most talented is also very great; but being undisciplined by a knowledge of the laws which govern composition in ornament, they are rather the producers of clever accidents in arrangement, than designers in the full sense of the term. On the whole, it seems probable that the japanning trade will not show more than a gradual approximation to finer styles of ornamentation for some time to come, and that the changes needed and gradually introduced will be rather the result of the improvements in other departments of ornamental industry being taken up from time to time, and adapted to the wants of the japanner and his employer, than from any determinate and well understood effort after original and artistic results as arising out of the study of the elementary principles of decoration.

From the individual character of the production of each of the leading houses in the japanning trade in Birmingham and Wolverhampton, there is evidence enough of an enormous scope, for any amount of art-knowledge, as applied to this industry; yet, strange to say, very few japanners know how to draw, and fewer still care to undergo a course of systematic training. So long as this state of things exists, employers may calculate upon little improvement in their manufacture; and with a beautiful material, great facilities in production, almost boundless variety in pigments, gold and silver powders, gold leaf, and pearl, the higher qualities of design will remain dormant for want of educated power in the worker.

The question of interior decorations of buildings does not come within the purpose of this paper, but the manufacture of wall-papers may very properly claim some attention. If anyone ever attempts to write a work upon "The Natural History of Ugliness," the paper-hangings manufactured in Great Britain and the United States would certainly stand in the first class of the genus *super-ugly*. Yet, even in this apparently almost hopeless manufacture, so far as regards the probability of anything like artistic influence being brought to bear upon it, a very decided improvement has taken place. Nor is this improvement manifested in the higher class of papers, which, in many respects, are as outrageous in form and colour as ever, as in the cheaper kind; those, in fact, which, being printed by machine, are adapted to the wants and means of the great mass of the people. In these, pretty and effective diapers have taken the place of the strange things which formerly disfigured the paper and the walls upon which it was hung, and in many instances persons of education and taste prefer these simple patterns, even for rooms in which they would desire to place a costly paper, because the result is so much more pleasing than the designs they would be compelled to take in a high-class article. Of course there are exceptions to this tendency to redundant ornamentation in gold and colour in the first-class paper hangings, and, as might have been expected, many of the leading houses of the metropolis take care that attention is paid to the character of the designs they employ, keeping in mind that, beside the carpet and the wall, there are other things in a room which have some little claim to be seen, and that the ladies do not care to be always compelled to dress up to the key-note of colour pitched by a wall-paper of intense brilliancy of tints and powerful self-assertion in the forms of the ornamentation. In fact, there is a lurking suspicion in the minds of upholsterers and paper-hanging manufacturers that, after all, "those fellows who write on art" may not be so far wrong, when they assert that a wall-paper when put in its place should form a decorated back-ground.

There are doubtlessly other manufactures, which attention might be called, hut it is feared with very little chance of indicating much progress. Some of these may possibly suggest themselves to others; if so, it is trusted that in the observations to which this brief summary of the present position of manufactures in their relation to art will give rise, these may be mentioned.

One great object of this paper has been to elicit a record of progress out of the remarks which it is to be hoped will be made by others; each, in his own speciality at least, more competent perhaps than the writer to give an opinion, either negative or affirmative. Finally, it is earnestly hoped that the result will be such a comparison of notes and experience as may enable all interested in the subject under consideration to arrive at a satisfactory conclusion,—first, as to what we have done; second, as to what we are doing; and, last, "though not least" in importance, as to what we *need* to do in design as applicable to the great staple industries of our country.

[Discussion followed]

Notes

1. See work table object W.2:3–1944 in the Victoria and Albert Museum.
2. R. S. Burn, *Ornamental Drawing, and Architectural Design, with Notes, Historical and Practical* (London: Ward and Lock, 1857), p. 38.
3. G. Wallis, 'Recent Progress in Design as Applied to Manufactures', *Journal of the Society of Arts*, 173, 4, 14 March 1856, p. 292.
4. G. Wallis, 'Recent Progress in Design as Applied to Manufactures', p. 299.
5. Ibid.
6. J. Lockett: Textile roller engraver, Strangeways Engraving Works, Manchester.
7. G. Wallis, 'Reply of Mr. Wallis', *Journal of the Society of Arts*, 174, 4, 21 March 1856, p. 320.
8. Madders: cloth dyed with the root of the plant *Rubia tinctorum*, a reddish-purple dyestuff.
9. Macclesfield: Cheshire town once a major centre of silk production and weaving.
10. Parian: Parian ware is a type of biscuit porcelain imitating the white marble of the Greek island of Paros. It was developed around 1845 by Mintons.
11. In 1852 Richard William Binns (1819–1900) and William Henry Kerr (1823–1879) took over the management of the Chamberlain & Co porcelain works in Severn Street, Worcester.
12. Wilkinson, John Rickuss & Charles Toft established c.1855 in Hanley, Stoke.
13. Felix Edward Pratt (1813–1894) and Richard Pratt's company was a manufacturer of domestic earthenware and polychrome transfer-printed items.
14. Osler: Messrs. F & C Osler of London and Birmingham, founded in 1807 by Thomas Osler, were important makers of glass chandeliers, lighting and glass furniture especially for the overseas market.
15. Heely: Noted by 1805 in a Birmingham directory as a maker of steel chains, beads, combs, gilt toys, hairpins & springs. Heeley & Sons evolved their manufacturing business to become metalworkers and platers. In 1851 the business was run by Francis Heeley and was listed as a Steel Toy Manufacturer.
16. Messrs. Hardman, of Birmingham, Skidmore, of Coventry, suppliers of medieval ecclesiastical metalwork of all kinds.
17. 1850 Copyright of Designs Act.

4

DENIS O'DONOVAN, 'THE USES OF ART & DESIGN IN MANUFACTURE'

Denis O'Donovan (1836–1911), was an Irish scholar, palaeontologist, and librarian, who developed important connections with the intellectual world of Europe. He moved to Melbourne in 1866, when he was invited to become the first Professor of Natural Science at the University of Melbourne, and he was later a founding director of the Melbourne Industrial and Technological Museum. The Museum was established in Melbourne in 1870 'as a means of public instruction' for the people of Victoria. In 1871, he delivered this lecture on industrial design that was subsequently published by the museum. This paper was delivered in the third series of lectures provide by the museum.

Initially, the Australian colonies were not encouraged to develop any industrial base, rather they were seen as a source of raw materials and agricultural products, and a market for British goods. By the mid-nineteenth century, the economy was changing, and the colonies began to develop British ideas around design education, within state-based technical education. The colonies exhibited at international exhibitions, so they were exposed to contemporary trends in design.

As this paper shows, they were clearly influenced by the writings of British reformers such as Owen Jones, Charles Eastlake, and John Ruskin. Indeed, the arts and crafts ethos was to have a considerable impact on Antipodean art and design culture.

At the end of his lecture, O'Donovan raised a call to arms for his now fellow Australian countrymen:

> In this great movement [union of art and design] which is now spreading over the whole earth, it is absolutely necessary that we should take our place. If we do not, the time will come when Victoria, which should be the great manufacturing centre of these southern lands, will have to import perhaps from some neighbouring colony many of the articles used by her own people. Far from us such a disgrace![1]

Denis O'Donovan, 'The Uses of Art & Design in Manufacture', In Frederick McCoy, *Lectures Delivered by Professor McCoy ... [et al.] in the Lecture Room of the Museum, During the Second Session of 1871* (Melbourne: Samuel Mullen, 1872), Extract, pp. 79–83

[. . .] But if art in general is useful to the craftsman, that development of it which enables him to determine the most suitable form of every object he has to make, and to inscribe on it, with truth and beauty, all the facts of its material, its construction and its uses, must in particular be needful. This is what is called the art of design. It is not distinct from other art, being merely a special application of it, and can no more be taught by any fixed rules than the art of Phidias or of Raphael. A good designer must be born an artist, he must moreover be a man of careful observation and of much experience, and his taste must be cultivated by the happy influence of beautiful things. This is not to say he can be taught nothing. He can be helped to a more intimate communion with nature by learning those secrets which her ardent lovers have ravished from her in every age and he can be taught those principles which are gathered from the accumulated observation of all those who have gone before him. The leading principles that have been hitherto established, and those about which alone authorities seem to be undivided, I shall now endeavour to lay before you in the shortest and simplest manner that I can. They will teach us better than anything else how useful, even how essential, is this art in almost every branch of manufacture.

All design is either constructive or ornamental. The first principle concerns both divisions. I give it in the words of Mr. Owen Jones—"Construction should be decorated, decoration should never be constructed;"[2] that is to say, that ornament should be subordinate to construction, and should not be designed without reference to it; for a designer might produce an ornament most beautiful in itself, and yet show the grossest stupidity in its application.

With regard to constructive design considered separately, the most important and best-founded principle is the very simple and common-sense one, that an object must fitly answer the purpose for which it is intended. This beauty of fitness is nothing more than truth, without which art would be degraded to a systematic misrepresentation. Utility is the characteristic attribute of the manufactures of all the great eras of art. Indeed, it would be difficult to find a single example amongst articles of classical workmanship, of which it might be said that it was tasteful and elegant, without being particularly adapted to the especial object for which it was originated. Nor is this quite as simple a thing as might at first sight appear, for it is not enough that an object should be useful for its purpose; every portion of it should be designed with reference to the end in view—that a water-jug, for instance, should not only be made so as to hold water, but should have the handle so placed that the water can be taken in and poured out with the greatest case.

Fitness is a quality demanded of ornamental design also. Perfect figure-drawing, or a beautiful landscape, would be out of place on a cup or platter; delicate tints and patterns of flowers would be inappropriate on the meaner kitchen utensils; and even the bellows that enters into the drawing room becomes a monstrosity when it displays a moonlight view in Venice, or the balcony scene in *Romeo and Juliet*. This much may be said without entering into the lists for or against either of the two bodies of disputants who occupy the arena of ornamental art. Whether room decoration should be by flat patterns and dead colours, or should be by natural art such as that with which Tintoret adorned the Council Hall at Venice—whether a wall should be merely a background to the living figures in the room, or should be alive with lovely children playing amongst the vineleaves, as Correggio would have made it—is a question which I need not, even if I were capable to do so, take upon myself to decide. Of one thing I feel certain: that decorative art, when wholly unconventional, may be dignified and beautiful, and wholly in its place in certain surroundings, and that in others it may be much less suitable than the inferior forms of a zigzag or a chequer. I am, therefore, no partisan of the extremists on either side of this dispute. The interiors of noble buildings—abodes of kings, and great edifices of the people—claim the highest efforts of art for their adornment; a spoon, or a snuff-box, or a coal-scuttle, arc objects with whose uses high art can have no possible connection. Between the palace and the coal-box there are, however, various fields for decoration, and in these I think the artist must be left wholly to his sense of fitness and his taste. Taking it, then, for granted that conventionalism is often necessary in ornamental art, let me remark here that even good conventionalism can never be produced by a workman who has received no training in the higher departments of art. It has ever been so from Egyptian ornament to the purest medieval of the thirteenth century; how conventional soever was any great school of decoration in the past, the knowledge of the human figure and the most skilled and perfect drawing are everywhere as distinctly to be traced as in the birds, and cherubs, and wreathed foliage of the cinquecento. The same holds good with regard to the drawing of plants, and fruit, and flowers. Even in conventionalism an accurate knowledge of their forms is essential, for every part of a plant or flower, if properly understood, each member of the vegetable organism, if properly delineated, is a veritable ornament; and when we consider there are about 100,000 species of plants, we may form some idea of the vastness of the treasury here awaiting the student. Nor is this all; the study of these delightful objects with which the great temple of nature is adorned, these "stars of the earth," and all the fair profusion of fruit and foliage that surround us, hold up for ever before us in their silent, fascinating beauty those great laws of repetition and alternation, on which much of the merit of good conventional design must always depend.

The conventional art finds its special place in the household—amongst the familiar and useful objects of our homes, but it would nevertheless be absurd to lay down the rule that all higher art should be excluded therefrom. In like manner, it may be said that the loftiest forms of art belong to the great public edifices, yet would it be an error to suppose that even here conventional art can find no place. The golden rule, therefore, is one of fitness. When decoration is beautiful and appropriate, it fulfils all the conditions of perfection. The statues of a majestic

Gothic cathedral, as they ascend from the eye into the distance, and lose themselves in the shadows of its lofty arches, are rightly and properly conventionalised for the sake of effect, while the girdle of carved stalls and stone bas-reliefs around the choir is of the highest and most exquisite finish. In the same way, a teapot, ornamented with cherubs in high relief, or a carpet, resembling a menagerie marvellous with strange and savage creatures, are specimens of art falsely applied; but a sideboard, substantial, massive in shape, richly sombre in colour, may not unworthily receive the noble decoration of living forms; and I know no well-founded canon of taste that is violated when a cabinet is beautified with the most elegant pictorial composition, the most finished enrichments of sculpture, and the subtlest chromatic harmonies which the skill of the colourist can produce.

Another principle closely connected with this is that every article of manufacture should be not only fit for its use, and fitly ornamented, but by its design it should indicate the purpose to which it is applied. and should never be allowed to convey a false notion of that purpose. All the traps for the eye, in the shape of boxes that have the appearance of well bound books, bells that look like inverted tulips, sideboards formed on the models of Grecian altars, and flower-stands treated as ruined castles, are false and vulgar in taste, thoroughly bad and irredeemably depraved in art.

And now, looking about for maxims for your guidance, I find the only remaining one about which there is no serious difference amongst authorities, is that concerning the fitness of design to the material to be used. "Every material (I give it in Sir Charles Eastlake's words) is restricted by the nature of its substance to certain conditions of form."[3] Thus glass or any other brittle substance should not be made into the form of a pillar, the obvious idea of which is strength. Neither should glass be used wherever transparency is not desired. Feathers, or trees, or hair, should not be cut out of marble. Freestone is unfitted for work that requires minute elaboration, and cast iron should never be made to imitate wrought-iron ornament, or stone carving.

These, which are the fundamental principles of design, prove by their bare enunciation how essential is this art in the production of every object of daily use. Fine art produces beauty and elegance, design weds them to utility and fitness, and thus we see in a general way the uses in manufacture of art and design. But it will be well to go a step further than generalities. I shall, therefore, devote the remainder of the time I have to speak to you to compressing into as narrow a compass as possible some definite notions concerning the particular relations between art in its various developments and each of the principal manufactures that supply our ordinary wants. [. . .]

Notes

1 D. O'Donovan, 'The Uses of Art & Design In Manufacture', Frederick M'coy, *Lectures Delivered by Professor M'coy . . . [Et Al.] In the Lecture Room of the Museum, During the Second Session of 1871* (Melbourne: Samuel Mullen, 1872), p. 10.
2 O. Jones, *Grammar of Ornament* (London: Quartich, 1868), Proposition 5, p. 5.
3 C. Eastlake, *Hints on Household Taste* (London: Longmans Green, 1869), p. 41.

5

JACOB FALKE, 'THE VIENNA EXHIBITION IN CONNEXION WITH ART-INDUSTRY. IX, FURNITURE'

Jacob Falke (1825–1897) was a German-Austrian cultural historian and museum curator who was closely involved in the design movements of his time. Falke was of the school of thought that argued that aesthetically good design was found in an object's function. This was achieved by consideration of purpose, material, and production. In 1860, he published *Das Kunstgewerbe*, (The Arts and Crafts) which reflected English ideas on the same topic, and in 1866, he published *Geschichte des Modernen Geschmacks* (History of Modern Taste). His important publication of 1871 *Die Kunst im Hause (Art in the House)* was translated and annotated by Charles C. Perkins in 1879 as *Art in the House: Historical, Critical, and Aesthetical Studies on the Decoration and Furnishing of the Dwelling*. Falke later published his *Aesthetik des Kunstgewerbes* (Aesthetics of the Arts and Crafts) in 1883.

The Viennese Weltausstellung (World Exhibition) was a celebration of both the twenty-fifth anniversary of the coronation of Emperor Francis Joseph 1 and the success of Vienna as a capital city. A magnificent set of buildings and an ambitious range of exhibits made this an important but financially disastrous exhibition. In the exhibition, Falke created an interesting display of Hausindustrie (house industry or peasant made objects) which he considered very important in relation to the developing Kunstindustire (art industry). The link was that the simply crafted utilitarian goods produced for local use were created on the basis of the nature of materials and application as required; this was in contrast to the often impractical and over decorated historically styled goods founds in the city shops.

More specifically, Falke, writing on the displays in the Vienna Exhibition and their connection with the art industry of English furniture commented: 'Although the English furniture has not moved in the same direction of reform as the German, Austrian and Italian, it has still made a grand step in advance as to its artistic importance, and so takes its part in that great progress of taste in all branches of art-industry to which our Exhibition bears the most undoubted testimony'.[1]

Related to this, Falke's commentary on the issue of national taste is of interest, as this topic was closely linked to the culture of world exhibitions of the latter half of the century. He said, regarding the Paris Exhibition of 1867, 'England is located, with France, at the top end of the pyramid of taste, and therefore we must not expect, neither in its nor in France's case, any national elements in the arts industries of those countries of the kind we have found in Russia, Scandinavia and elsewhere'.[2]

Falke's work on furniture history and design was consolidated in his 1871(1879) publication *Art in the House Historical, Critical, and Æsthetical Studies on the Decoration and Furnishing of the Dwelling*.[3] This work puts an unsurprising emphasis on utility over ornamentation, and the role of unity and proportion. It was well received by the trade press as it was both historical and practical. The English *Furniture Gazette* commented on the value of comparative examples. 'The study of "how not to do it" is often quite as profitable as that of the more positive side of the subject, and this in itself would justify the insertion in this book of some of the illustrations which have reference to ungainly specimens of furniture; but, moreover, the juxtaposition of good and bad, as here followed out, cannot but point its own salutary moral even to the least initiated'.[4]

This article is one of ten dedicated to analysis of the products of the exhibition that were published in *The Workshop*. The journal had a sub-title of 'A monthly journal, devoted to art-industry, and the elevation and progress of taste in manufacture, construction and decoration. The original German periodical *Gewerbehalle* was published in two English editions by James Hagger in London. The first was titled *The Workshop* (1868–1872), which was succeeded by *The Art Workman* (1873–1884). Both were direct English translations of the corresponding years' volumes of *Gewerbehalle* (Stuttgart: 1863–1897). The English language version was also published in New York.

Jacob Falke, 'The Vienna Exhibition in Connexion with Art-Industry. IX, Furniture', *The Workshop*, 7, 4, 1874, pp. 49–51

IX. Furniture

If we examine the Furniture in the Vienna Exhibition we cannot fail immediately to remark two things, first, the want of repose and stability, the fluctuation of the taste of the day; and secondly, the sudden manifestation of certain new tendencies struggling for the mastery. This is of course true only with regard to civilised states which follow the stream of the times, but these are not the only countries represented in the Exhibition by objects of this sort. The East has now not only contributed objects of domestic furniture, but has erected whole dwellings and separate houses.

In the enceinte[5] of the Exhibition there was a so-called Oriental quarter, consisting of a group of Egyptian buildings with a palatial mansion, a Morocco villa, a Persian building, which however is entirely artificial, and a Turkish residence with some smaller Turkish buildings. Apart from what is nailed and rivetted in these houses, and so does not come under the category of furniture, there is little of interest from our point of view, as it is well known that the all-important parts of oriental furniture consist of woven stuffs, carpets, divans, hangings, &c., of which we have already spoken. Their woodwork is very insignificant. At present indeed it is becoming more important in proportion as the manners and customs of Turkish and Egyptian magnates begin to assimilate to those of Europe. We see a proof of this in the rich drawing room of the Turkish house, in which every chair and sofa is of European type. Similar articles are also to be seen in the Egyptian department, while the Egyptian palace retains its more genuine and antique appointments. In upright articles of furniture, such as low tables, cabinets and chests of drawers, Turkey exhibits a few covered with a mosaic of mother of pearl, but even these have adopted European forms, and have no special importance or delicacy of execution.

Hence it is only European furniture that claims any great interest for us, and this is exhibited in such perfection with regard to the different countries and their peculiarities, that it leaves us nothing more to be desired in order to form an exact appreciation of its present standpoint. Austria naturally occupies the greatest space, not only because she is at home, and that of course she takes the lion's share, but also because her furniture manufacture is a very important branch of her industry. Next follow France, England, Germany and Italy, and even the smaller states of Denmark and Belgium are well represented. Some few specimens are contributed from Sweden, Spain and Portugal, and some from Russia.

With the exception of Russia, who displays a tendency to give to her more delicate articles of furniture the stamp of the national ornamentation of her wooden houses, all these countries show nothing but the modern type, either according to the till now prevalent French fashion, or to new efforts at Reform. But with what diversity and significance does each country display its peculiarities!

Let us first look at France, which till now has taken the lead in this department of industry just as much as she has done in the world of fashion. In our former notices of other branches of Art-industry, we have often had occasion to remark that the present French taste takes its motives from the eighteenth century, and notably from its second half. Thus its furniture, as well as the plastic decorations on doors, walls and ceilings, belongs especially to the style of Louis XV. and Louis XVI. One consequence or this is, that marquetry flourishes in the French cabinet work, just as at the end of the last century, delicately executed and decorated with floral, allegorical, antique and other ornaments of the same kind. The form of these tables, chests, étagères, bedsteads and chairs, is for the most part meagre and stiff, and like their models they are often mounted in gilded bronze. Guerre brothers, Göckler, Charmois and Lemarinier and others have contributed a rich selection of such articles. Diehl[6] has more of a speciality, using instead of wood marquetry intarsia of bronze relief, or ivory with paintings and devices.

As formerly, so now, the French, besides the gilt and inlaid furniture in the style of the eighteenth century, have taken up the carved work of the Renaissance period, and execute it with the greatest delicacy, and in the utmost perfection. These last are more adapted to the library, the dining and smoking rooms, while the former, which are specifically French in their genre, are suitable for the drawing room, boudoir and bedroom. The modern French follows thus two directions, one Renaissance, the other Rococo in style, as may be seen in the house of the French Commissioners, which is intended to be a kind of model house. Of these carved articles in the sixteenth century style, which are either black in ebony or in imitation of it, or brown in walnut and oak, there are numerous exhibitors, from whom we may select the names of Fourdinois[7] and Roubillon.

In the same manner the sofas, chairs &c., are divided into their separate styles, but those which belong to the Renaissance are far less numerous and quite distinct in character. Roubillon, and Levy and Worms have some very beautiful specimens. In these there reigns far more freedom and fantasy, and the whims or an ever-varying fashion play a much more important part, especially in the upholsterer's department. Hence the chairs or sofas which belong to the period of the eighteenth century, are less severe in their style. Those that come nearest to their models are those which are covered with Gobelins tapestry in figures and landscapes, a kind of decoration, which absurd as it is, has still many representatives in France, as, for example, Braguenié and Duplan. In addition to this, in order to give them a gayer and more variegated appearance, the imitation of the oriental divans is even gaining ground. To this must be attributed all those fauteuils and chairs in which the woodwork is concealed by upholstery and a textile cover. The best specimens of this style are exhibited by Lemoine, Pénon, Levy and Worms.

Next to the French furniture manufacturers are the Belgian, but their contributions, particularly with regard to their chairs, sofas &c. are not sufficiently numerous to warrant a conclusive judgement. But their articles of upright furniture, bed, cabinets, buffets connected with a panelled wall and carved in oak, display perhaps a more distinct and decided leaning to the Renaissance of the sixteenth century. In such imitations the French are not true to their models, but transform them according to their own taste; the Belgians, on the contrary, as is also the case with their ecclesiastical art, are faithful imitators of the old style. The chief exhibitors in this branch are Snyers and Rang of Brussels.

A still more decided homage is paid to the Renaissance by the Italians, but their furniture manufacture takes a peculiar standpoint, and is of two distinct kinds, one for the house, the other for art. Of the first, we see but little in the Exhibition, nothing in fact, but a few divans and armchairs covered with silk, remarkable for very unnatural upholstery and entirely of the modern French school; the other kind, which, as we have said, is artistic, is richly represented, and shows only objects remarkable for their carving, their composition, or their workmanship, and which are intended for an artistically appointed house, or for the cabinet. Originally they were produced to satisfy the taste of the antiquarian, being either altogether imitations or exact copies. At present they are considered in general as that which they really are, modern articles of furniture in the Renaissance style, but with a view to apartments appointed *à l'antique*. The manufacture of them has attained a certain importance through the agency of dealers by whom the business is chiefly carried on, and several cities, especially Venice, Milan, Florence, Siena and Rome have a great trade in this branch.

In style and *technique* the several kinds of the old Italian wood furniture are well represented. In foremost rank as to number stand the buffets, cabinets, chimneypieces, frames, bedsteads, &c., which as to their style represent the whole Renaissance period, from its early flat ornamentation and severe composition to the solid and naturalistic alto relievo[8] of the Rococo. All is produced in a vigorous and masterly style, sometimes rude and with a certain daring, by which the Italian works are characteristically distinguished from the tame and highly ornamental productions of the French. The principal exhibitors are Frullini, M. Guggenheim, Morini, Panciera, Truci, and Ferri and Bertolozzi.

The second rank must be assigned to the marquetry, especially to the ebony specimens inlaid with ivory, in which the modern Italians display the same perfection of workmanship as their predecessors of the seventeenth and eighteenth centuries, though the design and delicacy of form do not always attain the same point. There are many excellent specimens in the Exhibition, of which we may select for notice those by Pozzi of Rome and Pogliani of Milan. The wood marquetry is of an inferior quality, and is especially defective in design. A third or fourth kind is seen in the cabinets of ebony with stones of different colours and gilt ornaments and figures in bronze, such as were produced in the seventeenth century for the art-collections and mansions of princes. An excellent specimen of this kind or work has been contributed to the Exhibition from Guggenheim's Art-institute in Venice.

The German furniture also, as represented in the Exhibition, shows a very decided leaning to the Renaissance, enhanced by conventionalised wall-decorations. There are some companies, as in Berlin and Breslau, and some private firms as Heininger's in Mainz, Stövesand in Carlsruhe, who expressly devote themselves to the Renaissance style. They exhibit single pieces, whole suites, and even rooms with wainscoting. In these we recognise a double progress, first in the direction of Art, and secondly in their freedom from French taste and hitherto prevailing fashion. Most of these German works are good in their tendency, and several are very successful in an artistic point of view, but in general they suffer from too great stiffness, as if designed with a view to architectural display. The same defect exists in the fully furnished apartments as we see them in the German compartment; they have a very creditable look, but they are altogether without gracefulness or comfort. Much of the poor impression they produce is due however to the defective arrangement of the German department, in which all aesthetic considerations have been overlooked.

The Austrian furniture, and particularly that of Vienna displays in numerous specimens the same tendency as the German, but with better success. The Austrian exhibition is very comprehensive, and gives in itself a good idea of all the oscillations and opposing tendencies which now reign in this branch of Art-industry. We find among them many failures, especially with regard to the upholstery, much of which still shows the obsolete French standpoint. They even hang the walls with thick silk covered cushions, as if to hinder the visitors from running their heads against the wall; they cover floors and walls with carpets and paper-hangings representing basket work, they decorate whatever can be decorated with a dull grey, together with many other absurdities of the same kind. Among them, however, are some works of great beauty, by sculptors, decorators, furniture manufacturers and cabinetmakers, as Schönthaler, Fr. O. Schmidt, Dübele, Ludwig and several others; also many charming models of rooms by the above named, and before all by Philip Haas and Sons. Just what we look for in vain among the Germans, the union of a certain poetical charm and comfort, with elegance and beauty, we find in a high degree in the Vienna exhibitors. The best and most perfect specimen is beyond all question the Austrian Imperial pavilion, the interior decoration and appointments of which have been executed from the ideas and designs of Storck. If we inquire after the artistic tendency of the Austrian furniture, a great part of it seems to be as it were groping in the dark, but still there comes out with more and more distinctness, from the chaos of the different styles and ideas, a modern and freely treated Renaissance. To this belong all the works of a higher character, and they are by no means few in number. Corresponding to it also carved work plays a great part in the Austrian furniture, especially in frames for mirrors and pictures which seem to be on the point of giving up their old ways, and returning to the same direction in point of style. In this respect the Vienna manufactory of Ullrich jun. has the pre-eminence. Together with carving marquetry work is also more extensively used in its application to furniture, not so much in the style of Louis XVI., as is the case with the French work, as with a leaning to older models.

   The English furniture is less distinct in its artistic tendency. Since the commencement of the efforts at reform in the matter of taste it has in every way entirely changed its character. Formerly rude and clumsy, it is now especially distinguished by the delicacy of its form and ornaments; formerly priding itself on the costliness and solidity of the material it has now become more agreeable to the eye, with inlaid work of coloured woods and ivory. The English specimens of this kind, as well as those in ivory, with black or red designs of flowers, emblematical devices and figures rather in the style of Louis XVI., are, as to their workmanship, among the most beautiful and most perfect productions in the whole Exhibition. Cooper and Holt, Walker, Morant, Holland and Sons, Jackson and Graham seem to have endeavoured to outvie one another. There is also a second point to be noticed in these articles of furniture which must be considered as a rational progress in modern Gothic. It is well known that, within the last twenty or thirty years, the English have built or restored many gothic mansions and filled them up in the same style. But their architects of the present day have arrived at a due estimation of that mistaken kind of gothic furniture which founds its claims to style and beauty on the architectonic adjuncts of buttresses, pinnacles, pillars, arches and tracery, and have restricted themselves to the rational and especially the constructive principle which pervades the furniture of the middle ages. Instead of carved work, rich articulation and prominent profiling, they keep to a more picturesque ornamentation either by a modest marquetry, by colouring the incisions, or by the introduction of miniature pictures or painted porcelains. There are several specimens of this kind of English furniture to be seen in the Exhibition, by Morant, Collinson and Lock; the most important of all is a sideboard by Cooper and Holt.

Although the English furniture has not moved in the same direction of reform as the German, Austrian and Italian, it has still made a grand step in advance as to its artistic importance, and so takes its part in that great progress of taste in all branches of art-industry to which our Exhibition bears the most undoubted testimony. Although much still goes on in the old ways, and blindly follows the worn out traces of French taste; although there is much groping in the dark, and many mistakes brought to light, still we see that, by the interchange of ideas, fashions and styles a new and more distinct direction has been given to taste, which no country, not even France, can ignore; a direction which, though it may found itself on ancient models, we may pronounce to be independent and peculiar to the second half of the nineteenth century. Success seems already assured to it. And this result must unquestionably be attributed to the museums and the efforts generated by them.

Notes

1 J. Falke, 'The Vienna Exhibition in Connexion with Art-Industry. IX. Furniture', *The Workshop*, 7, 4, 1874.
2 J. Falke, *Die Kunstindustrie der Gegenwart: Studien auf der Pariser Weltausstellung 1867* (Leipzig: Quandt & Händel, 1868), p. 116.
3 J. Falke, and C. C. Perkins, *Art in the House Historical, Critical and Æsthetical Studies on the Decoration and Furnishing of the Dwelling* (Boston: L. Prang Co., 1879).
4 'Some Critical Observations on Furnishing', *Furniture Gazette*, 12, 362, 5 July 1879, p. 2.
5 enciente: an enclosure or the enclosing wall of a, usually, fortified place.
6 Charles-Guillaume Diehl (1811–1885), furniture maker, Paris.
7 Henri-Auguste Fourdinois (1799–1871), established his Paris workshop in 1835.
8 alto relievo: high relief carving.

6

TOM TAYLOR, 'THE STUDY AND PRACTICE OF ART'

Tom Taylor (1817–1880) was a comic playwright and journalist; art critic of *The Times* (from 1857) and of *The Graphic* (during the 1870s). He studied at Trinity College, Cambridge, and then moved to London to begin his journalistic career, writing for the *Morning Chronicle* and the *Daily News*. Taylor also had a long association with *Punch* magazine rising to become editor. He went on to publish and edit books on British painters, including works on Joshua Reynolds, Charles R. Leslie, and Benjamin R. Haydon. Taylor had important friendships with members of the acting and artistic world including Ellen Terry, E.W. Godwin, and G. F. Watts.

This passage is the text of a lecture given at the soirée and prize-giving at the Bradford Mechanics Institute, School of Art, in 1874. The Mechanic's Institute was founded in 1832 as a focus for adult education, and in 1848, a School of Industrial Design and Art was established, although this took some time to be successfully established. In 1863, the Institute established professionally run classes, including textile subjects. The 1870s depression and the shock of the poor response to Bradford textiles at the 1878 Paris Exhibition meant further action was necessary and a small weaving school was opened in the Institute in 1878. This was soon enlarged to form the Bradford Technical School.[1]

Something of Taylor's approach can be found in this report of his evidence in the famous lawsuit for libel brought by J.M. Whistler against Mr. Ruskin in 1878. The waspish conclusion is perhaps typical of his sense of theatrical humour.

> Mr. Tom Taylor – Poor Law Commissioner, Editor of Punch, and so forth – and so forth: – 'I am an art critic of long standing. I have been engaged in this capacity by the *Times*, and other journals, for the last twenty years. I edited the "Life of Reynolds," and "Haydon." I have always studied art. I have seen these pictures of Mr. Whistler's when they were exhibited at the Dudley and the Grosvenor Galleries. The "Nocturne" in black and gold I do not think a serious work of art.' The witness here took from the pockets of his overcoat copies of the *Times*, and with the permission of the Court, read again with unction his own criticism, to every word

of which he said he still adhered. 'All Mr. Whistler's work is unfinished. It is sketchy. He, no doubt, possesses artistic qualities, and he has got appreciation of qualities of tone, but he is not complete, and all his works are in the nature of sketching. I have expressed, and still adhere to the opinion, that these pictures only come 'one step nearer pictures than a delicately tinted wall-paper'.[2]

Perhaps not surprisingly, as a biographer of Haydon, Taylor supported the 'art' aspect of art and design teaching, particularly in his emphasis on the role of the human figure as the basis of design.

Tom Taylor, 'The Study and Practice of Art', *The British Architect: A Journal of Architecture and the Accessory Arts*, 1, February 1874, pp. 133–135

The following paper was read by Mr. Tom Taylor at the Art Soirée of the Bradford Mechanics' Institute.

Mr. Taylor said: The Romans had a saying, "In the clash of arms the laws are dumb." In the din of electioneering strife which now prevails, what chance is there of a hearing for the small voice of Art?[3] But electioneering is a momentary distraction, coming upon a society directed from Art by other distractions quite as powerful and more permanent. There is pleasure; there is labour, with its great object of money getting; there are the higher interests connected with industry— those of science, mechanical invention, organisation of all sorts, as applied in industrial life. How is Art to find room in minds filled with these? How, indeed! Looking at the fulness of the busy lives in places like this, at the ugliness of so much of that life, its feverish activity, its absorbing interest for those who live it, if not for those who look on, one may well, at first blush, be inclined to despair of ever winning for Art anything like a standing ground within its circle. And yet many indications show that Art does make her voice heard, even in these busy haunts, and confirm one in the reasons that on reflection suggest themselves why it should be so. The gradual growth of size, stateliness, and architectural decorations in your own public buildings; the evidence, so rife in your streets, that you have arrived at the conclusion that the city is bound to provide for more than mere living and working; the gayer coloring and freer fancy of some recent local ceremonials which, in spite of unkind skies, showed a brightness of invention of which one had supposed the secret had passed away for ever from reformed Town Councils; the pictures in the private houses of your rich; the spread of copies of these by engraving and photography among the less wealthy; the frequent collection into large public exhibitions of the master-pieces of many private collections; the gradual and partial but still unmistakable improvement of design in all kinds of manufactures; the growth of classes, like those in this building, and of studies such as are to be rewarded here tonight—all show that the demands of human nature for something besides food, labour, material pleasure, and for something intellectual besides science and literature, are making themselves felt in the shape of a craving, however partial, vague, or even erroneous in its present aims, for Art—that is, for the power and means that put into outward and visible form the mind's conception of and craving after beauty. The love of music and its wide culture and extensive popularity, always remarkable in the north country, and now more marked than ever, testifies to a sense of the same want. Men must, in short, have some food for the appetite which God has implanted in them for higher things than money and the lower pleasures of sense—an appetite which is not fully satisfied even with the study of science, the delightfulness of poetry, or the spell of fiction. And the harder, more naked, monotonous, and colorless our lives, the more we feel this want. Nowhere, perhaps, is it more likely to be felt—supposing any perception left of Nature's choice beauties and better influences—than in a region given over to such manufactures as occupy this large and hard-working county and its neighbours. The same cause which so often turns north country toilers, in the teeth of the direst disadvantages of situation and circumstances, into enthusiastic field naturalists of uncommon acuteness and attainment, and into masters of a knowledge of animal, vegetable, or mineral nature all the more genuine for its local concentration, is likely to turn toilers of different temperaments into lovers of Art, if not into artists. Not that this craving, however common, whether among masters or men, would ever have covered this country with Schools of Art. They grew mainly out of the conviction, gradually forced on thoughtful statesmen and writers, that without Art it would be impossible for this country long to hold her ground against the more and more formidable attacks of the industrial armies of Europe. Our continental rivals, unable to compete with us in command of raw materials, in iron, in coal, and in energetic labour, were able, in some branches of manufacture, to neutralise our advantages in these great points by their superiority in design, owing partly to natural and social conditions, partly to better Art-teaching, and partly to delicacies of eye and hand due to the inherited influence of such teaching. It was felt that they even threatened to extend this superiority further and further. It was hoped that by giving the English instruction in design through Schools of Art in connection with a central department we should in the long run add equality if not superiority in design to our more material advantages over foreign competitors. I cannot pretend to pronounce how far this hope has been already realised. In part, I believe, it has been. And all, I think, must be satisfied that very great improvement in manufactures involving design has been observable since these schools had been at work,—a period, be it remembered, of little more than thirty years; though such schools are far from sufficient in numbers, and still more incomplete as regards methods and means of teaching. Apart, then, from such Art teaching as schools like this are meant to give,—whether they give it or not is unfortunately another question,—in the way of opening the eyes and minds of those who study in them to the perception of beauty in the world, and training their hands to some expression of it in the way of Art. they command attention besides, as essential conditions of our manufacturing prosperity, without which we shall be fighting at a disadvantage with our rivals in the manufactories and markets of the world, who are becoming every day more numerous and more formidable. This is the utilitarian view of such schools. But it so happens that every claim to support founded on such material considerations strengthens, and is, indeed, inseparable from their higher claims. What is helpful to us as manufacturers is *essential* to us as men. The industrial purposes of such schools may for the present determine the class of pupils who resort to them, and the fashion of the instruction given in them; but it is probable that in so far as this consideration has been allowed to modify their teaching it has done so mischievously, that our Art Schools are worse schools for educating designers, just in proportion as they are insufficient for training artists, and that the only way of reaping a harvest of good industrial design is by sowing the seeds of good Art. There is, in point of fact, no separating industrial design—as regards the qualifying of men either to produce or to appreciate it—from good design of any other kind. Good design is essentially one in its essence, whether shown in a stone or a statue, a pipkin or a picture. The highest perfection in contour, lines, color, and light and shadow, whether for beauty or expression, is to be found in the human form. All the other elements which the designer employs—geometric, or linear forms, foliage, shells, animals, manufactured things; as vases, weapons, musical instruments, and so forth—only exhibit in simpler and less perfect forms the beauties which find their fullest, as well as subtlest expression in the harmonies and symmetries, the curves and surfaces, the relation of parts to the whole, the effect of the purposes and functions of the whole in the determination of parts, which are to be found in the human frame. This is a truth which, stated in the general and summary way alone possible in such remarks as these, may appear doubtful or even paradoxical; but it is capable, I believe, of the fullest demonstration in detail, and such demonstration is, indeed, to my notion, in some sense the sum and substance of the teaching of every efficient school of design. I do not think, however, that this truth has been sufficiently apprehended, or, if admitted in theory, enough kept in view in the practice, either in Art provincial schools or their centre. From a short-sighted desire for rapid visible fruit in the shape of industrial design, there has been too much disposition to treat the teaching of such design as something distinct from the teaching of pure art proper, with the result of encouraging chiefly in the works sent up for competition for prizes precisely the least valuable qualities—those which can be commanded by patient, brainless, higgling labour—useless, not because it is tedious, but because it is labour wasted on non-essentials. Now, it is not to be wondered at if there should have been great errors committed in the teaching of our Art Schools—nay, if such errors should have struck root and borne seed in high places. The whole business of Art education has had to be learnt before it could be taught, and so, perforce, teaching and learning have gone on together. Our industrial design is very bad still —a great deal of it—though infinitely better than it was thirty years ago. So a great deal of our teaching of design may be, I fear is, unsound; but all the sound teaching we have is through such schools as this, and even in our errors there is, let us hope, instruction. Till very lately, England had no even nominal Art teaching except that of the Royal Academy—always imperfect, and now, at best, as unsatisfactory, I fear, measured by any high and well-considered conception of what such teaching should be, as that of the worst of the schools of design. Now, we count our Schools of Design by the hundred, and their pupils by the thousand. The department on which they depend commands the finest museum of examples of design—textile and plastic, in glass and porcelain and pottery, in wood and stone and clay, in gold and silver, in steel and brass and iron—ever got together; instructs and examines large classes of teachers and pupils; spends large sums of public money; is, indeed, one of the most conspicuous and stirring agents in public education. It will go hard with us if out of all this apparatus and all this activity we do not, at least, evoke some sound knowledge on the subject of good Art, and how to produce it. But it will not be enough to produce good designers, unless we can, at the same time, find them employers and customers capable of knowing and appreciating good design when they see it. Our national middle-class schools must teach, at least, the rudiments of Art; that our universities must carry on these rudiments to their highest conclusions, through the Art professorships lately endowed in them. At present it has hardly dawned on us that Art is an element of education at all. In truth, more has been done for our working artisans in this way than for those who call themselves their betters. Our Schools of Design are doing something for their pupils, however far short they may fall of what we may think adequate results. How near us is the time when the notion of twenty such schools in England, much more 200, would have appeared the wildest chimera; when the getting together of such a collection of casts and examples as we see here—which, however it may fail to satisfy a critical and well-informed taste in such matters, is, in comparison with any provision formerly made of the same kind, rich and rare indeed—would have been an utter impossibility; when the idea of finding a school of 200 pupils, and such an audience as the present—a polling-night audience, too, in the good town of Bradford—would have seemed a mad enthusiast's fancy! And as we have advanced thus far, why may we not hope to advance further? Why may we not anticipate the time when a second theory of Art teaching, well established at South Kensington, shall be disseminating its fruits to hundreds of affiliated schools; when good designers shall be had for the asking; when beautiful forms and colors shall be the rule, and ugly ones the exception, in our pots and pans, our silks and calicoes, our chairs and tables, our carpets and wall-papers; when the artist shall be a workman, and the workman an artist; when the amenities and refinements of Art shall no longer be the luxury of the rich, but the cheaply supplied want of the poor; when the "thing of beauty" shall be a "joy" for all, as well as a "joy for ever?" One would fain hope that beyond this season of transition, where the pressure of grim realities is felt sometimes so heavily, lies some such halcyon time of serenity and refinement, not for the few only, but for the many. If Art has nothing in store wherewith to embellish, soothe, and elevate the lot of the millions, my interest in it—and, I fancy, that of most who hear me—would be sensibly diminished. It is as the common gift that I cherish it, and would fain see it sown broader, and mixing wider and higher and bearing more fruit. As the sense of the beautiful has been given to all, though in varying degrees, I would fain see the terrible barriers reared by our habits and present social and industrial conditions between beauty and common people's lives growing lower and weaker, and all helps to this end at work; and it is chiefly for what they may do in this way, for the influence that good design in things of common use and wear is like to have in aiding in this good work, that I feel so deeply interested in such schools as this. But these are considerations addressed rather to my audience as part of the public, than to the pupils of this school. As I came here to distribute the prizes of the school, I ought to direct my observations rather to the points which occur to me as demanding the special attention of the students, and requiring to be specially inculcated upon them. The most useful form of such an address, perhaps—were I competent to give it—would be a lecture on the prize drawings, their merits and demerits, with the practical conclusions for guidance thence deducible. But I could not do this, first, because I have not had time—even were I capable of it—to acquaint myself with the work done here; next, because if I had the time, I could not venture on such a task without laying myself open to the charge of presumption; and lastly, because had I both the time and capacity, I should unquestionably, in such a critical survey, become a nuisance and a bore. But presuming that the Bradford students are like other students—open to the like temptations, liable to the same faults, tickled by the same hopes, likely to be led away by the same will-o'-the-wisps, I may say a few words, before ceasing to inflict my tediousness upon you, on some common dangers to which students of Art—and I will not consent to draw any distinction between students of Art and students of design—are liable, and venture some hints which may be of use in guarding against them. Remember that all useful work must be brain-work. Without thought your most careful toil will be all but wasted. Never be satisfied with doing anything in the way of copying or imitation without learning the lesson that should be contained in the labour. There is many a student who sends up a beautifully elaborate drawing from an industrial example or an antique, and wins a prize with it, who yet has learnt nothing from the surface relations of the light and shadow he has stippled so carefully, nothing of the facts under the surface which determined the depressions and saliencies indicated by the light and shadow—who, at the end of months of work, could not reproduce accurately the example or figure he has been studying, or any part of it—who has in fact fished all day and caught nothing. That is labour misapplied. But a student may have turned out an infinitely less elaborate piece of stippling, and yet have learnt in the course of his comparatively rough work with the stump[4]—for I believe South Kensington and the Royal Academy have at length relaxed their veto on the stump—all that the stippler failed to learn, partly, perhaps, from his absorption in the mere mechanism of his point. The first may take the prize, but the second has mastered the lesson, and of the two he is to be congratulated, if not by the person who does the prize-distributing work for which I am here tonight, and in much of which, for its own sake, I confess I take little interest; indeed, I doubt whether, all things considered, prizes will not be one of the concomitants of our present system which will be found to have fallen off from the art school of the future. The student cannot labor too hard to represent the facts of the thing before him, be it alive or dead—flower, face, animal, or still life—decorative example, or bust or cast from some masterpiece of the antique. But let him study his model before he sets to work, and determine what are the facts he means to express—as the beauty or the character; for what lesson he is studying it—whether for color or hue, or light and shade; for distribution or balance of parts; for symmetry or variety. Let him mark the means by which these characteristics are conveyed—the leading lines—those most essential to the action or expression, and which tell most on the surface of what goes on under it; then the relation of all the lines to each other, which are principal and which subordinate; and then general distribution, in what kind of curves they move, whether as radiating or as parallel lines, and so forth; the distribution of light and shadow, and its shiftings with the sun, or the movements of the thing being copied. If the object be a natural one, as bird, or animal, or flower, let the student note, besides, the beauty of all combinations and juxtapositions of hue, the wonderful harmonies in the fur of animals, the feathers of birds, the colors of flowers and leaves, the wonders of forms in leaves and petals, in themselves and in their combination with the stem and with each other. All these are intellectual exercises fraught with instruction and profit to the student; and it is for the competent master to put him in the way of systematising such questionings of his subject. And his work should soon show the effect of such question and answer, in its accuracy of proportion, its right understanding of the relative importance of component parts, and their bearings on each other—its due presentation of the leading lines which determine structure and active intention and expression. Above all, don't let the student be discouraged at the drudgery and toil which must attend his first steps. In Art, as in all other forms of progress, we must learn to walk before we can run. Now, what the student comes here for is to learn to walk. This is why he must begin by learning to draw simple geometrical forms, make uninteresting studies of cases and cubes, and spheres and the simplest pots, until his hand and eye have learnt to walk; then he may come to studies from the mind, and so to the bust, and then the cast, and, finally, the life: and in time he may be permitted to combine color with form, and so on; but still he is only learning to walk. Perhaps he may never get beyond a walk in the school at all; but even that will be of more advantage to him in his journey of life than he is now aware of. Do not expect him to be able to make pictures either, without mastery of the elements out of which pictures are made. It is no business of this school to teach him to make pictures at all—only to put him in the way of learning that art and mystery if he has a special vocation for it. Here he comes not for pleasure but for work, though it is work which contains the germ of much and high pleasure, as well as profit—profit in his enhanced sense of proportion and color in all things around him, in his greater accuracy of eye and hand for his work; if he be a workman, the invaluable power of expressing his ideas with the pencil instead of the tongue; if an engineer, his power of understanding mechanical drawings; if he be a designer for the manufacturer, at every moment, and in all he does or designs. If picture-making comes, besides all this, whether as a pleasure or an employment, well and good; but don't suppose there is anything intrinsically better in making pictures than in making shoes. There is a great deal more truly worthy of respect in making honest shoes, good for their purpose, than in making dishonest pictures, good for no purpose of a picture, and useless for all other purposes. Study from nature independent of the school, for those who can command leisure and opportunity is invaluable; and hardly any object, leaf or flower, bud or blossom, grass or twig, shell, fish, bird, or beast, but it is fraught with lessons innumerable and suggestions without end. No labour occupied in recording these lessons can be thrown away, and perhaps all the lessons of art are latent in nature. But nature alone will not suffice for the instruction of the student, for art is, as Bacon defined it, "*Homo additus naturae*"— "man added to nature."[5] Unless there passes into the student's work something of the student's self, that work has no right to be called art;—mere imitation is not, and never was, and never will be, fine art. It is in the combining, shaping, and coloring process which the facts undergo in their passage through the artist's mind that the new creation called Art is called into being. I find in a very valuable volume of "Lectures and Lessons on Art," by F. W. Moody,[6] instructor on decorative art at the South Kensington Museum,—which only came into my hands recently, or I might have derived from it some more valuable hints for these remarks —a classification, which seems to me a very fair one, of the comparative value of expression, form, color, detail, and finish in the student's work. I am thankful to know that a teacher so catholic, and, as it seems to me, so sound and right-minded as the writer of these lectures, holds a position of such authority in the school of South Kensington, for I do not remember to have read any book with which I have found myself, as a rule, more cordially in agreement. And when all is said this is the best test one can appeal to in support of one's high opinion of a book, as a subject one supposes it within one's competence to form a judgment on. Mr. Moody calls expression the very soul of art, and puts it at the head of all qualities, but points out how impossible it is to teach the subtleties of expression. The power to give expression and character are special faculties, and though study may do much to develop these powers, as we see in the case of Hogarth, they are in the nature of a divine gift, not to be taught in the school, and little to be improved there. To perceive *form*, on the other hand, is essentially a faculty to be learned; so is the perception of color; though both require special natural aptitudes, they can be cultivated to the most important extent. Knowledge of *detail* is essential, but parade of it is offensive. The careful study of all detail is necessary in the earlier stages of study, that the master come to maturity may know what to discard and what to retain of his multitudinous minor facts. Last in merit among artistic qualities, says Mr. Moody and I quite agree with him, comes *finish*. But this word is used of two things of very different importance. There is the finish, not for the sake of expressing truth, but for the look of the thing, for neatness, for parade of dexterity and patience, and there is the finish which will leave out nothing important in the representation of nature; the second a virtue in art, though the artist must still retain in his hands the power of apportioning his record of facts to his purpose; the former a vice, to which scholars in schools of design are particularly prone, being encouraged thereto, too often, by the prize-giving, local and central. At the same time, be careful not to confound this trivial and unessential finish with well-directed care, and labour in the thorough expression of all these is essential to be expressed in your subject. That is the aim of the true artist always, though he may sometimes give this expression in the swiftest, most summary fashion, sometimes with a loving, but not a finical elaboration, according as the nature of the subject and the aim of the artist may dictate. Whatever you do, be honest in your work; scamp nothing; never try to show off, to push yourself to the front; never trust to short cuts or "cribs;" never be thinking how clever you can be, or how original, but do your honest best and leave the result to find its level. All this, like most good advice, sounds very commonplace. But the great rules of art, like those of life and health, intricate as may be the problems raised by all three, are really simple. It is perseverance in the practice of them, under discouragement, and against the temptation to earn applause, or even success, at the cost of violating them, that is difficult. It should be the object of those who teach to take care first that sound rules are laid down, and then that the observance of them is not made more difficult than continuance in a straight road proverbially is, by allowing the rewards due to intelligent study to go to unintelligent, and by encouraging finical and unmeaning finish at the expense of more solid and less showy qualities, on the chances that prizes may be unintelligently awarded to unintelligent work. In conclusion. I must thank those who have contrived to steal an hour from the excitement of their election contest to listen to what I had to say. In Bradford the subject should be a special interest, considering the active and intelligent part taken in the organisation of this, among other branches of education, by a Minister,[7] whose connection with Bradford has been so long, and I may trust may continue an honour to both representative and represented.

Notes

1 *History of the Technical College*; University of Bradford: Bradford Technical College Archive.
2 J. M. Whistler, *The Gentle Art of Making Enemies* . . . (London: Heinemann, 1892), Unpag.
3 A General Election was held in 1874 resulting in the first Conservative victory in a general election since 1841.
4 Stump: a short thick roll of leather, felt, or paper usually pointed at both ends, used for shading or blending a drawing in crayon, pencil, charcoal, pastel, or chalk.
5 Francis Bacon in his *Descriptio globi intellectualis* (chapter 2): 'Ars sive additus rebus Homo', later also known in the version 'Ars est homo, additus naturae'.
6 Francis Wollaston Moody (1824–1886), designer and art critic. Author of *Lectures and Lessons on Art* (London: Bell and Daldy, 1873).
7 William Edward Forster M. P.

Part 2

DECORATIVE AND APPLIED ARTS

7

JOHN STEWART, 'ART DECORATION, AN EMPLOYMENT SUITABLE FOR WOMEN'

In 1864, Stewart advertised himself as a 'consulting and practical decorator', and in another advertisement, as a picture dealer based in Ironmonger Lane, Cheapside London. His comment in his business announcement that suggests the 'Consulting Decorator qualified to advise in the Theory and Practice of Decoration, has become as indispensable as the Consulting Engineer or Architects in their respective departments' is revealing of a developing business type.[1]

The issue of women's employment in art and design was a contentious one. In general, middle-class women were brought up to be married and run households. Any art or design activity in which women engaged at this level was on an amateur basis and purely for leisure or domestic use. There were of course women whose circumstances did not fit this model and they were able to be trained for artistic work, rather than take up the inevitable roles of governess or teacher. In 1859, the political economist and author of *Female Industry*, Harriet Martineau, developed this position in the *Edinburgh Review*:

> We look to cultivated women also for the improvement of our national character as tasteful manufacturers. It is only the inferiority of our designs which prevents our taking the lead of the world in our silks, ribbons, artificial flowers, paper-hangings, carpets and furniture generally. Our Schools of Design were instituted to meet this deficiency: and they have made a beginning: but the greater part of the work remains to be done; and it is properly women's work. There is no barrier of jealousy in the case, for our manufacturers are eager to secure good designs from any quarter.[2]

However, a more typical response to women's work is found in a letter to the editor of *The English Woman's Journal* (1862) from a 'West End Housekeeper':

> My opinion is this, that if a woman is obliged to work, at once, she (although she may be Christian and well bred) loses that peculiar position which the word lady conventionally designates; and having once

been obliged to step from drawing-room dignity, she need not hesitate as to where she steps down. It is evident to all refined and logical people that there is no real intrinsic difference between artists and other workers for money, high or low.³

Nevertheless, according to Stewart, the genteel nature of the art industries made them suitable for women as they were not strenuous, the work offered a respectable renumeration, and its methods would not interfere with existing men's employment. Inevitably, these changes led to another form of discrimination between women factory workers and female artisans.

The issue of 'suitable' women's employment rumbled on. Towards the end of the century, Alice M. Gordon (née Brandreth) as Mrs J.E.H. Gordon wrote articles on several topics, including electricity and women's education. Although it was over fifty years after women were enrolled in Schools of Design, Gordon still considered the necessity of the establishment of a School of Applied Design in London that dealt with practical design rather than art-based approaches. Her model was the New York School of Applied Design for Women, instigated by Ellen Dunlap Hopkins, in 1892. This school's purpose was to enable working-class women to be trained so that they could earn a living by developing their skills in aspects of ornamental design work. Gordon explained her point, saying: 'South Kensington teaching, as far as it goes is excellent, but passing through a course of training there the designer wants further instruction, more practical, technical, up-to-date. She also wanted to be put into communication with the manufacturer, and through the criticism of able working designers, learn the technical requirements of the market: in fact, having been shown the theories of her *Art* she wants to master her *Craft*'.⁴

Stewart's paper was first read at the National Association for the Promotion of Social Science conference in 1859.⁵

John Stewart, 'Art Decoration, an Employment Suitable for Women', *Art Journal*, 6, 1860, pp. 70–71

When sewing-machines are destroying stitching as a trade, and straw-plaiting is threatened with annihilation, from the ever diminishing size of ladies' bonnets, it cannot be surprising that, among the specialities suggested by the committee of the National Association for the Promotion of Social Science,⁶ employments suitable for females should have held a prominent place. But why employment for women? A woman's position is, or ought to be, essentially domestic. The unerring Record shows us that in ancient Israel a virtuous woman, almost as a matter of course, became a wife—one whom the heart of her husband trusted, because she did him "good," and "not evil"—who looked "well to the ways of her household," and did not eat the "bread of idleness"—whose children rose up around her to "call her blessed;" "her husband also, and he praiseth her." There are what are called "strong-minded" women, above the pleasures of domestic enjoyment; and this strength of mind usually and happily increases with length of days. But the law of population alters not, and as honest Trotty Veck[7] drew meaning from the chimes, so ought we to extract lessons from the well-balanced births of boys and girls. It was not good for man to be alone, and therefore Providence gives the one sex to be care-taker of, the other to be provider for, the household. But this wise arrangement is disturbed. Fleets, standing armies, and wars frustrate the normal law of population, and entail not only the expense of war establishments upon nations, but burdens of destitution, crime, and anxiety, through the natural protectors of so many females being drafted away from the duties of social life, and the full responsibilities of citizenship. Those interested in the proper elevation and development of industries suitable for females may especially long for, and ought earnestly to work for, the time when men shall beat their swords into ploughshares, and their spears into pruning-hooks; for in no employment can woman be so suitably engaged as in the preparation for, and due discharge of, domestic duties and responsibilities.

But before much can be done for the employment of women in any work higher than drudgery, much more attention must be paid to woman's education; and all must heartily sympathize with the remark of Lord Shaftesbury in his address at Bradford,[8] that, while too much cannot be done for boys, far too little is done for girls, in the matter of common school education. For example: in school-books, to which my attention has recently been turned, among all the books used in the National or Foreign and British schools which have come under my observation—filled as many of them are with admirable lessons for all stages of advancement in learning—I have not found in a dozen different books, half a dozen of lessons which the acutest imagination could show to be directly relative to the duties, responsibilities, or profitable employment of women. There is much, of course, common to both; but while there are hundreds of lessons bearing on the specialities of men, I doubt if there can be pointed out more than one or two bearing on the specialities of women,—even if women could all become wives; and not one bearing upon the women-life of the three or four millions of females who, in this country, are doomed to the felicity of single blessedness. This is educationally and socially a suicidal course towards a class who must be supported by labour, extraneous to the true and proper domestic duties of women; and many of whom, in the form of unwomanly shame, are taking terrible vengeance on society for the neglect of education, and who must, as a matter of necessity, worthily or unworthily support themselves. The attention which has recently been devoted to the subject of female education and employment is, however, most encouraging, and leads to the hope that recognition of defects will be succeeded by palliatives, and ultimately overthrow evils which society has, by neglect, to a large extent inflicted on itself.

In attempting to secure new employments for women, these three conditions, at least—because they are not the only conditions desirable—should be looked on as essential to permanent success, or to more than a temporary diminution of social misery. First, such employments should not be physically deteriorating, either from their continuously exhaustive character, or from that greater burden imposed by uniform posture, as in sewing. The advantages of this condition are so obvious—although often sadly neglected—that they require no argument.

The second condition is, that employment for women must be based upon strictly commercial principles, yielding the employed sufficient for respectable maintenance, the employer a fair profit on the work done, and, at the same time, supply the public with what is wanted, at a price placing it within the reach of a large class of consumers. It is comparatively easy to find special employment for special individuals, but it is not so easy to find large wants, which either exist or might be created, and which females, otherwise unoccupied, might be specially qualified to supply. And yet there are wants of this character; as, for example, the entire range of paper-hangings manufacture. It is an undoubted fact, that the small number of men who follow this trade in England have signally failed in producing what is wanted; and the consequence is, that nine-tenths of all the best, or even good paper-hangings, used in this country are manufactured in France, and are bought here, at a price which would provide ample remuneration, as well as employment, for thousands of females. Moreover, the qualities which have made English workmen fail in this branch of trade, are precisely those which would enable English women to succeed,—their lighter and more delicate manipulation, and more careful attention to detail, being exactly what would remedy the more prominent faults of English as compared with French paper-hangings; and if some of the "strong-minded women" would take possession of this branch of trade for their sex, with something of the same vigour which Florence Nightingale took possession of the hospitals, the British public would soon be constrained to bow before a similar success.

The third condition of successful employment is, that it shall not interfere with the present employment of men. To substitute women's toil for men's, without opening up new sources of employment for the latter, is evidently a social loss, rather than a social gain, inasmuch as the families of the land are dependent on the productive industry of fathers, while unmarried women have only to support themselves; and notwithstanding the strong objections to what are called men-milliners,[9] only one side of this branch is too often looked at, and account is not taken of the fact, that the young men who now stand behind counters in our large towns, are there preparing themselves for becoming the future merchants and shop-keepers of the country. Nor will it do to expect that men shall teach girls, in whom they have no interest, to supersede themselves; and while we may stigmatise as selfishness the decision of the watchmakers of London, and the porcelain painters of Worcester, not to work with women, unless under conditions which rendered women working impossible, these men were only following the instinct of self-preservation. And it may be taken as a settled point, that employments now in the hands of men will not, without a hard struggle, be given up into the hands of women. Nor is it desirable that the sexes should be placed together in workshops; for what would be socially gained in one direction by such arrangements, would be lost in another.

It is not to be expected, nor is it desirable, that one individual should charge himself with the duty of looking after, by endeavouring to provide for, all the unprotected females, and I have no ambition to assume so grave a responsibility. The suggestions contained in this paper shall, therefore, be confined to that comparatively small but interesting portion of middle-class females who have been educated at the government schools of design.

It cannot be concealed that the original expectations formed from those schools have not been realized: some have scattered blame fully and freely over the Department of Science and Art, attributing failure to the unpractical character of the education given; and this class of wise-behindhand prophets now tell us they never supposed that girls could be trained to do what was expected from them. I shall not attempt, as I do not require, to defend the deeds or misdeeds of the Department. The good accomplished almost infinitely overbalances the mistakes committed. The expectation was that girls educated in schools of design would be able to earn a respectable maintenance as designers, or wood-engravers, or porcelain-painters, or in other similar occupations. These hopes have been frustrated from various causes. Wood-engraving was, at one time, a most feasible suggestion for the employment of women; but what was true fifteen years ago, when wood-engraving was confined to books, has ceased to be so now that it has become an integral portion of the weekly press. That once light and agreeable profession now requires, as a rule, greater power of mental and even physical endurance than women are capable of, and an artistic aptitude which very few men possess. This change of circumstances has dispelled all hope of securing employment from this source for women.

The failure in pattern-drawing has also been caused, to a considerable extent, by what nothing but experience could have satisfactorily developed: and failure here is itself one of the strongest proofs of our national progress in Art-industries; so that instead of being a symptom of the failure of the Department, it may rather be considered one of the strongest evidences of its success. The progress of Art-manufactures has created new demands in the manufactories. While at one period it was enough to get a new design, and have that worked out as best they could, manufacturers now find it essential to pay as strict attention to production as to design; and hence the principal pattern-drawer has not only to design, but to take the superintendence, to a greater or less extent, of those who are to work out the designs produced. Few women have this power of superintendence, and even when possessed, it cannot be successfully exercised over men; so that the great proportion of those who were inclined to give women a fair trial at such work, have been forced to the conclusion that, commercially, men who can design and superintend with authority, are cheaper than women who can only design.

Another case of failure is found, which applies more to porcelain-painting, japanning, and such trades. In the latter, women had long been employed in the neighbourhood of Birmingham on common work, such as "spriging,"[10] and lining cheap tea-trays. But girls brought up at the schools of design go out with ideas far above such work and its wages, although, from the want of technical knowledge and manipulative experience, whatever their theoretical knowledge, their labour is commercially of less value; and dissatisfaction on both sides soon separates the master who has been overpaying, and the pupil who considers herself underpaid. This is a difficulty which only time and circumstances will overcome, and which will decrease just in proportion as the population become educated in Art and its principles. When those having acquired more or less knowledge cease to be uncommon people, they will naturally come to recognise the commercial relations of supply and demand as the only regulator of wages.

But the greatest source of failure has arisen from the unreasonable expectations formed, engendered by the ardent enthusiasm of some, and the unthinking ignorance of others. It was absurd to expect that any large number of girls should become designers, for the very obvious reason that a good designer is a creator, and those endowed with this faculty have been, and probably always will be, few, both among men and women. More was expected from these girls than was expected from either boys or men; and this arose from a totally fictitious estimate of what education in drawing could produce. The ability to draw is important; but mere power of hand and correctness of eye have the same kind of relation to a good design, that a knife and fork have to a good dinner. They are helps to the use of food, just as drawing is a help to the use of thought; but the thought constitutes the design: and as no schools can do more than aid thinking-power where it exists, schools can teach drawing, but they cannot make designers. Nevertheless, this delusion of making designers has tainted the whole atmosphere of these useful seminaries; and instead of looking at their education as a means of bettering industrial pursuits, it has been more generally fancied by the girls to be a means, through them, of regenerating the national taste. They go to situations not as workers, but as teachers and authorities in Art. The vast majority fail, as a matter of course; and the failure disgusts them, and tarnishes the fame of the department. The reason of the failure is obvious: the branches which have generally been considered open to them have been such as only high talent could fill; and it is no disgrace for many girls to fail, where so few men succeed. What is wanted for girls, is work in which the knowledge of drawing can be turned to account, according to the capacity possessed, and which shall combine the substantial advantages of trade, with the mental enjoyments of Art; work which shall furnish scope for a dozen different capacities, presenting each with a continual stimulus to progress, and, as a consequence, increased remuneration.

Art-decorations are, therefore, suggested as being peculiarly fitted to give extensive employment to the female pupils of these schools of design, without taking from the labour of men, because decorations in the style proposed are practically and socially unknown among the people of this country. Believing that mere theories on such subjects, unless based on facts, are practically useless, I have reduced this theory to practice, and have ample illustrations to show, so far as first attempts can show, what these girls can do, and how their various degrees of ability may be employed upon strictly commercial principles, at wages reasonably remunerative. There is, first, the rough sketch of the design produced by a few charcoal scratches; then there is the working out of that design in detail, consistent with the general forms; both of which require a combination of thought and skill which only the better class of pupils can produce. But these accomplished, the humbler talents become as available as the higher, and the first operation is to make what is technically called the "pounce," that is, to prick the lines of the detailed drawing, so that, by a little dust or charcoal rubbed over the drawing, the lines may be left on the ceiling or walls sufficiently clear to be followed by a blacklead pencil. This pencilling can also be done by girls of inferior ability, because the design being there they have only to follow it. Then comes what is called the dead colouring, that is, the laying on of flat tints within the pencil marks, and in which keeping within these marks is the chief, almost the only, ability required. Then the forming of the leaves by light and shadow requires higher ability and training; the painting of the flowers, fruit, and birds, still higher attainments; while the figures in the centres present range sufficient for the very highest genius—Raffaelle and his contemporaries not considering the figures or designs for such decorations beneath the efforts of their lofty intellects. The variety, combined with harmonious unity, of which such decorations are capable, places them infinitely above paper-hangings as a style of higher-class decoration, while the scope they afford for the exercise both of design and execution, often removes them entirely from the routine of trade to the dignity of Art. They have, moreover, all the sanitary and lasting advantages of oil paintings, combined with that interest and pleasure which artistic manipulation so pre-eminently possesses over mechanical block-printing; while their forms can be adapted to suit any shape, without appearing as parts of broken wholes: the expense to the public being about double that of good French paper-hangings, and the remuneration to the girls being from fifteen to thirty shillings a week.

Practically, a severe test of this suggestion for the employment of these females has been successfully made on the hall ceiling of Admiral Sir Maurice Berkeley's[11] house, in London—perhaps the first ceiling in Britain which has been decorated by a lady in the ordinary course of business; and the execution of that work met with the approbation of the heads of the Art department. The work can therefore be done; and an uncultivated field is thus opened for an interesting and remunerative employment for females. The public must determine the extent to which this new ground shall be redeemed from waste. At present there are good reasons for believing that such a branch of industrial Art will prove of inestimable advantage to a considerable class of females who, from their tastes and education, are sure to feel privations more acutely, but to whom the means of self-support have hitherto been closed.

This, and kindred branches of Art industries, deserve attentive consideration from all interested in the extension of female employment.

Notes

1 *London Art Review*, 1864, pp. 28 and 36.
2 H. Martineau, 'Female Industry', *Edinburgh Review*, 109, July 1859, p. 172.
3 *English Woman's Journal*, October 1862, p. 139.
4 A. M. Gordon, 'Women as Students in Design,' *Fortnightly Review,* 55, 328, 1894, p. 523.
5 *Transactions of the National Association for the Promotion of Social Science* 1859, Social Economy Dept. (London: Parker, 1860), p. 729.
6 National Association for the Promotion of Social Science: A British social reformist group founded in 1857 by Lord Brougham. The Association published Transactions of its meetings. It was dissolved in 1886.
7 Trotty Veck: Toby "Trotty" Veck, is a disillusioned character in Charles Dickens 1844 novella *The Chimes*.
8 Lord Shaftesbury: Anthony Ashley-Cooper (1801–1885) a British politician, philanthropist and social reformer.
9 Men-milliners: Sellers of haberdashery and hats for women, May be derogatory as referring to a trifling, or effeminate man.
10 Spriging: To decorate with a design or motif resembling a sprig or sprigs of foliage, flowers, etc. often in embroidery.
11 Admiral Maurice Frederick FitzHardinge Berkeley, 1st Baron FitzHardinge, (1788–1867).

8

PROF. [J. H.] CHAMBERLAIN, 'THE PROGRESS OF DESIGN'

This article is a newspaper report on the text of a lecture given to the Midland Institute[1] that was the last in the series of lectures on the 1862 International Exhibition as it related to the manufacturers of Birmingham. Chamberlain was long associated with the art school, being on the Council then later as chairman.

Chamberlain was a Birmingham architect, familiarly known as 'professor', who worked mainly in the Gothic revival style. He promulgated these ideas in his essays on 'Gothic Architecture and Art' for the American Architect and Builder's Monthly in 1870 and 1871. He was interested in the ideas of John Ruskin and in 1853 gave the RIBA Silver Medal essay 'On the introduction of colour, including paintings in fresco, to promote or heighten the effect of architectural composition generally', that encouraged Ruskinian ideas of the use of colour. Ruskin later chose Chamberlain as one of the trustees of his Guild of St. George.[2] In addition to his work in civic architecture, especially in Birmingham, his designs for stained glass, metalwork, and furniture were also important.

Chamberlain's lecture was a survey of design since the 1851 Exhibition and covered several issues that reflected contemporary concerns. These included the principles of design generally; the division between the Classicists and Gothicists; examples of good works, especially in wrought iron, and a stinging critique of the Crystal Palace building as re-erected in Sydenham.[3]

Chamberlain's Ruskinian credentials were also evident in a later lecture, given at the Birmingham and Midland Institute on 22 October 1883, titled 'Exotic Art'. In that paper, he argued that exotic art, i.e. that which was imported from foreign climes was not, and never was, appropriate for England, and should not have been allowed to displace what he called 'native art'. His call was to 'resolve, even if at first we do it badly, to express that admiration [of native art] in our own way, by such means as we can find out or invent, and lay aside the supreme folly of clothing our own ideas in the worn-out garments of other nations'.[4] This meant revisiting the Gothic style, but not repeating it unthinkingly; instead to adapt it to modern times. This lecture concluded by commending what he saw as the modern and sincere love of nature that was growing in the country, and the good effect that this was having in combating perceived ills: 'We have actually dared to thwart the railway engineer, and his more dangerous accomplice the director. We have determined that, ere it is too late, some part of England shall be free from the kind of curse that has turned the once lovely country between this town and Wolverhampton into a loathsome desert'.[5]

Prof. [J. H.] Chamberlain, 'The Progress of Design', *Birmingham Daily Post*, 28 May 1863

On Monday evening Professor Chamberlain delivered the last of the Midland Institute series of lectures, on the International Exhibition,[6] as bearing upon the manufactures of Birmingham, in the lecture theatre of the building in Paradise Street. The subject of it was "The Progress of Design." With regard to the progress of design, as shown in the work exhibited in the last exhibition, the lecturer said, the press of the country had favoured the country with a great deal of congratulation, and certainly some amount of it might be considered to be well founded. But at the same time this estimate must in a great measure depend upon the position in which one stood to take it. As compared with the Exhibition of 1851 there was apparent a wonderful and notable advance, but if one took one's standpoint in distant time one would be disposed to take a very favourable view of the matter. But from whatever point of view the matter was regarded, persons who understood the matter could not fail to see that the subject of design as applied to manufacture was singularly misunderstood. The object seemed to have been to get as much ornament as possible from it did not matter what source, and to apply it indiscriminately to whatever turned uppermost. For instance Gothic church ornament was found applied to so-called Gothic furniture in the most absurd fashion imaginable. This was illustrated by a drawing on the black board. The square outline of a chair was shown, and, the object being to make it Gothic, in the approved style, a pinnacle was added to each of the uprights forming the back, an arch was thrown into the intermediate space, a pediment was made to surmount the top, and tracery being thrown in to fill up the interstices, the legs were buttressed to give strength to the superstructure and tear the dresses of the ladies. In this way, said the lecturer, ornament was heaped in without regard either to taste, comfort, or convenience. Another illustration was afforded in the matter of fenders, where the whole design was incongruous and inconvenient, and always had been. One of the first principles of design was that it should be suited to the purpose for which the article on which it was bestowed was intended. And the next was that it should be suited to the material on which it was used. This was constantly forgotten. He remembered going to Sheffield once to buy a Gothic fire grate, and being shown several, he ventured to submit that one was not Gothic at all, when the manufacturer, with a look that he should never forgot, said: "I really do not know what you would have; this was faithfully copied from a tomb in York Minster." That man evidently forgot that a tomb was usually a work in stone, and a fire-grate a work in iron. Design, when left to common sense, though not generally very elaborate, possessed, nevertheless, their fitnesses. A village carpenter, for instance, making a gate, knew that it must be made strong enough to bear the strain of swinging backwards and forwards, and that it must be so hung that there should not be an undue strain on the top hinge. He therefore passed a bar diagonally from one angle to the other. But in our house doors, in which there was the same requirements, fashion demanded that the cross timbers should be either perpendicular, or perpendicular and horizontal. The result was that in a very short time after our houses were built the doors were found to drop so that we could not open them. A carpenter was sent for, and a piece was shaved off the bottom. Then it was found that the draught came in at the top, and the door was straightway forced in that direction; and so matters went on, the counter operations causing some expense and great discomfort because the first principles of design were not attended to. But, supposing both the nature of the material and the necessities of the design were understood, then came the matter of ornament. And here came in a third rule-namely that the rude form was to be considered as the skeleton or ground work of the ornamentation; in other words, that the ornamentation must spring out of the original construction. All ideas of ornament were derived from the contemplation of the great world of nature; in fact, ornament was but the reproduction of what a man saw around him. But it was necessary to treat this ornament in a conventional form. He did not mean by this, that it should be treated unnaturally or absurdly, for conventionalism in the sense in which he used the word, was merely taking out of nature what one wanted to imitate, and using it in accordance with what one wanted to work upon. For instance, if one desired to represent an ivy leaf one would analyse the subject, and find that the form of the ivy leaf in nature was founded on five triangles, superimposed one on the other. Then, if the constructive form were the most severe of forms, a square, these triangular forms would be so far modified as that each line of the leaf should be square; but if the constructive form was founded on the line of beauty it would be proper to bring the leaves into the highly naturalistic at once—that was, to copy nature as nearly as possible. And out of this grew the next principle of design—that the more severe the form the more conventional must be the treatment of its ornamentation. This was exemplified in the Egyptian obelisks—and the Egyptians understood the principles of design as thoroughly as any nation—where the only ornaments were the pyramid at the top and the strange hieroglyphics that covered it. It was also exemplified in the Grecian column, when advancing from the more severe square to the less severe round the artist introduced more ornament, as shown in the fluted lines and in the capitals. The Gothic clustered columns went a step further, and then we got foliage introduced as an ornament to the columns. Having thus dealt with the principles of design, the lecturer went on to show how far they had been applied in late years, as shown in the late Exhibition. Taking architecture, he referred, first to the building in which the Exhibition was held. The first Exhibition building,[7] he said, though built in a hurry was in point of originality and adaptability certainly very meritorious. But the second was simply a piece of very bad engineering, looking for all the world like a row of railway arches with a series of photographic sheds on the top.[8] It was said there was not money enough to beautify it, but that was not his point. According to his notion the whole building was so radically false in construction that it would be impossible to render it beautiful. And then as to money, it had cost more than the old Exhibition building and that at Sydenham together; but even if it had not, his contention was that if an architect had money enough to build any building he had money enough to produce some amount of good looks with it. Well, the nation was going to buy it, and when once we had got it we should find that there would be an enormous sum of money required to make it look decent and keep the wet out. So that if one were to judge of the progress of design in architecture by the building in which the Exhibition was held, one must inevitably come to the conclusion not only that there had been no advance on 1851, but that there had been a deplorable falling off. But fortunately, we were not left to make that humiliating comparison; there were a vast number of architectural designs in the building, many of them very good, and all showing what was going on in the architectural world. They showed that the contest between the Classicists and the Gothicists was not yet decided; and they showed also that church architecture had fallen almost entirely into Gothic hands, and that though three-fourths of the domestic architecture was of the old sort, the lump was liberally leavened with Gothic. Besides which there were many specimens, mostly by young architects, representing the new school of neo-Gothicists, or, as they were sometimes called, the Victorian Gothicists. Altogether, however, if we were to compare architecture, as displayed in the Exhibition, with architecture a hundred years ago, we had reason to congratulate ourselves; but if we merely regarded it in itself, the contemplation of most of the architecture of the present day was not a very encouraging sight. Passing then, in review, the history of the Gothic revival, commenced towards the latter end of the last century, and directed into its proper channel by Augustus Welby Pugin, the lecturer went on to show how, since the death of the latter, there had been a wonderful impetus given to the study of the art. Cheap travelling and photography, he said, had brought us face to face with foreign examples, and the consequence had been a discovery that most of our modern Gothic buildings were merely correct copies of early English work, and that there were hundreds of forms of Gothic of which we had never dreamt. And thus the school of neo-Gothicism had been raised up much to the horror of the old Gothic professors. But this school was, in his opinion, right in a great many of its doctrines. In the first place he thought it was established that old Gothic, however well it was suited to its own time, was not suited to the wants of the present day; and, secondly, that many of these foreign forms were specially invented to meet requirements more like our own. If, then, we were to advance at all, we could only do so by taking the widest possible view of all that Gothic had done and was capable of doing and fuse these forms into a new style. For his own part, much as he loved Gothic and believed in it, he would, if he were convinced old Gothic could not be made suitable to our present wants be content to drop it altogether. But he believed it was capable of anything and everything required of it, and that in its expansion it improved, and in so far as a living art was preferable to a dead one because better. Passing on to speak of ecclesiastical furniture, the lecturer briefly referred, in terms of high commendation, to two organs designed by Mr, George Sedden,[9] and then went on to speak in similar terms of the revival of the old form of tomb, with the effigy of the dead person in a recumbent attitude. That, he said, was the ancient form, and in his opinion by far the best. It was not until the time of the Renaissance that these dead people seem to be afflicted with a desire to get up. First they raised themselves off the pillow, resting their head on their hand, and then, in the days of Elizabeth, they got up on their knees; so that one often saw the father and mother, with their seven or eight sons and nine or ten daughters, all kneeling one after the other on the top of their tomb. That was tolerable, but in a very short time these figures got bolt upright, and as if gifted with some sort of galvanic life, took to attitudinising on the top of their monuments. Surely this was all most unfit; nothing could be better than the repose of the recumbent figure or more expressive of the rest of death. And therefore, he was pleased to see a return to the old way of doing things in the exhibition of 1862. Speaking next of ironwork, he said the advance of design in that department was something wonderful, as compared with the exhibition of 1851. One thing in particular was noticeable, and must have been noticed with delight, and that was the greater prevalence of wrought iron work. It not only spoke well for the advance of art, but for the advance of the art workmen, for certainly there was more talent required, and that talent was better fostered in the man who saw a welcomed beauty growing gradually up under his hammer than him who simply saw it cast all at once in front of the furnace. The work, too, was far superior; there was life in it, and perfection of form, whilst in cast work always dead, ugly, and imperfect. If the latter were done honestly, it succeeded only in providing the simplest forms, and if it were done dishonestly it was vulgar and useless. Of all things that filled the mind with disgust the sight of a cheap gas fitting was about the worst. He regretted very much that he had not a drawing of Messrs. Hardman's gates[10] there, for if he had he would have had an example of all that was beautiful in design and excellent in workmanship as applied to artwork in iron. The largest piece of iron work, however, was the Hereford screen, manufactured by Mr Skidmore of Coventry,[11] but it stood in a bad light at the bottom of a flight of steps, and therefore could not be seen to advantage. Still one could not look at it without admiring it, and fixed in its place it was no doubt, allowing for some faults, a skilful piece of work. Mr Skidmore, too, had a metal shrine to the memory of Bishop Pearson,[12] designed by Mr Blomfield,[13] a son of the late Bishop of London, but this is thought to be a great failure. It was an attempt to do in iron what had formerly been done in stone. He was not going to argue that iron might not someday supersede stone, but what he contended for was that the form of work applied to the two materials must be different. And the neglecting of this rule, indeed, was the fault of all attempts to apply metal to architecture. The builder adopted the same forms that had been applied to wood and stone, entirely different materials. The Oxford roof for instance was a failure and for that very reason. In fact, taking New Street Station,[14] which was ugly enough, there was no doubt that if iron were to come into use as a roofing material this must be taken as in some sort the form to be used in applying it to the purpose. The right method of decorating that form would have to be found, and it would not be found until the material used, the construction of the building, and the purpose for which it was intended, had all been carefully considered and the design suited to them. He was sorry to see that more advances had not been made in this matter of metallic architecture; there were very few specimens in the Exhibition, and what there were not made with the primary object of seeing what could be accomplished in this matter. As stained glass had been treated so fully by Mr. Hardman Powell[15] only a week before, and as he differed from Mr. Powell in many respects, he should say but little about it. It seemed to him, however, that the great defect of modern stained-glass windows was that the artist forgot he was making a picture *through* which the light was to fall, and not a picture *on* which the light was to fall. And out of this grew all that false art which filled the picture with shadows and endeavoured to make it what it could not by any possibility become—a finished picture according as paintings on canvas were said to be finished. It seemed to him that the stained window was merely a method of decorating by colour, and that so long as there was variety and harmony of colour, the picture was a mere secondary matter. And this seemed to be the ancient theory, for in all old works of art of the kind, the figure did not stand out and stare at everybody who entered the building, but lay back, modestly allowing the window to be rather admired because of the effect of its colour, or the rest of the building, than because of the picture represented in it. After speaking highly of Messrs. Hardman's window, at Ely, the lecturer went on to speak of the progress of design as applied to furniture, or rather of the want of progress in that direction. He sweepingly denounced the present forms of furniture, said the object seemed to be to crowd as many incongruities together as it was possible, and particularly ridiculed the notion of decorating our floors with gay carpets, whose colours spoilt the effect of everything else in the room. He saw no hope for a better state of thing, he said, so long as furniture remained in the hands of the upholsterer, and the upholsterer know nothing of art and had no taste. There were certainly a few pieces of Gothic furniture, designed by Mr. Sedden and others, but they were very little regarded, because they had no crocketted pinnacles, were not buttressed, and had no tracery. In them the principles of Gothic art were adapted to the material and the purpose for which the article was intended, and people did not recognise that it was Gothic. Having thus dealt with design, as shown in English manufactures, the lecturer brought his lecture to a close with a hasty glance at the French side of the Exhibition. The difference between the two sides, he said, seemed to be remarkable chiefly in this—that the French side seemed to have been stocked by persons who had consulted their neighbours as to what they intended to make, and had worked together harmoniously to exhibit something which taken as a whole, should be creditable to the nation, while the English side seemed to have been stocked by persons who had determined not to work with their neighbours, but, if possible, to make a great show individually.

On the whole, however, he thought we might congratulate ourselves on the progress made since 1851, and he did hope that, if we ever had another, the works he had undertaken to review would be still better in design and execution.—The lecturer was frequently applauded during the progress of his lecture.

Notes

1 Midland Institute: Founded in 1854 as an early example of adult artistic, scientific and technical education in Birmingham.
2 Guild of St. George: Founded as the St. George's Company in 1871 by John Ruskin. It was formally constituted in 1878. Ruskin grew increasingly interested in social concerns and the scourge of industrial capitalism that he saw. The Guild was intended to counter these developments by linking pre-industrial ideals with contemporary social improvements.
3 The lecture was also précised in *Building News*, 12 June 1863, p. 446.
4 Reprinted in W. Harris, *The History of Our Shakespeare Club* (Birmingham: 'Journal' printing. office, 1903), p. 74.
5 W. Harris, *The History of Our Shakespeare Club*, p. 74.
6 The International Exhibition, London, 1862.
7 Refers to the Crystal Palace, Hyde Park, and later Sydenham London.
8 See the illustrated article by Betty Bradford, 'The Brick Palace of 1862', *The Architectural Review*, 132, July 1962, pp. 8, 15–21. The building was demolished soon after the exhibition closed.
9 John Pollard Seddon, (1827–1906) designer. 1862 Exhibition Catalogue Class, 30, items listed at 5815.
10 John Hardman and Co. 'Medieval Metal Manufacturers' exhibited both ecclesiastic and domestic metalwork in the Gothic style at the International Exhibition, 1862.
11 The Hereford Screen, designed by Sir George Gilbert Scott (1811–1878) was made by Coventry metalworking firm Skidmore & Co. for Hereford Cathedral choir, England in 1862. It is now located in the Victoria and Albert Museum.
12 Metal canopy for the tomb of John Pearson, Bishop of Chester, d. 1686.
13 Mr Blomfield: architect Sir Arthur William Blomfield (1829–1899).
14 The station was designed by Edward Alfred Cowper and built by Messrs. Fox, Henderson & Co. who had previously worked on the design of The Crystal Palace. When completed, it had the largest arched single-span iron and glass roof in the world, spanning a width of 211 feet (64 m) and being 840 ft (256 m) long.
15 John Hardman Powell, (1827–1895) followed Pugin as chief designer at Hardman and Co.

9

CHRISTOPHER DRESSER, 'HINDRANCES TO THE PROGRESS OF APPLIED ART'

Christopher Dresser was a British designer, design reformer and theorist, author, industrial adviser, and businessman. He trained at the Government School of Design in London between 1847 and 1854, and soon after was appointed as a lecturer in botany at the School of Design. This position lasted until 1860, when he established his own design practice. He was soon successful in becoming a designer and consultant for a wide range of art industries.

The theories that informed his practice are explained in his *The Art of Decorative Design* (1862) and later developed in other works including the *Principles of Decorative Design* (1873) and *Modern Ornamentation* (1886). The need to understand design in both its historical and cultural context was important to Dresser, and this attitude is found both in his writings and his practice. His well-known influences, derived from his time spent in Japan, acted as a catalyst for others but were also crucial to his own practice and business enterprises.

The commentary on Dresser's paper at the end of the lecture raised several points, including two ongoing and contentious issues; the apparent superiority of French designs, and the issue of drawing and the figure. In the ensuing discussion, the Chairman, Matthew Digby Wyatt, stated that French ascendancy in design 'arose from the fact that the workmen who produced those beautiful objects had been taught form and figure drawing, and to imitate all kinds of natural objects'. He went on to criticise the lack of drawing skills in English workers: 'The great complaint with regard to the ordinary English workman was, that if he had to produce anything beyond straight lines, or very simple scrolls, which got tiresome by repetition, he produced something which was repugnant to the eye. The fact was he could not draw the human figure, or animals, in fact he had never learnt to imitate the natural objects, representations of which he wished to introduce into his design'.[1]

Wyatt then went on to critique designs that were not ornamented, and was in clear dispute with Dresser's approach:

> He admitted that objects of a negative character might be perfectly pleasing; for instance, one of the vases before him was perfectly agreeable,

both in form and colour, but it was strictly negative – there was no design in it. Many examples of Indian work were very beautiful, both in form and colour, but there was no imitation in them, and therefore there was nothing on which the eye delighted to dwell.[2]

George Wallis also had his say after the lecture, in a comment refuting Dresser's idea about the South Kensington museum's object labels, that did have a wider significance. Dresser had suggested 'that it would be very valuable if, by the side of certain specimens, a description were given why the object was considered good, or why it was considered bad or defective, why it should be studied, or why avoided'. Wallis thought that there was labelling enough in the museum already, and if they did as was suggested, the student would complain that they gave him more tablecloth than dinner'.[3] Interestingly, Dresser responded to this criticism with further commentary about the 'Chambers of Horrors' that had once existed in the Museum to explain false design principles. He said: 'It was not reasonable that any manufacturer should be allowed to cater for the most ignorant and depraved taste and produce whatever abortions he thought fit. All things of this sort ought to be checked in the same way as debasing literature'.[4] In any event, Philip Cunliffe-Owen, the director of the museum, inaugurated the series of *South Kensington Museum Handbooks* published from the 1870s, that went into some depth to explain the collections.

Christopher Dresser, 'Hindrances to the Progress of Applied Art', *Journal of the Society of Arts*, 20, 12 April 1872, pp. 435–440

Before commencing our consideration of the subject which I have the honour of bringing before you this evening, I must ask you to call to mind a few facts, as these will enable us to see that all hindrances to the progress of applied art result in pecuniary loss to the nation. Notice, first, that England is essentially a manufacturing country; second, that it exports its manufactures to every part of the world; and, third, that the intrinsic value of the article produced is, in many cases, of less importance than the pattern which the article manufactured bears. Bad note paper in a handsome wrapper sells; bad carpet, if it has a graceful pattern, sells; bad jewellery of elegant design fills our shop windows, and secures to its producers large profits. Indeed, we everywhere meet with "shoddy" material, wrought into forms of beauty, selling as though it were of real worth. Art, then, has a commercial value!

I cannot too strongly urge upon your notice the fact that nearly every material may, by the agency of art, be rendered valuable, even if, as mere material, it be almost worthless. Clay is, of all substances capable of art treatment, perhaps the most common and the most valueless, yet in the hands of the artist it assumes forms which so exalt it as to render it both estimable and lovable, and of great commercial worth. One man forms it into bricks, another into works of art; thus the same quantity of the same material becomes in the one case worth a fractional portion of a penny, while in the other it will sell for many pounds. That man is of greatest value to his country who draws to it the largest amount of wealth with the least expenditure of material.

I might say much more upon the commercial value of applied art, and show that many of our vast manufactures depend for their success upon the art which the articles produced bear upon them. Window curtains—whether of lace or damask, wall-papers, earthen vessels of all descriptions, silversmiths' work, jewellery, carpets, and many other forms of goods, depend for their sale largely upon the form into which they are wrought or the pattern with which they are endowed, and these goods constitute the major portion of our exports and our wealth.

Having called your attention to the fact that decorative, or applied art, has a commercial value, I can proceed to my subject, as you now perceive that whatever hinders the progress of applied art stands in the way of our commercial success and militates against national progress. The hindrances to art prosperity, to which I am about to call your attention, are not such as concern the artist only, but are impediments to our manufacturing interest, and concern others to the same degree at least as they do the artist. A faithful treatment of my subject, then, would involve the expression of no merely personal grievances, but the discovery and revelation of whatever hinders the progress of applied art in our country, and if so treated my subject would clearly be within the province of the Society of Arts to introduce, and of its members to consider; but were I to express to you the hindrances impeding the progress of merely personal ideas, I should not be justified in standing before you in this institution.

In commencing my subject, let me say that while I shall express to you my feelings fearlessly, and with that boldness which a firm confidence in the truth of the opinions which I shall express induces, yet I know that, for lack of knowledge, I may err in my judgment, and that even my reasoning faculties may be misguided; yet having devoted myself earnestly to the study of applied art for more than five-and-twenty years, I may at least claim to have thought upon the subject which I now introduce to your notice; and if in this paper I am severe in my censures or harsh in my denunciations, believe me that all results from a sincere love of my art and an earnest desire to see removed whatever stands in the way of its progress.

One of the chief hindrances to the advancement of decorative art is to be found in designers themselves, for there are many pattern-drawers who are a disgrace to the profession, inasmuch as the works which they produce manifest only gross ignorance, and are, therefore, altogether unworthy of notice. Of these I will not speak, but I desire that they should understand that whatever is produced which is of debasing character tends to the extermination of decorative art, for who would not prefer a plain article to one covered with graceless forms and inharmonious colours.

Passing from these men, to whom the name of "artist" cannot be applied, to those designers who have a certain amount of art-ability, we notice that the works produced by these latter are often inconvenient to use while they are beautiful in form, and are thus of a character calculated to bring art into disrepute. An art object should be useful as well as beautiful, if it is intended to fulfil a utilitarian purpose, yet not one poker out of a hundred is so formed that it can be used with comfort, nor is one tea-pot out of fifty so made that it will admit of the tea being poured from it without an expenditure of force greater than is necessary in order to the support of the weight which has to be lifted. By leverage a pound may balance a hundredweight, as in the steel-yard; so in the case of a tea-pot, by leverage that which weighs four pounds may be as heavy to lift as that which weighs eight. Although the law which regulates the placing of handle and spout on all vessels from which liquids are poured is thoroughly understood, yet it does not appear to be known to one designer in a hundred, judging from the vessels which we see offered for sale in our shops. In like manner, pokers have become so inconvenient to use that it is impossible to break coal or even poke the fire with one without hurting the hand; hence ladies have begun to regard fire-irons as mere ornaments, and to keep a little second poker and tongs for use, which latter are hidden in some corner, as objects unfit to be seen. There is nothing which tends to retard the progress of applied art more than the production by designers of objects which are inconvenient to use; and be assured that the most perfect beauty may be combined with the most complete utility; in other words, that which is most beautiful may be perfectly useful. How is it, I ask, that designers will not inform themselves upon subjects which, to them, are all important, and without a knowledge of which they cannot produce acceptable works? I am often amazed at the ignorance of my fellow ornamentists upon subjects which they ought perfectly to understand; and yet many of these men can draw well, and combine forms in a truly artistic manner, but their works, through not being adapted to answer the end of their creation, only tend to bring the beautiful into disrepute, by leading persons to suppose that if a work is graceful and lovable it cannot be used with comfort.

Our worst enemies are those of our own household; so, in like manner, the worst enemies to the progress of applied art are ignorant designers. If we, as designers, will but educate ourselves, we shall thereby remove one of the chief hindrances that impedes the progress of applied art.

It is a strange thing that to this hour the great majority of the designers, or pattern-drawers, employed in our manufactories are men almost wholly without education, and chiefly from comparatively low life. The son of a weaver in a carpet-works or lace-factory, if he manifests any taste for drawing, is put in the designing-room and is trained to draw patterns, but as he is placed there at the age of from ten to twelve years, and is the son of parents who could not afford to have him educated beyond being taught to read and write, he has but little knowledge when he commences his art-training, and as, in the great majority of designing-rooms, he never sees a work on ornament, nor a good example of true art-work, he gains simply a technical knowledge of the manufacture, and acquires no insight into the character of true art. A man cannot help his origin, neither is he to be despised for being the child of poor parents; but if he remains in ignorance he cannot be expected to produce noble works, nor to exalt the manufacture which he strives to adorn with forms and colours, While a man is not to be blamed for being born of poor parents, he is open to censure if he does not strive to gain whatever knowledge is placed within his reach. Nearly every town in the kingdom has now its drawing-school, where a certain amount of art-knowledge may be gained, and connected with these schools there are frequently art-libraries. That youth who is worthy to be called an art-student will avail himself of whatever means are open to him, and even if he be employed for long hours in the factory, he will strive by reading, sketching, and, beyond all things, by thinking, and by the study of nature, to gain such knowledge as will lead him to draw patterns such as will please persons of education, by revealing to them the fact that he who addresses himself to them through the agency of form and colour is also a man of education.

If it is any consolation to you, my fellow-students of applied art, let me say that I, with you, have felt the want of education, and have known the poverty of small means, but by foregoing for a time the pleasures which others enjoyed, and by continued close application to the study of our beloved art, I gained the victory over that poverty, and that utter want of education under which I for a time suffered; and now I can say that I sit at the tables of rich men, and that men of learning honour my table with their presence. I would not for a moment say what I do were it not for the thought that these words may encourage some poor student to work on till he rises through his poverty to that position in which he can present, his works fairly before our notice, and charm us with his knowledge.

Certain manufacturers may truly be regarded as hindrances to art progress. Some men are honourable, others are dishonourable; some men are noble, others are ignoble; some men are pioneers of progress, others retard all onward movements. It is curious that there are many men who would not rob another of a farthing, and yet who eagerly look for every new pattern which more honourable manufacturers than themselves produce, with the view of copying them if they be good and are not protected by registration, or of producing others as nearly like them as they can if they be registered. Such men I regard as not only hindrances to the progress of art (for who likes paying a high price for a well-considered design if immediately it is issued others copy the idea, if not the actual design, and by saving the cost of the pattern are enabled to undersell the original producer), but as nothing more nor less than thieves, who should be engaged on the tread-wheel with others of their kind. This detestable piracy of new patterns, which is constantly carried on by those who are truly little men, is one of the great hindrances to art progress. Did it ever strike these detestable rogues, I wonder, that by every piracy they commit they not only degrade themselves but exalt both the manufacturer and the designer of the pattern which is stolen; the very theft acknowledges the want of power to produce what is of equal merit. To those noble men who continue to produce what is new and what is beautiful, while they constantly suffer from theft, I would say persevere, for the tribute which the mean pay to your nobleness and enterprise is sufficient in itself to build up in time your worthy reputation.

Much has been said respecting the unwillingness of manufacturers to issue designs of an art character, and to pay such prices for patterns as will fairly compensate the designer for producing a carefully considered work. I have had as much to do with manufacturers, I think, as most artists, and perhaps more, and I am bound to say that I have found most of them both willing to try new things and to pay handsomely for well-considered designs, but as the object of business is, in a sense, money making, the manufacturer cannot be expected to produce many patterns such as will not sell when placed on the manufactured article. Some men I could name who nobly contribute towards the education of the people by yearly producing a few works in good art which do not command a large sale, owing to their being too advanced for the public taste, but these men are few in number, yet they do exist amongst us. However, with the exception of a few mean hounds, such as we find in every class of society, I exonerate manufacturers from the charge of being hindrances to the progress of a true decorative art.

But I cannot regard those whom I may describe as *middle men* as free from blame, for no class of persons in our country so thoroughly obstruct the progress of applied art as these middlemen, such as the "buyers," as they are called, in our large retail houses. For the most part these are men utterly ignorant of even the first principles of art, and yet they are as proud and self-opinionated as they well can be. If you talk to them of a pattern being good, or just, or right, you are often met with the remark, "Do I not know what sells" haughtily expressed. My candid opinion is that these men very imperfectly know what the public wants, and that they in many cases fail to let the people have what they really desire, through standing between them and the manufacturer. Scarcely a week passes in which I am not asked, "Where can I get good artistic things?" and scarcely a week goes by without my applying direct to a manufacturer for art works, or fabrics, of some kind; but I do give these middlemen credit for being good salesmen. If they like a thing they buy it, and they sell it, however bad it may be; and if they don't like a thing they won't sell it, however good it is. The salesman introduces a pattern to a customer, and says, "this is just in. Within the last week I have looked through the patterns of the best manufacturers in England, and this was the best pattern that I anywhere found" (perhaps it really was the worst, but his want of taste led him to regard it as the best). This, if said to a weak-minded lady of title, secures its sale, and then, when the future customers are told the same tale, and, also, that Lady Weakmind purchased it, its sale is certain. It is only a few days since that I was told by one of these middlemen, as he spread before me the most miserable carpet I ever saw, that Lady So-and-so had purchased it. I looked at it, and then felt constrained to remark that her ladyship's art knowledge gave her no more claim to her title than "the claimant's" education gave him to the Tichborne baronetcy.[5] What we should do in order to check the baneful influence of these ignorant middlemen, I do not know. Some few of our art manufacturers have opened retail shops, in order that they may come in immediate contact with the people!

Where would our great works in silver, and gold, and jewellery have been, if our leading manufacturers had not shown their works direct to the public? If middle men had stood between the manufacturer and the public in these cases, the chief works would never have been produced, for the first made would still be left in the manufacturers' hands.

There are a few of these middlemen whom I know to be exceptions to the rule, and who have some art taste; hence we find in a few shop windows a certain proportion of things of good pattern. We must look to their conversion to the cause of art by their getting art knowledge in some way, and by the pressure which the public may put upon them on the one side, and the enterprising manufacturer on the other; thus they shall no longer remain as hindrances to the progress of decorative art.

The public, in some instances, impedes the progress of art. The public is of two classes—the educated and the uneducated. The educated, in many instances, seeks better art than is to be found on the goods procurable at most of our shops; but the utterly ignorant, having no art knowledge, are pleased with whatever is "loud" and showy. These latter undoubtedly hinder the progress of art, as some manufacturers will cater for the patronage of the most vulgar, but this hindrance will disappear with the increase of art knowledge.

Whatever is bad in art tends to vitiate taste. If a person whose taste is highly cultivated, and who is sensitive to every deformity both in colour and form, is obliged to contemplate what is ugly, he, after a time, ceases to feel the hideousness of what he views; thus, if he takes lodgings by the sea-side, and the walls of the room in which he sits are covered by a hideous paper, and the floor by an obtrusive carpet, and if every piece of furniture is uncomely, and every so-called ornament in the room a mere offence to good taste, however repulsive all this may be when first seen, it will become less and less offensive as he dwells upon it, until finally it ceases to impress the sense as that which is uncomely at all; and in order that its true nature be understood the judgment has to be appealed to; thus the sense which leads us to discriminate between the beautiful and the uncomely becomes deadened. This leads us to perceive the necessity for surrounding ourselves with beautiful objects if we would keep alive within us a quick perception of the beautiful; and to see that whatever is presented before us which is beautiful tends to exalt our taste, and sharpen our perception of the beautiful. But we also perceive that whatever around us is not excellent tends to degrade our taste and to deaden our perception of the refined and graceful. This brings me to consider the effect which museum objects have upon the taste of the country.

The museum the action of which upon public taste I have chiefly to consider is that of South Kensington, for the objects collected in the British Museum are gathered together chiefly on account of their antiquarian interest. The Indian Museum at Whitehall is small, and, I am sorry to say, is visited by the few only; and the Kew Museum is of a botanical character. On the two former of these museums—the British and the Indian—I may have a word to say incidentally; but as the South Kensington Museum is intended to furnish art-instruction to the people, we must especially look to its teachings, and consider their effect on the large mass of people who visit it.

This I must say, that of all the museums that I have visited, and they are many, that of South Kensington contains the largest number of well-decorated objects, and of worthy examples of applied art, fitted to lead public taste in a right direction; and, almost without exception, these objects are well displayed and carefully preserved; but there are also examples of indifferent art in this museum, which it is not desirable that we take as examples, and the museum is not free from illustrations of even bad art, for such, I am sorry to say, are numerous. I take it as granted by all, whether friends or enemies of the museum system, that the collections of which I speak embrace much that is good, that they afford many examples of excellent applied art, and that, taken as a whole, they are a credit and not a disgrace to us as a nation. But if I discern anything in them, or anything connected with them, that appears to me to retard the progress of applied art, it is my duty to point it out; and should all agree that the museum is not as useful as it might be, we should then be justified in asking that whatever is wrong be set right, or that whatever can be improved be altered for the better.

The South Kensington Museum is too fully an historical or antiquarian collection, yet in this respect it is far from complete. Egyptian art is well represented in the British Museum, but it is scarcely, if at all, illustrated in the Kensington collections; and the same may be said of Babylonian art; while the specimens of Greek and Roman manufactures illustrative of the applied art of these peoples are so meagre as to be unworthy of consideration, while they are numerous in the British Museum.

It is to be expected that such branches of art as are fully illustrated in the one collection should be sparingly illustrated in the other, and I cannot help feeling regret that the contents of each museum should not, as far as possible, be made subservient to the purposes of the other. If some of the fine art examples now in the British Museum could be transferred to the Kensington collection, and some of the merely antiquarian specimens of the Kensington Museum be transferred to the British Museum, I cannot but think that both would thereby be benefited.

I say that the South Kensington Museum is too antiquarian in its character. It must ever be borne in mind that, however interesting things may be, owing to their age, it does not follow that because a thing is old it is necessarily beautiful; and yet many—yea, very many—are so enamoured with what is old, that however ugly it may be, or inconvenient to use, they prefer it to that which is new and good. Such blind worship of the old can only totally retard the growth of a true art-judgment in all who indulge in it. A clumsy and ugly utensil, even if formed of the roughest material, and wrought in the rudest manner, may yet be an object of great interest if it illustrates a manufacture in its infancy, or even reveals certain customs connected with the domestic life of the people that produced it; but this is the interest which an antiquarian would attach to it; the artist, however, would feel no interest in this vessel; it is not a thing to be copied, nor even to be studied as suggestive of what we should do. We must be careful to discriminate between what is merely old, and what is beautiful as well as old.

Mr. Redgrave, in his report on design, says, "The ornament of past ages is the tradition of the ornamentist, and tradition ever hands down to us things good and bad, both equally consecrated to most minds by the authority of time. But a moment's reflection will show how necessary it is to discriminate before receiving anything on such authority. A church or temple built in a rude age remains undisturbed by some happy chance..... The ornamental details found therein are copied and illustrated by the notes of antiquarians, or published in the proceedings of learned societies, and are at once regarded as authorities for imitation, it being forgotten that they were, perhaps, the works of obscure provincial artists, or of a barbarous age perchance, or of a people with whom art, no longer studied for its principles, had ceased to progress, or had rapidly declined."[6]

If all who visit the South Kensington Museum would first read Redgrave's report on design, as prepared for the Commissioners of the 1851 Exhibition, from which I have just made an extract, there would be little danger of their confounding the good with the bad in art. Redgrave's report is an excellent work, but, unfortunately, the people who visit the museum do not first read this book, hence it appears to me necessary that some other means of instructing them be resorted to. I say that the museum contains many examples of really bad art, such as if regarded as examples to be copied must hinder the progress of ornamentation. As illustrations, I may name the two large pulpits in the inner open court near the fernery; one by Giovanni Pisano, and the other by Nicola Pisano; both from Pisa. In the first the weight of the platform on which the priest stands rests, to a great extent, on the backs of three naturalistically treated figures, who are bent, almost to deformity, by the weight of the superposed mass, and appear as though they must be in great pain; three such figures and three columns bear the entire weight of the upper portion of the pulpit. In the case of the other pulpit, every second column (three out of six) rests on the centre of the back of a lion, which, like the figures just spoken of, are naturally rendered.[7] The wooden-looking lions bearing the fountain in the Alhambra Court, which we are familiar with at the Crystal Palace at Sydenham, do not appear to be susceptible of pain; hence a weight may rest upon them without our feeling troubled. But even with such wooden-looking lions as these, a column standing on the back would appear to have a weak and insecure foundation; but in the case of the pulpit both the lions and the figures are in every way offensive as supports, and can only serve as illustrations of the worst form of art.[8]

I have given two illustrations of bad art from the South Kensington collections, but I might give many, for scores of works there preserved illustrate what should be carefully avoided in all decorated objects; but setting aside the debased character of some of the old examples, which we may regard as of antiquarian interest, we cannot help noticing that a large proportion of the comparatively recent purchases of modern works are bad, and embrace just such as Mr. Redgrave, in common with all true artists, condemn. This is the more strange as the prizes offered to the students of the government schools of art, throughout the country, are offered on the condition that the works sent in competition be in accordance with the principles enunciated in Mr. Redgrave's report, and Mr. Redgrave is named in all the papers issued from South Kensington as the art superintendent of the museum and schools. Hear what Mr. Redgrave says:—"The Renaissance itself arose mainly from the study of Roman remains, and those often of the worst period of the empire, when Greek science, skill, and pure taste had fallen before Roman magnificence and barbarism, and before modern discoveries had opened up the Athenian treasures of Greek art. It was introduced, however, by men of enlarged minds, most of them great constructive architects, and by them it was constructively adapted; they embodied in it many of the first principles of the ancient styles; and if the stream of tradition had brought down much rubbish as well as treasure, still, the master minds of the fifteenth century gradually separated them, and applied with unrivalled skill and a fertile fancy what was beautiful and good. It was, however, essentially pagan in its details, and its ornament conveyed no symbolic truths to the hearts of men."[9]

This is Mr. Redgrave's description of the Renaissance, and I ask you to notice it, for the South Kensington Museum contains much more numerous illustrations of Renaissance art than of any other. My opinion of the Renaissance is not so favourable, even, as that of Mr. Redgrave, for I fail to see in its best works more than a recast of the Roman spirit, with which I have no sympathy; its forms utter no sentiment—they are cold and dead. The best forms produced in the time of the Renaissance are graceless when compared with Greek ornaments, and poor in both colour and form when contrasted with the rich Eastern styles, or our own Gothic.

But Mr. Redgrave goes on to say, "In the hands of less skilful masters, it soon became decoration without a pervading spirit, ornament merely used as ornament, without propriety as without meaning; and thus, as the Tudor style, it succeeded in this country to the Gothic, that style dying out partly from the causes above stated and partly from the change of feeling consequent on the reformed opinions which then prevailed. This debased form of the Renaissance, in its decoration, had already cast off all constructive truth and consistency, much that was bad in the late style was retained and mixed with it; whatever was good was as certainly forgotten. Columns were reversed, the heavy and broad part being upwards, the small part below; they swelled alternately into enormous bands, and were contracted into severing rings, and sometimes they stood upon balls to give a further sense of insecurity. Terminal figures were introduced which had the weight of their entablatures borne on baskets of imitative fruits or flowers. The covering pediments were broken, contrary to all constructive application, or were placed successively one within another; entablatures were enlarged out of all proportion to the supporting columns; and the useful was superseded by the ornamental."[10]

Let me make a few other extracts from the same source, and then let us consider the recent works added to the Museum. "Design," says Redgrave, "has reference to the construction of any work both for use and beauty, and therefore includes its ornamentation also. Ornament is merely the decoration of a thing constructed. Ornament is thus necessarily limited, for, so defined, it cannot be other than secondary, and must not usurp a principal place; if it do so, the object is no longer a work ornamented, but is degraded into a mere ornament. . . . . . When commencing a design, designers are too apt to think of ornament before construction, and, as has been said in connection with the nobler art of architecture, rather to construct ornament than to ornament construction . . . The primary consideration of construction is so necessary to pure design that it almost always follows that, wherever style and ornament are debased, construction will be found to have been first disregarded; and that those styles which are considered the purest, and the best periods of those styles, are just those wherein constructive utility has been rightly understood and most thoroughly attended to."[11]

In speaking of furniture, Mr. Redgrave says:—"It will without difficulty be conceded that, in every kind of furniture having a specific purpose, the first consideration of the designer should be *perfect adaptation to intended use*. . . . Another consideration to be attended to is stability of construction, *apparent* as well as *real*; the first being necessary to satisfy the eye, the last being indispensable to excellence and durability. . . . The constructive forms, moreover, should not be obscured by the ornament, but, rather, brought out by it. . . . Over enrichment, indeed, destroys itself, and it would not be difficult to point out works of the greatest pretension, and the most costly workmanship, which are completely spoilt by this fault."[12] I might go on giving you quotations wherein Mr. Redgrave denounces the pediment broken in the manner of the Renaissance; the arch when used constructively in wood-work, floor coverings bearing a pattern pointing in one direction only, earthenware plates and dishes covered entirely with ornament, and wherein he extols the works of India, Arabia, and the east generally.

Yet how is it that all these principles are violated by the recent purchases of modern works, and by the very decorations themselves of the South Kensington Museum.

If we look at the cabinet of Fourdinois, which was purchased at the Paris Exhibition of 1867 for the large sum of £2,750, and apply to it the test of Mr. Redgrave's principles, which are undeniably correct, we find it wanting in every particular.[13] Thus the structural lines are broken or concealed; the arch, which Mr. Redgrave justly terms a true method when employed in stone construction, but a false structural feature for works formed of wood, is a leading constructive element; the drawers and cupboards are disguised; mouldings are divided; and instead of construction being ornamented, ornament has been constructed, for decorative children in low relief pass from the panels of the spandrils over mouldings till they in part cover the styles of the panels, and yet this work cost the nation nearly £3,000. If this cabinet be compared with the simple, yet beautifully constructed, sideboard, which now stands near it, designed by Mr. B. J. Talbert, and executed by Messrs. Gillow and Co., of Oxford-street (which could, undoubtedly, be purchased for a fourth of the money), the justness of the latter will be at once apparent; but, unfortunately, this good work is not purchased for the museum, but is only on loan there.[14]

It is strange, indeed, that so many works which have been added to the museum during the last few years, if not the majority of such works, should be of a character at variance with the written opinions of the Art Superintendent, and that all the decorations of the building, save the Oriental courts by Mr. Owen Jones, are of a character contrary to his expressed views of art.

It is strange, also, that nearly all the objects purchased for the museum, save the few Eastern things derived from the International Exhibition of 1851, are in the Renaissance style of art, while Mr. Redgrave justly prefers Eastern works to these—the beautiful Chinese and Japanese objects now exhibited being chiefly on loan; but what is the cause of this, we ask? and this question we have a right to ask if we consider that the inconsistency which we observe between the preaching and the practice of the South Kensington Museum is a hindrance to the progress of applied art, and I certainly do think that it is.

The answer will be found in the fact that those of the authorities of the South Kensington Museum that have art knowledge have knowledge of pictorial art only, and the Renaissance has the greatest amount of the pictorial element, while it has least of those true structural qualities which have always accompanied good design, as Mr. Redgrave justly says, and of pure ornamental principles. The cabinet by Fourdinois while badly designed, and structurally false, bears upon it some beautifully carved figure groups, and these, embracing as they do the pictorial spirit, would naturally be chosen by a pictorial artist; and if we examine the purchases for the museum generally we find that they are such as have parts which pictorial artists admire, while but few can be regarded as examples of a true style of decorative art.

I consider that while there are many objects in the South Kensington Museum which are of great interest as worthy examples of a true applied art, the whole teaching of the museum is not as beneficial as it might be, and that some of the objects therein stored are hindrances to the progress of a true form of ornamentation. How can these hindrances be removed? This is a question with which we are much concerned. It appears to me that the first step was taken in the right direction when a collection of articles of bad taste was formed at Marlborough-house at the time when the museum was first instituted, which collection was arranged in a vestibule that become known as the "room of horrors."[15] It will be remembered that to each article here exhibited a label was attached, stating why the article was in bad taste. This "room of horrors" did more, in my judgment, to advance taste in this country than any institution that we have yet established, and I am pleased to see a revival of the same idea, although it is on a very small scale, at the Kensington Museum, where a case may be seen in the entrance-hall containing some of the very things that were exhibited in the old room of horrors. I sincerely hope that this idea will have extensive illustration, for the public should see what is bad as well as what is good; and especially should they be told why each article is bad, and why, or in what respect, it is good.

I submit to you the suggestion that it is desirable that every article in the South Kensington Museum should be furnished with a label stating why it is there;

whether it is a thing of mere antiquarian interest; whether it is altogether a successful work; or whether Some of its features only are to be commended while others are to be avoided. If this were carefully done by competent architects and ornamentists the museum would at once cease to be in any way a hindrance to the progress of applied and decorative art.

But more still might be done. In connection with the interesting food collection at the South Kensington Museum, Drs. Lyon Playfair and Edwin Lankester[16] prepared enlarged labels, setting forth general physiological principles, smaller labels relating to special groups of substances, and individual labels having reference to particular specimens, and the result is, that from visiting this collection you may gain a fair amount of physiological knowledge. Why, I ask, could not the same thing be done with the art collection? For as things now are, you might visit the museum for years without gaining much knowledge of applied art. I should suggest that large labels be prepared, explanatory of the general principles of utilitarian or applied art, such as might be condensed from Mr. Redgrave's report, and that a secondary label be prepared, treating of each group of things generally. Thus, one might relate to Persian art, another to Indian art, another to that of the Renaissance period, and so on; while each individual object should be furnished with a label which should point out both its excellencies and defects. And even short explanatory remarks might, at stated times, be offered by competent persons on the objects most worthy of being regarded as fit examples for us to follow; but the opinions given must not be those of men merely learned in literature and antiquarian lore, or even those of pictorial artists only, but the views of educated practical architects and ornamentists.

I come, in the last place, to notice the effect of the South Kensington Museum School teaching upon the public, for here, it appears to me, we experience such a want of efficiency, or rather completeness, in some departments, that if these schools are not in some respects an actual hindrance to the advancement of applied art, they fail to do much that they might accomplish.

These schools were originally commenced as Schools of Design, and their purpose then was that of aiding our commerce by producing designers such as could draw good patterns, and thus give increased value to our manufactures, while only the same expenditure of material was involved; but since then they have become mere drawing schools, as it was found that art works were not appreciated by an ignorant public. I submit for your consideration that the time has now arrived when schools of design should be re-established such as shall concern themselves with the furnishing of advanced or high-class education in all that pertains to the production of true works of art fitted for application to our industrial manufactures.

Designing, it will be said, is taught both in the South Kensington Museum Schools in London and in its various branch schools throughout the country. But how is it taught, and by whom? Without an exception, the masters at the South Kensington schools are more pictorial artists than ornamentists, and, without any discredit to them, I say that there is not one amongst them who even professes to have a thorough knowledge of ornamental art; and how can a man have great knowledge of two branches of art so utterly opposed to each other in spirit as are ornamental and pictorial art; for the one in its highest forms, as I pointed out to you last year, is in part at least imitative, while the other is wholly creative.

The South Kensington masters, being pictorial artists, naturally infuse the ideas of a pictorial artist into the minds of the pupils, and the result is, if the student acquires a reasonable power of painting, he strives to become a pictorial artist, and often passes to the Royal Academy of Arts with that view. As there is no one in connection with the schools who, being devoted to applied art, and having knowledge of ornament, infuses into the students of the schools a feeling of its nobleness and greatness, it is but natural that these schools should rather hinder than foster the development of true ornamentists such as the vast manufacturing interests of this country require. There is scarcely a week in which I do not visit some of our large manufactories where art is applied to the fabrics, or works, made, and although I have intimate intercourse with the designers employed at most of these works, I yet rarely meet with such as have been students at the South Kensington, or branch schools, and if I do I am frequently informed that these men are the least useful designers that they have; and I could name repeated instances in which students from the schools have been tried in the designing-rooms of factories, and found of so little value that their services have been dispensed with. There are, of course, honourable exceptions to this rule; but I fear the rule is what I have portrayed.

I blame no one for this state of things; I offer no censures; but I do say that the time has come when this state of things should be altered, and when every facility should be offered to our young people for becoming great ornamentists, and to our manufacturers for endowing their goods with an ennobling art.

My suggestion is this. Let our drawing schools remain, and let all who will learn to draw there be taught. Let these schools furnish the Royal Academy with pupils, if any of their students desire to become pictorial artists, but institute a Royal Academy of decorative or applied art, wherein the highest knowledge of design in all its branches, as required by our various manufactures, be fully given. Let ornament be treated as a fine art, and as that which is ennobling and refining in its influence upon those who view it, if it is truthfully rendered; and let all technical knowledge necessary to the understanding of the application of pattern to fabrics, and various wares, be given, and let such instruction in science be afforded as is necessary to the understanding of the processes by which ornament is applied to manufactured articles. One great want of our designers is general knowledge. As a class, they are as ignorant upon science, and even upon the history of art, as they well can be; indeed, their hands are informed while the intellect remains uncultivated. The very knowledge necessary to the understanding of technical art processes would lead to thought, and thought would lead to knowledge, so in two ways would the student be gaining an advantage through this technical education.

This institution should have the power of conferring degrees equal with the membership and associateship of the Royal Academy, for without encouragement no art will prosper. It was only the other day that one of our best known sculptors said, "We do the work, but it often happens that the man who unveils the statue gets the honour." It is thus; and it is equally true that through law, which settles men's quarrels, through the cruel art of war, and through statesmanship, men can rise to the peerage, but to the ornamentist, however great or learned he may be, no title nor post of honourable, distinction is open; but if we institute a Royal Academy of decorative art which has the power of conferring degrees in applied art, as our universities do in science, and literature, a stimulus will even thereby be given to applied art which, in my opinion, would soon place us at the head of the world as manufacturers of art objects and art fabrics. To this Royal Academy of applied arts the drawing school should also contribute pupils. If, combined with this academy, we could have an art-workman's institution, in which the mechanic could learn to use the metal-chaser's tool in a truly artistic manner, and the china painter his metallic oxides in the manner of an artist (Messrs. Minton and Co. have now a class in connection with the South Kensington Museum schools for this purpose), and where the wood carver could pick up the true spirit of his art, and, indeed, where knowledge of all art-handicrafts could be gained, we should then have removed from us the chief hindrances to the progress of applied art and impediments in the way of our manufacturing prosperity. Upon the occasion of the reading of this paper, Dr. Dresser exhibited a number of valuable oriental art objects and a series of manufactured articles of his own designing.

Notes

1 C. Dresser, 'Hindrances to the Progress of Applied Art', *Journal of the Society of Arts*, 20, 12 April 1872, p. 442.
2 Ibid.
3 Dresser, p. 441.
4 Dresser, p. 443.
5 The Tichborne case was a cause célèbre at the time. It concerned the claims by a man usually termed "the Claimant", who claimed to be the missing heir to the Tichborne baronetcy. The claims were dismissed after a lengthy legal case.
6 R. Redgrave 'Supplementary Report on Design.' *Great Exhibition. Reports by the Juries on the Subjects in the Thirty Classes into Which the Exhibition Was Divided... In Two Volumes* (London: Spicer Bros. 1852), p. 1591
7 Both in Victoria and Albert Museum, Cast Court.
8 The Crystal Palace was re-erected at Sydenham in 1854, Owen Jones and Sir Matthew Digby Wyatt were responsible for the suite of Fine Arts Courts. Owen Jones devised the Court of Lions of the Alhambra Court.
9 R. Redgrave 'Supplementary Report on Design.' *Great Exhibition. Reports by the Juries on the Subjects in the Thirty Classes into Which the Exhibition Was Divided... In Two Volumes* (London: Spicer Bros. 1852), p. 1590
10 R. Redgrave 'Supplementary Report on Design' p. 1590.
11 R. Redgrave 'Supplementary Report on Design' p. 1589.
12 R. Redgrave 'Supplementary Report on Design' p. 1617.
13 Victoria and Albert Museum No. 721:1 to 25–1869. Henri-Auguste Fourdinois, of 46 rue Amelot, Paris, patented a new type of inlay in 1864. The 'inlay' was cut thicker than the wooden panel into which it was to be placed; a recess was cut right through the

ground panel, so that the inlaid work could fit in and not move with climatic changes. The exposed extra thickness was then carved with further detail, rather than being engraved.
14 Victoria and Albert Museum: No. W.44:1–10–1953.
15 See Chamber of Horrors, vol 1, 1.18 and 1.19
16 Lyon Playfair, 1st Baron Playfair (1818–1898) a British scientist and Liberal politician who advocated improved technical education. Edwin Lankester (1814–1874) was an English surgeon and naturalist.

10

EMMA LAZARUS, 'A DAY IN SURREY WITH WILLIAM MORRIS'

Emma Lazarus (1849–1887) was a Jewish-American author, poet, and activist. She twice travelled to Europe, firstly in 1883 and again from 1885 to 1887. On the first of these trips, Georgiana Burne-Jones introduced her to William Morris. She visited the Morris works on 1st July 1883. In a letter to her close friend Helena Gilder, she positively gushed over Morris:

> Oh Helena, William Morris, I shall have a million things to tell you about him— such a day as we had with him down at Merton Abbey where his works are— He is a saint – and is the only man I have ever seen who seems to be as good as Emerson- & I don't know but that he is better— for he is more of a republican & not an aristocrat as Emerson was—.[1]

The intellectual link between Emerson and Morris is evident in this annotation by Emerson's son, of a section related to works and workers in his paper of 1841 titled 'The Method Of Nature': 'Mr. Emerson would have rejoiced in William Morris's word about a work of industrial art, that it should be 'a joy to the maker as well as the user', and that the cotton, or whatever, would be the better, not worse'.[2]

In a letter dated 29 January 1884 to her close friend Rose Hawthorne Lathrop, Lazarus wrote to explain the background to this article:

> I have been trying to write a brief record of one of the interesting episodes of my trip to England last summer – an account of my visit to Morris' workshop while I was there. I thought nothing would ever induce me to follow the usual American fashion and report it for the benefit of the public – back to the scribbling instinct is irresistible, & I am doing the very thing I despised & abjured! My only excuse is that I have got Morris's consent to do it, and his promise to correct & authenticate the M.S. So I am in hopes it will have a certain value and it is such a delight to live over again those beautiful happy hours![3]

On 12 July 1883, Morris wrote to Miss Lazarus, thanking her for a present to the library at Merton Abbey, and making a revealing point about his thoughts on the influence of his business:

> I am really glad that you were pleased with your visit to so small and imperfect an establishment as our works are: a place which hangs doubtful between the past and the present, & is, I more fear, going to be of no influence on the future—However we must try our best, & at any rate be pleased that it pleases us'.[4]

The Century Magazine was first published in the United States in 1881 as the successor of *Scribner's Monthly Magazine*. Initially, it was very successful and was one of the leading American periodicals into the early twentieth century, finally closing in 1930.

Emma Lazarus, 'A Day in Surrey with William Morris', *Century Magazine*, 32, July 1886, pp. 388–394

Early in July the roses fairly run riot in the garden-like county of Surrey; all along the railway the little village stations are walled with thickly flowering vines, or hedged with blooming bushes. From one of these small, bevined stations in a deep cutting of the Croydon road, we started—a party of four—on a soft, gray midsummer morning for a day at Merton Abbey.[5] Merton Abbey—the very name suggests visions of venerable Norman arches and cloisters, the roofless aisles and topless columns of some ruined seat of ecclesiastical power. In point of fact the Abbey whither we were bound is merely a utilitarian factory that supplies the marketwares for Morris & Co.'s decorative art shop in Oxford street. "Tis five miles from Croydon, one mile from Wimbledon," Mr. Morris had said, in directing us where to find him; and we had chosen to take the shortest part of the little journey by rail, and to drive in an open carriage from Croydon to Merton. Here the enamored Nelson used to come to bask at the feet of his Delilah.[6] Merton Place, which he gave to Lady Hamilton after her husband's death, is close by the Abbey, and revives the memory of that passionate intrigue, with its dramatic interplay of glory, shame, and beauty. The drive was not remarkably picturesque, leading at first through dead-and-alive provincial streets lined with the various ugliness of the suburban villa, and then issuing beyond the town to pass through a flat and sufficiently commonplace landscape. But to American eyes no bit of rural England can be devoid of interest and charm; the most ordinary objects seem under a spell to bewitch us back into the dream-world of a previous existence. An ivied wall, a pebbled brook, a thatched and lattice-windowed cottage, a single-arched stone bridge, an English daisy, a field of blood-bright poppies, take on a glamour that is not their own, but is borrowed from a thousand haunting memories of Shakspere and Wordsworth, of Spenser and Shelley, of Milton and Keats. The American sentimental traveler in England could supply curious notes to the expounders of the doctrine of heredity or the believers in the transmigration of souls. Was it he, or his remote forefather, who stood centuries ago precise under this knotty-limbed oak, amid these crisply hedged, velvet swarded meadows, opposite that identical gabled cottage of stone, smothered in its wealth of black-green ivy? How intimately he knows it all, how inexpressibly dear to him is the soil beneath his feet, the ever-changing mist and cloud-veiled sky above his head, the atmosphere of luxurious repose, the half-tearful, half-smiling, maternal look in the eyes of Nature, welcoming him to his ancestral home! Thus we drove through the tame and level fields of North Surrey with that subdued thrill of perfect physical and emotional content, that "sacred and home-felt delight," which we had come to associate with the very grass and air of England. The English friends who accompanied us had grown used to our easily excited enthusiasm, and appeared themselves to enjoy the familiar landscape through the medium of our fresher transatlantic vision. Feeling that we must be nearing our goal, we began to inquire of the passers-by our way to the Abbey, and before long we approached a plain, low, double house set back and somewhat raised from the level of the road, where we saw, framed against the black background of one of the upper windows, the cordial face and stalwart figure of William Morris, clad in a dark-blue blouse. Before we had alighted he was at the gate to receive us, welcoming us with his great, hearty voice and warm hand-grip. "The idle singer of an empty day" might sit for the portrait of his own Sigurd. He has the robust, powerful form of a Berserker,[7] crowned with a tall, massive head, covered with a profusion of dark, curly hair plentifully mixed with gray. His florid color and a certain roll in his gait and a habit of swaying to and fro while talking suggest the sailor or the yeoman, but still more distinctly is the poet made manifest in the fine modeling and luminous expression of the features. An indescribable open-air atmosphere of freedom and health seems to breathe from his whole personality.

Merton Abbey was originally, as its name implies, a Norman monastery, but since the time of Cromwell it has been adapted to manufacturing purposes, and Mr. Morris, therefore, had no need to run counter to his art-instinct by transforming to business purposes a thing of pure beauty. For that matter, it is scarcely doubtful but that Morris the friend of the workingman would have ruthlessly overridden the compunctions of the author of "The Earthly Paradise,"[8] if necessary to give better facilities of air and sunshine to the artisan. The situation of Merton, within ten miles from London, as well as its command of water-power, eminently fits it for its present purpose and the only visible relics of its ancient character are the broken fragments of a wall overgrown with the rank vegetation of ruins. This wall, which surrounded the Abbey lands, bounded a space of sixty acres. Some thirty years ago there still remained a piece of the old buildings, not on Mr. Morris's but on the adjoining property of Mr. Littler, whose print-works are on the other side of the railway. Unfortunately, however this interesting relic was allowed to fall into complete decay, and to be finally swept away. The religious establishment dates back to the beginning of the twelfth century, when Gilbert Norman, sheriff of Surrey, built here a convent for canons of the order of St. Austin. upon the demesne granted him by Henry I. Merton Abbey, as it was then called, was patronized by Stephen and Matilda, and was amply endowed with rich gifts. It is closely connected with at least two events of historic importance. A parliament was held within, its walls in 1236, when the "Statutes of Merton" were enacted, and when was made the memorable reply of the English nobles to the prelates who wished to conform the civil to the ecclesiastical code: "We will not change the laws of England." (*Nolumus leges Angliae mutare*) In this house also was concluded the treaty of peace between Henry III. and the Dauphin. Upon the breaking up of the monasteries, after the Reformation it was leased out to private persons, and is said to have been used as a garrison during the civil war of Charles I. Today a branch of the "Democratic Federation"[9] is peacefully and busily installed within its precincts, and in this romantic old garden, haunted by ghosts of sovereigns and monks, of legislators and nobles, of soldiers and artisans, the poet-socialist loves to sit and dream, building a thousand beautiful hopes of freedom and happiness for the people,—on this little spot of soil in which English law and English liberty took such deep and early root.

We were interested to hear that the place is the cradle of textile printing in England. Lysons,[10] writing in 1726, says that two thousand men were employed within the boundaries of the Abbey, and he displays his "characteristic Philistinism" (as Mr. Morris termed it) by taking occasion to contrast this useful labor with the laziness of the old monks. "The block-printing industry still lives, or rather languishes" said Morris, "on the Wandle,[11] but is pretty much confined at present to silk-printing (mostly for the Indian market), and the occupation of the blockers is very precarious." Following the guidance of our host, we found ourselves in an old-fashioned country dwelling-house, almost bare of furniture. In a small room over the stairs was a little circulating library for the benefit of the operatives; the books were as richly bound as though intended for the poet's private shelves, in consonance with his theory that the working man must be helped and uplifted, not only by supplying his grosser wants, but by developing and feeding his sense of beauty.

The manufactory consists of a small group of detached buildings where the various processes of dyeing, stamping, and weaving fabrics of wool, cloth, and silk, and of staining designs upon glass, are carried on by male and female operatives of all ages, from fourteen or fifteen upward, and of different degrees of skill, ranging from the uneducated mechanic or dyer-mixer to the intelligent artist. In the first outhouse that we entered stood great vats of liquid dye, into which some skeins of unbleached wool were dipped for our amusement; as they were brought dripping forth, they appeared of a sea-green color, but after a few minutes' exposure to the air, they settled into a fast, dusky blue. Scrupulous neatness and order reigned everywhere in the establishment; pleasant smells as of dried herbs exhaled from clean vegetable dyes, blent with the wholesome odors of grass and flowers and sunny summer warmth that freely circulated through the open doors and windows. Nowhere was one conscious of the depressing sense of confinement that usually pervades a factory; there was plenty of air and light even in the busiest room, filled with the ceaseless din of whirring looms where the artisans sat bending over the threads; while the lovely play of color and beauty of texture of the fabrics issuing from under their fingers relieved their work of that character of purely mechanical drudgery which is one of the dreariest features of ordinary factory toil. Yet this was evidently the department that entailed the most arduous and sedentary labour for as we went out again into the peaceful stillness of the July landscape, Mr. Morris reverted with a sigh to the great problem, and asked why men should be imprisoned thus for a lifetime in the midst of such deafening clatter, in order to earn a bare subsistence, while the average professional man pockets in comfortable ease a fee out of all proportion to his exertions? The obvious answer, referring to the relative scarcity of intellectual as compared with physical capacity, seemed to lose much of its pertinence when addressed to a man who had tested both kinds of labor and could so accurately measure their relative claims. There is no branch of work performed in Mr. Morris's factory in which he himself is not skilled; he has rediscovered lost methods and carefully studied existing processes. Not only do his artisans share his profits, but at the same time they feel that he understands their difficulties and requirements, and that he can justly estimate and reward their performance. Thus an admirable relation is established between employer and employed, a sort of frank comradeship, marked by mutual respect and goodwill. In this relation, Mr. Morris seems to have borrowed all that was sound and admirable from the connection between the mediaeval master-workman and his artist-apprentices. The excellent custom, restored from the generally despised days that preceded the invention of the steam-engine, Mr. Morris has modified, by adding thereto that spirit of intimate, boundless sympathy which under the name of humanitarianism is the peculiar product, as it is the chief dawning glory, of our own age. The exquisite fabrics to be found in his workshop, which have so largely influenced English taste in household decoration, are intended to perform another service less conspicuous but still more important than the first. That the workman shall take pleasure in his work, that decent conditions of light and breathing-space and cleanliness shall surround him, that he shall be made to feel himself not the brainless "hand," but the intelligent cooperator, the *friend* of the man who directs his labor, that his honest toil shall inevitably win fair and comfortable wages, whatever be the low-water record of the market-price of men, that illness or trouble befalling him during the term of his employment shall not mean dismissal and starvation, these are some of the problems of which Mr. Morris's factory is a noble and successful solution. For himself, he eschews wealth and luxury, which are within easy reach of his versatile and brilliant talents, in order that for a few at least of his brother men he may rob toil of its drudgery, servitude of its sting, and poverty of its horrors.

Mr. Morris's work has two distinct moral purposes,—one in its bearing upon the producer, which we have just considered, and the other in its relation to the purchaser. In the latter connection his aim has been to revive a sense of beauty in home life, to restore the dignity of art to ordinary household decoration. So strong and wide has been his influence that he may be said to have revolutionized English taste in decorative art. Graceful designs reproduced from natural outdoor objects, fabrics of substantial worth, be they the simplest cotton stuff or the most exquisite silks and brocades, colors that shall stay fast through sunshine and shade,—these are the general characteristics of his manufactures. By a singular fatality, his very success has been in certain ways detrimental to him. His designs have been imitated by manufacturers less scrupulous as to quality and thoroughness, until their peculiar charm of individuality is almost lost sight of. They have been cheapened and *commonplaced* and so distorted from their original purpose as apparently to encourage indirectly that very taste for useless luxuries, sham art, and stupid bric-a-brac it has been his chief endeavor to destroy. His name has become for some people (more especially in America) falsely associated with that modern fashion, which is his detestation, of encumbering our rooms with silly baubles that, in his own words, "make our stuffy, art-stifling houses more truly savage than a Zulu's kraal or an East Greenlander's snow-hut."[12] He has a special proclivity for "frank colors," pure and solid, and yet, as he himself complains with whimsical despair, "he is supposed to have brought into vogue a dingy, bilious-looking yellow-green—a color of which he has a special and personal hatred." All this misunderstanding arises not from any lack of clearness or consistency in his expression, but simply because of the perversion of his ideas through copies, imitation, and misreport, and the unwillingness of many people to dispel their hazy notion of him by examining for themselves his actual work, whether in literature or in decorative art. No one insists more strenuously than he upon the necessity of simplifying our lives. "Nothing can be a work of art which is not useful, that is to say which does not minister to the body when well under command of the mind, or which does not amuse, soothe, or elevate the mind in a healthy state. What tons upon tons of unutterable rubbish, pretending to be works of art in some degree, would this maxim clear out of our London houses if it were understood and acted upon." For "London'" read New York, and the lesson comes home to us with tenfold force. "If you cannot learn to love real art, at least learn to hate sham art and reject it. Learn to do without—there is virtue in those words, a force that rightly used would choke both demand and supply of mechanical toil. . . . And then from simplicity of life would rise up the longing for beauty; and we know that nothing can satisfy that demand but intelligent work, rising gradually into imaginative work which will turn all operators into workmen, into artists, into men."[13]

In accordance with these ideas, one is not surprised to find his factory a scene of cheerful, uncramped industry, where toil looks like pleasure, where flowers are blooming in the windows, and sunshine and fresh air brighten the faces of artist and mechanic. After going through all the workshops, the best part of our visit has yet to come, in a walk through the enchanting old garden.

A fair, green close,
Hedged round about with woodbine and red rose.

>   ... And all about were dotted leafy trees,—
>   The elm for shade, the linden for the bees;
>   The noble oak long ready for the steel,
>   That in that place it had no fear to feel.[14]

Are there just such gardens anywhere out of England, with their careless profusion and variety, their delightful little accidental walks and lanes leading nowhither, their absence of all primness in the arrangement of flower and berry beds, of all formality in their freely expanding, generously blooming trees! Here we stood for some time beside the merry little Wandle, which is no less full of sparkle and music because it has been coaxed into turning the great mill-wheel below the dam. Growing thick along the water, the blue-gray willows etch their delicate tracing of boughs against the soft sky.

Over the leaves of the garden blooms the manyfolded rose.[15]

If the Surrey roses were rich and plentiful along railway and roadside, what shall be said of their abundance and splendor in this protected spot! They clambered along the ruined abbey wall, and started up from bush and vine on every side, making the air spicy with their sweetness. Under the direction of this poet-husbandman, even the orchard and kitchen-garden seemed to wear a certain spontaneous grace with the partly disguised regularity of their well-ordered rows. Here, besides ordinary edible roots and plants, flourish others which were not considered susceptible of cultivation in England until Mr. Morris introduced them in order to extract particular juices for his dyes. One of the clear, brilliant yellows frequently employed in his fabrics is produced from the bushes of his garden. At our feet ripe strawberries nestled under their dark leaves, and overhead tall, gently rustling trees screened us from the tempered heat of the English sun. All was freshness and grace, all spoke of loving sympathy with nature and intelligent command of her virtues and activities; all was impregnated with that free, large, and wholesome beauty which Mr. Morris seems to obtain from everything that surrounds him.

In making the personal acquaintance of one whose artistic work is familiar and admirable to us, the main interest must ever be to trace the subtle, elusive connection between the man and his creation. In the case of Mr. Morris. at first sight, nothing can be more contradictory than the "dreamer of dreams born out of his due time," and the practical businessman and eager student of social questions who successfully directs the Surrey factory and the London shop. Little insight is required, however, soon to find beneath this thoroughly healthy exterior the most impersonal and objective English poet of our generation. The conspicuous feature of his conversation and character is the total absence of egoism, and we search in vain through his voluminous writings for that morbid habit of introspection which gives the keynote to nineteenth-century literature. He has the childlike delight in telling a story for the story's sake of Chaucer, Boccaccio, and Scott, the plastic power or setting before us in simple and distinct outlines figures of force and grace entirely removed from his own conditions and temperament, the unmoralizing, hearty pleasure in nature and art which characterized an earlier age. He has succeeded in forgetting and in making us

> Forget six counties overhung with smoke,
> Forget the snorting steam and piston stroke,
> Forget the spreading of the hideous town,

and in setting before us

> A nameless city in a distant sea,
> White as the changing walls of faerie.[16]

The passion for beauty, which unless balanced by a sound and earnest intelligence is apt to degenerate into sickly and selfish aestheticism, inflames him with the burning desire to bring all classes of humanity under its benign influence. That art, together with the leisure and capacity to enjoy it, should be monopolized by the few, seems to him as egregious a wrong as that men should go hungry and naked. With this plain clew to the poet's character, there is no longer any contradiction between the uncompromising socialist and the exquisite artist of "The Earthly Paradise." If Mr. Morris's poetry have (as I think no one will dispute) that virginal quality of springtide freshness and directness which we generally miss in modern literature, and which belonged to Chaucer as to Homer, the cause may be found in his reproduction in methods and principles of life of certain conditions under which classic art was generated. He has chosen to be a man before being a poet; he has rounded and developed all sides of a well-equipped and powerful individuality; he has plunged vehemently into the rushing stream of current action and thought, and has made himself at one with his struggling, panting, less vigorous fellow-swimmers. He has not only trained himself intellectually to embrace with wide culture the spirit of Greek mythology, the genius of Scandinavian as of Latin poetry, but he has cultivated muscle and heart as well as nerve and brain. The result upon his art has been indirect, but none the less positive. He seems intuitively to have obeyed those singular rules for poetic creation formulated by Walt Whitman:

> Who troubles himself about his ornaments or fluency is lost. This is what you shall do: love the earth and sun and the animals, despise riches, give alms to everyone that asks, stand up for the stupid and crazy, devote your income and labor to others, hate tyrants, argue not concerning God, have patience and indulgence towards the people, take off your hat to nothing known or unknown, or to any man or number of men, go freely with powerful, uneducated persons, and with the young and with the mothers of families, . . . reexamine all you have been told at school or at church, dismiss whatever insults your soul,—and your very flesh shall be a great poem and have the richest fluency, not only in its words, but in the silent

lines of your lips and face, and between the lashes of your eyes, and in every motion and joint of your body.[17]

Mr. Morris's extreme socialistic convictions are the subject of so much criticism at home, that a few words concerning them may not be amiss here. Rather would he see the whole framework of society shattered than a continuance of the actual condition of the poor. "I do not want art for a few, any more than education for a few or freedom for a few. No, rather than that art should live this poor, thin life among a few exceptional men, despising those beneath them for an ignorance for which they themselves are responsible, for a brutality which they will not struggle with; rather than this, I would that the world should indeed *sweep away all art for a while*. . . . Rather than the wheat should rot in the miser's granary, I would that the earth had it, that it might yet have a chance to quicken in the dark."[18]

The above paragraph, from a lecture delivered by Mr. Morris before the Trades' Guild of Learning,[19] gives the key to his socialistic creed, which he now makes it the main business of his life to promulgate. In America the avenues to ease and competency are so broad and numerous, the need for higher culture, finer taste, more solidly constructed social bases is so much more conspicuous than the inequality of conditions, and the necessity to level and destroy, that the intelligent American is apt to shrink with aversion and mistrust from the communistic enthusiast. In England, however, the inequalities are necessarily more glaring, the pressure of that densely crowded population upon the means of subsistence is so strenuous and painful, that the humane on-looker, whatever be his own condition, is liable to be carried away by excess of sympathy. One hears to-day of individual Englishmen of every rank flinging themselves with reckless heroism into the breach, sacrificing all thought of personal interest in the desperate endeavor to stem the huge flood of misery and pauperism. Among such men stands William Morris, and however wild and visionary his hopes and aspirations for the people may appear to outsiders, his magnanimity must command respect. No thwarted ambitions, no stunted capacities, no narrow, sordid aims have ranged him on the side of the disaffected, the agitator, the outcast. As poet, scholar, householder, and capitalist, he has everything to lose by the victory of that cause to which he has subordinated his whole life and genius. The fight is fierce and bitter; so thoroughly has it absorbed his energies, so filled and inspired and illumined is he with his aim, that it is only after leaving his presence we realize that it is to this man's strong and delicate genius we owe the enchanting visions of 'The Earthly Paradise," and Sigurd the Volsung, the story of Jason, and "The Aeneids of Virgil."

Notes

1 Letter to Helena Gilder 1883, in B. R. Young, *Emma Lazarus in Her World: Life and Letters* (Philadelphia: Jewish Publication Society, 1997), p. 114. Ralph Waldo Emerson (1803–1882) was a prolific poet, essayist, lecturer, and an upholder of social reforms. He was influential in the transcendentalist movement.

2 'The Method of Nature', An Oration Delivered Before the Society of the Adelphi, in Waterville College, Maine, August 1841, in Ralph W. Emerson, *Complete Works of Ralph Waldo Emerson* (Boston: Houghton, Mifflin, 1876), p. 497, (referring to p. 193).
3 B. R. Young, *Emma Lazarus in Her World: Life and Letters* (1997), p. 199.
4 W. Morris, 'Letter 886', in *The Collected Letters of William Morris, Volume II, Part A: 1881–1884*. Ed. N. Kelvin (Princeton: Princeton University Press, 1987), p. 207.
5 Merton Abbey, Surrey. Now part of greater London, SW19.
6 Delilah: Emma, Lady Hamilton.
7 Berserker: elite Viking warriors who went into battle without traditional armour, rather they wore animal pelts.
8 William Morris. *The Earthly Paradise*. A lengthy collection of retellings of various myths and legends from Greece and Scandinavia, begun in 1868 and several later volumes followed until 1870.
9 Democratic Foundation: Original name for the Social Democratic Federation, established in 1881 by H. M. Hyndman.
10 Daniel Lysons (1762–1834), was an English antiquarian and topographer.
11 Wandle: since the early eighteenth century, printing works where established on the river banks.
12 William Morris, 'The Prospects of Architecture In Civilisation,' *Hopes And Fears For Art* (1882) (New York: Longmans, 1908) p. 213.
13 William Morris, *Hopes and Fears*, p 215.
14 William Morris, "The Oracle", *The Earthly Paradise*, 1868–70.
15 Unknown source.
16 William Morris, Prologue, "The Wanderers", *The Earthly Paradise*, 1868–70.
17 Walt Whitman, *Leaves of Grass*, (Brooklyn: W. Whitman, 1855)
18 William Morris, 'The Lesser Arts', *Hopes and Fears*, p. 35.
19 Trade Guild of Learning: The Trades Guild of Learning was founded in London, in 1873 by the Reverend Henry Solly to promote the vocational and further education of artisans.

11

ANON, 'A STUDIO OF DESIGN: AN INTERVIEW WITH MR. ARTHUR SILVER'

Arthur Silver (1853–1896) was a designer and founder of the design business, the Silver Studio. Following his education at the Reading School of Art, Silver was apprenticed to the furniture designer and decorator Henry William Batley, and it is likely that his interest in Japanese design stems from this period. The Silver Studio was then founded in 1880, with the aim of 'bringing together a body of men to establish a studio which would be capable of supplying designs for the whole field of fabrics and other materials used in the decoration of the home'.[1] The studio supplied pattern designs for textiles and wallpapers to many of the major national and international interior decorating suppliers, often in the Art Nouveau or Japonisme styles, between 1895 and the early 1900s. Arthur also exhibited at Arts and Crafts exhibitions between 1889 and 1896, but he was not drawn to the politico-social aspects of the movement. He was fully aware that he was running a commercial enterprise, which left little room for dreaming. In 1894, Arthur Silver contributed three chapters to Gleeson White's publication *Practical Designing*, namely those on printed textiles, woven textiles, and floorcloth design. The studio continued in business until 1963.

The studio employed designers including Harry Napper,[2] and John Kay,[3] their names being credited for various designs in European journals, such as *Der Moderne Stil*. Napper and Kay designed textiles in the Art Nouveau style. The studio was also closely associated with the Liberty & Co. business, in particular, with the metalwork ranges Cymric silver (1898) and Tudric pewter (1902). These were often designed by Archibald Knox,[4] who had been recruited by Arthur Silver in 1898.

The Studio was an internationally influential art and design journal published in Britain, founded in 1893 by Charles Holme, and its first editor, Gleeson White. Its content covered most aspects of art, craft, design, and architecture. Gleeson White was a friend of Arthur Silver, so it is no surprise to find mention of Silver's work in the pages of the journal. *The Studio* reported upon trends and developments in the art and design world and promoted the work of such luminaries as C. R. Ashbee, Aubrey Beardsley, Charles Rennie Mackintosh, C. F. A. Voysey, and James McNeill Whistler.

The growth of design studios, such as the Silver Studios, that developed as distinct entities that supplied patterns and designs to a range of manufacturers was a feature of the later nineteenth century. However, they were not without their critics. The textile designer Arthur Wilcock observed: 'Though sometimes a good creative artist is employed in [the producer's own] studio, it is, as a rule, given over to work of a more technical kind, such as contending with the difficulties in sketches made by outside artists with little or no technical knowledge'.[5]

Anon, 'A Studio of Design: An Interview with Mr. Arthur Silver', *Studio*, 3, 1894, pp. 117–122

At the first glance one saw that the material a designer accumulated round him was as typical as that gathered together by a pictorial artist. Photographs after Botticelli and other old masters, panels of lustrous enamels and gesso-work, scraps of fine fabrics, and books of Japanese drawings, with large schemes of original patterns in every stage of progress, hung on the walls of the large studio which occupies the lower floor of a house given up wholly to pattern-planning.

"I came here," I said, "to discuss commercial design, and to hear your opinion on the matter."

"I distinctly object to the phrase commercial design," replied Mr. Silver, "if by that term you mean drawing to order, for payment, in accordance with any whim of the manufacturer. If by it, however, you imply the production of schemes that are practical in their form and colour, and adapted peculiarly to the material for which they are planned, then the adjective conveys no indignity."

"Let us call it practical design, then, as opposed to merely theoretical fancies."

"By all means; that is the object for which I work, and the motive which it is the objects of the studio system to develop. When I found, as every successful designer must needs discover sooner or later, that one pair of hands could not execute the orders which fell to my share, I attempted to bring together a body of men and establish a studio which would be capable of supplying designs for the whole field of fabrics and other materials used in the decoration of the house."

"Had such a system been worked before?"

"No doubt many Continental artists had found it answered their purpose. Indeed, at that time the large amount of commissions sent abroad aroused in me an intense desire to discover whether such an establishment could not be worked in England to counteract this habit and lead to the employment of British designs. In proof of its success, I may say that now commissions are coming to England from the Continent."

"But why do you consider that a studio is better able to accomplish this than individual designers, each working for himself?"

"For several reasons. Apart from the saving of mechanical labour, in having commissions executed and despatched under one roof, there is a far more important reason. When all designs are criticised and studied by not merely the head of the studio, but others who are technically expert in their various specialities, there is less chance of unpractical details creeping in. I have designed and know the requirements of almost every fabric, yet, to give an instance, it must often happen that a designer who has devoted his attention to wall-papers, who was trained for that special industry, has a good idea for carpets that he cannot carry out perfectly owing to the want of mastery of his material. Then, again, the man who has a distinct gift for beautiful design and can create lovely forms and well-balanced repeating patterns, often lacks an eye for colour. So he employs a formula rather than the special combination which one trained to colour sees at once to be needful for the completion of the design. Thus the individual artist is freer to sketch out a scheme that he knows will be put into practical shape, before he expends the labour (often a question of days, sometimes of weeks) to produce the finished coloured cartoon. This is good in many ways; it is annoying to a manufacturer to find a design, attractive enough at first sight, hopelessly unpractical on further inspection. He either returns it to the artist, or has it mechanically corrected by his own craftsmen, with a result that is not likely to satisfy the artist, and entails much expense and worry on the manufacturer. Many merchants would not feel inclined to send commissions again to a designer who had once or twice put them to this trouble. Again, by constantly working under the limits imposed by his material, the young designer comes to think in the language he is compelled to speak; and almost without his own knowledge curbs his ideas from the first within the limits they must ultimately assume."

"Could he not do this alone ?"

"I do not say he could not. But the effort would be wearying, and there is something more to be studied than merely mechanical limitations. Familiarity with designs for manufactured objects, extending over many years, has led me to feel instinctively that certain ideas would be unsaleable. Yet their sale must needs be (from the manufacturer's point of view) the test of popularity which makes the designer successful. It is no use fighting against ascertained facts."

"Then you would deliberately plan designs with a view to the taste of manufacturers and the public, who are supposed to exercise a bad influence in art ?"

"Most certainly not; but as you cannot compel a manufacturer to produce things he believes would be failures, it is best to attempt to meet his views, and all the time to do the very best to make the design as artistic as possible within their limits. By this gradual effort he can induce the public to advance cautiously until they have compassed a great improvement almost without their own knowledge. There are manufacturers and manufacturers; generally speaking, the majority want good art which will also show a profitable return, they ought to have it. I do not think that the efforts of manufacturers, or the circumstances under which they work, are sufficiently considered. I frequently sell designs which can never hope to attain more than artistic success; the cost of the production of these should be evidence of the designer to manufacturers recognising art for art's sake. One must face the problem boldly, which is to supply saleable designs of artistic merit."

"Then you believe that, speaking generally, the taste of the public is towards debased art?"

"No; I should not like to say that, but knowing how many patterns and ambitious schemes have resulted in great loss to the producers, I must recognise that, whatever his personal taste, and a manufacturer cannot afford to go on producing unsaleable goods. The problem we must endeavour to solve, is to supply manufacturers with saleable popular designs that, even in the lowest class, do not offend the canons of artistic propriety, and in some cases are (if I may say so) as good as any effort can make them."

"Do you advocate designing as a paying profession?"

"A thousand times no; a designer feels somewhat responsible for all the failures his work may entail on the manufacturers, and cannot under the present system enjoy his successes beyond having the satisfaction that he has given good value for the money he has taken. A designer must have his chief reward in the enjoyment of his work."

"Then you consider that designing can be taught?"

"There are three classes of designers in the reverse order of merit; first, the 'designer' who cares not what he designs so long as it will sell; secondly, the possessor of the supreme gift of 'individuality,' combined with a sympathy for the teachings of tradition and a knowledge of practical working—this is the man who establishes the artistic status of his country; and lastly, one who combines both plus the faculty of embodying abstract ideas in concrete forms in a way intelligible to others. But designing, as it is popularly understood, is simply analysis and recombination, therefore pupils, with a fairly imaginative temperament and a taste for drawing, can learn how to apply these faculties in a practical manner."

"You are referring, of course, distinctly to commercial designing?"

"Yes. But it is entirely a question of degree. It is not reasonable to expect to obtain as much music from a tin whistle as from the organ at the Albert Hall; you have the student who will evolve scratches from his inner consciousness, and another who will only make variations of examples—the one will develop marked individuality, and the other may ultimately do better business through the very absence of it."

"How would he do this?"

"A man of this temperament is invariably consumed with the idea that the slight difference he is introducing into his patterns constitutes originality; the general public estimate him accordingly. The manufacturer dares not invest much on the purely imaginative or individualist designer; however anxious he may be to go ahead, the advance, as I said before, can only be in very short steps."

"And you feel this would not be sacrificing the artistic quality of individuality and advocating the mediocre?"

"Most decidedly not: I am merely stating facts. When a student has to rely on designing for his means of livelihood in the future, a teacher is bound in all conscience to put the matter clearly before him. With respect to 'individuality,' when it is consistent for the purpose aimed at, it should be cherished as the most precious gift; and rather than have it cramped in any way, I would scatter all 'principles' to the winds and let such a one exercise his own sweet will with absolute freedom, provided his plans show a promise of fitness to a purpose."

"You must see the work of many beginners?"

"Yes and the result is very disheartening, at all events from my point of view; the general impression I receive is that receptiveness and individuality have been entirely sacrificed to routine. Do they show any feeling for colour as colour? Since you put that question, which is of crucial importance, I must say that this is the very quality marked by deficiency. I am only speaking what I know in saying colouring is the weak point of the chain in our industrial progress; so far as the colouring of designs is concerned, the best manufacturers can teach the designer much more than he can teach them."

"But if designing is no good as a paying profession, ought one not to prevent many philistine parents of artistic progenies giving their children the advantages of artistic training."

"A pupil who has the imaginative temperament combined with a faculty for expressing forms need not always remain a designer; a short experience in a studio should be of immense value to intending manufacturers of artistic productions or high-class decorators. The revolutions caused in business show a tendency for centralisation, and you will shortly have only the Stores on the one hand, and, on the other, men who are specialists and who can produce material with impressed individuality, otherwise they will be sucked in by the influence and whirlpools of competition. A man who, in business, can take out his sketch-book and show a customer what he wants, can always stand without the circle of competition and command his price." [. . .]

Notes

1 Middlesex University: Museum of Domestic Design and Architecture, Archive.
2 Harry Napper (1860–1930), textile designer who became freelance in 1898.
3 John Illingworth Kay (1870–1950).
4 Archibald Knox (1864–1933), Manx designer of Scottish descent. Particularly known as one of Liberty's major designers.
5 Cited in P. A. Sykas, 'The Public Require Spots: Modernism and the Nineteenth Century Calico Designer', *The Journal of the Textile Institute*, 89, 3, 1998, pp. 3–15, p. 8. Wilcock attended the Lambeth School of Art and in 1883 started his career as a designer of textiles and wallpapers, he later worked for Liberty's as well as other manufacturers of art fabrics and wallpapers. Wilcock eventually emigrated to the United States.

Part 3

DRAWING

12

JACQUES-EUGÈNE ARMENGAUD, *THE PRACTICAL DRAUGHTSMAN'S BOOK OF INDUSTRIAL DESIGN*

Drawing for design tended to fall into two opposing camps. The naturalistic approach that was championed by Ruskin and Haydon and their followers, which was contrasted to the engagement with geometry and the scientific approach to the use of drawing, promoted by such as Dyce and the engineer Nasmyth. Although Dyce was concerned with applied ornament and design, rather than Nasmyth's emphasis on the technological language of drawing. Nasmyth wrote:

> Viewing abstractly the forms of the various details of which every machine is composed, we shall find that they consist of certain combinations of six primitive or elementary geometrical figures, namely, the line, the plane, the circle, the cylinder, the cone, *and* the sphere; and that, however complex the arrangement, and vast the number of the parts of which a machine consists, we shall find that all may be as it were decomposed and classed under these six forms; and that, in short, every machine, whatever be its purpose, simply consists of a combination of these forms[1]

This extract focuses on the technical aspects of drawing which can be reduced to three forms. Firstly, those drawings used to design and define shapes and activities; secondly, those intended for workshop use in production, and thirdly, the presentation drawing showing the finished object. In engineering terms, the growth of the drawing shop meant some centralised control over the whole design. In 1905, the engineer John Haldane explained:

> now, because first-class engineering firms get up their drawings so completely in every respect that the men work to them implicitly, whereas, long ago, a great many little details were left out of the plans to save expense in the office, and thus the foremen had often to use their own discretion in giving the necessary instructions to machine hands, fitters, etc., which caused considerable loss of time.[2]

Jacques-Eugène Armengaud (1810–1891) was an important French industrial engineer, patent agent, and Professor of Machine Drawing at the *Conservatoire National des Arts et Métiers* (CNAM). This work was first published in French in 1848 as *Nouveau Cours Raisonné de Dessin Industriel* and went into many editions during the remainder of the century. It was also later republished in part as the *Engineer and Machinist's Drawing Book* in 1855.

The Practical Draughtsman's Book, (as translated by William Johnson editor of the *Practical Mechanics Journal),* was commended by the *Mechanics' Magazine* reviewer: 'It has accordingly earned a wide popularity on the other side of the Channel, and it is fortunate that in England it has been ushered into existence by one who, having observed the wants of English designers and draughtsmen in attaining a perfect knowledge of their art, possesses the happy talent of administering to them with ease and success'.[3]

Armengaud's notion of informed draughtsmanship embraced elegant delineation, industrial design, and pattern making, and his instructions mainly concentrated on the 'geometrical demonstration [that is, the grasp of theory] embodied in the drawing' in addition to a consideration of the 'physical difficulties of making patterns for both wooden and cast iron construction'.[4] Therefore, drawing that emphatically includes links to pattern-making is defined as a kind of central cognitive activity between theory and material shaping.

Jacques-Eugène Armengaud, ***The Practical Draughtsman's Book of Industrial Design: Forming a Complete Course of Mechanical, Engineering, and Architectural Drawing Translated from the French of Armengaud Aîné and Armengaud, Jeune and Amouroux; Rewritten and Arranged with Additional Matter and Plate Selections from and Examples of the Most Useful and Generally Employed Mechanism of the Day by William Johnson* (London: Longman, Brown, Green, and Longmans, 1853), Preface, pp. III–V**

INDUSTRIAL DESIGN is destined to become a universal language; for in our material age of rapid transition from abstract, to applied, Science—in the midst of our extraordinary tendency towards the perfection of the means of conversion, or manufacturing production—it must soon pass current in every land. It is, indeed, the medium between Thought and Execution; by it alone can the genius of Conception convey its meaning to the skill which executes—or suggestive ideas become living, practical realities. It is emphatically the exponent of the projected works of the Practical Engineer, the Manufacturer, and the Builder; and by its aid only, is the Inventor enabled to express his views before he attempts to realise them.

Boyle[5] has remarked, in his early times, that the excellence of manufactures, and the facility of labour, would be much promoted, if the various expedients and contrivances which lie concealed in private hands, were, by reciprocal communications, made generally known; for there are few operations that are not performed by one or other with some peculiar advantages, which, though singly of little importance, would, by conjunction and concurrence, open new inlets to knowledge, and give new powers to diligence; and Herschel,[6] in our own days, has told us that, next to the establishment of scientific institutions, nothing has exercised so powerful an influence on the progress of modem science, as the publication of scientific periodicals, in directing the course of general observation, and holding conspicuously forward models for emulative imitation. Yet, without the aid of Drawing, how can this desired reciprocity of information be attained; or how would our scientific literature fulfil its purpose, if denied the benefit of the graphic labours of the Draughtsman? Our verbal interchanges would, in truth, be vague and barren details, and our printed knowledge, misty and unconvincing.

Independently of its utility as a precise art, Drawing really interests the student, whilst it instructs him. It instils sound and accurate ideas into his mind, and develops his intellectual powers in compelling him to observe—as if the objects he delineates were really before his eyes. Besides, he always does that the best, which he best understands; and in this respect, the art of Drawing operates as a powerful stimulant to progress, in continually yielding new and varied results.

A chance sketch—a rude combination of carelessly considered pencillings—the jotted memoranda of a contemplative brain, prying into the corners of contrivance—often form the nucleus of a splendid invention. An idea thus preserved at the moment of its birth, may become of incalculable value, when rescued from the desultory train of fancy, and treated as the sober offspring of reason. In nice gradations, it receives the refining touches of leisure—becoming, first, a finished sketch,—then a drawing by the practised hand—so that many minds may find easy access to it, for their joint counsellings to improvement—until it finally emerges from the workshop, as a practical triumph of mechanical invention—an illustrious example of a happy combination opportunely noticed. Yet many ingenious men are barely able even to start this train of production, purely from inability to adequately delineate their early conceptions, or furnish that transcript of their minds which might make their thoughts immortal. If the present Treatise succeeds only in mitigating this evil, it will not entirely fail in its object; for it will at least add a few steps to the ladder of intelligence, and form a few more approaches to the goal of perfection—

"Thou has not lost an hour whereof there is a record;
A written thought at midnight will redeem the livelong day"[7]

The study of Industrial Design is really as indispensably necessary as the ordinary rudiments of learning. It ought to be an essential feature in the education of young persons for whatever profession or employment they may intend to select, as the great business of their lives; for without a knowledge of Drawing, no scientific work, whether relating to Mechanics, Agriculture, or Manufacturers, can be advantageously studied. This is now beginning to receive acknowledgement, and the routines of study in all varieties of educational establishments are being benefited by the introduction of the art.

The special mission of the *Practical Draughtsman's Book of Industrial Design* may almost be gathered from its title-page. It is intended to furnish gradually developed lessons in Geometrical Drawing, applied directly to the various branches of the Industrial Arts: comprehending Linear Design proper; Isometrical Perspective, or the study of Projections; the Drawing of Toothed wheels and Eccentrics; with Shadowing and Colouring; Oblique Projections; and the study of parallel and exact Perspective; each division being accompanied by special applications to the extensive ranges of Mechanics, Architecture, Foundry-Works, Carpentry, Joinery, Metal Manufacturers generally, Hydraulics, the construction of Steam Engines, and Mill-Work. In its compilation the feeble attraction generally offered to students in elementary form has been carefully considered; and after every geometrical problem, a practical example of its application has been added, to facilitate its comprehension and increase its value.

The work is comprised within nine divisions, appropriated to the different branches of Industrial Design. The first which concerns linear drawing only, treats particularly of straight lines–of circles–and the application to the delineation of Mouldings, Ceilings, Floors, Balconies, Cuspids, Rosettes, and other forms, to accustom the student to the proper use of the Square, Angle, and Compasses. In addition to this, it affords examples of different methods of constructing plain curves such as are of frequent occurrence in the arts, and in mechanical combinations–as the eclipse, the oval, the parabola, and the volute; and certain figures, accurately shaded, to represent reliefs, exemplify in cases where these curves are employed.

The second division illustrates the geometrical representation of objects, or the study of projections. This forms the basis of all descriptive geometry, practically considered. It shows that a single figure is insufficient for the determination of all the outlines and dimensions of a given subject; but that two projections, and one or more sections, are always necessary for the due interpretation of internal forms.

The third division points out the conventional colours and tints for the expression of the sectional details of objects, according to their nature; furnishing, at the same time, simple and easy examples, which may at once interest the pupil, and familiarise him with the use of the pencil.

In the fourth division are given drawings of various essentially valuable curves, such as Helices, and different kinds of Spirals and Serpentines, with the intersection of surfaces and their development, and workshop applications to Pipes, Coppers, Boilers, and Cocks. This study is obviously of importance in many professions, and clearly so to Ironplate workers, as Shipbuilders and Boiler-makers, Tinmen and Coppersmiths.

The fifth division is devoted to special classes of curves relating to the teeth of Spur Wheels, Screws and Racks, and the details of the construction of their patterns. The latter branch is of particular importance here, inasmuch as it has not been fully treated of in any existing work, whilst it is of the highest value to the pattern-maker, who ought to be acquainted with the most workmanlike plan of cutting his wood, and effecting the necessary junctions, as well as the general course to take in executing his pattern, for facilitating the moulding process.

The sixth division is, in effect, a continuation of the fifth. It comprises the theory and practice of drawing Bevil, Conical, or Angular Wheels, with details of the construction of the wood patterns, and notices of peculiar forms of some gearing, as well as the eccentrics employed in mechanical construction.

The seventh division comprises the studies of the shading and shadows of the principal solids—Prisms, Pyramids, Cylinders, and Spheres, together with their applications to mechanical and architectural details, as screws, spur and bevil wheels, coppers and furnaces, columns and entablatures. These studies naturally lead to that of colours— single, as those of China Ink or Sepia, or varied; also of graduated shades produced by successive flat tints, according to one method, or by the softening manipulation of the brush, according to another.

The pupil may now undertake designs of greater complexity, leading him in the eighth division to various figures representing combined or general elevations, as well as sections and details of various complete machines, to which are added some geometrical drawings, explanatory of the action of the moving parts of machinery.

The ninth completes the study of Industrial Design, with oblique projections and parallels, and exact perspective. In the study of exact perspective, special applications of its rules are made to architecture and machinery by the aid of a perspective elevation of a corn mill supported on columns, and fitted up with all the necessary gearing. A series of Plates marked A, B, &c., are also interspersed throughout the work, as examples of finished drawings of machinery. The Letterpress relating to these Plates, together with an illustrated chapter on Drawing Instruments, will form an appropriate Appendix to the Volume. The general explanatory text embraces not only a description of the objects and their movements, but also tables and practical rules, more particularly those relating to the dimensions of the principal details of machinery, as facilitating actual construction.

Such is the scope, and such are the objects, of the PRACTICAL DRAUGHTSMAN'S BOOK OF INDUSTRIAL DESIGN.

Such is the course now submitted to the consideration of all who are in the slightest degree connected with the Constructive Arts. It aims at the dissemination of those fundamental teachings which are so essentially necessary at every stage in the application of the forces lent to us by Nature for the conversion of Her materials. For "man can only act upon nature, and appropriate her forces to his use, by comprehending her laws, and knowing those forces in relative value and measure."[8] All art is the true application of knowledge to a practical end. We have outlived the times of random construction, and the mere heaping together of natural substances. We must now design carefully and delineate accurately before we proceed to execute—and the quick pencil of the ready draughtsman is a proud possession for our purpose. Let the youthful student think on this; and whether in the workshop of the Engineer, the studio of the Architect, or the factory of the Manufacturer, let him remember that, to spare the blighting of his fondest hopes, and the marring of his fairest prospects—to achieve, indeed, his higher aspirations, and verify his loftier thoughts, which point to eminence—he must give his days and nights, his business and his leisure, to the study of Industrial Design.

Notes

1 'Remarks on the Introduction of the Slide Principle in Tools and Machines Employed in the Production of Machinery' in R. Buchanan, *Practical Essays on Mill Work and Other Machinery. Revised into a Third Edition with additions by George Rennie* (London: John Weale, 1841), p. 394.
2 J. W. C. Haldane, *Life as an Engineer; Its Lights, Shades and Prospects . . . with Many Plates, Etc.* (London: E. & F.N. Spon, 1905), p. 56.
3 *Mechanics' Magazine*, 19 February 1853, pp. 152–3.
4 *The Practical Draughtsman's Book of Industrial Design*, 1853, p. v.
5 Robert Boyle FRS (1627–1691), an Anglo-Irish natural philosopher, chemist, physicist, and inventor.
6 Frederick William Herschel, FRS (1738–1822), was a German-born British astronomer.
7 'Of Writing', M.F. Tupper, *Proverbial Philosophy* (The First and Second Series) (London Edward Moxon & Co, 1867).
8 Alexander Humboldt, *Cosmos,* Volume 1, (1845–1862).

13

WILLIAM DYCE, *THE INTRODUCTION TO THE DRAWING-BOOK OF THE SCHOOL OF DESIGN*

Originating from Scotland, Dyce (1806–1864) in a full, though relatively short career, managed to engage with being an artist, a theorist, a designer, and a reforming administrator. In 1837, his proposals for improving manufacturing in Scotland by the reorganisation of the Trustees' Academy in Edinburgh were noticed in London. He was subsequently appointed superintendent of the new Government School of Design. He was encouraged to make a fact-finding tour of the education of artists and designers in Germany and France and providing an important report on the topic. (See 1.44) Although later removing himself from the field of education, he remained interested in art and design and was appointed as a juror at the London International Exhibitions of 1851 and 1862.

Dyce's ideas on pattern drawing were rooted in his experience in Edinburgh and the perceived need for designers to understand the manufacturing industries for which they worked. He promoted the establishment of a standardised drawing curriculum that avoided drawing from casts of antique sculpture or indeed living models, and instead encouraged the drawing of simple linear shapes, then creating abstracted forms from nature to be used for pattern work. He explained how this worked: 'The ornamentist refers to nature for the purpose of learning the contrivances by which she has adorned her works, that he may be able to apply the same forms and modes of beauty to man's handicraft'.[1] (pp. xvii)

A harsh critique of the original work from the *Westminster Review* in 1843 observed that 'we cannot admit that it will serve as an elementary drawing book for schools. It will be useful in schools of ornamental design that are frequented by young men who are not altogether beginners and are willing to go through much dry hard work for the sake of future profit. . . . whatever merits this book might possess it could never become a general drawing book for juvenile public instruction, as its authors set forth'.[2]

C. L. Nursey, master of the school of art in Belfast, was likewise unhappy with Dyce's book. In his response to the committee, established to report on the progress of the Department of Science and Art in 1854, he noted:

> It has been found, from long experience, that abstract examples like Mr. Dyce's, are uninteresting and unintelligible to the pupil of a school of design at the commencement of his course. He usually fails in copying them, tires, gets disheartened and disgusted, and leaves the school after a short time, which would not have been the case if the examples had been from simple and familiar forms.[3]

Dyce's thoughts on drawing as being abstractive and reproductive, distinguish them from fine art's imitative approach. His ideas were developed further by reformers such as Owen Jones, as well as Christopher Dresser, whose six-part article for the *Art Journal* published in 1857, titled 'Botany as Adapted to the Arts and Art Manufactures'[4] expressed analogous ideas. Similarly, Richard Redgrave in his *Century of Painters of the English School*, published in 1866, commented favourably on Dyce's system:

> It consisted first in the ornamental analyses of plants and flowers, displaying each part separately according to its normal law of growth, not as they appear viewed perspectively, but diagrammatically flat to the eye; so treated, it was found that almost all plants contain many distinct ornamental elements, and that the motives to be derived from the vegetable kingdom were inexhaustible.[5]

William Dyce, *The Introduction to the Drawing-Book of the School of Design, Published in the Years 1842–3, Under the Direction of W. Dyce*, (Reprinted) (London: Chapman & Hall, 1854), pp. V–XXIV

Introduction

THE object of the following work is twofold: in the first place, to serve as an Elementary Drawing-book for schools, and in particular for those schools whose ultimate purpose is to educate young persons in the art of inventing and executing patterns and designs for the various branches of ornamented manufacture; and, in the second place, to be a hand-book of ornamental art, for the use and guidance of manufacturers and pattern-draughtsmen. The work will, accordingly, be divided into two principal parts; one having reference to the study of design, the other to its application to industry. The former will contain a series of progressive lessons in drawing, so far as the art may be taught, by means of copies on paper; and the latter, a collection of designs, which it is hoped will form a complete book of reference for examples of all the various modes and styles of ornamental art.* It is to be understood, however, that many—indeed most of the examples given in the first part of the work, as mere exercises in drawing, may, in respect to design and invention, be referred to the second part. Of this kind are the various ornaments of architectural mouldings used by the Greeks, Romans, and the builders of the middle ages, and of more recent times; and also the specimens of geometrical ornaments, i.e. ornaments drawn with the ruler and compass, which form the sequel to the first division of the elementary part of the work. These will not be repeated in the second part; and though the first part may be used alone for its specific purpose of elementary instruction, the second, considered as a collection of designs illustrative of all the various authentic forms of ornamental design, cannot be reckoned complete without the first.

Before giving detailed account of the examples contained in the drawing-book, it may be well to consider for a little the kind of instruction which the peculiar business of a School of Design requires. To understand this subject clearly, regard must be had, in the first instance, to the nature of the art to be cultivated; and in relation to this, the particular faculties in the pupil to be called into exercise,—the habits to be formed—the kind of skill to be imparted; and these points being agreed upon, we shall be enabled to define the species of education best calculated to prepare him for his future pursuits.

The art of the ornamentist may be considered in two points of view: first, as to its means and materials of operation, as an imitative art:—in regard to which it ranks midway between the fine art and art purely mechanical, and partakes of the nature of both; sometimes, like the one, working solely by the hand,—sometimes, like the other, by the aid of mechanism; or secondly, as to the end of its imitation:—by which it is essentially distinguished from fine art properly so called. On the nature of this distinction it is necessary that we labour under no misconception; for it is obvious, that if there be such an essential difference between the two kinds of art as is here affirmed, it must show itself more or less through every stage of the tuition, giving to it a specific character and purpose beyond that which it must have in common with every kind of elementary instruction in design. It is, of course, to be understood, that the distinction drawn between ornamental art and fine art is made in reference to some object towards which each stands in some manner related; for the fine arts, as dealing with history, poetry, and generally with moral expression, occupy a field into which the ornamentist has no claim whatever to enter: in that view, no comparison can be instituted between the two kinds of art. But in regard to the *beautiful* in the works of nature, they labour in common ground; and it is in their pursuit of this, and in the end arrived at by each in relation to it, that we discover their characteristic differences.

Now, the artist (and by artist is meant the painter and sculptor; for the architect, so far as imitative art is concerned, is really an ornamentist), in dealing with

---

* The work thus projected by Mr. Dyce was never completed, its publication having ceased on his retirement from the direction of the Schools in 1843.

beauty in the works of nature, never contemplates it apart from its natural subject. Beauty is with him an individual quality,—it is the beauty of a horse, of a man, of a flower; and hence the expression of his ideas is necessarily made by a fictitious resemblance of the object in which the beauty naturally resides. He imitates the beauty of nature, by making beautiful images of natural objects.

The ornamentist, on the other hand, proceeds by a method directly the reverse. Beauty with him is a quality separable from natural objects; and he makes the separation in order to impress the cosmetic of nature on the productions of human industry. Works of industry thus moulded into shape are not imitations of nature because they are covered with pictured or sculptured resemblances of natural objects, but because they are adorned on the same principles as the works of nature themselves. If a sculptor, for instance, seeks to convey to us his idea of the beauty of a *lily*, he produces a model of the flower itself;—more beautiful and perfect it may be than it is to be found in any single specimen, but still it is the image of a lily that he has modelled. Not so the ornamentist: in his hands, the same beautiful form reappears with all its essential characteristics, but with a new individuality; it is no longer the form of a lily but of a cup, a vase, the bowl of a candlestick. or of a hundred other articles of common use. The artist and omamentist are both imitators of nature, but in different senses. The works of each resemble those of nature: but in the one the resemblance is fictitious; in the other, so far as it goes, it is a reality. In the one kind, the pleasure we receive is always relative to the natural objects depicted or sculptured; in the other, the pleasure is immediately referable to the work itself;—the one, in short, is a figment that affords us pleasure, by suggesting some actual or possible beauty of nature; the other is a reality that, so far as it goes, pleases us in the same sense, and for the same reason, that nature itself does. Thus the ornamentist is an imitator of nature, in a sense very analogous to that in which the man of science may be termed so, who applies her operating and governing laws and the means and hints furnished by her to the accomplishment of new ends of convenience and utility; and the real position, accordingly, of ornamental design is side by side with practical science: its real use to hide, by a coating of beauty, *the skeleton-like*, contrivances of the latter, and thus to bring them into the condition of the works of nature, in which beauty and utility are always concomitant.

It will be seen from these observations that ornamental art is rather *abstractive* and *reproductive* than imitative, in the same sense as the fine arts are said to be so; and this characteristic is of great importance in the matter of education.

In the first place, the beauties of form or of colour abstracted from nature by the ornamentist, from the very circumstance that they are abstractions, assume, in relation to the whole progress of the art, the character of principles or facts that tend by accumulation to bring it to perfection. On this account the *inductive* method (if the term may be allowed in an artistical sense), though altogether inapplicable to fine art (every work of which is isolated and identified both with the object represented and the individual artist), becomes a necessary element in ornamental design. The accumulated labours of each successive race of omamentists are so many discoveries made—so many facts to be learned, treasured up, applied to a new use, submitted to the process of artistic generalisation, or added to. A language and a literature of ornamental design are constituted; the former of which must be mastered before the latter can be understood, and the latter known before we are in a condition to add to its treasures. The very first step, therefore, in the education of ornamentists, must be, their initiation into the current and conventional language of their art, and by this means into its existing literature.

In the second place, if the nature of ornamental design has been rightly stated, it is obvious that there is something very erroneous in the opinions of those who contend, on the one hand, that the power of imitating any object artistically ought to be the first, as it is supposed to be the only important requisite, in the education of ornamentists; and, on the other, that the exercise of this artistic imitation ought to begin on the human figure, since the mastery of this would render every minor attainment comparatively easy.

If the study of ornamental design might be taken up as it were at the beginning,— as if the art had made no progress or had no previous existence,—it might be conceded that the legitimate paths of the ornamentist and the artist would in some measure be identical; for it is by imitating nature anyhow that we learn how, and what, and wherefore to imitate. There is no one who doubts that nature must be held up as the source from whence, as much now as ever, all the forms of beauty applicable to the uses of the ornamentist must be derived. A new style of ornament, as it is termed, can only be invented by the old method of imitating the cosmetic art of nature; but it is precisely because the old forms of ornament were drawn from this source, and may be proved to be founded on the most accurate perception of the objective causes of natural beauty—because, in short, they are facts and conclusions already arrived at, that we must make an acquaintance with them our starting-point; and this acquaintance is only to be gained by practice, i.e. by copying these authentic models of ornament reduced to their elemental form.

But there is a more practical and evident objection to the opinions which have been noticed. The power of imitating objects artistically is not adequate to the ends which the ornamentist contemplates. Representations of natural objects, such as flowers or animals, are not ornaments in any other sense than works of painting or sculpture may be said to be so. The application of such representations to walls or articles of furniture, it is true, has often been made, and is daily made, for ornamental purposes, and constitutes a species of ornamental art: but it is only one among a thousand others in which artistic imitation is inadmissible. The artist and the ornamentist may choose out of caprice, as in the case of arabesques, to unite their two arts; but the arts are not the less essentially distinct, nor, as a general rule, the less incompatible in practice. The very name *grotesque*, applied to that kind of art by the painters of the middle ages, because the ancient specimens of it were mostly discovered in grottoes or ruins, is used by us to express anything very absurd or ridiculous; and in truth, since it is a matter of fact that arabesque painting or sculpture have always been the offspring of artists, they ought rather to be looked upon as a kind of beautiful nonsense than as a species of art to be reasoned about.

It is not meant to deny that an intermediate kind of art is often extremely pleasing; as, for instance, when a vase is decorated with sculptures of flowers or fruit: but in this case, and in every other similar, it will be found that the pleasure is referable to some of the causes that essentially belong to fine art, and that the work is judged of artistically. But the question is not how far artists may become ornamentists, but to what extent a strictly artistic education is proper to ornamentists; and to judge of this, reference must be made to the principles already adverted to. The artist, it has been observed, has for his drift the representation of beauty as it appears in its natural subject; the ornamentist, the application of beauty to a new subject. To the former, therefore, artistical imitation is an essential requisite, since he works by it, and by it alone: it is, in short, his language. To the latter it is not an essential, but only a useful acquirement. The reason of this is obvious: the painter deals solely with the apparent forms of objects; and it is by giving us true pictures of the apparent form that he suggests the reality. The ornamentist, on the other hand, in his use of nature sometimes selects the apparent, sometimes the real form; but in either case the forms or colours which he has abstracted assume a positive and real character, and if he avails himself of artistic effects, it is more for the sake of gaining variety and force than for identity and truth of mere resemblance. In few words, the ornamentist refers to nature for the purpose of learning the contrivances by which she has adorned her works, that he may be enabled to apply the same forms and modes of beauty to man's handicraft; and this purpose necessarily leads him, as it were, to anatomise her works and resolve them into elements, rather than to view them in the aggregate with the eye of an artist; and to deal with minute particulars of form and colour more as they really are than as they appear modified by visual laws. As he does not aim at that fictitious resemblance of nature which it is the purpose of fine art to effect, but, so far as he goes, at the identical repetition of natural forms and colours in some new material and for some new purpose, it is obvious that the power of representing objects in the form of diagrams is to him far more necessary and valuable than that of imitating them with all their effects of light and shade, of surface or of material, as an artist does. This acquirement, therefore, of drawing with precision and readiness every variety of superficial form in outline, which to the artist would be of little use, must be a prominent object in the education of ornamentists.

Besides, it has been already observed, that in practice the method of the ornamentist sometimes inclines to that of the artist, sometimes to that of the mechanic; and the reason is very plain. The forms of natural objects are of two species; one bounded by straight lines, such as all the variety of crystalline forms; the other by curved lines of various degrees of simplicity and regularity. The former kind lie altogether within the province of geometrical drawing, the latter partially so; and it is in relation to the latter that the necessity arises for a kind of practical skill, to the attainment of which artistical imitation lends no aid. The outlines, for example, of greater part of the ornaments of Grecian architecture seem to be referable to the curved lines produced by the sections of a cone, to the spiral, the cycloidal line, &c.; and, indeed, the same forms occur everywhere throughout animate nature. Now, though it might be possible to discover the rules for describing geometrically these authentic forms of ornament and their prototypes, the discovery would in practice be of little use, because there is less difficulty in drawing them with the hand accurately enough for all practicable purposes, than there would be in applying the rule if it were known. The outlines of Greek ornaments are only approximations to scientific forms; nor is more required in art. The eye is satisfied with a degree of approximation attainable by practice, and, were it possible to work with mathematical accuracy, would be unable to appreciate the difference between the truth and the approximation. But it is precisely because forms and lines of the kind alluded to must in practice be drawn empirically, that ornamentists must undergo a study which can neither be ranked under the head of artistical imitation nor of practical geometry. These forms and lines of beauty are all, it is true, to be found in the objects commonly placed before the artist; but artistical imitation, so far from leading directly to their discovery, is, on the one hand, calculated to inspire a distaste for the abstractive process by which they are made to assume a positive and independent character; and, on the other, is for beginners about as bad an exercise as can be conceived for the attainment of the sort of accuracy and precision of hand in the delineation of superficial form, or of the patience in minute details of execution, which are indispensable to ornamentists,.

It must not be imagined that in these observations the value and necessity of artistic imitation, as an element in the instructions of a School of Design, have been underrated; for the question has not been, whether it be simply necessary, but whether, having due regard to the nature of ornamental art, it ought to occupy the primary and even exclusive position which opinions now current have assigned to it.* As a means of developing the intelligence and taste of the student with respect to the general aspect of nature, and of enriching his fancy and supplying him with new materials for his art, it is the best that can be devised; but in this view it is obviously an exercise better suited to the more advanced stages of his progress than to its commencement.

On a review of the foregoing remarks, it appears that the difference between the instructions in a School of Design and ordinary tuition in drawing arises, in the first place, from the amount of accuracy, precision, and readiness in the delineation of superficial form, which is required in the practice of the ornamentist; and, in the second place, from the accumulative nature of his art, which consists, to a great extent, of a variety of abstract and, so far as they go, perfect and unalterable forms of beauty, that must be learnt; not as matter of theory, but of actual practice. In this view, therefore, though in one sense the outlines of ornament, of which the second division of the elementary part of the work consists, are preparatory to the third, which forms the introduction to the artistical study of nature: they are, at the same time, intended to serve the double purpose of imparting manual skill in linear design, and of making the student versed in the established models of

---

* These, it is hardly necessary to remark, opinions are now in a great measure obsolete. At the time these observations were written, the late Mr. Haydon was the most prominent advocate of the views which are here controverted.

linear ornament. This circumstance must always be borne in mind,—outlines of ornament do not necessarily hold the same relation to ornaments in a solid material, as the outline of a picture or of a statue does to the picture or statue; they may or may not be considered relatively to solidity, the representation of solid forms, or of forms depicted in colours, on a surface. The solidity or coloured effect of the ornament are matters connected with the application of the form, but the outline, as containing its principle, is in itself complete; and in becoming practically acquainted with this, the student has made a positive acquirement in ornamental design.

In conclusion, the course of instruction given in the following work, while, on the one hand, it affords materials for the three kinds of practical study necessary to the ornamentist, viz. that of geometrical drawing, of the drawing of linear ornament by the hand, and of artistical imitation of solid objects, on the other makes the attainment of manual dexterity a means of acquaintance with the established and classical forms of decorative art.

Notes

1   *The Introduction to the Drawing Book of the School of Design*, p. xvii.
2   *Westminster Review*, 39, 2 May 1843, p. 588.
3   *First Report of the Department of Science and Art* (HMSO, 1854), Appendix C, p. 58.
4   C. Dresser, 'Botany as Adapted to the Arts and Art Manufactures', *Art Journal*, new series 3, 1857, pp. 17–19, 53–5, 86–88, 109–11, 249–52, and 340–42.
5   R. Redgrave, and S. Redgrave, *A Century of Painters of the English School: With Critical Notices of Their Works, and an Account of the Progress of Art in England* (London: Smith, Elder, 1866), p. 565.

14

LEWIS FOREMAN DAY, 'OF DESIGNS AND WORKING DRAWINGS'

Establishing his own studio in London in 1870, Day designed for a wide variety of mediums and supplied numerous manufacturers. He wrote prolifically on design, and his readership included professional and amateur designers, students of design, and manufacturers. He addressed the technical aspects of pattern making and its correct application in books such as *Instances of Accessory Art* (1880), *The Application of Ornament* (1888), *The Anatomy of Pattern* (1889), and *The Planning of Ornament* (1889), while his other books discussed specific mediums, such as *Art in Needlework* (1900) and *Stained Glass* (1903). Day was a founding member of the Art Workers' Guild and the Arts and Crafts Exhibition Society. However, he also embraced modern technology and advised on how to achieve good design through industrial processes; an issue which is well demonstrated in his debate with Walter Crane in *Moot Points: Friendly Disputes on Art and Industry Between Walter Crane and Lewis F. Day* (1903).

By the time of this chapter, there was a clear range of distinctions within the genre of drawing; between sketches, shop drawings, architects' working drawings, and engineers' working drawings, cartoons, and presentation and competition drawings.

An early use of the term 'working drawings' is found in a 1785 advertisement for a subscription journal titled *Rural Architecture* published by John Place, architect and surveyor, who also offered 'Designs for public and private buildings; also directions and working drawings for executing the same at any distance'.[1] The term was also used in engineering circles. For example, in the 1820s, the Society of Arts offered premiums for 'the best working Drawings in Plan, Elevation, and Section of a Condensing Steam Engine, in its most improved state, &c'.

In 1860, *The Builder,* in a short notice about 'Mechanical Draughtsmen', made a further distinction between 'mere drawing' and draughtsmanship. 'Of mere copyists there are hundreds too many. Although mechanical drawing may be an art by itself, and although an excellent draughtsman may be always sure of employment, the demand for mere drawing is limited, and excellent draughtsmen have always been scarce'.[2]

In the 1880s, the architect and designer, John Dando Sedding spoke out against the modern working drawing in relation to architecture, maintaining that it was a fallacy to think that 'adequate working designs can be expressed on paper', as they neither fully addressed the craft of architecture nor allowed the artisan creative freedom. Sedding warned against the close controlling of all work done to the 'necessary full-size and detail drawings', as this would inhibit the skills of the craftsman that might enhance the building craft processes. In other words, the real loss was the close links that apparently once existed between architects and craftsmen.[3] This was a bone of contention in British engineering businesses where workers were trying to maintain craft skills in the face of standardisation and rationalisation. The opposite was the case in America.

Early in the twentieth century, the American engineer Earnest Child usefully explained the different forms of working drawings for mechanical designing and production. Firstly, the outline drawings, giving general dimensions, and space occupied but with no details. Secondly, were the assembly drawings, showing the entire machine, with all its parts in their proper positions. Thirdly, were the detail drawings, showing on a large scale the separate parts of the machine, with all the information necessary for completion. Fourthly, some machines are so complex that it is necessary to make a separate drawing to show all the special fittings, and in some cases, it is customary to make motion diagrams for each machine.[4] The complexity of working drawings is evident.

Lewis Foreman Day, 'Of Designs and Working Drawings', *Arts and Crafts Exhibition Society, Catalogue of Second Exhibition*, 1889, pp. 93–109

There is some difficulty in saying anything apropos to an exhibition yet to be formed—it is likely that these remarks on Designs and Working Drawings may be out of all proportion to the show of such drawings at the Arts and Crafts; but there can be little doubt that among them there will be more than enough to illustrate what is here said; and, on the other hand, what is here said may help towards their just appreciation. That is the occasion, as it is the one excuse, for this short article.

From the point of view of the craftsman the most interesting drawings are working drawings—just the last to be appreciated by the public, because they are the last to be understood. The most admired of show drawings are to us craftsmen comparatively without interest. We recognize the "competition" drawing at once: we see how it was made to secure the commission, and not with a view to its effect in execution (which is the true and only end of a design), and we do not wonder at the failure of competitions in general. For the man who cares least, if even he knows, how a design will appear in execution, is the most likely to perpetrate a prettiness which will gain the favour of the inexpert, with whom the selection is likely to rest.

The general public, and all in fact who are technically ignorant on the subject, need to be warned that the most attractive and what are called "taking" drawings are just those which are least likely to be designs—still less *bonâ fide* working drawings. The real workman has not the time, even if he had the inclination, to finish up his drawings to the point that pleases generally; the inventive spirit has not the patience. We have each of us the failings complementary to our faculties, and *vice versâ*; and you will usually find—certainly it is my experience—that the makers of very elaborately finished drawings seldom do anything more than what we have seen before; and that men of any individuality, actual designers that is to say, have a way of considering a drawing finished as soon as ever it expresses what they mean.

You may take it, then, as a general rule that highly finished and elaborate drawings arc got up for show, "finished for exhibition" as they say (in compliance with the supposed requirements of an exhibition rather than with a view to practical purposes), and that drawings completed only so far as is necessary, precise in their details, disfigured by notes in writing, sections and so on, are at least genuine workaday designs.

If you ask what a design should be like—well, like a design. It is altogether a different thing from a picture; it is almost the reverse of it. Practically no man has, as I said, the leisure, even if he had the ability, to make an effective finished picture of a thing yet to be carried out—perhaps *not* to be carried out. This last is a most serious consideration for him, and may have a sad effect upon his work. The artist who could afford thus to give himself away gratis, would certainly not do so; the man who might be willing to do it, could not; for if he has "got no work to do"—that is at least presumptive evidence that he is not precisely a master of his craft.

The design that looks like a picture is likely to be at best a reminiscence of something done before; and the more often it has been done the more likely it is to be pictorially successful—and by so much the less is it strictly speaking a design.

This applies especially to designs on a small scale, such as are usually submitted to catch the rare commission. To imitate in a full-sized cartoon the texture of material, the accident of reflected lights, and other such accidents of effect, is sheer nonsense, which no practical workman would think of. A painter put to the uncongenial task of decorative design might be excused for attempting to make his productions pass muster by workmanship excellent in itself, although not in the least to the point: one does what one can, or what one must; and if a man has a faculty he needs must show it. Only, the perfection of painting will not, for all that, make design.

In the first small sketch-design, everything need not of course be expressed; but it should be indicated—for the purpose is simply to explain the scheme proposed: so much of pictorial representation as may be necessary to that is desirable, and no more. It should be in the nature of a diagram, specific enough to illustrate the idea, and how it is to be worked out. It ought by strict rights to commit one, definitely to a certain method of execution, as a written specification would; and may often with advantage be helped out by written notes, which explain more definitely than any pictorial rendering just how this is to be wrought, that cast, the other chased, and so on, as the case may be.

Whatever the method of expression the artist may adopt, he should be perfectly clear in his own mind how his design is to be worked out—and he ought to make it clear also to any one with sufficient technical knowledge to understand a drawing.

In the first sketch for a window, for example, he need not show every lead and every piece of glass; but there should be no possible mistake as to how it is to be glazed, or which is "painted" glass and which is "mosaic." To omit the necessary bars in a sketch for glass seems to me a weak concession to the prejudice of the public. One *may* have to concede such points sometimes; but the concession is due less to necessity than to the, what shall we call it?—not perhaps exactly the cowardice, but at all events the timidity, of the artist.

In a full sized working drawing or cartoon everything material to the design should be expressed, and that as definitely as possible. In a cartoon for glass (to take again the same example) every lead-line should be shown as well as the saddle bars;[5] to omit them is about as excusable as it would be to leave out the sections from a design for cabinet work. It is contended sometimes that such details are not necessary, that the artist can bear all that in mind. Doubtless he can, more or less; but I am inclined to believe more strongly in the *less*. At any rate he will much more certainly have them in view if he keeps them visibly before his eyes. One thing that deters him is the fear of offending the client, who will not believe, when he sees leads and bars in a drawing, how little they are likely to assert themselves in the glass.

Very much the same thing applies to designs and working drawings generally. A thorough craftsman never suggests a form or colour without realizing in his own mind how he will be able to get it in the actual work; and in his working drawing he explains that fully, making allowance even for some not impossible dullness of apprehension on the part of the executant. Thus, if a thing is to be woven he shows the cards to be employed, he arranges what parts are "single," what "double," as the weavers call it, what changes in the shuttle are proposed, and by the crossing of which threads certain intermediate tints are to be obtained.

Or again, if it is for wall paper printing, he arranges, not only for the blocks, but the order in which they shall be printed; and provides for possible printing in "flock" or for the printing of one transparent colour over another, so as to get more colours than there are blocks used, and so on.

In either case, too, he shows quite plainly the limits of each colour, not so much seeking the softness of effect which is his ultimate aim, as the precision which will enable the block or card-cutter to see at a glance what he means, and that even at the risk of a certain hardness in his drawing; for the drawing is in itself of no account; it is only the means to an end; and his end is the stuff, the paper, or whatever it may be, *in execution*.

A workman intent on his design will sacrifice his drawing to it— harden it, as I said, for the sake of emphasis, annotate it, patch it, cut it up, do anything to make his meaning clear to the workman who comes after him. It is as a rule only the dilettante who is dainty about preserving his drawings.

There may be some temptation to an artist very much in repute to be careful of his designs, and to elaborate them (himself, or by the hands of his assistants) because, so finished, they have a commercial value as drawings—but this is at best pot boiling; and the only men who are subject to this temptation arc just those who might be proof against it. Men so much in repute that even their working drawings are in demand, have no such urgent need to work for the pot; and the working drawings of men to whom the pounds and shillings must needs be a real consideration, are not sought after.

In the case of very smart and highly finished drawings by comparatively unknown designers—of ninety-nine out of a hundred, that is to say, or nine hundred and ninety-nine out of a thousand perhaps—elaboration implies, either that having little to say a man fills up his time in saying it at unnecessary length, or that he is working for exhibition.

And why not work for exhibition, it may be asked. There is a simple answer to that: the exhibition pitch is in much too high a key, and in the long run it will ruin the faculty of the workman who adopts it.

It is only fair to admit that an exhibition of fragmentary and unfinished drawings, soiled, tattered and torn, as they almost invariably come from the workshop or factory, would make a very poor show—and the Selection Committee of the Society have to keep that in mind. It is for this reason that they insist upon some sort of frame to all drawings exhibited; for what is not worth a frame of some kind is probably not worth showing; and anyone who proposed to frame a drawing would naturally concern himself as to its appearance in its frame, and would endeavour to make it presentable. That is a very different thing from working it up to picture pitch; and no one who thinks about it, however slight his experience, will confound the two.

When all is said, designs exhibited appeal primarily to designers. *We* all want to see each other's work, and especially each other's way of working; but it should not be altogether uninteresting to the intelligent amateur to see what working drawings are, and to compare them with the kind of specious competition drawings by which he is so apt to be misled.

Notes

1 *Morning Post and Daily Advertiser*, May 12, 1785.
2 'The Mechanical Draughtsmen', *The Builder*, 7 January 1860, p. 7.
3 J. D. Sedding, 'On the Relation of Art and the Handicrafts', *The Builder: Supplement*, 7 May 1887, pp. 693–4.
4 E. T. Child, 'Mechanical Drawing', *Amateur Work* (Boston), January 1902, p. 62.
5 Saddle bars: horizontal metal bar that support the lead work of leaded lights or stained glass windows to add stability and prevent bowing.

Part 4

DESIGN PRINCIPLES

15

GEORGE WALLIS, 'THE PRINCIPLES OF FINE ART AS APPLIED TO INDUSTRIAL PURPOSES'

George Wallis (1811–1891) was an artist and art educator, who particularly promoted education in industrial art. He was associated with design schools, acting as headmaster of the Birmingham School of Design, and later as keeper of the art collections at the South Kensington museum. His writings helped to popularise the issues surrounding art education for industry. This was the fourth in a series titled 'Art Education for the People', written for the *People's Journal*.

In this paper, Wallis discussed the distinctions between fine art and industrial art, and the issues that arise from this. He claimed that the fine artist 'records by idealised imitation', whereas the industrial artist 'aims at the embellishing of the works of man'. Wallis went on to explain the difficulties in this latter process. 'With some, to *draw* is to *design*. With others, to *design* is to *invent*. With a third party, to *draw* means merely to copy, and to *design* means *dovetailing* together in congruous or incongruous mixture certain things already done by somebody else'. A little later he elucidates how the industrial artist will adapt 'the natural type to a new material [that] compels him to *reproduce*, almost *create*, as well as *imitate* - *invent* as well as *copy* - design as well as *draw*!'[1]

Wallis was unhappy with the direction of the centrally directed School of Design curricula. So in 1845, he wrote a 'Letter to the Council of the Manchester School of Design, on the System of Instruction pursued in that School'. The Council later published this letter as a pamphlet. *The Athenaeum* reviewed it and noted initially that 'the title of this pamphlet is a misnomer: it is not a letter on the System pursued in the Manchester School of Design, but a very formal and authoritative enunciation of the system that ought to be pursued everywhere else'. However, the review continued with a sarcastic blast at Wallis and his outspoken methods, and mocked his apparent pretensions to have all the answers to design education: 'The self-veneration of this gentleman is brought so constantly to the attention of the reader, the word "I" is so frequently and so pregnantly used that the question must be asked, Who is Mr. Wallis: What has he done in Art, in the literature of Art, as "an artist educator" (to use his own phraseology), that he should venture to put forth a manifesto of such inordinate pretensions?'[2]

An unusual source, a travel guide to England, entered the discussion with a supportive commentary on Wallis's role in the Manchester School.

> In two years from the time of Mr. Wallis taking the charge, the funds of the school were flourishing; the interest taken in it by the public was great, and nearly half the Institution was occupied by the pupils, while the applications for admission were more numerous than could be accommodated. Under this management, the public, who care little for abstract art, were taught the close connexion between the instruction of the School of Design and their private pursuits. This is what is wanted in all our towns. It is not enough to teach boys and girls, —the manufacturers and purchasers need to be taught by the eye, if not by the hand . . . While matters were proceeding so satisfactorily, the Somerset House authorities (who have since been tried and condemned by a Committee of the House of Commons),[3] proceeded to earn their salaries by giving instructions which could not be carried out without destroying all the good that had been done. The Manchester Committee and Mr. Wallis protested against this *red-tapish* interference. It was persisted in; Mr. Wallis resigned, to the great regret of his pupils and manufacturing friends in the managing council.[4]

George Wallis, 'The Principles of Fine Art as Applied to Industrial Purposes', *The People's Journal*, 3, 1847, pp. 230–233

ART-EDUCATION FOR THE PEOPLE. By George Wallis, Late Principal Master of the Manchester School of Design. No. IV. THE PRINCIPLES OF FINE ART AS APPLIED TO INDUSTRIAL PURPOSES. (With Illustrations designed and drawn on wood by the Author.)

If we doubted for a moment the identity or great principles, as applied to every department of Art, this paper would have been entitled—"The reproductive principles of Industrial Art, compared with the Imitative and Ideal of Fine Art;" but, as no such distinction is recognised, our current essay merely involves an attempt to show in what particular the principles of Art, as applied to Industrial Purposes, are *practically* different in their technical uses to those same principles as applied to historic composition, either in painting or in sculpture. In developing principles, the rules, or various modes of applying those principles, cannot necessarily be illustrated in a series of brief essays like the present: these are rather the immediate subject of the intelligent teacher and apt pupil, the professor in his chair, with his chalk and demonstration board, or the author with his special work and careful student-reader.

It would be a mere waste of time and argument to say anything here of the importance of a thorough knowledge of first principles as the only true and efficient means by which any art or science can be properly understood or successfully practised; nor is it to be supposed that any really sincere and disinterested man can be found who, whilst acknowledging this point in the abstract, would in practice so far limit its exercise, as to say that a superficial knowledge of general principles, without caring as to their practical application, is sufficient for even the humblest Art-student. In maintaining the oneness of Art, and the general identity of its first principles, however, it is not to be forgotten that false conclusions have been drawn therefrom; and that it has been erroneously supposed and strenuously argued, that when once a knowledge is attained of those principles which govern productions of an elevated character —which, from their aims, must ever be regarded as the highest development of imitative and ideal power—the artist may at once deal, without further consideration, in an artistic sense at least, with those more mechanical departments which enter so largely into the productions and embellishments of every-day life, and which, for the sake of distinction, we have already characterised as the results of Industrial or Ornamental, in contradistinction to Fine Art.

The fallacy of such an assumption is best known, indeed, can only be truly known, to those who have aimed at practising both; for it is by no means an uncommon occurrence, to find that highly intelligent artists in the departments of portrait and landscape, nay, of history itself, are totally unacquainted with the simplest method by which an arabesque or an ornamental accessory to their pictures may be produced. Nor does this arise from any want of talent on their part, but simply from a misconception of the value of the power to do such things, and from a want of a knowledge of those first principles which govern the treatment of NATURE as applied to *ornament*, compared with the treatment of that same NATURE as applied to *pictorial effects*.

It will be our purpose, therefore, to explain in as simple and concise a manner as the subject will permit, this distinctive difference in the practice of Historic and Ornamental Art, and to illustrate, without elaboration of example or multiplicity of verbiage, those *reproductive* principles of Industrial Art which replace, or are combined with, the *imitative* and *ideal* principles of Fine Art when applied to actual practice. Nor can we insist too strongly on this point being clearly and distinctly understood, and constantly borne in mind in the education of youth, or overrate its importance as a primary consideration in the enunciation and working out of any system of Art-Education, whether governmental or otherwise; inasmuch as it lies at the very root of that question of *originality* about which people talk so loudly, for which they affect to be willing to pay so liberally, but which, when it appears, they do not understand, because they test it by obsolete standards instead of natural principles.

Maintaining the necessity for sound education in every department of Art— alike to the artist-painter or sculptor on the one hand, and to the artist-manufacturer of decorated articles on the other—it would be a mere affectation of acquiescence not to denounce as a delusion any plans of Art-Education which did not embrace the study of nature, in its true application to practical purposes, as one of its most important objects, if, indeed, it should not be its very highest aim. By the term *study,* as used here, we do not mean mere copying, but the investigation of those peculiarities of physical construction as developed in external form, the true adaptation of which gives nature its greatest charm, and constitutes its truest beauty.

But it is only by a clear and distinct perception of the true functions of each department of Art, that the artist can expect to arrive at correct results, when called upon to act therein; and nothing appears more strange to any intelligent mind, viewing this question as it were from an elevation, than the confusion of ideas,—the utter absence of true systematic arrangement in the development of the powers of the Art Student, which has hitherto prevailed, and which confusion is still further perpetuated in the notions engendered in the minds of that same student as he progresses. All this arises out of the non-reduction of the true purposes and functions of Art, to clear and definite principles. With some, to *draw* is to *design*. With others, to *design* is to *invent*. With a third party, to *draw* means merely to copy, and to *design* means *dovetailing* together in congruous or incongruous mixture certain things already done by somebody else. Again, Fine Art, *par excellence*, is the "be all, and end all" of student practice with some,—with others, it is only the beginning; whilst it is not infrequently most determinedly insisted upon by another party, that as regards manufactures, Fine Art has nothing at all to do with the matter! And all this "confusion of tongues" comes, as before stated, of the want of a definite idea of the true function of each department of Art, and in the work of education a clear and distinct perception of what it really is which the student ought to learn, how he ought to learn it, and the purpose to which he wants to apply it after he is taught. Let us endeavour, therefore, to ascertain what it really is which the student is required to do, the nature of the knowledge he seeks, and what his aims should be?

The direct mission of Fine Art is to teach, by the vivid representation of great and noble acts, how good men have laboured and battled for humanity. It pictures before us, in all the truth of expression, in all the force of form, and light and shadow, with all the splendour of colouring, the deeds of the worthies of the past whom we are most taught to revere, and we are led upward in imagination to their personal identity, and see them again in their habits as they lived, deservedly held up as exemplars to the rising generation.

It seeks, too, to embody the *ideal* of the poet; and to give palpable form and real expression to his creations. Nay, the painter is himself, in his highest vocation, a poet; expressing by form and colour, that which the writer-poet expresses by words.

Fine Art then, records by *idealised imitation* the glorious works of good men, whilst it holds those of bad men up to our abhorrence—it gives to posterity their images, either on the tinted canvass or the sculptured marble—it imitates the beautiful effects of nature as seen in the glowing landscape or the rising storm, and perpetuates the appearance of those beauteous gems of the seasons—flowers and fruits, which, though fading whilst the painter catches their tints, yet live after decay by and through his genius.

Industrial Art, on the contrary, aims at the *embellishment of the works of man*, by and through that power which is given to the artist for the investigation of the beautiful in nature; and in transferring it to the loom, the printing machine, the potter's wheel, or the metal worker's mould, he *reproduces* nature in a new form, adapting it to his purpose by an intelligence arising out of his knowledge as an artist and as a workman. In short, the adaptation of the natural type to a new material compels him to *reproduce*, almost *create*, as well as *imitate*—*invent* as well as *copy*—design as well as draw!

The question very naturally arises, "But how is he to do this?" "Study the antique!" says one. "Study nature!" says another. "Study neither," says a third, "but study my *pattern books* !" We say, "study them all;" but let it not be surface-study.

It should be for the investigation of principles for which the antique should be studied; not for the mere power to copy it. It should be for the discovery of new types nature should be studied; and if possible, as we fully believe it is, for the enunciation of new principles! It should be for the proper understanding of those mechanical difficulties and peculiarities of material so essential to the successful practice of industrial design, that the manufacturer's *pattern book* should be studied; in other words, the adaptation of the material to the purposes of decoration. In Fine Art there is an analogous process of study, for the artist must learn the use of his materials, oil or water colours, fresco or encaustic, before he can produce a picture, and study the peculiarities of marble working or bronze casting, before he can produce a statue.

Again, the abstract principles of Industrial and Fine Art are the same, and, at the outset must be studied in a similar manner. Those laws of form, size, and proportion, of the classification of colours, as also of projection or light and shadow, are identical, and the thorough investigation of these principles are alike necessary to full success in each. There is, however; a very distinctive difference in their actual practice, which it is our purpose to illustrate.

In Fine Art, he who produces the best *ideal imitation* best succeeds. His object is strictly to imitate what he sees, in the first instance; but in doing so he endeavours to *elevate* his subject, and thus to a certain extent acts upon a principle analogous to that of the Industrial artist, and *reproduces* the object in appearance with such an infusion of his own mind as will give it force and originality; but the reproduction is an *aesthetic* not a *material* one. In short, he *idealises* as well as *imitates*. Take a portrait, for example. If the artist has simply the capacity to *imitate* every detailed point of the original, and in doing so aims at nothing but a stark likeness, the result will be anything but satisfactory. If, on the contrary, the mental qualities of the original are aimed at, the painter possessing that perceptive and ideal power so essential to their transfusion into his work, then the portrait becomes something more than a mere likeness—it is an idealised representation, an aesthetic reproduction of the individual represented. A photographic portrait is ever wanting in this latter quality; hence its unsatisfactory aspect.

The painter, however, is untrammelled by those peculiar difficulties which beset the industrial application of the original type, for he has simply to contend, so far as the agency of his materials go, with those artistic technicalities which arise out of the representation of his subject in all its peculiarities of form, light and shadow, and colour, upon a plane surface; but the sculptor approaches the Industrial artist more closely, because he has the physical characteristics of his materials to study whilst working out his idea. Thus, in marble, his figure must be posed in such a manner as to permit of its representation on every side, although the one point is ever present to the artist, as most expressive of his idea. The arrangement of the details of the form, so as to support each other against the weight of material, is likewise a matter of grave consideration. In metal, the difficulty is increased in one respect, because of the necessity of moulding for the purpose of casting; whilst it is diminished in another, by the greater strength of the material. The friability of the marble being replaced by the ductility of bronze. Thus the sculptor is more of an Industrial artist than the painter.

In Industrial Art, though *imitation* is the basis, yet reproduction in a new form and material is the object. Thus, if the artist takes a flower, the *Malope Grandiflora*[5] for instance, as a painter, he draws the best imitation he can of it in all its forms, proportions, light and shadow, and colour; but for the purposes of Industrial Art he treats it very differently.

Thus, if he is desired to use it for the purposes of the porcelain manufacture, or to treat it as a cup for metal work, though each of these would require certain technical modifications, yet, as a general adaptation of the original type, the treatment would be not unlike the illustration.

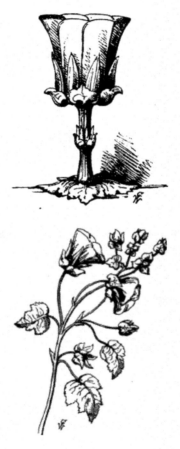

The corolla of the flower gives the hint for the body of the cup. the calyx forming its base. The foot is formed by the leaves of the plant arranged geometrically, and the stem is decorated in the middle by an adaptation of the bud of the flower in its partially developed state.

Adapting the same type for another manufacture, the treatment again varies. Thus, if the branch of a chandelier is required, we have two materials to contend with, glass and metal, with certain uses for each, according to their natural qualities: the metal to convey the means of illumination, whilst it supports the glass for the diffusion of the light. The branches of the flower are here converted into spirals, the stem is thickened and decorated with the leaves and buds of the plant, whilst the corolla and calyx are not unlike, in treatment, to the cup.*

The use of the same type for the decoration of a plane surface requires another kind of reproduction. Thus, if it be used for textile fabrics, whether the pattern be woven or printed, the requirements of the design would necessitate some arrangement by which the forms would readily repeat themselves, and these forms would be arbitrarily confined to a given space, technically called a *repeat*. The arrangement here given is a simple one, and might be easily adapted to a variety of surface decorations.

---

* In the hurry of drawing the illustrations, the writer— unfortunately or fortunately, the reader must judge which — committed one of those oversights so common in designing for Industrial Art. The light of the chandelier branch, as drawn, would illuminate the ceiling and walls only of a room. Owing to the calyx of the flower being much too large, the metal of which it would be constructed would obstruct the light in its passage downward. He prefers, therefore, pointing out the error himself, to having it discovered by anyone else; and gives the accompanying illustration of a treatment by which the light would be more completely diffused. A more palpable illustration could scarcely be conceived of the necessity for understanding and considering the purpose and mode of construction of the article designed. A drawing may be in the abstract very beautiful — in practice quite useless.

Elaboration has been avoided, so as to give the eye of the uninitiated an insight into the mode by which a series of simple lines are carried over any amount of surface. The original forms are the same as those of all the former illustrations, the treatment being varied to suit the requirements of the material on which, or in which, it is supposed to be wrought. The natural type is strictly kept in view in each case, nor departed from except for adaptation to the requirements of each manufacture.

It must never be forgotten, however, that much depends upon the selection of a fitting type; and in this respect, the same principle would govern the industrial artist in the choice of his type, as would be observed by the historic artist in the selection of *his* model. The painter does not choose as the *sitter* for his hero or heroine any commonplace individual who may present himself or herself; but selects those who possess the marked characteristics which belong to his *beau ideal* of that same hero or heroine. Just so with the Industrial artist—he takes not any plant, flower, or object which he may chance to meet with, but carefully considers the capabilities of each, and how far it is adapted to his uses in a particular way, for a particular purpose in a particular manufacture. Forgetting, or not knowing, these principles of selection, adaptation, and reproduction, he is ever aiming at something he cannot attain to, or contents himself with becoming a mere reproducer of hackneyed types found in the antique, instead of natural images; a ringer of the changes upon an everlasting acanthus, or an ever-enduring, and never-to-be-used-enough, honeysuckle!

The educational importance of attention to or neglect of these principles must receive future consideration, but we fearlessly affirm as a proposition for intermediate thought, that—

> *Ornamental Art depends upon the reproductive adaptation of the forms of Nature for its greatest beauties and most sterling qualities, and that true originality can only be arrived at through this source; whilst all ornament not based thereon, is simply the result of slavish copyism, and a mannerism arising out of the study of misunderstood authorities—the fragmentary remains of ages—whose manners and requirements were essentially different to our own.*

Notes

1 Wallis, 'The Principles of Fine Art as Applied to Industrial Purposes', *The People's Journal*, 3, 1847, p. 231.
2 *Athenaeum*, 349, 3 January 1846, p. 17.
3 *Report from the Select Committee on the School of Design: Together with the Proceedings of the Committee; Ordered, by the House of Commons, to Be Printed, 27 July 1849*, (London, 1849).
4 S. Sidney, *Rides on Railways Leading to the Lake & Mountain Districts of Cumberland, North Wales* (London: William Orr, 1851), pp. 171–2.
5 Malope is a genus of three species in the mallow botanical family (Malvaceae).

16

[ANON], 'UNIVERSAL INFIDELITY IN PRINCIPLES OF DESIGN'

The reports on the Great Exhibition published in *The Times*, and the *Morning Chronicle* newspapers that critiqued the display of goods yet gave praise to the Crystal Palace building itself and the machinery exhibits therein, were used as the basis for this article. This is not surprising since the newspapers were reflecting Henry Cole's own ideas on design reform and the need for the establishment of principles of design.

Intended as both didactic and dogmatic, this article used these newspaper reports as inducements to help the author's cause. *The Times* did not hold its punches, proclaiming that 'The sins committed against good taste are confined to no single people, but, as we send to the Crystal Palace the largest number of contributors in each section, our faults and short-comings are unavoidably the most glaring'.[1]

Like other critics, *The Times* saw that machinery, through the 'stringent application of mechanical science to the material world . . . and in the truthfulness, perseverance, and severity [of machine design] . . . there is developed a style of art at once national and grand'.[2] The newspaper equally praised the Crystal Palace building itself, noting that 'there are no pillars that could be dispensed with, no architectural mannerisms, no effort at effect unsubordinated to the general design. All is plain, simple and mathematically severe'.[3]

The Morning Chronicle was equally scathing about the lack of good design and summed up in a nutshell the issue as they saw it: 'what we want are canons of taste—laws of beauty—principles and axioms of propriety'.[4] This was music to Cole's ears, as he pushed for exactly this. Utility and a positivist approach had won the day.

Cole, contemplating the results of the Great Exhibition in his autobiography, made two important points that were quite prescient in relation to this issue of canons or principles of design.

> It was from the East that the most impressive lesson was to be learnt. Here was revealed a fresh well of art, the general principles of which were the same as those in the best periods of art of all nations — Egyptian,

Grecian, Roman, Byzantine, Gothic. And turning from artistic to industrial objects, and speaking generally, I venture to submit whether our American cousins did not, in their reaping and other machines adapted to new wants and infant periods of society, teach us the next most valuable lessons.[5]

The whole issue of principles of design in relation to taste, beauty, and propriety remained a contentious issue for the rest of the century.

[Anon], 'Universal Infidelity in Principles of Design', *Journal of Design and Manufactures*, V, August 1851, pp. 158–161

The absence of any fixed principles in ornamental design is most apparent in the Exhibition[6]—not among ourselves only, but throughout all the European nations. Many other nations shew better faith and better practice in design than those of Europe. Does the progress of civilisation and the increased value put upon knowledge and labour destroy principles of taste? It might seem so. Ponder thereon.

If we were to collect the most elaborate works of ornamental design from each European nation, it would be found that they resembled each other so much that it would be difficult, if not impossible, to identify the nationality of them, and every class of manufacture would be found to have some features not only inconsistent with its use, but actually warring against it. It appears to us that the art-manufactures of the whole of Europe are thoroughly demoralised, and destitute for the most part of correct principles. France, to which the world gives the *pas*, seems to us to be only the leader in what should rather be avoided than imitated in manufactures, and it is when England attempts to plagiarise from France that she appears to the greatest disadvantage. The most serious violation of principle common to both nations is the negation of utility as paramount to ornament. All European nations at the present time begin manufacture with ornament and put utility in the background. The very best things in the Exhibition are the least ornamented. One of the most faultless pieces of furniture is Mr. Snell's writing-table,[7] and one of the most faulty is the Austrian bed.[8] We have recently seen some observations on the state of design as presented in the Exhibition, which have been published in *The Times* and *Morning Chronicle*, and which appear to us, in the main, so sound and so suggestive that we transfer them to our pages; and we entreat manufacturers and students of design to read them again and again and reflect upon them. We commence with those in *The Times*:—

"Our potters have sent contributions to the Exhibition which illustrate every known style of the manufacture. Some delight in Etruscan shapes and colours, others take the bronzes of Pompeii for their model. The influence of China is of course prominently seen, and medieval art also showers down its suggestions. Then we have bad imitations of Sèvres and worse of Dresden. Every day we are adding to the number of our reproductions; and, no sooner is Parian introduced for modelling statuettes, than Cupids and other juvenile indelicacies are perpetually smiling at us under glass shades, or sitting in very uncomfortable attitudes upon projections of dishes, or balancing themselves miraculously upon the summits of lids. But pottery is by no means the only or the most flagrant case of this imitative rage, which is so strongly marked at the Exhibition. Take the section of carpets, and you will find it almost, if not quite, as strong. Here partly, probably, in obedience to the dictates of the Berlin wool-workers,[9] and partly in deference to the tastes of the Brussels and French makers, we have got into a habit of covering the floor we tread upon with a luxuriance of vegetation and a lavish expenditure of colours which it is quite wonderful quietly to contemplate. Let anyone look along the girders of the western nave, from the sides of which our carpets are suspended, and we are much mistaken if even the Chiswick shows[10] have any longer the slightest charm for him. He will there see flowers, and leaves, and fruits, of a size such as was never seen in this world before, and we conscientiously hope may never be seen in this world again. He will find his eyes dazzled and perplexed by moss-roses that give him a headache with their brightness, and he will wonder how he could ever make up his mind to walk over a material so decorated. The uses of a carpet are no mystery, and any sensible person who examines the subject will have no great difficulty in deciding what style of ornament is unsuitable for such an article. In the first place, he will say, make your carpet the background for setting off your furniture appropriately and well. Now is that to be done by broad and startling contrasts of colour, which are constantly drawing the eye-sight painfully downwards, instead of allowing it to rest agreeably upon other objects? Again, no one will contend that flowers represented as real, and fruit rounded off so that you are tempted to stoop down and gather it, and vegetation that threatens the foot with hopeless entanglement, are proper designs to tread upon. Yet that is what not only England, but all Europe, judging by the Exhibition, does in this matter—and why? Because when tapestry became no longer useful, the love of large patterns and real effects which it suggested were imported into carpet-making, while the monstrosities of Berlin wool-work came in aid of the mania. The English section of carpets has imitations of Indian, of Brussels, of French, of parqueterie and tessellated pavements, and of the medieval style of manufactures. In one article that is a pretty long list of reproductions, and reminds us that in industry, as in the drama, we are rather addicted to borrowing other people's ideas, and not very choice in the selection of them. Let us take another branch of production, where it seems less likely that we could err. It is that of grates, lamps, candelabra, chandeliers, candlesticks, and such-like objects, for the heating and illumination of our dwellings. In these undoubtedly there are a few very fine productions, and with respect to some of them our pre-eminence is undoubted; but let any person of ordinary taste examine the whole collection carefully, and he will retire from the survey with a painful impression of the ignorance displayed in the use of really beautiful materials. He will find grates, exquisite in the quality of their workmanship, but totally unsuited for the uses they are intended to serve, which must necessarily break the hearts of servants in the effort to keep them clean, with Greek, Gothic, Moorish, and Elizabethan architectural arrangements introduced which are totally unnecessary, and figures of human beings in unhappy proximity to an element which must inevitably destroy them. The English manufacturer never abandons the idea of vegetation, and wreaths of fruits and flowers that would puzzle the horticultural acumen of Mr. Paxton[11] himself are fearlessly suspended over the receptacle for the glowing embers, or disposed upon the fender as if it was meant that they should be toasted. Again, in lamps, candelabra, chandeliers, and such-like, the greatest atrocities in taste are committed; all reliance upon the materials employed and the purpose they are intended to serve seems to be thrown overboard, and the study of the makers has evidently been to render their products as little as possible like what they were intended for. Some seize upon the idea of trees with curiously entangled branches, and which have neither art nor nature to recommend them; others get a human figure patiently to support upon its head a weight of metal which would sink the stalwart frame of an Atlas; then animals and birds of all kinds are represented doing physical impossibilities in the cause of light, and, to crown the absurdities perpetrated, Cupids and the other adjuncts of heathen mythology are lavishly interspersed among chandeliers and brackets with a disregard of simplicity and elegance in design which is truly surprising. . . . . Some sections, and especially that of machinery, feeling their pre-eminence secure and undoubted, have been content to be plain and unpretending, in consequence of which they develop a high degree of artistic excellence. The most refined taste will gather pleasure and satisfaction from a survey of our machinery department; for there, in the forms and the arrangements, strict attention to the proprieties and requirements of each machine may be readily traced. The only beauty attempted is that which the stringent application of mechanical science to the material world can supply, and in the truthfulness, perseverance, and severity with which that idea is carried out, there is developed a style of art at once national and grand. We may quote, as remarkable illustrations of this, Whitworth's[12] tools and the cotton machinery of Hibbert and Platt.[13] So, again, in the building which enshrines this vast collection of human industry there are no pillars that could be dispensed with, no architectural mannerisms, no effort at effect unsubordinated to the general design. All is plain, simple, and mathematically severe; yet who can enter that vast interior and not feel his heart swell within him at the solemn and majestic impression which it creates? We do not for a moment contend that the unbending precision which produces such great results in the cases quoted would be equally applicable to the manufactured products made available for our every-day and domestic wants and comforts, but unquestionably it shews that there are limits to the decorative art prescribed by the uses and the material of the objects on which it is exercised, and that we cannot with impunity attempt to recall defunct or foreign styles of ornament. Whether we shall ever have a school of design incorporated with our manufactures original, characteristic, and meritorious, it is impossible at present to foretell, for the Exhibition throws no very hopeful or decided light upon that subject. New tastes are not formed and old habits, of subserviency are not dismissed in a day. The power of cheap production and the advantages of excellent material, turning the scale of the market, blind our eyes to defects which would not otherwise escape notice if competition pursued us more closely. Then it must be remembered that the sins of which we complain are shared with England in pretty equal proportions by every other European country. In some branches we are in advance, in others we are behindhand; and the French undoubtedly twist about the ideas which they gather from the past with a freedom and playfulness which we with our literal faithfulness of rendering cannot always equal. But, on the whole, the vein of art in connexion with manufactures seems well-nigh exhausted all over Europe. What, then, is to be done, and where shall our industrial classes look for inspiration to guide them? Undoubtedly they will learn most from a careful study of the Indian collection. There they will find developed in its greatest known excellence the harmonious combination of colours in textile fabrics. Such a thing as vulgarity in design seems unknown in our Eastern dominions except when clearly imported by ourselves. They appear to have the secret of being minute in their patterns without any confusion or indistinctness, and, however great the elaboration of ornament in which they indulge, *the uses and materials of the article* which they decorate are considered paramount. We do not, in pointing out these things, by any means recommend that our manufacturers should cultivate long beards, rush into the productions of Cachmere shawls and Masulipatam carpets, go about in palanquins, and, forswearing Christianity, become Mahommedans or Brahmins; but they may supply defects and correct faults in the decorative art as practised among them from a careful elucidation of those rules upon which the instinctive genius of Eastern nations in such matters depends. They may at length penetrate the secret of that happy ease and grace of style which makes Indian productions magnificent without, being in the least degree staring or pretentious."

These are doctrines which we have again and again insisted on. Our manufacturers should affix throughout their workshops, for the edification of all, "Decoration must be subordinate to the uses and materials of the article." The *Morning Chronicle* justly points out that,—

"In all former stages of society—in other periods of our own English history, and in other countries—production, in whatever branch, or under whatever sky, was self-interpreting, told its own story, and carried with it its own credentials. A single glance ranked it under all the categories. Its *where* and its *when* were unmistakeable. It needs but the veriest tyro in art to settle the date or the place of a church, or a medal, or a dagger, or a piece of earthenware, or a manuscript, or a jewel, or a fragment of embroidery, of metal work, or of bookbinding. There is not a handwriting extant, of any antiquity, which even a slight familiarity with the subject would not readily assign to its century—perhaps to its city. But how stands the case among ourselves? We design and execute in every conceivable style. We imitate every extant school. We are equally at home in the reproduction of classical and of Byzantine art—Etruscan ware and Majolica; we can execute Chinese or Athenian with the same facility; we can forge—perhaps that is the most appropriate term—an Egyptian obelisk or a Corinthian capital, a so-called

Gothic moulding, or a Sèvres cup. We are not just at present contending that all this is wrong—we only say that it is a fact, and a new fact.

"But we will go further, and say that it must be wrong—perhaps even morally wrong—injurious to, if not destructive of, a healthful sense of propriety—to allow one shop-front to be the reproduction of a scrap of an hypaethral temple,[14] and the very next door to exhibit an adaptation of a pointed arcade. At this very moment the three most remarkable buildings of our own days exhibit the following jumble:—in the Palace of Westminster, a medieval design; in the British Museum, a severely classical model; in the Queen's Palace, a something like Louis Quatorze. The buildings themselves have no special affinities to the respective styles adopted. There they are, and conjointly they exhibit sufficiently the state of public taste. And these vagaries and inconsistencies are not confined to ourselves. Germany can shew its Valhalla, and its synchronising Byzantine church, erected under the auspices of King Ludwig of Bavaria. This state of European taste is most forcibly illustrated by the contents of the Great Exhibition. It proves that art and manufacture in the nineteenth century are not their own historians. They are perfectly incapable of any chronology. Side by side, from the same manufacturer—perhaps from the same artist, certainly in the same material—are the stiff processional treatment of a frieze, the flowing capriciousness of an arabesque, and the literal imitation and transcript of nature itself. Naturalism and conventionalism find an equal advocacy, and often from the same critic. Mr. Dyce is beautiful—Mr. Etty is beautiful. It scarcely crosses our minds as incongruous that the furniture of a single room exhibits specimens of work, of intention, and of execution and adaptation, ranging over twice ten centuries, and of national taste and climatic purpose, extending from Mexico to St. Petersburgh."

Every student in design should learn the following by heart:—

"What we want are canons of taste—laws of beauty—principles and axioms of propriety. It was once considered false heraldry to place metal upon metal; but it is now thought no solecism to aim at producing exactly the same effects in wax, in silver, in stone, in wood, in iron, in smashed paper, in pounded gypsum, in leather, in silk, and in cotton. A goldsmith is thought an equally good artist whether he makes a candlestick in the shape of a branch of fuchsia, or of a monolithic column, or even if he combines the two in one design. A bunch of roses or a dead fish we think alike beautiful, and equally so whether raised on a porcelain dish, or cast on a silver tankard; we do not complain whether we get festoons or quatrefoils carved on a chimney-piece, embroidered on a veil, woven into a carpet, or printed on paper-hangings. Can each of these be equally right? Is the standard of prettiness a sufficient account of, or reason for, the proceeding? For ourselves, it seems something like a debasement of human intelligence to look with equal favour on a group of prancing horses and a model of the *Victoria Regia*,[15] as alike suitable for a centrepiece! If the dining-room carpet is the transcript of the Bellerophon mosaic,[16] in flat tessellation, ought the drawing-room carpet to present us with vases and bouquets of poppies and lilies, in all the colours and lights and shades of a Covent Garden flower-stall? May a painted window imitate a landscape by Claude as legitimately as an interlaced diaper?

"We are quite aware of the answer to all this—it is urged that tastes vary, and that manufacture must follow taste. But our question is, whether there is any taste in this variableness of taste—whether taste ought so to vary—whether, if its rules were discovered, or rather elucidated, taste is not as fixed a thing as truth—whether beauty has not laws. It cannot be that aesthetics, to use the hard word of the day, which covets so much ignorance and falseness—is only 'what I like,' as Horne Tooke[17] said that 'truth was only what the individual troweth.'" It may be that at present this difficulty overlies the whole region of modern thought and belief; but what we urge is, *that art has its dogmas and its orthodoxy*, which are as severe as any other axioms. It is not unnatural that we should find ourselves at sea in this great flux of things. Ours is an age of transition; we are in the midst of the breaking up of the great deep of the past, and we are perhaps struggling after a wider and more distinct range of truth. We are, perhaps, labouring out great principles for the future; it may be that we are on the way to re-construction after the deluge. But ours is certainly a chaotic period. The Exhibition shews that we are most skilful mimics—that we know how to reprint classics—that we can restore everything. But what do we create? Is there not something more truthful, more really artistic —more calculated to impress us with the fact that the workman had a feeling and interest in his work and a clear adaptation of his means to this end—in the Indian niellos and its solid metal-work, in the dull, stately grandeur of the carpets of Tunis and Turkey, nay, even in the Sioux embroidery, than in Bright's flashy "tapestry carpets,"[18] in Hunt and Roskell's[19] silver capriccios, or in the miserable rococo of our Oxford-street sideboards? Is it not a fact that we are living in something like a Claudian age of art-feeling? The very greatest work which the Exhibition can achieve—one which it is very likely to achieve, if rightly read—one for which, among its many high purposes, we gratefully hail it—is that of giving us a decided and acknowledged national taste, and of creating a defined style in English art, which shall embody a distinct historical character of our own age, a homogeneity of feeling, a truthfulness of conception and adaptation, and a clear estimate of the worthlessness of mere individualism in art. We ask to be taught by the Exhibition what is mere capriccio and *tour de force*—what is sound invention and artistic truth. The Exhibition, we trust, will teach us to reject unreality. Painted slate is a very clever thing—so is a casting in *carton-pierre*; but one touch of human nature, one stroke of the chisel, one original blow of the hammer which comes from the soul, and speaks to the soul, is worth all our imitations and reproductions, however correct and elaborate."

Truly "art has its dogmas and its orthodoxy," which our Schools of Design have yet to learn and teach.

Notes

1 *Times,* 1 July 1851, p. 5.
2 Ibid.
3 Ibid.
4 *Morning Chronicle*, 8 July 1851, p. 4.

5 H. Cole, *Fifty Years of Public Work* (London: G. Ball, 1884), p. 252.
6 Great Exhibition of all Nations, London, 1851.
7 Snell & Co. 27 Albemarle St, London. No mention of a specific writing table found in the Official Catalogue, although a library table is listed.
8 Austrian bed: large carved wooden bed with lush red hangings. See View of the installation of the Austrian Pavilion at the 1851 London Exhibition: Austria No 1 Plate from Dickinsons *Comprehensive Pictures of the Great Exhibition of 1851* (1854).
9 Berlin wool-work: A form of needlework that is particularly associated with mid-nineteenth century. Based on the ancient *opus pulvinarium* it is usually worked in a cross-stitch. It was mainly produced by amateurs using imported German brightly-coloured woollen yarns that were worked into a square meshed canvas using cross or tent stitches. The novelty was the use of printed and coloured paper patterns which showed a grid plan of the threads which could be counted out.
10 Chiswick shows: From 1827 the Horticultural Society's (later Royal Horticultural Society) held fêtes at their Chiswick, London, garden, and from 1833, shows with competitive classes for flowers and vegetables. The last was in 1857.
11 Mr. Paxton: Sir Joseph Paxton (1803–1865) English gardener and architect.
12 Whitworth: Sir Joseph Whitworth Company, Manchester, Manufacturers of machine tools.
13 Hibbert and Platt: Oldham, Manufacturers of textile machinery.
14 Hypaetheral: Wholly or partly open to the sky:
15 *Victoria Regia* (now Amazonica): a species of flowering plant, the largest of the *Nymphaeaceae* family of water lilies.
16 Bellerophon mosaic: Roman mosaic depicting Bellerophon and Chimera, found in Autun, France in 1830. See *Illustrated London News* 20 July 1850.
17 Horne Tooke: John Horne-Tooke (1736–1812), a politician and philologist. 'Troweth' meaning belief.
18 John Bright's tapestry carpets: John Bright, the Liberal Statesman, was one of the principals of John Bright and Sons carpet manufacturers, Rochdale, from 1839. The method of weaving Tapestry is a combination of weaving and printing, producing a multi-coloured surface effect.
19 Hunt and Roskell: Hunt & Roskell, a firm of manufacturing and retail jewellers and silversmiths, was founded by Paul Storr in 1819, New Bond Street, London.

17

'EXAMPLES OF FALSE PRINCIPLES IN DECORATION'

In 1852–3, the Museum of Ornamental Art, Marlborough House, (now the Victoria and Albert Museum) featured a short-lived gallery of 'Examples of False Principles in Decoration'. This so-called chamber of horrors exhibited 87 ornamental manufactured objects, which were considered to exhibit false principles of decoration. This allowed visitors and students to compare the selected items with those defined as being in good taste. *The Spectator* was in favour of the displays. Their contemporary review discussed it in some detail and made a point about the contrasts between good and bad taste.

> A word of this Chamber; which we regret to find has now, from scantiness of space, ceased to be kept together for public inspection. Here were gathered examples of false principles in decoration; and nothing could be more impressively instructive to the public tastelessness than such a display. Save to those who come furnished with abstract notions of beauty and a refined eye for its manifestations, taste is most readily taught by contrasts, and defined by negatives'

They went on to comment on the impact of the displays and the public reactions:

> Practically, too, we believe that it was the section of the Museum which collected the greatest throng and excited the most lively interest. Respectable families stared to see their pet article of ornament or item of gentility gibbeted for public reprobation, and, regretfully pondering, perhaps—we only venture to say perhaps —discarded it'.[1]

Over twenty-five years after its closure, Charles Phelps Taft in his in 1878 lecture to an audience in Cincinnati on the South Kensington Museum, explained the value of the 'Chamber of Horrors':

> It served as a foil for the beautiful objects in the adjoining rooms and instructed the people as to the kind of trash prepared for them by ignorant and avaricious manufacturers. For instance, one manufacturer thought

the human form would make a good candlestick, with the candle inserted in the top of the hat, or directly into the cranium. In another instance, a weaver had adopted for a plaid cloth a pattern so large that it required two persons to display the entire pattern at once. Such a department in our new museum would be instructive.[2]

However, for J. C. Robinson, the South Kensington Museum's first Superintendent of the Art Collections, reminiscing in 1880, thought that the display was not successful in its aims: 'The results, however, were not satisfactory, for setting aside the angry reclamations of indignant manufacturers whose productions were thus gibbeted, the British public showed a most conservative leaning towards the old accustomed "horrors" or at best treated the experiment as a somewhat incomprehensible joke. This crude and ridiculous episode at any rate served to show that there was no royal road to the acquisition of good taste in art'.[3]

Interestingly, the idea was revived by the German art historian and museum director Gustav E. Pazaurek, who recommended that every museum of arts and crafts should add a 'chamber of horrors' to present examples of bad design to educate the public in matters of good taste and design. In 1909, Pazaurek put the idea into practice in the Stuttgart Museum, where he set up a 'Cabinet of Bad Taste'. The continually updated collection was on display until the early 1930s with more than 900 objects collected. Pazaurek developed a particular and intricate system to classify all kinds of design errors that were represented in the collection. The classification scheme was based on four major headings – Material errors, Design mistakes, Decorative mistakes, and Kitsch, which he published in 1912 as *Guter und schlechter Geschmack im Kunstgewerbe* (Good and Bad Taste in the Applied Arts).

'Examples of False Principles in Decoration', *A Catalogue of the Articles of Ornamental Art, in the Museum of the Department, for the Use of Students and Manufacturers, and the Consultation of the Public. With Appendices, Third Edition* **(London: Printed by George E. Eyre and William Spottiswoode for Her Majesty's Stationary Office, 1852), Appendix C, pp. 22–32**

APPENDIX (C.)

EXAMPLES OF FALSE PRINCIPLES IN DECORATION.

Whilst the Museum offers to the students specimens of ornamental art, most of which illustrate correct principles in decoration, it has been deemed advisable to collect and exhibit to the student examples of what, according to the views held

EXAMPLES OF FALSE PRINCIPLES IN DECORATION

in this Department, are considered to illustrate wrong or false principles. The chief vice in the decoration common to Europe at the present day is the tendency towards direct imitation of nature, which in respect of ornamental art is opposed to the practice of all the best periods of art among all nations. On this point, as well as on others to be observed in the treatment of various materials, Dr. Waagen,[4] Mr. Dyce,[5] Mr. Pugin,[6] and Mr. Redgrave[7] make various remarks, which are herewith appended and illustrated by examples.

IMITATIVE STYLE.—"There has arisen a new species of ornament of the most objectionable kind, which it is desirable at once to deprecate on account of its complete departure from just taste and true principles. This may be called the *natural* or merely imitative style, and it is seen in its worst development in some of the articles of form.

"Thus we have metal *imitations* of plants and flowers, with an attempt to make them a strict resemblance, forgetting that natural objects are rendered into ornament by subordinating the details to the general idea, and that the endeavour ought to be to seize the simplest expression of a thing rather than to imitate it. This is the case with fine art also: in *its* highest effort mere imitation is an error and an impertinence, and true ornamental art is even more opposed to the merely imitative treatment now so largely adopted. Let anyone examine floral or foliated ornament produced in metal by electrotyping the natural object, whereby every venation and striation of the plant is reproduced, and compare it with a well and simply modelled treatment, where only the general features of the form are given and all the minutest details purposely omitted; and if this latter has been done with a true sense of the characteristics of the plant, the meanness and littleness of the one mode will be perfectly evident, compared with the larger manner of the other. But this imitative style is carried much further: ormolu stems and leaves bear porcelain flowers painted to imitate nature, and candles are made to rise out of tulips and China asters while gas jets gush forth from opal Arums. Stems bearing flowers for various uses, arise from groups of metal leaves, standing tiptoe on their points, (See Nos. 81, 83) and every constructive truth, and just adaptation to use, is disregarded for a senseless imitative naturalism. In the same way, and doubtless supported by great authority, past and present, enormous wreaths of flowers, fish, game, fruits, &c. imitated *à merveille* dangle round sideboards, beds, and picture frames. Glass is tortured out of its true quality to make it into the cup of a lily or an anemone (see No. 34); not that we may be supposed to drink nectar from the flower, but that novelty may catch those for whom good taste is not piquant enough, and chaste forms not sufficiently showy. In fabrics where flatness would seem most essential, this imitative treatment is often carried to the greatest excess (see Nos. 4, 5); and carpets are ornamented with waterlilies floating on their natural bed, with fruits and flowers poured forth in overwhelming abundance in all the glory of their shades and hues (see Nos. I, 2); or we are startled by a lion at our hearth, or a leopard on our rug, his spotted coat imitated even to its relief as well as to its colour, while palmtrees and landscapes are used as the ornaments of muslin curtains. Though far from saying that imitative ornament is not sometimes allowable, still it will at once be felt that the manner wants a determined regulation to exclude it in most of the above-mentioned cases from all works aspiring to be considered in just taste, and to leave it to be adopted by those only who think novelty better than chaste design, and show preferable to truth."—REDGRAVE.

Woven Fabrics, &c. Decorated on False Principles

Carpets

"The use of these fabrics suggests the true principle of design for their ornamentation, which is governed by the laws for flat surfaces, where the object is rather to treat the whole as a background than to call particular attention to the ornamentation. Flatness should be one of the principles for decorating a surface continually under the feet: therefore all architectural relief ornaments (see Nos. 4, 5, 6), and all *imitations* of fruit, shells, and other solid or hard substances, or even of flowers, strictly speaking, are the more improper the more imitatively they are rendered (see Nos. 1, 2, 3). As a field or ground for other objects, the attention should hardly be called to carpets by strongly marked forms or compartments, or by violent contrasts of light and dark, or colour; but graduated shades of the same colour, or a distribution of colours nearly equal in scale of light and dark, should be adopted; secondaries and tertiaries, or neutralized primaries, being used rather than pure tints, and lights introduced merely to give expression to the forms. Under such regulations as to flatness and contrast, either geometrical forms, or scrolls clothed with foliation in any style, leaves, flowers, or other ornament, may be used, which with borders and compartment arrangements, and the use of diaper treatments, leave ample room for variety and for the inventive skill of the artist. It may be thought impossible or unnecessary to confine the designer too strictly by such laws, and they are, indeed, rather stated from a sense of their truth than with an immediate hope of their thorough acceptance; but at any rate they may serve as curbs to extravagance of design, and as guide marks to lead back the errant designer to the path of consistency."

—REDGRAVE.

"The primary law of all such designs is, that they must not disturb the flatness of the surface on which they are drawn, but only diversify it with lines agreeable to the eye, and with harmonious masses of colour. Hence no foreshortenings should be attempted in such designs, and all perspective views are to be absolutely rejected, as at variance with the principles of a true style of ornament. It is obvious that the

EXAMPLES OF FALSE PRINCIPLES IN DECORATION

character of the pattern will be essentially affected by the quality of the materials and the purpose for which it is intended. Thus, for instance, shawls, though of a yielding texture, rather follow the movements of body in a general sense; hence the patterns of shawls should be of considerable size with soft flowing outlines. Cottons, on the contrary, and other similar clothing fabrics, which cling more to the body require smaller and more symmetrical patterns."—WAAGEN's *Report on Exhibition of 1851.*

No. 1.—CARPET.

> *Observations.*—Direct imitation of nature; flowers out of scale; architectural ornament in imitation relief; inharmonious colouring.

No. 2.—CARPET.

> *Observations.*—Direct imitation of nature; flowers out of scale.

No. 3.—FRENCH PORTIERE.

> *Observations.*—Direct imitation of nature; stripes running vertically, contradicting the lines of the folds in the use of such fabrics.

No. 4.—CARPET.

> *Observations.*—Imitation of a ceiling; architectural mouldings and ornament in relief.

No. 5.—CARPET.

> *Observations.*—Direct imitation of nature; flowers, &c. out of scale; representation of a landscape, sky water, &c.; architectural scrolls in high relief; bright blue shadows on a neutral coloured ground.

No. 6.—CARPET.

> *Observations.*—Want of meaning and unity in the pattern; the helter-skelter distribution of the lines are like productions under the influence of nightmare.

No. 7.—CARPET.

> *Observations.*—Cornucopiae filled with flowers, resting upon nothing; want of general leading lines.

No. 8.—CARPET.

> *Observations.*—Imitation of pierced Gothic panelling in oak; representation of a moulded surface.

No. 9.—CARPET.

> *Observations.*—Imitation of natural leaves in relief, with shadows; want of unity and general leading lines.

Chintzes

"The consideration of chintzes comes under the head of hangings; and upon these fabrics it is quite necessary to make a few remarks, since their decoration seems at present to be of the most extravagant kind. Overlooking the fact that the lightness and thinness of the material will not carry a heavy treatment, and that, in addition to all the principles which have been shown to regulate design for hangings, the use of imitative floral ornament is peculiarly unsuitable on account of the folds, the taste is to cover the surface almost entirely with large and coarse flowers, dahlias, hollyhocks, roses, hydrangeas or others which give scope for strong and vivid colouring, and which are often magnified by the designer much beyond the scale of nature (see Nos. 11 to 16). These are not only arranged in large groups, but often cover the whole surface, in the manner of a rich brocade. Nothing can be more erroneous, or more essentially vulgar as would at once be evident did not fashion blind us for a time, and a feeling of costly labour and difficult execution prevail over truth and good taste.

"Moreover, it is scarcely possible in such distributions of colours, whether printed or woven, to arrange them according to just or scientific laws; for although this is attainable when colour is in simple flat tints, and subordinated geometrical groupings, when the tints are broken up and graduated into shades and distributed with regard to flowing and naturally dispersed form alone, the due quantities for harmony, the juxtaposition of complementary and harmonizing tints, and true balance of parts, easy in any simple or symmetrical arrangement becomes difficult or impossible. The present mode of ornamenting these fabrics seems to have arisen from the false spirit of imitation—a desire to rival the richness of silk; but it is overlooked that the texture, naturally light, requires lightness and elegance of form and colour; that, as a *summer* fabric, richness and of hue, as tending rather to a sense of warmth, is out of place, and that on the contrary, fresh and cool light grounds, with flat ornamental forms, either 'all over' or in 'up and down' bands, or diapers of floral ornament on a simple textural ground, are the true principles for the decoration of chintzes."—REDGRAVE, *on Design*.

Nos. 10, 11, 12, 13.—FURNITURE CHINTZES.

> *Observations.*—Direct imitations of nature; branches of lilac and rose trees. made to bend to the forms of sofa cushions and chair arms. In No. 11, the ground, which should be light in chintzes, entirely obscured by the pattern. General gaudiness and want of repose.

No. 14.—FURNITURE CHINTZ.

> Observation.—Wreaths and festoons of natural flowers, tied together with imitations of ribbon.

No. 15.—FURNITURE CHINTZ.

> *Observations.*—Imitation of one fabric upon another—ribbon upon chintz; the design of the ribbon composed of direct imitations of natural flowers.

EXAMPLES OF FALSE PRINCIPLES IN DECORATION

No. 16.—FURNITURE CHINTZ.

Observations.—Imitation of ribbon upon chintz; direct imitation of moss roses and stalks to bend round the arms of chairs, sofa cushions, &c.

No. 17.—SILK HANGING.

Observations—Imitation of one fabric upon another; festoons of ribbon upon silk; direct imitations of nature, in roses and tulips.

Nos. 18, 19.—SILK HANGINGS.

Observations.—Direct imitations of nature; architectural ornaments in relief.

No. 20—SILK HANGING.

Observations.—Direct imitation of nature; detached bunches of natural flowers; want of unity and general lines.

Paper and Other Hangings

"Those papers which are shaded are defective in principle; for, as a paper is hung round a room, the ornament must frequently be shadowed on the light side. The variety of these miserable patterns is quite surprising: and, as the expense of cutting a block for a bad figure is equal if not greater than for a good one, there is not the shadow of an excuse for their continual reproduction. A moment's reflection must show the extreme absurdity of repeating a perspective over a large surface with some hundred different points of sight."

—PUGIN'S *Christian Architecture.*

"If the use of such materials is borne in mind, the proper decoration for them will at once be evident, since this ought to bear the same relation to the objects in the room that a background does to a picture. In art, a background, if well designed, has its own distinctive features, yet these are to be so far suppressed and subdued as not to invite special attention, while as a whole it ought to be entirely subservient to supporting and enhancing the principal figures—the subject of the picture: The decoration of a wall, if designed on good principles, has a like office; *it is a background to the furniture, the objects of art, and the occupants of the apartment*. It may enrich the general effect, and add to magnificence, or be made to lighten or deepen the character of the chamber: it may appear to temper the heat of summer, or to give a sense of warmth and comfort to the winter; it may have the effect of increasing the size of a saloon, or of closing in the walls of a library or study; all which, by a due adaptation of colour, can be easily accomplished. But, like the background to which it has been compared, although its ornament may have a distinctive character for any of these purposes, it must be subdued, and uncontrasted in light and shade: strictly speaking, it should be flat and conventionalized, and lines or forms harsh or cutting on the ground as far as possible avoided, except where necessary to give expression to the ornamentation. Imitative treatments are objectionable on principle, both as intruding on the sense of flatness, and as being too *attractive* in their details and colour to be sufficiently retiring and unobtrusive."—REDGRAVE, *on Design*.

No. 21—PAPER HANGING.

> *Observations.*—Direct imitation of nature; detached bunches of flowers; want of general lines and parent stems.

No. 22—PAPER HANGING.

> *Observations.*—Imitation of festoons of ribbon; direct imitation of natural flowering and vulgar colour.

No. 23—PAPER HANGING.

> *Observations.*—Natural objects in unseemly positions; horses and ground floating in the air; objects much out of scale.

No. 24—PAPER HANGING.

> *Observations.*—Imitation of a picture.

No. 25—PAPER HANGING.

> *Observations.*—Mere imitations of nature; want of colour to balance the blue ground.

No. 26—PAPER HANGING.

> *Observations.*—Direct imitation of nature; imitation of ribbon in festoons upon paper.

No. 27—PAPER HANGING.

> *Observations.*—Perspective representations of a railway station, frequently repeated and falsifying the perspective.

No. 28—PAPER HANGING.

> *Observations.*—Perspective representation of the Crystal Palace and Serpentine; with flights of steps and architectural framework causing the same error as in 27.

No. 29—PAPER HANGING.

> *Observations.*—Imitation of ribbon upon paper; direct imitation of nature.

No. 30—PAPER HANGING.

> *Observations.*—Direct imitation of nature upon a ground of architectural elements

EXAMPLES OF FALSE PRINCIPLES IN DECORATION

No. 31— PAPER HANGING.

Observations.—Perspective representation of architecture.

No. 32—PAPER HANGING

Observations.—Imitation of a picture repeated all over wall, although it could be correctly seen from only one point.

Nos. 33, 34—PAPER HANGINGS.

Observations.—Direct imitations of nature. No sense of harmony in the distribution of colour.

No. 35—PAPER HANGING.

Observations.—Horses, water, and ground floating in the air; landscapes, racecourse, &c. in perspective.

No. 36—PAPER HANGING.

Observations.—Objects in high relief; perspective representations of architecture employed as decoration for a flat surface.

Garment Fabrics

"The design applied to apparel must exercise a great influence over the general taste of the public; and persons who have been accustomed to consider gaudy, florid, and large ornament suitable for articles of clothing, will hardly be capable of judging correctly of what is true, beautiful, and appropriate in the ornament of the domestic utensils and furniture of their dwellings. The great sources of error in designing for garment fabrics are over ornamentation, and attracting undue attention to the ornament which may arise from many causes; thus from the violence of contrast either of light and dark or of colour, from overcharging the colour (see Nos. 40, 42, 55, &c.), or from the ornament being too large for the fabric. All these causes, however, are modified by the material. Thus muslins and barèges will bear more pronounced contrasts than the more solid or more absorbent textures of jacquonet muslins or de-laines. Silks and de-laines, again, will bear greater fulness of colour than the drier surface of cotton; while woven patterns in silk, formed by tabby and satin in a self-colour, will bear much larger figures than are applicable to either woven patterns in varied colours, or the same printed on cottons or silk. These observations will show the necessity of the designer carefully attending to texture, lustre &c., in preparing his design, and illustrate the difficulty of adopting without adapting the ornament of one fabric to the decoration of another. The flowing lines, agreeable distribution, and flat treatment of the details will illustrate other points in these remarks.

"In reverting to the general question of design for garment fabrics, it may be remarked, that the making up of such goods for use should have due consideration in the general direction of the pattern. Thus, while "up and down" treatments in stripes and trails are proper, the horizontal direction of pronounced forms is not to be admitted, since, crossing the person, the pattern quarrels with all the motions of the human figure, as well as with the form of the long folds in the skirts of the garment. From this reason, large and pronounced checks, however fashionable, are often in very bad taste, and interfere with the graceful arrangement of any material as drapery.

> "If we look at the details of the Indian patterns we shall be surprised at their extreme simplicity, and be led to wonder at their rich and satisfactory effect. It will soon be evident, however, that their beauty results entirely from adherence to the principles above described. The parts themselves are often poor, ill-drawn, and commonplace; yet, from the knowledge of the designer, due attention to the just ornamentation of the fabric, and the refined delicacy evident in the selection of quantity and the choice of tints, both for the ground, where gold is not used as a ground, and for the ornamental forms, the fabrics, individually and as a whole, are a lesson to our designers and manufacturers, given by those from whom we least expected it. Moreover, in the adaptation of all these qualities of design to the fabrics for which they are intended, there is an entire appreciation of the effects to be produced by the texture and foldings of the tissue when in use as an article of dress, insomuch that no draught of the design can be made in any way to show the full beauty of the manufactured article, since this is only called out by the motion and folding of the fabric itself. An expression of admiration for these manufactures must be called forth from every one who examines them, and is justly due to merits which are wholly derived from the true principles on which these goods have been ornamented, and which result from perfect consistency in the designer."
>
> —REDGRAVE, *on Design.*

No. 37—COTTON HANDKERCHIEF.

Observations.—Perfect unsuitableness of the ornament to the use; large, coarse, and vulgar pattern; inharmonious colouring.

No. 38—PRINTED CALICO.

Observations.—Coarse contrast of stripes; mixture of principles, imitation of nature and Indian treatment.

No. 39—MIXED FABRIC.

Observation—Imitation of marble.

No. 40—MOUSSELINE-DE-SOIE.[8]

Observations.—Vulgar and inharmonious colouring; want of geometrical distribution; mere imitative arrangement; landscapes in perspective.

EXAMPLES OF FALSE PRINCIPLES IN DECORATION

No. 41—MOUSSELIN-DE-LAINE.

Observations.—Inharmonious colouring; want of geometrical distribution; mere imitative treatment.

No. 42—PRINTED CALICO.

Observations.—Violent contrasts; bad geometrical forms; imitation of floor-cloth or parquetage.

No. 43—FRENCH BARÈGE.[9]

Observations.—Total want of geometrical distribution; mere imitative treatment; strange conceit in the pattern; pattern much too large for the material.

No. 44—SILK.

Observations.—Imitations of nature; perspective; violent contrasts.

No. 45—MOUSSELINE-DE-LAINE.

Observations.—The commonest geometrical form forced into notice by violent contrast; overcharged size of pattern; bad contrast of colour.

No. 46—SILK.

Observations.— Imitation of a vase; the red and green both cold colours, instead of the red being warm in proportion to the coldness of the green.

No. 47—MOUSSELINE-DE-LAINE.

Observations.—Imitation of one fabric upon another,—lace upon muslin; extremely coarse geometrical basis of the form; imitation of coral.

No. 48—JACQUONET.[10]

Observations.—Mere adoption of Indian forms; false appropriation of Indian principles.

No. 49—CALICO FOR SHIRTS.

Observations.—Perspective representation of a summer house and trees in stripes.

Nos. 50, 51, 52—CALICO FOR SHIRTS.

Observations.—Direct imitation of figures and animals; ballet girls, polka dancers, and race horse in various attitudes.

Nos—53, 54, 55, 56.—PATTERNS FOR TROWSERS.

Observations.—Geometrical forms totally unfit for the garment for which they are intended; interfering with the form of the wearer.

No. 57—MUSLIN CURTAIN.

>*Observations.*—Coarse architectural scroll; and imitation of lace folded upon lace.

Nos. 58, 59, 60—POCKET HANDKERCHIEFS.

>Observation.— Direct imitations of landscapes, animals, and vessels.

Porcelain, Glass, Metal Work, &c., Decorated on False Principles

Porcelain

"Landscapes and pictures are almost always out of place in pottery, and it certainly is objectionable to cover the centres of plates and dishes with pictures and views; not only because it hides the surface, which it has been before said it is desirable to retain, but because utility would be better served by the absence of any decoration in the part which receives the viands, to satisfy that sense of cleanliness, only to be obtained by the white unchanged surface of the material.

"There is still another subject to be referred to, which consists in the imitation of the ornament peculiar to one age and one purpose on the utensils of another age, and which are intended for totally different usages: or applying the ornament of one material to the decoration of another, which last fault, in speaking of other manufactures, has already been often strongly animadverted upon. The revivals of Wedgwood were, in a degree, in this spirit; and although they produced a vast change for the better in the forms of our pottery, and placed a salutary curb on the extravagance of the style that then obtained, they were but the resurrection of a dead art (see No. 70); and the funeral urns of Etruria, being inconsistent with modern uses, have a cold formality quite inconsonant with the feelings of the time."—REDGRAVE, *on Design.*

No. 61. —DESSERT PLATE. (Painted at Sèvres.)

>*Observations.*—The beauty of the material entirely lost; pictures of flowers placed to an unseemly use, and hidden when used.

Glass

"Brilliancy of surface and transparency should ever be preserved with the greatest care in all right treatment of glass. And yet, strange to say, these qualities are not only often disregarded, but there is a strong tendency to contradict and destroy them: thus we see wine-glasses and decanters, water-bottles, carafes, and drinking-vessels of many kinds, not only with the surface covered with ground ornament, but sometimes wholly and entirely changed and obscured by grinding, so as to render them perfectly opaque: or, we have colour most injuriously applied to destroy purity, and prevent a proper enjoyment of the glowing lustre of the liquid contents; whilst sometimes the material is wholly or partially opalized; in the one case making it into a spurious porcelain in the other into a species of japanned hardware, without the toughness and tenacity of that manufacture. Another excellence of glass is its lightness as compared with its power of containing: the maintenance of this quality is opposed to the heavy and deep surface-cutting to which glass is now so frequently submitted, especially in water-jugs and decanters, and in the pieces of dessert-services. This cutting is intended to enhance the jewel-like and prismatic effect of glass, but it is opposed to its true qualities for such purposes, and should only be resorted to in handles stems, or bases, where transparency is unimportant, where constructive thickness is necessary, and the grasp in holding may be aided by the facets of the surface. Yet it has been the fashion to carry this practice of cutting to an extreme, tending to vulgarize, as far as possible, the simple and beautiful material: in some of the works exhibited it has been applied even to the bowls of wine-glasses.

The more simple mode of manufacturing glass is productive not only of the most beautiful shapes, but of its best qualities: and blown glass unites thinness, translucency, and pure surface, to forms which combine the greatest symmetry with varied curves; that is, the sphere, resulting from the circular motion of the workman's instrument, elongated by the breath and weight, into the ellipse and its combinations. These blown forms may be ornamented by narrow bands of engraved ornament, of which flatness and symmetrical distribution are requisite qualities: in wine-glasses and drinking vessels it ought to be reserved for those parts of the bowl which do not interfere with a perfect sight of their contents. Any gilding or enamelling can only be admissible under the same rules. In all cases, elegance of form should be the first consideration, to which cutting, gilding, or engraving should be entirely subordinate. The relation of the stem to the bowl in wine-glasses is another point of some importance. The practice has of late obtained of making them of such extreme tenuity as to produce a sense of fragility and insecurity, which is quite as great an error in taste as the contrary fault of heaviness and thickness."—REDGRAVE *on Design.*

No. 62—GLASS BUTTER DISH. No. 63—WINE GLASS. No. 64—JELLY GLASS.

> *Observations.*—In each of these articles the natural outline of the glass when blown destroyed by the surfaces being cut.

No. 65—GLASS GOBLET, OPAL.

> *Observations.*—Coarse and vulgar in form; the transparency of the material sacrificed to imitate alabaster.

No. 66—GLASS GOBLET (FLASHED WITH OPAL AND ENGRAVED).

> *Observations.*—The general form coarse and heavy; transparent appearance of the material entirely destroyed, thereby rendering it impossible to see the contents.

No. 67—GLASS GOBLET.

Observations.—Use disregarded by a conceit in causing the vessel to shrink in the middle. This glass could not be emptied without raising the foot considerably above the mouth

No. 68.—CORNUCOPIA FOR FLOWERS

Observations.—The constructive line very bad,—the base appearing as if stuck on, instead of forming part of the whole; transparency of the material destroyed.

No. 69—GLASS FLOWER VASE.

Observation. —The general outline entirely destroyed by the horizontal cuttings.

No. 70—EARTHENWARE VASE.

Observations.—The nature of the material obscured by the colour employed, giving the vase the appearance of being japanned; ornaments copied from a funeral vase, and inappropriate.

No. 71—FLOWER POT

Observations.—Imitation in earthenware of reeds, painted blue, bound together with yellow ribbon.

No. 72—PAIR OF SCISSORS.

Observations.—Imitation of a stork; the beak opening the reverse way; the body of the bird made to open in the direction of its length.

No. 73.—WATER JUG.

Observations.—General form ungraceful and broken by ornament, consisting of grapes, leaves, and infant bacchanals.

No 74—STONE JUG, FIGURED.

Observations.—Mixture of styles; direct imitation of nature.

No. 75—SMALL EWER.

Observations.—General form disregarded; ornament suggestive of Louis XV. style; graceless imitation of natural forms.

No. 76.—JUG.

Observations.—The general form totally disregarded; it is a rude imitation, in blue earthenware, of the trunk of a tree, on which are applied figures, vine leaves, and grapes, all out of scale with one another; this jug has been one of the most popular ever manufactured.

No. 77.—FRENCH SCENT BOTTLE.

> *Observations.*—Total disregard of utility; the handle incapable of being grasped; the base resting upon points of metal.

No. 78.—SLAB FOR FIREPLACE.

> *Observations.*—Nature as adapted to Berlin wool work transferred to porcelain.

No. 79.—PAPIER MACHÉ TRAY.

> *Observations.*—An example of popular but vulgar taste, of a low character, presenting numerous features which the student should carefully avoid:— 1st, the centre is the piracy of a picture; 2d, the picture, on which most labour been bestowed, is thrown away. It is wrong to hide a picture by putting a teapot upon it: if a picture is wanted it should be placed where it can be seen, and will not be destroyed by use; 3d, the scroll lines of the ornament, instead of following the form, are directly opposed to it, and are scattered, as if by chance anywhere; 4th, the glitter of the mother-of-pearl is the most prominent feature of the whole, and, being spread about, creates the impression that the article is slopped with water or perforated with holes.

Metal Work

"It has before been remarked that the figures introduced into the ornament of metalwork are too often merely applied or stuck on, not arising out of the work as a constructed whole, and this more especially in those works which have been usually committed to the skill of the artist; but if not to be tolerated in these works, in objects of utility they are far more out of place, and ornament requires that figures should have an ornamental construction. It cannot be too often repeated, that imitative trees and foliage, flowers that are like the growth of the hothouse electrotyped, and which dangle and shake with every movement, as much almost as would their prototypes on their natural stems, are not ornament, are in the worst possible taste for any useful purpose, and have a flimsy and tinsel-like appearance, as much beneath the impressive effect in metal of even mere plain surface, as they are wide of any pretensions to fitness or propriety as works in metal at all. (See No. 82). This naturalism is evidently a heresy of the artist's, and should have no quarter at the hands of the ornamental designer. In the section devoted to hardware, the treatment of metallic surface has already been the subject of remark; much of which will apply here also; but in connexion with this imitative art, it may be remarked that the frosting, which it renders almost necessary for its display, is even more opposed to the brilliancy of metal than that ovidation[11] so useful in showing art-treatment. —REDGRAVE *on Design.*

"It is impossible to enumerate half the absurdities of modern metalworkers; but all these proceed from the false notion of disguising instead of beautifying articles of utility. How many objects of ordinary use are rendered monstrous and ridiculous, simply because the artist, instead of seeking the *most convenient form, and then decorating it, has embodied some extravagance to conceal the real purpose* for which the article has been made!"

—PUGIN'S *Christian Architecture.*

No. 80—BRACKET FOR CURTAINS.

> *Observations.*—Direct imitation of nature; and unfitness for the purpose. Yet this, of its kind, has been one of the most successful articles of manufacture in respect of sale.

81.—LAMP.

> *Observations.*—This glittering article is of French manufacture, and in all its parts, without exception, illustrates some false principle. Its general constructive line is bad, the heavy top totters upon an unsubstantial base; it rests upon the points of leaves, which seem ready to give way under the load; these leaves are direct but bad imitations of nature. The porcelain vessel for holding the oil, with its coarse gilding, affects to look like metal; the upper portion of the metal work is entirely out of scale with the lower, whilst the gaudy imitation of network is made further to disturb the composition.

82—JUG FOR WASHHAND STAND.

> *Observations.*—Imitation of one material in another—marble in earthenware.

83—GAS BURNER.

> *Observations.*—Gas flaming from the petal of a convolvulus!—one of a class of ornaments very popular, but entirely indefensible in principle.

84—GAS BURNER.

> *Observations.*—Manifests all the faults of the *natural* style —is totally without a sense of construction, the opal flower has no relation to the fuchsia, and this latter is treated quite at variance with its growth, the strange stamen supporting the globe giving the finish to the absurdities of the *style*.

Notes

1 *Spectator*, 22 October 1853, p. 17.
2 C. P. Taft, *The South Kensington Museum, What it is, How it Originated, What it has Done and is Now Doing for England and the World: and the Adaptation of Such an Institution to the Needs and Possibilities of this City*: a Lecture Delivered at Pike's

Opera House in Cincinnati, Friday Evening, April 5, 1878 (Cincinnati: Robert Clarke, 1878), p. 18.
3. J. C. Robinson, 'Our National Art Collections and Provincial Art Museums', *Nineteenth Century*, vii, 1880, p. 987.
4. G. F. Waagen. *Reports by the Juries on the Subjects in the Thirty Classes into Which the Exhibition was Divided.* [4] (London: Spicer, 1852).
5. William Dyce (1806–1864)
6. A.W.N. Pugin, *The True Principles of Pointed or Christian Architecture*, (John Weale: London, 1841).
7. Redgrave: R. Redgrave, and G. R. Redgrave. *Manual of Design*, (London: Published for the Committee of Council on Education by Chapman and Hall, 1876).
8. Mousseline: A thin silk fabric with a texture like that of muslin. Woven in silk or wool.
9. Barége: A light, silky dress-fabric, resembling gauze, originally made at Baréges.
10. Jacquonet: A cotton fabric originally imported from India, aka jaconet.
11. Ovidation: a form of heat treatment linked to oxidation.

18

[ANON], 'THE PRINCIPLES OF DESIGN ESSENTIAL TO THE CONSTRUCTION OF ARTISTIC FURNITURE'

The label 'art furniture' or 'artistic furniture' is widely used to describe specific late nineteenth century products of mainly Britain and America, often seen in conjunction with, and under the umbrella of, either the arts and crafts or the aesthetic movement. While this makes some sense stylistically, there are other reasons for the label, its introduction, and eventual ubiquity during the period.

Art furniture was the commercial development of the design reforms that had begun in the 1840s and continued throughout much of the nineteenth century. Initially, building on the opinions and products of the early reformers such as A. W. N. Pugin and William Burges, 'art furniture' eventually became a blanket term for merchandise made in a wide range of styles. Nikolaus Pevsner suggested succinctly that during the nineteenth century a split 'had occurred during the second third of the nineteenth century between art and craft, and art and manufacture'.[1] One of the aims of the design reforms was to reunite utility with beauty, in a variety of manufactured products, thus linking arts, crafts and manufactures. Although the application of the 'art' prefix to various industries and product types was initially rather exclusive, it eventually developed into a wide range of commercial responses.

Art furniture had two phases. Initially, it referred to the architect-designed products of a limited number of specialist companies employing a skilled workforce. The bywords of early art furniture were taste, beauty, and individuality. This in part represented a revolt against the prevailing tastes of furniture that critics considered overblown and meretricious. The changes were driven by an educated and increasingly sophisticated middle class who, from the mid-1870s, were reading art journals and advice books and were increasingly aware of the opportunities for self-expression through a harmonious interior. The second phase, fully developed by the 1880s, saw the term art furniture become a catch-all for a wide range of commercial furnishing products sold to a middle-class market across the United Kingdom and North America. The word 'art' had become as much a sales pitch as an ideal.

The Furniture Gazette was an illustrated furniture trade journal 'treating of all branches of cabinet-work, upholstery and interior decoration'. The main thrust of this set of articles was to argue that good taste was not impulsive and based on personal perception, rather it was based on sound principles. The intended 'to deal with those laws which relate to beauty and fitness; to the harmonious combinations of forms and colours; and to the adaptation of the design to the material, the parts to the whole, and the whole to its own special and proper purpose'.[2]

[Anon], 'The Principles of Design Essential to the Construction of Artistic Furniture', *Furniture Gazette*, 3 May 1873, p. 51, 17 May 1873, pp. 84–6, 31 May 1873, pp. 115–6, 7 June 1873, pp. 132–3

Of late years many able writers have taken up the subject of furnishing from an artistic point of view, and heaped ridicule upon the prevalent bad taste of upholsterers and furniture manufacturers. But there is much to be said on both sides.

Upholsterers and manufacturers are here very like the players, of whom it has been said, that if they please to live, they must live to please. The whole taste of a nation cannot be educated and refined in a day, any more than Rome could be built in that short time; and if we look back to the many horrors of ugliness and vulgarity which not long since were common and are now unknown, we shall find no reason to be dissatisfied with the artistic progress which even these much-abused tradesmen have made within a very short period of time.

To their credit be it said, that without any special training in art, and despite all the worst and strongest traditions of their trade, furniture has improved in usefulness, in beauty, and in artistic taste. That it will continue so to improve, we have the best guarantee in the increasing public appreciation and knowledge of artistic principles, and the consequently fast increasing demand for really artistic furniture. That which the public demand, the manufacturers and tradesmen will certainly supply; the taste of their workmen will therefore be educated, and in the cultivation of that taste everybody concerned will find a pleasurable source of mental activity and aesthetic refinement to which most of them may now be almost, if not entire, strangers. Progress creates progress.

To aid this movement the present series of papers has been projected, and it will be the earnest aim of their author to explain in clear and simple language those principles of form, colour, sentiment, and feeling, on which a vast range of artistic effects depends. To do this effectually each branch of his subject must receive systematic study, and the reader who seeks information and instruction, with a view to the practical application of such principles, must therefore not be impatient if he finds the author a little too anxious to make him understand the theory of a given effect before he proceeds to describe the means which usually tend to its attainment.

In the other columns of this paper the materials used in the construction of furniture receive due attention; in these columns it is our intention to deal with those laws which relate to beauty and fitness; to the harmonious combinations of forms and colours; and to the adaptation of the design to the material, the parts to the whole, and the whole to its own special and proper purpose.

We say laws, advisedly, for we must not fall into the common error of imagining that taste is a mere thing of caprice or opinion, governed by no known principles, and distinct from everything like scientific exactness. On the contrary, the laws of art are as clearly and distinctly defined by scientific investigation as are the laws which govern the more mechanical arts of chemistry and optics. The chemist combines and mixes for the production of a vast range of new effects, but the principles governing the effects remain unchanged and unchangeable. The musician does the same with his notes, but every new concourse of sweet sounds obeys the established laws of harmony. The architect has a wide range of effects in Classic and Gothic art, with all their divisions of Ionic, Corinthian, Tuscan, and Composite, or Anglo-Saxon, Early English, Norman, and Tudor; their sub-divisions, &c. But the laws governing proportion, symmetry, chiaroscuro, subordination, a balance of lines and masses, and so on, remain ever the same, and can never be violated with impunity. It is just so in the application of these laws to the industrial arts. We may find it difficult to establish rigid rules for special applications where the applications are capable of such endless diversification, but the primary laws remain for our guidance, resting safely upon scientifically demonstrated principles, which are intimately associated with the invariable laws of Nature.

But these are laws in which there is nothing to cramp the imagination of the inventive. They are those of a wise and beneficent government, which leads, but does not drive; which suggests, but does not command; provides many pleasant roads to one good end, and leaves the wayfarer to select his own. "The arts," says Sir Joshua Reynolds, "would be open for ever to caprice and casualty, if those who are to judge of their excellencies had no settled principles by which to regulate their decisions."[3]

It was not long since the custom to treat as entirely distinct those arts which appeal to the mind and heart through the eye, and those other arts which are associated with life's common everyday ordinary necessities. Then a piece of furniture was made to serve only its meanest use, and no one dreamed of it as a possible means of also conveying pleasure to the mind, and serving important moral purposes. As a building was once erected merely for the warmth and shelter it provided, so chairs and tables were once merely regarded as things to sit upon or eat from. The idea of fancy, imagination, feeling, or intellect having anything in common with these vulgar necessities would have been held up to scorn and ridicule. Artists would then have indignantly resented the idea of mere mechanics studying art, while the fact of their absolutely applying its principles to trades in honourable rivalry for the palm of excellence, acquiring celebrity, and converting the shops in which their works were displayed into veritable museums, would have been scouted as the day-dream of a madman. Yet, nowadays, thanks to a growing love of art inspired by fine-art lectures, exhibitions, and Government art-schools, which have sprung up and flourish in every direction, that dream is on the eve of realisation, and those who have not already recognized the fact, must speedily do so, or prepare to relinquish their places to a generation of more active, enterprising, and noble workers and thinkers.

There is no doubt that a powerful and lasting stimulus in this direction was given by the Great Exhibition of 1851, which has been kept up by the succession of international and annual exhibitions ever since. These periodical gatherings of the productions of industrial art first awakened in the minds of our manufacturers, as well as in those of the public, a sense of our prominent short-comings in the matters of artistic taste and design. Hence came the first glimmering of a dim idea that such things had their uses. Even those who valued more highly the penny they put into their pocket than the thought they put into their mind on seeing the furniture of France, Germany, Italy, and Belgium, could not blind themselves to the fact that the highest excellence of workmanship and materials received increased commercial value from their combination with artistic knowledge and taste. It was not enough to say that "the doors fit with the nicest accuracy, the drawers move with perfect smoothness, and the wood is so well seasoned that a faulty panel or shrunken joint is out of the question," if with such admirable qualities we had ugly forms, incongruous ornament, and a display of generally bad taste which pained the artistic eye and conveyed uncomfortable sensations into every mind susceptible to impressions conveyed through the sight. As this dawning light strengthened a change came; the beautiful was no longer always remorselessly denied access to the useful; and from that time forth until now, when a rooted interest in art pervades all ranks of the community, we have had constantly accumulating evidence of a far better state of things to come.

But it is still to come. Therefore it befits us all to be active in the noble work of culture and refinement. We must no longer pause to ask of what use is art? That question was long since answered in every thoughtful mind. Our mechanics are no longer content to be machines. They desire to invest thought, feeling, and intelligence in their work, and to look far beyond mechanical excellence in the technical requirements of their trade. They must carry us back to the time when the highest art gave its impulse to the lowest, and received in return an impulse of no mean value from the lowest; for "it is a law in the arts, a law imposed by their community of origin and end, that they mutually assist and support each other."

We conclude this our introductory paper with a few remarks offered by Peter Graham, Esq., of the well-known firm of Jackson & Graham:—"The knowledge, thought, and care required to be exercised in the conception and production of articles of decorative furniture, are greater, perhaps, than many suppose who look at them in their complete state. The style and principle of construction have first to be studied, then the proportions of all the parts, the materials to be used, whether various woods with the introduction of marbles, metal enrichments, bronzed or gilt, ivory, paintings on porcelain, buhl, or marquetrie, inlaying or carving. It will be thus seen that some knowledge of architecture is required to be united with that of sculptor, painter, and ornamentist, &c, with the technical skill of the cabinet-maker, in the completion of an article of decorative furniture; and just in proportion as their combined works have been well executed, and directed by good taste and judgement, will be the pleasure that may be derived from the possession, or contemplation, of the completed work. Some articles may depend mainly upon form and construction for their decorative character, and others require aid from the art of the sculptor or ornamentist only; but, generally, the manufacture of decorative furniture may be said to be the application of fine art to articles of utility, and no department of industry affords wider scope for its application."[4]

The True Rank of Decorative Art

Before proceeding to treat of the fundamental principles which govern the successful practice of decorative art as applied to furniture, it will be as well to prepare the ground by considering its real rank and importance as a means of expressing taste, feeling, and sentiment, affording sensuous gratification, and conveying ideas to the mind. In our day ornament is so intimately associated with the fine arts of painting, sculpture, and architecture that we are a little apt to overlook its importance when it is connected with the humbler branches of industrial art.

The influence of external objects in the impressions they make upon the senses, and the extent to which the mind is influenced by such impressions, has been a prolific source of theories and controversies from time immemorial. More especially has it been so in connection with the fine arts, and hence, perhaps, that element of confusion and uncertainty in the minds of their students which has been so unfavourable to the general development of artistic taste.

The swarthy dirty carpet-weaver of the East, who, poverty-stricken, ragged, stolid, and ignorant, squats on his floor of clay, and in his ill-made loom weaves carpets so gorgeous and harmonious in colour, so admirably fitted in design for their purpose, and so complete in their luxuriant feeling and the expression of a perfect sense of beauty, never heard of these theories and would probably scorn such controversies. The New Zealander, who, in the decoration of his paddle, or war-club, surpasses our most accomplished, educated professors of decorative art in the perfection and fitness of his designs, knows as little of such abstruse questions. The Chinese or Japanese ivory carver, patiently and lovingly producing the most delicate and elaborate work in the midst of the filth and squalor of his wretched hovel, is as ignorant. And again we remember the wonderful skill of the workers of metal in Abyssinia. Noting these things we ask: are the minds of such ignorant men, placed in the midst of all that stupefies and degrades, more susceptible to impressions of the beautiful in form or colour than we, with all our boasted progress in art and science, are? Or is all decorative art in reality merely sensuous and instinctive?

It is by no means easy to answer these questions.

If we determine to regard decorative art as sensuous, resulting from feelings rather than ideas, we are then driven to the conclusion that perfection in that art must be a question of race. And for this view there is much to be said and much evidence to be advanced. But the evidence on the other side is not less powerful. For instance, we ourselves are still the descendants of that old Keltic race which in its savage condition so greatly excelled in decorative work, and we want neither models, nor teachers, nor patronage, and yet in such work we are even now far behind the excellence attained by our savage ancestors. Why should the instinct which survives in the one race die out in the other?

It has been urged that the power which enables the savage artist to excel in ornament, is the same as that which, applied to the less sensuous arts of more civilized nations, leads to successes of a higher and more intellectual character; and that thus, inferior phases of art being left to inferior instincts, do not attain the same pitch of perfection. In reply to this, we have but to glance backward to ancient Greece. Wonderful and glorious in the perfection of all its loftier art manifestations, Greek art was not less glorious or wonderful in the perfection of its very humblest species of decoration.

But is not the real source of our non-success in decorative art to be traced to the contempt with which through generation after generation it has been the fashion to treat it? Are we not even now, probably, in error in regarding it as so purely sensuous and instinctive? It is very difficult to separate feelings and ideas, or to trace the extent to which certain impressions are due to the one or to the other. We all know that the mind imbibes ideas unconsciously; nothing is more common.

We all know how thoughts and feelings act and react one upon the other. Thus certain sounds will convey ideas and feelings of martial grandeur. Other sounds are invariably plaintive and melancholy in the ideas and feelings they suggest. Some appeal to the discordant feelings, and are suggestive of hate and strife; others are as powerful in their suggestions of love and tenderness.

Hans Christian Oersted, in one of his "Dialogues on the Fundamental Principles of Beauty,"[5] referring to the secret connection between ideas and tones of music, says when you see a person draw a number of careless strokes in the sand, you conclude that his thoughts are unoccupied. But when you see him draw a circle or an equilateral polygon, you think there must be some thought in his mind about the composition of the figure; for mathematical figures are representations of ideas. If you say that a circle is a figure the circumference of which is everywhere equally distant from the centre, you certainly have an idea of the circle; and if you describe a circle, you may also be said to have constructed this idea. The circle being produced, you find associated with it other ideas. Two diameters, standing perpendicularly on each other, divide the circle into four quadrants. "You see that the angles which the radii enclose must always stand in proportion to the arcs belonging to them; that the circumference must always be in a certain proportion to the diameter: in short, you see countless properties which, regarded from the one side, are different; while, from the other, on the contrary, they are the same as the nature of the circle. This variety in oneness now stands before you, although in an unconscious manner, when you behold a circle; and you find it beautiful, although you are not aware, or at least you do not think, of all these properties." These thoughts united give an idea, in the Platonic sense, which exists in the circle, even if we cannot describe it in words. The infinite symmetry, the completeness, variety, and unity of the circle affect us with a sense of its beauty without our knowing why it does so. We cannot find one thought in which all these thoughts may be included; but yet we have the full perception that the circle we have apprehended by intuition is a totality of thoughts. "The Beautiful pleases us as the image of an idea, without our being at the same time conscious of the idea itself." In the same clever way Professor Oersted traces the beauty of other forms to the ideas which they express acting unconsciously on the outward and inward sense, proceeding from the straight lines and angles of inorganic nature to the endless combinations of curves which appear in constantly increasing variety as we ascend in the ranks of organization.

Referring, as we have done, to the beauty of musical sounds, the Professor still finds the same laws; but, deprecating the idea that the existence of such laws has a tendency to render art mechanical and the artist a machine, who puts his work together as the carpenter puts a box together, says, "We may account for our enjoyment of art, without at the same time depreciating that which is divine in it. For what can be a higher and worthier pursuit than to produce works of art which harmonize with the most profound reason," even if we do so, as we must suppose our savage ancestors did, without calculation, or receive the impressions of pleasure they give without requiring such calculation?

Regarding his occupation from this point of view, the artisan decorator in our furniture factories may be encouraged to bring some thought and ambition to bear upon his work, and not deliver himself up to the endless monotony of slavish repetition. He may give expression to his love of art for art's dear sake; and begin to feel that it is his mission, in conjunction with the loftiest and noblest artists, to elevate, refine, and purify the lives of others as well as his own. The study of nature in all her varieties of beauty will open to him never-ending sources of learning and delight.

In this way pearls, and shells, and flowers, birds, insects, and quadrupeds, the geometrical wonders of the world of crystals, grasses and weeds, the changes of the seasons, the hours of the day, each and all will present him with ever-changing novelties of the most delightful character, and suggestions which shall give him the crowning pride and joy of being nobly creative instead of servilely imitative. Let them:—

> Scatter the germs of the Beautiful
> In the holy shrines of home:
> Let the pure, and the fair, and the graceful here
> In the live'iest lustre come:
> Leave not a trace of deformity
> In the temple of the heart;
> But gather about its hearth the germs
> Of Nature and of Art.[6]

II. Fitness

The fitness of an object for the purpose it is intended to serve is so obviously a source of pleasure, that it is difficult to understand how those who seek to please by artistic decoration can so frequently overlook it. Beauty and utility are indeed so intimately associated that they might frequently be used as interchangeable terms.

Adam Smith, in his "Theory of the Moral Sentiments," pointing out a person annoyed by seeing his chairs all placed in the middle of the room, where they looked ugly, and angrily putting them into their places against the wall, where he considered they looked handsome, says, "The whole propriety of this new situation arises from its superior conveniency in leaving the floor free and disengaged. Yet it is this conveniency alone which may ultimately recommend that arrangement, and bestow upon it the whole of its propriety and beauty in the eyes of the owner of the apartment."[7] From the same principle, he further argues, arise those national institutions which promote the general welfare. It is the same regard for the fitness of objects to their end, the same regard for the beauty of order, art, and contrivance; in short, the same study of utility in all its appliances, which results in the perfection of a government and the happiness of a nation,—things of beauty which are a joy for ever. Another writer, going even farther than Adam Smith, ingeniously resolves our whole approbation of virtue into a perception of that species of beauty which results from the appearance of utility, pointing out that no qualities of the mind are approved of as virtuous but such as are useful or agreeable either to the person himself or to others; and that no qualities are disapproved of as vicious but such as have a contrary tendency.

As with the owner of the chairs so was it with Copernicus, who perceived a want of fitness for the end attained in the Ptolemaic system of astronomy,[8] and so set to work to displace it. Pythagoras, so enraptured by discovering the beauty of proportion in simple triangles, that he celebrated the event with a sacrifice of one hundred cattle on the altar of his gods, had in his eye the vast practical utility of a truth on which, simple as it is, the earliest foundations of astronomy and navigation rest. What is more beautiful than the idea that every particle of matter in the universe attracts more or less every other particle, yet what law of nature serves greater uses than that of gravitation? What wonderful beauty we find associated with utility throughout all nature! The glorious sunlight which gives a charm to the meanest and most degraded object in creation, is the source of nearly every important blessing we possess, including our lives, health, and the joy of seeing. The atmosphere in which we live and move and have our being, the weight of which is so enormous that its pressure shivers iron like glass, although the tiniest insect waves it with its fragile wings, is as useful as it is beautiful. We marvel at the magnificent colours of the sunrise and sunset, and we know that these are due to that assemblage of gases, the utility of which is so immense that we cannot overrate it. With reverence be it remembered that the great Creator of all things within this vast universe of worlds has always associated with the greatest as with the smallest of his works, that glorious element for which we here plead with you—the beautiful. He has blended beauty with every possible degree and kind of usefulness so intimately that we cannot say whether the useful arises from the beautiful or the beautiful from the useful.

These thoughts have induced me to place first in my list of chapters on artistic beauty as applied to articles of every-day use in our homes, the principle of Fitness. No matter what species of decoration you are engaged upon or what purpose the article decorated is to serve, the leading idea in your mind should be that of Fitness. To this subordinate every other consideration. Novelty is a very good quality, imagination and ingenuity in design are not of course to be underrated. Beauty of colour, of form, of light and shade, are all desirable. But there is no high quality of beauty in any of these things if in their applications the principle of fitness is ignored. We should see fewer discordant masses of ugly building materials in our streets, if, instead of a feverish craving for novelty and attractiveness, the architect had subordinated every other quality to the first principle of his art—Fitness. The practical upholsterer would never have introduced that huge brass pole with its gigantic and ugly brass flowers hanging stiffly down from either end of it, if he had once given a thought to its real purpose and its fitness for serving it. The idea of bending or bulging out would never have influenced the designer of certain popular legs for chairs, if the purpose of chairs and the idea of fitness in designing them had held sway in his mind. The wood-carver, who like poor old Caleb, with his barking toy-dogs,[9] likes to go "as close to nature" as he can for the price he receives, does so without the slightest idea of also studying nature in connection with the purpose of the object his work is to decorate. No, he regards Fitness as something with which he has nothing to do. Nay, he often designs without even the most remote idea of the purpose to which his design is to be applied. It is simply so much ornament to be stuck on a chair, a sideboard, or a table, a cabinet, or a cornice, he knows not, cares not, what, as whim or caprice, governed by no just idea of suitability, may dictate. The same ornament serves all purposes and for all is most likely equally unfit. As for use, it has literally none. Florid scrolls, fruit, and flowers, griffins and dragons, columns and pilastres, &c, &c, they are all turned out one after another, all alike, and all without a single wholesome human thought or feeling in whole acres of them.

Take our wall papers and judge them by this idea of Fitness. How seldom we see anything that we can regard as really artistic. Bear in mind the purpose of these hangings. We do not erect walls for the sake of paper-hangings, as some pretentious designers really appear to think we do. The room is for furniture, for objects of art, for comfort, and to produce a pleasant general effect on our minds and feelings. There are, therefore, many things in a room more important than its walls, and, therefore, paper-hangings should be fitted for a subordinate position, in other words for their uses, all of which are in antagonism with the glaring colours, staring patterns, and pretentious, but absurdly feeble attempts at the picturesque in which so many of our designers indulge.

Again, look at the cheaper styles of decoration, the mouldings, and ornaments which we manufacture from plaster, terra cotta, composition, gutta-percha, putty, papier-mâché, carton-pierre, &c, and at the way in which we commonly use such things. Sticking them on thickly, gilded and coloured, a mass of barbarous splendour, to disguise ugly forms, in much the same way as some vulgar tasteless woman patches herself with jewellery and finery under the impression that she is making herself beautiful in the eyes of admirers. She is only making her ugliness more conspicuous and depriving it of its last chance of escaping comment and observation. How little again is the question of fitness considered in the production of stained glass, in the designing of carpets, of bedsteads, of window blinds, of fenders and fire-grates. Some of the latter are often more fitted to go into glass cases than to have their polished and dainty beauty destroyed by fire and smoke. So it is with many other things coming under the head of furniture. Who has not seen tables and sideboards, ay, and even chairs and couches, so bristling with the projecting points of carved, or imitations of carved work, that it was positively dangerous to go near them? If tables and sideboards were made to tear clothes, we could praise the fitness of such decoration, not otherwise. All these things are crimes against the great leading principle of all true decorative art,—namely, Fitness. (To be continued.)

Our last article was written to point out how a sense of pleasure is generated in every mind by the idea of fitness; how in Nature's works, from the humblest to the most magnificent and sublime, beauty and fitness are invariably associated; and in conclusion, how little attention this primarily important idea of fitness has received from certain unfit designers in branches of furniture, upholstery, and decorative trades which we represent. The fact is that most of our designers have not been properly trained to their work, or in other words fitted for it, and this is likely to remain the case until the demand for really artistic furniture and decoration becomes more common, and the principles of design in its construction are more widely understood and appreciated. In the meantime, however, we do not stagnate, and within the last ten or fifteen years we have really made great strides towards our hoped-for end. For this end we must all continue to strive. The meaningless admiration of the ignorant must not lead us astray; our standard must be so high that, even if we cannot hit it, the shaft of our intention shall go higher than it would if our mark had been less elevated.

The decorative workman must first fit himself for his work before he can hope to fit his work for its uses. When he becomes familiar with the principles governing good work, he will be capable of doing good work, and in doing it the happy result will give happiness to others and to himself. Ruskin says "In order that people may be happy in their work, these three things are needed: They must be fit for it; they must not do too much of it; and they must have a sense of success in it—not a doubtful sense, such as needs some testimony of other people for its confirmation, but a sure sense, or rather knowledge, that so much work has been done well, and fruitfully done, whatever the world may say about it. So that in order that a man may be happy it is necessary that he should not only be capable of his work, but a good judge of his work"[10]

Next to the consideration of fitness as a moral sentiment, fitness for use in construction and decoration, and the fitness of the workman for his work, comes the consideration of another element—that of fitness to the material in which the work is executed. This, too, is a matter of considerable artistic importance.

In the Russian Court of the Great Exhibition of 1851 were exhibited some doors of costly malachite, made with panels, &c, in the style of decorative wooden doors, and hung to pilasters utterly disproportioned to their support.[11] Even those who were loudest in admiring the great beauty of this material could not refrain from expressing, more or less definitely, a sense of its unfitness for such uses. It will be apparent at once that extreme weight is not the idea which is likely to give pleasure in connection with a door, however handsome it may be in forms or colours. It will be seen at once that, whereas panelling arises in wood naturally enough from the mode of construction suitable for such a material, in stone it arises from nothing but the parrot and monkey's paltry little quality of slavish, meaningless imitation. There was no fitness in it; and without fitness the other elements of beauty were simply wasted, or, at the best, were very badly used. Take painted glass as another illustration of this defect. To paint on such a material as you would paint upon wood or canvas, neglecting the idea of its use, and merely aiming to produce a good picture, would be a blunder, however beautiful the drawing, colouring, and realistic effect might be in themselves. The main idea of the artistic painter on glass being harmony and transparency, he does not wish to shut out the light, but merely to subdue it, and to give it an effect of solemn richness or cheerful brilliancy which shall best aid and accord with the general effect of the room or building to which it is subordinated.

In the construction and decoration of wrought iron we often see shapes which have been cut out of flat pieces of metal and bent into elegant curvilinear forms, with surfaces gradually melting from convex into concave, forming a combination of harmoniously varied lines and surfaces very beautiful and in perfect accordance with the idea of fitness. But apply the same lines and surfaces to stone and the ideas of their beauty are at once brought into antagonism with the ideas of their unfitness—the result is a discord. Instead of thinness and flexibility, we here have solidity and inflexibility, a material which we all know cannot be readily bent or moulded, one which must be laboriously cut and chiselled away. Therefore, massiveness and boldness are felt to be in greater harmony with the obvious character of such a material than contrary qualities would be, such as are in accordance with the nature of the other material. Heavy iron garden furniture frequently offends against this principle of fitness by being constructed in imitation of rustic woodwork, the yielding curves and flexible twistings of which are out of harmony with the evident natural rigidity and solidity of the material.

In wood-carving a great effect of fitness between the material and the carving is ensured when the ornament is so designed and adapted as to give the grain of the wood its fair value. But this is not often possible. Where the light and shade of a piece of wood-carving are interfered with by the light and dark forms given by the partly-coloured grain of the wood, the carver loses the full effect of his work, consequently, the material should always either be selected because it is free from such effects of colour, or the grain should be allowed to display itself to the greatest advantage by being associated with the design. Never allow one kind of beauty to act in antagonism to another. Let the effect of the one strengthen that of the other to the utmost possible degree, not weaken it, whatever the material may be, wood, stone, glass, or metal. The task is often one of great difficulty, but necessity has in this way often been the mother of invention in the works of our most original designers.

In the next place, look how frequently the designs woven into our carpets are unfitted for the material in which they are executed. Every footfall which tells us so unobtrusively and pleasantly that they are soft and yielding, as for their use they should be, is often contradicted by the inartistic designer's noisy suggestions of a false and very uncomfortable idea of unyielding hardness. We know that carpets are flat, and that they ought to be so, but the designer often insults our common sense in just the same way, by suggesting that they are not and ought not to be flat. In the carpets of Turkey and India, as in some of those by our own manufacturers, we see both designs and colours in perfect unison with the material, being neither suggestive of inlaid wood nor of mosaic stone-work. The forms and colours of such carpets have no such clear-cutting distinctness of outline, they blend softly one into the other. The designs are fitted to the use which the article is intended to serve, and to the material in which it is manufactured.

In curtains the design should in the same way be in keeping with the nature of the material. For a thick material, which falls into broad massive folds, large bold designs are appropriate. Silk draperies falling, on the contrary, into numerous small folds, should bear a small pattern, such as, when hanging, it can display to advantage. And as the sheen of silk is its chief beauty, the design should be one that will not interfere with its lustre. Lace draperies should also be treated by the designers with due regard to the nature of such a material. In short, in every case the error of applying to a material a design for which it is unfitted, must always be scrupulously avoided. Professor Dresser, in one of his works on ornamental art, says:—"As a principle, it will be found that whenever the true susceptibilities of a material are sought out, and the endeavour is to produce beauty which is most befitting to the peculiar mode in which the material is worked, that the manufacture progresses in art; but whenever a treatment is adopted which disguises the true mode of production, or is at variance with it, the manufacture becomes coarse and degraded."[12]

Fitness of design must not only be regarded in connection with use and material, but it must also govern the association of part with part. If the parts are not in keeping one with another, the design may be fitted to the particular object the article is designed to serve, and each part may be fitted in design to the material of which it is composed, and yet the result be unsatisfactory. For instance, suppose we have an article of furniture in which the main characteristics are costliness of material and richness of ornament, with delicacy and gracefulness of design, it would be obviously unfitting to associate with these ideas those of boldness, massiveness, extreme simplicity, and cheapness; yet this has been done. An artist who is better known as a journalist and author, Mr. George Augustus Sala[13]—his non-admirers call him George Dis-gustus,—gave expression to this feeling when objecting to the association of terra-cotta decorations with delicate ornamental woods, with which "ivory, or gilt, or silvered bronze, Parian, or porcelain, would more fitly and gracefully serve," said, "A staring mass of red terra-cotta—as in

Mr. Gillow's trophy side-board (at the Paris Exhibition of 1867)—otherwise a noble piece of work—reminds one of the vulgar saying about "putting a beggar on a gentleman." Who would fill up a Florentine picture-frame with a hodful of bricks ? Yet this is precisely the effect produced by the importation of a ponderous mass of baked earth into the midst of most delicate and graceful carved work."[14]

Notes

1. N. Pevsner, 'Art Furniture of the Eighteen Seventies', *Architectural Review*, III, January 1952, pp. 43–50.
2. 'Principles of Design Essential to the Construction of Artistic Furniture', *Furniture Gazette*, May 3, 1873, p. 51.
3. Sir Joshua Reynolds, *Seventh Discourse. Delivered to the Students of the Royal Academy on the Distribution of the Prizes*, December 1776.
4. Peter Graham, 'Furniture', *The Record of the International Exhibition 1862* (Glasgow: Mackenzie, 1862), p. 490.
5. Hans Christian Oersted (1777–1851). Danish physicist and chemist who also wrote aesthetic essays such as *Dialogues on the Fundamental Principles of Beauty*,
6. From a hymn "Scatter the germs of the Beautiful."
7. Adam Smith, *Theory of the Moral Sentiments*, 1759 and later editions.
8. Ptolemaic system starts by assuming that the Earth is stationary and at the centre of the universe.
9. Charles Dickens, *The Cricket on the Hearth*, c. 1868. Caleb is a toymaker.
10. John Ruskin, *Pre-Raphaelitism. by the Author of Modern Painters* (Smith, Elder & Co: London, 1851) p. 7.
11. Demidoff factory exhibit. See illustration in *Exhibition of the Works of Industry of All Nations, 1851: Reports by the Juries on the Subjects in the Thirty Classes into Which the Exhibition was Divided* (London: W. Clowes and Sons, 1852), Vol III.
12. C. Dresser, *Development of Ornamental Art in the International Exhibition: Being a Concise Statement of the Laws Which Govern the Production and Application of Ornament with Reference to the Best Examples* (London: Day and Son, 1862) p. 117.
13. George Augustus Sala (1828–1895), an author and journalist.
14. G.A. Sala, *Notes and Sketches of the Paris Exhibition* (London: Tinsley Brothers, 1868), p. 344–55. Sideboard is shown in *Illustrated London News* 7 December 1867.

19

LUCAS BAKER, *THEORY OF DESIGN*

Lucas Baker was one-time Supervisor of Drawing in the public schools of the city of Boston, working under Walter Smith, and was later associated with the art school that was linked with the Metropolitan Museum of Art, New York. It is worth noting Walter Smith's comments on the role of art schools, in connection with the teaching of drawing which would have influenced Baker:

> A school of art, then, should be designed upon the assumption that the knowledge of elementary drawing in such subjects as free-hand, model, geometric, and simple linear perspective drawing has already been acquired; and its mission is to take up the student upon his leaving the day-school, and carry on his general art education to a higher level firstly, and guide it in a special direction afterwards. The school should be to artisans what the university is to the professional man; and to such professions as those of the architect and engineer it should be a professional school also.[1]

A brief notice in the American *Journal of Education* commented that Baker's *The Theory of Design* . . . 'gives a masterly presentation of the true principles of inventive art. The work is divided into three parts: (1) the text proper, liberally illustrated; (2) a series of original designs made by a class of pupils under the instruction of the author; and (3) a collection of plant forms (natural and conventional) for use as elements of design.'[2]

Baker's attitude to decoration is evident in this passage from the book, which is very reminiscent of comments made by reformers thirty years earlier.

> With reference to the use of real pictures of birds, beasts, fishes, landscapes, and human figures in the decoration of dinner-services, there seems to be an evident impropriety in roast meats and gravies swimming over a sunset sky, . . . or a thicket where unsuspecting quail are feeding. Such have the sanction of use in high quarters, though the want of great wealth will prevent the mass of the people from indulging in such questionable taste'.
>
> (p.87)

In his conclusion, Baker reiterates the role of laws and principles of design: 'We have endeavored to present the subject of design in its dependence upon certain fixed laws which govern the mind with reference to its inevitable action in the contemplation of the beautiful'.[3]

In 1885, Jane C. Croly's *Needlework* used Baker's text to explain conventionalising to 'the embroiderer who wishes to attempt her own construction of patterns'. She explains how the issue of conventionalising 'a flower or figure, is an expression of hidden significance to many. Its true definition, we have found, is this: "When the general or geometrical form of a leaf, or flower, or sprig, is drawn, with many of the minor features and accidental markings omitted, the leaf, flower, or sprig is said to be conventionalized; that is to say, the natural form has been converted into a form suitable only for ornament."'[4]

The positivist origins of Baker's ideas are clearly found in the earlier work of Dyce and others. In his other major publication, *The Science and Art of Model and Object Drawing* Baker makes his ideas very explicit. 'The subject of Object-Drawing has a basis of fact throughout. There is no guess-work; mathematical precision pervades the whole; every question can be settled by reference to fundamental principles'.[5]

Lucas Baker, *Theory of Design: A Treatise on the Theory and Practice of Design and the Methods of Instruction Suited to Teachers, Designers, and Art-Students, and a Text-Book for Schools* (New York: Ivison, Blakeman, Taylor, and Co, 1883), pp. 5–13

Utility and Beauty

> This love of beauty is taste.
> The creation of beauty is art.
>
> EMERSON.[6]

There is a general demand for that which is accounted beautiful. We are not satisfied with utility alone, but we must have beauty combined with it. "Every man," says Emerson, "values every acquisition he makes in the science of beauty above his possessions." Again the same author says, "The most useful man in the most useful world, so long as only commodity was served, would remain unsatisfied. But, as fast as he sees beauty, life acquires a high value."[7]

All men desire the beautiful as they desire wealth; and nature seconds the desire, and giveth beauty to everything of life. It is evident, that, if it were easy to set down categorically the principles of beauty, it would not be so difficult to make beautiful objects by following them. But these principles are neither easy to define, nor to understand, and to put into practical application when defined. Hogarth imagined that he had found *the line* of beauty. Many philosophers have tried to define beauty; but they do not agree whether it is a thing, a principle, a process, a manifestation, or a combination: and it may be, after all, that there are many kinds and many degrees of beauty.

It is evident, however, that, to produce a beautiful design, we must know upon what fundamental principles we can proceed, in order to work out our results with any degree of certainty.

We shall find that beauty depends very much upon a variety of ideas, distinct from the purely useful, and does not inhere in a simple or in a single quality.

To design beautiful things, we must proceed upon the fundamental principles of beauty,—a method of arrangement and association, according to certain fixed rules; and these accord with certain psychological necessities of every cultivated mind. We must then become acquainted with the aesthetic law of distribution and arrangement. "Beauty," says Emerson, "is the form under which [the] intellect prefers to study the world."[8] We must study the necessities of the mind with reference to what it demands in the beautiful, so as to fulfill the conditions it imposes upon us.

The Nature of Beauty

The ultimate art principle is the law for the production of the beautiful. Beauty is the combination of the qualities we love. It is not a thing, but an effect. Beauty is the external sign of conformity to the internal law of harmonic construction. With reference to organic law it is the stamp of excellence, hence it approximates virtue as to moral qualities. "Beauty is the mark God sets upon virtue."[9]

Ideas of beauty accompany and are co-ordinate with the desire to attain the perfect ideal. Not to love the beautiful is to be content with the uncultured. As all true culture tends to human perfection, and the attainment of the ideal; so it tends to create in man the love of the beautiful.

Art is the effort of man to express this love. Utility feeds, warms, clothes, and defends; but beauty satisfies the heart, engages the affections, exalts the mind, as it hallows the soul. It is the source of poetry, music, and art.

"Ideas of beauty," says Ruskin, "are among the noblest which can be presented to the human mind, invariably exalting and purifying it according to their degree."[10]

In nature utility and beauty are one; that is, they are produced by the same cause: and so the laws of utility and beauty are one. The shell of the fish is not only useful as a house and a hidingplace, but it is also beautiful in its color and structure and texture. Autumn-leaves must needs go through the whole gamut of warm colors in passing from the green of summer to the sear, dry state in which November winds find them. The decaying log or stump must become a garden for thousands of beautiful lichens and mosses, more beautiful than anything which art can create. The snow must appear white, green, blue, red, or purple, according as it is in sunlight or shadow, or as the light of the sky is one tint or another. Even a white house appears green against a purplish eastern sky at sunset. Nature is lavish of her luxuries, and beauty is the greatest luxury. It costs her nothing, because it is an *incident* of her utilities. Nature does nothing without adornment. She is the engineer and the artist in one; and her ornaments are not "applied," but are inherent in all her activities. Therefore we act in the line of nature when all our acts and works become beautiful as well as useful.

The Law of Construction

If the subject of design has no basis of law to which its methods may be referred, and which may form the basis of true criticism, then all opinions as to excellency are mere opinions, worthy of no attention whatever; and the whole subject must be given over to the sport of mere fashion, caprice, or fancy: and the limit of his imagination is the only restraint placed upon the designer. In that case criticism will be useless, and conduce to no end. But if, on the contrary, there is a basis of fundamental law, which has its sanction in psychological necessities, then the whole subject is no longer one of chaos and contradiction, but one of order and sequence; and its principles and rules can be set down and defined, and a system of just criticism may exist, and certainty may take the place of doubt.

The forms under which design appears are very numerous, and the application varied; yet a few classes will comprehend the whole. First, there is design as applied to structural forms with reference to the distribution and form of masses, individual and concrete. Under this head all architectural forms would be included, and also landscape gardening.

Second, we have design as applied to surface decoration. This again divides itself into two parts,—*a*, the decoration of surface or mural space by forms in relief; and *b*, the decoration of surface by forms in the flat. There is still another application of design in higher art, where questions of composition and arrangement in pictures and statues arise. But, as all these forms are amenable to precisely the same laws of composition, there is no necessity that they should be considered apart.

We propose, then, to study the distribution of forms in surface decoration. For purposes of ornament, a surface is supposed to be broken into various masses. There is to be the act of segregation before we come to the act of arrangement. Literally the surface is to be broken into pieces before we can arrange the fragments. The laws of design determine the relative size and forms of the associated magnitudes, and their co-ordination and distribution. These laws we propose to investigate with reference to their relation to and dependence upon certain psychological principles.

Every simple element used in design must have each of the following qualities magnitude, form, position, direction, relation. Each of these qualities must be graded and co-ordinated with each other according to the laws of rhythmical* and

---

* All good composition is rhythmical in this sense, that there are at certain intervals constantly recurring masses which are emphatic from the fact that they possess superior magnitude to those immediately preceding and succeeding. These emphatic masses become the resting-places for the eye in its movement over the design.

harmonic arrangement. The harmonizing of all the attributes of the elements used in design constitutes the essential art principle.

Hence design is the art of arranging forms, magnitudes, lines, and colors (where colors are used) in such a manner as to produce a pleasing effect upon the mind of the beholder. Or, we may say that design is the art of breaking a given surface into different magnitudes and forms, arranged to express harmony, rhythm, unity, fullness, richness, and all other qualities which we like, and which can be conveniently expressed; so that the whole space produces a pleasing effect upon the mind. If it is rhythmical and harmonic, it is music to the eye. Schelling called architecture "frozen music."[11] The quality of the ideas expressed determines the quality of the design.

If, for any reason, a design does not please, it shows that the work is a failure; as the object has not been attained. As designs for ornament, like pictures, are intended to please *all* cultivated persons alike, it becomes important for the designer to know upon what mental and psychological conditions pleasure and displeasure depend; *and if it is* found that certain qualities and conditions are always liked by all cultivated minds, and that certain other qualities are always disliked by the same minds, he will have a sure guide to his efforts, and can proceed on sure grounds to accomplish what he has undertaken.

The Conditions of Pleasure

It will be perceived, then, that the study of design begins with the study of conditions of our likes and dislikes.

The question is, then, by what is the mind pleased, and by what is it displeased? Let us set down some of the characteristics in external objects which are pleasing to the human mind. We delight in the evidences of forethought and invention. We like fullness, roundness, diversity combined into symmetry, system, unity, harmony, rhythm, relationship, broadness (or breadth), vastness, grandeur. We like justice and propriety, and fitness and adaptation, likeness in things dissimilar, contrast and picturesqueness. We are pleased with strength and durability. These are some of the principal qualities which always give pleasure to the mind.

The opposites of these qualities we do not like in anything, except where utility makes them indispensable. We dislike hollowness, barrenness, meagerness, incompleteness, poverty, spareness. So also disorder, disjointedness, and chaos; incongruities, alienation, unjustness, narrowness, and littleness in a certain sense. We all dislike monotony. We do not like to see the evidence of thoughtlessness, foolishness, or imbecility.

Now, we are all agreed in liking the one class of these qualities, and in disliking the other class. So, too, we shall agree in liking those works of art which show the one class, and in disliking those which exhibit the other class.

Let us state here a principle to be observed in all *art*: it is, that *no quality or excellence, however good or lovely when in its true place and relation, can satisfy the mind when often repeated out of its true place and relation, and left without sufficient contrast by opposing qualities.* Without it, all is chaos. In other words, every element in art must have its true *setting* or environment to give it value. No quality is good of itself. The curve of beauty, or "Hogarth's curve,"[12] if often repeated without proper contrast, becomes anything but the curve of beauty. Beauty comes by combination, and does not inhere in special forms.

The harmonic arrangement of magnitudes and forms, of colors and lights and shades, must prevail in every design, to cover space, however much the design may be influenced by special ideas of style, motive, or peculiarity of any kind. These ideas of style, and the like, are superadded to the rhythmical and harmonic arrangements, without in any way superseding or disturbing them. There are many possible ideas which may enter into a design without in any way affecting the general law of construction as above stated, such as picturesqueness, grotesqueness, surprise, contrast, harmoniousness, oddities, conceits of fashion; expressions of softness, smoothness, roughness, or ruggedness; lively and exciting, or quiet and reposeful; ideas of forms which are modern or ancient, foreign or domestic, and native; paradoxical, comical or funny, or staid and commonplace. These, and other ideas of significant character, may find place or expression in ordinary surface decoration, independent of the laws of distribution.

The comprehension of these fundamental laws of design will enable the student to understand the meaning of his work, and give a broader application to the ever varying fancies of his mind.

All good pictures are wrought out by the distribution, over the surface of the canvas, panel, or paper, of certain related forms, magnitudes, lines, and colors.

There are these four separate kinds of qualities to be harmonized into a united result, and there are certain methods by which they may be combined so as to produce the desired effect.

Hence harmonious arrangement in design requires that these elements should be so grouped that they will present to the eye and mind a family likeness and relationship; so that it will seem the most natural thing in the world for them to belong to each other, and to be brought together in that place, and for that particular purpose.

It will be seen, therefore, that an ingenious compound of unrelated elements does not make a design, but that a complete understanding of the laws of combination is essential in order to make it possible to give expression to the grand and the beautiful.

Notes

1 W. Smith, et al., *Art Education, Scholastic and Industrial* (Boston Mass.: James R. Osgood and Co., 1872), p. 76.
2 *Journal of Education*, 17–18, 1883, p. 410.
3 L. Baker, *A Treatise on the Theory and Practice of Design and the Methods of Instruction Suited to Teachers, Designers, and Art-Students, and a Text-Book for Schools* (New York: Ivison, Blakeman, Taylor, and Co., 1883), p. 107.
4 J. C. Croly, *Needle Work: A Manual of Stitches and Studies in Embroidery and Drawn Work* (New York: A. L. Burt, 1885), p. 126.

5 L. Baker, *The Science and Art of Model and Object Drawing: A Text Book for Schools and for Self-instruction of Teachers and Art-students in the Theory and Practice of Drawing from Objects* (New York: Ivison, Blakeman, Taylor, and Company, 1883), p. 6.
6 R. W. Emerson, 'Nature', *The Prose Works of Ralph Waldo Emerson; in Two Volumes* (Boston: J.R. Osgood and Co, 1878). p. 15.
7 Emerson, 'Beauty', *The Prose Works of Ralph Waldo Emerson; in Two Volumes*, p. 471.
8 Emerson, *Beauty*.
9 Emerson, *Nature*.
10 J. Ruskin, *Modern Painters*, Vol. 1, Chapter 6, "Ideas of Beauty" 1843.
11 Friedrich von Schelling (1775–1854), German philosopher, author of *Philosophie der Kunst* (1809) (Stuttgart: Cotta, 1859), p. 593.
12 Hogarth's curve: According to his theory, described in his 1753 book *Analysis of Beauty*, the S-shaped curved lines signify liveliness and activity as opposed to straight lines, which signify inactivity and inertness.

20

WALTER CRANE, 'DESIGN IN RELATION TO USE AND MATERIAL'

The book was published in 1892 with a second English edition in 1898, followed by a German edition in 1902, then a Dutch translation in 1903, demonstrating the interest in Crane's work in Europe. Indeed, Crane was a friend of Hermann Muthesius, the author of *The English House* which espoused many Art and Crafts ideas: indeed, some of Crane's work was published in this book. An American edition of the *Claims of Decorative Art* was published in 1922.

In the introduction to his volume Crane argues for a unity of arts, under the umbrella of architecture: 'While maintaining the first importance of the arts and crafts of design as contributing to the formation of a fine sense of beauty —a sense which grows by what it feeds on, I have dwelt upon the necessity of harmonious relation in all the arts, and a return to their primal unity in architecture. In this fraternal unity none is before or after the other, none is greater or less than the other'.[1]

Not surprisingly, with Crane's involvement in the socialist movement, one of the chapters in this book is titled 'The Prospects of Art under Socialism', and another is titled 'Art and Social Democracy'. This was enough to infuriate some critics. *The National Observer*, a Conservative (Tory) British (1888 to 1897) magazine published a cutting review of the book, attacking Crane's socialist leanings in particular. Having acknowledged that 'the worthless is always popular', the reviewer goes on to say:

> The decorative artist on the other hand is never so happy as when he is denouncing, in the most turbulent English, the "rapacity of competitive commerce" and falling the loquacious tear over "the sympathetic work of associated workers". For Mr Crane, "all things are absorbed in the organisation of labour"; and, therefore, with an exquisite logic he labels his essays which deal with vague history and vaguer economics "The Claims of Decorative Art".

The review adds 'in spite of the Fabian Society [art] is still the toy of wealth, or of culture, which is only an intellectual expression of wealth . . . we are weary of this eternal confusion of art with politics, of the wearisome and circular argument that Socialism is a short-cut to artistic achievement'.[2]

To balance this, the reviewer in the *Pall Mall Gazette* was much more supportive, noting 'An interesting chapter on design in relation to use and material [which] could easily bear expansion, and we hope that Mr Crane may someday devote a full volume to his analysis of decorative forms and their relation to material'.[3]

He did indeed publish more work, including *The Bases of Design* (London: Bell & Co., 1898); *Line and Form* (London: George Bell & Co., 1900), and *Ideals in Art* (London: George Bell & Co., 1905).

Walter Crane, 'Design in Relation to Use and Material', *The Claims of Decorative Art* (London: Lawrence and Bullen, 1892), pp. 90–105

THE fundamental importance of design, and its claims to consideration, will hardly be disputed, particularly at a time when the advancement of art in its application or relation to industry is so much sought for. There is not a single thing we use but involves this primal necessity of design in some degree, which has not demanded some exercise of human thought, some measure of ingenuity, some kind of plan, to fit it for its purpose, or to commend itself to our sense of beauty. And here it may be said, although art in this sense is generally termed "applied art," strictly speaking, all forms of art, properly understood, come under this head, and that there is no such thing as *un*applied art—or, if there is, we may say then it is not art at all.

The gist of the whole matter lies in this application. Design in all its forms is governed by the relative spirit. In making a design, even of the simplest kind, important considerations and questions immediately arise—questions of *scale*, of *treatment*, of *material*, of *position*, of *use*, which finally decide its character; and in the solution of such questions lie at once the business and the success of the designer and craftsman.

Now the first of these considerations is SCALE. This is determined by the size of the object or surface we deal with, its use, and its relation to its surroundings: as the relation of the axe-head to its handle, the unit of a pattern, the height and proportions of a chair—what, in short, we may call architectural considerations. Fitness of scale is of course primarily determined in relation to the scale and proportions of man himself, who is naturally the standard and measure by which all work for the use and pleasure of humanity is finally checked. You would not, for instance, carve colossal heads on chair backs; or, on the other hand, try to make a chimney-pot look like a miniature cathedral spire! These, of course, are extreme instances.

There is a certain natural logic and common sense of proportion which keeps us tolerably straight in these matters, while it allows a sufficiently indefinite margin for individual taste and variety of character.

There exist obvious reasons, as well as natural feeling, in favour of decoration intended to be near the eye, or upon objects to be handled or used, being small in scale and finely worked; and though, in that perpetual readjustment and inventive adaptation in the control of the designer there is always scope for variety, behind all he is conscious of the pressure of relative considerations—of natural law, in fact.

Then we come to the great question of TREATMENT, in which lies folded, as it were, like the flower in the bud, the very virtue and essence of art.

To begin with, the designer, in the application of his art to material and use, has to put away from him the allurements of imitative naturalism, except in so far as they can be made to contribute and be subordinated to the effect and purpose of his work as a whole. He soon perceives the natural cleavage between nature and art—between the accidental picturesqueness of confused detail, broken surface-lights, and shadows, and definite, selected, related, and expressive forms and lines. He may be likened to a child with a handful of wooden letters out of which he has to construct words and sentences. Nature and the history of art is the vast encyclopaedia of fact and form and phase out of which the poet and the artist have to choose the materials for their work.

A painter pure and simple is, of course, much less restricted, much less weighted with relative considerations, than the designer, and is at liberty, governed only by the necessary internal relation of his work, to avail himself of effects beyond the scope of the maker of tapestries or mosaics, the painter of glass, or the carver. Yet, curiously enough, in our industrial century the influence of the easel-picture painter has been paramount. He has ridden (I will not say in triumph) over our household furniture, he has trampled on our hearthrugs and carpets, he has left his impress on our napery and antimacassars; his influence, in fact, can be traced from our faience to our fish-slice; and this perhaps because, owing chiefly to industrial and economic conditions, the term art and artist came to be limited to pictorial work and its producer,—since the modern easel-picture painter was until lately the only form of craftsman working independently, and with anything like complete control of his own work.

We are recovering, however, I think. We are realising the difference between pictorial and decorative art, between *imitative* and *constructive* design. It will do us no harm, as a corrective to our pictorial excesses, to draw the line very sharply between the two,—to put, metaphorically, the decorative sheep on the one hand, and the pictorial goats on the other. For we must remember there are two sides to art, with distinct aims. They may be characterised as "*aspect*" and "*adaptation*": the one seeking rather to imitate planes and surfaces, accidental lighting, phases and effects; the other constructive, depending on its beauty, on qualities of line and form and tint, unaffected by accidental conditions, seeking typical rather than individual forms, and ornamental rather than realistic results.

The first necessity in designing is Definition. Hence LINE is all-important. Let the designer, therefore, in the adaptation of his art, lean upon the staff of *line,—* line determinative, line emphatic, line delicate, line expressive, line controlling and uniting. It cannot lead him wrong; it will never deceive him. He will always know where he is weak, and where he is indecisive, where he has hesitated, and where he has been confident. It will be the solid framing of his structure—the bones and marrow of his composition.

In line alone, having regard to all its different degrees of tenuity, the designer possesses a means of expression of considerable force and sympathetic range. It lends itself to the most sensitive and delicate definition in a fine pen, pencil, or silver-point drawing, and it is capable of the utmost strength and architectural solidity, as in the emphatic outlines necessary to express the pattern and bring out the qualities of the material in large mosaic decorations and stained glass; where, too, other considerations come in, as the tesserae (Fig. 20.2) of the one, and the lead lines (Fig. 20.1) and color scheme in the other.

Fig. 20.1

Fig. 20.2

And here we come to another essential element in designing: we cannot touch what may be called the exigencies of particular materials, or begin to define our cartoon or pattern in line without perceiving the necessity of proceeding upon some kind of system in the treatment of form and detail.

In purely pictorial work, of course, this is not felt to the same degree, though the necessity *is* present even there, since we cannot work with Nature's own materials. We cannot dip our brush in liquid sunshine on the one hand, or have the blackness of night upon our palette on the other. We have not her greens or her reds, and gold and blue, in our boxes; we cannot command the full colours of the sunset or the dawn; so that with the most uncompromising realist the result is after all a compromise, a question of translation, adjustment to a scale, and more or less figurative expression. The same as regards minuteness of detail. Do we paint for the eye at such and such a distance, the photographic lens, or the microscope? A little nearer or a little farther, and all the conditions are changed. The fact is, as I have said, *all* art is conditioned; it is only a question of degree, and it is the successful demonstration and determination of these degrees which mark the difference between one kind of art and another, between one artist and another.

There is of course no absolute determination of rules for all cases. There is nothing absolute in art. *Art is not science.* The way is perpetually open for new experiments, for new expositions, and new adaptations and applications, which makes the pursuit of art in all its forms so peculiarly fascinating, and ever fresh and inspiring.

But to return to the question of System. Now supposing we wanted to make a pattern of a rose for a wall-paper. We might pick one from our garden (if we had one, as indeed every designer ought to have) and sketch it exactly as we found it—a portrait, as near as we could make it, of an individual rose with all its accidental characteristics. Well, we might make an interesting study, certainly, but when we came to apply it we should perceive that it made, however good as a study, a very poor pattern, and its virtue and interest as a drawing would be at once destroyed directly our pictorial rose was repeated—which we should be driven to do. We should practically get the repetition of a more or less shapeless blot, a *formal* and *regular repetition* of an *informal* and *naturalistic drawing*—a contradiction in terms, in fact. Yet it is a thing that has been attempted over and over again. A sentimental public perhaps likes roses, in season and out of season, and considers perhaps that a rose in any material would, if not smell, at least look as sweet. It may be so, but if it be not sweet and clear in line and disposition, and organic as a pattern, its sweetness is wasted on the desert air of false art and taste and failure in decoration.

Therefore it is that the designer, having regard to the conditions of ornamental effect and relation to use and material, proceeds in a very different way. He finds that a certain formalism is an essential condition of his work, seeing that his aim is to adorn a space pleasantly, to construct a pattern that will bear repetition, or rather demand it, as another essential condition of its existence. He finds therefore that typical and abstract forms are of more value for the purpose than accidental ones; that suggestion is better in decoration than naturalistic or pictorial imitation. He would naturally, in taking a rose as his theme, recur to the primitive and fundamental type—to the simple flower as we see it on the parent stem of the wild rose of our hedges (Fig. 20.3). With such a type as this he could safely make a diaper or simple sprigged arrangement which would be satisfactory as far as it went. (Fig. 20.4)

Fig. 20.3

Fig. 20.4

Nor, let it be observed, is the designer, in following such principles, departing from nature necessarily. Nay, in his way he may be expressing as much natural truth even as the pictorial artist: as we have seen that truth of aspect is one thing, and truth of construction and detail another; while in following the necessities of adaptation to use and material the designer is only carrying out in the region of art the great principle of Nature herself, which rules through all forms of life,—that necessity of adaptation to conditions, which, as we have learned, has led to the endless variety of development in both plant and animal form that we see on every side.

The necessity of plan in designing next makes itself felt, and is of course very important, and capable of almost any degree of extension and complexity, although designs for extension on walls or hangings generally fall into recognisable classes with different variations. Starting with our diaper, square or diagonal, which may be considered the simplest, we may build our pattern upon a great variety of foundations (Fig. 20.5). But we shall find it necessary to build upon *some* plan, as a plan is as essential to a pattern as the skeleton to the human figure, though you may eventually conceal it as much as the skeleton is concealed by the human form, or more, by superadded enrichment, detail, and intricacy. How far to go in this way the nature of the material and its uses will generally decide.

Fig. 20.5

As to colour treatment, again, the best decorative effect does not demand the use of heavy shading or relief. The colours should be pure and fair, and the true local colours of all things should be sought, unaffected by accidental lights and shadows, as if we saw everything in an evenly diffused or flat light.

In modelling, or any treatment where the means of expression and ornamental effect is by relief, of course the question is different, though here again the gist of the matter lies in treatment, and there is all the difference in the world between one treatment and another.

Now of course the strictest observance of such principles in designing as I have indicated will not necessarily ensure an interesting pattern, though they would suffice to produce a workable one. Other considerations come in as we advance. Plan involves the consideration of the proportion and relation of our masses, and beauty of silhouette. Draw a figure with a big head, and it at once looks ridiculous (this seems so taken for granted by the many, that comic draughtsmen have subsisted upon it for years), while with a head of the natural proportion it may have grace and dignity. The same principle holds good in ornamental designing, and a beautiful result very largely depends upon a due recognition of the importance of proportions. It does not follow that these proportions are those of nature, as in a naturalistic picture. In a decorative design, to serve our ornamental purpose, one may depart widely from them, as in the relative size of trees and figures and flowers and animals, etc., where there is no approach to naturalistic representation, as in designs for textiles and other things.

DESIGN IN RELATION TO USE AND MATERIAL

The important thing to preserve is the relation of masses, the organic and necessary connection arising out of the constructive necessities. In pattern work *three proportions* are generally felt desirable. You cannot jump at a bound from large to small, therefore an intermediate scale is useful as in illustration (Fig. 20.6).

Fig. 20.6

The masses of the tree and the pot are combined by the forms of the birds, and further, by the thin stems and leaves behind.

Silhouette, again, is a very important consideration in designing. It is a very good practice to block out one's design in silhouette in the first instance, as this will afford the best test of the relations and proportions of its masses possible, and of its variety. One does not seek to arrange a figure exactly symmetrically, (as at A Fig. 20.7) except under very formal conditions. That at B is felt to be a more agreeable treatment. The more variety in contour, the more beauty we get.

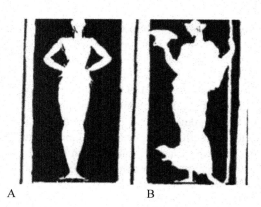

Fig. 20.7

The best practice in effective and ornamental use of silhouette is to be found in designing patterns for stencilling, where everything depends upon it. You block out a pattern in flat color—light on dark, or dark on light—in such a way that it is capable of being cut out of a sheet of card or zinc without breaking, so that by painting over the perforated part, which is the pattern, it is transferred to any ground you desire. Fig. 20.8 shows two sketches of stencil patterns; the halves to repeat.

Fig. 20.8

Another important consideration in designing is the adequate filling of the space for which your design is intended.

Now here again pictorial proclivities have been very misleading. They have led us, in illustrating books for instance, to that inorganic way of loosely vignetting a subject—splashing a landscape upon or across a page without regard to its mechanical conditions, and ignoring its necessary relation to the type. Instances of this kind of treatment are to be found notably in our illustrated magazines of Continental or American origin, which have been setting the fashion in so-called page decoration of late years. But this inorganic, unrelated kind of designing has not confined itself to books. You may find it anywhere and everywhere almost,— dabbed upon fans, dragged across cupboard doors, and generally upset over the unconsidered trifles of everyday life.

I am afraid, too, that something is traceable to Japanese influence. But it does not at all follow that, because a Japanese artist, with his wonderful knowledge of nature and precision of touch, can throw a flowering branch, or bird, or a fish across a sheet of paper, or a panel, with such consummate skill as to delude us into the belief that he has decorated the space, therefore any one, with very inferior powers of draughtsmanship, can go and do likewise with equal *éclat*. It is somewhat like attempting tightrope dancing before one can walk properly on the ground.

The truth is that all the solid and determinative motives in design are traceable to the influence of architectural style. In the absence of a living style in architecture, the arts of design, which are really its offspring, languish, and lose at once their fitness, monumental dignity, and importance.

For style is strictly the sum of considerations like the foregoing—with individual feeling superadded. It is the quality which collects and concentrates, as it were, the virtue and essence of the past, and fuses it with the present. It consists in that highly selective impulse or instinct which gives an artist's work its own peculiar and distinctive character, without isolating him or disconnecting him from the work that has gone before, or the work of his own day, so that a great design is in fact a link, or a luminous point or jewel, in a long golden chain, and necessarily dependent upon its continuity.

Style, of course, is a very different thing from what are known as "styles." It is the difference between the quick and the dead. We can get decorations "in any style" nowadays to order. We can be Ancient Egyptian, or Greek, or Roman, or Pompeian, or Byzantine, or Celtic, or Italian, or German, Gothic or Renaissance, whichever we please, Louis Quatorze or Louis Seize—worse luck,—but none of them seems to please for long, perhaps because their designers and producers are only "pleasing to live," as is the proverbial fate of those who "live to please." Ours is the age for masquerading, because we have no particular *reality* of our own—no style, in short. But we cannot be always masquerading, however amusing it may be once in a while, and whatever superior advantages we possess for getting at the best authorities. The motley and fantastic crowd palls at last, and we are glad to get back to everyday, if plain, habiliments, wherein we can at least feel at home.

It is this feeling "at home," too—which is so important in design—which marks the difference between artist and archaeologist. Ease and mastery of expression in any material is the aim of the designer, while keeping strictly within the limitations of that material.

In making a working drawing the designer should be mentally, if not actually, the craftsman also: the conditions and necessities of the material ever present to his mind; its very limitations suggesting new motives, and stimulating invention, as it never fails to do when the designer and the craftsman are one.

So, too, where there has been no conscious aim at decorative beauty, we find beauty of result, at least as regards the all-important quality of line, which goes to prove that organic lines, or lines of construction, at least where the construction is simple and evident to the eye, are usually beautiful lines, as in the sickle, the scythe, plough, ship, bridge, and wagon, for instance, and that this relation to material and use is a fundamental and necessary quality of all design.

Mistakes are usually made in the attempts to beautify by superadded ornament, unrelated to the object, use, and material, instead of treating it as a natural outgrowth, so that the absence of ornament is preferable to ornament not beautiful, or to ornament, however beautiful in itself, which does not decorate. And indeed, unless ornament is organic in this sense, we had much better be without it, and trust to the simple beauty of constructional lines alone.

Now this decline of organic design, it can hardly be doubted, is traceable in a great measure to the economic conditions and the development of machine industry in the interests of a commercial system of centralisation and a world-market which have characterised our century, and which have succeeded the system of division of labour developed in the last, as that succeeded, as Mr. Morris has often pointed out, the older system of local production for use; and this *because* its effect has been to *separate the designer and the craftsman*, and to turn both more or less into machines. The effect of this is to throw the designer out of sympathy with the use and material of his design, to cut him off from the suggestive and inventive stimulus of the material, while, under the pressure of competition, forcing him to the constant production of so-called novelties, while it turns the craftsman or mechanic into an indifferent tool. The results are precisely what might have been expected, and what we have seen. In fact, the only wonder is they are not worse; but humanity has always been better than its systems.

As to the craftsman, the workman, he, perhaps, relegated to the performance of one monotonous function—a unit in a long sum of industrial production,—becomes but a part of a machine, his personality merged in the general description of 'hands' (a designation, by the way, which does not encourage the development of brains), and, in short, all personal interest and identity with his work as a whole taken away, and leaving him with no prospect of winning public and personal appreciation—even if a "fortythousandth part," as Carlyle would have said,[4] of a product could reasonably hope to win such things—since all credit for the finished result is practically claimed by the employer.

These things being so, I say it is not wonderful our "industrial art," as we call it, *is* what it is.

What then should we aim at? If this is the *real* condition of affairs, what is the *ideal*? For unless we consider we are living under the best possible arrangements—social, political, and industrial—we must entertain an ideal of some sort, even if it be a stranger, like an angel unawares.

Well, then, if so far you are disposed to agree with me (firstly) as to the necessary conditions and considerations for the production of well-designed decorations and accessories of daily life, from the roof which shelters us to the cup we drink out of; (secondly) as to the relation of the designer and producer of these necessities—for I claim that beautiful things are a necessity of any reasonable and refined human life; and (thirdly) as to the condition of the producer of such things himself,—then we shall have reached the conclusion that for the production of beautiful and thoughtful work you must have conditions of life wherein beauty and thought have opportunity to germinate and grow naturally, and as a matter of course, out of the conditions of daily life and work, as naturally as the apple-tree blooms in the spring. But this means no less than that the conditions of health and refinement, of a vigorous and full if simple life, be open to *all*, both men and women, without distinction; and before such conditions can be realised it evidently implies that something like fundamental changes must take place in the constitution of society.

Then it comes to this, that all we have to make up our minds about are two things:—(1) Whether we consider art as an utterly unrelated, individual, and accidental matter; or (2) whether we consider it and its beautiful results as the highest outcome of life, and as necessarily dependent upon the character, ideals, and conditions of that life. If the latter, then it may be worthwhile to take such steps as may be within our power and mental vision to co-operate towards the realisation of such a life and such an ideal, which, strange and roundabout a method as it appears, will yet prove the shortest way to our goal, namely, a true revival of design in its relation to material and use.

Notes

1. W. Crane, *The Claims of Decorative Art* (London: Lawrence And Bullen, 1892), p. vi.
2. *National Observer*, 8, 185, 4 June 1892, pp. 69–70.
3. 'Some Recent Art Books', *Pall Mall Gazette*, 2 July 1892.
4. Carlyle: "Is not Carlyle perfectly right when he sneers at that kind of 'liberty' which consists in having, as a voter has in our country, a forty-thousandth part of a Talker in our 'National Palaver?' And even that Talker, though he is called my representative, may not, to that infinitesimal fraction represent me". Cited in L. Gronlund, *The Co-Operative Common-Wealth in Its Outlines: An Exposition of Modern Socialism* (London: Sonnenschein, 1886) p. 160.

21

SELWYN IMAGE, 'OF DESIGN AND THE STUDY OF NATURE'

The National Association for the Advancement of Art and its Application to Industry was founded in 1887. A. H. Mackmurdo, the editor of this work, was the Honorary Secretary, so he was able to promote the ideals of the arts and crafts movement, as well as the beliefs of the individuals involved. The movement was seen as probably the best bridge between art and industry. This work was published in association with the National Association for the Advancement of Art, with essays from leading practitioners including W.R. Lethaby on Cabinet-making, E. Roscoe Mullins on Modelling and Carving, Ernest W. Gimson on Plaster-work, Reginald Blomfield on Metal-work, May Morris on Embroidery, and Heywood Sumner on Stencil-plates.

Selwyn Image (1849–1930) was an artist, designer, writer, and poet associated with the Arts and Crafts Movement. He was particularly associated with design work for stained glass windows, furniture, and embroidery, and he was also an illustrator of books. Selwyn Image was the first Slade Professor of Fine Art at Oxford from 1910 to 1916. He was also involved in the establishment of the Century Guild and was an active member of the Art Workers' Guild. Like many other artist/designers turned commentators, he had his own opinions and was clear in his definition of design:

> design implies two things: it implies, first of all, that we are acquainted with the essential characteristics of the natural object upon which we found our design; and, secondly, that we have imaginative cunning enough to employ these essential characteristics in an arrangement of masses and lines, which fill the space satisfactorily.[1]

None other than Oscar Wilde commented on a lecture given by Image on 'Modern Art'. Wilde particularly noted his emphasis on the role of nature:

> To stand apart from the world of nature is fatal, but it is no less fatal merely to reproduce facts. Art, in a word, must not content itself simply with holding the mirror up to nature, for it is a re-creation more than a reflection, and not a repetition but rather a new song.

Wilde completed his review in characteristic style: 'Everybody, however, was extremely pleased to learn that it is no longer the duty of art to hold the mirror up to nature, and the few Philistines who dissented from this view received that most terrible of all punishments the contempt of the highly cultured'.[2]

Image's emphasis on the links between the study of nature and design is also clear in a different article titled 'On Designing for the Art of Embroidery' where he stated:

> Learn your business in the schools, but go out to Nature for your inspirations. See Nature through your own eyes, and be a persistent and curious observer of her infinite wonders. Yet to see Nature in herself is not everything, it is but half the matter; the other half is to know how to use her for the purposes of fine art, to know how to translate her into the language of art.[3]

The British Architect also refers to this work in an 1892 article about the revival of handicrafts. 'It is a capital antidote to the sort of teaching hitherto usually available, and comprises a series of essays by artists, setting forth the principles of design and established methods of workmanship'.[4]

Selwyn Image, 'Of Design and the Study of Nature' in A. H. Mackmurdo (Ed.), *Plain Handicrafts: Being Essays by Artists Setting Forth the Principles of Design and Established Methods of Workmanship; A Guide to Elementary Practice* (London: Percival & Co., 1893), pp. 1–6

I. The present volume consists of a series of practical papers on several forms of decorative art. This paper I have been asked to write as a kind of introduction to the others: it will deal, that is to say, with matters common to them all, common to every form of fine art from the simplest to the highest; for I am asked to write about Design, and about The Study of Nature. I shall not attempt, however, to discuss these important matters exhaustively, or even at any length: I shall be content merely to put down a few thoughts by the way, which may serve, I hope, to clear the ground a little, and help you to go on working at the questions for yourselves.

II. Nowadays the word Design is constantly on our lips. It is an excellent rule not to use words, more than we can help, without having a clear sense of what we mean by them. If somebody, then, came up to me and said, "Tell me, as shortly as you can, what it is you mean by Design," I should try and answer him somewhat after this manner: "I mean by Design, the inventive arrangement of lines and masses, *regarded for their own sake*, in such a relation to one another, that they form an harmonious whole a whole, that is, towards which each part contributes; and is in such a combination with every for their own sake, in such a relation to one another, that they form an harmonious whole: a whole, that is, towards which each part contributes; and is in such a combination with every other part, that there results an unity of effect, which completely satisfies us."

In this definition let me call your attention specifically to two things. It says, that the material of Design is lines and masses regarded for their own sake: it implies, that the excellence of a design depends upon these lines and masses being so arranged as to form an harmonious or complete whole. Let me say a word or two under both these heads.

(a.) *Lines and masses regarded for their own sake*. All art is suggested to us by some natural appearance: all design is suggested by certain natural forms. The artist may have before him, let us say, a shell, a flower, a landscape, a human figure. These things are in an ascending scale of interest; the emotions, which they are capable of arousing in us, are increasingly complex and fine. But to the artist, thought of simply as a designer, simply as exercising upon them his faculty of design, they are all one and the same: he thinks what lines they give or suggest to him, what masses they give or suggest to him; he thinks of this, and of nothing more.

You will not, of course, misunderstand me. I am not asserting, that any artist can regard a beautiful human figure with no more feeling than he regards a beautiful flower. But that is, because every artist, however great a designer he may be, is necessarily, as a human being, much more than a designer. Regarding the matter, however, purely from the point of view of thought (and it is necessary to regard it thus for the purposes of analysis), just in so far as he is a designer, just in so far as he is exercising his perception and faculty of design both flower and figure are alike to him; they are simply the objects, that is to say, which give or suggest fine lines and masses.

Now, those kinds of art, in which the mere lines and masses are of obvious and supreme importance, in which pattern and shape are clearly the essential elements (as, for instance, in wall-papers, or iron-work, or pottery), have come in popular language peculiarly to be associated with the idea of Design; and those artists, whose business it is to be employed in the production of these things, are spoken of specifically as Designers. You must not imagine, however, that Design does not enter into, and is not of the greatest importance in the more complex and higher forms of art as well; in sculpture, for example, and in picture-painting. In these, also, it is of the greatest importance: so that no one can be a fine sculptor or a fine picture-painter, who is not a fine designer. But in sculpture and picture-painting there are so many other fine interests besides the interest of design, that of this latter we often in these forms of art do not take sufficient account, greatly to our loss: and in popular language we come to appropriate the terms Design and Designer to such works only as have their main interest and excellence in the character and arrangement of their lines and masses.

(b.) Secondly, the excellence of a design depends upon its lines and masses being so arranged as to form an harmonious or complete whole. It is not sufficient, that is to say, that the individual lines and masses should be in and by themselves fine: they are this, certainly, but they are more than this. They stand in a determined relation each to each, and each to the entire effect of all of them. A fine design is not a mere sequence of isolated, charming details; it is a body, as it were, composed of many members, of many necessary members, not one of which is without significance in respect of the entire effect; not one of which could be spared or altered without damage to the whole. Where everything is entirely in its right place and proportion, it is not till you come to analyse the whole that this strikes you. It is the mountain, first of all, which asserts itself; by and by you take notice of its separate rocks and stones, and of the exquisite flowers that grow round them.

III. Now let me say a few words about the study of Nature, especially about the study of it for the purposes of decoration. It is, however, with a general remark on the relation of Art to Nature that I will commence for it is very necessary, to start with, that we should have our ideas about this relation clear, whatever particular branch of art it may be that we ourselves practise.

(a.) You sometimes hear it said that art is the mirror of nature; that the sole, or at any rate the highest, end of art, that is to say, is to make a facsimile of natural appearances. This is not the place in which to enter upon an elaborate discussion of so interesting and delicate a question: I shall content myself, therefore, with asserting that such a view of the matter seems but a very superficial and misleading view; one which the more widely and deeply you consider the matter will prove itself unsound, whether you examine it by the light of reason, or by the example and teaching of the great masters of art in all countries and times. I think, then, you will find it much more correct to say, not that art is but the mirror, or facsimile, or imitation of nature, but that nature is the storehouse of materials, the storehouse of suggestive symbols, from which art draws its inspirations for the purpose of inventing its own fresh arrangements of form and colour. For art, indeed, is not, in the finest sense of it, an imitative, but a creative thing, it does not merely reflect the appearances of the world around us, but fashions out of the suggestiveness of these appearances a new, a peculiar, world of its own.

(b.) Still, nature certainly is the fountain-head; the source of inspiration, the storehouse of materials. If a man throws off the popular and superficial idea that his aim as an artist is simply to reproduce, as literally as he can, natural appearances, and says, "Never mind about nature, I shall invent out of my head," he is not only the victim of folly, but of a folly that will show itself quickly and bring him to naught: for very soon he will have exhausted his store of ideas and fancies; and then he can only live on by repeating himself, growing more and more mannered and uninteresting. No; a student of nature he must be, certainly, though not its slave; a quiet, continuous, discerning student of nature, intent upon its secrets, intent upon discovering its methods; storing up in his mind the fundamental principles which characterise nature, keeping record of its endlessly various, surprising manifestations.

(c.) In this last paragraph you will see that I have given you your clue to the proper manner of studying nature, as well as insisted on the necessity for such a study. The first, the great thing, is to look for the essential characteristics of any object before us, to understand the make of it, its anatomy and constant qualities. The present volume is concerned altogether with the purely decorative arts, but does not touch upon the use of the human figure. Let me illustrate what I mean, then, by a single and simple instance. Suppose we are going to design a pattern for embroidery, and that this pattern is to be founded on a wild rose, and that we have got a spray of wild rose in front of us for the purpose of studying it. To begin with, we deliberately will pay no attention to whatever in this spray is accidental, to any merely individual details of form or colour. We look at the typical number and shape of the petals, the typical shape and growth of the leaves, the way these join on to the stem, the growth of the stem itself, the placing of the thorns on it. When we know these things thoroughly, we know the idea, so to say, upon which all species of the wild rose are founded, and of which they are but so many various developments. Till we know these things thoroughly, we are not in a position to make a wild-rose design; we have not sufficient material to work upon, not sufficient material for our imaginative cunning to play with, and shape into a decorative pattern over the space given us to fill. For design implies two things: it implies, first of all, that we are acquainted with the essential characteristics of the natural object upon which we found our design; and, secondly, that we have imaginative cunning enough to employ these essential characteristics in an arrangement of masses and lines, which fills the space given us satisfactorily. If we have not the imaginative cunning, we simply cover the space with an inadequate and inappropriate representation of a natural object: if we have not the acquaintance with nature, we simply cover it with masses and lines that are nonsensical. Upon both these points it is impossible to lay too much emphasis.

(d.) And here I will bring this paper to an end, a paper which professes to be nothing more than suggestive. But, if you have any gift for decorative art, a suggestion or two will be of service, will open your eyes and set you along the right path. If you have no such gift, I fear that the most elaborate instructions. in the world will never make you design a single thing worth looking at; so that you had better turn your attention, without further waste, to some more appropriate and profitable industry.

Notes

1 S. Image, 'Of Design and the Study of Nature', in *Plain Handicrafts.* Ed. A. H. Mackmurdo (London: Percival & Co., 1893), p. 6.
2 'Art at Willis's Rooms', *Sunday Times*, 25 December 1887, cited in O. Wilde, *Miscellanies* (Boston: Luce, 1909), p. 89.
3 *Arts and Crafts Essays* (London: Rivington, 1893), p. 419.
4 'The Revival of the Handicrafts', *British Architect*, 1892, p. 187.

Part 5

ELEMENTS OF DESIGN

5.1

COLOUR

22

JOHN GARDNER WILKINSON, *ON COLOUR AND ON THE NECESSITY FOR A GENERAL DIFFUSION OF TASTE AMONG ALL CLASSES*

Sir John Gardner Wilkinson (1797–1875) was an explorer, Egyptologist and antiquarian, who like many others of his generation was interested in other cultures. One reviewer of the book commented how 'In common with all travellers in the East, Sir Gardner Wilkinson bears testimony to the singular taste displayed by the Eastern nations, especially the Arabs, in the choice and arrangement of colours'.[1]

The book's intention was to present 'canons of taste', which Wilkinson had developed in his conclusions following a tour of continental museums, and it incorporated some articles that he had already contributed to *The Builder* journal in 1855. He proposed a range of changes to the current situation in design teaching, including the development of artistic principles, by trying to reveal 'aesthetic errors', and encouraged the Sunday opening of museums and galleries so that taste could be more widely diffused. He also, like some of his contemporaries such as Owen Jones, suggested the use of Islamic sources that advocated the abstraction of nature for use in the design of British manufactured goods.

In another part of the book Wilkinson explains how he thought it was often the consumer who needed educating in terms of good taste and design:

> [He] stated that the chief impediments to the general progress and extension of taste are more attributable to the purchaser than to the makers of ornamental works. . . . It is the universal remark that those things which are bad in style find a more ready sale than the good, and that not from the price being lower, but solely from the choice of the public. If the bad happens to be attractive, it meets with admirers; and high finish, minuteness of detail, and whimsical shape, are greater recommendations than good form and purity of design.[2]

Wilkinson also takes the contemporary idea of learning by comparison, by including illustrative examples of 'good' and 'bad' taste placed in contrast.

In terms of colour, a review of this book in *The Gardeners' Chronicle* (1859) discussed the colouration of plants and their uses and considered the limits of Chevreul's[3] colour theory. They pointed out that 'Beautiful arrangements of colour depend upon taste and not upon arbitrary colour theory. This has been excellently pointed out by Sir Gardner Wilkinson'.[4]

The location of this review is less surprising when the sub-title of Wilkinson's book 'With remarks on laying out Dressed or Geometrical Gardens' is known. Incidentally, Gertrude Jekyll was later to be influenced by Chevreul's colour theories and went on to produce gardens in the opposite style to Gardner's geometric suggestions.

A very supportive review in the *Art Journal* suggested that

> Sir Gardner Wilkinson is an authority upon certain classes of artistic works, whose opinion ought not to be lightly esteemed. His long residence in the East, and the study which he gave to the ancient arts of the people among whom he dwelt, as his previous publications show, well qualify him to become an instructor at home on matters which have again induced him to appear as an author.

The garden analogy mentioned above is also made in this review. Wilkinson suggests that

> from the general arrangement of an English flower-garden and borders, [it can be seen] how universally defective is this faculty as regards colour, and he follows these remarks with several pages treating of coloured glass windows and glass mosaics, and points out the mistakes which many artists in stained glass of our own day make, when they copy, as they are apt to do, the faulty drawing or the inelegance of the figures of an early period, for the sake of giving an antique character to their work.[5]

John Gardner Wilkinson, *On Colour and on the Necessity for a General Diffusion of Taste Among All Classes, with Remarks on Laying Out Dressed Geometrical Gardens. Examples of Good and Bad Taste Illustrated by Woodcuts and Coloured Plates in Contrast* (London: J. Murray, 1858), pp. 1–4

Part 1. On Colour

§ 1. It has been generally remarked by foreigners, and as generally admitted by ourselves, that the English are very indifferent to the effect of colour for decorative or ornamental purposes. We take little pleasure in studying the harmonious arrangement of colours, either in dress, furniture, or architecture; and when the attempt is made to compose coloured designs we frequently tolerate and even admire discordant or anomalous combinations. Indeed, we sometimes maintain that bright colours not only fail to please, but are even disagreeable; and advocate the use of compound hues, neutral tints, greys, and other so-called "quiet colours," in preference to any combinations of the primaries, red, blue, and yellow, and other colours of the prism. These we often pronounce to be "gaudy." But bright colours are not necessarily gaudy. It is when bright colours are put together without due regard to their suitableness to each other, their relative quantities, or the arrangement they require, that they appear gaudy and glaring. Gaudy colours we may, in fact, define to be the union of bright hues without harmony; and no wonder the effect should be disagreeable. But this is the result of want of skill in their combination; the fault is not in the colours, but in the arrangement. Any face which is deformed, however perfect the individual features, would fail to please; while the same features, properly put together, would make it beautiful; and certain musical notes, incorrectly combined, would produce a discord, though the same properly adjusted would produce harmony. So too with colours; and we find that some, even of those who have always been indifferent to colour, or averse to the use of bright hues, are ready to acknowledge the beauty of certain harmonious combinations, and are surprised at the effect, which they expected to be gaudy and offensive. There are, however, some who are as completely insensible to the effect of such harmony as they are to that of musical sounds; others, again, have a perverted or false taste; and others are unable to distinguish colours, being affected by what is called "colour-blindness." To these three it is useless to appeal; as it would be to expect a person incapable of discovering discordant notes to have an appreciation of harmony in music. But for those who are *capable* of understanding the harmony of colour, and who only require proper instruction, it is essential that correct examples should be provided, which should be constantly set before them, as the perceptive faculties may be improved or misled by the frequent contemplation of perfect or imperfect models. It is therefore of great importance that those who give instruction in the harmony of colours should be thoroughly imbued with the true feeling for it, and should possess that natural perception which, though it may be improved, cannot be obtained by mere study.

It is not by forming a theory on some fanciful basis, that a *perception* of the harmony of colours is to be acquired. Like a correct ear for music, it is a natural gift. Theory will not form it, as theory will not enable any one to detect a false note. The power depends on the perceptive faculty; and unless anyone possess this, he will vainly attempt to lay down rules for the guidance of others. Yet we find that some have based their notions of the proper arrangement of colour *solely* on theory; and others, who might have had a proper feeling for it through their own perceptive faculty, or from the study of good models, have occasionally allowed themselves to be led astray by some plausible assertions, founded upon a fanciful basis, and supported by false *reasoning*.

The same hasty attempts have been made to lay down rules for colour as for form and proportion. These are all dependent on the perceptive faculties; and it is certainly not by *beginning with a theory* that any of the three can be taught. The Italians have a remarkable perception of true proportion, but they did not learn it from a theory, nor do they teach it by rules; and how would it be possible to define every variety of form and make them all amenable to rules ? When we hear a false note, it is not to a theory that we have recourse in order to prove it; and we can no more help seeing a discord (if we have a true *perception* of colour) than we can help being struck by a discord in music. If the ear is correct, it will detect the latter; if the eye is so, it will perceive the former. Neither the eye nor the ear can do otherwise. Theory will not supply the place of those organs; and it would be as hopeless to attempt to teach the ear to discriminate between sounds, or the nose to distinguish scents, by rule, as to substitute theory for the perceptive faculty in judging of colour. Mr. Ruskin, in his "Elements of Drawing",[6] observes that composition is unteachable, and "no one can invent by rule, though there are some simple laws of arrangement," for which he gives some very useful instructions. So too the agreement and disagreement of particular colours must depend on the power of perceiving them; and, as in judging of form and proportion, the eye can only be *assisted* by certain facts which are the result of observation, but which can never be obtained by mere theory. It is hopeless to begin by teaching this through the ear. The harmony of colour must first be learnt through the eye; and those who teach it must possess the faculty of perceiving it; but to begin with a theory is writing the grammar of a language before the language is understood. Nor is it, *at any time*, possible to reduce it to rules, like a language. And yet instances of this precipitation are constantly occurring; and instead of *guiding the eye*, which is to be the judge in such matters, there is an attempt to substitute the memory for the perception, and to charge it with rules founded upon some plausible and imaginary data. Because such and such colours stand in a certain relationship to others, or are compounded in a particular manner, it is affirmed that they must *therefore* accord or disagree with some other one; and the question asked is not whether they *do* or *do not* agree, but whether they *ought* or *ought not* to agree. [. . .]

Notes

1 Review, *British Quarterly Review*, 58, April 1859, p. 555.
2 J. G. Wilkinson, *On Colour and on the Necessity for a General Diffusion of Taste Among all Classes* (London: J. Murray, 1858), p. 359.
3 M. E. Chevreul (1786–1889), a French chemist, well known for colour theories particularly around the concept of simultaneous contrast.
4 *Gardeners' Chronicle*, 5 March 1859, p. 192.
5 Review, *Art Journal*, 1 January 1849, p. 48.
6 J. Ruskin, *Ruskin*, (Boston: Dana Estes & Co, 1856), p.358.

23

LUCY CRANE, 'COLOUR'

Lucy Crane (1842–1882) was an English writer, art critic, musician, and translator, who like many women from a similar background maintained herself by working as a teacher and governess. She wrote children's stories and nursery rhymes, and lectured in England on fine art. Her lectures were gathered and published posthumously by her brothers Thomas and Walter Crane, both providing illustrations for the book. John Ruskin, Thomas Carlyle and William Morris influenced her, and like her brothers, she held socialist views on the relationship between art and society. While she thought that Ruskin was despondent about the future of art and design, she saw Morris as being ever hopeful of change. On the topic of design, she declared, 'as Mr. Morris says, that the best designed and constructed things in a house are generally found in the kitchen; but that is because they fulfil their use, and are appropriate to their place, both of which qualities they lose when transported to the drawing-room'.[1]

Art and the Formation of Taste originated as a series of lectures that were initially delivered to pupils of her friend the teacher, Miss Janion of Harold House, Lansdowne Road, Notting Hill, then later for private courses of lectures across England. The main theme was in a typical arts and crafts manner – the application of art to everyday life.[2]

The Magazine of Art gave faint praise in its review: 'Her precept on such matters as form and colour, and her example on such homely affairs as the decoration of the fireplace, are unexceptional and though she is a little weak and uncertain when speaking of Michelangelo and Raphael, in the main her hints are good and her opinion safe'.[3]

The American author and poet Charles Goodrich Whiting in writing a preface for the American edition published in 1887 stated glowingly; 'Of teaching ill adapted to American life, there is scarcely a trace in this book. Indeed, the Cranes are of the people, and have done their beautiful work for the people'. However, he had one sharp criticism in defence of American design:

> Miss Crane finds nearly her worst example of unfitness in design in an American toilet-jug; and this is almost the sole instance of the British insular spirit in the book, since it is certain that no nation has a monopoly of vulgarity in such matters, and British designs are apt to be the clumsiest that are seen in the international expositions.[4]

Lucy Crane, 'Colour', *Art and the Formation of Taste* (London: Macmillan 1882), pp. 97–101

III.—Decorative Art—Colour, Dress and Needlework

[. . .] The principles [of colour harmony] which will be found safe guides both in house-decoration and dress may be arranged under five heads —Analogy, Contrast, Variety, Delicacy, Repetition.

To explain what I mean by Harmony of Analogy, I will suppose a lady of fair complexion and delicate colouring to be seeking harmonious tints for an entire costume. Her hair is light brown, so she may choose a darker fuller brown for the dress; her complexion will bear a delicate pink, so the brown of her dress must incline more to dove than to russet, and in the brown bonnet that matches her dress there may be a delicate pink feather and lining; and in the lining of her parasol, and the gloves, the pink should be repeated, perhaps of a slightly fuller pink, but still not deeper than the pink of the under side of a mushroom.

I have seen a drawing-room furnished in similar tones, only with a somewhat wider range. The brown was a little warmer, and in stamped velvet for the chair-coverings; some of the cushions and the mantel-border embroidered with wild roses and yellow centres; the walls pink, of two shades; the curtains of brown figured silk lined with pink; and the carpet a blending of all these tints together.

Thus, by beginning with some colour having natural fitness to recommend it, and using one or two of its modifying tints taken separately, by the union of the whole we get a harmony of analogy.

Harmony by contrast is on a different principle; we must suppose a brilliant complexion, and dark hair and eyes, or brown eyes and red-gold hair. The natural colouring already offers strong contrasts, so pale, soft, and subdued tints seem out of place and ineffective. Cardinal red, gold, cream colour, and black, would perhaps suit the dark hair and eyes; and blue and flesh coloured brocade of Louis Quinze might suit the red-gold hair and brown eyes. It seems to me a sure rule that persons whose natural colouring is in a low key, one tint nearly assimilating with another, should wear soft tones of colour in dress, also nearly assimilating with each other; and where the natural colouring offers strong contrasts, the colouring of the dress should be full and strong also. I cannot think that strong contrast can ever be good in the colouring of a room, where it seems to me repose and softened light are always needed. Here is an arrangement of contrast in colouring, however, which still seems simple and harmonious. Two full blues, two rather greener ones, and two shades of a flesh-colour-like pink. This colouring may be seen in brocades of the time of Louis Quinze.

The next principle I would suggest is *variety*. It is an immemorial custom that dining-room curtains should be red, with leather chairs, red tablecloth, and Turkey carpet in which red prevails. There is not much variety in this time-honoured fashion; nor is there sometimes in the manifestations of the new. I saw a drawing-room the other day with a peacock feather patterned wallpaper, dado and wood work of peacock blue, and curtains and chair-coverings of peacock patterned chintz, exactly matching the wallpaper. The result was flat and monotonous, in my opinion. Both these are instances of want of variety. I would never recommend chairs to be covered with stuff like the curtains, or the walls to be like either. The walls of the dining-room may be a brownish yellow; the curtains of a mixed red and yellow-the yellow a little pinkish; and the chairs plain red, and the carpet brown and yellow and red, and a little green. A great deal of pleasure can be felt in the variety of these tints, which, nevertheless, produce a unity of effect when regarded as a whole. It is a good rule, if the walls have a pattern on them, that the curtains should be plain, and *vice versa*, so a dress should not be entirely figured or embroidered, but only in portions, that the design may show all the more richly.

To come to the next point—*delicacy*—by delicacy I do not necessarily mean paleness; delicacy of effect is gained by suiting exactly the colour to the material. To muslin and such like filmy substances full bright tints are most unsuitable; pale tender hues, and light tracery of pattern belong to them; still, delicacy in these does not involve insipidity, which poverty of tone and design would cause. For richer stuffs, in silk and satin and velvet, fuller hues are quite suitable. The shimmer, the shifting of lights and shadows, the bloom of the texture, modifies the effect of a full colour, which in a dull and common stuff would be flat and heavy. This principle should lead us not to offend the delicate tints of flesh and hair by surrounding them with coarse hues and hard masses, but to blend and tone down all our adornments according to the example of Nature, who so carefully softens tints and outlines—for example, where the hair begins on the temples and the eyebrows, and the colouring of cheek and lip. We instinctively avoid clothing an infant in dark and hard colours; it would seem unsuitable and discordant. Do not let us treat ourselves so very much worse.

The senses do not recognise a weak impression at the same time as a stronger one. We cannot listen properly to music going on in a room when people are talking and laughing loudly. A strong flavour in a dish, such as garlic or onions, overpowers every other it may possess; so strong colours in dress and room-decoration catch the eye, and fill it to the exclusion of every softer and more delicate one.

The fourth principle is *repetition*. Never have a colour concentrated in one spot, but take care to repeat it in others. If you have blue and white chintz in one corner of your room, put some in another corner to balance it. If you have a pink feather in your bonnet, wear pink gloves or a pink parasol. To isolate a colour is to draw the eye to that particular point, and to keep it there, instead of gently leading it on from one to another. [. . .]

Notes

1 L. Crane, *Art and the Formation of Taste* (London: Macmillan, 1882), p. 67.
2 *The Illustrated Queen Almanac and Lady's Calendar*, 1883, p. 292.
3 'Art in March', *Magazine of Art*, March 1883, p. 24.
4 L. Crane, *Art and the Formation of Taste* (Boston, Chautauqua Press, 1885) p. v-vi.

24

JOHN D. CRACE, 'THE DECORATIVE USE OF COLOUR'

John Dibblee Crace (1836–1919) was an important English interior decorator and author. He was part of the well-known Crace family that had been in the decorating business since 1768. The Crace family were one of the most significant firms of interior decorators of the nineteenth century. They worked for every British monarch from George III to Queen Victoria and decorated various buildings ranging from royal palaces to exhibition halls. J.D. Crace was noticed for the work he undertook assisting his father in the decoration of the 1862 exhibition halls in London.

James Ward was supportive of John Gregory's Crace's work at the Great Exhibition. Writing in his comprehensive review of the displays in the Exhibition, he noted that

> In this class [of English decorators] we may safely assume that Crace holds the highest position; though there are others, eminent in their peculiar styles, whose taste is equally conspicuous. Messrs. Crace were the first, we believe, who elevated decoration to a branch of the fine arts; for they alone, on an extended scale, have introduced order, harmony, and uniformity of character in their works.[1]

J.G. Crace was involved again in exhibition work when he became the Superintendent of Decoration for the Great Exhibition building of 1862 where he used a colour scheme that avoided repeating Owen Jones's 1851 use of primary colours.[2] The 1862 exhibition building, designed and built by Captain Francis Fowke (1823–1865) of the Royal Engineers, used pale bronze green columns with maroon red circular parts and a separating gold line. In 1862, the satirical magazine *Punch* could not resist making fun of Fowke's building, along with a gibe at Crace's decorations:

> With him [Fowkes] the daring decorator Crace
> T'was his to make with polychromatic skill
> What first was ugly uglier still.[3]

A fortnight later, they relented a little, in a piece entitled 'Punchii Cracem Pacem Petentis Palinodia:'

> So *Punch* begs hereby to cancel
> What he said of CRACE's stencil,
> And owns he's been fairly ta'en to task for it;
> But reserves leave, *pace* CRACE,
> To regret FOWKE's ugly face,
> Should in CRACE's cunning colour find a mask for it.[4]

A version of this paper was published as J. D. Crace, 'The Decorative Use of Colour' (*British Architect*, 29 20, 1888, pp. 354–363). Crace remained interested in the academic and historic aspects of decoration publishing an article on 'Household Taste' in the *Furniture Gazette* (17, 11 March 1882 pp 167–9 and 1April p.23), as well as a paper on 'Pugin and Furniture' (RIBA Journal 5, 1894, pp. 517–9).

John D. Crace, 'The Decorative Use of Colour', *The Journal of the Society of Arts*, 36:1851, 1888, pp. 696–704

The title of this paper is intended to indicate the limits which I propose to myself in dealing tonight with a subject which admits of consideration from several points of view, and covers a very wide field. Of the scientific side of colours I propose to say little or nothing; and of that side of the subject which relates to the pictorial use of colour I am also desirous of saying no more than is incidental to my own branch of the subject. My wish is to draw your attention to those principles which should, in my opinion, regulate and underlie all purely decorative work, when applied to forms and surfaces which—whether they appertain to buildings or to moveable objects, made by the hand of man—are not presentations of natural objects.

Unlike the works of Nature, the things which man invents and constructs for his own use, have their design based upon simple geometrical forms; and, in the majority of instances, these are in some direction symmetrical.

In all parts of a building, and in a vast number of other products of man's invention, stability is the first requirement; and precisely in the degree to which this condition is important to the structure, is it important also that any colour, used decoratively on that structure, should assist and confirm the idea of stability or of strength.

In considering the lessons to be derived from nature in the matter of decorative colouring, we must never lose sight of the great distinction between the forms to be coloured. In the case of Nature we may almost say that the forms to which beautiful colouring has been applied are never simple geometrical forms, and rarely have stability as a characteristic. Nature is always moving, always presupposes motion. Animals, birds, insects, foliage, flowers; these are the objects on which her most exquisite harmonies are lavished. All move, either actively of their own volition; or passively, by the action of wind or wave. If, therefore, we may seek in them instruction in the combination of harmonious colours, as we undoubtedly may, we must not look to them for instruction in the distribution and arrangement of colour upon objects and structures which are intended to be immoveable. We can follow them in colouring a fan, not in colouring a dome.

I lay stress on this distinction at starting, because I strongly advocate constant recourse to Nature; and to reap advantage from her teaching, you must beware against misapplying it. Moreover, the true lessons to be derived from natural objects are not to be fully learned from those objects detached from their natural accessories or surroundings. Something may be so learned; yet it is but a fraction of the whole, a word or two out of the poem.

We may certainly go pretty directly to Nature for lessons in one form of decorative art—I mean the art of dress—so far as the distribution and harmony of colour are concerned. I do not know to what extent the fashionable dressmakers make it a practice to study the combinations of colour in flowers, birds, and other living things, but I am quite sure that they can go to no better school; and I feel pretty sure that the most artistic designers of women's attire draw their best inspirations from these sources. After making the necessary allowance for complexion and other special circumstances, there is considerable resemblance in the conditions which would regulate the arrangement of colour in a lady's dress to those which are found in the plumage of birds. There are the same easy curves, the same variety of attitude, which render geometrical or very regular and symmetrical division unsuitable, and which, on the contrary, invite irregular forms, with the occasional piquancy of a suddenly accentuated contrast. In graceful movement or in graceful repose there is no symmetrical arrangement of the limbs, nor of the curves of the human body; nor, indeed, in animal form of any kind. Hence those surface divisions of colour are best which are independent of any one attitude; which, in fact, are not liable to distortion by each change of position.

But how different is every condition when we come to deal with a solid and inanimate structure. It is difficult to follow the rapid—and, to a great extent, unconscious—workings of the mind in matters of taste, and in the exercise of the critical faculties; difficult to distinguish what is due to discrimination, and what to association with some previous experiences. But there is one circumstance indispensable to the enjoyment of the beauty of any work of art. It is this. The mind must have no doubt—no misgiving—as to the objects stability; to that extent the mind must be satisfied at a glance. That amount of repose attained, it will (unconsciously) seek knowledge of the general form and outline; and only after that, will it settle into such a reposeful condition as to allow of the examination and enjoyment of detail. So long as any perplexity remains, the sense of beauty will be dormant, or nearly so, where the handiwork of man is concerned. Man must understand his brother man's work, or it troubles him. Now, it is just at this point that colour comes in with a few words of rapid explanation—if properly used. Colour will explain form at first sight (if used to that end), with a clearness and rapidity quite unattainable by form alone, and especially by form alone in a diffused light.

The reason why the exterior of a building is comparatively independent of colour for the expression of its proportion and of its structural lines is, that the stronger and more direct effects of light at once throw into relief the salient features. It is the reduced and diffused light of the interior which renders the explanatory help of colour so valuable, I was going to say indispensable. True, colour serves other and less simple ends; but that is its first purpose; and to so use it as to explain simply and effectively the structure and proportion of the interior, and the direction and nature of its surfaces, whether plane or curved, convex or concave, is the first duty of the architectural colourist.

Be the ultimate object the richest splendour, the most elegant elaboration, or the most austere simplicity, the first consideration in the use of colour to any interior, or to any part of a building, must be that it shall assist and in no way confuse, that sense of repose which comes of a prompt recognition of its main forms and structural lines.

Now before proceeding to consider by what methods this object may be accomplished, I will here just anticipate a comment which will no doubt have occurred to many of you on this postulate. "This may be true," you say, "of such buildings as have architectural expression and structural features to deal with; but what of the numberless interiors and structures which have no such features and no such expression?"

To this I reply that, so far as the want of such expression is perceptible, the colourist's first aim in treating such structures must be to offer such a substitute as will afford the same mental repose. In other words, he will so distribute his colour that the forms brought into prominence may assist the idea of stability, and go to counteract any sense of apparent weakness or confusion.

It is, however, more convenient to deal first with that part of the subject which relates to buildings having defined structural expression. Now such buildings vary immensely in the extent to which they may be said to rely on their architectural detail for effect, or to be dependent on colour. Broadly speaking, one may say, "the more moulded surface the less colour," and the greater the necessity for extreme care in its use. In an interior which is already elaborately treated by the architect with mouldings and carving, and the surfaces subdivided into panels, simple "explanation " must be the aim. To distinguish the really important structural features from the mere subdivision of intermediate space, and to do this without detaching them, is the first object. There must be the same sort of relation between the major and minor structural lines that there is between the trunk and its branches.

Take the case of a vaulted hall or church, with arches and vaulting springing from piers or columns. A relationship must be maintained (whatever the extent or scale of colour) not only between piers, architraves, cornices, and archivolts, but between these and such minor divisional features as subdivide the surfaces between them. Subdued in tone these last may be, but not removed nor sharply contrasted. The broad contrasts must be between the structural forms generally and the spaces or surfaces between them; whilst the sharper, more vigorous relief of colour must be within the limits of—and expressing the direction of—the structural features themselves.

But, again, there are many buildings which having the same main constructive features as that which we have been considering, have no such minor or secondary moulded divisions. Each bay of the vaulted roof may be a blank surface. We have then to consider what alternatives may be adopted in treating these blank spaces.

Firstly. It may be contemplated to devote them to a decorative pictorial treatment, without actual subdivision. This will rarely be quite satisfactory; because any pictorial representation, straying, as it were, over a large area of curved surface, produces some confusion as to the form of the surface, and what is architecturally more important, leaves the structural lines too detached from what they should support—standing in fact like the bare bones of the whole. In such a case, however, this ill effect may be much moderated by interposing, between structure and panel, a band or bordering of such colouring as will, while supporting and spreading out the constructive arch or rib, ally it in some measure with the colouring of the panel.

But, however excellent may be the pictorial work, it will be seen to far more advantage if it be framed and supported by such dividing margins as will serve at once to suggest the contour of the surface, and to limit each pictorial area to such space and form, as can well be seen from one point of view. It is not necessary that these minor dividing bands should represent actual or possible structure. It is sufficient that the major lines of construction are expressed, and that the contour or section of the spaces between is explained by lines which become the equivalent of the minor construction—and suggest the ramification or network of support.

There is yet another type of internal structure, which may be founded upon the same general lines as those we have just considered, but is divested almost entirely of mouldings, or moulded relief. Such buildings are dependent for their effect entirely on their coloured decoration, and are, perhaps, so built with the express object of affording scope for such treatment. Firmly expressed lines, and borders of colour, take the place of mouldings; and these must have sufficient force to make clear the structure, and to define the limits of the several areas of surface.

It is upon interiors of this last type that mosaic decoration may be most advantageously employed. This magnificent method of decoration by colour does not accord well with the use of mouldings, except to the most limited extent. Its nature demands exceptionally bold treatment, and the very strength and brilliance of its effects destroy all perception of the delicate shadows and roundings of good mouldings. It demands large surfaces, and is most effective where the surfaces are curved, these affording that variety of angle to the light which gives such splendour of effect to the gold grounds. It is under such conditions that mosaic is used in St. Mark's, at Venice; in the churches at Ravenna; and in many other of the best examples.

In the course of the foregoing remarks I have repeatedly spoken of the need for lines or divisional margins to "explain" the contours or planes of large surfaces. It is perhaps necessary to show why they are required, and how they serve the purpose.

It will be obvious to anyone who considers the matter that it is only by *its external limits,* or by some indication of shadow or other incident, that we feel at all sure whether any large surface of one tint is perfectly flat, uneven, or curved. We can see that a plastered wall is bulged if we look at it edgeways against the sky or against some vertical line; but if we stand facing it, and the light be diffused (that is to say, if there be no cast shadow), we can form no true opinion as to whether the wall is a true plane, or bulged, and out of upright. But if, instead of being plastered, it be a brick or stone wall, with straight horizontal courses, every joint which is above or below the sight-line will at once betray the curve of the bulge, and will indicate whether it be convex or concave. These horizontal joints will not, however, tell us whether the wall leans bodily in or out, or is "hollow" from top to bottom; we must look for some continuous vertical joint, or to some door or window opening, to betray this. We must, in fact, have the means of comparison which a straight line, or a line of known direction. will afford.

Now let us see how this applies in decoration. We will take a feature over the treatment of which there has been much discussion during the last few years—the "cupola" or interior of the dome. Suppose that we are standing under and looking up into a plain undecorated cupola, what do we know at a glance as to its form? What remains in doubt?

Well, we know, at once, that it is circular in plan; we learn that from the cornice, from which it springs; but beyond that, and some chance indication that its vertical section is curved, we know nothing. Whether that vertical curve is high or low, elliptical, semi-circular, or segmental we do not know, and cannot so much as guess, until, by dropping a series of vertical lines on its surface, we exhibit its vertical section. Then doubt disappears, and the eye, relieved from perplexity, and satisfied as to the stability of the vault soars up the curved line, grasping the whole meaning of the noble form, and ranges. tranquilly among such detail as may occupy its surface.

Now, as the cupola is explained by these vertical lines, so is a barrel vault explained by the archivolts which divide it into bays, and by the other framing lines between them; whether they be in colour or in relief only. So groined vaulting is explained by its ribs; and where the builder has already provided such explanation, the decorator must confirm it;. where it does not exist, he must supply it.

Let us now consider what is to guide the colourist in dealing with interiors which have no structural features to emphasise; which, in fact, cannot be regarded as architecture at all. If such be of a size, and for a use, which seem to call for some attempt at imparting dignity to its effect, it will probably be desirable to suggest, by the decoration, some structural division. In some cases the addition of a frieze will establish more agreeable relations between the walls and ceiling; in others some vertical division of the walls—which may form points of departure for division of the ceiling—may greatly enhance the dignity, and improve the proportion of a plain room. In any case, if there be any strength of colour in the ceiling, there should be, at some points, strength of colour leading up to it. In rooms for domestic use, these are often practically supplied by the window hangings, and in the majority of such rooms the dimensions are so limited that the want of constructive features is not felt.

And it may here be remarked that one very broad distinction divides most domestic interiors from those which are intended for some public or special use, when the question of coloured decoration arises. In the latter there are no draperies, nor carpets, nor any of those accessories, such as furniture, which all play so important a part in the colouring of a private house. Consequently, in the absence of these, the decorative colouring of the building itself has to be more complete, its harmony more carefully balanced, more thought out as to the purpose and result of each tone used. The absence of the accessories of a house, with all their variety and irregularity, leaves the colouring of the building more exposed to view, and more directly challenging criticism. A firmer, surer, and more purposeful hand is needed for the colouring of a bare public building than will serve for the domestic interior, in which picturesque arrangement, suggestions of historical association or foreign travel, or the collector's taste, may often play a more important part than either architecture or decorative colour. Nevertheless, much may be done, even in a room of moderate size, to improve or make the best of its proportions, and to impart an interest to it as a whole, by the distribution and management of the colour. The flat ceiling which, being the largest unbroken surface in the room, always has a tendency to appear weak, may be lifted and supported by the lines or grounds of colour which form the framework of its ornamentation, being so arranged as to throw strength into the sides and angles; and these leading forms and lines may themselves be made interesting and suggestive by their combinations of curve or angle. It is a common error to suppose that colour will "bring down" a ceiling. This will only happen where the tones are too strong or too crude for those which occur on the walls and in the draperies. All ornament must be kept subordinate in strength of contrast to the tones of the framework or controlling lines. If this be neglected, a sense of confusion will mar the effect, and destroy the repose essential to success.

The use of polychromy for external decoration demands very careful attention; and the extent to which it is desirable, as well as the best methods for its exercise, have been much debated during the last thirty years.

I would venture to say, on this subject, that, in a building which has any pretence to architectural design, the polychromy of its structural features should be confined to that presented by its constructive materials. Yet, even such buildings present occasionally features or surfaces which may be so treated in colour (whether by mosaic, or even by the painter), as greatly to enhance the effect and value of the whole. I could point to numerous examples, both ancient and modern, of the successful use of colour in this way. Of modern instances, I may quote the great frescoes outside the Berlin Museum,[5] where colour is used pictorially; or the merely ornamental colouring of the window reveals in the Chateau de Blois; or, again, the very skilful introduction of mosaic ornament in the brickwork of the

THE DECORATIVE USE OF COLOUR

Trocadero at Paris[6]—all of which must, I think, be admitted to contribute largely to the effect and value of the buildings themselves.

But there is another class of building, of which we have only too many examples here, which afford occasional opportunity for some amount of colour treatment. I mean the stucco-fronted houses, in which design can hardly be said to have a place. Their "architectural symptoms'" are of the slightest, and they, in any case, have to be painted in some way, periodically, to preserve them from decay. Here there would seem to be a fair field for careful schemes of colour, and I have observed a few very able instances of the external treatment of such buildings. Certainly, there is a growing taste for some application of colour to such houses, even where they are private residences. One such residence near me has recently had its ground story (including the front door and area railings) pointed the colour of red sealing-wax. After this, I feel that it is not timidity that restrains us in this matter. What we seem to want is judgment—a knowledge of how to compensate, by simple means, for the want of beauty and interest in the structural form.

There is, again, the detached villa, which, being less prominently exposed to public view, might often be made a much more attractive and more refined looking building, and be brought into better harmony with its small pleasure garden by a little skilful colouring than it is when its stucco surface is left with the usual two coats of "light stone colour." Many a small suburban house in the outskirts of Paris has so been treated, with the result of presenting as much outward charm as if many hundred pounds had been lavished on architectural refinement.

True it is not so permanent; but is our leasehold tenure so permanent as to offer much inducement to us to spend money on permanent adornment? The great majority of us think ourselves lucky if our interest in the house we live in extends to 20 or 30 years; at the end of which time our ground landlord swoops down on us with a bill of dilapidations, with an extra rent-charge, and probably a demand for premium based on our own improvements. It is quite a question whether the house will last another such term; for it must be admitted that, however charming, your stucco villa is not a very long-lived piece of work. Not that I join in the abuse of stucco, for under the short-lease system you probably get a better and more weathertight house for your money, if it be of the modest "stuccoed" order, than if you attempt one, at the same rent, in sculptured freestone or ornamental brick. Only it is better to treat it as stucco, and to do your best with the paint pot, than to make believe it has a noble stone frontage.

The same general rules which should regulate the distribution of coloured form on parts of a building apply, with reasonable modifications, to smaller objects. Take pottery. If a vase or cup has a graceful contour, it is obviously desirable that any variety of colour used in its decoration should assist in showing its form, not disguise it. Very beautiful art is often expended on such articles with the result of actually detracting from their beauty of outline. I am not speaking of modern English pottery in particular. It is a mistake common enough in the finest manufacture of other countries, and it seems to me a quite unnecessary mistake. Of course, very exquisite painting will charm, even when used to poor advantage, but its merit of execution does not altogether justify its misapplication. In our own time, and in our country, it is a great misfortune that all our best artists learn to paint for a gilt frame alone, and are, for the most part, absolutely untrained in thinking out their subjects for any other application. I cannot but think that in this matter our Royal Academy of Arts might effect much reform, and give an immense impetus to the artistic excellence of the productions of this country, if, from time to time, they admitted to their exhibitions some proportion of objects of applied art of a high standard. It would encourage the best men to throw some, at least, of their best work into branches of art that can never rise to the highest level unless they draw to their service the best men. It was these branches of art that went to build up the fame of the greatest artists that the world has known; and I confess to the opinion that, so long as our highest art training has no other object than the production of detached pictures, destined to no special purpose or position, painted to no requirement. having for object chiefly to catch the eye of the buyer, so long the standard of art will drift right or left, to this or that particular fashion of excellence; but, being without purpose, will never attain to any very noble rank.

I am afraid that my discourse tonight may provoke the criticism that, being "on the use of colour," it has mentioned no single colour, has suggested no harmonics, has indicated no contrasts. I must plead that these omissions were intentional, not because I think these things in themselves less important than the matter I have spoken of, but that they are now frequently and ably treated, and are daily better understood. I was desirous so to limit my subject as not to divert attention from my main proposition, which is, that whatever the tones of colour employed, whatever the scale of harmony, no "decorative use of colour" can be really successful which is not based on the intention to do the best possible for the thing decorated. And then I go a little further, and say that no art can really attain the highest excellence if it has no broad purpose, no alliance with its sister arts. The art which is shut up in itself, whose masters have neither trained knowledge of, nor sympathy for, its allies, whether humble or noble, can never be progressive. In art, as in life, man's noblest work is most often produced in the earnest effort to ennoble and complete the work of others.

[Discussion followed]

Notes

1 J. Ward, *The World in its Workshops: A Practical Examination of British and Foreign Processes of Manufacture, with a Critical Comparison of the Fabrics, Machinery, and Works of Art Contained in the Great Exhibition* (London: Williams S. Orr and Co., 1851), p. 171.
2 See J. G. Crace, 'On the decoration of the international exhibition building', *Journal of the Society of Arts*, 10, 1861–2, pp. 339–45.
3 'The Opening of The Great Exhibition,' *Punch,* 42, 3 May 1862, p. 179.
4 *Punch,* 42, 17 May 1862, p. 201.
5 Wilhelm von Kaulbach (1804–1874), created the frescoes for the Neues Museum, Berlin.
6 Trocadero: Jean-Antoine-*Gabriel Davioud* (1824–1881) was the French architect who designed the *Palais du Trocadéro* for the Exposition Universelle of 1878.

25

ROBERTS BEAUMONT, *COLOUR IN WOVEN DESIGN*

An expert on textile manufacturing, Roberts Beaumont (1862–1922) was appointed Instructor in the Department of Textiles, Leeds University in 1875, and later became Professor and Head of Department from 1889 until his retirement in 1913. His father, John Beaumont, was the first director of the Leeds Textiles Department. Roberts was also responsible for some of the organising and examining work of other technological educational authorities, including the City and Guilds of London Institute and the Royal Society of Arts, both of which rewarded his works with the conferment of medals on him.

Roberts Beaumont was also engaged in inventing new techniques for textiles production, as well as publishing several works on the industry and its processes. These books included standard works on textile subjects, such as *Woollen and Worsted Manufacture, Colour in Woven Design,* and *Union Textile Fabrication.* He also promoted the study of contemporary design in the university, through a teaching collection of photographic plates, and a departmental museum. During 1888, *The Textile Recorder* published a series of articles written by Beaumont on the topic of 'Design and Colour in Fancy Vestings'.[1] It is interesting to note that most of his illustrations used to demonstrate his ideas on colour harmony were drawn, like many other contemporary authors on colour, from Turkish carpets and Indian shawl examples.

A rather cutting review of this book, published in the journal *Nature* during 1891, critiqued the tone of the language and phrases as being rather overblown and obscure, but more importantly, they felt that they could not fully endorse Beaumont's theories of colour. They pointed out that

> For instance, he contrasts what he calls the "light theory of colours" with the "pigment theory," and then, speaking of the latter, says: "Scientifically, it is no more a correct scheme than the light theory is applicable to the industries or to the mixing of paints." But surely the theory of Young, Maxwell, and Helmholtz[2] is as applicable to the results obtained by mixing pigments or coloured fibres, as it is to the results of mingling coloured lights.[3]

Beaumont is clearly more at home discussing the technical aspects of textile design around issues of forms and their combinations, construction, or weave and the use of color in textiles, as this passage shows.

Roberts Beaumont, *Colour in Woven Design*, (London: Whittaker and Co., 1890), pp. 1–5

Theories of Colouring

1. *Elements of Woven Pattern.*—Weave, Combinations of Forms, and Blends of Colours, are the three primary elements of textile design. They enter, either separately, or in conjunction with each other, into every species of loom effect. Weave relates specifically to the build or structure of the fabric, and is an indispensable factor in any type of cloth, whether plain, twilled, or ornamental in character. It may be defined as the system or plan of crossing the warp and weft yarns which constructs the fabric. In some makes of textiles weave is merely a simple principle of interlacing which produces a compact, substantial texture, being entirely subordinate in effect to other constituents of the style, such as colour, and decorative design resulting from intricate adjustments of form and figure. Though weave may thus be regarded in textile designing as generally being a constructive and not an ornamental component of the pattern, yet there are numerous examples in which it possesses both these characteristics. Textures of this description are neither embellished with figure nor colour, and therefore derive their design from the structural plan employed in the process of weaving. Schemes of inter-crossing that give these results are devised in such a manner as to form in one operation an even and firm cloth, decorated with a type of pattern that usually consists of minute parts, but which is pronounced and decided in composition.

Combinations of Forms, on the other hand, have no relation whatever to the structural or architectural arrangement of the fabric. The sphere of form in woven design is not constructive, nor even utilitarian, but in the amplest sense ornamental. It is surface decoration obtained by amalgamating, on defined principles, linear and curvilinear lines. Even in the development of figured patterns, in which this element of design plays an important part, weave is a useful factor. Ornament, comprising combinations of geometrical and floral figuring, is liberally applied to various types of loom textures, including styles for ladies' robes, dresses, mantlings, silk goods, damasks, and quilts; and Brussels, Kidderminster, velvet pile, and other carpets. It is almost an invariable law for both weave and colour to be introduced into this kind of textile decoration; hence the importance of first acquiring a knowledge of these principles of woven pattern before attempting to apply elaborate ornament to the surface of a loom product.

Colour, the third element of all classes of designing, is very differently related to textile effects from either Weave or Form. Its specific province is to brighten and improve the qualities of the design due to the two latter principles. While in decorative arts generally it imparts boldness, unity, and richness of tone to the ornament resultant, in textiles it may be either the main constituent of the pattern or the developer of its integral parts. Any discarding of the use of fancy or coloured shades would diminish the elegance of design, impoverish its appearance, and all but annihilate some branches of woollen industry.

2. *Occurrence and Utility of Colour in Loom Products.*—

It is only necessary to anatomise woven design to trace the extensive use of colour in textiles. Commencing with woollen fabrics, in every class of these cloths, whether tweeds, flannels, and light textures for ladies' robes, or thick figured mantlings, rugs, wraps, and shawls, it forms one of the main characteristics of the pattern. In the first three of these textures colour is the distinguishing element of the style. To remove it from such fabrics would result in a complete erasure of all design or ornament. Whether the pattern be stripe, check, figure, or intermingled effect, it obtains its outline and detail from the method of colouring adopted. But colour is not confined to woollens, it is also an important factor in design produced in worsted, silk, cotton, and jute yarns. There is in worsteds a larger diversity of weave design than in woollen, or carded-yarn textures; but still colour is very extensively employed to develop the effects due to Weave and Form, and also to impart a cheerful and lustrous appearance to the cloths. Patterns in dress fabrics, shirtings and other articles, made entirely of cotton, are frequently mere combinations of fancy shades; while, if the fabrics composed of silk and jute materials are considered, including—in silk—ties, handkerchiefs, and various kinds of matelassés;[4] and—in jute—simple carpets, mats, and coarse rugs, it will be discovered that the colour element of the design largely predominates. This brief summary of the cloths in which fancy shades are used shows that colouring, and the combinations of colours, in all branches of woven products embellished with design, are the elements which give tone and character to the styles. Though the cloths produced may be soft to the touch, substantially made, uniform in structure, and skilfully finished, yet a lack of brightness and elegance in colouring so powerfully detracts from the merit of the pattern that these qualities, in themselves, are not sufficient to give the fabric an attractive appearance—particulars which demonstrate the importance of choice and tasteful colouring in designs produced by the loom. Evidently colour has a twofold part to play in the development of woven effects: for it may, firstly, be the sole constituent of the pattern; and, secondly, a supplementary element which affords precision and beauty to the composition of the design.

3. *Treatment of Colour in Relation to Textiles,*—Though, to a considerable extent, the principles of colouring are similar in all types of decorative design—harmonious blending and contrasting combinations possessing like qualities in whatever materials they obtain—still there are several reasons why some of the recognised canons of the science of colours are inappropriate, if not inapplicable, when textiles are the media of development. Foremost of these is the technical difficulties which arise in the employment of colour in woven pattern. There is not the same facility nor means for its application here, as in the treatment of ordinary surface decoration. The make of the cloth, and the principles of its structure,

determine the system of distribution; while the general aspect of the entire body of colouring varies according to the nature of the materials employed. If the same colourings which appear harmonious, neatly toned, and cheerful in arrangement in a velvet pile carpet, were reproduced in a silk texture, many points of dissimilarity would be noticed in the general effect obtained, though the tint and hue of the shades combined might be identically the same in the respective fabrics. Why is this? Are not the apparent modifications in the colourings—of such they appear when thus compared—due, first, to the difference in the nature of the materials composing the textures; second, to the dissimilitude of their structural character; and, third, to the distinct principles of weaving practised in their production? The pile of the carpet—full, erect, and compact—gives breadth, force, and richness to the colours; whereas the fine and bare texture of the silk article imparts a more precise effect to the shades, causing the whole blend to possess an aspect which, while harmonious, lacks that desirable quality of bloom so characteristic of the pile production. It is clear, therefore, that colour in textiles requires to be studied as a special art. Its functions and effects in woven goods are so various and distinct from what they are in ordinary decorative work, that it can only be effectively treated when the nature of textile materials, and the diverse structural arrangements of woven goods, are considered. In a word, there are not only recognised principles of woven design which have no place in purely ornamental art, but also schemes and laws of colouring which simply apply to the development of pattern in woven fabrics. Any exposition, therefore, of the theory and practice of colouring, to be useful to the textile technologist, must be given in relation to the varied technicalities of the weaver's craft.

Notes

1 *Textile Recorder*, October, November, December 1888.
2 The Young–Helmholtz Theory (the trichromatic theory) is a theory of trichromatic colour vision, which examines the human visual system that creates the experience of colour. Maxell proved the theory in 1857.
3 *Nature*, 43, 1891, p. 343.
4 matellassé: A double or compound textured fabric with a quilted appearance.

5.2

FORM

26

HORATIO GREENOUGH, 'AMERICAN ARCHITECTURE'

The American sculptor Horatio Greenough (1805–1852) is best known for his theories and observations that were published in his 1852 work *The Travels, Observations, and Experience of a Yankee Stonecutter*. Greenough's well-known concept of 'form following function' was explained in this work: 'If there be any principle of structure more plainly inculcated in the works of the Creator than all others, it is, the principle of unflinching adaptation of forms to functions'.[1] This idea of adapting to the requirements of the environment was developed into a discussion of the architectural form:

> Instead of forcing the functions of every sort of building into one general form, adopting an outward shape for the sake of the eye or of association, without reference to the inner distribution, let us begin from the heart as a nucleus and work outward.[2]

It was also in this article on 'American Architecture' that Greenough explained his ideas more fully in a passage that had clear Darwinian overtones:

> The law of adaptation is the fundamental law of nature in all structure. So unflinchingly does she modify a type in accordance with a new position, that some philosophers have declared a variety of appearance to be the object aimed at; so entirely does she limit the modification to the demands of necessity, that adherence to one original plan seems, to limited intelligence, to be carried to the very verge of caprice.

Greenough then critiques contemporary obsessions with fashion, by noting how 'The domination of arbitrary rules of taste has produced the very counterpart of the wisdom thus displayed in every object around us'.[3]

Another interesting point among many, coming from Greenough's analysis of architecture, was his idea that buildings intended for people to use, may be classified as machines based on type-forms associated with the users' needs and wants.

> The edifices in whose construction the principles of architecture are developed may be classed as organic, formed to meet the wants of their

occupants, or monumental, addressed to the sympathies, the faith, or the taste of a people. . . . In the former class [organic] the laws of structure and apportionment, depending on definite wants, obey a demonstrable rule. They may be called machines, each individual of which must be formed with reference to the abstract type of its species.[4]

Finally, his comments on beauty have a similar resonance. He suggests that 'The normal development of beauty is through action to completeness. The invariable development of embellishment and decoration is more embellishment and more decoration. The *reductio ad absurdum* is palpable enough'.[5] He concludes that 'Beauty is the promise of function'.

Horatio Greenough, 'American Architecture', *The United States Magazine and Democratic Review*, New York, 13, August 1843, pp. 206–210

We have heard the learned in matters relating to art, express the opinion that these United States are destined to form a new style of architecture. Remembering that a vast population, rich in material and guided by the experience, the precepts, and the models of the old world, is about to erect durable structures for every function of civilized life, we also cherished the hope that such a combination would speedily be formed.

We forgot that though the country was young, yet the people were old, that as Americans we have no childhood, no half fabulous, legendary wealth, no misty, cloud-enveloped background. We forgot that we had not unity of religious belief, nor unity of origin; that our territory, extending from the white bear to the alligator, made our occupations dissimilar, our character and tastes various. We forgot that the Republic had leaped full grown and armed to the teeth from the brain of her parent, and that a hammer had been the instrument of delivery. We forgot that reason had been the dry nurse of the giant offspring, and had fed her from the beginning with the stout bread and meat of fact; that every wry face the bantling[6] ever made had been daguerreotyped, and all her words and deeds printed and labelled away in the pigeon-holes of official bureaux.

Reason can dissect, but cannot originate; she can adopt, but cannot create; she can modify, but cannot find. Give her but a cockboat,[7] and she will elaborate a line of battleship; give her but a beam with its wooden tooth, and she soon turns out the patent plough. She is not young, and when her friends insist upon the phenomena of youth, then is she least attractive. She can imitate the flush of the young cheek, but where is the flash of the young eye? She buys the teeth —alas! she cannot buy the breath of childhood. The puny cathedral of Broadway, like an elephant dwindled to the size of a dog, measures her yearning for Gothic sublimity, while the roar of the Astor-house,[8] and the mammoth vase of the great reservoir, show how she [America] works when she feels at home, and is in earnest.

The mind of this country has never been seriously applied to the subject of building. Intently engaged in matters of more pressing importance, we have been content to receive our notions of architecture as we have received the fashion of our garments, and the form of our entertainments, from Europe. In our eagerness to appropriate we have neglected to adapt, to distinguish,—nay, to understand. We have built small Gothic temples of wood, and have omitted all ornament for economy, unmindful that size, material, and ornament are the elements of effect in that style of building. Captivated by the classic symmetry of the Athenian models, we have sought to bring the Parthenon into our streets, to make the temple of Theseus work in our towns. We have shorn them of their lateral colonnades, let them down from their dignified platform, pierced their walls for light, and, instead of the storied relief and the eloquent statue which enriched the frieze, and graced the pediment, we have made our chimney tops to peer over the broken profile, and tell by their rising smoke of the traffic and desecration of the interior. Still the model may be recognized, some of the architectural features are entire; like the captive king stripped alike of arms and purple, and drudging amid the Helots[9] of a capital, the Greek temple as seen among us claims pity for its degraded majesty, and attests the barbarian force which has abused its nature, and been blind to its qualities.

If we trace Architecture from its perfection, in the days of Pericles, to its manifest decay in the reign of Constantine, we shall find that one of the surest symptoms of decline was the adoption of admired forms and models for purposes not contemplated in their invention. The forum became a temple, the tribunal became a temple, the theatre was turned into a church; nay, the column, that organized member; that subordinate part, set up for itself, usurped unity, and was a monument! The great principles of Architecture being once abandoned, correctness gave way to novelty, economy and vainglory associated produced meanness and pretension. Sculpture, too, had waned. The degenerate workmen could no longer match the fragments they sought to mingle, nor copy the originals they only hoped to repeat. The mouldering remains of better days frowned contempt upon such impotent efforts, till, in the gradual coming of darkness, ignorance became content, and insensibility ceased to compare.

We say that the mind of this country has never been seriously applied to architecture. True it is, that the commonwealth, with that desire of public magnificence which has ever been a leading feature of democracy, has called from the vasty deep of the past the spirits of the Greek, the Roman, and the Gothic styles; but they would not come when she did call to them The vast cathedral with its ever open portals, towering high above the courts of kings, inviting all men to its cool and fragrant twilight, where the voice of the organ stirs the blood, and the dim-seen visions of saints and martyrs bleed and die upon the canvass amid the echoes of hymning voices and the clouds of frankincense, this architectural embodying of the divine and blessed words "come to me, ye who labor and are heavy laden, and I will give you rest!" demands a sacrifice of what we hold dearest. Its cornerstone must be laid upon the right to judge the claims of the church. The style of Greek architecture as seen in the Greek temple, demands the aid of sculpture, insists upon every feature of its original organization, loses its harmony if a note be dropped in the execution, and when so modified as to serve for a custom house or a bank, departs from its original beauty and propriety as widely as the crippled gelding of a hackney coach differs from the bounding and neighing wild horse of the desert. Even where, in the fervor of our faith in shapes, we have sternly adhered to the dictum of another age, and have actually succeeded in securing the entire exterior which echoes the forms of Athens, the pile stands a stranger among us! and receives a respect akin to what we should feel for a fellow-citizen clothed in the garb of Greece. It is a make believe! It is not the real thing! We see the marble capitals; we trace the acanthus leaves of a celebrated model—incredulus odi![10] It is not a temple.

The number and variety of our experiments in building show the dissatisfaction of the public taste with what has been hitherto achieved; the expense at which they have been made proves how strong is the yearning after excellence; the talents and acquirements of the artists whose services have been engaged in them are such as to convince us that the fault lies in the system, not in the men. Is it possible that out of this chaos order can arise? that of these conflicting dialects and jargons a language can be born? When shall we have done with experiments? What refuge is there from the absurdities that have successively usurped the name and functions of architecture? Is it not better to go on with consistency and uniformity in imitation of an admired model than incur the disgrace of other failures? In answering these questions let us remember with humility that all salutary changes are the work of many and of time; but let us encourage experiment at the risk of license, rather than submit to an iron rule that begins by sacrificing reason, dignity and comfort. Let us consult nature, and in the assurance that she will disclose a mine, richer than was ever dreamed of by the Greeks, in art as well as in philosophy. Let us regard as ingratitude to the author of nature the despondent idleness that sits down while one want is unprovided for, one worthy object unattained.

If, as the first step in our search after the great principles of construction, we but observe the skeletons and skins of animals, through all the varieties of beast and bird, of fish and insect, are we not as forcibly struck by their variety as by their beauty: There is no arbitrary law of proportion, no unbending model of form. There is scarce a part of the animal organization which we do not find elongated or shortened, increased, diminished or suppressed, as the wants of the genus or species dictate, as their exposure or their work may require. The neck of the swan and that of the eagle, however different in character and proportion, equally charm the eye and satisfy the reason. We approve the length of the same member in grazing animals, its shortness in beasts of prey. The horse's shanks are thin, and we admire them; the greyhound's chest is deep, and we cry, beautiful! It is neither the presence nor the absence of this or that part or shape or color that wins our eye in natural objects; it is the consistency and harmony of the parts juxtaposed, the subordination of details to masses, and of masses to the whole.

The law of adaptation is the fundamental law of nature in all structure. So unflinchingly does she modify a type in accordance with a new position, that some philosophers have declared a variety of appearance to be the object aimed at; so entirely does she limit the modification to the demands of necessity, that adherence to one original plan seems, to limited intelligence, to be carried to the very verge of caprice. The domination of arbitrary rules of taste has produced the very counter part of the wisdom thus displayed in every object around us; we tie up the camel leopard to the rack; we shave the lion, and call him a dog; we strive to bind the unicorn with his band in the furrow, and to make him harrow the valleys after us!

When the savage of the South Sea islands shapes his war club, his first thought is of its use. His first efforts pare the long shaft, and mould the convenient handle; then the heavier end takes gradually the edge that cuts, while it retains the weight that stuns. His idler hour divides its surface by lines and curves, or embosses it with figures that have pleased his eye, or are linked with his superstition. We admire its effective shape, its Etruscan-like quaintness, its graceful form and subtle outline, yet we neglect the lesson it might teach. If we compare the form of a newly invented machine with the perfected type of the same instrument, we observe, as we trace it through the phases of improvement, how weight is shaken off where strength is less needed, how functions are made to approach without impeding each other, how the straight becomes curved, and the curve is straightened, till the straggling and cumbersome machine becomes the compact, effective and beautiful engine.

So instinctive is the perception of organic beauty in the human eye, that we cannot withhold our admiration even from the organs of destruction. There is majesty in the royal paw of the lion, music in the motion of the banded tiger; we accord our praise to the sword and the dagger, and shudder our approval of the frightful aptitude of the ghastly guillotine.

Conceiving destruction to be a normal element of the system of nature equally with production, we have used the word beauty in connection with it. We have no objection to exchange it for the word character, as indicating the mere adaptation of forms to functions, and would gladly substitute the actual pretensions of our architecture to the former, could we hope to secure the latter.

Let us now turn to a structure of our own, one which from its nature and uses commands us to reject authority, and we shall find the result of the manly use of plain good sense so like that of taste and genius too, as scarce to require a distinctive title. Observe a ship at sea! Mark the majestic form of her hull as she rushes through the water, observe the graceful bend of her body, the gentle transition from round to flat, the grasp of her keel, the leap of her bows, the symmetry and rich tracery of her spars and rigging, and those grand wind muscles, her sails! Behold an organization second only to that of an animal, obedient as the horse, swift as the stag, and bearing the burden of a thousand camels from pole to pole What Academy of Design, what research of connoisseurship, what imitation of the Greeks produced this marvel of construction? Here is the result of the study of man upon the great deep, where Nature spake of the laws of building, not in the feather and in the flower, but in winds and waves, and he bent all his mind to hear and to obey. Could we carry into our civil architecture the responsibilities that weigh upon our ship-building, we should ere long have edifices as superior to the Parthenon for the purposes that we require, as the Constitution or the Pennsylvania is to the galley of the Argonauts. Could our blunders on terra-firma be put to the same dread test that those of ship-builders are, little would be now left to say on this subject.

Instead of forcing the functions of every sort of building into one general form, adopting an outward shape for the sake of the eye or of association, without reference to the inner distribution, let us begin from the heart as a nucleus and work outward. The most convenient size and arrangement of the rooms that are to constitute the building being fixed, the access of the light that may, of the air that must, be wanted, being provided for, we have the skeleton of our building. Nay, we have all excepting the dress. The connexion and order of parts, juxtaposed for convenience, cannot fail to speak of their relation and uses. As a group of idlers on the quay, if they grasp a rope to haul a vessel to the pier, are united in harmonious action by the cord they seize, as the slowly yielding mass forms a thorough-bass to their livelier movement, so the unflinching adaptation of a building to its position and use gives, as a sure product of that adaptation, character and expression.

What a field of study would be opened by the adoption in civil architecture of those laws of apportionment, distribution and connexion, which we have thus hinted at. No longer could the mere tyro huddle together a crowd of ill arranged, ill lighted and stifled rooms, and masking the chaos with the sneaking copy of a Greek façade, usurp the name of architect. If this anatomic connexion and proportion has been attained in ships, in machines, and, in spite of false principles, in such buildings as make a departure from it fatal, as in bridges and in scaffolding, why should we fear its immediate use in all construction? As its first result, the bank would have the physiognomy of a bank, the church would be recognized as such, nor would the billiard room and the chapel wear the same uniform of columns and pediment. The African king standing in mock majesty with his legs and feet bare, and his body clothed in a cast coat of the Prince Regent, is an object whose ridiculous effect defies all power of face. Is not the Greek temple jammed in between the brick shops of Wall street or Cornhill, covered with lettered signs, and finished by groups of money changers and apple women, a parallel even for his African majesty?

We have before us a letter in which Mr. Jefferson recommends the model of the *Maison Carrée* for the State House at Richmond.[11] Was he aware that the *Maison Carrée* is but a fragment, and that too of a Roman temple? He was. It is beautiful!—is the answer. An English society erected in Hyde Park a cast in bronze of the colossal Achilles of the Quirinal, and changing the head, transformed it into a monument to Wellington.[12] But where is the distinction between the personal prowess, the invulnerable body, the heaven shielded safety of the hero of the Iliad, and the complex of qualities which makes the modern general? The statue is beautiful!—is the answer. If such reasoning is to hold, why not translate one of Pindar's odes in memory of Washington, or set up in Carolina a colossal Osiris in honor of General Greene?[13]

The monuments of Egypt and of Greece are sublime as expressions of their power and their feeling. The modern nation that appropriates them displays only wealth in so doing. The possession of means, not accompanied by the sense of propriety or feeling for the true, can do no more for a nation than it can do for an individual. The want of an illustrious ancestry may be compensated, fully compensated; but the purloining of the coat of arms of a defunct family is intolerable. That such a monument as we have described should have been erected in London while Chantry[14] flourished, when Flaxman's[15] fame was cherished by the few, and Bailey and Behnes[16] were already known, is an instructive fact. That the illustrator of the Greek poets, and of the Lord's Prayer,[17] should in the meanwhile have been preparing designs for George the Fourth's silversmiths, is not less so.

The edifices, in whose construction the principles of architecture are developed, may be classed as organic, formed to meet the wants of their occupants, or monumental, addressed to the sympathies, the faith or the taste of a people. These two great classes of buildings, embracing almost every variety of structure, though occasionally joined and mixed in the same edifice, have their separate rules, as they have a distinct abstract nature. In the former class, the laws of structure and apportionment, depending on definite wants, obey a demonstrable rule. They may be called machines, each individual of which must be formed with reference to the abstract type of its species. The individuals of the latter class, bound by no other laws than those of the sentiment which inspires them, and the sympathies to which they are addressed, occupy the positions and assume the forms best calculated to render their parent feeling. No limits can be put to their variety; their size and richness have always been proportioned to the means of the people who have erected them.

If from what has been thus far said it shall have appeared that we regard the Greek masters as aught less than the true apostles of correct taste in building, we have been misunderstood. We believe firmly and fully that they can teach us; but let us learn principles, not copy shapes; let us imitate them like men, and not ape them like monkeys. Remembering what a school of art it was that perfected their system of ornament, let us rather adhere to that system in enriching what we invent than substitute novelty for propriety. After observing the innovations of the ancient Romans, and of the modern Italian masters in this department, we cannot but recur to the Horatian precept—

exemplaria Graeca Nocturna versate manu, versate diurna![18]

To conclude. The fundamental laws of building found at the basis of every style of architecture, must be the basis of ours. The adaptation of the forms and magnitude of structures to the climate they are exposed to, and the offices for which they are intended, teaches us to study our own varied wants in these respects. The harmony of their ornaments with the nature that they embellished and the institutions from which they sprang, calls on us to do the like justice to our country, our government, and our faith. As a Christian preacher may give weight to truth, and add persuasion to proof, by studying the models of pagan writers, so the American builder, by a truly philosophic investigation of ancient art, will learn of the Greeks to be American.

The system of building we have hinted at cannot be formed in a day. It requires all the science of any country to ascertain and fix the proportions and arrangement of the members of a great building, to plant it safely on the soil, to defend it from the elements, to add the grace and poetry of ornament to its frame. Each of these requisites to a good building requires a special study and a life-time. Whether we are destined soon to see so noble a fruit, may be doubted; but we can, at least, break the ground and throw in the seed.

We are fully aware that many regard all matters of taste as matters of pure caprice and fashion. We are aware that many think our architecture already perfect; but we have chosen, during this sultry weather, to exercise a truly American right—the right of talking. This privilege, thank God! is unquestioned,—from Miller,[19] who, robbing Béranger, translates into fanatical prose, "Finissons en! le monde est assez vieux!"[20] to Brisbane,[21] who declares that the same world has yet to begin, and waits a subscription of two hundred thousand dollars in order to start. Each man is free to present his notions on any subject. We have also talked, firm in the belief that the development of a nation's taste in art depends on a thousand deep-seated influences beyond the ken of the ignorant present; firm in the belief that freedom and knowledge will bear the fruit of refinement and beauty, we have yet dared to utter a few words of discontent, a few crude thoughts of what might be, and we feel the better for it. We promised ourselves nothing more than that satisfaction which Major Downing[22] attributes to every man "who has had his say, and then cleared out," and we already perceive pleasingly what he felt, and what he meant by it.

Notes

1. H. Greenough, *The Travels, Observations, and Experience of a Yankee Stonecutter* (New York: G.P. Putnam, 1852), p. 162.
2. H. Greenough, 'American Architecture', *The United States Magazine and Democratic Review*, New York, 13, August 1843, p. 209.
3. Greenough, p. 208.
4. Greenough, p. 209.
5. H. T. Tuckerman, and H. Greenough, *A Memorial of Horatio Greenough* (New York: Putnam & Co., 1853), p. 136.
6. bantling: a young child.
7. cockboat: a small boat towed behind a larger vessel.
8. Astor House: Astor House was the first luxury hotel to be built in New York City. It opened in 1836.
9. helots: a class of serfs in ancient Sparta, intermediate in status between slaves and citizens.
10. Latin: 'I detest it' (Horace).
11. The Virginia state house or Capitol was conceived by Thomas Jefferson and was based on the Maison Carrée in Nîmes. It was constructed between 1785 and 1788.

12 Wellington Monument: Erected in 1822 and designed by Richard Westmancott. In fact the head was not changed to represent Wellington. In 1814 Lady Spencer started a subscription among 'the Ladies of Great Britain' to fund the statue.
13 General Greene: Nathanael Greene (1742–1786) was a major-general of the Continental Army in the American Revolutionary War.
14 Sir Francis Legatt Chantrey (1781–1841), British sculptor.
15 John Flaxman RA (1755–1826), British artist.
16 Bailey and Behnes: Edward Hodges Baily (1788–1867), and William Behnes (1795–1864)-British sculptors.
17 Reference to Flaxman.
18 *[Vos] exemplaia Graeca etc.,*: "For yourselves, handle Greek models by night, handle them by day." Horace.
19 William Miller (1782–1849), who prophesied a second coming in 1844. His sect were called Millerites.
20 Finissons en!: "Let's finish! the world is old enough."
21 Albert Brisbane (1809–1890), American utopian socialist who is remembered as the chief populariser of the theories of the French utopian thinker Charles Fourier.
22 Major Downing: A pseudonym under which Seba Smith, (1792–1868) an American writer, wrote a series of humorous and popular letters on the politics of the United States. First published collectively in 1833, they were written in the Yankee dialect.

27

DAVID R. HAY, *THE NATURAL PRINCIPLES AND ANALOGY OF THE HARMONY OF FORM*

David Ramsay Hay (1798–1866) was a Scottish artist, interior decorator, and colour theorist. In April 1820, he worked for Walter Scott on the decorations at Abbotsford, and in 1850, he decorated Holyroodhouse for Queen Victoria, and then in the 1850s, he designed interiors for the National Gallery of Scotland. He called himself house-painter and decorator to the Queen, Edinburgh.

Hay took a strong interest in the theoretical aspects of his work, for example, publishing: *The Laws of Harmonious Colouring in House Painting* (1828); The *Natural Principles and Analogy of the Harmony of Form* (1842); *Proportion: or the Geometric Principle of Beauty Analysed* (1843); *First Principles of Symmetrical Beauty* (1846); and *The Science of Beauty* (1856).

In relation to form, Hay suggested that 'Forms are therefore analogous to sounds and colours in their effects upon the senses, and through the senses upon the mind. But the proving of this analogy would do little in the formation of an intelligible system of harmony of form: it must be shown that the perfect analogy also exists in the component parts producing these effects'.[1] Hay then argued that as there are three primitive colours (red, blue and yellow), so also there are three primitive sounds; the tonic, the median and the dominant, and also three primitive forms, the circle, the triangle, and the square. He argues that harmonies depend upon a predominance of one and a subordination of the other two in any composition.

Hay was a corresponding member of the Society for Promoting Practical Design, &c. and in the fourth edition of his *The Laws of Harmonious Colouring in House Painting* he dedicated the work to 'The Chairman and Members of the Committee of The Society For Promoting Practical Design, And a Knowledge And Love of The Arts Among The People'. (See 1.43)

Hay also developed rules of visual beauty based on Greek theories of musical harmonies, which divided up forms in the same proportions and partitions found in these sounds. Hay considered that harmony was found in the proportion and arrangement of the elements of abstract form that led to the 'geometric poetry of the graphic art'. He went on to say 'When forms are combined merely to produce a pleasing effect, as in ornamental design, or even in architecture, where the subjects are not in imitation of any natural objects, such compositions may be assimilated to those of melody or harmony in music, independently of the analogy of their elements. It has, however, been shown, that the elements of abstract form are in many respects similar to those of abstract sound'.[2]

The Court Gazette newspaper was genuinely impressed:

> The author is one of the individuals peculiarly endowed with that rich gift which constitutes the sculptor, the architect, and the painter; and hence the ingenious theory developed in this work, which logically associates sight with sound, geometry with acoustics. It is the developed theory of Plato, who eloquently commented on the music of beautiful forms; a theory which Darwin, the Platonic poet, in a note to his 'Temple of Nature', practically carries out, by suggesting the construction of a machine which, while producing the varied notes of the gamut to the ear, should, at the same time, present to the eye the 'various modulations of the prismatic colours. Mr Hay's theory is somewhat like this; but practically developed for the painter, the sculptor, and the architect'.[3]

David R. Hay, *The Natural Principles and Analogy of the Harmony of Form*, 3rd Edition (London: W. Blackwood and Sons, 1842), pp. 1–6

Introduction

It will not be disputed that the effect of forms upon the eye is either harmonious or discordant, agreeably to certain modes of arrangement of the lines which circumscribe them, or divide their parts. All writers on taste, architecture, landscape-gardening, and other subjects where discussions on the beauty of form are necessarily introduced, admit this fact. At the same time it is allowed, that as yet there has existed no system, or development of fixed principles, by which forms may be harmoniously arranged, but that judgment in such matters depends upon an abstract idea of beauty not easily defined. One of the latest and best writers upon taste says—"In the greater part of beautiful forms, whether in nature or art, lines of different descriptions unite. The greater part of the forms of nature and art possess an union, or composition of uniformity and variety, of similarity and dissimilarity of forms. But were such a combination in itself beautiful, it would necessarily follow, that, in every case where it was found, beauty would be the result. This is not the case, however."[4] And in support of this fact, the author in question quotes Mr Alison, who says—"Every one knows that the mere union of similarity and dissimilarity does not constitute a beautiful form;" and proceeds to say, that it is only when we perceive or imagine a correspondence among the part—a relation and harmony—that we are enabled to say, "that nature has been kind in combining different circumstances with so much propriety for the production of one effect."[5]

One of the latest and most eminent writers on architecture observes, in an excellent essay upon that subject, that—"It may be asked what standard of beauty there is in this art on which taste may be formed; though it must be obvious, that like other children of the imagination, such as poetry and music, no other can be assigned than such compositions and modes of arrangement as, by their harmony and simplicity, attract the attention of the rudest mind, which is pleased without being conscious why, and of the most learned or practised, which discovers in them those proportions and peculiarities of form which always produce the most pleasing impression, and appear to be dictated by nature."[6] Quotations to a similar effect might be given from innumerable works; but the above are considered sufficient to prove, that our general knowledge of the important subject of the harmony of form is open to improvement. If, therefore, it can be shown, that the impressions made upon the eye by forms are really founded on natural principles, and that the proportions and peculiarities of form which produce the most pleasing impressions, are in reality, as well as appearance, dictated by nature, being a response to these principles in the human mind, a desideratum in the arts will be obtained. And further, if it can be shown that, agreeably to the boundless analogy by which the sciences and arts are connected, forms are in all respects analogous to sounds, and that consequently a system of linear harmony can be established, similar to that which regulates the arrangement of musical notes, a knowledge of this important branch of art may also become a part of elementary education.

There can be no doubt that the effect produced by the harmony of sound, colour, and form, are equally the result of a susceptibility of the human mind, which renders it capable of appreciating an adherence to certain natural principles by which harmony in every case is produced. These principles are clearly understood in regard to the harmony of sound, from its having occupied the attention of the most eminent natural philosophers in all ages. Colours, likewise, since the discoveries of Sir Isaac Newton, have in their combinations been reduced to something like system. But the harmony of form has been left out of those enquiries, as a matter depending upon opinion alone, unless in regard to architecture, where the works of the ancients have in some measure supplied the want of general principles.

As a knowledge of the natural principles which regulate the arrangement of musical sounds tends to improve the general understanding and practice of that particular art, without producing a musical ear, or enhancing the pleasure derivable from an intuitive perception of "the melody of sweet sounds;" so may a knowledge of the natural principles of harmony in form improve our judgment in architecture, sculpture, and painting, without rendering us fit to follow any of those arts as a profession, or enhancing the pleasure conveyed to the mind by the visual organ.

A person is said to have an ear for music, in the ratio of the sensibility of that organ to the relative gravity and acuteness of sounds; and when this is accompanied by an intuitive appreciation of the natural principles which regulate their combination, he will, according to the extent of this talent, have a genius for musical composition. So, likewise, in the ratio of the sensibility of the eye and intuitive appreciation of the natural principles of form, will an individual possess a facility in producing harmonious arrangements, independently of any other knowledge of these principles. Thus works of art in all ages have occasionally displayed the most perfectly harmonious combinations of form. These are, however, of rare occurrence, being the works of men of great genius; and although they may be models for the careful study of those who follow such arts professionally, they cannot supply the place of natural principles in forming the public taste. Had the arrangement of musical sounds depended, like that of forms, upon the works of the ancients. without a knowledge of the natural principles upon which the excellence of these works depends, music could not have become a part of polite education.

It is not, therefore, assumed that this attempt to develop the principles of linear harmony, whatever its success in other respects may be, can have any effect in raising the standard of excellence, by improving the practice of professors of genius in the various arts which owe their excellence to beauty of form. Its object is more the improvement of the public taste in judging of such productions; and it is believed the fact will be readily admitted that such an attempt is not uncalled for. Neither can a knowledge of these principles tend, in any way, to add to the number of professors of the arts of design: it will rather lessen it; for as the public taste improves, untalented pretenders in all such professions will be detected, and sterling genius will meet the encouragement it alone deserves.

Notes

1 D. R. Hay, *The Natural Principles and Analogy of the Harmony of Form*, 3rd Ed. (London: W. Blackwood and Sons, 1842), p. 10.
2 D. R. Hay, *Proportion: Or the Geometric Principle of Beauty Analysed* (London: W. Blackwood and Sons, 1842), p. 58.
3 *The Edinburgh Review*, 82, 1845, cited in advertising back matter.
4 T. D. Lauder, *An Essay on Taste by Sir Thomas Dick Lauder, accompanying the Third Edition of "Sir Uvedale Price on the Picturesque,"* (Edinburgh: 1842), p. 33.
5 Lauder, *An Essay on Taste* p.33.
6 W. Hoskins, *A Treatise on Architecture by William Hoskins, F.S.A., Architect* (Edinburgh: 1835). Footnote in Hay.

28

LUCY CRANE, *ART AND THE FORMATION OF TASTE*

Lucy Crane (1842–1882) was an English writer, art critic, and translator who wrote children's stories and nursery rhymes. She was influenced by John Ruskin and Thomas Carlyle and held socialist views on art and society.

Art and the Formation of Taste originated as a series of lectures that were initially delivered to pupils of her friend, the teacher Miss Janion of Harold House, Lansdowne Road, Notting Hill, and later for private courses of lectures across England. The theme was the application of art to everyday life.[1] The book contained six lectures with illustrations by her brothers Walter and Thomas Crane. In this essay on *Form,* she makes a simple request for plainness and simplicity in the design of objects. Basing her plea on the ideas of Ruskin and Morris, she suggests that appropriateness is the key to good design. Appropriate materials, appropriateness for a particular place, and a form that is appropriate for usage. She then gives a number of examples of inappropriate design including 'a tea-kettle in the form of a drum, with the sticks for handles; a toast-rack formed of wreaths of ivy (what has ivy to do with toast?), or rifles piled in a very unmilitary manner; a biscuit-box in the shape of a coal-box; gilt chain cables for holding back curtains'.[2] *The Art Journal* was not really satisfied:

> the teaching is, in the main, of the usual orthodox cast – implications of the dicta of Ruskin, Pater, Morris, and others. Everyone nowadays will allow that 'to expend labour in disguising use and falsifying material shows an utter misconception of heart'; but we suspect that there be those who would handle rather roughly such 'axioms' as 'nothing is ornamental unless it is also really useful,' quoted approvingly from Mr Morris. The old bill of indictment—now quite undefended – against our furniture, our fire-irons and the rest, is repeated much in the old manner. But we are not furnished with what we chiefly want – some clear guidance towards better things. 'The hungry sheep look up and are not fed'.[3]

Although Lucy Crane identified three simple 'points of general application' that were the basis for her discussions, they were simply statements of principle, although they clearly reflected mainstream thinking about the role of art and design in society:

1. That the general aim of Art is Beauty, and the appreciation of that Beauty and the true enjoyment of it is Taste.
2. That there are certain principles by which Taste may be formed and guided.
3. That these principles are worthy to be studied, since we cannot escape from the necessity of exercising a choice.[4]

This extract is taken from her lecture titled 'Decorative Art – Form' where the author initially critiques the division of labour that she suggested created an over-finish to a surface. Although she acknowledges that there was a role for machinery to produce some items on a large scale, she puts it in a nutshell by stating 'Division of labour is good for pins, but bad for works of art'.[5] Crane goes on to say 'The ornament (I quote from a long-since printed magazine article) which begins with the mere draughtsman and ends with the mere salesman, deteriorates at every stage, in its change of hands from the original design'. She then goes on to critique the division of labour again, this time in relation to jewellery works. 'According to the ordinary system of producing jewellery, the design has been made by one man, the dies sunk by another, the striking up by a third, some foliage and filigree work added by a fourth, and some shallow, scratchy engraving to complete the pattern by a fifth, and it becomes what the accomplished shopman who sells it calls "a truly sweet thing in bracelets of the newest and most original design."'[6]

See also 3.23

Lucy Crane, *Art and the Formation of Taste* (London: Macmillan, 1882), pp. 61–68

II. Decorative Art—Form

"For," says Mr. Morris, "whereas all works of craftsmanship were once beautiful, unwittingly or not, they are now divided into two kinds—works of art, and non-works of art. Now nothing made by man's hand can be indifferent; it must be either beautiful and elevating, or ugly and degrading."[7] Can we not carry about us in the world; can we not be guided in our purchases by some such thoughts as these? and take care never to buy a cheap, ill-made, useless article, merely because it catches our fancy. Let us consider if there is good work in it,—honest material, actual use,—and if so, let us pay for it a fair price, and we shall be doing what we can to help on the good cause of promoting happy toil and successful labour; in short, of making Decorative Art to be again what it once was, "An Art made by the people and for the people, a joy to the maker and user."[8]

In Mr. Ruskin's "Two Paths" I find a principle laid down that I am convinced is perfectly sound, and easy of application in these matters.

"The true forms of conventional ornament consist in the bestowal of as much beauty on the object as shall be consistent with its Material, its Place, and its Office."[9]

Every object, then, that we admit into our houses should be able to sustain with credit the following inquiries:

> Does it appear to be made of the Material of which it really is, or ought to be made?
> Is it appropriate to the Place for which it is intended?
> Does it declare its Use or Office, and seem fit for it?

Let us examine a little into the application of each separate requirement. The first, you see, condemns all imitations of a substance, especially when the object is not likely to have been made of that substance. Such are doors painted in bronze, sham jewellery, paper flowers, glass coloured to look like china, plaster to look like iron and bronze, and many more. It seems a very strange thing, when one reflects, that it should be supposed that we all take pleasure in a thing that pretends to be something else than it appears, and that the deception should be pointed out to us as a recommendation. The advertisement that assures us that Paris diamonds and Abyssinian jewellery[10] cannot be distinguished from the real thing, the shopkeeper who tells us that some stuff of mixed material has quite the appearance of silk, and that a silk-finished velveteen could easily be mistaken for velvet; all this is intended to appeal, and really does appeal, to the tastes and wants of a large class. But how much better and more honest is it to know what the especial article we want *ought* to be made of, and to see that we get it—silk honestly silk, and woollen honestly woollen, and cotton honestly cotton, and linen really and truly linen; and when the manufacturers find what is expected of them they will supply it accordingly. It must have been inappropriate and perishable material that first put it into the careful housewife's mind to provide an extra case or cover for various household objects—oil-cloth or drugget to cover the stair-carpeting, holland covers for the furniture, and antimacassars over them again, oil-cloth to cover tables, and table-covers to cover the oil-cloth, and mats to save the table-cloth, and much more of the same kind. In the first place, the materials used should be appropriate and serviceable, and in the second, people should not be ashamed of the signs of honest wear in them. Still, for my part, if I must cover things up at all, I would cover them when they were really shabby than while they were fresh. And when this system of covers extends itself to paper-covers for flower-pots, china-cases and covers for sardine-boxes, silvered perforated cardboard cases for matchboxes, and such like, it seems to express a dislike to the honest plainness and simplicity, really right and appropriate, of the things themselves, and a false refinement and love of disguise. It is the same feeling that leads people to call shops repositories and emporiums, and florists to call themselves "horticultural furnishers." Simplicity and plain dealing in the material of household goods and appliances will lead us a long way in the direction of taste. And we have high authority for feeling the dignity and admirableness of even a very humble function well performed. Does not George Herbert say:

> Who sweeps a room as for Thy laws
> Makes that and the action fine.[11]

Now as to the second requirement. The various rooms in our houses are intended for various uses and occasions, and natural instinct for convenience leads us to furnish them in accordance with these uses and occasions—the dining-room solid and severe, with large and steady furniture adapted to serious needs; the kitchen, full of useful homely appliances, kept bright and clean; and the drawing-room, with its books and pictures and elegancies, suited for leisure and social purposes, and therefore rightly the most decorated room in the house. So bearing the different functions of each room in mind, and furnishing them in accordance with each, we get a general sense of order and appropriateness. All this is obvious enough, and is generally sufficiently well carried out. Only very often in minor appliances, the want of the feeling for appropriateness makes itself felt. A coalscuttle is an excellent and useful thing in its way, and in its appropriate place; but why have it in miniature on our tables, and scoop salt or sugar out of it? Wheel-barrows and buckets, rink-skates and perambulators, used for similar purposes are really less convenient than a small dish or bowl really designed for use, without any ulterior notion of ingenuity or conceit. A tea-kettle in the form of a drum, with the sticks for handles; a toast-rack formed of wreaths of ivy (what has ivy to do with toast?), or rifles piled in a very unmilitary manner; a biscuitbox in the shape of a coal-box; gilt chain cables for holding back curtains; are examples of the same thing that occur to me, but a large and very astonishing list could very soon be collected. It is true, as Mr. Morris says, that the best designed and constructed things in a house are generally found in the kitchen; but that is because they fulfil their use, and are appropriate to their place, both of which qualities they lose when transported to the drawing-room.

Now, as to the third requirement, which in its application is closely connected with the second. All things of common use have their appropriate form, which, when once discovered, should be used and repeated without disguise. Thus a salt-cellar is most really convenient when made of glass, of a simple oblong shape, so as not to be easily upset, that the spoon may comfortably rest in it, and the salt be easily renewed; and there, are many modifications of form, and even colour, that might be introduced without hindering use in any way, or making the thing seem other than it is; and so may this principle be carried out indefinitely; and I cannot see, except for the love of novelty and pretentious conceit, why anything more should be wanted. It cannot be a very lasting pleasure to shake pepper out of an owl's head, or help yourself to butter out of a beehive; but it is a lasting pleasure to have a thoroughly useful and soundly-constructed thing made out of a right and good material, appearing in its appropriate place, and declaring and fulfilling its proper use and office. Without directly referring to these three conditions at every moment, I would be understood as keeping them in mind as I go on.

Notes

1 *Illustrated Queen Almanac and Lady's Calendar*, 1883, p. 292.
2 L. Crane, *Art and the Formation of Taste* (London: Macmillan, 1882), p. 66.
3 Review, *Art Journal*, April 1883, p. 132.
4 Crane, p. 48.
5 Crane, p. 56.
6 Crane, p. 56.
7 W. Morris, *Hopes and Fears for Art*, 'The Beauty of Life'. Delivered before the Birmingham Society of Arts and School of Design, February 19, 1880.
8 W. Morris, Lecture, 'The Art of the People' delivered before the Birmingham Society of Arts and School of Design, 19 February 1879.
9 J. Ruskin, "Modern Manufacture and Design", *The Two Paths* (Orpington: George Allen, 1886), p. 82.
10 Both imitations of the real object; diamonds and gold respectively. Parisian diamond Company made paste jewels. Abyssinian gold was a substitute for gold, being of varying compositions but typically consisting of an alloy of copper, zinc, and aluminium plated with gold.
11 G. Herbert (1593–1633), Welsh poet; *The Elixir* (1633).

29

HENRI MAYEUX, *A MANUAL OF DECORATIVE COMPOSITION FOR DESIGNERS, DECORATORS, ARCHITECTS AND INDUSTRIAL ARTISTS*

Henri Mayeux, (1845–1929) was a French architect and professor of decorative art at the National School of Fine Arts. The work was originally published as *La Composition Décorative* (Paris: Quantin, 1884) with this edition being translated by J. Gogino.

In this work, he warned against trying to create beauty by simply applying complicated or rich decoration. He argued that it would be better to leave an object unadorned than to cover it with a richness that adds nothing to it. The old argument about decorating construction, rather than constructing decoration is still evident. Indeed, nearly half of the book is given over to a discussion of the wide range of materials use in decorative arts and design, with a view to ensuing the 'fitness' of design to the chosen material, thus avoiding unfortunate imitations.

This edition was praised by the *Saturday Review* because 'the young student in design, may learn, from the specimens of good and bad work depicted what errors of form and composition to avoid'.[1] However, in its book review of a slightly later edition in 1895, *The Academy* was very critical of the translator and the effect on the reader:

> we fear the skill of the translator has not been equal to the task of rendering it into English which will clearly be 'understood'. For instance, it is not every cultivated Englishman (to say nothing of the ordinary artisan) who will see at once what is meant by the following sentences: 'A pleasing shape is essential in forms not dependent upon their thickness for their expression'.

The article goes on with other examples and then says, 'We present our respectful sympathy to the author, M. Mayeux, on this wretched translation of his book'.[2]

Henri Mayeux, *A Manual of Decorative Composition for Designers, Decorators, Architects and Industrial Artists* (London: J.S. Virtue and Co, 1889), pp. 1–4

Introduction

I. Decorative Art Composition

Decorative, or as it is sometimes called, *ornamental* art, is too often considered as occupying an inferior position in the hierarchy of the Fine Arts; as having nothing in common with them, except in outward appearance. This is, however, a mistake which it is necessary to correct, since that word *decorative* is applicable to all the arts, when they are used to satisfy certain conditions of usefulness with reference to surroundings or position.

There is little difficulty in classifying arts applied to industry or industrial arts,* such as working in bronze, wood, iron, ceramics, enamels, mosaic, tapestry, glass, etc., for decorative or architectural purposes, the latter being readily recognised as one of its finest and noblest expressions; but confusion is apt to exist when we approach painting and sculpture, no matter how decorative their chief object may be. Do not the frescoes which cover our walls, the pier-glasses, and doors, as well as the bas-reliefs, medallions, busts, and statues, associated with a fine architectural building, and forming part of it, all belong to decorative art? This, their essential characteristic, is not met with in works of art conceived without reference to their surroundings, and consequently susceptible of being displaced at will.

There are works, however, which have been, by common consent, called *decorative,* although they were not executed with a view to any definite destination; but in this case they are possessed of special qualities, and, if necessary, they may be introduced in general decoration; whilst we see works conceived in view of a particular site wanting in such qualities, and thus unfitted for the part assigned to them. The main object, therefore, in *decorative composition* is the study of those qualities whereby balance between the various parts of a work, whether of *form* or *decoration*, is secured, and a whole, attractive in itself and in harmony with its surroundings, is obtained.

But before entering into these complex questions we wish to note one or two points: First, with regard to industrial products, we would observe, although they have no bearing upon art, that the practical use for which they are intended should be well kept in view. Are we not right, for instance, to demand that the mouth of a vessel shall allow of water being poured easily, that the handles shall be

---

* The expression *industrial arts* has been criticised on the plea that art is debased when applied to industrial ends, and has been replaced by *art industries* which is in no way more logical. We shall not enter into a mere question of words: what is important is that, which expression is used, it be understood.

convenient; and the various openings of a piece of furniture disposed with regard to their practical use? Exceptions will naturally be made of objects fashioned solely to please the eye, with no reference to domestic uses, such as decorative plates and ornamental metal-work. Even practical usefulness, to be complete, should be accompanied by a certain degree of beauty, so as to give to its embodiment something more than mere mechanical value.

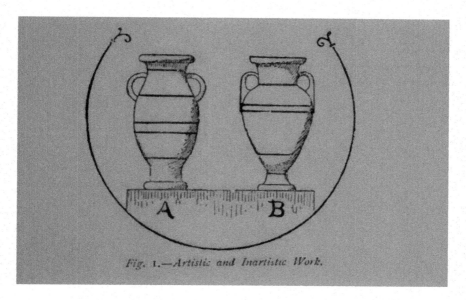

Fig. 1.—*Artistic and Inartistic Work.*

There is, unfortunately, a prevalent idea abroad that the beautiful is attained by complicated forms overloaded with elaborate ornamentation. That this is an error will be made apparent to the most inexperienced eye by the following very simple example. Fig. 1 represents two vessels of the same height, made of the same clay, and we may assume that the same care was bestowed upon the execution of each. They are each furnished with two handles, and decorated with an equal number of brown stripes painted on the outer surface; A is the work of a simple potter, without artistic education, whilst B is the work of one of those Greek workmen, whose refined taste is too well known to need comment. There is no one but will feel the superiority of vase B over its companion A; the purity of outline, the finish of the handles, the division of the stripes, at once establish a wide difference in the artistic value of the two pieces.

It will be seen from this example that a knowledge of the laws both of *form* and of *decoration* will raise the standard of any work, from the lowest grade of industry to the highest standard of art. *Clearness* is another quality which it is no less important to bear in mind, and which will be dealt with in our chapter on decorative composition. The best guide for the attainment of *clearness* is common sense. In a composition, for instance, it will not be satisfied unless all the component parts, however complicated, can be viewed at a glance, and without effort even at some distance. An undecided method, profuseness of detail, want of truth in the part assigned to the subject of the work, i.e. all the defects most opposed to distinctness (and, alas! too frequently seen in current composition), cannot be too severely or too often stigmatized, if it is wished to raise the standard of our art industries from the mere routine which seems to have taken permanent root in our studios.

Notes

1 *Saturday Review*, 5 January 1889, p. 26.
2 *Academy,* 15 June 1895, p. 509.

30

HUGH STANNUS, 'SOME PRINCIPLES OF FORM-DESIGN IN APPLIED ART'

The interest in the concept of form as a basic part of design continued to be discussed and analysed by theorists and practical designers turned authors. Hugh Hutton Stannus (1840–1908) was a pupil at the Sheffield School of Art. He then joined stove makers Hoole and Co., in the city, working under the sculptor Alfred Stevens, who was the chief designer there at the time. Stannus was also one-time chief assistant to upholsterer and decorator Leonard Collmann, who was also a friend of Alfred Stevens. Stannus designed a piano for Collmann that was displayed at the 1871 International Exhibition.[1] Later, Stannus became a lecturer on applied art at the National Art School, in South Kensington. He was subsequently appointed professor of applied art in University College London and was a teacher of Architectural Ornament at the Royal Academy. He had links with the Arts and Crafts movement and was a FRIBA. In addition to his teaching and studio practice, Stannus revised Franz Meyer's *A Handbook of Ornament* (1892) and he also wrote *The Decorative Treatment of Natural Foliage* (1891), as well as *The Theory of Storiation in Applied Art* (1893). He also published a memoir of his mentor as *Alfred Stevens and His Work . . .* (1891).

Stannus had a particular interest in metalwork design and especially ironwork, in which he seems to have been successful. The *Athenaeum,* in a report on the 1862 International Exhibition, noted that 'Mr. Hugh Stannus is amongst the few who study the true character of design needful for metal-works. [His] *Design for Iron Gates,* are admirable in the constructive richness of their composition'.[2]

Twenty years later, Stannus delivered a paper to the Royal Institute of British Architects on the topic of 'The Artistic Treatment of Constructional Ironwork'. His concluding remarks were a call for eclecticism as the most hopeful path of progress towards true independence of design:

> At the same time, the iron style of the future must be logically deduced, as well as eclectic. It should possess the purity of line and mathematical proportion of Greek architecture, the distributed surface decoration of the Mahommedan, the rich modelling of the Roman, the simplicity of

the component parts of the Romanesque, and the economy of material, together with the constructive truth of the Gothic.[3]

The article on form design reproduced here is one of a series of four Cantor Lectures delivered to the Society of Arts during the session 1898/9. It considered broad principles of form and then focussed on functionality as an issue. The discussion included considerations relating to the use of anthropometric data: The provision of a handle or handles that he referred to as ansation (an obscure Latin borrowing); and the practical issues of designing with considerations such as the cleaning of objects, and the avoidance of injury to both the user and the object.

Hugh Stannus, 'Some Principles of Form-Design in Applied Art', *Journal of the Society of Arts*, 46, 14 October 1898, pp. 885–889

Lecture 1

ART may be defined as that branch of mental activity the intention and result of which is to make the material Environment-of-life more pleasant. When the things and acts which constitute this environment arc most pleasing to minds of most intelligence—then they are said to be "beautiful". The Beauty may appeal through any of those channels of communication from the Environment to the Mind, which are termed "the five Senses"; and may be beauty in Sight, Sound, Smell, Touch, or Taste. And, according to the particular Sense it affects, it will be beauty in:—Shape or Form and Colour, Sound, Odour, Taction, Savour. Opinions are divided on the question—of the intellectual order in which these should have precedence; and they are here arranged on the principle of Distance v. Proximity, it being assumed that those Senses which require *nearness* are more personal to the animal portion of the observer, and those which can be exercised on *distant* objects are appreciated by the intellectual faculties.

There is an Art (or several Arts) which appeals to each particular sense; thus:—Architecture, Sculpture, Painting, &c., to sight—Poetry, Music, &c., to sound—Perfumery, &c., to smell—Texture to touch—and Gastronomies to Taste; but only the first three, which appeal to the sense of Sight, are included in this present course.

A further subdivision is made—between the art that is produced without special reference to the surroundings, which is independent, isolated, unapplied, and sometimes heterogeneous or unsuitable—and the art which is made *for* its place and *in* its place, is applied, and should be homogenous, and appropriate. The former may be termed "Independent-art"; and the latter is "Applied-art".

SOME PRINCIPLES OF FORM-DESIGN IN APPLIED ART

The INDEPENDENT ARTS are:—Sculpture, when the examples were made, each for its own intrinsic beauty in line and mass, without reference to the positions that they may afterwards occupy, but generally intended to be, each of them, the dominant feature of the Collection or Shrine. Some of these examples like the Aphrodite of Knidos, the Nike of Melos, and the Apollo of the Belvedere are among the noblest achievements man—Painting, when, similarly, the pictorial artist shows his mastery over drawing, colour and chiaroscuro, in subjects chosen to display those qualities without reference to or knowledge of any subsequent positions that may be dignified by the easel pictures; and, here again, it would not be difficult to name works which are immortal—Music, when the tone-artist feeling the throbbing of interwoven melodies, is impelled to score them without reference to any words— and so with the other Independent Arts: each of them is independent of any useful objects; and arises mainly out of the worker's joy in his powers.

The APPLIED ARTS are:—Architecture, when interesting Variety, well-considered Proportion, refined Detail, and expressive Features are added to structures (as is so well shown in Fergusson's History of Ancient and Mediaeval Architecture, 1893, page 13, and in Mr Statham's Architecture for General Readers, 1895, page 17) which without such graces would be only Building—Sculpture, when the relief Frieze and Panel are applied as the decoration of the Cabinet—Painting, when the beauty of foliage is applied to a Wall—Music, when the rhythmic beat of the military March is utilised to keep the soldiers in proper "step" —and so with the other Applied Arts: each of them owes its existence to the fact that it is *applied*.

This course is on Applied Art. Sir Edward Poynter P.R.A. in his fine scholarly and searching "Ten Lectures on Art" first published in 1879, has classified Applied Art into the two kinds, which are here termed:— Form-design and Decoration-design.[4]

FORM-DESIGN (or constructive design as he terms it)—"has its simplest expression in the form that savage gives to the ordinary objects of his daily use; • • • to his hatchet, or to the rude vessels in which he cooks his food".

DECORATION-DESIGN is seen "in the patterns which he cuts on the prow of his boat, or traces with a stick on his pottery, or the mud walls of his hut".

The FORM of an object, and the DECORATION of that Form—are often conceived together or simultaneously in the Artist's mind, analogously to the close relation between the PLAN of a Building, and the ELEVATIONS of the walls that enclose that Plan. Practically, however the Plan for accommodation is first considered; and the Wall-design depends upon it; and similarly in Art: the Form (or, at least, the general Mass-form) is primary, and the Decoration is secondary. Thus a Pot is: (firstly) thrown on the wheel, in which operation it receives its Form; and (secondly) scratching, painting, or modelling, is added or applied, in which operation it receives its Decoration.

There are cases, in which:—(a) the Function of the object does not permit of Decoration, or (b) the Beauty of the form does not require any further addition;

but these will be considered, generally, as they arise. For the present, it will be well for the Student to consider the two operations as distinct; and to deal firstly with FORM, and secondly with DECORATION.

In Form-design the artist considers the design for the intended object, after the general conditions have been formulated according to the requirements of Fitness (i.e. fitness to the Function or intended purpose and use of the object, to the Material of which the object is to be made with its capabilities and limitations, and to the particular Construction or methods of joining-together that he intends to adopt); and, always subject to these Conditions, he adds, according to his artistic individuality or "taste", such further qualities as—Variety in the Mass-form, and Proportion of parts to each other and to the whole object.

These two qualities—Variety and Proportion—when superadded to the Fitness are sufficient in themselves to render an object beautiful. Further artistic work may impart other qualities, e.g.:—Richness, Refinement, Accent, &c.; but they are not absolutely necessary. One Vase with Variety and Proportion superadded in the Form, though without any decorative detail, may shew a high order of Beauty; while, in another of bad Form, the faults may be a little disguised by judicious Decoration, but they cannot be eradicated; and it will always be low in the scale.

The two Branches of any treatise on Applied Art are: (1) the Elements, and (2) the Principles which govern the application of those elements. In the sister art of Gastronomies, the Cook manipulates and mingles certain Ingredients according to certain Recipes; and the student will perceive the analogy between the Ingredients and the Elements, and between the Recipes and the Principles.

The ELEMENTS of FORM are the Geometrical Solids, e.g.: the Cylinder, Prism, Sphere, Ovus, Cone, Hyperboloid, Parallelepiped, &c., and many Irregular forms which need not be particularised here.

The ELEMENTS of DECORATION are Geometrical Lines and Figures, Ornament (see the author's second course of Cantor Lectures on "Artificial Foliage"), Natural Foliage (see the author's first course of Cantor Lectures on "Natural Foliage"), Artificial Objects (e.g. the Garland, Shield, Festoon, Tablet, &c.), Parts of Animals (e.g. the Lionhead for the Water-spout, the Lion-leg for the Foot-stool, &c.), Animals and Compound-animals (e.g. the Lion, Gryphon, &c.), and, lastly, the Human-figure, which is the noblest of all. All of these, except the Human-figure, will be seen in Meyer's "Handbook of Ornament" (2nd English edition, Batsford, 1894).

A PRINCIPLE, in ordinary language, is the underlying universal consideration which governs conduct in Daily-life, e.g. the "Golden Rule". The essence or spirit of this is expanded, embodied, and applied in detail to particular Places; and this application is termed a By-law. It is further expanded, in more detail for particular Persons; and this is termed a Rule of Etiquette.

The PRINCIPLES in APPLIED ART are analogous; but, by an unfortunate looseness of idea, in some lists of Principles, there has been no distinction made between the universal Principle (that is right under all conditions) and the local Law (that is limited in application, and subject to be suspended in operation by the higher); nor between these and the minor Rule (that is applied only to the small details in their "personal" relation to each other);* and the undiscriminating Dogmatism, that makes the less of as much importance as the greater, has caused a hostile feeling against all principles, and a desire to "kick over the traces" in the restless and capricious search for so-called "Novelty".

These Principles are:—Fitness, Variety, Proportion, Sympathy, Expression, &c. It is impossible, within restricted limits, to do more than mention their importance; and it may perhaps be more useful to the student if his attention is directed to the Laws.

The FUNCTION of any object or feature of an object is the intended Purpose or Duty that it is arranged to serve or sustain, e.g. the retaining of the Stems in a vertical attitude, by the Flower-vase—or the permitting of an easy flow of Liquid, by the Teapot-spout. Sometimes several Functions arc served by the same object, e.g. in the Greek water-vase termed the Hydria (the first sketch in figure 30.2) a vessel that—(a) the women carried in a horizontal attitude resting in an annular pad on their heads, in going to the Spring; hence its largeness and roundness of profile at the centre of gravity (empty) near the widest part of the vessel—(b) was held by the women under the bubbling flow; hence the large and strong single Handle attached to the neck—(c) had to catch as much water as possible; hence the wide Mouth—(d) had to be lifted by each woman to her head; hence the two Sidehandles—(e) had to be steady when carried in a vertical attitude on the head; hence the strong wide Foot—(f) had to prevent splashing as the woman walked; hence the contraction from the vase-shoulder to the vase-neck. So, also, in the oil-vase termed the Lekythos (the second sketch in figure 30.2), the vessel was—(a) small and suspended from the girdle; hence the small strong Handle—(b) was used by the athletes for anointing themselves; hence the swelling out of the neck for the purpose of forming a Cup (as shown by the dotted lines) from which the finger might easily extract a small quantity as required. The Greek Vases, of the great period, are so perfectly beautiful in their Form that the spectator is liable to overlook or not to appreciate the no less perfect fitness for their Function.

Objects are FUNCTIONALLY DESIGNED when all the Purpose or Duties for which they am intended arc properly considered and provided for. The quality, that is thereby conferred upon the object, is termed Functionality.

The Law of FUNCTIONALITY is the first and the most important in Applied-Art. It prescribes that the Form shall be such as will best serve the intended Purpose of each object. No desire for Variety, in bulk, curvature, or texture, may be permitted to interfere with this. Nor should *Vis inertia*[5] or indolent Pleading of Custom be allowed to prevent the student from searchingly considering

---

* See this beautifully expressed in "The Education of the World," by Dr. Temple (the present Archbishop of Canterbury) published in "Essays and Reviews."

each function of each part. In a competition for a Foot-scraper to be executed in cast-iron, some years ago: one of the models showed two cupids, about 6 inches high, holding *a piece of drapery* like two maids shaking a carpet, against the upper edge of which the foot was to be scraped! The two Cupids were very good examples of modelling: but the artist appeared to have overlooked the fact that the problem was:—not to model a cupid, but to design a Foot scraper. The result was ridiculous as a design and disastrous for him; and many of the objects that vulgarise houses result from a similar ignoring of this first and greatest Law– Functionality.

DISREGARD of Functionality is shewn in the sketch (The first in Fig. 30.1)

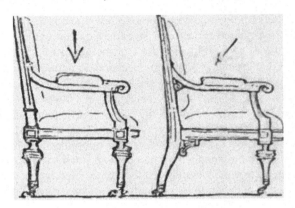

Fig. 30.1

The artist may have thought that the strain on the chair was only *vertical* (shewn by the arrow) as it is on a Stool or a seat without a back. But, when a Back is provided, and the sitter leans against it, the strain becomes *oblique*; and this should be provided for (as shewn in the second sketch). The first is from a set of chairs, beautiful in other respects, in one of the French palaces: perhaps they have not been much used, (now they are merely Show-objects): if they had to undergo the wear and tear of daily life, they would soon exhibit, in the loose joints and ricketyness, the neglect of the artist.

FUNCTIONALITY includes considerations relating to the Anthropic-size: the Ansation[6] and the Cleaning of Objects, and also to the avoidance of Injury to the user and of Injury to the object.

ANTHROPIC-SIZE is the average size of Man as governing the size of Objects that he uses. Thus:—that of the whole body is necessary for the opening-space of Doors, &c., both in height and width—the height of his Breast is necessary for that of Parapets—the height of his Knee-joint is necessary for that of Seats—the height of his Hand is necessary for that of Door-handles and Chair-backs—the size of his hand for that of Handles of Doors, &c.—the size of his fingers for that of Teacup handles, &c.—the length of his foot for the breadth of a Stair-tread—and

SOME PRINCIPLES OF FORM-DESIGN IN APPLIED ART

the length of his down-hill Step is taken for that of the Stair-riser and Stair-tread together.

DISREGARD of Anthropic-size is seen in the Steps round the Parthenon, and in other Temples. The height of the Riser and the breadth of the Tread are too great; hence, in some Temples, smaller Steps of anthropic-size were cut-out or interpolated at the entrances. When the Anthropic-size is considered in a building, in the Steps, the Seats, the Doors, and other parts: then the spectator can better assess and appreciate the Size of the building. The church of St. Peter's, on the Vatican Hill, at Rome is an instance of the manner in which the colossal size of the building loses its impressiveness by reason of the colossal size of the details and disregard of Anthropic-size.

ANSATION is important in all objects that are carried. The artist takes this into his thought, considering the number, position, attitude, &c. of the Handles; and so making them characteristic and expressive features in his design. M. Viollet-le-Duc, in the sixth of his fine analytic and suggestive "Entrétiens", 1860,[7] shews the arrangement of handles when a Vase must be reversed for draining. Dr. Christopher Dresser, in his useful books: "The Art of Decorative Design", 1862, at pp. 133 et seq., and "The Principles of Decorative Design" (about 15 years later), at pp. 139 et seq., has reasoned-out the application of the Handle in relation to the distributing of liquid from the vessel. Two sketches of Fig. 30.2 are adapted from his illustrations.

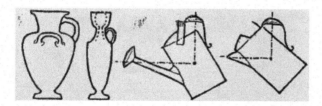

Fig. 30.2

The third sketch is for a *pip*espout Water-can; and the fourth sketch is for a *lip*-spout Water-can. In each case-the Centre-of-gravity of the vessel (when full) is found, as marked by the Dot in the two sketches. A Line (termed the Delivery-line) is drawn, from this Dot, to the lowest point at which the liquid is delivered. From this Dot, and at right-angles to the Delivery-line, a Line (termed the Suspension-line) is drawn in an upward direction. When the Distributing-handle is on this Suspension-line, then the vessel is most easily manipulated.

DISREGARD of Ansation is seen in most Tea-pots: all who have to pour-out tea will have felt the great disadvantage of the Position of the handles. Another example is shewn in Fig. 30.3 in which the Vase, described (among others) as being "in the highest-sense original generally from admirable designs by the great artists of Germany",[8] is furnished with attached extraneous pieces of Ornament in such a manner that the would-be user cannot hold it to drink from, either by the Sidehandles or the Stem-handle.

Fig. 30.3

Fig. 30.4

The Vase is shewn in fig. 30.4 with the Ansation corrected. (It is necessary here to explain that this and nearly all the figures arc from *rough sketches* such as were made on the black-board; and, beyond elucidating the Law involved, make no pretension to be Designs.)

ALL MOVABLE OBJECTS, which have to be lifted from one position to another, should either be ansated or be provided with some conspicuous knob or plain portion that may be grasped with efficiency and comfort. When the maid is uncertain what she should take hold of for the purpose of lifting the chair or pulling down the chandelier—then the artist is in fault.

CLEANING, or provision for efficient and easy cleaning, is important in all objects that are used. The inside of the Jug, and face of the Mirror, will occur to everyone.

DISREGARD of this is seen:—in the elaborately-chased chamber-candlestick, that becomes clogged with overflowing wax—in the pot Jug with neck too small to admit the hand (if the artist plead that the smallness of the neck gives character to his design and that he cannot do without it: then he has mistaken his vocation)—in the carved Mirror-frame "decorated" by the Swag-festoons that overhang the Glass, causing the leaving of dirty places or the risk of breakage as each weekly Cleaning-day comes round—and more examples will occur to every Housewife.

INJURY to the USER must be foreseen and prevented, by the avoidance of sharp edges and spikey relief-work, and generally by the introduction of smoothness and softness, so far as is practicable, in all places within reach of Traffic or Use. Without going so far towards the other extreme as to provide Padded-rooms, the artist may yet take care, in these days of feverish hurry and rushing-about, that, in the mouldings of Passage-ways, &c., and in the Metal-fittings of Doors, &c., there shall be no projecting blocks to "bark the shins" or "skin the knuckles" of the user.

DISREGARD of this will be seen:—in the Chair-back that tears the Lady's dress by its prickly ornament—in the wrought-iron support to the Wash-bason that becomes entangled in the dress—in the Screws of the Door-handle that are not "driven-home"—&c.

INJURY TO THE OBJECT by the Use must be equally avoided. An interesting example of this is seen at Pompeii, where the arrisses[9] shewing an angle of about 100° to 120° between the flutes of the Greek Doric columns were damaged by the Traffic; and where, consequently, the flutes are filled up with cement making facets only, with arrisses of 157½, which is much more obtuse, and therefore less liable to injury.

Notes

1 *Illustrated catalogue, International Exhibition, London* (1871–72), p. 19.
2 *Athenaeum,* 13 September 1862, p. 346.
3 H. Stannus, 'The Artistic Treatment of Constructional Ironwork', [Paper read to RIBA], *Builder,* 28 January 1882, p. 96.
4 E. Poynter, *Ten Lectures on Art* (London: Chapman and Hall, 1879), p. 2.

5 *Vis inertia*: a body at rest or inactive.
6 Ansation: The provision of a handle or handles.
7 E. E. Viollet-le-Duc, *Entretiens Sur L'architecture* (Paris: Morel, 1858).
8 *The Illustrated Catalogue of the Universal Exhibition Published with the Art Journal* (London and New York: Virtue and Co, 1868), p.6.
9 arris is the sharp edge formed by the intersection of two plane surfaces.

5.3
MATERIALS

31

EMIL BRAUN, 'ELECTROTYPING APPLIED TO ART MANUFACTURES'

Electrotyping (galvanoplasty) is a technique used to reproduce metal components through a chemical process, invented by both Mr. Thomas Spencer of Liverpool, and Moritz von Jacobi in 1838 in Russia. The process created facsimiles of any irregular surfaced objects. The important distinction between electro-typing and electro-plating is that in electroplating, the deposited metal acts as coating to the object whereas in electroforming the object is produced through the process of electrodeposition on a mould of the original, so that metal deposits are attached directly to the moulds in the plating vats. When the buildup of metal was enough to create an autonomous copy, the mould was removed. The *Art Journal* was very enthusiastic about the process they saw at Elkington's during an 1846 tour:

> On the other hand, the electrotypes are perfect: the finest lines, the most minute dots, are as faithfully copied as the boldest objections. We have found reproduced in the electrotype the scratch of a needle, which could not be seen in the original without the aid of a microscope; hence, if we have a perfect model or mould, the electrical process will ensure a perfect copy or cast.[1]

To produce the electrotypes, firms like Elkington and Franchi and Sons sent specialist mould makers to the locations of fine historic examples. The moulds were made from gutta-percha or similar material and then used to produce copper patterns that were the master model for numerous subsequent copies. These copies could be then be finished in several ways to reproduce the original.

These models were planned to develop Britain's design skills by providing students in schools of design with the best examples of historic design, as well as providing the viewing public in museums with examples of good taste. As they were often modelled on famous originals, they were valuable as didactic, as well as artistic examples. Not surprisingly, the process that clearly married art and industry was supported by Prince Albert, who not only engaged with Elkington and Co., but also provided models for the process, and purchased examples for his collection.

The process of manufacture, like many others during the period, was also of interest to the lay public, as well as to manufacturers. In 1884, Knight's *Penny Magazine* published a lengthy article titled 'A Day at an Electro-Plate Factory describing the processes of production in some detail'.[2]

August or Auguste Emil Braun (1809–1856) was a German archaeologist, who in the autumn of 1833 went to Rome, where he became Secretary to the German Archaeological Institute. Later he apparently established a galvanoplastic workshop in Rome, where reproductions of antique art objects were produced. In 1846, Emil Braun introduced himself to George Elkington, asking about the galvano-plastic process and requesting a machine and an experienced workman to operate it. In response, Elkington asked Braun to become a designer for the company and to provide source material for their electrotypes.

In 1850, Emil Braun wrote the text for Ludwig Gruner, *Specimens of Ornamental Art, selected from the Best Models of the Classical Epochs*, (London: T. McLean, 1850). The book was intended to provide examples of ornamental designs for the use of industry. It was dedicated to Prince Albert, who was a great supporter of the electrotyping process and its products. Indeed, Braun had met Prince Albert when he visited in Rome and introduced him to the treasures of the city.

Braun also published an article titled 'Sideboard Plates' in the *Art Journal*, (1850, pp. 113–114) pointing out that the role of metal plate on display in a dining room was more than just a show of wealth but was also an indicator of the owner's knowledge and appreciation of art.

Emil Braun, 'Electrotyping Applied to Art Manufactures', *Art Journal*, 12, 1 July 1850, pp. 205–207

Electrotyping is one of the most successful applications of the discoveries made in the domain of science to the Fine Arts. It involves the possibility of transferring the forms created by sculpture to a noble and solid material, without destroying by such a process, the freshness and bloom of the original in the slightest degree. Those who are not aware how hard is the struggle which, for thousands of years, has been carried on between artists seeking to embody their ideas in the firm and sharply defined forms conferred by bronze casting, and those physical conditions which impede the settling of the floating metal in the moulds, prepared with anxious care, will not be able at once to appreciate the incomparable value of such a discovery. But artists who have gone through the trials to which the uncertainties of casting subject them, and who have seen, totally wasted away in the process, all the refinements of their carefully studied modelling, have been struck by the results of this new method, as by a miracle. Thorwaldsen,[3] who saw only the first experiments made, when this mode of workmanship was yet in its infancy, hailed the discovery as one of the greatest that has ever been made in the department of technical reproduction. He, whose teeming imagination had busied, during his long and active life, the hands of numerous artists in reproducing in marble the creations of his genius, in a style which afforded him little satisfaction and which rendered, indeed, but little justice to his merit, foresaw at a single glance how immense, how incalculable an advantage, was to be derived by great sculptors from this new manufacturing process. To this great artist, however, befel that which was the fate of many men of distinguished talent, and which is so touching in the fatal destiny of Moses, who was allowed to cast his eyes upon the fertile plains of Canaan, but not himself to enter the promised land. With his cooperation, this branch of Art would rapidly have shot up into a mighty tree, while it is still even at the present moment regarded as a weakly sapling, little cared for, without promise of fruitfulness, and considered by many amateurs of Art, as of an equivocal and even suspicious origin.

Prejudices have stifled in their prosperous commencement more than one useful invention. We may mention as an instructive instance, and one well adapted to our case, the anecdote of Nero who ordered the man to be put to death who presented him with a cup of transparent glass, which was elastic like metal, fearing lest gold and silver should lose their value by such a discovery.

Electrotyping has encountered a reception nearly as chilling. The political disturbances of Europe, it is true, have contributed much to withdraw the attention of the public from the astonishing results obtained by this process; but still more than these unhappy circumstances have the false notions current respecting its true character, contributed to throw it into the shade and to rob it of the favour of real protectors and lovers of Art.

What in former times would have been the greatest recommendation, the very moderate price at which such reproductions of the finest workmanship can be presented to the public, has been perverted into an objection against their real value. The wealthy have been told that this description of workmanship is wanting in solidity, and the many find it always dearer than plaster, papier mâché, and such like worthless and perishable materials.

Perhaps, however, the public has not been alone in the wrong, and the proportionably small encouragement which this manufacture has met with, may be attributed in great measure, to the not always successful choice of models selected for production. Not every subject that looks well in marble or clay, presents a similar fine or striking appearance in bronze, the smooth untransparent surface of which displays the whole form with such a hard distinctness, that finishing touches sufficiently sharp for any other material, here seem to have entirely lost their power. The laws of style, and the conditions under which modelling associates itself in a suitable and harmonious manner with such a material, must therefore be thoroughly studied, before that success can be attained which is aimed at in such a process of artistic reproduction.

Every attempt to acquire a clear understanding of what is meant by style, in reference to Art-manufactures, would be vain and useless without the help afforded by a comparative glance at the history of Art. Here we learn at the first view, how important is, not the material itself selected as the medium of ideas to be artistically expressed, but the specific manner in which it is treated. The striking effect of Egyptian sculptures depends entirely upon the assimilation of the forms created by the plastic hand of man with those huge masses of rock employed for this purpose, which still continue to exercise a peculiar power over our imagination as products of nature. The moment that the artist ceases to consider these indestructible qualities of the substance made use of, the latter enters into a hard conflict with the forms impressed upon it by the human mind, and it happens, not unfrequently, that the whole artistical effect is entirely destroyed by such a contradictory action of the maltreated and offended material. A comparison made between a statue of Bernini and any sculpture of Egyptian, Indian, or Greek Art, will bring immediately before the eyes of our readers the difference to which we allude. Whilst in the Art-productions of the ancients the idea grows out of the dead masses themselves, as leaves and blossoms burst out from the stem of an old tree after a night of spring rain, the sculptures of the modern artist leave upon us the impression, as though the subjects represented by them were entangled in some harassing conflict of passion, and the lively movements they display are those of a convulsive state of agony rather than the free action of an organic development.

This radical defect, which appears in the most striking manner in the works of the seventeenth century, is, however, a general quality of the sculpture of modern times; and not only Michael Angelo's Moses partakes of it, but even Ghiberti's gates of the Baptistry at Florence, which the former declared worthy to be the gates of Paradise, are open to censure in this respect. Although they are of so elevated an order of beauty and so masterly a perfection, that no bronze of the classical epochs which has come down to our times, can be compared with them either in excellence of workmanship or in the overflowing riches of a sublime and poetical conception, these same sculptures, as works of bronze, are surpassed by the most common Art-manufactures of the Greek and Roman epochs, which bear almost without exception, the stamp of genuine plastic workmanship. Is it not as if a magic spell had transformed the figures put into action by the Florentine artist, into beings which have become strange to themselves, and therefore ill at ease and seeming to be in a perpetual struggle with the material with which they are associated! With the bronzes of the ancients we find precisely the contrary. The figures adorning the bas-reliefs of Siris,[4] in the British Museum, are to such a degree amalgamated with the metal, that, were we desirous of bringing them down to the level of actual life, they would appear like beings belonging to a higher sphere in the midst of this common and low existence. We should immediately be aware that they are not composed of the same clay as our own bodies, but of a nobler material; and as a bird, whose lungs are fitted for inhaling the pure and rarefied atmosphere of the higher regions of the empyrean, is unable to inhabit the denser element for which a fish is adapted by its inferior organisation, so, the metal figures of a Greek sculpture seem to require quite a different medium for their more subtle and merely poetical existence.

This is not the place to enter farther into the details of such a question, the solution of which requires great experience in matters of Art, and an uncommon delicacy in the perception of different degrees of artistic excellence, and perfection of style. Here we are interested in it only in a practical point of view. We can, therefore, refer directly to the experience made by all those who have been occupied in electro-typing, that it is not sufficient to convert any monument of Art whatever into metal, but that the success of galvanoplastic reproductions depends entirely upon the subjects chosen. The contrast between form and material we alluded to above, becomes much more striking when all the details of artistical execution reappear in a material for which they are not intended. This unexpected result has been frequently so startling in effect, that many electrotypers have been disappointed by it to such a degree as to be induced entirely to abandon a process presenting in itself advantages not to be obtained from any other mode of mechanical reproduction. Mismanagement of the most useful of scientific discoveries threatens, therefore, to rob our century of the glory of having made it, and it is strange enough to see how the story of the inventor of the application of steam-power is repeated even on this occasion. Whilst Napoleon was inclined to shut up in a lunatic asylum the man who offered him steam-vessels, our artists are disposed to wish for zealous electrotypers a fate perhaps even more cruel.

It is not my intention to give, on this occasion, any description of the chemical process or technical improvements which have been introduced into the electrotyping manufacture. Such things are now universally known and afford little interest to those who do not concern themselves about the means by which a work of Art is produced, but who wish only to enjoy good workmanship on the best terms. The question which occupies us at the present moment, regards, exclusively, the results obtained by the application of a scientific discovery, which has done wonders in other branches of industry. For although even the gilding and plating process does not always receive full justice, this newly established branch of trade has struck deep root and will not easily be abolished by the old fire process, which offering only apparently greater advantages, has ruined the health and destroyed the lives of so many persons, and is far from being able to enter into competition with electro-plating. If the credit of the latter has suffered in any quarter, the fault is entirely due to bad workmen and not to the process itself, the perfection of which depends of course on the method adopted in its application, and on the conscientiousness with which it is put in practice. Manufacture-spoilers end at last by spoiling only their own reputations.

The finest philosophical instrument put into the hands of a savage will soon become an object for laughter and ridicule, and mere matter-of-fact men cannot be forced to acknowledge the most evident results of science, even when placed before their eyes. I remember that when Sir Humphrey Davy[5] in his journey through Italy was kind enough to explain one of his wonderful discoveries to some Roman chemists, after having pointed out the result of the experiment perceptible only to the scientifically educated eye of the philosopher, he exclaimed joyfully at the appearance of the magic spark—" L'hanno viduto!" " Did you see it?" He was afterwards ridiculed by a sceptical professor of chemistry, who in a spirit of malicious mockery frequently repeated the words of the great founder of electro-chemistry, whom he ignorantly looked upon as a visionary. Thus we see, that one of the branches of galvanoplastic industry, which affords the greatest advantages for the diffusion of knowledge, has been cultivated within very narrow limits only, whilst its usefulness, if properly understood, ought to have assured it an universal application. We speak of the reproduction of engraved copper-plates, which on the Continent, in Germany at least, has an astonishing success, whilst in England it is scarcely practised at all. The cause of such neglect is the same as in the case of other useful inventions, which lose their character only by mismanagement. Failure is followed by discouragement and the latter by indifference, which has always a most injurious effect upon national industry. I know an establishment where several thousand copper-plates have been reproduced in this manner, and where *the number of engravers, instead of being diminished, has been considerably increased by it.* The workmanship is enabled by this means to improve, while the prices of such productions become cheaper in proportion, and Art itself, as well as the public, is benefited in the highest degree. A reformation in trade of the most advantageous character takes place, which is profitable both to the producer and to those who enjoy what is produced, without injury to either party. Yet in spite of this it is difficult to persuade even a practical man of business that progress is insured by so admirable an invention, and this, for no other reason, than because it has been subject to mismanagement.

If prejudices are so great an obstacle to the improvement of the most useful methods, we cannot wonder that these difficulties should be still greater in the higher regions of Art, where the machinery is much more complicated, and where fashion exercises a potent sway. When the first notices of the application of electro-typing to sculpture reached the present director of the royal foundry of Munich,[6] he immediately went to Paris to assure himself of so powerful a means, promising to supersede the fire process, the imperfection of which was known to no one so well as to this clever and experienced artist. The opinion, however, which he laid before the public after his return to Munich, was quite opposite to the results afterwards obtained by long practice. His impression was that this process would never be applicable to works of large size, whilst now every electrotyper knows that small sized objects occasion sometimes much greater trouble than can be made to answer in a commercial point of view. Mr. Müller produced a bust about the size of life to show that he was well acquainted with the process, of which he had entertained such bright hopes, and in which he had found himself suddenly so disappointed. To those, however, who are initiated in the secrets of the manufacture, he has only offered a positive proof that he did not sufficiently understand it. The copper produced by him in fact deserved the blame, whilst he endeavoured to lay the fault upon a method, upon which he had bestowed so little time and patience, and the study of which requires as many years as he had allotted weeks to it. It is indeed to be regretted that this skilful and zealous artist should have so hastily abandoned the process, as he, in all probability, with the aid of scientific men, would soon have been enabled to bring it to that degree of perfection which others have at last attained at a far greater expense of means and time, than he would have required for the purpose. The artistical execution was masterly, and of all persons who have occupied themselves with electrotyping, perhaps no one had so decided a vocation for it as he.

It is generally supposed that the scientific is more essential than the artistical part to insure success in this branch of technical reproduction, but this is a great mistake. As the most accurate knowledge of the theory of fire-casting would enable no one successfully to establish a foundry dedicated to Art-manufacture, so it is quite as hazardous to look for great results in electrotyping from the theoretical knowledge of electro-chemistry alone. It is true that a galvanoplastic workman cannot dispense with the study of the primary elements of galvanic action, but I have frequently seen those, who had a large store of patience and skilful perseverance, succeed much better than those who could boast of considerable scientific attainments. Even here the old saying of a practical philosopher holds good, that "a part is greater than the whole," as it is frequently more essential to apply a very small portion of scientific knowledge than to aim at becoming master of the secrets of nature, by peeping into her laboratory for a few moments. Only an apple falling from a tree enabled Newton to discover those laws which the whole apparatus of science could not so easily have made evident; and thus we find, that in the improvement of great inventions, those have succeeded best who have endeavoured to simplify the means and to reduce the problem to a matter-of-fact question, the solution of which has not unfrequently been discovered by a child.

Those who have no confidence in this new method of converting artistic models into a noble and enduring material, usually allege in support of their scepticism, that, as yet, almost all the establishments of this kind have come to an untimely end, with the exception of the few sustained by means not derived from commercial resources. This, indeed, cannot be denied. There is scarcely a capital in Europe where one or more electrotypers do not deplore their folly in having gone too far in this branch of speculation. Although the political disturbances of Europe may have had some share in so complete a failure of success, it must still be confessed, that even in more favourable times they would have gone to ruin, as the practical direction chosen by them could not lead to any good result. The fault lies, however, not in any defect of the method, but exclusively in the wrong application of it.

To explain our meaning, we may venture to say, that had the art of copper-engraving been discovered in our own times, it would probably have met with the same result. And has it not been so with lithography? The inventor of this incomparable multiplying process, to which our century is indebted for the unlimited propagation of cheap and useful knowledge, of instruction and amusement, ended as a bankrupt, as many electrotypers have done, who deserved a better reward than the malicious ridicule with which the thoughtless many have saluted them. The invention succeeded, however, immediately after having passed from the hands of the man of genius to those of dry but shrewd and practical men of business, who availed themselves of this powerful means for satisfying the wants of the million. The history of discoveries and inventions is not less rich in tragical combinations than that of political events. Ungrateful are the many, and therefore we must not wonder if those who make a fortunate discovery should endeavour to derive some immediate personal advantage from it, without much considering the common good. The world *will* be deceived, " therefore," says the man of business, " you *must* deceive it." This maxim is carried into practice perhaps more in Art-manufacture than in any other branch of human industry, with the exception always of medicine, where the most clever and conscientious physicians are compelled to adapt themselves to the folly and credulity of mankind by assuming a mask either of charlatanism or of exterior roughness. To prove what we have ventured to assert, it will be sufficient, for the present, to direct the attention of those who have any capacity for appreciating correctness and refinement in Art, to the small-sized bronzes which are manufactured, in enormous quantities, at Paris, at Rome, and in England. Without speaking of the artistical treatment, which is, of course, subject to the caprices of fashion, we shall allude only to the style of workmanship generally displayed by them. And here we must be, in the first instance, just, in acknowledging the astonishing progress made by fire-casting since the bright epoch of the sixteenth century. Frequently these Art-manufactures of the present day are so perfect, that they seem to be made with the same facility as plaster-casts. Such reproductions, however, as they do not attain the sharpness of the latter, are not fitted for catching the crowd, and are therefore condemned to undergo a process much more cruel than that to which Marsyas and Bartholomew were subjected.[7] The artists who are commissioned to put such bronzes into a condition for sale, are generally unable to model a single object, but are acquainted with the means requisite for tricking out works of this description in a seductive manner. They obtain what is desired, principally, by two contrivances. The first consists of a mode of execution which throws over them a veil, not allowing the eye of the spectator clearly to distinguish any details of form, and the second gives a deceptive effect to some prominent parts. The former is obtained by a particular kind of file, by means of which the whole surface is rubbed over, without any regard to the modelling; the latter is produced by the chisel, commonly used in the most arbitrary manner. Both modes of treatment proceed upon the attempt to produce a false illusion, and their striking effect arises from mutual contrast. The file-rubber has no other intention than that of converting the whole surface of the sculpture into one smooth plane, by destroying the modelling wherever the casting process has left any trace of it; and he succeeds with the multitude in making them believe that every part of the work is of the same perfection; the chiseller endeavours to revive the plastic expression, on those parts, at least, where even the inexperienced eye of the unreflecting amateur would discover that the pith and marrow of the original are entirely gone, and that the whole has lost all character.

This system of imposition in Art-manufacture is accomplished by the skilful management of picturesque accessories, without which no sculpture can hope to obtain the applause of the many. This is even acknowledged by the ancients, who assigned to those statues of Praxiteles the highest value, which were painted by Nicias.[8] But this fact proves clearly that the utmost discretion and a very subtle refinement are required to associate advantageously the two branches of Art. This requisite delicacy is far from being observable in the present mode of colouring our bronzes, by giving them a kind of patina, which *imitates*, it is true, that bestowed upon ancient bronzes by the effects of time, but only in a manner setting taste and common-sense at defiance.

With such an apparatus of seductive means have those to contend, who hailed, in electrotyping, the rising star of a better era in Art-manufacture, relying with bright hopes upon a process which would enable the workman, to whom is confided the reproduction of a master-piece of sculpture, to preserve the expression of every individual touch coming from the plastic hand of the inspired artist as the expression of the soul within. The first experiments proved that these prospects were not mere delusions. A general cry of astonishment was heard all over Europe; artists and connoisseurs expressed the most entire satisfaction at the results obtained; but electrotypers soon became aware that they could not continue to work upon praise alone, and that to sustain the new art in successful rivalry with her older sister, they stood in need of some means of competing with that outside gloss and polish, without which even the prostitute children of the latter would fail to achieve success.

In despite of such difficulties electrotyping has still held on its course. Large bronze works have been executed, and the thoroughly satisfactory result yielded by them has shown to the world that science has presented Art with an offspring of real genius, which has not only talent, but also courage and perseverance enough to fight its own way. Artists of impartial judgment have gone farther, and have declared, that should they be required to execute their works in bronze, electrotyping must be the process, and no other, this method being alone worthy to be entrusted with the reproduction of a finely executed model.

If the life-and-death question with reference to a method presenting the brightest reflection of the most astonishing discoveries made in the highest regions of science may be considered as decided, the practical question respecting its useful application to industry and commerce is as yet barely touched. Although there is scarcely any branch of manufactures that does not derive great advantages from the galvano-plastic process, there are, on the other hand, very few men engaged in business acquainted with the real resources which it affords, and whose ideas are sufficiently clear to enable them to know what opinion to form of it. As it is not so easy a matter to obtain the information necessary for an authentic statistic account, I thought that it might prove useful to lay my own experience, and the convictions derived from it, before the public, partly to destroy prejudices, partly to show what powerful means have been placed in our hands, and how ungrateful a return has been made for it during the last ten years.

To do full justice to the argument, we must begin by pointing out the limits which electro-typing, as a branch of manufactures, is not allowed to transgress but at its own risk. Whoever undertakes to conduct such a power in the hope of benefit, must endeavour to know how far it is able to reach, or, still better, what are its boundaries. The latter may be, on one side, very near, nay, so close at hand, that a feeble-minded man will shrink back and lose all courage, whilst in another direction the far-reaching eye of a prophet will scarcely be able to determine whither the combinations of which such a discovery is capable, may lead us. And has not the experience of a few years shown, that the sphere of this branch of industry is almost unlimited? Certainly it is so; but it has happened not unfrequently that the instrument dropped from the hand of one, proves to be most valuable in that of another. Was it not Minerva who flung aside the flutes which did not suit her expressive mouth, while in the hands of Marsyas[9] they became an enchanting instrument, the magic effects of which it required Apollo himself to neutralise? This significant story is daily repeated, and it would be highly advisable and useful to pay some attention to the lesson of practical truth which it conveys.

Electrotyping was invented nearly at the same time with the different photographic processes, which offered likewise a means of aid so full of promise to artistic reproduction. These prospects have, however, proved illusory, the latter not having approached the boundaries of real Art. We have learnt by photography how far this merely naturalistic process is able to go, and know now, that common reality, fixed mechanically by a mirror, without having passed through the poetical and reproductive medium of an artistic eye, soon becomes destitute of interest. On their first exhibition we see such shadowy images surrounded by a gaping crowd, but we soon perceive in those who do not speedily make their escape, evident tokens of mortal weariness. With creations of real power and meaning such disappointments do not occur, and artists may learn by this great experiment the full force of the influence which they possess. *Mind* can alone stir and touch the many, and the most brilliant outward accessories cannot long continue to affect the multitude, although it is often caught at first by bright colours and attractive forms. Retzsch,[10] with his slight outlines has, as well as Flaxman,[11] electrified whole nations, while the most elaborate works of Art have not exercised half the effect produced by the sight of these figured poems.

From such a fact the electrotyper may learn what he is able to expect from his reproductive power. He will not raise the dead by it, but he may be sure that the sculpture of the present days will make the most extensive and varied use of his assistance. Products of nature covered with a film of copper or silver, even repetition of ancient monuments, will not move the public; but if he succeeds in embellishing our daily existence by the introduction of poetical elements adapted to every-day use, he will be able to effect a reform, and in many respects even a revolution such as has been hitherto unknown in the history of industry.

In the following articles we shall, without entering into any merely vague schemes, give an account only of those departments of sculpture where electrotyping has already met with an unrivalled success, and whence Art has derived not only an enlargement of her domain, but, what is of much more value, a real and solid improvement. Such a review will be not less interesting to the sculptor and Art-manufacturer, than to those who indulge in the elevating pleasures afforded by plastic means. Sculpture possesses in a higher degree than any of the sister Arts the power of amalgamating itself with those objects which the ingenuity of man has devised in aid of the organs bestowed upon him by nature, and exercises therefore a more widely diffused influence upon habitual and practical life.

Notes

1 'Illustrated Tour of the Manufacturing Districts, Birmingham', *Art Journal*, 8, 1846, p. 62.
2 *Penny Magazine of the Society for the Diffusion of Useful Knowledge*, 13, 806, October 26, 1844, pp. 417–424.
3 Bertel Thorvaldsen (1770–1844), Danish sculptor.
4 "Bronzes of Siris" (4th century BCE; British Museum, London).
5 Sir Humphry Davy (1778–1829), chemist and inventor.
6 Ferdinand von Miller (1813–1887), a German bronze caster and director of the Royal Foundry, Munich.
7 Both were flayed.
8 Nicias: 4th century BCE Athenian painter. noted for his skill in chiaroscuro.
9 Marsyas: a Phrygian Satyr renowned for flute playing.
10 Moritz Retzsch (1779–1857), German artist.
11 John Flaxman (1755–1826), British sculptor and draughtsman.

32

GEORGE DODD, 'PAPIER MÂCHÉ'

Papier-mâché is a malleable, mouldable substance that has been used for a variety decorative applications and objects since the seventeenth century. Henry Clay is credited with producing papier mâché goods, including furniture, on a commercial scale in England. In 1772, Clay took out a patent for making 'high varnished [paper] panels for rooms, doors, cabins of ships, cabinets, bookcases, screens, chimney-pieces, tables etc'.[1] The ornamenting of papier mâché was an integral part of the process and was the subject of several further patent applications.

In 1840 Charles Bielefeld noted 'that Papier mâché is applied to the enriched cornices of bookcases and cabinets, to the mouldings and corners and centre ornaments of panelling[sic] on their doors and sides; to the enriched scroll legs of cabinets and pier tables in the old French style . . . '[2] Whilst his work was mainly directed at architectural applications, more domestic designs were also being produced on a large scale.

Although papier mâché was popular, the designs used were often criticised. In a lengthy article, *The Art Journal* discussed the exhibits shown at the 1851 exhibition where they particularly called for patterns that were too derivative to be re-developed, and designs to be used that reflected the scale of the objects to which they were applied.[3] Three years later, George Wallis, discussing the displays at the New York Exhibition of 1854, noted that the papier-mâché furniture designs were 'all below mediocrity, being chiefly imitations of the worst style of pearl inlaying and japan work executed in England. Everything approaching to purity of design, or in the inlaid work, to geometric arrangement of the parts, is as carefully avoided as it generally is in Europe'.[4]

The Birmingham japanning firm Jennens and Betteridge, were aware of the criticisms, as seen in the evidence of Samuel Wiley, an employee of the firm to the Select Committee on Arts and Manufactures. Wiley was a japanner with the firm to whose energies he attributed a great improvement in japanning: 'being men of taste and stimulating their apprentices and teaching them the art of drawing, they have taken great pains.'[5]

Despite already providing training to their workers, Thomas Howell, a factory inspector, who had visited Jennens and Betteridge, reported to the Select Committee that the firm was 'extremely anxious for any institution that the state might furnish that would encourage art in Birmingham, with reference to their own particular manufacture'.[6] Designs clearly improved, as the *Art Journal* reported how current products may be favourably compared to those of twenty years ago 'when masses of huge gaudy colours with unmeaning splashes of gold were considered essential to make a work look valuable'.[7]

George Dodd (1808–1881) was an English journalist and writer, who wrote articles on industrial art in the *Penny Cyclopædia*, the *English Cyclopædia* and supplements. He edited and wrote in the *Cyclopædia of the Industry of all Nations* (1851). Some of Dodd's articles on productions and materials were collected and published in volumes, under the titles of *Days at the Factories* (1843) and *Curiosities of Industry* (first published 1852) and the well-known *Where do we get it, and how is it made?* [1862]. Dodd also wrote for Dickens's *Household Words* on occasion, using some of the material in his other works.

George Dodd, 'Papier Mâché', *Curiosities of Industry* (London: George Routledge and Co, 1858), pp. 17–22

Papier Maché and Carton Pierre

The very pretty and useful material which bears the name of Papier Maché does not always deserve that name. The brilliant display which Messrs. Jennens and Bettridge,[8] and other manufacturers, made at the Great Exhibition ought to have been designated by some more significant and correct name; it is *pasted* paper and *moulded* paper, but not *mashed* or *pulp* paper, as the French name *maché* indicates. There are two distinct branches of industry here involved, which we must separate in order to speak of the notabilities of each.

And first for the real, the true papier maché, that which was introduced about twenty-five years ago, and from which Mr. Bielefeld[9] produces such a wondrous variety of decorative ornaments. This is almost entirely paper; there may be a small percentage of other material to impart certain minor qualities, but it is essentially paper. And if we enquire what kind of paper is thus used, we find that it is any and every kind. All is "fish that comes to this net." Nothing is refused, nothing laid aside, whether linen or cotton or hemp be the fibre from which the paper was originally made: all is available, whether it be black or white, bleached or unbleached, plain or figured; whether it be fine as 'extra satin wove,' or coarse as tough wrapping paper; whether in large sheets or small fragments; whether new and unused, or old and worn;— all will be welcome to the *maché* vat. Of course, in a practical point of view, where all kinds are useful, the manufacturers look about them for cheap miscellaneous lots, instead of appealing to the bran new stock of a wholesale stationer. Bankers have sometimes tons' weight of old account books by them, which have ceased to be of use, but which they are unwilling to place in the hands of the trunk-maker or the butterman,[10] on account of the private transactions to which the writing on the pages of such books relate; and as it is a task of no little difficulty and danger to burn these books, the bankers are glad to find a receptacle for them in the vat of the papier-maché manufacturer, under a pledge that they shall really and promptly be so used, without exposure to public gaze. Thus the banker may perchance see the relievo decorations of his own drawing-room made from his own old account books; a ledger may find a new home as part of a cornice, or a cash-book as a frame for a looking-glass, or a day-book as a ceiling ornament. Nay, these transformations may extend wider; for in years gone by, the banker's old shirt may have been transferred to the rag-bag, thence to the paper-mill, and thence to the account-book maker, and thence to the bank, and thence to the papier-maché factory, and thence to the drawing-room of the banker's residence—where his admiring gaze may rest upon a graceful ornament, some fibres of which once clothed his own back.

The cuttings of paper, produced by the principal applications of that material, form a very large portion of the supply whence papier maché is made. Bookbinders, pasteboard-makers, envelope-makers, account-book and pocketbook-makers, printsellers, paper-hangers, all accumulate heaps of shreds and cuttings; and the papier-maché vat may receive them all, unless better prices can be obtained elsewhere. Whatever may be the source whence the supply is obtained, it is certain that paper has now reached that commercial point which gold and silver reached long ago—that is, none need be wasted, for a market can be found for all the odds and ends.

The kind of papier maché which is now under notice is a paste-like mass formed of paper-pulp, and pressed in moulds to any desired form. Mr. Bielefeld, the leading manufacturer in this branch, has an establishment in the country where water power can be commanded, and where machines, moved by this power, bring the paper to the required state. The paper, be it of what kind it may, or of as many different kinds as it may, is moistened, and chopped, and minced, and routed about until it becomes a perfectly homogeneous pasty mass, or rather a mass having a consistency like that of dough or of putty. A trifling portion of other substances is, as we have said, introduced, but not sufficient to change the general character of the mass as a paper substance. Then comes the moulding or pressing. The material is too thick to be poured into a mould like plaster of Paris, or like molten metal; it is pressed into flattish moulds, like clay, or composition, or gutta percha. A piece is cut off, about enough for the article to be made, it is pressed well into the mould, a counter-mould is placed upon it, and the force of a powerful press is brought to bear upon it, so as to drive the material into every minute crevice of the mould.

And here we come to the artistic department of such a manufacture as this. To command anything like a leading position in decorative art, there must be an untiring attention to new designs, new artistic ideas, new combinations of form, and colour, and material. Hence, in such an establishment as the one now under notice, the moulds (made in metal from plaster models) are constantly increasing in number and value; they accumulate not merely by hundredweights, but by tons; the designer, the carver of wood moulds, the engraver or sinker of metal moulds, are all adding to the store. It may be that a new design does not 'take' sufficiently to pay the expense even of making the mould, but this may be counterbalanced by another which has a long run, and by degrees an extensive manufacturer becomes able to strike a balance, to establish an average which shall determine the probable returns to be expected from each new mould. Among our large establishments, where mechanical skill and fine art meet hand in hand, those which produce the most continuous run of new designs are those which generally rise to the uppermost place; and it is here that the artistic education of the artizan becomes a matter not merely of individual but of national importance.

The articles made of this material are chiefly architectural ornaments for interior use, such as ceiling ornaments, cornices, and so forth; but they are becoming every year more and more widely spread in their application. The theatres afford ample scope for the display of papier-maché ornaments; because the material is so tough that it will scarcely break, and so light that it requires much less fastening than the whiting and glue composition ornaments of former times. The countermould imparts to the ornament a hollowness at the back which economizes material and lessens the weight. The surface which the paper or papier presents is of a nondescript colour, arising from the mixture of various colours in the pulp, but it is fitted to receive any decorations in gold, oil-paint, size-colours, or varnish. Thus, an ornate frame for a looking-glass, made of papier maché, may be gilt with a degree of perfection nearly equal to that of a carved frame. But it is also capable of assuming a sculpturesque form. There were in the Great Exhibition, as many of our readers may remember, two statuettes after Michael Angelo, a copy of the noble horse's head from the Elgin marbles, and a bust of some celebrated man, all formed of papier maché, and deriving therefrom a toughness which defies almost any power of breakage. The Corinthian capital in this material, set up on a pillar in the western nave, was an example of the more ordinary application for ornamental purposes.

There is another modem decorative material, still more recent than papier maché, but like it honoured with a French name: we mean *carton pierre*, which may be interpreted *stone cardboard* or *pasteboard*. This more nearly resembles plaster than papier maché; it has a little paper in it, a great deal more plaster, and one or two other substances; the mixture thus produced is fashioned in moulds and is applied to various ornamental purposes, but it is much heavier than papier maché. The beautiful internal decorations at the Lyceum Theatre are, we believe, made of carton pierre. Carton pierre is manufactured in England chiefly by Messrs. Jackson,[11] but it appears to have been a French invention, and to be made in France and Germany more largely than in England. The *carton pierre* of the one country, and the *stein pappe* of the other, seem to be pretty nearly the same material: viz., a kind of liquid plaster combined with other materials, poured instead of pressed into moulds, and backed with a stratum of paper to give strength. Some of our French neighbours displayed beautiful specimens of friezes, vases, pilasters, and bas-relievos, in carton pierre, at the Great Exhibition; while the Prussian exhibitor, Gropius,[12] displayed some dozens of neat little statuettes in the same material. The noble chandelier for sixty lights, exhibited by Messrs. Jackson, was perhaps the best specimen of carton-pierre work.

But to return to papier maché. That the pulpy or maché paper is susceptible of being made into beautifully even flat surfaces, is exemplified in the thick *millboard* used by bookbinders. Time was when all such millboard was essentially pasteboard, produced by pasting together a large number of sheets of paper to the required thickness; but now the pulp is used. In the first place there is a flat table or slab, with a raised edge all round to form a sort of shallow mould. Into this mould the pulp is laded, to a depth depending on the thickness of the millboard to be made, and. this pulp, by drying between felted cloths, by drying in the open air, by gentle pressure in a press, and then by powerful pressure between rollers, assumes at length that hard, tough, strong, smooth uniform consistency which distinguishes millboard, and which makes that material so invaluable to the bookbinder. Mr. Bielefeld is about to introduce an important modification of this process in the production of panels for artists. He has produced panels eight feet by six, made entirely of papier maché half an inch thick, mounted on a skeleton wood support or frame; and the surface of these panels appears as if it would be admirably fitted for paintings, more durable than canvas, and less likely to split than wood panel; indeed, splitting is out of the question in respect to such a material. The bulkheads and the cabin partitions of some of the fine steamers of our day have been made of this material; it is tough and strong, and admits of any degree of ornamentation. The material is said to be a bad conductor both of sound and of heat, and has thus a twofold recommendation for room partitions. It seems to have been some such material as this which Mr. Haddan[13] contributed to the Great Exhibition, in the form of panels for railway carriages, or rather for the whole broadside. It is alleged that such panels do not shrink, and do not require grooves for fixing; whether they will bear being 'run into' better than other railway panels, has probably not yet been tested.

Now we may turn our glance to that which, though not really papier maché, is much more extensively known by that name than the material just described. The gorgeous contributions to the Hyde Park collection must be in the recollection of most persons. That paper, even with the adventitious aid of painting, and varnishing, and polishing, and gilding, and inlaying, should be wrought into such beautiful forms, might well excite the wonder of those to whom the manufacture was new. It was no small triumph of skill to produce, out of such a substance, the pearl inlaid pianoforte and music stool; the Victoria Regia cot, designed by Bell, the sculptor, and decked with emblematic devices in gold and colours; the pearl-and-gold inlaid loo-table; the Lotus work-table, designed by Bell; the pearl-inlaid and gilded work-table, in a form suggested by Benvenuto Cellini's vase; and Bell's chess-board for his "Parian" chessmen—to say nothing of the chairs, tables, sofas, cabinets, secretaries, screens, vases, writing-desks, blotting-folios, work-boxes, papetières, inkstands, envelope-cases, card-boxes, flower-stands,

PAPIER MÂCHÉ

teatrays, coffee-trays, wine-trays, standishes, crochet and netting-cases, and the numberless things which modern refinement has rendered familiar to us. The Furniture Courts in the Exhibition certainly glittered with these productions.[14]

It would give a better idea of the manufacture (although somewhat lowering to its dignity) if these productions were called pasteboard, for pasteboard they certainly are, as the reader will presently see. It was towards the close of the last century that iron tea-trays began to be imitated or superseded by papier maché, and from these trays has gradually sprung up an important department of Birmingham industry, a department in which it is pretty generally admitted, we believe, that Birmingham excels all other places.

Although the real papier maché snaps up all kinds of paper indiscriminately, with most impartial fairness, the tea-tray paper (if we may so term it) is not so easily satisfied; it requires whole sound sheets to work upon, and these sheets must have a certain definite quality to fit them for their destined purpose.

Let us watch, in thought, the making of a papier-maché tea-tray. In the first place we see that the paper employed has a grayish colour, and looks like thick blotting-paper; and in the next we see that a mould or form is employed to give shape to the tray. Artists or designers are constantly at work producing new patterns; but we are here supposing that a tolerably simple tray is to be manufactured. A model of the tray is prepared, giving the exact form and shape; and from this model a mould is cast in iron, brass, or copper, the surface of the mould corresponding, of course, with the interior of the tray to be made. Women and girls, seated at tables, cut up the rough gray paper into pieces of the requisite size, and these pieces are handed to the pasters, who are also women—for it is worthy of remark that this very pretty art is one which is capable of being conducted in many of its branches by females. These pasters have beside them a plentiful supply of paste, made of flour and glue dissolved and boiled in water. The mould is greased to prevent the paper from adhering. The first sheet is pasted on both sides, and handed to another woman, who lays it on the mould, pressing and rubbing and adjusting it until it conforms to the shape. Another and another are similarly applied, and the mould, with its threefold garment, is put into a drying room, heated to a high temperature, where it is brought to a dried state. It is removed from the stove-room, filed to give it a tolerable smoothness of surface, and then clothed with three more layers of paper, in the same mode as before. Again is the stove-room employed, again the pasters ply their labour; a third time the stove-room, again the pasters; and so on, until thirty or forty thicknesses of paper have been applied, more or less, of course, according to the substance intended to be produced. For some purposes as many as a hundred and twenty thicknesses are pasted together, involving forty stove dryings, and of course carrying the operations over a considerable number of days. A mass of pasteboard, six inches in thickness, which is occasionally produced for certain purposes, is perhaps one of the toughest and strongest materials we can imagine. If a cannon-ball, made of such pasteboard, were fired against a ship, would not the ball itself escape fracture?

The mould being covered with a sufficient layer, a knife is employed to dexterously loosen the paper at the edges; the greased state of the mould allows the paper to be removed from it. Then are all imperfections removed; the plane, the file, and the knife are applied to bring all 'ship-shape' and proper.

Next come the adornments. The pasteboard itself is not beautiful, so beauty is sought in other ways. Shell-lac varnish of very fine quality, coloured according to circumstances, is applied coat after coat, until a thickness is obtained sufficient for the purpose. The black polished surface of ordinary papier-maché trays is produced by black japan varnish, applied by women with a brush. But whether the varnish be black or coloured, it usually undergoes a rubbing and polishing to such a degree as to equal in brilliancy anything produced in the arts. It is said that the finest polishing instrument used to give the last finishing touch after all the 'rotten-stones' and 'emeries' have done their best, is the soft palm of a woman's hand; and that those females employed in this art, who are gifted by nature with the much-coveted charm of a soft and delicate hand, find it commercially advantageous to preserve this softness and delicacy by a degree of gloved carefulness not usual in their rank in life. What will the poets say, when woman's hand is thus spoken of?

Then ensue the painting and the gilding, the bedizenment with gaudy show, or the adornment with graceful device, according as the goods are low or high priced, or the manufacturer a man of taste or no taste. A kind of stencilling is employed in cheap work, but in better specimens the real artist's pencil is brought into requisition.

The inlaid-work exhibited in the higher class of papier-maché goods is very curious. A sort of imitation tortoiseshell is thus produced. A thin transparent varnish is laid on the prepared tray, leaf silver is laid on the varnish, the two are dried, and varnish is laid thickly over the silver, and pumice-stone is skilfully applied to grind away so much of the varnish at particular spots as will give to the whole the mottled appearance of tortoiseshell. Every day's experience tells us that imitations themselves are imitated. Not only is varnished silver made to imitate tortoiseshell, but varnished vermilion is made to imitate varnished-silver. A method of decorating papier maché with imitative gems has been recently introduced, in which some kind of foil or varnish is applied to the back of glass, and the glass employed as an inlaying. But perhaps the most striking ornamentation of this kind is pearl-inlaying, of which Messrs. Jennens and Bettridge's pianoforte was such a brilliant specimen. Here real mother-of-pearl is employed. A design is painted on the thin pieces of pearl with shellac varnish, a strong acid is applied, all the shell is eaten away except those parts protected by the varnish, and thus the pearl is brought into an ornamental form. The pearl is placed upon the wet japan of the papier maché, to which it adheres; and it is then coated with such a thick layer of varnish as to equal the thickness of the film of mother-of pearl. It is varnished, dried, and rubbed with pumice over and over again, until a level surface is produced. It may be easily conceived how excellent the varnish and the mode of application must be to render such a thickness of applied varnish durable. The firm lately mentioned have made a complete suite of papier-maché drawing-room furniture for the Queen of Spain, decorated in this remarkable way.[15]

But it is doubtful whether this excessive glitter of polish and pearl will have a permanent reputation. Something more sober will probably live longer. At any rate, when we find Mr. Owen Jones supplying Alhambraic designs, and other artists pictorial designs, for tea-trays, we find a nearer approach to fine art. The papier-maché contributions to the Great Exhibition from the Messrs. Spiers of Oxford[16] were remarkable, inasmuch as the two or three hundred specimens contained views of about a hundred and fifty public buildings and interesting places in and near that city. There is in many of these specimens a medieval taste in ornament fitted to the medieval state of feeling in Oxford.

Notes

1. H. Clay, Patent no. 1027, 1772.
2. C. F. Bielefeld, 'On the Use of the Improved Papier Mâché in Furniture', in *Interior Decoration of Buildings and in Works of Art* (London: The Author, c.1840), p. 6.
3. R. Hunt, 'Papier-Mâché Manufacture', *Art Journal*, November 1851, pp. 277–278.
4. J. Whitworth, and G. Wallis, *The Industry of The United States in Machinery, Manufactures, and Useful and Ornamental Arts: Compiled from The Official Reports of Messrs. Whitworth And Wallis* (London: G. Routledge & Co., 1854), p. 60.
5. S. Wiley, *Select Committee on Arts and Manufactures* (1835), Q 751, p. 52.
6. T. J. Howell, *Committee on Arts and Manufactures* (1836), Part II, Q 119, p. 14.
7. 'Exhibition of Art-Manufacture in Connection with the Department of Science and Art', *Art Journal*, 44, 1858, p. 251.
8. Jennens & Bettridge (A partnership between Theodore H. Jennens and John Bettridge between 1816 and 1864) of Birmingham and London, were appointed Papier Mâché Manufacturers to King George IV, William IV, and Prince Albert, and exhibited a variety of wares at the Great Exhibition in 1851.
9. Charles Frederick Bielefeld (1803–1864), *On the Use of Improved Papier Mâché in Furniture, in the Interior Decoration of Buildings, and in Works of Art*, 2nd ed. (London: Papier Mâché Works, No. 15, Wellington Street North, Strand, 1850).
10. Trunk maker or the butter man: discarded paper was used to line travelling trunks and wrap butter.
11. George Jackson (1766–1840) founded George Jackson & Sons Ltd. in London in 1780 to produce decorative plaster ornaments.
12. "Paul Gropius, proprietor of the Diorama at Berlin, next exhibits a collection of ornaments and figures formed of stone-paste", *A Guide to the Great Exhibition: Containing a Description of Every Principal Object of Interest: with a Plan, Pointing out the Easiest and Most Systematic way of Examining the Contents of the Crystal Palace* (London: George Routledge and Co, 1851).
13. John Coope Haddan, civil engineer.
14. See *Official Descriptive and Illustrated Catalogue of the Great Exhibition of the Works of Industry of All Nations, 1851* (London: Spicer 1851).
15. "A suite of papier mâché boudoir furniture, of great splendour and elegance, it is said, has just been completed by Messrs. Jenners and Bettridge, of Birmingham, for the young Queen of Spain. It consists of eighteen reclining chairs, a sofa, the largest ever made in this material, sofa-table, light ornamented tables, conversation chairs, and ottomans. The ornaments are chiefly of burnished gold and mother of pearl, in the ornate style of Louis the Fourteenth, with groups of birds, fountains, and festoons." *The Builder*, 5, 1847, p. 192.
16. Spiers of Oxford: Richard James Spiers (1806–1877) established his business in 1834 as a stationery and fancy goods shop and subsequently specialised in objects made of papier-mâché. The business closed in 1890.

33

[ANON], 'DESIGN IN RELATION TO MATERIAL'

The debates about the use of sham or imitation materials in design raged in varying degrees throughout the nineteenth century. Whether in relation to materials such as stone, wood, iron, (wrought or cast), plaster, or processes including veneering, marbling, graining, and electroplating, the arguments exercised many of the most well-known minds of the time. For most critics, it was a matter of morality and the apparently perceived intention to deceive that were the main issues. On the other hand, imitations were often seen as cheaper, cleaner, easier, and more modern and progressive. Nevertheless, from Pugin to William Morris, the voices of condemnation were strong.

Pugin for example contended that 'Cast-iron is a deception: it is seldom or never left as iron. It is a mere trick, . . . better is it to do a little substantially and consistently with truth than to produce a great but false show'.[1] John Ruskin went further in his *Seven Lamps of Architecture*. In the 'Lamp of Truth', he proclaimed: 'Touching the false representation of material, the question is infinitely more simple, and the law more sweeping; all such imitations are utterly base and inadmissible'.[2] He went on to make a further point:

> The last form of fallacy which it will be remembered we had to deprecate, was the substitution of cast or machine work for that of the hand, generally expressible as Operative Deceit.
> There are two reasons, both weighty, against this practice: one, that all cast and machine work is bad, as work; the other, that it is dishonest. Of its badness I shall speak in another place, that being evidently no efficient reason against its use when other cannot be had. Its dishonesty, however, which, to my mind, is of the grossest kind, is, I think, a sufficient reason to determine absolute and unconditional rejection of it.[3]

Eight years later, in 1857 the architect, Sir George Gilbert Scott, in a chapter titled 'On the Boundaries of Truth and Falsehood in Architecture' used the analogy of knowing the boundaries of right and wrong:

> As in morals nothing is so certainly indicative of a degraded state of society as the decline of truthfulness and the prevalence of deceit, so in

art the surest signs of degradation are the decay of reality and truth, and the general adoption of systems of deception and sham.[4]

In relation to papier mâché products, the *Art Journal* mentioned how 'Producers of this class of goods have found that if it not be a fraud, it is at all events a mistake, to make purchasers pay for an accumulation of cost that is worthless'.[5] In 1878, *The Builder* returned to the issue in an article titled 'Truth about Shams'.

> "Thou shalt have silver and gold on thy table, and if it be too costly for thy purse thou shalt sham it"; that is the verdict of modern society, and consequently, on the moment, there is nothing else to be got, for the verdict of the majority rules the manufacturers and dealers. . . . But if we go out of the groove of habit and come to exercise our own unbiassed tastes, would not good taste and "common sense" any day pronounce in favour of an earthenware teapot of good design, and a horn spoon with a little mounting of real silver on it, in place of mock-silver articles of either kind. And we believe the same feeling holds good, and is perfectly in accordance with "common sense", as well as with aesthetic taste, when we turn to the development of shams on a larger scale, which are more directly connected with architectural adornment.[6]

The concept of 'good taste' and 'common sense' in designed objects was both an antidote to shams and an expression of integrity. This idea is well shown in this 1881 extract about school buildings: 'She [Art] may suitably mark a great social movement if invited to be present in its buildings, may show what can be done in the merest plain brickwork if her fundamental principles of truth and common sense be adhered to throughout'.[7]

This anonymous essay was published simultaneously in *The Builder* (2 January 1869), and the *Morning Post* acknowledges this source. The same article was later published in *English Mechanics and the World of Science*.[8]

[Anon], 'Design in Relation to Material', *Morning Post*, 2 January 1869, p. 3

Among the anomalies resulting from the system of architectural reproduction which has now for so long a time prevailed among us, the rehabilitation of this or that extinct form or manner of design in place of thoughtful original invention, it has come to pass that we have become singularly indifferent as to the relation which should subsist between the texture and peculiar capabilities of any given material and the artistic form which is to be impressed upon it. During the cold reign of the pseudo-classic tendency, when the mere repetition, in any material, of the leading features of Greek architecture formed the Alpha and Omega of our art, it was, of course, all in the natural order of things that there should be columns formed from channelled segments of wood glued together into a cylinder, and that imitation of stone-coffered ceilings should be arduously attained by the aid of plaster and bracketing. These things were openly done, and no one raised an eye-brow or lifted a shoulder at them. But when there arose the spirit of modern Gothic, mighty, as we were assured, to the pulling down of the strongholds of plaster capitals and wooden plinths, *et id genus omne*,[9] then was it confidently prophesied that the spirit of 'sham' had been demolished, and great were the paeans sung over the demolition. Nor let us by any means question, in the main, the received opinion that much good fruit has been borne by that notable movement. If it was connected with much of blind and bigoted exclusiveness and copyism, it at least brought us back to study a style which on the whole was verily a style of building design, of design capable of due accomplishment nowhere save in building, and in no material save stone; and so far as the treatment of this grandest of architectural materials was concerned, the teaching of the medieval monuments was unexceptionable. They belonged to a time when men may be said to have literally thought in stone, and had come to know and sympathise with their material to a degree never attained since. Yet from this very fact it arose that the stone type of design took such possession of the minds of the old builders that they could not shake it off even when working in other material, and much of their treatment of woodwork became only so much stone design lignified, if we may coin a word. To the enthusiastic revivers of medievalism there could be no such thing as error in Gothic work, and accordingly they complacently intimated and reproduced the wooden buttresses which resisted no thrust, the wooden arches cut from the solid, and all the other little anomalies consequent on the translation into this material of design formed in a totally different one. The style was to be reproduced with reverence, faults and all, just as it was found. The particular result just alluded to is, however, only a single instance of the manner in which this enthusiastic copying militated against thoughtfulness in design. It is to be feared that, independently of such partial and inevitable results, the copying system which has so long prevailed has acted much more widely than this, in inducing a carelessness and want of thought as to the aesthetic use of materials, and habituating us to a sort of routine method of treating them, rather in accordance with pre-existing examples than with considerations of the nature and quality of the material, and the special treatment demanded thereby. The effects of this want of consideration are apparent all round us. We may endeavour, however, to indicate some of the forms in which it is most prominent.

Stone, which may be considered, in spite of all newly-applied material that are coming into fashion, to be, *par excellence*, the architect's medium for design, is a material best used under compression, very weak under cross-strain, and which in general can only be used in super-imposed blocks of a limited size. These conditions would seem to indicate unmistakably enough the proper and architectural method of using stone. We should naturally conclude that an arched form of construction should be the rule in a stone building, or that if a lintel form only be adopted, the width of the opening should not only be limited, but that as much as possible of the material should be left in the lintel, which should on no account be weakened by cutting away from it for so-called ornamental purposes. Yet we constantly see buildings in which both these obvious conditions are utterly disregarded. There are positions, indeed, in which a lintel construction becomes desirable in stone, as when no sufficiently secure abutment can be obtained, or when a row of window-heads are ranged immediately under a horizontal cornice. But a fashion has now sprung up, and is gaining ground greatly among the architects of the new Gothic school, the absurdity of which cannot be too strongly insisted upon. A lintel construction is adopted, but in order to assimilate the lintel with what is supposed to be the Gothic spirit, it is cut up into the form of a shallow arch, pointed or otherwise. Thus the lintel is materially weakened, and a large portion of the stone literally goes to waste, along with the labour expended on it. We have actually seen a full half of a stone lintel cut away in this manner, to a horizontal soffit, the ends being left in the form of brackets turning down upon the brick jambs of the opening. Where a soft stone is used, this may increase the supply in the grit and rubbing stone market, but what other good effect it is to have it would be difficult to say. One of the very worst forms in which we have seen this absurdity was in the case of a building where the lintel was cut into the form of an ogee arch (a very bad form, be it observed, at the best), the point of the ogee sitting up the centre of the stove, of course, in a charming manner; we almost expected to see the split go right through the lintel as we looked at it. The capabilities for effect, again, resulting from the necessity for arranging the material in courses, are not nearly enough considered in walling. There is hereby a natural opportunity presented for the use of a quiet and unobtrusive external polychromy, by the selection of stone of varied tints, but of similar texture and formation; and also for obtaining a picturesque character in the walling, which can be imparted by varying the depth of the courses, or by here and there a thinner course, exactly in the manner best calculated to bond the walling securely; so that here construction and effect go hand-in-hand, as in all true architecture they almost invariably do. The capabilities of wall-surface, in this kind of way, are not by any means made the most of at present. A current vulgarity in wall-treatment, on the other hand, is the use of panelling, which is also an example of the sin of appropriating a method of treatment originating in the qualities of another material. When we see a panelled wooden cabinet or sideboard, or a panelled door, the system appears perfectly natural and satisfactory; because we know then that we are dealing with a substance of a fibrous texture, sufficiently tough to cohere even when sawn into very thin layers, and which will consequently bear joining by tenons and other such contrivances. A panelled door, therefore, is a fitting and economical method of applying the material used; but it is an absurdity to apply panelling, merely as such, to a wall-surface, thus conveying to the eye the idea that it is framed of thin slabs and angle-pieces, when we know the material is, in fact, too friable for any such treatment. The only legitimate application of panelling to stone wall-surface is when a flush or raised panel of marble veneer is introduced (a proceeding, however, which on some grounds is questionable), or when the panel mould is merely introduced as the boundary-line of some decorative carving, in which case the sinking should not be so deep as to conceal any part of the ornament, but merely sufficient to mark it off from the plain wall-surface adjoining. But the placing of mere panelling over the surface of a building, as ornament, is always evidence of poverty of designing power and want of perception of the true requirements of architectural design. The constant use of it was one of the great blots on the Italian Renaissance, many of the best buildings of this school being deprived of a great deal of their effect, and almost taken out of the category of architecture altogether, by their being covered over with a feature which masked their real construction and gave to the whole building a sort of tea-caddy or cabinet appearance quite alien from the effect which a construction of solid blocks of bonded stone ought to present. A similar error is the employment of that hideous feature, as it appears to us, a rusticated column. Where the column is really built up of isolated parts in shallow courses, this method is constructively far inferior to the use of a monolith where one can be obtained; and if the column is really a monolith, artificially rusticated, the case is worse, as involving a waste of material to produce a sham.*

As to wood, there is no end to the misuse that has been made of this useful and pliable material; the misuse in the majority of cases resulting from the imitation of stone treatment. It is made into sham plinths and surbases,[10] put together with much careful joinery; inch pieces are 'boxed' into the imitation of a solid cornice or soffit; it is twisted round, under the influence of steam, into sham arches; forms foreign to its very nature. The absurdity is, that a kind of erection of separate pieces is often made, when a single solid piece would have both looked better and been more durable. In erecting large stone gate piers, it is a natural plan to foot the shaft of the pier on a plinth stone larger than itself, and to crown it with a heavy projecting cap. But for smaller piers, where a monolith is easily obtainable of sufficient size, it is an absurdity to do this, as the monolithic gate-pier on this scale will be far stronger than a built one and the absurdity is still greater when (as we have seen) a monolith is used, and the greater part of the surface chipped away 2in. deep all round, in order to get a sham plinth at the base. The same sort of blunder is constantly made with stair numerals. A newel[11] should be a solid piece of wood, to receive the handrail and notch board, and should be so treated, any ornamental finish at the top or pendant at the bottom being worked out of the solid. But in many cases it seems to be considered the thing that a newel should imitate a large pier, and so a cap and plinth there must be, and the plinth is nailed round the bottom, and the tap nailed on at the top. In due course of time the plinth shows signs of separating from the core, to which it is attached, and the head gets loose; whereas the simple post might have lasted for generations. A common misuse of wood is found in such erections as summer-houses and conservatories, especially in buildings of a classical tendency; where, instead of the upright stiles being treated as wood and moulded solid, they are developed into

---

* We speak of course of columns of moderate dimensions, such as would occur in an entrance porch– a situation in which rusticated columns have been a good deal used.

apparent pilasters, composed of 1¼in. stuff with all the insignia of caps and bases, and 'everything proper.' We have actually seen such a thing as a kind of bandbox pedestal elaborately framed round iron columns, which, in fact, went through the door on to a template on the wall underneath— a regular hollow square box with plinth, surbase, and all adroitly put together. This is perhaps a flagrant case but the shams that have been perpetrated in wood are much as to make one doubt sometimes whether there is such a thing as architectural principle at all. The Gothic school are certainly foremost in deprecating such things as we have just alluded to, but they have their own little shams in the treatment of woodwork too. The wooden buttress is now indeed going out, but in the 'firework' designs for bookcases and organ-cases, with inlaid and variously-coloured wood, which we constantly see, there is frequent use made of the shaft and arch, on a small scale, which is simply a stone feature translated into wood. In such pieces of furniture the quality of wood as a material, its resistance to cross-strain, and its comparative softness and facility for carving, point to its suitable employment in square and diagonal moulded bracing, and in carved brackets, while its cohesiveness in thin layers authorises, as we before remarked, a panel construction; and panels, let us note may be made highly ornamental in cases where *bona fide* carving is too expensive, by being simply pierced through in some carefully-designed flat pattern,—a source of decoration which might have been made more of and been more artistically developed than it has been. As to the 'centre-bit' style of decoration, so much in fashion, formed by piercing round holes in the wood everywhere, it is only worthy of very young children. We say nothing of designs for roofs, for there timber is, so to speak, master of the situation; if you do not treat it on true 'wooden' principles, the roof will revenge itself upon it clumsy constructor by falling, and pushing out the walls. The sententious ejaculation of Butler,—

Ah, me, what perils do environ
The man who meddles with cold iron ![12]

may apply to architectural as well as to military aspirants. So far as construction is concerned, we need scarcely, we hope, at this time of day, urge that iron when used constructively in the form of girders, or columns, should be shown as such, and not be masked by a quasi stone or wood construction. Nor does the treatment of wrought iron in ornamental work call for special comment here, so far at least as principles of design are concerned. Wrought iron is so peculiar a material, and demands so much arduous labour in the treatment of it ornamentally, that there is little fear that it should ever be used except to produce those effects which are peculiar to it, and which nothing else can well imitate. It is when we come to that too often pernicious compound, cast-iron, that our critical spirit is aroused: *hoc opus, hic labor est*[13]— or rather the saving of labour. As to the use of cast-iron for ornament generally, perhaps the best advice to those about to use it would be comprised in one word — "Don't." There are cases, however, where much money cannot be spent on ornament, and where a certain amount of decorative effect can be attained by the aid of cast-iron; but then it must be designed with due regard to the deficiencies of the material. Let no one suppose that highly ornamental carved work, when once executed in wood, can be reproduced *ad infinitum* in cast-iron with any but the most lamentable and poverty-stricken results. It is from the attempt to get too much out of cast-iron that the material has been so vulgarised and misused. It must be remembered that we are here dealing with a material coarser than sandstone, which is utterly incapable of giving sharp cuttings and under-cuttings, delicate surface-work, or anything which goes to produce that crispness necessary to the proper effect of elaborate carved design; yet we see foliated capitals and leafage ornament perpetually attempted in this material, sometimes cast from models themselves coarsely executed in lead, the coarseness being necessarily exaggerated in the casting. This sort of cast-iron ornament is alone sufficient to remove the stamp of art from a building, and throw over it a flashy, tradesman-like appearance. What can legitimately be attempted with cast-iron in the way of ornament is whatever depends on simple lines and square decided sections, without aiming at delicacy of surface-work. Brackets, for instance, with pierced ornamental spandrels, the ornament produced merely by the flat perforation in the material, without any attempt at a moulded edge, will generally have a satisfactory result. Similarly, capitals to cast-iron columns may be designed, consisting of simple flat leafage forms, defined only by the sinking between them, and not attempting to take the place of the carved foliage ornament, which can only be satisfactorily executed in wood or stone. In designing capitals of this kind, suitable for the material, there would be scope for some novel treatment of the crowning feature of a shaft or column. As to the kind of so-called ornament we meet with on our iron lamp-posts and area-railings, the leaves and wreaths and festoons, with their details only half made out, struggling, as it were, to show themselves through the course material, year by year more choked and filled up with paint and dust,—with regard to such things the only consolation (if it can be called so) is that the design is generally worthy of the material in which it is attempted.

What we have said about cast-iron will also apply in great measure to that other material for cast ornament, plaster. A growing distaste for this perishable though showy vehicle of ornament is one of the main things for which we have to thank the modern mediaeval movement, though the pioneers of this movement carried the matter too far, in the inclination which they showed to ignore even the efficacy of plaster in rendering the interior of a building comfortable and warm, and to return to bare brick or stone walls. And plaster has also its legitimate uses as an ornamental material—uses which in a future number we may endeavour to define more minutely. But, though more ductile than cast-iron, it can never have the sharpness and crispness of actual carving; and therefore all attempts to execute elaborate and delicate ornament in this material must result in a sort of pie-crust effect, and be classed with that sort of ornament which may be designated generally as flummery.[14]

We have indicated a few of the leading and most obvious points in which the relation between material and design appears to us to be habitually and constantly overlooked; to those among our readers who are accustomed to think before they work, many others will doubtless occur. We would draw attention, in conclusion, to the importance of such considerations as regard the future of architectural art. The simplest path in art is often the truest, and leads most directly to the goal, and we cannot but think that in the present day there would be less diversity as to what really constitutes good architecture, less confusion and jumbling of old styles, and a better chance of arriving at the "new style"—that mirage constantly hanging before the eyes of the modern architect, and ever receding from his grasp —if architectural designers would oftener adopt the simple plan of considering, first, what material will be practically best for the building they are to erect; and, secondly, what is the nature and property of that material, in what method it can be constructively used so as to insure its utmost efficiency, and what class of ornament its peculiar texture and surface render it fitted to give full value to.

Notes

1 A. W. N. Pugin, *True Principle of Christian Architecture* (London: Henry Bohn, 1853), p. 27.
2 J. Ruskin, *Seven Lamps of Architecture: Lamp of Truth* (London: Waverley Book Co., 1849), p. 50.
3 Ruskin, p. 55.
4 Sir G. G. Scott, *Remarks on Secular & Domestic Architecture, Present & Future* (London: J. Murray, 1857), p. 235.
5 'Exhibition of Art Manufacture', *Art Journal*, 44, August 1858, p. 251.
6 *Builder*, 36, 23 September 1878, p. 1004.
7 E. R. Robson 'Art as Applied to Town Schools', *Art Journal*, May 1881, p. 137.
8 *Builder*, 2 January 1869, 27, pp. 3–5 and *English Mechanics and the World of Science*, 8–9, 26 February 1869, p. 507 and 19 March 1869, p. 573.
9 *et id genus omne*: and everything (else) of this kind.
10 surbases: the uppermost part, such as a moulding, of a pedestal, base, or skirting.
11 newel: a post at the head or foot of a flight of stairs, supporting a handrail.
12 Samuel Butler, *Hudibras*, 1732.
13 *hoc opus, hic labor est:* In this the task and mighty labour lies.
14 *flummery:* meaningless or insincere flattery or conventions.

5.4

MANUFACTURING METHODS

34

ADAM SMITH, AND DUGALD STEWART, *THE WORKS OF ADAM SMITH*

Adam Smith (1723–1790) was a Scottish economist, philosopher and author, as well as a moral philosopher, a proposer of free industry and trade, a pioneer of political economy and a key figure during the Scottish Enlightenment.

Arnold Toynbee in his *Lectures on the Industrial Revolution of the 18th Century* summed up the importance of Smith's most famous work *The Wealth of Nations:* 'No wonder that every page of the Wealth of Nations is illumined with an illimitable passion for freedom of industry and trade. In the spirit of that book still more than in the facts contained in it, the dawn of a new epoch is visible. The Wealth of Nations is the great proclamation of the rights of industry and trade'.[1]

Apart from his philosophical works, Smith also showed an interest in the arts and design. He was an advisor to the Foulis School for the Art of Design in Glasgow that was established in 1753, in matters of organisation, as well as practice. He also considered aspects of design including colours and finishes. In his *Theory of Moral Sentiments,* Smith suggested that 'Certain colours are more agreeable than others and give more delight to the eye the first time it ever beholds them. A smooth surface is more agreeable than a rough one. Variety is more pleasing than a tedious undiversified uniformity'.[2] Smith's statement underlines how the ability to select and purchase a range of colours and finishes would not only give the owner 'more delight' but would also often distinguish them from those who could not afford such luxuries and had to rely on plain often naturally coloured and rough objects. Nonetheless, Smith was dismissive of contemporary flippant attitudes towards colour and the impact of changing tastes, as explained in his *Lectures on Jurisprudence*, delivered in the 1760s:

> These Four distinctions of colour, form, variety or rarity and imitation seem to be the foundation of all the minute, and to more thoughtful persons, frivolous distinctions and preferences in things otherwise equal, which give in the pursuit more distress and uneasiness to mankind than all the others, and to gratify which a thousand arts have been invented.[3]

In terms of design, Smith is well known for his example of the division of labour in the production of pins. For Smith, the division of labour was the primary facilitator for improved productivity. He wrote in *The Wealth of Nations* that the value of the division of labour was 'first, to the increase of dexterity in every particular workman; secondly, to the saving of the time which is commonly lost in passing from one species of work to another; and lastly, to the invention of a great number of machines which facilitate and abridge labour'.[4] Finally, he argues that it is the 'great multiplication of the productions of all the different arts, in consequence of the division of labour, which occasions, in a well-governed society, that universal opulence which extends itself to the lowest ranks of the people'.[5]

Although the idea of 'universal opulence' might have been attractive, the division of labour was to become a bugbear of later socialist design reformers. Indeed, Ruskin used Smith's pin example to denounce the practice of division of labour.

> We have much studied and much perfected, of late, the great civilized invention of the division of labour; only we give it a false name. It is not truly speaking the labour that is divided; but the men; – Divided into mere segments of men broken into small fragments and crumbs of life; so that all the little piece of intelligence that is left in a man is not enough to make a pin, or a nail, but exhausts itself in making the point of a pin or the head of a nail.[6]

In this example, Smith analyses the progress of a woollen coat to demonstrate the networks and interdependence of various players in the design and production of ordinary domestic objects.

Adam Smith, and Dugald Stewart, *The Works of Adam Smith* (London: Printed for T. Cadell, 1811–12), pp. 15–19

All the improvements in machinery, however, have by no means been the inventions of those who had occasion to use the machines. Many improvements have been made by the ingenuity of the makers of the machines, when to make them became the business of a peculiar trade; and some by that of those who are called philosophers or men of speculation, whose trade it is not to do anything, but to observe everything; and who, upon that account, are often capable of combining together the powers of the most distant and dissimilar objects. In the progress of society, philosophy or speculation becomes, like every other employment, the principal or sole trade and occupation of a particular class of citizens. Like every other employment too, it is subdivided into a great number of different branches, each of which affords occupation to a peculiar tribe or class of philosophers; and this subdivision of employment in philosophy, as well as in every other business, improves dexterity, and saves time. Each individual becomes more expert in his own peculiar branch, more work is done upon the whole, and the quantity of science is considerably increased by it.

It is the great multiplication of the productions of all the different arts, in consequence of the division of labour, which occasions, in a well-governed society, that universal opulence which extends itself to the lowest ranks of the people. Every workman has a great quantity of his own work to dispose of beyond what he himself has occasion for; and every other workman being exactly in the same situation, he is enabled to exchange a great quantity of his own goods for a great quantity, or, what comes to the same thing for the price of a great quantity of theirs. He supplies them abundantly with what they have occasion for, and they accommodate him as amply with what he has occasion for, and a general plenty diffuses itself through all the different ranks of the society.

Observe the accommodation of the most common artificer or day-labourer in a civilized and thriving country, and you will perceive that the number of people of whose industry a part, though but a small part, has been employed in procuring him this accommodation, exceeds all computation. The woollen coat, for example, which covers the day-labourer, as coarse and rough as it may appear, is the produce of the joint labour of a great multitude of workmen. The shepherd, the sorter of the wool, the woolcomber or carder, the dyer, the scribbler, the spinner, the weaver, the fuller, the dresser, with many others, must all join their different arts in order to complete even this homely production. How many merchants and carriers, besides, must have been employed in transporting the materials from some of those workmen to others who often live in a very distant part of the country! how much commerce and navigation in particular, how many ship-builders, sailors, sailmakers, rope-makers, must have been employed in order to bring together the different drugs made use of by the dyer, which often come from the remotest corners of the world! What a variety of labour too is necessary in order to produce the tools of the meanest of those workmen! To say nothing of such complicated machines as the ship of the sailor, the mill of the fuller, or even the loom of the weaver, let us consider only what a variety of labour is requisite in order to form that very simple machine, the shears with which the shepherd clips the wool. The miner, the builder of the furnace for smelting the ore, the feller of the timber, the burner of the charcoal to be made use of in the smelting-house, the brick-maker, the bricklayer, the workmen who attend the furnace, the mill-wright, the forger, the smith, must all of them join their different arts in order to produce them. Were we to examine, in the same manner, all the different parts of his dress and household furniture, the coarse linen shirt which he wears next his skin, the shoes which cover his feet, the bed which he lies on, and all the different parts which compose it, the kitchen-grate at which he prepares his victuals, the coals which he makes use of for that purpose, dug from the bowels of the earth, and brought to him perhaps by a long sea and a long land carriage, all the other utensils of his kitchen, all the furniture of his table, the knives and forks, the earthen or pewter plates upon which he serves up and divides his victuals, the different hands employed in preparing his bread and his beer, the glass window which lets in the heat and the light, and keeps out the wind and the rain, with all the knowledge and art requisite for preparing that beautiful and happy invention, without which these northern parts of the world could scarce have afforded a very comfortable habitation, together with the tools of all the different workmen employed in producing those different conveniences; if we examine, I say, all these things, and consider what a variety of labour is employed about each of them, we shall be sensible that without the assistance and co-operation of many thousands, the very meanest person in a civilized country could not be provided, even according to, what we very falsely imagine, the easy and simple manner in which he is commonly accommodated. Compared, indeed, with the more extravagant luxury of the great, his accommodation must no doubt appear extremely simple and easy; and yet it may be true, perhaps, that the accommodation of an European prince does not always so much exceed that of an industrious and frugal peasant, as the accommodation of the latter exceeds that of many an African king, the absolute master of the lives and liberties of ten thousand naked savages.

Notes

1 A. Toynbee, and B. Jowett, *Lectures on the Industrial Revolution of the 18th Century in England* (London: Longmans, 1894), p. 188.
2 A. Smith, *The Theory of Moral Sentiments: To Which is Added a Dissertation on the Origin of Languages* (London: Printed for A. Millar, A. Kincaid and J. Bell in Edinburgh, 1767), p. 302.
3 A, Smith, R. L. Meek, D. D. Raphael, and P. G. Stein, *Lectures in Jurisprudence* (Oxford: Clarendon Press, 1978), p. 337.
4 A. Smith, *An Inquiry into the Nature and Causes of the Wealth of Nations* (1776), Book 1, Chapter 1.
5 Smith, (1776), Book 1, Chapter 1.
6 J. Ruskin, *Stones of Venice*, 2nd Ed. (London: Smith Elder, 1867), p. 195.

35

WILLIAM COOKE-TAYLOR, 'THE MUTUAL INTERESTS OF ARTISTS AND MANUFACTURERS'

William Cooke-Taylor (1800–1849) was a prolific Irish author and advocate of the Anti-Corn Law League. He wrote widely on Irish history, on the British factory system, and was editor of the Anti-Corn Law League's journal and a campaigner for copyright laws.

In this article, Cooke-Taylor argues that the mutual benefits of artists and manufacturers were in tune, in terms of developing the economy, the taste, and morals of the country. He talks of artists and manufacturers as being friends and allies in an important project to achieve these goals. Cooke-Taylor's article also addressed the issue of artisans and the stultifying aspects of the division of labour, which he argues might be alleviated by ensuring an artistic element is introduced into the manufacturing processes, wherever possible.

In 1877, *The Art Journal,* in a retrospective article that looked at changes in the relationship between art and manufacture, quoted from Cooke-Taylor's article that lamented the state of design in 1848. They then went on to comment upon the improvements as they saw them:

> Is there a firm in Manchester now, or in Kidderminster, or in any one of the producing centres, that has not its artists room, where a score (often more) of artists sit regularly at their work, to supply the artistic wants of the establishment? There is no leading establishment in England, Scotland, or Ireland that does not entertain a staff of artists, while many of them have imported, not the designs, but the designers.[1]

This apparent improvement of taste in art and literature was a 'silent revolution' and thus seemed to confirm Cooke-Taylor's argument that the development of 'artistic taste, will afford the philanthropist [the] most powerful leverage for securing the moral and social elevation of the British people'.[2] However, for Cooke-Taylor, this 'social elevation' remained strictly within the existing hierarchies of society.

William Cooke-Taylor, 'The Mutual Interests of Artists and Manufacturers', *Art-Union*, 10, 1 March 1848, pp. 69–70

We know the Fine Arts originated in that love of ornament which is inherent in our nature, and of which distinct traces can be found in the lowest depths of barbarism and the most unintelligent forms of savage life. We cannot trace their progress from the cradle to maturity, because their infancy was coincident with the infancy of general humanity; tradition alone preserves imperfect memorials of a time when the art of recording was unknown. It is also singular, that the most fragile specimens of ancient Art been more perfectly preserved than those of the most solid and durable materials; we have Egyptian vases of greater age than granite statues, and Etrurian pottery more antique than Etrurian tombs. Comparing the relics of the past with the discoveries made in lands revealed to us at different stages of civilisation, we are led to conclude that the moulder preceded the statuary; that sculpture was in its origin merely a plastic art, and that utility had more influence over its early progress than the realisation of ideality.

There appears to us, then, a natural and early connection between the pursuits of the Artist and the Manufacturer. In the primary ages both were combined in one person; through periods of progress they advanced concurrently; and to ensure the perfection of both, the bonds by which they are united, instead of being relaxed, should be drawn closer together in mutual alliance. The Artist offers to the Manufacturer the conception which is sure to command the homage of the public; the manufacturer enables the artist to give his conception not merely a local habitation in material reality, but an existence which admits of its being known, appreciated, admired and applauded. We have abundant evidence that the greatest artists of their day furnished designs for the vases and bronzes of Greece, Etruria, and southern Italy. The Cartoons of Raffaelle testify that the greatest of modern painters did not disdain to become a designer for the workers at the loom and the embroidery frame; Benvenuto Cellini developed the purest conceptions of statuary with the chasing tool; and the revolution which our Wedgewood worked in the English potteries, was most effectually aided by Fuseli and Flaxman.

There is, then, nothing derogatory to the highest Art in lending its aid to decorate objects of utility. The sculptor does not lower his position when he supplies a model for the moulder in iron, brass, statuary-porcelain, or any other substance in which casts may be taken. The painter no way derogates from his dignity when he furnishes beautiful patterns to the manufacturer of furniture cottons, of muslins, of chintzes, or of paper hangings. Artists are public teachers; and it is their duty, as well as their interest, to aim at giving the greatest possible extent and publicity to their instructions.

Now a great but silent revolution has been taking place in the production and reproduction of works of Art for more than a century. The whole tendency of modern invention is to facilitate the multiplication of copies, and to perfect accuracy in copying. Even within our own memory these inventions and discoveries have wrought a wondrous change in the tastes and habits of the people; in their power of appreciating works of Art, and their readiness to concur in securing adequate renumeration to artists. We all remember Goldsmith's description of the humble ornaments that decorated the mantel-piece of the ale-house in his "Deserted Village"—

> "The broken tea-cups wisely kept for show,
> Placed o'er the chimney, glisten'd in a row."[3]

But it would be hard to find an ale-house now in which the ornaments are not of a more ambitious, and we may add of a more instructive, character. Plaster-busts of popular favourites, bisques, statuettes and other pieces of ornament, as suggestive of thought as they are conducive to true decoration, are fast increasing in the rooms where the rustics congregate, even in our most remote districts. The Italian boys with their plaster of Paris casts have been the precursors to a new school of English manufacturing Art; they have fostered a taste beyond their capabilities to satisfy, and generated a demand beyond their power to supply.[4] Steel engraving has produced still more marked and more happy results. In Goldsmith's day the decorations of the walls of the cottage were

> "The twelve good rules, the royal game of goose;"[5]

in our own memory, paltry wood-cuts, most detestably coloured, such as might suit the taste of the subjects of the king of Dahomy, or the aborigines of Australia, were a profitable ware at rural fairs and markets. They have, for the most part, been driven out of the field; the improvement of taste has generated a more intense thirst for knowledge; there is a natural desire to know the history of the event or place delineated in a favourite picture, and to search into the biography of the person represented in any portrait which we may chance to possess.

Now the moral result of this silent revolution has not, we apprehend, been fully appreciated, even in regard to cheap Literature, which as yet has out-stripped cheap Art. We doubt if there are many who have even set themselves to inquire into the number of seditious and immoral ballads which have been forced to remain in cold obstruction by the cheap publications of Chambers, Knight, Parker, and others. We doubt whether enough of attention has been paid to the mass of sedition, blasphemy, and obscenity, which has been annihilated by the presence of sound instruction and interesting information attainable at an easy rate. It is a subject to which unexpected circumstances have directed our attention, and we feel as convinced as we do of our own existence, that the extension not merely of literary information, but, at least in an equal degree, of artistic taste, will afford the philanthropist, most powerful leverage for securing the moral and social elevation of the British people.

We trust in the high and generous feelings of British artists; we know that no mere pecuniary reward, no title of worldly honour, would be dearer to them than the conviction, that, while they laboured for fame with posterity they were also contributing to the intellectual and moral advancement of the generation in which they live and move and have their being. If we suggest other motives, lower in kind, but still not destitute of practical importance, it is not because we despair of the efficacy of the nobler influences, but because we are anxious to show, that what we urge is not only desirable, but also feasible and practicable.

The multiplication of the copies of a work of Art is an extension of the fame of the artists, from the applause of some score of amateurs, to the honest appreciation of some thousands, and perhaps millions of his countrymen. While the noble and wealthy possess the splendid original in marble, alabaster, or bronze, the value of that original is not deteriorated to the possessor by the multiplication of statuette copies; while the fame of the artist is infinitely extended, and his share in the education of his countrymen proportionately increased. His chances of future gain are equally enlarged; in a country like England, where skill, education, and intelligence, are constantly raising men from the ranks to social position and fortune, a future patron of Art, and perhaps of the artist, is in course of training, when the aspiring operative is enabled to purchase a copy of some of the rising artist's early productions at a moderate rate. Wilkie[6] could tell, and used to tell, the story of a munificent patron who had bought a cheap engraving of one of his first pictures, when but a humble mechanic, and who, when he became a capitalist, was anxious to make the most liberal offers for originals.

As artists rarely trouble themselves with a study of the arts of reproduction, they are very liable to the error of introducing details into their works, which add little, if anything, to the general effect and beauty of the whole, but which interpose many serious obstacles to the process of modelling and casting. Now, we are anxious that artists should think sometimes of copyists; that the sculptor should recognise the existence of the modeller, as the painter does of the engraver. Copyright in design secures to him a more certain, and a more honourable remuneration, than any that could have been gained from the lavish liberality of the Medicis, or the extravagant caprices of the Bourbon. In Art, as in Literature, it will be found that small profits on an extensive circulation afford, eventually, better remuneration than large profits from a very limited demand. Let us not be misunderstood; we do not wish artists to become the servants of manufacturers; we do wish them to become their friends and allies; their partners in educating the people; in improving the tastes, and consequently, the morals, of the community; in developing the intellectual strength and the intellectual resources of the United Empire.

Art has its high and holy mission; genius and talents, whatever may be their form, are given to the favoured few, that they may work out the sublime purpose of Divine Providence—the advancement of "Glory to God in the Highest," by the promotion of "Peace upon Earth, Good Will towards Men." Community in the admiration of any excellence is a strong bond of peace; union in the love of any ennobling exertion of the human faculties is, above all things, efficacious in developing and fostering good will. The civilising and humanising effects of Art are upon record; they did not escape the notice of the Roman poet, whose words, though rather hackneyed, we must be excused for quoting:

> "—Ingenuas didicisse fideliter artes
> Emollit mores, nec sinit esse feros."[7]

Heathen Art recognised its great mission of civilisation; Christian Art in the middle ages was keenly sensible that it had the same high and holy mission; we should be "dull as the fat weed that rots on Lethe wharf,"[8] if we doubted that the Art of the nineteenth century, with all its superior means and appliances, surrounded by wonders which Science has achieved, and miracles which mechanical skill has accomplished, should fail to perceive duties, and perform functions, that were felt and discharged in ages of comparative darkness.

The multiplication of the copies of superior Art, so far from degrading the artist, elevates him to that position in the hierarchy of social intelligence and utility, from which he would inevitably be degraded, if he did not suit the operation of his influences on the community to the altered circumstances of the age. The parliamentary orator of the last century was little known beyond the precincts of the House; a few disjointed fragments of his eloquence alone crept surreptitiously into circulation, indistinctly proving his patriotism, and still more feebly representing his ability; Chatham[9] himself is to us little better than a name; now, the night on which the Statesman speaks has hardly gone down the sky, the sun of another day has scarcely peeped upon the heaven, when the records of his words are in the hands of thousands of his countrymen, travelling, as with falcon-flight, to the remotest corners of the land. What was the influence of the author in the days of Shakspeare? He, the greatest of philosophic poets, he, who

> "Scatter'd from his pictured urn,
> Thoughts that breathe, and words that burn,"[10]

depended so little on readers, and had so little reliance upon any public, save that which could be congregated within the walls of a theatre, that there is good reason to doubt of his ever having intended to collect his immortal dramas for publication. Compare the position of Shakspeare in the reign of Elizabeth with that of Dickens in our own, and the enormous power which authors have gained, from the wondrous increase of the facilities for multiplying copies of their works, will be so apparent to everyone, as to preclude the necessity of farther comment,

Now, we desire for the artist the same means of general and extensive influence over his countrymen, the same share in contributing to the moral and social elevation of his country and his age, which the progress of mechanical improvement has conferred upon the orator and the author. Phidias contributed as much to the glory, the instruction, and the intellectual development of Athens, as Aeschylus, or Pericles; but we should be guilty of gross adulation to any modern artist, if we placed him, in this respect, on a level with Dickens and Macaulay. We depreciate not the artist, but we deplore his limited means of extension and multiplication; he has fallen back, not absolutely, but relatively; he retains his intelligence, but he does not keep his influence; his school increases not with the increase of population.

Now, we ask artists to aid us in redeeming for Art its due proportion and rightful share in the intellectual agencies, by which the national mind is moulded, formed, and developed. To obtain that influence, they must establish such a connection between the studio and the factory, as exists between the study and the printing press; they must extend the range of their genius, and widen the circle of popular appreciation. All restriction is adverse to the genius of the age, and should Art perversely adhere to restriction, it will be lost in the undistinguished multitude, from want of strength or followers to make a perceptible party. There is not an artist in England who does not feel that Art holds not the place it merits in public estimation. But can any man wonder at this, who reflects on the few opportunities which the great bulk of the nation has for acquiring a knowledge of the excellences of Art? Our National Gallery is of comparatively little worth; our annual exhibition of sculpture is displayed in a dark cellar, or rather, is hidden there, to prevent its being displayed; and in sober fact, the chief instruction in Art attainable by the English public is derived from the display of statuettes, and copies in shop-windows.

But it has been said, "there is no use in giving the people of England patterns of High Art in their manufacture, for they cannot appreciate their excellence, and they will not pay the price of their production." This reminds us of an anecdote told of Addison[11] and a celebrated diplomatist of his day. The diplomatist doubted whether TRUTH would be appreciated in political discussion, just as some people doubt whether taste would be appreciated in various forms of manufacture. Addison asked the diplomatist, "Did you ever try truth?" and we ask the sceptical manufacturer, "Did you ever try taste?" Our own experience as journalists enables us to contradict those doubts so injurious to the character of the English people. Our readers are aware that we have added largely to the artistic attractions of the ART-UNION, and that this increase of expense has necessitated some increase of price.* There were many sceptical advisers ready with warnings as to the hazard of the experiment. We were told that the English taste for Art was of that kind which

---

* It may not be uninteresting to our readers to know that the circulation of our Journal has gradually increased with that increase of taste, which we have laboured to advance; and that our own advantages have augmented in proportion to the improvements it was our duty to promote. The circulation of the Art-Union during the first year of its existence—nine years ago—was under 1000; it varied between 1000 and 2000 during the four succeeding years; it then increased to 4000; in the year 1846, it was raised to 7000; in the year 1847, it had much more than doubled that amount; and we commence the year 1848 with a still more largely augmented circulation. Much of this advance is no doubt attributable to the improved, and greatly more expensive, character of the Publication; but much of it is unquestionably owing to enlarged interest in the subject, to the added power of appreciating excellence, and the increased desire to produce, and to procure, improvements in every branch of Art.—Ed.

is satisfied with the most inferior article, provided it can be had at a very low price; but we trusted to the continuance of that improvement in the public taste by which we have hitherto been borne onwards, and to which, without vanity, we may boast that this Journal has largely contributed; and our confidence has been rewarded by a large addition to the number of subscribers.

English manufacturers cannot hide from themselves that the neglect of Art has been the chief cause of the notion of inferiority by which English fabrics have long been branded. We grant that within the last few years most gratifying evidences of improvement have been brought before us. English porcelain, for instance, has been advanced as much beyond the stage in which Wedgewood left it, as he raised it above the state in which he found it. Two years ago we should not have compared any flower painting of our potteries with a flower painting from Sevres, or any of our raised floral decorations with a similar production from Dresden; now we should court the comparison, and seek the rivalry without any dread of the issue. It is no great effort of memory to recollect a time when, if any man talked of setting up a casting in English iron as a rival to a French bronze, he would be saluted with shouts of laughter as inextinguishable as those of Homer's gods; but no one who has seen the castings of Coalbrookdale would shrink from inviting competition with the iron of Berlin or the bronze of Paris. Not less marked is the advance in our embroideries and textile fabrics, in our printed muslins and furniture cottons, in our carpets and our paper-hangings, in our cabinet-work and in our modes of domestic decoration. Such progress would not have continued, as it obviously and undeniably has done, if improvement had not been practically found to pay. Every exertion to increase artistic excellence has been remunerated by public appreciation and patronage, and would have been still more amply remunerated had the artistic education of the public eye been more perfect and complete.

Artistic improvement in manufactures has created an entirely new school of Architecture in London. Assuredly there are few whose memory cannot carry them back to the old shop-fronts of the Metropolis. They remember the small dingy panes, the heavy frame-work, like the gratings of a prison, and the miserable attempts at display of wares, more calculated to repel than to invite purchasers. Now that shopkeepers have got some things worth showing, they have become eager to display them.* Does any man imagine that the plate-glass, rich

---

* Already there are several shops in the metropolis established for the express purpose of exhibiting, with a view to sale as well as show, the more attractive productions of British Manufacturers; combined in some cases with those of the foreign manufacturer: we may instance the shops of Mr. Cundall and Mr. Eldred, both in Bond Street; in each of them will be found a collection of remarkable works from several British and Continental manufactories. We may safely state that in these cases the experiment has been very eminently successful; we believe we may claim the merit of having set them the example: indeed they have publicly stated as much; the objects we exhibited in our Office window having been largely inquired for, and not being procurable through our means, naturally suggested to active and enterprising tradesmen the policy of obtaining them for sale; and

mouldings, and splendid pillars in the shops of Regent Street, the New Strand, and Ludgate Hill, would ever have been erected but for the confident belief that repayment would be derived from the gratification afforded to the improved and improving taste of the people? We may be assured that, if the shopkeeper found his association with the architect a losing concern, the march of plate-glass and gilt mouldings would long since have been arrested. Its continued progress is a conclusive proof that taste pays; no one, indeed, can doubt the fact who walks through the streets of London with his eyes open.

If we are asked in what branches of manufacture artists may most beneficially be consulted for the improvement of production, we should be much more puzzled to name those to be excepted from a very lengthened list, than those which ought to be included. Art is not less extensive in its range than Science, and we should be glad to know the name of any branch of English production which has not benefited by scientific discovery. Chemistry has marked traces of its progress in every article of our dress, from the hat that covers our head, to the patent sole which protects our feet; it has given patent tiles to our roofs, and concrete to our foundations; it has brightened the candle which lights us to bed, and hastened the fire which cheers us in the morning. Yet we can, though not very distinctly, remember a time when there was as much doubt of the remunerative application of chemical discovery to the improvement of production, as there is now of the application of Art; when the hatter shrunk from all intermeddling with his dye-furnace and his glue-pot; when the shoe-maker feared all manner of danger to his sole; when water-proof hats were deemed as visionary as the cap of Fortunatus,[12] and water-proof boots or shoes as romantic as the slippers of swiftness. Science had to win its way against doubts and fears; the progress of Art must be attended with the same impediments, but every step in advance is not only so much gained from the past, but also a pledge and assurance of further gain from the future. Of Art, as of Fame, it may truly be said,

"Mobilitate viget, viresque acquirit eundo."[13]

But in speaking of the importance of Art to the manufacturer, and of the beneficial results, which may reasonably and surely be expected from the formation of more

---

thus originated these shops, which will, no doubt, multiply: when we find they have multiplied sufficiently, we shall consider that our task has been fulfilled; that there will be no longer any necessity for a public exposure of such articles at our Office;—leaving the duty of procuring and supplying them to those who will do so in the ordinary exercise of trade. We receive proofs, daily, of the avidity with which manufacturers avail themselves of the means of obtaining publicity for their works; such was by no means the case a very few years ago: this is mainly attributable to the advancing spirit of the age, with which all classes are compelled to keep pace; and it is in some degree no doubt owing to the Designs' Registration Act, which, however imperfect it may be, affords some security to the inventor or improver. Upon this subject we shall have much to say when bringing under notice the approaching Exhibition at the Society of Arts.-Ed.

intimate relations, and a closer alliance, between the artist and the manufacturer, we must not forget that there is another large and important class most deeply interested in the issue,—we mean the operatives. To them we are persuaded that every enlargement of the sphere of artistic production, and every consequent extension of artistic influence, is fraught with greater and more decisive advantages than to any other class of the community. Art affords the best antagonistic force to the dementalising and almost demoralising results which are, to some extent, necessarily involved in the excessive division of labour. There is a stupefying tendency in a sameness of mechanical employment, not always curable by showing the connection between occupation and utility of result, but most assuredly remediable by establishing a connection between occupation and intellectuality of result. No one who has had an opportunity of seeing both at work can mistake the difference between the man employed in filing the parts of a gun-lock, and preparing a decorative casting. The former is degenerating into a mere mechanism of thews and sinew; the latter is developing his intelligence and exercising his judgment.

All who are acquainted with the locality are aware of the great intellectual and moral change which has taken place in the Potteries since the Fine Arts have become more closely associated with the manufacture of porcelain and earthenware. A similar result, equally connected with the progress of the Arts applied to Manufactures, has been witnessed in Coalbrookdale,[14] and other similar establishments. No one who reflects on the matter can doubt that such consequences may reasonably be expected from a larger diffusion of artistic information, because no one can doubt that the most prolific source of vice and crime in this country is stupefied and brutalised intelligence. The progress of Art in manufactures will necessarily raise the wages of labour. Skill and training must always command their price in the market, and the greatest service that can be rendered to the operative is to show him how intelligence can most largely be combined with industrial pursuits. On this subject we should be disposed to dilate at greater length, but that we have already trespassed on our assigned limits, and it is, besides, one of such great importance as to demand consideration in a separate article.

Here then for the present we shall conclude, convinced that such an alliance as we have recommended, so far from lowering the position of the ARTIST or diminishing the net returns of the MANUFACTURER, will largely increase the fame and profits of both, and also confer large benefits on all whom they employ and on all whom they supply.

Notes

1 S. C. Hall, 'Art and Art-Manufacture', *Art Journal*, April 1877, pp. 101–104.
2 W. Cooke-Taylor, 'The Mutual Interests of Artists and Manufacturers', *Art Union*, 1 March 1848, p. 69.
3 Oliver Goldsmith *The Deserted Village,* 1770.
4 Immigrant Italian workers came to London and would sell plaster figures on the streets. In 1827 the artist Flaxman 'kept a large shop in the Strand, for the sale of

plaster figures, which was not then so hackneyed a trade, as it has now become by the large importation of Italians.' See https://www.npg.org.uk/research/programmes/plaster-figure-makers-history.

5 Oliver Goldsmith, *Deserted Village*.
6 Sir David Wilkie (1785–1841), artist.
7 *Ingenuas didicisse*: a faithful study of the liberal arts refines the manners and corrects their harshness (Ovid)
8 Shakespeare *Hamlet* Act 1. Sc.5.
9 William Pitt, 1st Earl of Chatham.
10 Thomas Gray *The Progress of Poesy: A Pindaric Ode*, 1757.
11 Joseph Addison (1672–1719) English essayist.
12 Fortunatus, in a medieval story, had an inexhaustible purse and a wishing-cap, which would transport him instantly to any place he desired, but these gifts proved the ruin of himself and his sons.
13 *Mobilitate etc.*: increases with travel and gains strength by its progress, (Virgil).
14 Coalbrookdale: A village in the Ironbridge Gorge in Shropshire, England, that was noted for its decorative ironwork.

36

JAMES WARD, *THE WORLD IN ITS WORKSHOPS*

James Ward (who also published under the pseudonym Philoponos) was quite jingoistic in his writing, rather oddly suggesting that Britons were superior to all other nations because they lived on an island. This concept was picked up by *The Literary Gazette* review which thought his book useful but reflected that 'we cannot but fancy that a very strong national prejudice runs through all that author writes; he appears determined to see no merit in anything which is not English, and he too frequently hides or perverts a fact which may appear to him to prove the superiority of any foreign manufacture'.[1]

Ward's main thrust in this book was to discuss the manufactures and machinery on display at the Great Exhibition. Early in the introduction he says 'What is the most significant feature of the Exhibition? Indisputably the machinery, its beautiful structure, and the altered tone in relation to its bearing on human labour'.[2] He then went on to say 'Machinery, it will be found, is the true source of moral progress and industrial improvement'.[3]

Inevitably, perhaps, Ward also addressed the issue of artistic design. He wrote: 'We excel in administering to the ordinary wants and comforts of the world, but it must be confessed that our manufacturers and artisans are deficient in beauty of design, in high artistic conception and skill, and in decorative art, as compared to the foreigner'.[4] The seemingly inevitable comparison with the French and their apparently superior products seems to be somewhat at odds with the attitude expressed by the *Literary Gazette*'s review above. Later in the book, Ward has some more things to say about the nature of design and its teaching.

> Practice and perseverance are necessary to make a designer, but, after all, designing is a natural gift, in the same way as painters, poets, and composers are gifted. A youth may be taught to draw, and copy the designs of his instructor, to perfection, but it is a different thing for him to produce an original design.[5]

He goes on to stress the role of education for design which should inculcate knowledge of 'sciences of perspective and of the five orders', and the need for a sense of 'beauty of outline, which consists in correctness and congruity, [which] is the acme of perfection in any drawing of an article of taste'.[6] Ward also reserved some terse comments for the British working man; 'They committed the logical absurdity of protecting imperfection, and of condemning perfection'.[7] and argued that, rather like William Morris, a little later, 'If then the artisan had not only a pair of hands but a head also to be employed, his situation would be most happily reversed. Instead of waiting in the labour market for the chance of being the lowest bidder for employment, he would go to the capital-market to find the highest bidder for his services'.[8]

James Ward, *The World in Its Workshops: A Practical Examination of British and Foreign Processes of Manufacture, with a Critical Comparison of the Fabrics, Machinery, and Works of Art Contained in the Great Exhibition* (London: Williams S. Orr and Co., 1851), pp. 1–16

Introduction

"Have I made up my mind upon the Exhibition?" you enquire. I have not; nor, indeed, can I at present. I have scarcely recovered from the bewilderment and confusion of mind which is incident to such a singular sight. In that wondrous structure there is study for a month, reflection for a year, and instruction for ever. At present I can merely discern a few outlines of its great industrial features, and the filling up of each outline is a world within itself. Look at that machine, for example; simple as it seems, it is the epitome of man's industrial progress—of his untiring efforts to release himself from his material bondage. And how many thoughts, ideas, and experiments have been expended upon that apparently simple structure—how many brains puzzled, pained, ay, even paralysed, to bring it to its present usable state? However, let us leave the comparative anatomy of that industrial phenomenon to some mechanical Cuvier[9]—he alone can do justice to its illustration. Nevertheless, just analyse that fabric on the opposite side of the building; it is so delicate in texture, and so beautiful in colouring. It would sorely puzzle even a practical mind to enumerate the processes through which it must have passed ere it arrived at its present finished state. Look where you may, in fact, the same difficulties present themselves; the mind is barely able to take more than a skin-deep glance at the varied and surrounding objects, unless it happen to have been instrumental in the production of either one or other. And even if we make this concession, how much have we diminished the difficulty? "I made that piece of silk down at Manchester, in a Jacquard loom, so I know all about it," exclaims some well-meaning but dogmatic weaver, if you will only encourage him to speak his mind. Indeed, so my dear man, because you wove that piece of silk you conclude that you know all about it. You received, for instance, the warp in a dyed state, of which, I presume, you know little or nothing, for dyeing involves a knowledge of the rather mysterious science of chemistry, which requires a special study. That is only one stage preceding your operations upon it. Next comes the "throwing" of the silk, which you probably never saw; still it is a study of itself, requiring considerable mechanical skill, great knowledge of the raw material, and the capacity to make the most of both. Then there is the raw material itself. What know you whence it came, how cultivated—whether by Christian, Mahommedan, or Chinese? We need go no further. *What you do know is invaluable*; but it is only a tithe of the knowledge comprised in that simple piece of silk. You know how to throw the shuttle, perhaps to put the warp in the loom, to pick off the *fluff*, if there chance to be any, to weave so many shoots to the inch, and to take home the work when finished for your pay. That is about the extent of your knowledge; however, it is as much as can be expected, and is very creditable to you. *Ex uno disce*.[10] This simple but dogmatic weaver is a fair type of the majority of what are called "practical" spectators.

"Do I mean to say that practical minds are not capable of availing themselves of the improvements they may see in the Exhibition?" I really do. Take the mass of what are called " practical" minds, as a body they are nearly as inapt to appreciate and apply improvements as the mere loungers and idlers who saunter through the treasure-stored avenues of the building. They will look with perhaps a shrewder eye at the several objects upon the production of which they may have been partially engaged; but the result, in a majority of cases, will prove little more than a negative; they must wait for the thinking few to lead them, from whom all practical knowledge of a valuable nature is derived. These few are the stars that guide the many in the true path of improvement; but as yet they are below the horizon, gathering light, as it were, to shine steadily and clearly on the future course of their humbler "practical" brethren.

You remember the picture which political economists delight to draw when they want to demonstrate one of their favourite theorems.* They paint a man brought up in civilized life as cast upon a desert island; he is without food, without clothes, without fire, and without tools. "We see the human being," they say, "in the very lowest state of helplessness. Most of his preceding knowledge would be worse than useless, for it would not be applicable to his new position." By way of alleviating his case they say, " Let the land upon which he is thrown produce spontaneous fruits, let the climate be most genial, still the man would he exceedingly powerless and wretched." No doubt. But why? "The helplessness of this man's condition," they tell us, "would principally be the effect of one circumstance: *he would possess no accumulation of former labour, by which his present labour might be profitably directed.*"[11]

---

* "Capital and Labour;" Charles Knight.

This is a somewhat fanciful picture, you will say; but has it no pendant in practical life? Place the same individual, for instance, in the Grand Transept of the Crystal Palace, with the prodigies of art, of science, and of labour before him, where the resources of human ingenuity are displayed in every variety of substance and form, and the chances are that he would experience a perplexity of mind fully equal, if not so painful as though he were upon the desert island, and the presumed destitution staring him in the face. What could he look at first, and how would he look at it, seeing that his preceding experience, or, to use the precise term of the sages just cited, his accumulation of knowledge, would be of comparatively little avail? On the one hand, he would scarcely know how to provide against the destitution staring him in the face; on the other, he would be equally puzzled to worm his way rightly and instructively through the intellectual zig-zag in which he must naturally find himself. Look where he might, his eye would soon become embarrassed by the novelty of the scene, both in form and material—

"A scene so various that would seem to be
Not one, but all the world's epitomé."

His first sensation—and it must have been that of thousands who have visited the Exhibition—would be that of wonder and surprise at the overwhelming mass of beautiful objects which the skilled industry of the age had ranged before him; when he had partially recovered from this state, his imagination might chance to take a turn in such a region of fairy revelry, but some time must necessarily elapse ere reason could exercise her influence, and calm down his mind to sit quietly on its judgment seat, to enable him to view things in a clear and truthful light. His state of mental helplessness, in fine, would be equally conspicuous whether contemplating the *embarras des richesses* in the great ark of industry, or placed in the supposed lowest state of human existence on the desert island. He would lack the necessary instruction in both instances.

In the retreat from Moscow—"what has the retreat from Moscow to do with the Exhibition?"—Simply this, that the human mind, under the most opposite circumstances, sometimes exhibits a similarity of action, however the motives may vary. In the retreat from Moscow some of the soldiers were heavily laden with the spoils of the city, and Segur, in his account of that terrible event, gives a painfully ludicrous description of their embarrassment when compelled by fatigue to abandon a portion of their treasures.[12] There must have been a strange conflict in the minds of those harassed troopers—a fearful struggle between greed, on the one hand, and the apprehension of death on the other—as to what they should retain and what abandon in their hurried, uncertain, and melancholy route. A similar feeling, it is fair to presume, pervades the multitude of spectators while wandering through the wondrous avenues of the Exhibition, from the sheer want of a simple and judicious direction; and the majority must leave those trophies of a peaceful conflict with the painful impression that they are utterly incapable of estimating the relative merits of the industrial combatants. Like the soldiers of Napoleon, the spectators are compelled to leave the *spolia opima*,[13] if we may be allowed the phrase, behind them—not solely from the fatigue they endure to acquire it, but principally from incapacity to form a correct notion of its value. And it is in the nature of things that it should be so. Did you ever experience a similar sensation when your young feet first paddled along the sea-shore? Had you then no difficulty in making a choice of the objects everywhere around you? We had. At the first sight of that multitude of shells and stones, which were so beautiful and diversified in appearance, so clear and so bright, the receding waves having just washed over them, our young mind was strangely perplexed. At length we picked up one, then another, then a third, and so on, the last always appearing the most beautiful, until we had gathered so large a quantity that we could scarcely carry them. Then came the time for ultimate selection—the most difficult of all tasks to our youthful fancy and taste, until reason determined the point to lie between our strength, on the one hand, and our choice on the other. The question, therefore, was partially settled, and we reduced our quantity to a comparative few, which appeared to our wondering and uninitiated eyes as the most rare and beautiful specimens of their kind. Nevertheless, we were guided more by caprice than by judgment; and showiness of appearance rather than intrinsic beauty and utility, which instruction alone can discern, were the prevailing qualities of our choice.

"What notion have I formed, then, of the Exhibition, after all my bewilderment and perplexit?"

I will endeavour to tell you. I think that its friends are a little too sanguine, and that its enemies are a great deal too doleful and condemnatory. It is much more likely to effect the good anticipated on the one hand than it is to inflict the evil so gloomily depicted on the other. Let us avoid extremes.

"Premature, do you say?" Not in my opinion; it has taken place at precisely the right time; it is a natural consequence of a preceding cause. The error on the part of several of its opponents consists in mistaking it for a cause instead of a consequence. The elements to produce such a result have been long at work, and something of the kind has been quietly and gradually developing itself in the practical and calculating mind of the world for these years past, although the latter may be, in some degree, startled at its peculiar aspect and hearing. In fine, I view the Exhibition as natural a complement to the preceding movements of material industry, as a field of battle is to the concentration of armies, for

" Coming events cast their shadows before."[14]

"The comparison is strained, is it?" In what way is it strained. Has not all Europe been strenuously endeavouring, for the last quarter of a century, to bring each other into closer connection? Have not railways enabled the Englishman to visit Vienna and Berlin, Paris and Dresden, as easily as he could Manchester and Edinburgh some twenty-five years ago? And have not the same lines of communication enabled the several inhabitants of those cities to pay England a similar compliment? Having visited those great central points of civilisation, and finding something in each different to our own, it is natural that we should treasure that something in our minds, and also endeavour to realise it for the gratification of our senses. We see, for example, a piece of furniture, a pattern of silk, a porcelain vase, or any other object which strikes the eye as differing from what we are accustomed to, and the desire is naturally awakened to possess it. It is purchased, brought home, and most likely admired; others do the same, until the whole circle of society, both here and abroad, becomes more or less influenced by similar feelings. The possessors of these exclusive objects naturally prize them, and in several instances unduly vaunt their excellence, which creates a feeling of rivalry on the part of others who are not so fortunate, but who are also equally desirous to obtain them. The dealer then steps in, and with the cunning belonging to his craft, turns the public weakness to account, by flattering the *few* who possess these rare and exclusive objects in order that he may supply the *many* who desire them. This dealer is no better judge of the relative excellence of foreign and home manufactured objects, nor in many instances so good as those who possess them, but with the turn-a-penny tact which he has acquired, he assumes a thorough knowledge of both. The dealer, in this instance, becomes, as it were, the arbiter of home and foreign productions, utterly regardless of every feeling but one—"which will yield me the most profit?" The result inevitably follows—our manufacturers complain, our artisans complain, and our general producers complain at what they call, and justly, too, in many instances, the undue preference given to foreign commodities. Under these circumstances what would common sense suggest? Unquestionably a fair, a just, and an equitable comparison between the objects manufactured abroad, and the objects manufactured at home, in order that there should be no delusion as to relative excellence. And how could you obtain such a comparison but through the medium of the Exhibition, or something analogous to it? Endure me for a moment. You have not only railways to whisk mankind about the world, but you have the incomparably quicker instrument—the electric telegraph. When you see the charged-wire obedient to the commands of man, not only to move as he directs, but to speak as he bids, when, in short, he has reduced by this powerful agent time and space to an almost incomputable quantity, is it not natural to expect that everything within the sphere of human influence should be proportionally affected. The momentum once given to the elements of man's social existence, it never ceases until the whole is perceptibly influenced and homogeneously directed. When the quick-footed step on quicker than is their wont in the race of life, those of slower pace must make a proportionate measure in their footsteps, or they will be grievously worsted in the race, if indeed they do not entirely drop off, and even lose sight of the rear. If one portion of mankind adopt the spirit of improvement with greater aptitude than another—if they enrich themselves ere the other have made up their minds to even recognise its existence, one of two things must ensue—either the sluggards must quicken their mode of action, or they will be thrust aside by others of more resolute aim and more determined energy. It is not in the nature of things that the active and stirring minds of our workshops and counting-houses should sweep round the world in search of new materials and new wants without disturbing those of a more sluggish and sleepy disposition; but, happily for the latter, it is so arranged in the providential government of human affairs that what frequently appears contrary to our interests, ultimately proves to be beneficial; and seeing also that change is a condition of our existence, it is much more salutary and judicious to prepare for it, than blindly attempt to resist its progress. In a council of owls you would naturally expect the proposal to reduce the light to the dimness of their orbs, but in an assembly of rational minds, the suggestion would rather be to enlarge the power of the eye—to improve its visual faculty—so that the full blaze of intelligence might beam upon it.

However "strained," then, the comparison may be between the Exhibition as a sequence to the industrial movements of mankind, and the field of battle as a sequence to the concentration of opposing armies, there are one or two points of resemblance that surely must strike you. Let us quietly examine the phenomena as they present themselves on both sides the comparison. The industrial forces of the world have long been moving to a single point, just as much so as the military forces of Europe were, preceding a great single result; and the only perceptible difference between yon dark column of machinery (the metaphor allowed), which has marked a line for itself right through the territories of industry—tumbling, tossing, uprooting, and whisking settled interests about as though they were old rags only fit to be pulped into new forms; and the armed battalions of troops is simply this—that one leads to a victory over the moral forces of man's nature, while the other leads to a conflict of the evil passions of his nature, as though man was born for mere savage and destructive pastime. The one, it is true, is a sustaining and creative rivalry; the other a destructive and desolating conflict. The first teaches man, though the instruction is somewhat roughly given, how he may improve his moral and social condition by augmenting his productive power; while the latter has no other effect but to inspire him with brutal feelings, and to inflame the savage instincts of his nature. The operation of the industrial and moral forces of man's nature must therefore naturally terminate in some such scene as the Exhibition in Hyde Park; and such a terminus is just as appropriate as is that of his evil passions in the scenes enacted on the plains of Leipsic or of Waterloo. Certes, the peaceful trophies of the one are a more soul-cheering sight than the sanguinary results of the other, so that the Exhibition, if the comparison may be continued, simply denotes a change in the ordinary strife of the world; and in lieu of fabricating weapons for mutual destruction, mankind seem tacitly agreed to rival each other in the manufacture of commodities essentially requisite for their mutual advantage.

It is simply a transfer of skill and industry—from bullets of lead to bales of cotton, and in lieu of conflicting armies we are destined, for some time at least, to endure conflicting tariffs. The movements of the industrial and military forces of the world have, therefore, been in nearly parallel lines; and there is this condition attached to the movement, that those who wish to do justice to themselves and to their fellow-members of the community must become thoroughly prepared for the industrial conflict, or they will be thrust to the rear, or trodden down by their more disciplined competitors.

" What good do I expect to accrue from the Exhibition?" This. The manufacturer, the artisan, and the consumer, now know in what relation they stand to the foreigner, as regards their respective interests. The first will naturally direct his energies to the improvement of his fabric; the second will endeavour to augment his skill; and the third will be enabled to see more clearly how to guide his judgment to a right selection in his choice of objects. Many misconceptions will be obliterated, and many errors removed; the whole circle of the producing and consuming world stand then on a perfectly fair footing to justly appreciate and understand each other. This, indeed, is a great good. Great and inestimable, however, as this good appears, the Exhibition presents another of equal importance in relation to our social and moral well-being. It is a great advantage to have our eyes opened; it is still greater to have them opened in a right direction. The English artisan now knows in what degree he is inferior to the foreign artisan, and in what degree he is superior; and not only has the artisan acquired this important knowledge, but the manufacturer and the consumer know likewise. So that the former need not be deterred from improving his skill by the prejudiced ignorance of the one, or the too easy credulity of the other. The artisan, for the first time in the history of the world, has obtained a clear stage and no favour; it will depend, in a great measure, upon himself whether he be capable of turning so excellent an opportunity to good account.

"Wherein do we excel, and wherein are we deficient?" We excel in administering to the ordinary wants and comforts of the world, but it must be confessed that our manufacturers and artisans are deficient in beauty of design, in high artistic conception and skill, and in decorative art, as compared to the foreigner. The following remarks, in the first edition of the *Wealth of the World in its Workshops*, have been fully borne out by the fruits of the Exhibition, and explain, in some measure, the reason why we are inferior to the foreigner in these several respects. In speaking of the British manufacturer, we observed .—"That in those branches of operative skill and art, which are peculiarly British, they will prove unrivalled; and that, even in some in which the superiority of our continental neighbours is rather a lingering tradition from the past than a reality of the present, they will be able to assert an equality of excellence which has hitherto been injuriously denied them. There are others, however, in which we can scarcely hope to find them pre-eminent—in those principally in which the perfection of the art of design is an indispensable element. There are many reasons for the present superiority of, at least, our French neighbours in this respect, and it will not be uninteresting or uninstructive to discuss the chief of them briefly in this place.

"There is in France, as compared with England, so little employment for juvenile labour, that the rising generation has ample leisure for some preliminary instruction before it is summoned to the active duties of life. In and around all our great seats of manufacturing industry, a child can be put to some use, so as to contribute something towards the support of the family, at a very early age; and hence we find that, when grown up, they have acquired no accomplishments in the way of education, farther than such as enable them to read a newspaper and (with some difficulty) to write a letter. For the peculiar occupation to which they are destined they receive no preparatory education at all; they take to it, when very young, nothing more than their natural strength and mother wit; and they grow up as nothing more than the motive power of the tools they are taught to use, or the tools of the motive power which it is their business to attend to. They thus become most expert workmen—and, perhaps, they owe a portion of their excellence in this respect to all their mental energies being concentrated in what may be called the manipulation of the task they are performing. To that task they daily apply themselves without troubling their heads about how their labour might be abridged, or how the product might be improved. But in France, a contrary system is prevalent, arising from the different circumstances of the two countries. Children, as we have said, have there a few years for education before they are called to contribute to their own support; and the State has wisely provided that this education shall be such as will be of some service to themselves and to society in after-life. The art of design is a principal feature in it—though not to the exclusion of the ordinary rudiments of reading and writing—and thus it may be truly said, that the child is made the father of the man, for he acquires in childhood that which will be most serviceable to him in manhood, and which can rarely be acquired after the cares of manhood have begun, and the habits of self-satisfied ignorance have become confirmed. It is this early and appropriate education which renders almost every operative in France an *artist* likewise in the branch of manufacture to which he has been devoted. Hence he has a superior *taste for the beautiful* to what the English operative can boast; and the fruits of this elevation in the capacity and imagination of the French operatives are naturally observable in the greater delicacy or grandeur of French designs, as the occasion may require. We do not mean that the French operatives universally supply the designs for the productions upon which they are engaged; but when they do not, it is a necessary consequence of their being such *respectable* masters of the art of design, that those who make the art of design a profession, must be very superior masters of it indeed, and that the operatives themselves, from their capacity to appreciate the ideas of the designer, must be capable of interpreting and expressing them in the execution of the work more effectually than if they had no more sense of their beauty than the scene-painter, however expert in the use of the brush, may he supposed to have of the beauty of a Claude or Canaletti.

* * * *

"But the Exhibition, while it cannot fail to prove highly instructive to our skilled artisans, by the *studies* which it will bring before them for the enlargement of their conceptions and the improvement of their taste, will also undoubtedly conduce, in another manner, to the elevation of their calling in an intellectual, and of their condition in a worldly, sense. It has generally been assumed, as we have before remarked, that the inferiority of the British artisan in design is a natural defect, and that taste is a gift which has been but very moderately vouchsafed to him. But this theory will not bear a philosophic examination. Always and everywhere the development of any faculty, and its progress towards perfection, have depended upon the demand for its employment, and the rewards offered for its exercise. If the great body of the people do not appreciate, or have no relish for, any particular kind of excellence, the talents which could otherwise display it will remain dormant. Thus, while the people of this country had no taste for music of a refined and elevated character, we had no native composers in the higher walks of the art; but since the public taste has been educated in this respect, and the great body of the people can enjoy and require what their forefathers had no ear for, we have had a galaxy of composers, scarcely inferior to the brightest stars of Italy. And so it has been, and will be, with our skilled artisans. If they have not hitherto shone in the higher walks of ornamental art, it has been because the mass of the community has not appreciated it, and that there has therefore been no sufficient demand for its production to reward its cultivation. But let the public taste become educated in this respect—and what means so powerful to this end as such Exhibitions as that intended?—let there thus arise a demand for greater excellence in decorative works than those which satisfy the ignorant simplicity of the present day, and latent talent will be evoked to supply it. Elegance in dress, in furniture, in household fixtures, in every requisite for personal and domestic enjoyment, will conventionally become one of the prime decencies of life; and who can doubt that such a consummation would greatly elevate the worldly condition of the skilled artizan; while, as callings are always estimated according to the intellect required in their exercise, it would equally elevate him in the scale of society.

"We must also solicit attention to another consideration. The skilled artisan in this country will always possess one great advantage over the artisan of any other, namely, the vast abundance of capital which in this country is always ready to avail itself of his talents. It will be said that the artisan has not found this to be invariably the case; but this seeming contradiction to the assertion is easily explained. Hitherto our artisans have had little more than mere manual skill to offer, and the capitalist has regarded them, according to the different branches of employment for which they are fitted, as being all nearly equal to each other in this respect, that it has not been worth his while to make any discrimination between them. If he required a hundred hands, he went into the appropriate labour-market, and took those out of the number competing for work, who were willing to work, on the lowest terms. This practice is very injurious to the artisans as a body, for not only have the best been excluded from employment by the competition of the worst, but the rate of remuneration became fixed by what the very worst hands were willing to accept. This has arisen from the difficulty of discovering beforehand any difference in the value of the mere manual labour of individuals. The artisan has had nothing to offer to the competition of capitalists, for the competition has been the other way, manual labour competing for employment. But how different would be the case, if the artisan was an artist also—one not only with hands to execute, but with a head to design? This would at once do away with the equality in the value of the services of all, which has reduced all to the necessity of contending amongst themselves for employment, the strange principle of their rivalry for the notice of the capitalist being, not who can do the best work, but who will sacrifice himself for the worst wages. Let the artisan, we repeat, become an artist also, and this would be done away with; for though there may be no difference between the value of one pair of hands and that of another pair of hands, there will always be a difference between the value of one man's intellectual gifts and those of another man. If then the artisan had not only a pair of hands but a head also to be employed, his situation would be most happily reversed. Instead of waiting in the labour-market for the chance of being the lowest bidder for employment, he would go to the capital-market to find the highest bidder for his services. Capitalists would then be the competitors for high-priced talent, and not artisans the competitors for low-priced work.

"Lastly, let none be so near-sighted and narrow-minded as to urge that the Exhibition will be a stimulus to foreign nations to excel in the industrial arts. We trust that it may be so, and that it may conduce to their rapid progress in prosperity. We wish to see them rich and flourishing; for what reason have we, even on the score of selfishness, to desire that they should remain in poverty or fall into decay? We are—with our great natural advantages, our unbounded supply of coals and of all the useful metals, the energetic and never-tiring industry of our population, the enterprising spirit of our Anglo-Saxon blood, our peculiar climate which renders bodily and mental activity a condition of healthy existence, and our insular position, so pre-eminently favourable to commerce—we are, by these and other great natural advantages, and for an indefinite term must continue to be, the great manufacturing and mercantile nation of the world. What, therefore, have we to fear? Not that other nations may grow rich, but that they may grow poor; *for poor countries must ever be poor customers to us*. Let our artisans ever remember this."

" What is the most significant feature of the Exhibition?" Indisputably the machinery, its beautiful structure, and the altered tone in relation to its bearing on human labour. This, you will acknowledge, is a step in the right direction, and its importance is equally recognized by the foreigner as by ourselves. Here and there, it is true, a lingering prejudice or so may be entertained, but it finds little countenance from the great bulk of our artisans. One and all of the more intelligent and really influential among that useful class of men are convinced that machinery is a powerful adjunct, and that the more perfect it becomes the more powerful is its agency, and, also, the more valuable its assistance to their manual labour.

We have frequently laboured to impress this great truth upon the minds of the working classes;* and under trying circumstances too, therefore feel a more than ordinary pleasure at perceiving its recognition. We addressed the workmen employed on the French railways, whose hatred to machinery was evinced rather inconveniently on one or two occasions, in the following terms, which may not be inappropriately applied to the present time:—

"What is a machine? A contrivance by man to increase his power over matter. If the power of man, then, to subdue matter be a good, which, we presume, no one will deny, the increase of that power must be a greater good, and its

---

* Vide "Machinery, is it a Good or an Evil." Paris, 1844.

ultimate perfection the greatest of all goods. The mind may conceive, as it frequently does, the grandest projects for human improvement, but the hand alone cannot execute them. There have been thousands of instances of this kind, which the world has never known, and which must have died away in the brain that conceived them. One of the great causes, if not the principal, of man's advancing so slowly in the path of amelioration, has been the incapacity of his hand to execute the conceptions of his head; it follows, therefore, that the nearer the power of the hand approximates to that of the head, the more rapid will be his advance.

" Man is the creature of machinery in a civilized state; deprive him of it and he instantly becomes helpless and unprotected. Man himself is a magnificent machine, and God, his creator, exclaims the pious and eloquent Barrow,[15] is the first of mechanicians. Look at the form of man, either in repose or in activity, and you cannot but admire its beauty. What a majestic pile is that bony construction!—how ingeniously devised and how exquisitely formed !—how true in principle and how admirable in practice!

"Man, know thyself," says the Scripture, which may be interpreted, without the slightest irreverence, "contemplate thine own frame, examine its construction, and imitate its perfection, in thy works!" The nearer man, therefore, approaches to the perfection of his own frame in his mechanical contrivance, the nearer he approaches to divine wisdom. And without violating the implicit reverence which is due to the Creator, may we not imagine some superior spirit whispering in the ear of earth's first-born—"Man, make a machine, and your condition shall be improved, and the more perfect you get in machinery, the happier, the better, your state of existence, and the only possible way to obtain absolute dominion over the earth is mechanical perfection. There is one thing, however, very clear, that man *has* partially emancipated himself from his material slavery by his mechanical inventions; and when the spade first assisted the power of his hand, and the plough first followed the direction of his head, the beginning of his emancipation must practically have commenced."

Could the holy army of martyrs, who were literally hunted out of existence for displaying the inventive powers with which the Creator had endowed them, once more revisit their earthly habitations, how strange must be their sensations! William Lea[16] here would see millions depending upon his stocking-frame for their daily bread, though he wandered from place to place with that sacred treasure, heart-broken and starving, without meeting with a single soul capable of recognizing its wondrous utility; and Hargraves[17] would find some consolation for the bitterness of his existence in the fact of his invention being universally cherished and improved; nor would the delight of Jacquard[18] be less could his spirit quietly contemplate the improvements of his loom, whereby the use of cards is altogether dispensed with. Poor Jacquard thought that he had attained all that was requisite, by the substitution of cards for the old cords and pedals; but were he to examine the loom now in the Exhibition—the first of the kind, and the invention of a Belgian—his benevolent heart would leap with delight. The ingenious Frenchman diminished the number of unsightly cripples by his comparatively easy process of weaving the fabric; and the Belgian, carrying improvement a step further, has greatly facilitated the power of production, by diminishing the complication and weight of labour. Thousands of other instances might be adduced, were we to enumerate, even partially, the progressive stages of improvement which one and all of the mechanical contributions to the Exhibition present. Each machine, in short, is little more than a *monument of mental martyrs.*

An old writer, whose name we have forgotten, pithily remarks, that "what is man's calamity in his ignorance, is his blessing in his intelligence." This remark may be applied, more or less, to the whole range of human actions, but to none more closely than to man's treatment of his mechanical inventions. Some few years ago, the bulk of artizans were much opposed to machinery, and did all they could to arrest its improvement. The machines they were in the habit of using were thought sufficiently perfect; and those that had the slightest tendency to interfere with them were uniformly condemned. They committed the logical absurdity of protecting *imperfection*, and of condemning *perfection*.

Happily for themselves, and for mankind at large, our artizans have become more enlightened, and view the rich treasure of mechanical skill in the Exhibition with feelings of almost affectionate admiration. Of all the changes in the industrial relations of the world we deem this the most important, therefore have considered it as the prominent feature of the Exhibition. Machinery, it will be found, is the true source of moral progress and industrial improvement.

Another feature equally deserving of notice, however, is the contributions of raw materials. As the latter compose the basis of all our manufactures, it is indispensable that we should form a correct judgment of their relative excellence, and not depend upon caprice or accident for our supplies. Hitherto this has been the case, for the merchant has made the latter dependant upon his exports, and not shaped his exports so as to bring back the best specimens of the raw material. For instance, we export a great quantity of manufactured articles to the Brazils, and to secure a return cargo our ships are laden, perhaps, with rosewood, although a finer quality of that material may be found elsewhere, which would prove highly advantageous to our cabinetmakers. The same remark is partially applicable to the bulk of raw materials, which materially retards the excellence of our general industry. The Exhibition has evoked from every quarter of the globe the finest specimens of its raw productions, and has afforded an opportunity of examining them "cheek by jowl,"—an opportunity of immense utility to the industrial interests of the country. The consumer now will not content himself with receiving comparatively bad timber from Canada, inferior bark from France, and mediocre linseed from Prussia; but as he ranges his eye round the Exhibition he will immediately detect the whereabouts of the finest qualities of each of these important articles. The same remark may be applied to the iron, the lead, the copper, the ores, the minerals, and, indeed, to the whole range of our contributions. If the Exhibition has effected only this good, it has amply repaid the time, the trouble, the anxiety, the expense, the annoyance, and every other *the*, that a disturbed imagination, a narrow judgment, and a malevolent disposition, could attach a disparaging and contemptuous epithet to. Taking even this microscopic view of the Crystal Palace we can discern sufficient materials for the commendation of those who have been more immediately instrumental in its erection, but this is a theme upon which we have no desire to dwell. Let it suffice that we recognise the Exhibition as *un fait accompli*, and shall treat it accordingly; and we can the better afford this, seeing that we were about the first in the field to anticipate the benefits which have already accrued from it. "There is nothing succeeds like success," says the French proverb, and we have a lively recollection of the strange and gibberish notes that were rife in many quarters when the idea of the Crystal Palace was in embryo, which contrast somewhat strangely with the Io Peans[19] now so lustily shouted in its favour. *N'importe;* we shall continue in the same strain, and simply repeat our thanks to the Prince, whose moral courage never for a moment flagged, and whose practical sagacity must have astonished even his friends. Every obstacle—and their name is legion—was quietly overcome by patient endurance and untiring perseverance, in spite of the cold discouragement of many, and the positive obstruction of the few.

One word more. In a somewhat hasty glance at the varied and valuable collection of objects, it is natural to suppose that many of a highly interesting nature must have escaped our notice. The following fact is an instance in point:—The American revolving pistol is noticed under its proper head, with a due acknowledgment of the originality of the invention, and its powers of destruction; but, since these observations were committed to type, we have derived some information which leads us to modify our first impressions. The originality of the invention is questionable,—it being a simple improvement upon a preceding production. Some thirty years ago the Messrs. Evans and Son, of Wardour Street, the eminent machinists, manufactured 200 revolving barrels, enclosing lesser barrels, exactly like the pistol in the Exhibition, and the only difference between the two inventions is simply this—the cylinder of the original was pressed back by the finger and thumb of the left hand, while the pistol revolves by means of a click after each discharge. In almost every other respect the productions are the same. It is somewhat singular that the order was given to Messrs. Evans and Son by a Mr. Collyer, an American; and if he were the inventor of the revolving barrel, it is equally creditable to the ingenuity of our transatlantic brethren.

In presenting the second edition of the "Wealth of the World in its Workshops" to the reader, we have simply to remark that the illustration of the useful rather than the ornamental, in industrial art, has been our principal aim, believing with Milton that—

". . . . that which before us lies
in daily life is the prime wisdom,"[20]

Notes

1 *Literary Gazette: A Weekly Journal of Literature, Science, and the Fine Arts*, 13 September 1851, p. 628.
2 J. Ward, *The World in Its Workshops* (London: Williams S. Orr And Co., 1851), p. 12.

3 Ward, p. 15.
4 Ward, p. 8.
5 Ward, p. 108.
6 Ward, p. 108.
7 Ward, p. 14.
8 Ward, p. 12.
9 George Cuvier (1769–1832), French naturalist and zoologist.
10 *Ex uno disce*: from one (example), learn all.
11 C. Knight, *Capital and Labour Including the Results of Machinery* (London: C. Knight, 1845), p. 9.
12 Segur: Phillippe-Paul, Comte de. Ségur, *History of the Expedition to Russia, Undertaken by the Emperor Napoleon, in the Year 1812* (London: Treuttel and Wurtz, Treuttel and Richter, 1825).
13 *spolia opima*: rich spoils of war but only those which the commander-in-chief of a Roman army removed from the leader of the foe in a field of battle .
14 Thomas Campbell, *Lochiel's Warning* (1801).
15 Isaac Barrow (1630–1677) mathematician and theologian.
16 William Lea: William Lee of Calverton near Nottingham invented the stocking frame in 1589.
17 James Hargreaves invented the 'spinning jenny' in 1764 in Oswaldtwistle, Lancashire England.
18 Jacquard: Joseph Marie Charles Jacquard (1752–1834) a French weaver and merchant who developed the earliest programmable loom.
19 Io Peans: songs of joy and praise.
20 J. Milton: *Paradise Lost, Eighth Book.* (1667).

37

JOSEPH WHITWORTH, AND GEORGE WALLIS, *THE INDUSTRY OF THE UNITED STATES IN MACHINERY, MANUFACTURES, AND USEFUL AND ORNAMENTAL ARTS*

The two authors of the report were well qualified to describe the developments in machinery design and production in the USA. Sir Joseph Whitworth, (1803–1887) was an English engineer, entrepreneur, inventor, and philanthropist. In 1841, he devised the British Standard Whitworth system, which created an accepted standard for screw threads. George Wallis (1811–1891) was an artist, and art educator who particularly promoted education in industrial art. He was associated with design schools, acting as headmaster of the Birmingham School of Design and later as keeper of the art collections at the South Kensington Museum.

In 1853, the two men were appointed as British Commissioners for the New York International Exhibition. Together, they visited a number of different industrial locations to assess American methods. The report, *The Industry of the United States in Machinery, Manufactures, and Useful and Applied Arts*, was the result.

Their report was impressed by the standardisation of large-scale production that produced items with a low unit cost, all with the aid of specialised machinery. However, in matters of taste and design, Wallis was often unimpressed:

> There is no appearance of any attempt to strike out a national style, although the many peculiar features of the country, the habits of the people, and the undoubted originality in the mechanic arts, would lead to the inference that a gradual repudiation of European modes and forms will take place . . . At present the co-mingling of totally different styles of decoration in architecture, and the adoption of European designs for totally different purposes to those for which they were originally intended, are among the least of the errors committed in a vague seeking after novelty.[1]

Some fifteen years after the report was published, George Wallis commented most disappointedly that 'Much of the information embodied in these reports has not been utilized in this country to this hour, for it happened that they came before the public at the period when the Crimean War was about to commence'. He went on to critique the lack of adaptation of the American system of manufactures that employed templates and jigs, machine tools, and interchangeable parts. He particularly lamented the fact that 'the system reported upon as in full work at Springfield, [the Armory] in Massachusetts, by Mr. (now Sir Joseph) Whitworth, was treated as a chimera, utterly impracticable; and that, too, by the producers of small-arms in this country, who, a few years afterwards, founded a public company to adopt this very system and carry it out at Birmingham'.[2]

Joseph Whitworth, and George Wallis, *The Industry of the United States in Machinery, Manufactures, and Useful and Ornamental Arts: Compiled From the Official Reports of Messrs. Whitworth and Wallis* (London: G. Routledge & Co., 1854), pp. III–XI

Preface

The close relation which subsists between the kingdom of Great Britain and the Republic of America, arising from community of origin, of language, of civil and religious freedom, and to a great extent from the similarity of the laws under which both countries are placed, renders it natural that the people of these countries should regard each other with the deepest interest, and maintain a friendly rivalry in all that relates to social progress.

The American citizen is eminently a man of facts and figures, and there is very little in our arts and manufactures which escapes his keen observation. For reasons sufficiently obvious, it is most desirable that the British subject should be furnished with the means of knowing the state of manufacturing industry on the other side of the Atlantic, and of acquiring the lessons of practical value which may be learned from comparing these matters as they are presented in the Old and the New World.

It must be confessed, on all hands, that the means of such comparison which were anticipated from the Exhibition in Hyde Park,[3] were not furnished in such a manner as to lead to any just and satisfactory results. The industry of the United States cannot be properly exhibited under a glass case. To be estimated aright, it must be witnessed *in situ*. It must be inspected in its gigantic manufactories, erected on the banks of rapid rivers; its vast and ingenious machinery must be seen in operation supplying the want of human hands and arms; and for this end, the intelligent traveller must allow himself to be transported for thousands of miles, from State to State, and over rocky mountains, availing himself of the cheap "cars," which are at his service in all directions.

Peculiar facilities for obtaining an adequate acquaintance with the industry of the United States were afforded to the deputation sent out from this country on occasion of the Industrial Exhibition at New York.[4] That deputation consisted of gentlemen eminently qualified in their various departments to appreciate the subject brought under examination, and to report thereon. The delay in completing the arrangements for the Exhibition led to the determination to "visit the various localities in which raw materials were most abundant, mechanical skill most largely applied, manufacturing industry fairly established, and art and science most perfectly developed."[5] Mr. Whitworth undertook to examine a report on machinery, and Mr. George Wallis on manufactures, decorative art, and kindred subjects; and it will be seen in the following pages with what great ability these gentlemen have discharged the duties with which they were intrusted.

The present volume contains the essential parts of the report presented to our government, somewhat reduced in bulk, but retaining everything supposed to be important, and published at a price which places it within reach of the many.

The volume, therefore, presents to the mechanics, the artisans, the inventors, the manufacturers, the capitalists, and the general public in this country; the result of extensive and careful investigations made under the most favourable circumstances, and is issued in the confidence that it will supply a want which is extensively felt.

The industry of the United States has to be estimated by the peculiar circumstances of the country to which it has been devoted. In the States the labour-market is higher than with ourselves, especially as respects skilled labour. It has, therefore, been a principal aim as much as possible to apply machinery for the purpose of supplying this want, and, as the consequence, it will be seen that some of the principal achievements of American inventors have been acquired in this department. To this very want of human skill, and the absolute necessity for supplying it, may be attributed the extraordinary ingenuity displayed in many of their labour-saving machines, where automatic action so completely supplies the place of the more abundant hand-labour of older manufacturing countries.

Of this we have an illustration in the machine for the manufacture of the seamless grain-bags, the loom for which is described as a perfect self-actor, or automaton, commencing the bag, and continuing the process until the work is turned out complete.[6]

For another curious illustration or this automatic action we have the manufacture of ladies' hair-pins at Waterbury.[7] A quantity of wire is coiled upon a drum or cylinder, and turns round upon its axis, as suspended from the ceiling of the workshop. The point of the wire being inserted into the machine, and the power applied, the wire is cut off to the requisite length, carried forward and bent to the proper angle, and then pointed with the necessary blunt points, and finally dropped into a receiver, quite finished, all but the lacquering or japanning. These pins are made at the rate of 180 per minute.

The reader is referred also to the automaton machine for shanking buttons. The blanks being cut in thin brass, are put into a curved feeding-pipe, in which they descend to the level of the machine, by which a hole is stamped in the centre of each. Then the shank is formed by another portion of the machine, from a continuous wire carried along horizontally, the wire being shaped into the shank, and pushed up into its proper place. These operations are completed at the rate of 200 a minute, the only attendance required being that of one person to feed this automaton with the blanks and the wires, which he is so well able to work up to the satisfaction of his masters.

There is, of course, nothing to boast of on the ground of superiority on account of these inventions; but it is much to the credit of the American inventor, that he is able so to meet the necessities of his case, and supply the want of fingers, which are at present so scarce.

Another peculiarity observable in American industry, is the want of that division of labour which is one of the great causes of excellence in the productions of our own and other of the older countries in which art is carried to a high point of perfection. With us, trades and manufactures branch out into a variety of subdivisions, from which, besides the perfection noticed, we have a great economy of time, and, consequently, of expense. The citizen of the United States knows that matters are different with him, and seems really to pride himself in not remaining over long at any particular occupation, and being able to turn his hand to some dozen different pursuits in the course of his life.

This knowledge of two or three departments of one trade, or even the pursuit of several trades, by one individual, does not interfere so much with the systematic division of labour as may be supposed. In most instances the change of employment is made at convenient periods, or as a relief to the workman from the monotony of always doing the same thing. This change and variety of occupation is, in many respects, favourable to the man, as distinguished from the operative or the artist. In many cases our economic laws enhance the work or the value of time, when they degrade the workmen, between whom and the perfection of their works a singular contrast exists. While our American operative is a man and a citizen, he is often found wanting in that perfect skill of hand and marvellous accuracy which distinguish the workmen of this country. So much is there to check the national tendencies of self-gratulation and boasting on either side of the Atlantic, and to promote respect and good-feeling among us all.

The machinery of a country will naturally correspond with its wants, and with the history and state of its people. Testing the machinery of the United States by this rule of adaptation, the mechanical appliances in use must call forth much admiration. A large proportion of the mechanical power of the States has, from its earliest application, been, from the circumstances of the country, directed to wood, this being the material on which it has been requisite to operate for so many purposes, and which is presented in the greatest abundance. Stone, for a similar reason, has been subdued to man's use by the application of machinery, of which we have an instance in the fact that one man is able to perform as much work by machinery in stone-dressing, as twenty persons by hand. In common with our own and other great manufacturing countries, the Union presents remarkable illustrations of the amazingly productive power of machinery, as compared with mere manual operations. Into the details of these triumphs of machinery it is unnecessary here to enter. It may suffice to refer to the improvements effected in spinning-machinery, by which one man can attend to a mule containing 1,088 spindles, each spinning three hanks, or 3,264 hanks a day; so that, as compared with the operations of the most expert spinner in Hindoostan, the American operative can perform the work of 3,000 men.

The Law of Limited Liability, which is now engaging public attention, is an important source of the prosperity which attends the industry of the United States. This law affords the most ample facilities for the investment of capital, and has led to a much greater development of the industrial resources and skill of that country than could have resulted under other circumstances for many years to come. In the United States, the agent or secretary, manager, treasurer, and directors being also shareholders, are held by the law responsible to the extent of their means for the results of the management intrusted to them. The limited responsibility is confined to the nonmanaging shareholders only. It will be seen from the several illustrations given in the following pages, that this law works well in America; and these facts will strengthen the case of those who advocate its application to our country.

The comparative density of the old and the new countries, differing as they do, will account for the very different feelings with which the increase of machinery has been regarded in many parts of this country and the United States, where the workmen hail with satisfaction all mechanical improvements, the importance and value of which, as releasing them from the drudgery of unskilled labour, they are enabled by education to understand and appreciate. This statement is not intended to disparage the operatives of our own country, who in many respects are placed in a position different from that of their class in the United States, where the principles that ought to regulate the relations between the employer and the employed are thoroughly understood, and where the law of limited liability, to which we have just referred, affords the most ample facilities for the investment of capital in business, and where the skilled labourer is in many respects furnished with many opportunities of advancement which he has not among us. Particularly it should be noticed that no taxation of any kind is suffered to interfere with the free development of the press, and that the humblest labourer can indulge in the luxury of his daily paper, so that everybody reads, and intelligence penetrates through the lowest grades of society.

Practical men will have the opportunity of deriving some useful suggestions from the descriptions of machinery and tools, of factories and their operations, given in the following pages; while the intelligent observer and inventor will probably discover many deficiencies which his ingenuity will enable him to supply for the good of the republic and his country, and withal to his own advantage.

But, *à propos* of inventions, we are very much disposed to remonstrate against the unequal method with which the "plural unit"[8] deals with our countrymen, and with other foreigners; and we should be glad to hear what can be said, at the other side of the Atlantic, in defence of the invidious distinctions that prevail. A citizen of the United States, or an inchoate citizen, may obtain his patent for £6;

a foreigner of any country except Great Britain for £63; and a subject of our own country for £105.

It will be seen thus, that a foreigner applying to the United States for his patent must pay ten times as much as an American citizen; and that, if he should be an Englishman, or Scotchman, or Irishman—one really of kith and kin with his cousins in America—he must pay half as much again as the subject of any other foreign power, and about seventeen times as much as is paid by a citizen of the States.

It is alleged, that these distinctions are made on a principle of retaliation, our charges to an American citizen being so much out of proportion with those he has to pay for in his own country.

In the first place, we reply that we make no such invidious distinction as is here made between other countries and our own. A citizen of the United States stands, and always has stood, on the same level with ourselves. Why, then, when we make no such distinction in our own favour, should this distinction be made against us? *Mrs. Malaprop*[9] tells us that "comparisons are odorous;" and we certainly do not like the bad odour in which we find ourselves in relation to these patent laws, when we find that our own flesh and blood on the other side of the Atlantic will not sell us for less than £105 what they will sell to a Frenchman or an Austrian for £63.

Then, secondly, we have recently greatly altered the standard of our fees for patents in favour, not of ourselves only, but of all comers, provisional protection (including agency) being reduced to £10. 10s., and the total cost of a patent to £31 10s.; so that they are reduced to terms compared with which the fees of the United States, to an Englishman, are enormous. Surely, after the changes which we have effected, and of which America has the benefit, it cannot be intended to retain the high, and in most cases, prohibitory tariff which now operates so much against free trade in invention between this country and the United States.

We hope that the government of the United States will listen to the remonstrance which we feel ourselves called upon to make, but in no hostile and unfriendly spirit. And we are sure that this suggestion is one which will be cordially sustained by the inventors of our own country, as we hope it will be kindly entertained on the other side of the Atlantic.

On the subject of the good understanding which prevails between employers and their people, a very interesting and instructive illustration is given in the description of the Bay State Mills[10] in the Appendix.

Our attention might be profitably directed to a peculiar application of the electric telegraph, for the purpose of conveying signals of alarm in cases of fire. The city of Boston is divided into seven districts, the stations of which are all connected with a central office. By a very ingenious mechanism, in cases of fire, signals are conveyed to the central office, and by striking the signal-bell a certain number of times, intelligence is conveyed as to the district in which a fire has broken out, and an alarm is sounded at short intervals until the requisite assistance is obtained.

The object of this publication is to aid these two great countries by the careful study of each other's progress, and thus to afford mutual instruction. The question to be decided from these comparisons is not that of the relative amount or quality of talent in either country, but simply how that talent has been called into exercise, and to what diversified results it may lead.

Notes

1. J. Whitworth, and G. Wallis, *The Industry of The United States in Machinery, Manufactures* (London: G. Routledge & Co., 1854), p. 67.
2. G. Wallis, 'The International Exhibition,' *Art Journal Catalogue of the 1871 International Exhibition* (London: Virtue & Co., 1871–2), p. 9.
3. The Great Exhibition of 1851, London.
4. The Exhibition of the Industry of All Nations was held New York in 1853.
5. *The Industry of The United States in Machinery, Manufactures, and Useful and Ornamental Arts: Compiled from the Official Reports of Messrs. Whitworth and Wallis* 1854, p. iv.
6. Seamless grain bags were invented by Cyrus Baldwin of the Stark Mills, Patent 8533 of 1851.
7. Messrs, Blake and Johnson of Waterbury Conn.
8. "Plural unit" refers to the United State of America.
9. Mrs Malaprop: A character in Richard Brinsley Sheridan's 1775 comedy-of-manners *The Rivals* known for using incorrect words in a sentence, resulting in nonsense.
10. Bay State Mills: Lawrence, Mass. A woollen textile mill.

38

WILLIAM MORRIS, 'THE REVIVAL OF HANDICRAFT'[1]

William Morris (1834–1896) was a polymath who turned his hand to designing and making in a variety of processes, as well as poetry and novel writing, socialist activism, and publishing, among other achievements. Morris also had a lifelong interest in the Middle Ages, both in terms of art and society. Indeed, Morris's novel *A Dream of John Ball* (1888) with the famous lines 'When Adam delved and Eve span, who was then the gentleman?' demonstrates this historic interest as well as the socialist implications.

Although considering himself first and foremost an artist, he was also a businessman, founding Morris, Marshall, and Faulkner & Co. in 1861. Indeed, it was this business that was an example of his failure to deliver what he preached, in that most of his clients were not from the working classes. This, along with influences from Carlyle and Ruskin, was to affect all his work. It is therefore impossible to exclude the radical questions of the day from any consideration of his designs and products. Indeed, he said as much in this chapter: 'it is impossible to exclude socio-political questions from the consideration of aesthetics'.[2]

Posthumously printed, *Architecture, Industry and Wealth* is a selection of lectures and articles that reveal the variety of Morris's artistic interests which range from architecture, design and textiles, to the connections between the arts and socialism. Topics included in the book include 'History of Pattern Design'; 'The Lesser Arts of Life'; 'Art and Socialism'; 'The Revival of Architecture', and 'The Inference of Building Materials upon Architecture'. This chapter, 'The Revival of Handicraft' was first published in the *Fortnightly Review* in November 1888.

In the article, Morris points to the crafts, whereby the unselfconscious craftsperson is at one with the product, while he sees the industrial labourer as alienated from the object that he produces. He also sees a conflict between the effects of machinery versus handicraft upon the arts; 'Almost all goods are made apart from the life of those who use them; we are not responsible for them, our will has had no part in their production, except so far as we form part of the market on which they can be forced for the profit of the capitalist whose money is employed in producing them'.[3] Furthermore, he makes it plain who he thinks is to blame: 'The cultivated middle class is a class of slave-holders, and its power of living according to its choice is limited by the necessity of finding constant livelihood and employment for the slaves who keep it alive'.[4]

Nevertheless, he was not completely against the machine and its role in society: 'I have spoken of machinery being used freely for releasing people from the more mechanical and repulsive part of necessary labour; it is the allowing of machines to be our masters and not our servants that so injures the beauty of life nowadays'.[5]

Despite this pessimistic outlook, Morris ends on a cheerful note saying 'It is my firm belief that we shall in the end realize this society of equals, and also that when it is realized it will not endure a vicarious life by means of machinery; that it will in short be the master of its machinery and not the servant, as our age is'.[6]

William Morris, 'The Revival of Handicraft', *Architecture, Industry & Wealth; Collected Papers* (London: Longmans Green, 1902), pp. 214–227

VIII

The Revival of Handicraft

For some time past there has been a good deal of interest shown in what is called [in] our modern slang Art Workmanship, and quite recently there has been a growing feeling that this art workmanship to be of any value must have some of the workman's individuality imparted to it beside whatever of art it may have got from the design of the artist who has planned, but not executed the work. This feeling has gone so far that there is growing up a fashion for demanding handmade goods even when they are not ornamented in any way, as, for instance, woollen and linen cloth spun by hand and woven without power, hand-knitted hosiery, and the like. Nay, it is not uncommon to hear regrets for the hand labour in the fields, now fast disappearing from even backward districts of civilised countries. The scythe, the sickle, and even the flail are lamented over, and many are looking forward with drooping spirits to the time when the hand plough will be as completely extinct as the quern,[7] and the rattle of the steam-engine will take the place of the whistle of the curly-headed ploughboy through all the length and breadth of the land. People interested, or who suppose that they are interested, in the details of the arts of life feel a desire to revert to methods of handicraft for production in general; and it may therefore be worth considering how far this is a mere reactionary sentiment incapable of realisation, and how far it may foreshadow a real coming change in our habits of life as irresistible as the former change which has produced the system of machine production, the system against which revolt is now attempted.

In this paper I propose to confine the aforesaid consideration as much as I can to the effect of machinery *versus* handicraft upon the arts; using that latter word as widely as possible, so as to include all products of labour which have any claims to be considered beautiful. I say as far as possible; for as all roads lead to Rome, so the life, habits, and aspirations of all groups and classes of the community are founded on the economical conditions under which the mass of the people live, and it is impossible to exclude socio-political questions from the consideration of aesthetics. Also, although I must avow myself a sharer in the above-mentioned reactionary regrets, I must at the outset disclaim the mere aesthetic point of view which looks upon the ploughman and his bullocks and his plough, the reaper, his work, his wife, and his dinner, as so many elements which compose a pretty tapestry hanging, fit to adorn the study of a contemplative person of cultivation, but which it is not worth while differentiating from each other except in so far as they are related to the beauty and interest of the picture. On the contrary, what I wish for is that the reaper and his wife should have themselves a due share in all the fulness of life; and I can, without any great effort, perceive the justice of their forcing me to bear part of the burden of its deficiencies, so that we may together be forced to attempt to remedy them, and have no very heavy burden to carry between us.

To return to our aesthetics: though a certain part of the cultivated classes of today regret the disappearance of handicraft from production, they are quite vague as to how and why it is disappearing, and as to how and why it should or may reappear. For to begin with the general public is grossly ignorant of all the methods and processes of manufacture. This is of course one result of the machine-system we are considering. Almost all goods are made apart from the life of those who use them; we are not responsible for them, our will has had no part in their production, except so far as we form a part of the market on which they can be forced for the profit of the capitalist whose money is employed in producing them. The market assumes that certain wares are wanted; it produces such wares, indeed, but their kind and quality are only adapted to the needs of the public in a very rough fashion, because the public needs are subordinated to the interest of the capitalist masters of the market, and they can force the public to put up with the less desirable article if they choose, as they generally do. The result is that in this direction our boasted individuality is a sham; and persons who wish for anything that deviates ever so little from the beaten path have either to wear away their lives in a wearisome and mostly futile contest with a stupendous organisation which disregards their wishes, or to allow those wishes to be crushed out for the sake of a quiet life.

Let us take a few trivial but undeniable examples. You want a hat, say, like that you wore last year; you go to the hatter's, and find you cannot get it there, and you have no resource but in submission. Money by itself won't buy you the hat you want; it will cost you three months' hard labour and twenty pounds to have an inch added to the brim of your wideawake;[8] for you will have to get hold of a small capitalist (of whom but few are left), and by a series of intrigues and resolute actions which would make material for a three-volume novel, get him to allow you to turn one of his hands into a handicraftsman for the occasion; and a very poor handicraftsman he will be, when all is said. Again, I carry a walking-stick, and like all sensible persons like it to have a good heavy end that will swing out well before me. A year or two ago it became the fashion to pare away all walking-sticks to the shape of attenuated carrots, and I really believe I shortened my life in my attempts at getting a reasonable staff of the kind I was used to, so difficult it was. Again, you want a piece of furniture which the trade (mark the word, Trade, not Craft!) turns out, blotched over with idiotic sham ornament; you wish to dispense with this degradation, and propose it to your upholsterer, who grudgingly assents to it; and you find that you have to pay the price of two pieces of furniture for the privilege of indulging your whim of leaving out the trade finish (I decline to call it ornament) on the one you have got made for you. And this is because it has been made by handicraft instead of machinery. For most people, therefore, there is a prohibitive price put upon the acquirement of the knowledge of methods and processes. We do not know how a piece of goods is made, what the difficulties are that beset its manufacture, what it ought to look like, feel like, smell like, or what it ought to cost apart from the profit of the middleman. We have lost the art of marketing, and with it the due sympathy with the life of the workshop, which would, if it existed, be such a wholesome check on the humbug of party politics.

It is a natural consequence of this ignorance of the methods of making wares, that even those who are in revolt against the tyranny of the excess of division of labour in the occupations of life, and who wish to recur more or less to handicraft, should also be ignorant of what that life of handicraft was when all wares were made by handicraft. If their revolt is to carry any hope with it, it is necessary that they should know something of this. I must assume that many or perhaps most of my readers are not acquainted with Socialist literature, and that few of them have read the admirable account of the different epochs of production given in Karl Marx' great work entitled "Capital." I must ask to be excused, therefore, for stating very briefly what, chiefly owing to Marx, has become a commonplace of Socialism, but is not generally known outside it. There have been three great epochs of production since the beginning of the Middle Ages. During the first or medieval period all production was individualistic in method; for though the workmen were combined into great associations for protection and the organisation of labour, they were so associated as citizens not as mere workmen. There was little or no division of labour, and what machinery was used was simply of the nature of a multiplied tool, a help to the workman's hand labour and not a supplanter of it. The workman worked for himself and not for any capitalistic employer, and he was accordingly master of his work and his time; this was the period of pure handicraft. When in the latter half of the sixteenth century the capitalist employer and the so-called free workman began to appear, the workmen were collected into workshops, the old tool-machines were improved, and at last a new invention, the division of labour, found its way into the workshops. The division of labour went on growing throughout the seventeenth century, and was perfected in the eighteenth, when the unit of labour became a group and not a single man; or in other words the workman became a mere part of a machine composed sometimes wholly of human beings and sometimes of human beings plus labour-saving machines, which towards the end of this period were being copiously invented; the fly-shuttle may be taken for an example of these. The latter half of the eighteenth century saw the beginning of the last epoch of production that the world has known, that of the automatic machine which supersedes hand labour, and turns the workman who was once a handicraftsman helped by tools, and next a part of a machine, into a tender of machines. And as far as we can see, the revolution in this direction as to kind is complete, though as to degree, as pointed out by Mr. David A. Wells last year (1887), the tendency is towards the displacement of ever more and more "muscular" labour, as Mr. Wells calls it.[9]

This is very briefly the history of the evolution of industry during the last five hundred years; and the question now comes: Are we justified in wishing that handicraft may in its turn supplant machinery? Or it would perhaps be better to put the question in another way: Will the period of machinery evolve itself into a fresh period of machinery more independent of human labour than anything we can conceive of now, or will it develop its contradictory in the shape of a new and improved period of production by handicraft? The second form of the question is the preferable one, because it helps us to give a reasonable answer to what people who have any interest in external beauty will certainly ask: Is the change from handicraft to machinery good or bad? And the answer to that question is to my mind that, as my friend Belfort Bax[10] has put it, statically it is bad, dynamically it is good. As a condition of life, production by machinery is altogether an evil; as an instrument for forcing on us better conditions of life it has been, and for some time yet will be, indispensable.

Having thus tried to clear myself of mere reactionary pessimism, let me attempt to show why statically handicraft is to my mind desirable, and its destruction a degradation of life. Well, first I shall not shrink from saying bluntly that production by machinery necessarily results in utilitarian ugliness in everything which the labour of man deals with, and that this is a serious evil and a degradation of human life. So clearly is this the fact that though few people will venture to deny the latter part of the proposition, yet in their hearts the greater part of cultivated civilised persons do not regard it as an evil, because their degradation has already gone so far that they cannot, in what concerns the sense of seeing, discriminate between beauty and ugliness: their languid assent to the desirableness of beauty is with them only a convention, a superstitious survival from the times when beauty was a necessity to all men. The first part of the proposition (that machine industry produces ugliness) I cannot argue with these persons, because they neither know, nor care for, the difference between beauty and ugliness; and with those who do understand what beauty means I need not argue it, as they are but too familiar with the fact that the produce of all modern industrialism is ugly, and that whenever anything which is old disappears, its place is taken by something inferior to it in beauty; and that even out in the very fields and open country. The art of making beautifully all kinds of ordinary things, carts, gates, fences, boats, bowls, and so forth, let alone houses and public buildings, unconsciously and without effort has gone; when anything has to be renewed among these simple things the only question asked is how little it can be done for, so as to tide us over our responsibility and shift its mending on to the next generation.

It may be said, and indeed I have heard it said, that since there is some beauty still left in the world and some people who admire it, there is a certain gain in the acknowledged eclecticism of the present day, since the ugliness which is so common affords a contrast whereby the beauty, which is so rare, may be appreciated. This I suspect to be only another form of the maxim which is the sheet anchor of the laziest and most cowardly group of our cultivated classes, that it is good for the many to suffer for the few; but if any one puts forward in good faith the fear that we may be too happy in the possession of pleasant surroundings, so that we shall not be able to enjoy them, I must answer that this seems to me a very remote terror. Even when the tide at last turns in the direction of sweeping away modern squalor and vulgarity, we shall have, I doubt, many generations of effort in perfecting the transformation, and when it is at last complete, there will be first the triumph of our success to exalt us, and next the history of the long wade through the putrid sea of ugliness which we shall have at last escaped from. But furthermore, the proper answer to this objection lies deeper than this. It is to my mind that very consciousness of the production of beauty for beauty's sake which we want to avoid; it is just what is apt to produce affectation and effeminacy amongst the artists and their following. In the great times of art conscious effort was used to produce great works for the glory of the City, the triumph of the Church, the exaltation of the citizens, the quickening of the devotion of the faithful; even in the higher art, the record of history, the instruction of men alive and to live hereafter, was the aim rather than beauty; and the lesser art was unconscious and spontaneous, and did not in any way interfere with the rougher business of life, while it enabled men in general to understand and sympathise with the nobler forms of art. But unconscious as these producers of ordinary beauty may be, they will not and cannot fail to receive pleasure from the exercise of their work under these conditions, and this above all things is that which influences me most in my hope for the recovery of handicraft. I have said it often enough, but I must say it once again, since it is so much a part of my case for handicraft, that so long as man allows his daily work to be mere unrelieved drudgery he will seek happiness in vain. I say further that the worst tyrants of the days of violence were but feeble tormentors compared with those Captains of Industry who have taken the pleasure of work away from the workmen. Furthermore I feel absolutely certain that handicraft joined to certain other conditions, of which more presently, would produce the beauty and the pleasure in work above mentioned; and if that be so, and this double pleasure of lovely surroundings and happy work could take the place of the double torment of squalid surroundings and wretched drudgery, have we not good reason for wishing, if it might be, that handicraft should once more step into the place of machine production?

I am not blind to the tremendous change which this revolution would mean. The maxim of modern civilisation to a well-to-do man is, Avoid taking trouble!

THE REVIVAL OF HANDICRAFT

Get as many of the functions of your life as you can performed by others for you! Vicarious life is the watchword of our civilisation, and we well-to-do and cultivated people live smoothly enough while it lasts. But, in the first place, how about the vicars, who do more for us than the singing of mass for our behoof for a scanty stipend? Will they go on with it for ever? For indeed the shuffling off of responsibilities from one to the other has to stop at last, and somebody has to bear the burden in the end. But let that pass, since I am not writing politics, and let us consider another aspect of the matter. What wretched lop-sided creatures we are being made by the excess of the division of labour in the occupations of life! What on earth are we going to do with our time when we have brought the art of vicarious life to perfection, having first complicated the question by the ceaseless creation of artificial wants which we refuse to supply for ourselves? Are all of us (we of the great middle class I mean) going to turn philosophers, poets, essayists, men of genius, in a word, when we have come to look down on the ordinary functions of life with the same kind of contempt wherewith persons of good breeding look down upon a good dinner, eating it sedulously however? I shudder when I think of how we shall bore each other when we have reached that perfection. Nay, I think we have already got in all branches of culture rather more geniuses than we can comfortably bear, and that we lack, so to say, audiences rather than preachers. I must ask pardon of my readers; but our case is at once so grievous and so absurd that one can scarcely help laughing out of bitterness of soul. In the very midst of our pessimism we are boastful of our wisdom, yet we are helpless in the face of the necessities we have created, and which, in spite of our anxiety about art, are at present driving us into luxury unredeemed by beauty on the one hand, and squalor unrelieved by incident or romance on the other, and will one day drive us into mere ruin.

Yes, we do sorely need a system of production which will give us beautiful surroundings and pleasant occupation, and which will tend to make us good human animals, able to do something for ourselves, so that we may be generally intelligent instead of dividing ourselves into dull drudges or duller pleasure-seekers according to our class, on the one hand, or hapless pessimistic intellectual personages, and pretenders to that dignity, on the other. We do most certainly need happiness in our daily work, content in our daily rest; and all this cannot be if we hand over the whole responsibility of the details of our daily life to machines and their drivers. We are right to long for intelligent handicraft to come back to the world which it once made tolerable amidst war and turmoil and uncertainty of life, and which it should, one would think, make happy now we have grown so peaceful, so considerate of each other's temporal welfare.

Then comes the question, How can the change be made? And here at once we are met by the difficulty that the sickness and death of handicraft is, it seems, a natural expression of the tendency of the age. We willed the end, and therefore the means also. Since the last days of the Middle Ages the creation of an intellectual aristocracy has been, so to say, the spiritual purpose of civilisation side by side with its material purpose of supplanting the aristocracy of status by the aristocracy of wealth. Part of the price it has had to pay for its success in that purpose (and some would say it is comparatively an insignificant part) is that this new aristocracy of intellect has been compelled to forgo the lively interest in the beauty and romance of life, which was once the portion of every artificer at least, if not of every workman, and to live surrounded by an ugly vulgarity which the world amidst all its changes has not known till modern times. It is not strange that until recently it has not been conscious of this degradation; but it may seem strange to many that it has now grown partially conscious of it. It is common now to hear people say of such and such a piece of country or suburb: "Ah! it was so beautiful a year or so ago, but it has been quite spoilt by the building." Forty years back the building would have been looked on as a vast improvement; now we have grown conscious of the hideousness we are creating, and we go on creating it. We see the price we have paid for our aristocracy of intellect, and even that aristocracy itself is more than half regretful of the bargain, and would be glad if it could keep the gain and not pay the full price for it. Hence not only the empty grumbling about the continuous march of machinery over dying handicraft, but also various elegant little schemes for trying to withdraw ourselves, some of us, from the consequences (in this direction) of our being superior persons; none of which can have more than a temporary and very limited success. The great wave of commercial necessity will sweep away all these well-meant attempts to stem it, and think little of what it has done, or whither it is going.

Yet after all even these feeble manifestations of discontent with the tyranny of commerce are tokens of a revolutionary epoch, and to me it is inconceivable that machine production will develop into mere infinity of machinery, or life wholly lapse into a disregard of life as it passes. It is true indeed that powerful as the cultivated middle class is, it has not the power of re-creating the beauty and romance of life; but that will be the work of the new society which the blind progress of commercialism will create, nay, is creating. The cultivated middle class is a class of slave-holders, and its power of living according to its choice is limited by the necessity of finding constant livelihood and employment for the slaves who keep it alive. It is only a society of equals which can choose the life it will live, which can choose to forgo gross luxury and base utilitarianism in return for the unwearying pleasure of tasting the fulness of life. It is my firm belief that we shall in the end realise this society of equals, and also that when it is realised it will not endure a vicarious life by means of machinery; that it will in short be the master of its machinery and not the servant, as our age is.

Meantime, since we shall have to go through a long series of social and political events before we shall be free to choose how we shall live, we should welcome even the feeble protest which is now being made against the vulgarisation of all life: first because it is one token amongst others of the sickness of modern civilisation; and next, because it may help to keep alive memories of the past which are necessary elements of the life of the future, and methods of work which no society could afford to lose. In short, it may be said that though the movement towards the revival of handicraft is contemptible on the surface in face of the gigantic fabric of commercialism; yet, taken in conjunction with the general movement towards freedom of life for all, on which we are now surely embarked, as a protest against intellectual tyranny, and a token of the change which is transforming civilisation into socialism, it is both noteworthy and encouraging.

Notes

1. Originally published in *Fortnightly Review*, November 1888.
2. W. Morris, 'The Revival of Handicraft', *Architecture, Industry & Wealth; Collected Papers* (London: Longmans Green, 1902), p. 215.
3. Ibid.
4. Morris, p. 226.
5. Morris, 'How We Live and How We Might Live', *Commonweal 3,* July 1887, p. 210.
6. Morris, 'The Revival of Handicraft', p. 226.
7. A simple hand mill for grinding corn, typically consisting of two circular stones, the upper of which is rotated or rubbed on the lower one.
8. *wideawake:* a hat with a low crown and a very wide brim.
9. David A. Wells, "The Economic Disturbances Since 1873," *Popular Science Magazine*, XXXI, 1887.
10. Ernest Belfort Bax (1854-1926), an English barrister, socialist, and historian.

39

FREDERICK W. TAYLOR, *THE PRINCIPLES OF SCIENTIFIC MANAGEMENT*

Frederick Winslow Taylor (1856–1915) was an American mechanical engineer who developed methods to improve industrial efficiency. Taylor collected his experiments and efficiency techniques together and published them as *The Principles of Scientific Management*. His contributions combined the ideas of homogeneous tasks, specialised workforce training, the planning, and instruction of tasks based upon the explicit division of labour and management, thus encouraging assembly line processes for large scale-production. The oft-quoted example of the redesign of a standardised shovel is instructive. Taylor reduced the number of people shovelling at the Bethlehem Steel Works from 500 to 140; in addition, they were able to increase the daily weight shovelled from 16 to 59 tons. This example puts his methods in a nutshell. As a by-product, Taylor's revised shovelling method also reduced the physical wear for the person.

His ideas were used in the design of operations, workspaces, and job routines, all of which have often been criticised for making workers rather machine-like, leaving them as simple operators, abrogating any thinking to management. Contemporary reviews of the book picked up this very issue. *The Economic Journal* reviewer concluded in 1912 that 'What scientific management seems to do, by its time-studies and stop-watches and simplification of movements and efficient monotony, is to reduce the minds of all its workmen to that of a squirrel perpetually revolving in a cage'.[1] This undermining of concepts, such as craft knowledge which had once been a powerful bargaining tool for workers, was clearly intentional.

In an editorial of 1915 titled 'Modern Industry and Craft Skill', the *International Molders Journal* offered a refutation of 'scientific management' and explained the value of crafts.

> The one great asset of the wage worker has been his craftsmanship. We think of craftsmanship ordinarily as the ability to manipulate skilfully the tools and material of a craft or trade. But true craftsmanship is much more than this. The really essential element in it is not manual skill and dexterity but something stored up in the mind of the worker.

This something is partly the intimate knowledge of the character and uses of the tools, materials and processes of the craft which tradition and experience have given the worker. But beyond this and above this, it is the knowledge which enables him to understand and overcome the constantly arising difficulties that grow out of variations not only in the tools and materials, but in the conditions under which the work must be done.[2]

The impact of scientific management on design was to bear considerable fruit in the early decades of the twentieth century. Whether it was in factory layout and design, such as in Henry Ford's motor car business, or the ideas of standardisation and abstract forms that influenced the design of objects, the ideas behind scientific management were seen as a virtue to be developed. The adaptation of these ideas to changing social, technical, environmental, and organisational thinking was crucial to the development of modernism in the twentieth century. Scientific management possibly encouraged links between art, architecture, and design, based on the concepts of engineering, rationality, and order, but at what expense?

Frederick W. Taylor, *The Principles of Scientific Management* (New York: Harper & Bros., 1911), pp. 9–15

Fundamentals of Scientific Management

The principal object of management should be to secure the maximum prosperity for the employer, coupled with the maximum prosperity for each employé.

The words "maximum prosperity" are used, in their broad sense, to mean not only large dividends for the company or owner, but the development of every branch of the business to its highest state of excellence, so that the prosperity may be permanent.

In the same way, maximum prosperity for each employé means not only higher wages than are usually received by men of his class, but, of more importance still, it means the development of each man to his state of maximum efficiency, so that he may be able to do, generally speaking, the highest grade of work for which his natural abilities fit him, and it further means giving him, when possible, this class of work to do.

It would seem to be so self-evident that maximum prosperity for the employer, coupled with maximum prosperity for the employé, ought to be the two leading objects of management, that even to state this fact should be unnecessary. And yet there is no question that, throughout the industrial world, a large part of the organization of employers, as well as employés, is for war rather than for peace, and that perhaps the majority on either side do not believe that it is possible so to arrange their mutual relations that their interests become identical.

The majority of these men believe that the fundamental interests of employés and employers are necessarily antagonistic. Scientific management, on the contrary, has for its very foundation the firm conviction that the true interests of the two are one and the same; that prosperity for the employer cannot exist through a long term of years unless it is accompanied by prosperity for the employé, and vice versa; and that it is possible to give the workman what he most wants—high wages—and the employer what he wants—a low labor cost—for his manufactures.

It is hoped that some at least of those who do not sympathize with each of these objects may be led to modify their views; that some employers, whose attitude toward their workmen has been that of trying to get the large amount of work out of them for the smallest possible wages, may be led to see that a more liberal policy toward their men will pay them better; and that some of those workmen who begrudge a fair and even a large profit to their employers, and who feel that all of the fruits of their labor should belong to them, and that those for whom they work and the capital invested in the business are entitled to little or nothing, may be led to modify these views.

No one can be found who will deny that in the case of any single individual the greatest prosperity can exist only when that individual has reached his highest state of efficiency, that is, when he is turning out his largest daily output.

The truth of this fact is also perfectly clear in the case of two men working together. To illustrate, if you and your workman have become so skilful that you and he together are making two pairs of shoes in a day, while your competitor and his workman are making only one pair, it is clear that after selling your two pairs of shoes you can pay your workman much higher wages than your competitor who produces only one pair of shoes is able to pay his man, and that there will still be enough money left over for you to have a larger profit than your competitor.

In the case of a more complicated manufacturing establishment, it should also be perfectly clear that the greatest permanent prosperity for the workman, coupled with the greatest prosperity for the employer, can be brought about only when the work of the establishment is done with the smallest combined expenditure of human effort, plus nature's resources, plus the cost for the use of capital in the shape of machines, buildings, etc. Or, to state the same thing in a different way: that the greatest prosperity can exist only as the result of the greatest possible productivity of the men and machines of the establishment, that is, when each man and each machine are turning out the largest possible output; because unless your men and your machines are daily turning out more work than others around you, it is clear that competition will prevent your paying higher wages to your workmen than are paid to those of your competitor. And what is true as to the possibility of paying high wages in the case of two companies competing close beside one another is also true as to whole districts of the country and even as to nations which are in competition. In a word, that maximum prosperity can exist only as the result of maximum productivity. Later in this paper illustrations will be given of several companies which are earning large dividends and at the same time paying from 30 per cent. to 100 per cent. higher wages to their men than are paid to similar men immediately around them, and with whose employers they are in competition. These illustrations will cover different types of work, from the most elementary to the most complicated.

If the above reasoning is correct, it follows that the most important object of both the workmen and the management should be the training and development of each individual in the establishment, so that he can do (at his fastest pace and with the maximum of efficiency) the highest class of work for which his natural abilities fit him.

These principles appear to be so self-evident that many men may think it almost childish to state them. Let us, however, turn to the facts, as they actually exist in this country and in England. The English and American peoples are the greatest sportsmen in the world. Whenever an American workman plays baseball, or an English workman plays cricket, it is safe to say that he strains every nerve to secure victory for his side. He does his very best to make the largest possible number of runs. The universal sentiment is so strong that any man who fails to give out all there is in him in sport is branded as a "quitter," and treated with contempt by those who are around him.

When the same workman returns to work on the following day, instead of using every effort to turn out the largest possible amount of work, in a majority of the cases this man deliberately plans to do as little as he safely can—to turn out far less work than he is well able to do—in many instances to do not more than one-third to one-half of a proper day's work. And in fact if he were to do his best to turn out his largest possible day's work, he would be abused by his fellow-workers for so doing, even more than if he had proved himself a "quitter" in sport. Underworking, that is, deliberately working slowly so as to avoid doing a full day's work, "soldiering," as it is called in this country, "hanging it out," as it is called in England, "ca canae," as it is called in Scotland, is almost universal in industrial establishments, and prevails also to a large extent in the building trades; and the writer asserts without fear of contradiction that this constitutes the greatest evil with which the working people of both England and America are now afflicted.

It will be shown later in this paper that doing away with slow working and "soldiering" in all its forms and so arranging the relations between employer and employé that each workman will work to his very best advantage and at his best speed, accompanied by the intimate cooperation with the management, and the help (which the workman should receive) from the management, would result on the average in nearly doubling the output of each man and each machine. What other reforms, among those which are being discussed by these two nations, could do as much toward promoting prosperity, toward the diminution of poverty, and the alleviation of suffering? America and England have been recently agitated over such subjects as the tariff, the control of the large corporations on the one hand, and of hereditary power on the other hand, and over various more or less socialistic proposals for taxation, etc. On these subjects both peoples have been profoundly stirred, and yet hardly a voice has been raised to call attention to this vastly greater and more important subject of "soldiering," which directly and powerfully affects the wages, the prosperity, and the life of almost every workingman, and also quite as much the prosperity of every industrial establishment in the nation.

The elimination of "soldiering" and of the several causes for slow working would so lower the cost of production that both our home and foreign markets would be greatly enlarged, and we could compete on more than even terms with our rivals. It would remove one of the fundamental causes for dull times, for lack of employment, and for poverty, and therefore would have a more permanent and far-reaching effect upon these misfortunes than any of the curative remedies that are now being used to soften their consequences. It would insure higher wages and make shorter working hours and better working and home conditions possible.

Why is it, then, in the face of the self-evident fact that maximum prosperity can exist only as the result of the determined effort of each workman to turn out each day his largest possible day's work, that the great majority of our men are deliberately doing just the opposite, and that even when the men have the best of intentions their work is in most cases far from efficient?

There are three causes for this condition, which may be briefly summarized as:

> *First.* The fallacy, which has from time immemorial been almost universal among workmen, that a material increase in the output of each man or each machine in the trade would result in the end in throwing a large number of men out of work.
>
> *Second:* The defective systems of management which are in common use, and which make it necessary for each workman to soldier, or work slowly, in order that he may protect his own best interests.
>
> *Third.* The inefficient rule-of-thumb methods, which are still almost universal in all trades, and in practising which our workmen waste a large part of their effort.

This paper will attempt to show the enormous gains which would result from the substitution by our workmen of scientific for rule-of-thumb methods.

To explain a little more fully these three causes:

First. The great majority of workmen still believe that if they were to work at their best speed they would be doing a great injustice to the whole trade by throwing a lot of men out of work, and yet the history of the development of each trade shows that each improvement, whether it be the invention of a new machine or the introduction of a better method, which results in increasing the productive capacity of the men in the trade and cheapening the costs, instead of throwing men out of work makes in the end work for more men.

The cheapening of any article in common use almost immediately results in a largely increased demand for that article. Take the case of shoes, for instance. The introduction of machinery for doing every element of the work which was formerly done by hand has resulted in making shoes at a fraction of their former labor cost, and in selling them so cheap that now almost every man, woman, and child in the working-classes buys one or two pair of shoes per year, and wears shoes all the time, whereas formerly each workman bought perhaps one pair of shoes every five years, and went barefoot most of the time, wearing shoes only as a luxury or as a matter of the sternest necessity. In spite of the enormously increased output of shoes per workman, which has come with shoe machinery, the demand for shoes has so increased that there are relatively more men working in the shoe industry now than ever before.

The workmen in almost every trade have before them an object lesson of this kind, and yet, because they are ignorant of the history of their own trade even, they still firmly believe, as their fathers did before them, that it is against their best interests for each man to turn out each day as much work as possible.

Under this fallacious idea a large proportion of the workmen of both countries each day deliberately work slowly so as to curtail the output. Almost every labor union has made, or is contemplating making, rules which have for their object curtailing the output of their members, and those men who have the greatest influence with the working-people, the labor leaders as well as many people with philanthropic feelings who are helping them, are daily spreading this fallacy and at the same time telling them that they are overworked.

A great deal has been and is being constantly said about "sweatshop" work and conditions. The writer has great sympathy with those who are overworked, but on the whole a greater sympathy for those who are *under paid*. For every individual, however, who is overworked, there are a hundred who intentionally underwork—greatly underwork—every day of their lives, and who for this reason deliberately aid in establishing those conditions which in the end inevitably result in low wages. And yet hardly a single voice is being raised in an endeavor to correct this evil.

Second. As to the second cause for soldiering—the relations which exist between employers and employés under almost all of the systems of management which are in common use—it is impossible in a few words to make it clear to one not familiar with this problem why it is that the ignorance of employers as to the proper time in which work of various kinds should be done makes it for the interest of the workman to "soldier."

The writer therefore quotes in the appendix from a paper read before The American Society of Mechanical Engineers in June 1903, entitled 'Shop Management,' which it is hoped will explain fully this cause for soldiering.

Third. As to the third cause for slow work, considerable space will later in this paper be devoted to illustrating the great gain, both to employers and employés, which results from the substitution of scientific for rule-of-thumb methods in even the smallest details of the work of every trade. The enormous saving of time and therefore increase in the output which it is possible to effect through eliminating unnecessary motions and substituting fast for slow and inefficient motions for the men working in any of our trades, can be fully realized only after one has personally seen the improvement which results from a thorough motion and time study, made by a competent man.

To explain briefly, owing to the fact that the workmen in all of our trades have been taught the details of their work by observation of those immediately around them, there are many different ways in common use for doing the same thing, perhaps forty, fifty, or a hundred ways of doing each act in each trade, and for the same reason there is a great variety in the implements used for each class of work. Now, among the various methods and implements used in each element of each trade there is always one method and one implement which is quicker and better than any of the rest. And this one best method and best implement can only be discovered or developed through a scientific study and analysis of all of the methods and implements in use, together with accurate, minute, motion and time study. This involves the gradual substitution of science for rule of thumb throughout the mechanic arts.

This paper will show that the underlying philosophy of all of the old systems of management in common use makes it imperative that each workman shall be left with the final responsibility for doing his job practically as he thinks best, with comparatively little help and advice from the management. And it will also show that because of this isolation of workmen, it is in most cases impossible for the men working under these systems to do their work in accordance with the rules and laws of a science or art, even where one exists.

The writer asserts as a general principle (and he proposes to give illustrations tending to prove the fact later in this paper), that in almost all of the mechanic arts the science which underlies each act of each workman is so great and amounts to so much that the workman who is best suited to actually doing the work is incapable of fully understanding this science, without the guidance and help of those who are working with him or over him, either through lack of education or through insufficient mental capacity. In order that the work may be done in accordance with scientific laws, it is necessary that there shall be a far more equal division of the responsibility between the management and the workmen than exists under any of the ordinary types of management. Those in the management whose duty it is to develop this science should also guide and help the workman in working under it, and should assume a much larger share of the responsibility for results than under usual conditions is assumed by the management.

The body of this paper will make it clear that, to work according to scientific laws, the management must take over and perform much of the work which is now left to the men; almost every act of the workman should be preceded by one or more preparatory acts of the management which enable him to do his work better and quicker than he otherwise could. And each man should daily be taught by and receive the most friendly help from those who are over him, instead of being, at the one extreme, driven or coerced by his bosses, and at the other left to his own unaided devices.

Notes

1 *Economic Journal*, 22, 87, September 1912, p. 475.
2 Cited in J. P. Frey; 'Modern Industry and Craft Skills', *The American Federationist*, 23, May 1916, p. 365. Frey was editor of the *Molder's Journal*.

5.5 CRAFT MACHINE AND DESIGN

40

CHARLES R. ASHBEE, 'DECORATIVE ART FROM A WORKSHOP POINT OF VIEW'

Charles Robert Ashbee (1863–1942) was a British architect and designer and an important figure in the Arts and Crafts movement. He was instrumental in establishing the Guild of Handicraft and was a keen supporter of the workshop approach to design and making that embraced the socialist ideals of William Morris and the craft ethic of Ruskin. The aim of the Guild was to

> seek not only to set a higher standard of craftsmanship, but at the same time, and in so doing, to protect the status of the craftsman. To this end it endeavours to steer a mean between the independence of the artist – which is individualistic and often parasitical – and the trade-shop, where the workman is bound to purely commercial and antiquated traditions, and has, as a rule, neither stake in the business nor any interest beyond his weekly wage.[1]

The Guild included a range of crafts including metalwork in silver and iron, jewellery, furniture, and book production. The Guild was recognised as an interesting force in design within the pages of journals such as *The Studio* and through exhibitions such as those run by the Arts & Crafts Exhibition Society.

For Ashbee, the workshop was the preferred place of production in comparison to either the studio or the factory. For him, the studio represented the triumph of the individual genius of art over society, whereas the factory represented the triumph of society over art, through large-scale production. The workshop, by contrast, was a place of integration in all respects: A place of social solidarity and unity, and the production of objects and wares that were necessary for life.

> In the Guild it is sought to encourage the workman's individuality; in the School the designing class is regarded as the backbone of the School. Each pupil is taught first to conceive the design, and then to apply it through the help of the other classes to the different materials, the wood, the metal, the clay, the gesso, the flat surface for painting. The effort here, therefore, is not to emulate the ordinary Technical School but to

follow in the lines laid down by the leading artists who have the encouragement of the Handicrafts at heart, in the belief that the modern cry for the education of the hand and eye can only be fully achieved in the education of the individuality of the workman.[2]

His attitude is evident in the text which compares and contrasts the studio and the workshop. Ashbee made some concessions to machinery, but they were limited. He said

> I have no objection to using the dental fret for modelling in silver, or a steam drill, for boring and punching, still less do I mind the polishing lathe, or belting it to the engine, but if the doing of these accessories ... disorganised the economy and inventive power of my workshop, then as a silversmith I am better off without them.[3]

The paper was given to the second conference of The National Association for the Advancement of Art and its Application to Industry held in Edinburgh.

Charles R. Ashbee, 'Decorative Art From a Workshop Point of View', A Paper Read at the Edinburgh Art Congress, November 1889, pp. 1–11

THE key to the study of most things nowadays is the social question; hence if we want to study the art question in any other than its immediate bearing on ourselves, we must approach it from the same point of view. Every artist or craftsman works out, consciously or not, some portion of what might be termed the art problem in its social aspect, in painting, in architecture, in handicraft alike. In his line portraiture, the spirit forces in the portraits of Watts will appeal to him. Does he affect Burne Jones, he will see the nineteenth-century hero in the head of Perseus: is it church architecture he is dealing with, there will come home to him the sense of two conflicting forces, living vulgarity and dying antiquarianism. If he be bitten with Paris, there are the confessions of George More[4] for a stumbling-block. As for Naturalism it will bring with it its honest acceptance of modern ugliness. In Impressionism the great moments of our civilisation may be flashed upon him. While the lower forms of art will reveal a still closer bearing on social questions; beauty-in-use will be brought before him, cheap-and-nasty will be his bugbear; and transcending all questions of style or school, the great question of the life of leisure will come upon him with silent insistence. How much leisure have I, how has it come to me, what justifiability is there for it in my case; to what purpose of communal service am I placing it?

THIS Congress[5] is in itself a recognition of the fact that the social question is the key to the artistic. Its purpose is, as far as I conceive it, to popularise, to organise, to socialise art.

THE object of this paper, starting with the recognition of the social bearings of art, is to suggest the application to the art problem, and to the question of art development, the ideals and practicalities of an ordinary nineteenth-century workshop, in the belief that a purer and healthier condition both of industrial activity, and artistic sensitiveness can only be attained by a combination of the two.

TO start with the aphorism that art must be carried on in the workshop and not in the studio, in the face of the fact that all the great art work of the present day has been carried on in the studio and not in the workshop, appears at first sight a paradox; but it is easy of explanation. In the first place, we are dealing with art as a whole, and not with picture-painting; in the second place, we are dealing with decorative art, in which the painting of a picture is a matter of minor importance: this accepted, the aphorism will not be difficult of establishment.

I do not wish it to be taken as in any sense for or against either, but I should draw the distinction between the workshop and the studio somewhat in the following manner.

THE studio is a happily situated nest, somewhere in the region of villas and top hats; it is built of red bricks, even if cheaply. It is fitted with all the apparatus necessary for the lighting, lifting, and wheeling to and from exhibitions of the large masterpiece; and it is ornamented with all the conventional gusto of the prevalent Queen in Anne-ity.[6] Within there are scraps of damask silk, bartered from Roman curiosity shops, divers 'subjects' under way, various Madonnas of the future, suggestions of decorative work sprayed upon the odd moments of panels. There is a cast from Pheidias, a photogravure of Millet, a skeleton and a lay figure.[7] In the corner a pair of embroidered slippers, and on the mantel-piece pipes and tobacco. The inmate for whom these things have their being, works hard, appreciates the silence and solitude of his surroundings, and is comfortably conscious of his Bohemianism. In the afternoon there are lady visitors, and the servant brings in five o'clock tea.

THE workshop is almost as light as the studio, though less pleasantly situated, and near the racket of some big thoroughfare. But what matters noise ? if there be noise without, there is noise within; hammering and sawing, and what not. Nor are the internal surroundings as pleasant to look on. Blue whitewash takes the place of damask fragments, and moveable gas jets of patent reflectors. The place is in a condition in which no housewife would enter it, and the glue pot is simmering on the stove pipe. As to the fittings, there are benches, and racks for tools, also possibly a small furnace, and a good deal of grime. To hang up prints there would be inadvisable, though a photo-lithographic advertisement assists in telling the days of the week, and offers an appropriate quotation for the better committing them to memory. As to the rest the furniture consists of rows of pegs on which hang hats, coats, and aprons; here and there a teapot with a broken spout, and an occasional coloured kerchief containing two plates bound face-wise. The inmates of the workshop pursue their avocation with the regularity of clock-work;—a light in their faces perhaps, of an armed resistance to something,—and the dinner hour at twelve o'clock is enlivened with the perusal and discussion of racy paragraphs from a halfpenny radical print.

THESE to my mind are the two pictures; but I hold that in the higher sense the proper place of decorative art is the latter; and I repeat the aphorism that art must be carried on in the workshop, not in the studio.

CRAFT MACHINE AND DESIGN

IN the first place, the right understanding of forms of ornament,—elements of design, is only possible in their direct bearing on forms of material,—elements of construction. You need your basis of matter wherein to engender the spirit. You must understand the stone, the wood, the pigments, the clay, what each can do, what its limitations are; and this means an understanding, if, merely for the sake of conceiving our own incapacity to use them, of the tools that are the guardians of these limitations. 'Rivingtons,'[8] that famous tome on building construction, whose pyramidal ascent of facts has to be scaled before youthful architects pass Royal Institute examinations, would lose half its value if it were not for the fact of the isolation of the architect's studio, euphemistically termed his office; but a half-hour in the workshop would save days of fruitless drudgery over its pages. I received the other day from the head-master of a provincial board-school, a letter saying that his board desired him to teach the use of tools; could I assist him, what text-books was he to read up, and could a list of the tools be provided? I recommended, not ' Rivingtons,' but a carpenter to take the head-master's place.

THE ways are innumerable in which the workshop alone can instruct in the limitations of material, and the functions of the tool; every hour in the workshop reveals something, whether it be so small a matter as the pressure of the sable which produced the favourite form of the Gothic painted leaf, or so great a matter as the thrust of the arch which produced that identical ogeeval curve in architectural construction. The study of these limitations is complex enough for us, without our losing the accumulated benefit of workshop experience and practicalities. We may go home to our studios and copy realistically if we will; but given the knack, it always remains easier to copy realistically than to master the limitations of material.

A historical study of art forms is perhaps one of the most fascinating things possible, and would be calculated to throw much light on decorative art from the workshop point of view. If we were to tell an every-day artist that his shoddy stucco frame is, in the eyes of the Creator, more of a work of art than his own landscape painting which it contains, the remark would savour of blasphemy: or if we were to point out to him that the same painting was actually a development of the frame itself, and that the genesis of the picture in the frame could be traced to the days when Margaritone[9] illuminated the frameworks and crucifixes of Umbrian Altars with toilsome conventionalisations of the Christ, it would appear to him a mere antiquarian vagary, but none the less both statements might safely be asserted.

THUS much for the artistic principles contained in the ideas of studio and workshop respectively; and if the recording angel have even not yet thrown the chased goblet into the heavier scale of the latter, we have still all the human and vital elements in the being of each, to take into account.

WE might call the studio in its nature subjective; it fosters that refined sensuality of nineteenth-century art, self-introspection, whereas the workshop has in it the elements of the human and objective. In the coming together of men, in the magnetic affinities that spring up between them, are the forces that engender art creativeness, just as in academical life they give rise best to speculation and literary creativeness. Ideas may be conceived in solitude, but they are brought to birth by co-operation. Men take creative force from each other. Those psychical moments of which we now hear so frequently, imply men in the union of number, in their combined readiness to accept the new idea. The ancients would have stated the case between the workshop and the studio in the terms of Pantheism. Narcissus had a studio by the brookside, and he perished in the contemplation of his own loveliness; Vulcan had a workshop under Etna, and all men and gods marvelled at it, for it was grand and awful by virtue of the united and rhythmical ringing of its hammers.

WHEN we set to work, however, to produce decorative art in the workshop, there is forced upon us the problem of the subdivision of labour; how unsatisfactory and uneconomical any present system is, and how necessary a re-arrangement. But the question is, on what basis. The exigencies of the market determine the supply of the decorative commodity; certain goods are wanted, and have to be provided rapidly and largely; alter these exigencies, and you alter the conditions. As soon as people begin to feel the true connection between construction and design, the designer will at once be brought nearer the workshop. Architects will no longer build houses with half timber masks, nor designers paint landscapes on coal-scuttles. A newer division of labour will set in, by which the designer will work less on paper, and the workman less without it.

BEARING in mind that the great problem of the modern workshop is organisation, there seems a curious fitness in the application of its ways and methods to the question of decorative art, for decorative art from the very fact of its being so impersonal, admits of organisation. That ceaseless fund of willing labour with which mankind is endowed, finds scope in it. The labour by which historical schools grow up, labour unoriginal, imitative, conscientious, diligent and humble; the labour which produced the intricacies of the monastic manuscript, and the thousand crockets[10] on the Gothic cathedral. For decorative art on any large scale implies repetition, implies method, and the constant dwelling on and development of some one idea. It is as the variation on a theme in a symphony; for one man to do it is an impossibility; you need a hundred with different instruments, before you can give your decorative theme its full value in variety.

AND further, your organisation, just like your decoration, must have a soul in it. The thousand men who carve the crockets must have the sense of concerted action, even as the thousand crockets must artistically express unity; and so our next question is how this can be got, what is to be our substitute for the monastic ideal, or the creative enthusiasm of the guilds? There again the modern workshop can come to our aid. Apply the militant spirit of trades' unionism which more or less pervades most of our principal workshops—apply the growing instinct for co-operative action whether for the purposes of attack, of distribution, or of production—and we have a like spirit to that by which the Athens of Pericles was perfected, or the England of William of Wykeham[11] made beautiful.

THE basis of the new subdivision of labour must therefore be a sound one socially. In the Greek and Mediaeval times, labour was divided in a manner which we neither can nor need seek to copy; we have merely to study results, and emulate with means and methods of our own. And so if we take the workshop as our basis of action, we have, as I conceive it, to reorganise the subdivision of labour from an anti-class point of view. We have first to recognise the dignity of all labour—dignity in service; we have secondly to recognise the equality of all labour—equality in service, but differing according to merit and capacity. We have, even as a wise collector does, to give equal rights to the Sevres vase, and the chap book of hawkers' cries.[12] True, they appealed to different publics in their day, but in the cupboard—each a work of decorative art—they stand as man to man.

AT present the class disunions are acute in proportion to their nearness; the workman dispises the clerk, the clerk the workman; the wage of each is to all intents and purposes fixed and the same; the labour of one is as valuable to the community as the labour of the other; it is the artificial class barrier that does the mischief. A regards B as a snob or a renegade, B looks on A as an inferior being. None the less, however, the workshop is ready for the reorganisation, only another force has to be introduced, and that is community of action. Community of action is already partially accomplished in our great armies of industry and distributive agencies; the co-operative principle has only to be more fully applied. In decorative art, where men are working to a creative purpose, and where their labour is in itself educational, this community of action can be more keenly felt, for it is a union not only of pockets, but of hands and hearts. And its highest outcome will be style—style in workmanship, style in design, in decoration, in architecture, and ultimately, national style. Put your decorative art in the workshop; united action is the steel, workshop needs, and ingenuities are the flint, and from their contact the living spark will spring. We should regard decorative art as a new heraldry; let our pupils, our workshops, and our communities have badges, devices, trade marks of their own. For there are great principles involved in the emblematic treatment of decorative art. It implies an understanding of ornament in its repetition and development. It implies a soul within, which may have prompted its creation, and it implies community of action, because it can exist only where men are banded together for some common purpose. The signature of Turner on a picture is a personal matter, but the hand on the prentice's column, the collar of S.S.,[13] the badges of the old guilds, the mark of P.R.B.,[14] imply an art principle within a co-operative force.

SOLVE the question of style in art, and we are at once brought to the solution of a still harder problem—that of our standard of criticism, the bane of every most enlightened and judicious hanging committee. We may, since the days of Sir Joshua, have produced schools of painting, but we have produced no schools of craft. Given the style, the schools' outcome, and at once we have the standard. At present the workman's only canon is technical excellence, and that of the average Englishman, so far as he can be said to have any at all, is a shallow realism. A landscape of Hunt's he judges good if it be like what he, in some beefy moment, has seen; a figure of

Burne Jones, in purposeful convention, is to him an affectation and an enigma. 'I'm a plain man, and I know what I want':—admirable aphorism! but fitly paraphrased as follows: I'm an ignorant man, I know what suits my ignorance, and I'm very proud of it.' And that was why Watts in his solemn picture of Mammon[15] has applied to the modern god, the old Greek fable of Midas with the ass's ears.

TO come now to a further point, the direct application of these ideas to industry, we have to work by a decentralising process. It is only in their application to each special industry in its own district, it is only by a frank acceptance of the ways and methods of the workshop as the men of the workshop in those districts have in the course of generations created them, and by a full recognition of the organising solidarity of these ways and methods, that any healthy growth or glory in decorative art can be achieved. Is it the industry of silk or cotton which we want to benefit, we must teach our workmen and designers, the evolution of pattern from the East, the sweetness of the Sicilian damask, the virtue of the Flemish diaper, and we must show them how the social conditions of each art epoch had reference to the design in its manifold developments. Is it the industry of furniture and wood-work, we must trace step by step the historical sequence of church fittings, the Gothic screen, the Jacobean pulpit, we must show how the art of architecture in England, or the art of painting in Italy, fashioned the art of cabinet-making; whether in the reredos, or the wedding chest, and we must trace the intricacies of construction and design, from the solid carpentry of the Norman into the veneer of Louis Seize. If our industry be iron we have the relation of the wrought to the cast; the work of those nameless artists whose craft adorns the fireplaces of English country houses, or the cunning workmanship of the Canterbury screens and the Hampton Court gates. Is the local industry silver—that most degraded of all modern English crafts,—we can trace the history of its decline under the Georges, through the art of Holland into the splendour of the Spanish renaissance and back to its crowning glory in the Middle Ages—the sacramental cup. If we are dealing with the industry of colour-making, it is our business to apply the craft of the Van Eycks, of Cennino Cennini, to modern manufacture, and not only to bring to bear scientific skill to purity of making, but artistic sensitiveness to the development of lights and tones of colour in their decorative significance. But in each and every instance if it is the workman we want to train, it is of the workman we must tell; each school, each epoch, the industry produced in each country must be treated in its relation to the social conditions of the men whose impress is left upon it. This I hold is the only way of ultimately applying English decorative ability to English industry, and it is this that I should call the application to decorative art, as far as education goes, of the workshop of the nineteenth century.

AS to the ways and means, they are ready to hand. This Congress is our ventilating machine; exhibitions like those of the Arts and Crafts are the agencies for bringing the public in touch with the workshops; then there is the instinct for cooperation growing up in these workshops, and there is the movement for the establishment of polytechnics and other technical institutions, which should give the element of school and educational dignity.

WHETHER these ways and means are being developed aright is another question, and one which it is scarcely within the scope of this paper to take into consideration; but, as the experience which has supplied its material and given birth to its confidence has been drawn from the growth and development of workshops, schools, the artistic creativeness and the general labour movement in East London, it might not be out of place to point to a few of the special movements which have been tending in the direction indicated, especially as East London has in many matters of the kind in late years been taking the lead.

INDEED, I should hold it needless on my part to speak as a theorist on these points, or even to speak at all, were I not myself engaged in constructive work. The days of artistic speculation are gone by, all that concerns us now is the method of applying those truths which most artists and thinkers concur in holding. The work which my colleagues and I are doing in East London, strives in a certain measure to realise the healthier conditions of decorative art, of workmanship, and of industry in general, to which this paper has given attention. By the creation in the Guild of Handicraft of a co-operative workshop on the one hand, implying the recognition of the reorganisation and redivision of labour, and on the other by the creation of a school of Handicraft which shall be grafted on to this workshop and thus serve as a field from which to draw its future workmen, and as a storehouse for its artistic traditions, we have striven to revive in some small way that spirit which created the great craftsmanship of Tuscany, of Normandy, or of Bavaria. We are seeking in short to apply the workshop to decorative art.

AS an instance of the way in which this work is being developed on its educational side, I am proposing in the following term to start a further series of lectures and classes for the purpose of linking the education of the school to the industry of the district. East London is the great centre of the English cabinet-making trade, and thus I am intending to give from my professional point of view as an architect, and in conjunction with the technical skill of one of the leading workmen in the guild workshop, a historical and practical course on the history and development of the industry of the English cabinetmaker.

TO continue the question of the workman's interest and the workman's education in these ways and means, I hold you can do nothing unless you give him representation. You accuse the workman of a want of ideas and a want of interest, but he has one all-absorbing idea, one over-mastering interest; and that is the problem of industry and its reorganisation. If you want him to grow interested in art matters you must put them to him in his own terms. Offer him the art problem as a problem of workshop organisation, and he will solve it for you. Here, again, the workshop steps in. You cannot work out the problem of technical education in the teeth of the opposition of the Trades' Unions: regard it merely as a means for benefitting English industry to the interest of the masters, and it will be ephemeral; regard it as a national matter, and it will live. And this holds good not only of our workshops, but of our exhibitions and of polytechnics and technical schools. The problem which, to my mind, is in the immediate future before the Arts and Crafts Exhibition Society—if it would more fully, even than it has already done, realise those pretty little devices on its note paper of workmen shaking hands, 'decoratively,' with artists—is the problem of the methods of representation from the English workshops, trade unions, and clubs, on the body [of] the Society; it is a question of what we risk—is it to be a vulgar democracy or an exotic art? For my part, speaking as an artist, I should say trust in the democracy, for the art can only be worked out through its agency.

EXACTLY the same applies to polytechnics, whether in representation or in education. Polytechnics and technical schools can only develop by becoming, in the fullest sense, People's universities; by being brought to bear directly on the industries of the locality in which they are situated, and by having on their governing bodies the representation, loyally and frankly given, of the working men who through their trade societies and clubs are seeking to re-organise English industry within the workshops.

TO take the case of the People's Palace,[16] another of the young institutions of East London, and one whose fair prospects in many ways have made it the model from which the other polytechnics are being created: nothing from a workman's point of view can be more out of sympathy with the conditions of East London labour and workshops than its complete absence of representation: nothing from an artist's point of view more hopeless for the ultimate improvement of the industries of the district or of industry in general, than its method of art education. You cannot win your workmen's sympathies unless you work through them; offer them endowments from above, and they will leave them to the middle class, give them representative power, and they are with you. And as for education in art, it must be of the best, or not at all. Art, in any direct bearing on industry, can only be taught by men who can themselves create, whether in design or in workmanship. Better than make of our schools and polytechnics South Kensington Cram Shops, let us give up the idea of art teaching altogether, for the destinies of English handicraft and industry will assuredly be worked out without them.

TO sum up. The points I have insisted on are these: The art problem must be worked out through the social problem. The home of decorative art must be the workshop, not the studio. In working our decorative art on a large scale we must reorganise the subdivision of labour, and we must reorganise it on an anti-class basis. We must apply to decorative art the principles of the workshop, especially those co-operative ideals growing up in our midst, and we shall find in the development of the workshop the solution of the problems of style and criticism in art and craft. Finally, we must have in our exhibitions, schools, and polytechnics complete representation from workmen in their societies. Thus alone can a genuine workshop and a noble national art be created. The great question of the consumption of its commodities—the question from the point of view of the public outside, I have left for a future paper; but the workshop from within may suggest ways and means for this also. The destinies of British art and industry must eventually be decided by the British working classes; even as they are at present slowly and surely solving our social and economic questions, and in the end it may yet be told how from the obscene bulb of the plutocracy sprang the tulip of the new civilisation.

Notes

1. See https://www.chippingcampdenhistory.org.uk/content/history/people-2/arts_artists_and_craftspeople/c_r_ashbee accessed July 2020.
2. B. G. Burroughs, 'Three Disciples of William Morris, 2. C. R. Ashbee', *Connoisseur*, 172, October 1969, p. 88.
3. Cited in A. Crawford, *C. R. Ashbee: Architect, Designer & Romantic Socialist* (New Haven & London: Yale University Press, 2005), p. 215.
4. *The Confessions of a Young Man* (1886 in French; 1888 in English) a memoir by Irish novelist George Moore.
5. Congress of the National Association of the Advancement of Arts, Edinburgh, 1889.
6. Reference to the taste for architectural design in a so-called Queen Anne style.
7. Lay figure: a small jointed manikin of a human body used by artists and designers.
8. *Notes on Building Construction Arranged to Meet the Requirements of the Syllabus of the Science & Art Department of the Committee of Council on Education, South Kensington* (London: Rivingtons, 1875).
9. Margarito or Margaritone d'Arezzo (fl. c.1250–1290), Italian painter.
10. crocket: a carved ornament in the form of a curled leaf or cusp. A hook-shaped decorative element common in Gothic architecture.
11. William of Wykeham (c.1320–1404), was Bishop of Winchester and Chancellor of England.
12. Chap-book: a form of popular literature circulated by itinerant dealers or chapmen, mainly consisting of small pamphlets of popular stories, ballads, tracts, etc.
13. Collar of S. S (Sesses): is one of the oldest and best-known jewelled livery collars. They have been in continuous use in England since the 14th century as insignia of a guild or a symbol of fealty to a noble house.
14. PRB: Pre-Raphaelite Brotherhood.
15. G.F. Watts, 'Mammon' 1884–5.
16. The People's Palace for East London, built in 1886, was intended to improve the lives of the local community by providing locations for 'technical education and rational recreation'.

41

JOHN DANDO SEDDING, 'DESIGN'

John Dando Sedding (1838–1891) was a successful designer and ecclesiastical architect who worked in a Gothic-revival style. He was influential amongst Arts and Crafts architects and designers, including Ernest Gimson and Edward Barnsley. His publications include *Garden-Craft Old and New* (1891; repr. 1903) and *Art and Handicraft* (1893).

The *Arts and Crafts Essays* from which this article is taken was a compilation of essays by members of the Arts and Crafts Exhibition Society in London. The topics included furniture, stained glass, textiles, wallpaper and metalwork, as well as design practice and colour theory. The forward by William Morris concluded with this statement that succinctly explains part of the ethos of the Arts and Crafts and the Exhibitions:

> It is this conscious cultivation of art and the attempt to interest the public in it which the Arts and Crafts Exhibition Society has set itself to help, by calling special attention to that really most important side of art, the decoration of utilities by furnishing them with genuine artistic finish in place of trade finish.[1]

Walter Crane, in the same publication, also explained some of the ideas behind the Arts and Crafts movement: 'It is a protest against turning men into machines, against artificial distinctions in art, and against making the immediate market value, or possibility of profit, the chief test of artistic merit'.[2] *The Saturday Review* was supportive of the Arts and Crafts initiatives which were published in this work. The reviewer made the point that the Arts and Crafts movement was being attacked from two sides.

> Hitherto, in their manifestos, we have seen the army which Mr. Morris commands fighting back the Victorian gimcrack and the Georgian 'brown brick box': unfortunately, a foe has now appeared on the opposite side, and the Impressionists come forward 'loudly proclaiming their enmity to beauty'. It is to stem these converging streams of hostility that

the members of the Arts and Crafts Exhibition Society have drawn their forces together; and we recommend to all who are interested in a most pressing problem of the age to see what it is that they have to say for themselves.[3]

While the main thrust of the paper was to discuss embroidery and its design issues, Sedding also touched on the favourite topic of the part that nature might play in the inspiration of designers. In fact, the last paragraph of this extract, on the role of nature in design, was quoted in full, in Lethaby's obituary for Sedding in *The Builder*.[4]

John Dando Sedding, 'Design', *Arts and Crafts Essays* (London: Rivington Percival, 1893), pp. 405–413

"Drink waters out of thine own cistern, and running waters out of thine own well."
—SOLOMON,

"Produce; produce; be it but the infinitesimalest product, produce."
—CARLYLE.

FOR the last sixty years, ever since the Gothic Revival set in, we have done our best to resuscitate the art of embroidery. First the Church and then the world took up the task, and much admirable work has been done by the "Schools," the shops, and at home. And yet the verdict still must be "the old is better."

Considering all things, this lack of absolute success is perplexing and needs to be explained. For we have realised our ideals. Never was a time when the art and science of needlework were so thoroughly understood as in England at the present moment. Our designers can design in any style. Every old method is at our fingers' ends. Every ingenious stitch of old humanity has been mastered, and a descriptive name given to it of our own devising. Every traditional pattern—wave, lotus, daisy, convolvulus, honey suckle, "Sacred Hom" or tree of life; every animal form, or bird, fish or reptile, has been traced to its source, and its symbolism laid bare. Every phase of the world's primal schools of design—Egyptian, Babylonian, Indian, Chinese, Greek, Byzantine, European—has been illustrated and made easy of imitation. We are archaeologists: we are critics: we are artists. We are lovers of old work: we are learned in historical and aesthetic questions, in technical rules and principles of design. We are colourists, and can play with colour as musicians play with notes. What is more, we are in terrible earnestness about the whole business. The honour of the British nation, the credit of Royalty, are, in a manner, staked upon the success of our "Schools of Needlework." And yet, in spite of all these favouring circumstances, we get no nearer to the old work that first mocked us to emulation in regard to power of initiative and human interest.

Truth and gallantry prompt me to add, it is not in stitchery but in design that we lag behind the old. Fair English hands can copy every trick of ancient artistry: finger-skill was never defter, will was never more ardent to do fine things, than now. Yet our work hangs fire. It fails in design. Why?

Now, Emerson has well said that all the arts have their origin in some enthusiasm. Mark this, however: that whereas the design of old needlework is based upon enthusiasm for birds, flowers, and animal life,* the design of modern needlework has its origin in enthusiasm for antique art.

Nature is, of course, the groundwork of all art, even of ours; but it is not to Nature at first-hand that we go. The flowers we embroider were not plucked from field and garden, but from the camphor-scented preserves at Kensington. Our needlework conveys no pretty message of

"The life that breathes, the life that lives,"

it savours only of the now stiff and stark device of dead hands. Our art holds no mirror up to Nature as we see her, it only reflects the reflection of dead periods. Nay, not content with merely trifling the *motifs* of moth-fretted rags, we must needs turn for novelty to an old Persian tile which, well magnified, makes a capital design for a quilt that one might perchance sleep under in spite of what is outside! Or we are not ashamed to ask our best embroideresses to copy the barbaric wriggles and childlike crudities of a seventh-century "Book of Kells," a task which cramps her style and robs Celtic art of all its wonder.

We have, I said, realised our ideals. We can do splendidly what we set ourselves to do—namely, to mimic old masterpieces. The question is, What next? Shall we continue to hunt old trails, and die, not leaving the world richer than we found it? Or shall we for art and honour's sake boldly adventure something—drop this wearisome translation of old styles and translate Nature instead?

Think of the gain to the "Schools," and to the designers themselves, if we elect to take another starting-point! No more museum-inspired work! No more scruples about styles! No more dry-as-dust stock patterns! No more loathly Persian-tile quilts! No more awful "Zoomorphic" table-cloths! No more cast-iron-looking altar cloths, or Syon Cope[5] angels, or stumpy Norfolkscreen saints! No more Tudor roses and pumped-out Christian imagery suggesting that Christianity is dead and buried! But, instead, we shall have design *by* living men *for* living men—something that expresses fresh realisations of sacred facts, personal broodings, skill, joy in Nature—in grace of form and gladness of colour; design that shall recall Shakespeare's maid who

"with her needle composes
Nature's own shape, of bud, bird, branch, or berry,
That even Art sisters the natural roses."[6]

---

* A strip of sixteenth-century needlework in my possession (6 ft. by 2 ft. 6 in.) figures thirty different specimens of plants, six animals, and four birds, besides ornamental sprays of foliage.

For, after all, modern design should be as the old—living thought, artfully expressed: fancy that has taken fair shapes. And needlework is still a pictorial art that requires a real artist to direct the design, a real artist to ply the needle. Given these, and our needlework can be as full of story as the Bayeux tapestry, as full of imagery as the Syon Cope, and better drawn. The charm of old embroidery lies in this, that it clothes current thought in current shapes. It meant something to the workers, and to the man in the street for whom it was done. And for our work to gain the same sensibility, the same range of appeal, the same human interest, we must employ the same means. We must clothe modern ideas in modern dress; adorn our design with living fancy, and rise to the height of our knowledge and capacities.

Doubtless there is danger to the untrained designer in direct resort to Nature. For the tendency in his or her case is to copy outright, to give us pure crude fact and not to *design* at all. Still there is hope in honest error: none in the icy perfections of the mere stylist. For the unskilled designer there is no training like drawing from an old herbal; for in all old drawing of Nature there is a large element of design. Besides which, the very limitations of the materials used in realising a design in needlework, be it ever so naturally coloured, hinders a too definite presentation of the real.

For the professional stylist, the confirmed conventionalist, an hour in his garden, a stroll in the embroidered meadows, a dip into an old herbal, a few carefully-drawn cribs from Curtis's *Botanical Magazine*,[7] or even—for lack of something better—Sutton's last Illustrated Catalogue,[8] is wholesome exercise, and will do more to revive the original instincts of a true designer than a month of sixpenny days at a stuffy museum. The old masters are dead, but "the flowers," as Victor Hugo says, "the flowers last always."

Notes

1 W. Morris, Preface, *Arts and Crafts Essays* (London: Rivington Percival, 1893), p xii.
2 W. Crane, 'Of the Revival of Design and Handicraft: With Notes on the Work of the Arts and Crafts Exhibition Society', *Arts and Crafts Essays* (London: Rivington Percival, 1893), p. 13.
3 'Arts and Crafts', *Saturday Review of Politics, Literature, Science and Art*, 76, 1981, 14 October 1893, p. 448.
4 *The Builder*, 10 October 1891, p. 207.
5 Syon Cope: Embroidered ecclesiastical cloak, (1310–1320, made); Victoria and Albert Museum, London.
6 Shakespeare: *Pericles*, Act V.
7 *The Botanical Magazine; or Flower-Garden Displayed*, was an illustrated publication which began in 1787 and is widely referred to by the subsequent name *Curtis's Botanical Magazine*.
8 *Sutton's Illustrated Catalogue:* a catalogue of a seed company established in 1806.

42

FRED MILLER, 'DESIGN AND CRAFTSMANSHIP'

The British artist and naturalist, Fred Miller, was also a widely published author on arts and crafts topics. He explains his entry into the world of design and crafts, which incidentally gives an interesting impression of art school training.

> The training I received at the West London School of Art was of a very rule-of-thumb character – drawing from uninteresting casts in a heated, fetid underground cellar, where the tuition, meagre as it was, was of as mechanical a character as the work during the day, and so deadening was it that after a while I dropped going to the school. During my pupillage I developed a certain amount of technical facility, but I was sadly deficient in knowledge of form . . . It was like reciting in a language one did not understand'.[1]

This publication was the amalgamation and development of a series of articles. Miller contributed to the *Art Journal* on art, crafts and craftsmen.[2] Miller's attitude to design teaching is clear in the following passage:

> I am inclined to think that old work has hitherto been thrust too prominently before the student to the exclusion of all else, with the result that he wearies of it, and would consign it to its fitting burial-place, the gloomy recesses of a museum. The same old casts which for years have hung up in schools of art have bred contempt because of one's familiarity with them. The work that is being wrought by our contemporaries is, as it should be, of a more stimulating and vivid interest to a student than any efforts of a bygone age, and I have therefore excluded old examples in this work, save in a few instances, so that the reader may learn, if he will, of his contemporaries by seeing what they are doing.[3]

A poor review in *The Academy* educational supplement pointed out that 'Although we are quite willing to allow that Mr Fred Miller is a practitioner of no mean ability in several different departments of art industry, it is clear that the literary gift is not to be reckoned among them'.[4] Another reviewer concurred but also lamented the design of the book: 'It is, upon the face of it, lamentable that the author of an otherwise meritorious work should have concerned himself so little with, or have been so little able to effect, the production of a decently "got up" book. Mr. Miller has produced one that is singularly distasteful in *format* and that is equally lacking in literary distinction'.[5]

The British Architect's anonymous reviewer of the book was more conciliatory and even supportive of some of the ideas: 'design and craftsmanship, [as] Mr Miller very properly maintains, are one, and should be indivisible. Design in its relation to a handicraft cannot be properly considered apart from the limitations of material and method of working. And therefore "the only training worth anything is working under a practical man," in fact taking a course in the workshops and studios now offering such cheap facilities to all who are willing to learn'.[6]

Miller published a number of books on woodworking, glass painting, and interior decoration and also wrote numerous articles on arts and crafts topics including many for *The Girl's Own Paper*.[7]

Fred Miller, 'Design and Craftsmanship', *The Training of a Craftsman* (London: J.S. Virtue & Co Limited 1898), pp. 24–35

Chapter II

Design and Craftsmanship

The two are one, and should be indivisible, for no craftsman can be full statured who is not an artist, and no designer can succeed in applied art who is not something of a craftsman, and for this reason. You must know what are the particular qualities to be brought out in each craft before you can design for it. We will assume that you are going to use the Oriental poppy as the *motif*, and it has to be adapted to three different purposes—a repoussé cup, a painted tile, and a piece of embroidery. Now, it might be imagined that to make one design would be sufficient, and that it could be used with slight modifications for the three crafts. As a matter of fact, that is what would have been done in my apprenticeship days, for anything was good enough *then* for decorative art; but now that the art crafts have been recognised as taking quite as high a place in man's handiwork as any other art (so-called *fine*), a more reasonable practice is followed, and the student beating a cup would seize upon certain characteristics of the poppy because the beaten metal will render some feature of the poppy better than could be obtained by a painted tile, while the embroiderer, again, would develop some other characteristic of the plant to suit the requirements of his work. The first thing, therefore, is to study the requirements of your craft, so that you may develop them to the utmost, and your design is therefore conditioned by the necessity of bringing out the qualities of the material you work in.

Let us look at the matter a little closer. In repoussé work your effect is produced by beating some parts of the metal in high relief, and throwing others back, and this breaking up of the surface to produce light and shade is the first and chief point to be aimed at. Now, an oriental poppy has a hairy surface, but this is a peculiarity which the metal-worker can hardly, if at all, take into account, because beaten metal would not be helped by having the surface broken up minutely to give the effect of hair: it is a feature of the plant he can afford to ignore. But the tile painter might easily hint at the hairy surface if he chose to, because he is using a much more flexible material than the metal-worker—one in which greater delicacy of manipulation is possible. The embroiderer, again, has a much less flexible material to deal with than the tile-painter. To obtain the effect of roundness or relief is almost an impossibility, or, at all events, would be a matter of excessive labour, out of all proportion to the effect produced, and further, embroidery does not depend for its effect upon the quality we find in repoussé work, but upon a pleasing disposition of lines where form is only hinted at and not simulated.

It will be noticed that I have been assuming that one man is called upon to make designs for three different crafts, not necessarily for himself to carry out; on the contrary, the work is split up between two classes of workers, the design being the work of one and the execution of another. This is making the worker a mere finger machine, and the designer the so-called thinking machine, and is just what we want to avoid. The craftsman should be his own designer; in fact, design should be developed out of finger dexterity. To show his skill as a metal-worker, and his appreciation of the quality of the material he works in, should suggest the design. The relationship is so *intime* between the material and the design wrought upon it that the two are, as I said at the beginning of this chapter, one, and should be indissoluble. It is practically impossible to make a design on paper, say, for a repoussé cup, which shall bear any close relationship to the cup when beaten, and even a design for embroidery bears only a slight affinity to the same when wrought with the needle, for a line on paper has none of the value of the same made up of stitches on a woven surface; and unless this is borne in mind, the apparent poverty of a working design induces the designer to endeavour to obtain richness by elaborating the design on paper, with the result that, when carried out, the work is wanting in simplicity, doesn't seem to fit the material or the material fit the design, and this because the design is made independent of the method of reproduction, instead of being developed out of it.

A student should train himself as a designer at the same time that he is acquiring the *techne* of his craft, and there should never be a time when the one is thought more of than the other, for the reason I have given that the two play into each other and do not exist separately. This is no arbitrary statement, for if we consider the matter, the tyro has so limited an amount of skill that only a very simple design can be attempted by him, but as his hand cunning increases, his desire for more elaborate work will manifest itself; and though it may take a wrong direction at times and lead him to do what should never be attempted, he will by degrees learn the class of effect his material most adequately renders, and within the conditions imposed upon him by his craft work to the best end.

It is some time before the student sets the full value upon his material and directs his energies to developing its particular qualities. In this connection I may mention that in my early days as a glass painter I was shown on one occasion a highly naturalesque piece of glass-painting. It was a head after Guido, and looked not unlike an indifferent oleograph.[8] I had hitherto only seen glass painted in the severe manner of the fourteenth century, and this rococo piece of glass painting delighted me because it looked *so much like a picture*. No reason was given me why this highly enamelled glass picture was not worthy the praise I bestowed on it. I was merely snubbed and laughed at for admiring it, whereas, had it been pointed out to me that to attempt to paint a picture on glass was putting the material to the worst possible use, and was not developing its resources, but, on the contrary, was doing quite the opposite, it would have saved me some misdirected energy later on. It is the duty of the teacher to direct the student's attention quite as much to what is most worth doing as it is how best to do it, and this should be done by appealing to the student's reason rather than by sneering at his prejudices. The student can be helped, too, by being shown good examples of old and modern work in which the resources of the particular craft are developed on right lines. As to what these right lines are the following chapters will make some attempt at showing.

How entirely design is controlled by method of reproduction is seen in the economy of means to end. Human labour is a valuable thing, and should be highly prized and reverently and economically employed. To use it inadequately by misdirecting it or undervaluing it is thriftlessness or worse. A designer unacquainted with the technique of the craft he essays to work for is almost certain to fall into one or both errors. I hold strongly that the maximum of effect should be produced with the minimum of effort. Craftsmanship is the result of a series of well-directed single efforts, each representing so much physical and mental power. Each of these efforts, therefore, should be valued, so that no waste takes place, and the beauty of hand labour is seen largely in the "trick of the tool's true play." Machine work cannot have this, as a machine can only facsimile a particular piece of work the required number of times. It can therefore secure you great accuracy, and give you work which is "faultily faultless, icily regular, splendidly null."[9] It were surely wrong, therefore, to try to make machinery give you the nervous irregularity of the hand as to put the hand to do what a machine so unerringly accomplishes. These remarks are truisms I know, and yet how constantly we see them disregarded. It is only quite recently that the beauty of beaten silver in spoons, for instance, has been recognised, simply because our eyes had grown accustomed to the highly polished surface which we grew to think indispensable to plate. Habit and custom largely govern taste, because so few of us think independently and act for ourselves. Yet it is in the breaking away from the established order of things that our personality finds expression, and an original turn is given to work. You use tradition and are guided by precedent, but are not bounded by it. You must avail yourself of the past or you get no further than the painted mask outside a wig-wam, but from what is known and has been accomplished you stretch out to the unknown and reach forward to that which is waiting for you to do.

Mr. George Frampton[10] put this to me very graphically by roughly sketching on the back of a letter the two diagrams I have redrawn, as they better explain what one means than many words. You have a long narrow space to decorate let us say. One very familiar plan is to have an undulating line with scrolls springing from it, and flowers and leaves to fill up (Fig. 42.1). The man who first hit upon this certainly succeeded in filling his space in a very admirable way so admirable, indeed, that many of us have not troubled to think out any other way, but content ourselves with small modifications of it.

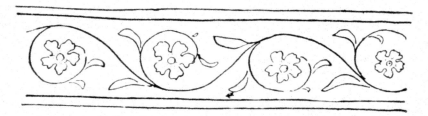

Fig. 42.1

But a craftsman might come along who, disregarding this scrolly arrangement, took two such well-known forms as he cabbage and daisy, and, arranging them something as in Fig. 42.2, broke away at once from tradition, and showed us that there was one other way at least of decorating a long narrow space.

Fig. 42.2

The same sculptor, referring to a memorial to Mitchell, the shipbuilder,[11] which he was working at the last time I was in his *atelier*, told me that people have grown so accustomed to pillars and capitals in architecture. that when he divided his panels with conventionalised tree trunks, and foliage, they felt almost outraged, and one architect expostulated with him on the enormity of his proceeding. Yet because pillars have been used for so many centuries, it does not follow that there is no other way of supporting an arch or dividing a series of architectural spaces or niches, and yet the man who breaks away from tradition is certain to bring down a storm of criticism upon him from those who cannot open their minds to a new impression.

The very original treatment of a wooden capital to a pillar in the handsome fireplace exhibited at the "Arts and Crafts" in 1896 was condemned by some architects, because it did not follow custom or conform to rule—was not a "capital" in their sense, in fact!

The one thing craftsmen have to fight for is liberty to express themselves in their own way. It will take time to effect, but events hasten at certain periods in the world's history, and I foresee that as the public is much more ready to accept new departures than it was in the days of my pupilage, it will before long demand originality, or, at all events, personality, in all work: the crafts will have to be steeped in the ego of those who wrought them, instead of being cut out to some pattern which custom has termed the style of so and so. Style will not then mean some arbitrary arrangement, and the craftsman treated as a piece of cloth pinned to a paper pattern by which to shape him, but will be recognised as individuality, the expression of a trained mind and skilled fingers rejoicing in its work.

That division of art into "Fine" and that which is not fine is of course a wholly misleading one, and shows a great lack of appreciation as to what constitutes art on the part of those who make such a division. No such distinction can be made, for the same impulses are stirred, whether you paint a portrait or carve a pew end. Thought, imagination, an eye for proportion, hand cunning, the result of long training, are required wherever art is produced. The artist should throw himself just as strongly into his work, whether he choose to carve, work in metal, or paint on canvas. The idea that anything will do because the work is not bounded by a gilt frame is happily dying out. There is no higher or lower art; it is all to be judged from the same platform. As Ruskin says, "The only essential distinction between decorative and other art is the being fitted for a fixed place; and in that place, related, either in subordination or in command, to the effect of other pieces of art. And all the greatest art which the world has produced is thus fitted for a place, and subordinated to a purpose. There is no existing highest order art but is decorative. The best sculpture yet produced has been the decoration of a temple front—the best painting the decoration of a room."[12]

The tendency to specialisation which comes of the sub-division of work in these days is very detrimental to the development of a craftsman. Physically, change of work is rest, and an artist tired of one work can by change of labour achieve what idleness cannot. The great men of the past did everything in their calling, and some of the marked personalities in the present day are all-round workers. Witness, Alfred Gilbert,[13] George Frampton,[14] and Alex Fisher,[15] to take three names occurring to me, and the reproductions of the work of the last two in these pages.

Before taking up some of the more prominent art crafts individually, I wish to make it clear to the reader that what follows is not a series of "lessons" on these crafts, but an examination of the principles underlying the successful practice of them, with special reference to the work of modern craftsmen. The only training worth anything is working under a practical man, for technique cannot be imparted successfully by written directions, and training in the art crafts can be obtained much more easily now than it could a few years since. At the end of the book will be found a few of the schools in London where instruction is given in the crafts, with some of the teachers engaged; but instruction in hand-cunning, however thorough it be, is not the only teaching necessary. Work must exhibit taste as well as skill, and harmony between means and end, by which I mean that every craftsman should so work that the utmost is made of the particular quality inherent in each craft. Wood should not be carved as though it were stone, or glass painted as though it were a canvas; and it will be my endeavour to point out what is the direction one's work should take to secure the best results—best, that is, from the point of view of the craft itself, for on the question of "design" dogmatism is *de trop*;[16] besides, what little of a definite nature I have had to say on that subject has already been said.

Notes

1. F. Miller, *The Training of a Craftsman* (London: J.S. Virtue & Co. Limited, 1898), pp. 8–9. The West London School of Art was established under the Department of Science and Art in 1862 at 204 Great Portland Street, London.
2. See for example, F. Miller, 'Women Workers in the Art Crafts', *The Art Journal*, 58, 1896, pp. 116–118.
   F. Miller, 'Some Gold, Silver, and Coppersmiths', *The Art Journal*, 58, 1896, pp. 345–349.
3. F. Miller, *The Training of a Craftsman*, p. 4.
4. *Academy* Educational Supplement, January 15, 1898, p. 69.
5. 'The Training of a Craftsman', *The Artist: An Illustrated Monthly Record of Arts, Crafts and Industries*, 1898, p. 114.
6. 'Architect and Craftsman', *British Architect*, 49, January 7, 1898, pp. 2–4.
7. See for examples https://www.victorianvoices.net/topics/crafts/miller.shtml. Accessed 12 June 2020.
8. Oleograph: A type of coloured lithograph which has been impressed with a canvas grain effect and varnished, so as to make it look like an oil painting.
9. Alfred Lord Tennyson, *Maud*.
10. Sir George James Frampton, (1860–1928), sculptor.
11. Memorial to Charles Mitchell (1820–1895) ship builder and munitions manufacturer, 1898. North aisle of St. George's Church, Jesmond, Northumberland.
12. J. Ruskin: *The Two Paths*, 1859, Lecture III.
13. Alfred Gilbert (1854–1934), English sculptor and goldsmith.
14. George Frampton (1860–1928), English sculptor.
15. Alex Fisher (1864–1936), English silversmith and painter active in the Arts and Crafts movement.
16. *de trop*: unwelcome.

43

THORSTEIN VEBLEN, 'PECUNIARY CANONS OF TASTE'

Thorstein Veblen (1857–1929) was a Norwegian-American economist and sociologist, who, during his lifetime, emerged as a well-known critic of capitalism. An academic for most of his career, Veblen's first appointment was in 1892 when he was selected for a post in the economics department of the University of Chicago. Here he produced two significant works, *The Theory of the Leisure Class* (1899) and *The Theory of Business Enterprise* (1904). Veblen left Chicago in 1906 and after two other appointments he moved to New York in 1918, where he was an editor at *The Dial* and assisted in the foundation of the New School for Social Research. Veblen was also managing editor of the *Journal of Political Economy* between 1895 and 1906.

In terms of design, his interest in anthropological approaches to economic problem that addressed issues of aesthetics and material cultures is valuable. Veblen's idea of 'economic beauty' laid emphasis on the aspects of utility, minimalism, and low budget over the aesthetic aspects that he saw as expressing class distinctions. These aims were best achieved using machinery and large-scale production methods. His concept of a new commercial as well as ethical basis for design and production of consumer goods rejected expensive hand made products and replaced them with simple, unadorned, machine-assisted productions that would be widely available. His concept seems quite close to the discussion around the form should follow function discussion already established by the sculptor Horatio Greenough and the contemporary American architect Louis Sullivan.

In this work, *The Theory of the Leisure Class* (1899), Veblen created the familiar notions of conspicuous consumption and conspicuous leisure. His comments on aesthetic beauty and pecuniary beauty are of interest in relation to design, whereby aesthetic beauty is seen as functional, whilst pecuniary beauty is considered ostentatious and 'wasteful'. In other words, the more complex an item is, the more it becomes simply a symbol of affluence. This apparently functionalist ethic is evident in this passage:

> So far as the economic interest enters into the constitution of beauty, it enters as a suggestion or expression of adequacy to a purpose, a manifest and readily inferable subservience to the life process. This expression of economic

facility or economic serviceability in any object – what may be called the economic beauty of the object – is best served by neat and unambiguous suggestion of its office and its efficiency for the material ends of life.[1]

In terms of design and craft, Veblen explained his theory in relation to William Morris's Kelmscott Press printed products. He saw them as examples of the conspicuous waste that symbolised the prevailing attitudes to consuming.

> The Kelmscott Press reduced the matter to an absurdity – as seen from the point of view of brute serviceability alone – by issuing books for modern use, edited with the obsolete spelling, printed in black-letter, and bound in limp vellum fitted with thongs. As a further characteristic feature which fixes the economic place of artistic book-making, there is the fact that these more elegant books are, at their best, printed in limited editions.

On top of this, his argument about the apparent 'exaltation of the defective' suggested that these superior products were probably less serviceable and readable than modern examples, but they bestow upon the owner not only a pecuniary distinction but apparently are also examples of superior aesthetic taste. The botanist and sociologist Lester Ward, also the first president of the American Sociological Association, pointed out in a review of *Theory of the Leisure Class* that taste is often irrational:

> No biologist can fail to observe parallels in the organic world to many of the facts set forth in this book. Space forbids their enumeration, but one can scarcely refrain from noting among nature's many wasteful ways the phenomena of secondary sexual characters, typified by the antlers of the stag and the gaudy tail of the peacock. These may be compared to wasteful human fashions, such as are enumerated in the chapter on 'Pecuniary Canons of Taste.' The principal difference is that nature, in producing these useless and cumbersome organs, has really given them a high degree of intrinsic beauty, even as judged by human tastes, while the products of human fashion, based on the canon of ' pecuniary beauty,' or costliness, are useless impediments to activity without the slightest claim upon any rational standard of taste.[2]

Thorstein Veblen, 'Pecuniary Canons of Taste', *The Theory of the Leisure Class: An Economic Study of Institutions* (New York: The Macmillan Company, 1899), pp. 157–165

Chapter 6: Pecuniary Canons of Taste

The habit of looking for the marks of superfluous expensiveness in goods, and of requiring that all goods should afford some utility of the indirect or invidious sort, leads to a change in the standards by which the utility of goods is gauged.

The honorific element and the element of brute efficiency are not held apart in the consumer's appreciation of commodities, and the two together go to make up the unanalysed aggregate serviceability of the goods. Under the resulting standard of serviceability, no article will pass muster on the strength of material sufficiency alone. In order to completeness and full acceptability to the consumer it must also show the honorific element. It results that the producers of articles of consumption direct their efforts to the production of goods that shall meet this demand for the honorific element. They will do this with all the more alacrity and effect, since they are themselves under the dominance of the same standard of worth in goods, and would be sincerely grieved at the sight of goods which lack the proper honorific finish. Hence it has come about that there are today no goods supplied in any trade which do not contain the honorific element in greater or less degree. Any consumer who might, Diogenes-like,[3] insist on the elimination of all honorific or wasteful elements from his consumption, would be unable to supply his most trivial wants in the modern market. Indeed, even if he resorted to supplying his wants directly by his own efforts, he would find it difficult if not impossible to divest himself of the current habits of thought on this head; so that he could scarcely compass a supply of the necessaries of life for a day's consumption without instinctively and by oversight incorporating in his home-made product something of this honorific, quasi-decorative element of wasted labour.

It is notorious that in their selection of serviceable goods in the retail market, purchasers are guided more by the finish and workmanship of the goods than by any marks of substantial serviceability. Goods, in order to sell, must have some appreciable amount of labour spent in giving them the marks of decent expensiveness, in addition to what goes to give them efficiency for the material use which they are to serve. This habit of making obvious costliness a canon of serviceability of course acts to enhance the aggregate cost of articles of consumption. It puts us on our guard against cheapness by identifying merit in some degree with cost. There is ordinarily a consistent effort on the part of the consumer to obtain goods of the required serviceability at as advantageous a bargain as may be; but the conventional requirement of obvious costliness, as a voucher and a constituent of the serviceability of the goods, leads him to reject as under grade such goods as do not contain a large element of conspicuous waste.

It is to be added that a large share of those features of consumable goods which figure in popular apprehension as marks of serviceability, and to which reference is here had as elements of conspicuous waste, commend themselves to the consumer also on other grounds than that of expensiveness alone. They usually give evidence of skill and effective workmanship, even if they do not contribute to the substantial serviceability of the goods; and it is no doubt largely on some such ground that any particular mark of honorific serviceability first comes into vogue and afterward maintains its footing as a normal constituent element of the worth of an article. A display of efficient workmanship is pleasing simply as such, even where its remoter, for the time unconsidered outcome is futile. There is a gratification of the artistic sense in the contemplation of skilful work. But it is also to be added that no such evidence of skilful workmanship, or of ingenious and effective adaptation of means to end, will, in the long run, enjoy the approbation of the modern civilised consumer unless it has the sanction of the canon of conspicuous waste.

The position here taken is enforced in a felicitous manner by the place assigned in the economy of consumption to machine products. The point of material difference between machine-made goods and the handwrought goods which serve the same purposes is, ordinarily, that the former serve their primary purpose more adequately. They are a more perfect product—show a more perfect adaptation of means to end. This does not save them from disesteem and depreciation, for they fall short under the test of honorific waste. Hand labour is a more wasteful method of production; hence the goods turned out by this method are more serviceable for the purpose of pecuniary reputability; hence the marks of hand labour come to be honorific, and the goods which exhibit these marks take rank as of higher grade than the corresponding machine product. Commonly, if not invariably, the honorific marks of hand labour are, certain imperfections and irregularities in the lines of the hand-wrought article, showing where the workman has fallen short in the execution of the design. The ground of the superiority of hand-wrought goods, therefore, is a certain margin of crudeness. This margin must never be so wide as to show bungling workmanship, since that would be evidence of low cost, nor so narrow as to suggest the ideal precision attained only by the machine, for that would be evidence of low cost.

The appreciation of those evidences of honorific crudeness to which handwrought goods owe their superior worth and charm in the eyes of well-bred people is a matter of nice discrimination. It requires training and the formation of right habits of thought with respect to what may be called the physiognomy of goods. Machine-made goods of daily use are often admired and preferred precisely on account of their excessive perfection by the vulgar and the underbred who have not given due thought to the punctilios of elegant consumption. The ceremonial inferiority of machine products goes to show that the perfection of skill and workmanship embodied in any costly innovations in the finish of goods is not sufficient of itself to secure them acceptance and permanent favour. The innovation must have the support of the canon of conspicuous waste. Any feature in the physiognomy of goods, however pleasing in itself, and however well it may approve itself to the taste for effective work, will not be tolerated if it proves obnoxious to this norm of pecuniary reputability.

The ceremonial inferiority or uncleanness in consumable goods due to "commonness," or in other words to their slight cost of production, has been taken very seriously by many persons. The objection to machine products is often formulated as an objection to the commonness of such goods. What is common is within the (pecuniary) reach of many people. Its consumption is therefore not honorific, since it does not serve the purpose of a favourable invidious comparison with other consumers. Hence the consumption, or even the sight of such goods, is inseparable from an odious suggestion of the lower levels of human life, and one comes away from their contemplation with a pervading sense of meanness that is extremely distasteful and depressing to a person of sensibility. In persons whose tastes assert themselves imperiously, and who have not the gift, habit, or incentive to discriminate between the grounds of their various judgments of taste, the deliverances of the sense of the honorific coalesce with those of the sense of beauty and of the sense of serviceability—in the manner already spoken of; the resulting composite valuation serves as a judgment of the object's beauty or its serviceability, according as the valuer's bias or interest inclines him to apprehend the object in the one or the other of these aspects. It follows not infrequently that the marks of cheapness or commonness are accepted as definitive marks of artistic unfitness, and a code or schedule of aesthetic proprieties on the one hand, and of aesthetic abominations on the other, is constructed on this basis for guidance in questions of taste.

As has already been pointed out, the cheap, and therefore indecorous, articles of daily consumption in modem industrial communities are commonly machine products; and the generic feature of the physiognomy of machine-made goods as compared with the hand wrought article is their greater perfection in workmanship and greater accuracy in the detail execution of the design. Hence it comes about that the visible imperfections of the hand-wrought goods, being honorific are accounted marks of superiority in point of beauty, or serviceability, or both. Hence has arisen that exaltation of the defective, of which John Ruskin and William Morris were such eager spokesmen in their time; and on this ground their propaganda of crudity and wasted effort has been taken up and carried forward since their time. And hence also the propaganda for a return to handicraft and household industry. So much of the work and speculations of this group of men as fairly comes under the characterisation here given would have been impossible at a time when the visibly more perfect goods were not the cheaper.

It is of course only as to the economic value of this school of aesthetic teaching that anything is intended to be said or can be said here. What is said is not to be taken in the sense of depreciation, but chiefly as a characterisation of the tendency of this teaching in its effect on consumption and on the production of consumable goods.

The manner in which the bias of this growth of taste has worked itself out in production is perhaps most cogently exemplified in the book manufacture with which Morris busied himself during the later years of his life; but what holds true of the work of the Kelmscott Press in an eminent degree, holds true with but slightly abated force when applied to latter-day artistic book-making generally,—as to type, paper, illustration, binding materials, and binder's work. The claims to excellence put forward by the later products of the book-maker's industry rest in some measure on the degree of its approximation to the crudities of the time when the work of book-making was a doubtful struggle with refractory materials carried on by means of insufficient appliances. These products, since they require hand labour, are more expensive; they are also less convenient for use than the books turned out with a view to serviceability alone; they therefore argue ability on the part of the purchaser to consume freely, as well as ability to waste time and effort. It is on this basis that the printers of to-day are returning to "old-style," and other more or less obsolete styles of type which are less legible and give a cruder appearance to the page than the "modern." Even a scientific periodical, with ostensibly no purpose but the most effective presentation of matter with which its science is concerned, will concede so much to the demands of this pecuniary beauty as to publish its scientific discussions in old-style type, on laid paper, and with uncut edges. But books which are not ostensibly concerned with the effective presentation of their contents alone, of course go farther in this direction. Here we have a somewhat cruder type, printed on hand-laid, deckel-edged paper, with excessive margins and uncut leaves, with bindings of a painstaking crudeness and elaborate ineptitude. The Kelmscott Press reduced the matter to an absurdity—as seen from the point of view of brute serviceability alone—by issuing books for modern use, edited with the obsolete spelling, printed in black-letter, and bound in limp vellum fitted with thongs. As a further characteristic feature which fixes the economic place of artistic bookmaking, there is the fact that these more elegant books are, at their best, printed in limited editions. A limited edition is in effect a guarantee—somewhat crude, it is true—that this book is scarce and that it therefore is costly and lends pecuniary distinction to its consumer.

The special attractiveness of these book-products to the book-buyer of cultivated taste lies, of course, not in a conscious, naïve recognition of their costliness and superior clumsiness. Here, as in the parallel case of the superiority of hand-wrought articles over machine products, the conscious ground of preference is an intrinsic excellence imputed to the costlier and more awkward article. The superior excellence imputed to the book which imitates the products of antique and obsolete processes is conceived to be chiefly a superior utility in the aesthetic respect; but it is not unusual to find a well-bred book-lover insisting that the clumsier product is also more serviceable as a vehicle of printed speech. So far as regards the superior aesthetic value of the decadent book, the chances are that the book-lover's contention has some ground. The book is designed with an eye single to its beauty, and the result is commonly some measure of success on the part of the designer. What is insisted on here, however, is that the canon of taste under which the designer works is a canon formed under the surveillance of the law of conspicuous waste, and that this law acts selectively to eliminate any canon of taste that does not conform to its demands. That is to say, while the decadent book may be beautiful, the limits within which the designer may work are fixed by requirements of a non-aesthetic kind. The product, if it is beautiful, must also at the same time be costly and ill adapted to its ostensible use. This mandatory canon of taste in the case of the book-designer, however, is not shaped entirely by the law of waste in its first form; the canon is to some extent shaped in conformity to that secondary expression of the predatory temperament, veneration for the archaic or obsolete, which in one of its special developments is called classicism.

Notes

1 T. Veblen, 'Pecuniary Canons of Taste', *The Theory of The Leisure Class: An Economic Study of Institutions* (New York: The Macmillan Company, 1899), p. 152.
2 L. F. Ward, Review, 'Thorstein Veblen the Theory of the Leisure Class', *American Journal of Sociology,* 5, 6, May 1900, pp. 829–837.
3 Diogenes of Sinope: the embodiment of the Greek philosophical sect- the cynics- that stressed stoic self-sufficiency and the spurning of luxury.

44

ESTHER WOOD, 'HOME ARTS AND INDUSTRIES EXHIBITION'

Esther Wood (1866–1952) was a British art critic, author of *Dante Rossetti and the Pre-Raphaelite Movement* (1894), and an early member of both the Fabian Society and the Independent Labour Party. She married J. W. Wood in 1893 and then followed him in joining the Social Democratic Federation.

The Home Arts and Industries Association founded in 1884 by Eglantyne Louisa Jebb as the 'Cottage Arts Association' changed its name in 1885. The organisation sought to revive traditional rural crafts which were threatened by the mechanisation of production and by increasing urbanisation. In conformity with the thinking of John Ruskin and with Arts and Crafts philosophy, supporters believed that flourishing traditional crafts helped sustain rural communities and provided workers with far more personal satisfaction than was possible for factory workers. The Association funded schools and organised marketing opportunities for craftspeople. By 1889 it had 450 classes, 1,000 teachers and 5,000 students.

The first of the Associations' annual exhibitions took place in July 1885 and by 1888 were large enough to take place annually in the Royal Albert Hall, until 1913. In 1904 the *Art Workers' Quarterly* explained that the association, 'is a society for teaching the working classes handicrafts such as wood carving, inlaying, metal repoussé, basket weaving, leather work, book binding, and for encouraging these and others such as lace, embroidery spinning, weaving, pottery etc., by means of an annual exhibition'.

A report published in *The Edinburgh Review*, October 1906,[1] used the annual exhibition to discuss the nature of the Home Arts and Industries Association's displays. The reviewer concluded that, as examples of design, the items on display were often lacking in any understanding of aesthetic excellence or design principles, although it was acknowledged that the association promoted a useful purpose in local cottage industry. The review was linked to another review of a book on Greek art, which allowed the reviewer to make comparisons between the two.

The *British Architect,* in a supportive review of the Association, made the point that 'Good work and clever design, however produced, is urgently needed in England to compete with foreign production, and if associations will help to this end they are to be most cordially welcomed'. The journal expressed the need for the association to recruit 'teachers who knew *how* to teach and *what* to teach'. In relation to this schooling, they went on to say 'Mere daintiness, prettiness, and fineness of manipulation will, we trust, be left to take care of themselves, and the main facts of sound artistic design, and direct expressive workmanship kept always to the fore front, as the main things to aim at'.[2]

Esther Wood was pleased to report that women's work was rising above the level of bazaars and home-made fancy work: 'One of the healthiest symptoms of progress observable amongst the exhibits was the increased production of useful commodities, and the corresponding decrease in merely ingenious ornaments and bric-à-brac'.[3] Oddly, this same paragraph was repeated verbatim two years later in *The Studio* review of the 1901 Glasgow Exhibition.[4]

Esther Wood, 'Home Arts and Industries Exhibition', *The Studio*, 17, 1899, pp. 99–109

Those who have visited the exhibition of the Home Arts and Industries Association[5] year by year will quickly recognise those features of interest which have become associated with certain class-holders and the districts they have worked. We know, for instance, that we may expect good metal *repoussé* from Keswick and Five-mile-town, and from Mrs. Waterhouse's pupils at Yattendon;[6] from these also sound joinery and wood-carving, as well as from the large class at Southwold.[7] We shall look for wood-inlay from Stepney and Pimlico, and from Bolton-on-Swale, through the efforts of the Hon. Mrs. Carpenter and the Hon. Mabel de Grey; for good textiles and tapestries from Ashridge, Aldeburgh, Windermere, and from the Haslemere industries[8] organised by Mr. and Mrs. Godfrey Blount; and for leather-embossing from Miss Bassett's and Miss Baker's classes at Leighton Buzzard and Porlock Weir; while the little group of workers inspired by Mr. and Mrs. G. F. Watts at Compton and Limnerslease[9] may be counted on for something worthy in the direction of terra-cotta modelling and the minor decorative branches of church architecture. The mortuary chapel in their own village (described in the STUDIO for September last), on which these students have been engaged for some time, should now be near completion. Judging from the beautiful little altar [. . .], and other portions that have already been seen, the building should be a monument of what sincere and patient craftsmanship can do with limited resources under teachers like these. The altar is of terra-cotta, modelled in small panels, each by a different member of the class. The designs, by Mrs. G. F. Watts, are simple, but full of delicate symbolism, and vary from each other just sufficiently to interest without wearying the worshippers' eyes. The decoration of the reredos consists of a copy of Mr. Watts's well-known picture, *The All-pervading*.

Passing along the stands laden with handiwork from all manner of obscure and quaintly-named corners of the British Isles, the previous standard of excellence seemed well maintained, and even challenged by some of the newest classes. One of the healthiest symptoms observable amongst the exhibits was the increased production of useful commodities, and the corresponding decrease in merely ingenious ornaments and bric-a-brac. Hence we were spared that most mischievous development of industrial shows, the "utilisation of waste," in which ingenuity and patience are exhausted in applying remnants of material to purposes for which they are wholly unfit; and there were fewer of the bazaar like "fancy articles" in which fancy of the most vagrant sort has closed all doors by which true imagination might enter and fire the godhead of art. A very encouraging number of exhibitors reached that point of vision at which "the hand refrains," and through the discipline of reticence and sympathy "the soul attains" some measure of its ideal.

The workmanship in most of the classes improves steadily year by year. The Southwold cabinetmakers still rank high in this respect; their splendid technique has already been commended in these pages. In the metal-work there was greater homogeneity of construction and design, and there were very few good things spoilt by bad setting. A handsome repoussé plaque from Five-mile-town came rather dangerously near this mishap with its commonplace fluted edging; and the little screen from Yattendon, [. . .] did not sit quite comfortably on its frame, though its lightness and daintiness of execution in no way belie the traditions of the class. But the oak chest and cupboard from Mrs. Waterhouse's design were thoroughly admirable pieces of craftsmanship, and their steel hinges and fittings, simple in form and unspoilt in surface, made a rich harmony with the natural surface of the wood. The honours of the execution of the works are divided between Charles and George Allum, G. Bastow, Tom Green, Tom Matthews, Alfred Pizzy, Charles Kent, and Charles King.

A very promising class of metal-workers is to be welcomed from Newlyn, whence came the excellent fender we illustrate, made by R. Hodder from J. B. Mackenzie's design. The construction was conspicuously good.[10]

Another very attractive fender came from the Keswick class,[11] and illustrated very happily the proper use of natural forms in decoration. It was of flat pierced brass, with three cats couchant—as the heraldists would have it—broadly outlined in the cutting. This fender, admirably constructed by Joseph Spark, is from a design by Harold Stabler, to whom further praise is due for three beautiful hot-water jugs, [. . .], made in hammered brass and copper by Thomas Spark. In designing for pewter and for somewhat heavier applications of brass and copper, John Williams is still the tutelary genius of Five-mile town.[12] The designs of so able and judicious an artist must be invaluable alike to the novice and to the more advanced craftsmen, for they have a breadth and dignity of line which cannot fail to react well upon the growing style of the executant. The exhibits of this prolific little Irish community included a very pleasing copy of an old lantern by Patrick Roche, a door-plate in hammered copper by Thomas Adams, the plaque in hammered brass above referred to, from a design of mushrooms by John Williams, executed by J. B. Wilson, and a number of mugs, candlesticks, and other light decorative furniture by Robert Mitchell, W. J. Walker, T. Cumberland, and Arthur Adams. In the Christchurch class J. Early showed some simple but unconventional sconces with hanging extinguishers in hammered brass. There was very little wrought-iron work; the best was by Edward and Ernest Edwards, of East Wretham, Norfolk.

In the wood-carving classes held under the Kent County Council in ten villages, the difficulty as to design was very apparent. The work was prolific and ambitious, but poor in ideas. A visiting designer or organiser might be of great service during the coming year. The vigorous little classes at Southwark—Red Cross and Bankside, S.E.—are hampered by the same problem. It must be admitted that some of the best work in wood, metal, and leather is done from stock designs which come as old friends to the annual reunion. Only those who have struggled with mixed classes of beginners know the difficulty of getting original forms or decorations from the students themselves. In the present state of industrial art, a new idea—which should be the starting-point of every creation—is the last thing attained even by the skilled and intelligent mechanic; and this defect is not covered by sacrificing quality to variety, and giving beginners too much licence, either in the invention or the choice of a task. The more experienced teachers have frankly recognised this, and with admirable modesty and good sense have restricted their pupils to copying good models, existing in public collections or supplied by competent modern designers. It requires no little judgment to apportion these in such order as to make for genuine progress in the class; in short, to circulate set designs among average students without falling into something like the boarding-school routine, in which we know that the young lady who exhibited *Dignity and Impudence* at Christmas will achieve *The Sanctuary* in the midsummer term. But the committee are fortunate in having among the class-holders themselves designers of rare and delightful ability, such as Miss Mabel de Grey, Mrs. Carpenter, and Mrs. Hodgson, whose taste and enthusiasm in the art and craft of wood-inlay sustains the work of this branch at a notably high level. In the Pimlico and Stepney classes and at Bolton-on-Swale some very careful and effective pieces of decoration have been done. The best items were a dainty little workbox in which unimpeachable craftsmanship by Edward Ford does due honour to Miss de Grey's design; a panel for a dining-room overmantel by the same artist, laid in rich but mellow-coloured woods by Lewis Ford; and a letter-box with a bright little design of turkeys by Mrs. Carpenter, carried out by Nathan Fawell. In the same group must be mentioned two benches well-constructed and decorated by Arthur Toyer, Geo. Butler, W. and N. Fawell, and a bookcase by Walter Smales, all from Mrs. Carpenter's designs; also an oak chest with a very original and humorous design called *Scandal*—a group of old women sending gossip by the birds—designed by Miss de Grey and executed by John Reason; and an eggcup-stand with a decoration of cocks and hens, designed by Miss May Barker and inlaid by Herbert Shaw. From Little Gaddesden the simple and well-built cupboards inlaid with designs by Mrs. Hodgson were conspicuous for breadth of treatment and richness of colour. The executants were A. Johnson, G. Clifton, W. Fountain, and W. Fenn.

Among the textiles, the Haslemere peasant tapestries deserve especial praise for steady development on bold yet wisely unpretentious lines. Under the tuition of Mrs. Godfrey Blount the villagers have learnt to set simple applique patterns with accurate finish, and often with surprisingly rich effect. Their work should be greatly helped by Mrs. Joseph King's weaving industry in the same district, through which some very fine and substantial fabrics are now being produced. Mrs. Denison's spinning and dyeing classes at Ashridge are doing excellent things, and furthering the use of vegetable pigments. The same praise of colour applies to Miss Garnett's large class at Windermere, who have made some very successful experiments in a mixture of linen and silk. In embroidery and other fancy needlework the London classes show deft and conscientious hands, especially in the Honor Club and the Soho Club for Girls.

The girls trained by Miss Bassett at Leighton Buzzard have achieved a quite enviable reputation for embossed leather, equalled if not surpassed by their friendly rivals, the fishermen of Porlock Weir. One of the most interesting exhibits in this group was the binding of an edition-de-luxe of Spenser's "Shepheard's Calendar," designed by Miss Bassett and executed by Minnie King, who also made the praiseworthy copy of a leather casket at South Kensington Museum. A similar box by Arthur Smallbones, and a smaller one by Ada Coster, were very well decorated and put together. The work of Philip Burgess was the most distinguished product of Miss Baker's class at Porlock Weir, notably in some large embossed panels for a hall, and a handsome travelling writing-case with a decoration of flying seagulls, and the inscription "As cold water to a thirsty soul, so is good news from a far land." Both these exhibits were of Miss Baker's design.

A word may be permitted on a point of order. There is a tendency to ignore the origin of a design which has become the property of the association, and is described on the labels as "H.A.I.A." This hardly seems an adequate acknowledgment to such helpers as Mr. Voysey, Mr. Cave, Mr. Spooner, Mr. Benson, and the ladies who have from time to time supplied original designs. There appears no reason why any piece of art should cease to be duly attributed to its author because he has generously given the copyright for the members' common use.

In such an exhibition much creditable work must perforce remain unnoticed; there was, for instance, a considerable show of Mr. Harold Rathbone's "Della Robbia" pottery from Birkenhead; and in the humbler paths of industry the sound and durable work of the Saxmundham basketmakers certainly deserves mention. One conscientious craftsman may often in this way become the starting-point of a new industrial life; and it is in this light that one sees the wisdom of the committee in maintaining the geographical classification of the work. In the present century the association of places with particular industries has become almost a farce. We know that a great deal of our "Sheffield cutlery" is now made elsewhere, and that the same degeneration has affected our textiles, from Kidderminster carpets to Honiton lace. One of the first battles of industrial reform is surely for the principle of honesty in the naming of goods. and the Home Arts and Industries Association are undoubtedly right in trying to restore the just and reasonable pride of place to their craftsmen. The cultivation of this spirit will raise the whole movement to a more professional level, and redeem it from any lingering reproach as to the charity that covers a multitude of aesthetic sins. The organisation does undoubtedly help a number of capable but variously handicapped amateurs, who could not otherwise compete in the market. But whatever be the motives which sustain devoted teachers amid the discouragements of their task, neither to these nor to any incidents of its fulfilment must the critic lend a sympathetic ear. This way lies the sentimental cul-de-sac into which the sweepings of the art-world have been gathered from all time, by such as cherish little Tommy's painting-book because he is such a beginner, or find a subtle charm in a bad basket because its maker was blind. To judge a piece of art upon its merits is the first principle of criticism, and to invite such judgment is the wish of every serious artist and craftsman. It remains for those who sympathise with the aims of the association to convince the ordinary purchaser that home-made goods of genuine value already await him in the market, and to encourage him by all means to seek and prefer them. There should no longer be any excuse for an English lady to clothe herself in shoddy material, or for her lover to buy her engine-turned jewellery at the ordinary trade shop. How far more gracious is the gift that bears the stamp of humanity in all its parts—a free, sincere, and intelligent utterance of the joy of living!

Notes

1 *Edinburgh Review*, October 1906, pp. 204, 418, 424–446.
2 *British Architect*, 25, 23 June 1886, p. 653
3 E. Wood, 'Home Arts And Industries Exhibition', *The Studio*, 17, 1899, p. 100.
4 *The Studio*, September 1901, p. 169.
5 HAIA was founded in 1884 by Eglantyne Louisa Jebb. The first annual exhibition was held in July 1885 and by 1888 they were in the Royal Albert Hall, an annual occurrence until 1913.
6 The Yattendon (Berkshire) metalworking class was started in 1890 as a brass working course by Mrs Alfred Waterhouse, (wife of the architect Alfred Waterhouse),
7 The Southwold School of Industrial Art established 1894 in Suffolk.
8 Haslemere Peasant Industries, Surrey, was an umbrella organisation for a number of small workshops reviving craft traditions and employing local skilled labour set up by Mr and Mrs Blount.
9 In 1895 Mary Watts ran evening classes at Limnerslease, the Watts nearby residence and studio at Compton, Surrey.
10 The Newlyn Industrial Class was established in 1890 in Cornwall.
11 Keswick School of Industrial Art was founded in 1884 by Canon Rawnsley and his wife Edith as an evening class in woodwork and repoussé metalwork.
12 Fivemiletown, Northern Ireland. In 1892, Mary Montgomery, set up metal craft classes for local men and boys. She had trained in London in repoussé metalwork.

45

OSCAR LOVELL TRIGGS, 'ROOKWOOD: AN IDEAL WORKSHOP'

Oscar Lovell Triggs (1865–1930) was an instructor in English at the University of Chicago from 1895 to 1903. Triggs was the author of several books and edited an 1892 edition of Walt Whitman's *Leaves of Grass*. He was founder of the Saugatuck Press and editor of the 'Bulletin of the Morris Society of Chicago'. His ideas on Arts and Crafts that he called Industrial Art were influential amongst craftspeople. His Industrial Art League (1899–1904) was an unsuccessful attempt to merge education and production into workshops on socialist principles based on his readings of Tolstoy, Whitman, Ruskin, Carlyle, and Morris.

Triggs had many links to Art and Crafts and was a frequent contributor to Stickley's *Craftsman* magazine. Triggs's ideas on industrial socialism were more ambivalent toward the machine than many of his colleagues. He drew on the work of J.A. Hobson and his *Evolution of Modern Capitalism* (1894), arguing that machines could complement handwork in specific ways: 'Order, exactitude, persistence, conformity to unbending law, these are the lessons which must emanate from the machines'.[1]

The Rookwood Pottery that Triggs uses as an example in this text was founded in 1880 in Cincinnati, Ohio, by gifted china painter Maria Longworth Nichols (later Storer) (1849–1932). As well as being involved in the design process, Longworth Nichols ran the business side of the pottery. The Rookwood Pottery went on to be one of the most successful producers of Art Pottery in the United States, winning international acclaim at the 1889 Paris Exposition Universelle and winning more medals at later world's fairs. As might be expected, the business avoided mechanised production and gave the artists wide scope for expression, and importantly, employed many women artist–designers. In line with arts and crafts thinking, the pottery was promoted as being 'an Artist's Studio, not a Factory'.

In a review of this book, the sociologist Charles Richmond Henderson endorsed its values:

> In any case it is refreshing to have our American Philistines, adorers of exports of raw products and steam-driven machinery, stung through

thick and leathery skins by the satire of the artist; to hear them told that we may sell watches and engines in Europe and yet fall short of being quite civilized. And it is wholly sane and inspiring to remind us that it is not the material output of a factory or mill which gives glory to a nation; but that the decisive factor is the kind of men and women who get their living in the factory and mill, and whose blood and flesh are ground up to make 'profits'.[2]

However, not all saw this glory. Thorstein Veblen was critical of the movement and responded to Triggs in an article published soon after. Veblen argued that sentimentality is not economically sensible. He again argued that the 'machine issue' refers to modernity and therefore does have some role in the development of taste.[3]

Oscar Lovell Triggs, 'Rookwood: An Ideal Workshop', *Chapters in the History of the Arts and Crafts Movement* (Chicago: The Bohemia Guild of the Industrial Art League, 1902), pp. 157–162

V. Rookwood: An Ideal Workshop

"The social question," said Mr. Ashbee, in his fifth aphorism, "has prior claim to the artistic."[4] The world slowly adjusts itself to the truth of this statement. The question of art is altogether a question of social reform. Art must grow out of the life. If the life is not so ordered that art will appear as its crown and fulfilment it is idle to foster and upbuild it. To give it independent development is to preserve the empty form and overlook the informing and vitalizing spirit. Those who prate most of art are not the true promoters so much as the thinkers, the social reformers, who are trying to reach a status of true liberty, to destroy slavery of every kind, to humanize industry, and to introduce other motives into production than the commercial and mechanical ones. Hence the Arts and Crafts movement, with its principle of co-operative individualism, is brought into harmony with some of the deepest thought tendencies of the times; with such books as George's "Progress and Poverty," Kropotkin's "Farm, Field, and Factory," Tolstoy's "The Slavery of Our Times," Edward Carpenter's "Angels' Wings," and "Towards Democracy," Whitman's "Leaves of Grass," Crosby's "Plain Talk in Psalm and Parable,"[5] and the writings of Bolton Hall.[6] For when the present system is outworn, and a more just and equal order is established, the order for which these writers are laboring, industry will be the crown of life, and art the crown of industry. Art on any other terms than the contentment of a well-ordered and consistent life is undesired and undesirable.

So long as the factory is organized to the end of making profits for some owner and director, an issue of production in art is practically impossible. The wage slavery of the factory forbids art; the machine forbids it; competition forbids it; the methods of designing and executing by division of labor are against it. The factories that are so constituted that their products rise to the plane of art may be counted on the fingers of one hand. These few, conducting business within the present system, but with higher motives, may be referred to as indicating also the tendency toward workshop reconstruction. Chief among the factories that undertake production from the instinct for beauty—and which enjoy also commercial success—may be counted the Rookwood Pottery at Cincinnati. Instituted as a private industrial experiment by Mrs. Maria Longworth Storer in 1880, it has grown in twenty years to a position of public importance and of far-reaching influence. The aspects of its organization and work that bear upon our present theme may be briefly considered. Three factors evidently conspire to make the Rookwood Pottery what it is—the founder, the workmen, and the public.

The Rookwood Pottery has—so to speak—a soul. A woman's intelligence and affection went to its upbuilding. It is established upon a person. Upon this fact all other features of the factory depend. The motive that controlled the enterprise from the beginning was the desire to produce a perfect product. Below this must have been the intention to perform a social service in perfecting a given product. But perfection is fugitive—how secure [is] it in a workshop involving many hands and minds.

Though the management of the business is centered in a board of directors, the fullest possible freedom is given to the workmen; they are encouraged to experiment, to express their own individuality, and to increase their culture by study and travel. The spirit of the factory is that of co-operation and good fellowship. Mr. Taylor, the genial director, calls himself "the arbiter," expecting initiation from his associates. From the first the problems have been solved as they have arisen from the inside. The factory consequently has its traditions, and its products represent organic growth. Its art is as indigenous as that of the first potter. The principle of construction is to adjust design sympathetically to shape and material. No printing-patterns are permitted, and no copying or imitation is allowed. Division of labor is practiced sufficient to insure technical skill but not to the extent of destroying unity of design. This one fact, unity of design, that for which Rookwood is especially noted, is itself an evidence of the unity of the workers, their absorption in a common purpose. Let discord enter or dissatisfaction be felt, or let the pride of any worker assert itself, or the authority of the director be unduly exercised, and the effect is recorded at once in the product. The problem of uniting a workshop of large membership would seem to be solved here by the cultivation of human sympathy—that delicate something that is the source of all high endeavor.

But the pottery is not merely a workshop; it is in a sense a school of handicraft, an industrial art museum, and a social center. The craftsmen, creating and initiating on their own ground, constantly improve in skill and character. By the employment of apprentices the workshop could be at once transformed into a school. A portion of the building is now devoted to exhibition. By means of lectures, and other entertainments at the pottery, the public participates in some degree in the enterprise, and by reaction shapes the product. Here are all the elements needed for the ideal workshop—a self-directing shop, an incidental school of craft, and an associative public. Standing high on the edge of Mt. Adams, an attractive building in a fair environment—the building an interesting example of Early English architecture, with roof of tile and walls of cement decorated by scratchwork—it is even now a model factory. Its motive, its management, its principles of work, its fine artistic production—all distinguish it from contemporary factories. With only slight changes, by the development of forces already implicit, such a workshop as the reformers have dreamed of could be here and now created.

Notes

1 J. A. Hobson, *Evolution of Modern Capitalism* (London: George Allen and Unwin, 1894), p. 348.
2 C. R. Henderson, 'Chapters in the History of the Arts and Crafts Movement. Oscar Lovell Triggs', *American Journal of Sociology*, 8, 1, July 1902, pp. 138–139.
3 T. Veblen, 'Arts And Crafts', *Journal of Political Economy*, 11, 1, 1902, pp. 108–111.
4 C. R. Ashbee, *A Few Chapters in Workshop Reconstruction and Citizenship* (The Guild and School of Handicraft. 1894), p. 16.
5 H. George, *Progress and Poverty: An Inquiry into the Cause of Industrial Depressions and the Increase of Want with Increase of Wealth; the Remedy* (New York: United States Book Co, 1879)

P.A. Kropotkin, *Fields, Factories and Workshops* (New York: G.P. Putnam's Sons, 1901).

L. Tolstoy, *The Slavery of Our Times* (New York: Dodd, Mead & Company, 1900).

E. Carpenter, *Angles' Wings, A Series of Essays on Art and Its Relation to Life* (London: S. Sonnenschein & Co., 1899).

E. H. Crosby, *Plain Talk in Psalm and Parable . . . Third Edition* (London: Francis Riddell Henderson, 1901).
6 Bolton Hall (1854–1938), American lawyer and activist.

46

J. SCARRATT RIGBY, 'REMARKS ON MORRIS' WORK AND ITS INFLUENCE ON BRITISH DECORATIVE ARTS TODAY'

J. Scarratt Rigby was a designer of textiles and wallpapers in the arts and craft mode for well-known companies including GP & J Baker, A.H. Lee of Birkenhead, and Liberty and Co., and was the honorary secretary of the Society of Designers.[1] In that capacity, he represented them as the Institute of Decorative Designers to the Committee on the Law of Copyright 1900, where he advocated a term of life plus 30/50 years for design copyright. He also railed against the design registration system whereby multiple protection applications were needed to be made for different classes of products (textile, wallpaper etc) He also wrote several reviews and articles on design for the journal *Artist* and this article for the *Art Workers' Quarterly*.

The Art Worker's Quarterly sub-titled 'a portfolio of practical designs for decorative and applied art' was edited by artist and designer, W.G. Paulson Townsend (1868–1941), who was quite widely published in decorative arts subjects. Townsend explained that the journal was intended 'to supply designs in a readily applicable form to those who do not invent, plan, or adapt ornament, and who find difficulty in obtaining good and suitable suggestions for their work. Further, it is his aim to assist those who may have some knowledge of the principles on which ornamental design is constructed, by publishing specimens of good work from the best historical and contemporary examples'.[2]

The journal covered a range of topics including pieces on art schools, craft organisations, exhibitions etc., with useful articles on a range of decorative and applied arts and crafts. The works of major figures in the English Arts and Crafts movement were illustrated and discussed, and a number of them also supplied articles for the journal. It was published in five volumes by Chapman & Hall, London, between 1902 and 1906, and had two further editions. *The Bookman* recommended the journal, when bound in volume form, as its collection of designs and examples of art works would be of interest to craftspeople and the artistic public, and be an ideal 'gift book' for any family which cares that its surroundings shall be in the best taste.[3]

This article is a rather hagiographic résumé of William Morris and his firm's contribution to art crafts and design.

J. Scarratt Rigby, 'Remarks on Morris' Work and Its Influence on British Decorative Arts Today', *The Art Workers' Quarterly: A Portfolio of Practical Designs for Decorative and Applied Art*, January and April 1902, pp. 2–5, 61–63

The impossibility of dealing with the subject of present-day decorative arts without constant reference to the work of William Morris will readily be admitted by most people. Some of these arts almost owe their existence to the prodigious mental force and untiring vigour he brought to bear upon them; in others his work, if examined and compared with that of today, will be seen to be, the direct parent of some important phases; while many which even his enormous capacity was unable to cope with have received inspiration directly from him or from the group of men of whom he was the acknowledged centre of radiation. For William Morris not only worked himself with an unswerving force such as few men are gifted with, but his generous energy inspired those around him with an enthusiasm in his aims which made it possible for him to produce and influence a mass of creative work usually far beyond one man's power.

The beginning of the whole thing was co-operative. Morris found himself at a time when English decorative arts seemed to have just passed its lowest ebb—in the decade following the exhibition of 1851—among a group of artists remarkably and happily in unison in their desire to bring more colour and interest into such work. The outcome as most of us are aware, was the establishment of the firm of Morris, Marshall, Faulkner & Co., which was not so much a firm, as we understand the word, as a co-operative society in the broadest sense of the term. Originally, the aim of this association was simply to supply themselves and their friends with furniture and decoration which would satisfy their artistic taste; it was later when the scheme met with such success, that business premises were opened and the firm launched as a commercial undertaking. In the early days Madox Brown, Rossetti, Burne-Jones, Philip Webb, and others of the group, with Morris himself, supplied designs for furniture, decoration, stained-glass, etc., and assisted in various ways as the need for their work arose, sharing, according to the original scheme, the profits that remains after the firm's expenses, including payment for their work, had been met.

It is not the object here to go into the history of the firm or of Morris work generally, but some account of the latter is necessary to elucidate the theme of the article. In the nature of things, given William Morris's strong and direct individuality it was not long before his became the guiding hand and central influence of the association, a fact which was freely and formally recognised by his partners some years after the formation; and until his death he remained the head of the firm which has now a world-wide reputation.

Addressing themselves to the gigantic task of reforming the decorative art of the time, the association found themselves compelled to face and deal with a number of distinct crafts. Possibly, but for Morris's untiring energy in research and accomplishment, his original methods of thought and exquisite sense of color and composition, and his absorbing love the actual work of creation and production, they might never have been a decorative firm. They would have done some stained-glass and furniture, but in the direction in which they attain success and mostly influenced decorative art, little or nothing would have been done without him. With him, however, the firm's history presents the picture of the inception or revival and serious undertaking of a number of decorative crafts, one after one being attacked, and, within the limits of his strong likings in style, brought to successful issue.

There is no need here to dilate upon the facts of these preferences having become one of the most salient characteristics of the firm. Many of the tentative efforts of the early days of the association showed little sign of breaking away from the traditions of Gothic work; but Morris's grip soon began to make itself felt. The medievalism which appears to be universally recognised as the keynote of his work seems to have been more a matter of temperament than of critical selection. The last of men to be bound by laws he did not like, he instinctively chose only the themes and the styles of work that interested and suited him, caring little so that by their means he could give expression to his ideas and clothe them in the bold form and beautiful colour that were a necessity to his nature.

Easily traceable as it is in many instances to earlier work, and varied as it is, the "Morris" style, therefore, soon became a thing accomplished and distinct; and, to set aside the many imitations which were its inevitable penalty, became the foundation on which some of the most interesting types of the work of today are based. These have been very largely modified from their prototype to suit different methods of work or production, and, moreover, different requirements. For, being the expression of a temperament differing widely from the average temperaments of the day, it follows that its best and most enduring effect upon our work must be indirect rather than direct.

It is in the decorative crafts—as distinct from those that may be termed structural or architectural —that Morris mostly worked, and it is in that direction that "Morris work" has more obviously influenced the work of to-day. Morris himself never designed any considerable quantity of furniture, for instance. In the early days some of the firm's output of furniture was designed by J.P. Seddon and Madox-Brown. Some of the latter's design attracted considerable attention at the early Arts and Crafts Exhibitions, where it was exhibited probably more on account of the interest of the associations surrounding its production than as representing the contemporary work of the firm. But from the commencement of the association Mr. Philip Webb was the designer of practically all the cabinet work, and of whatever had a distinctly architectural character; his place being taken in later years by his pupil Mr. George Jack. A certain amount of painted decoration on furniture passed in early days under Morris's hands; but the bulk of this was done for friends, and does not appear to have been followed up in later times. The firm's cabinet work, as we know it now, is the work of Mr. Philip Webb and his pupil, and expresses, as nearly as anything may be said to do so, the refined development of the ideas that inspired the early group. It is worthy of note that the translation of the rush-bottomed chair from the kitchen to the parlour, where it yet retains a respectable position, was undoubtedly due to the influence of these ideas.

Decorative metal work, a craft which has a position of so much importance today, Morris did not touch, neither has it ever been one of the branches of art practised by his firm. The same may be said of mosaic and enamelling.

From the beginning of the firm the production of the stained glass was essentially co-operative. Madox-Brown, Rossetti, and Morris himself in the early days all made a number of cartoons for this purpose, while in later times the figures in all "Morris" stained glass were supplied by Burne-Jones. Morris himself always took the responsibility of superintending the production of the design in glass, having, at the beginning, gone into the matter with his accustomed thoroughness, labouring at and investigating for himself all the details of glass making, firing, etc., studying from old books ancient methods and aims, and commencing afresh for himself where the workmen of his favourite periods left off. He, if any one person, should be called the "designer" of the glass; the planning, the ornamental work and backgrounds of the figures, and, above all, the colouring were due to him. The details of the ornamental work it was soon found possible to entrust to artists trained in his methods; but the colouring, to him always the most important element, he always kept under his own eye, and to the last was master, and from all accounts conspicuously shone in the work. Burne-Jones's figure cartoons for the glass were more black-and-white drawings than designs, treated, of course, in a perfectly decorative manner but equally adaptable in many cases to, say, tapestry and painting (many of them, indeed, being turned later into pictures). For instance, it was not his practice to show even the lead lines, so essential in design for glass.

Taking as their standard the full, rich, harmonious colouring of mediaeval glass, the association revolted absolutely against the crude and feeble colours of the glass in vogue at the time, and against the practice of over-painting, which they considered directly opposed to the principles which should govern such work. I do not know if they were the first to introduce the glass of the varied and pleasing qualities which we are now accustomed to see used in the best work, but their consistent use of it undoubtedly had much to do with its more general adoption. This glass was used, as in mediaeval work, in small pieces, carefully selected as to colour and quality, with broad lead lines supplying the darks and giving the necessary roundness and definition to the figures, with the minimum of the brown shading that obscures the light. From their published utterances we learn much of their methods, and the principles are undoubtedly those of much of the best work of today. The "white" which was never quite transparent, was used as foil for the rich colours of the pot-metal, the system of relief being always the heraldic one—light upon dark, or dark upon light. The lead lines were therefore part of the background in the one case, part of the figure in the other. Invention, expression, and good dramatic action, with strong and simple drawing, were essential qualities of the design.

REMARKS ON MORRIS' WORK AND ITS INFLUENCE

Tapestry making is one of the latest and one of the most important of the Morris revivals, though probably one that has less direct influence than most on the work of today, for the simple reason that the great expense of the finished work puts it out of the reach of any but the most wealthy. Taking the best of fifteenth-century Flemish tapestries as his models, Morris laid himself out as usual to study and practise for himself all the details of old methods of production, and was not content to call in assistance until he had with his own hands woven a piece to a design of his own of birds and foliage. The early designs were confined to these elements; for the later work Burne-Jones supplied the figures.

This is a craft that Morris valued greatly as the highest expression of textile art, needing great artistic skill, and nothing that could "fairly be called a machine." To use his own words. he looked upon it as "a mosaic of pieces of colour made up of dyed threads. and capable of producing wall ornament of any degree of elaboration within the limits of duly considered decorative work. • • • The first thing to be considered • • • is the force, purity, and elegance of the silhouette of the objects represented, and nothing vague or indeterminable is admissible. • • • Depth of tone, richness of colour, and exquisite gradation of tints are easily to be obtained in tapestry; and it also demands that crispness and abundance of beautiful detail which was the especial characteristic of fully developed mediaeval Art."[4] He rejected totally alike the later historical styles of design and methods of production, considering the open backgrounds and pictorial character of these most unsuitable. The figures, birds, and flowers in his own work, though as lifelike as may be, are designed without shadow, but simply relieved as light on dark, simply shaded as by a front light, and in most cases further definition being given to the principal objects by a firm outline.

The well-known masterpieces, the "Star of Bethlehem" and the set of pieces at Stanmore Hall[5] representing incidents from the "Quest of the Holy Grail," are of course the highest expression this art has ever obtained in this country, or maybe in all time. The work is still in progress at Morris & Co.'s works at Merton Abbey, under the direction of Mr. Dearle, Morris's pupil; and I do not know of any competitors. The great expense involved in labour and in training artists to do the work—some of the pieces have taken two or three workers as many years to complete—prohibit any general use being made of the art.

On the subject of Morris's painted decoration for walls, etc., it is perhaps not necessary to speak at great length. In the early days of the association it was practised to a certain extent for his own and his friends' uses, and in later times the painted decoration at St. James's Palace[6] and Stanmore Hall may be taken as representing the artist's maturer tastes in this direction. In these instances the decorated spaces are covered with pattern-work of scrolls and foliage and flowers of the type with which we are familiar in his manufactured pattern work, executed always in bright and soft colourings. In this work he indulged his love of a profusion of bold form to an extent to which any one less closely wedded to such tastes in art would hardly have ventured. But hand-painted decoration is necessarily costly, and it must soon have become apparent to him that a decoration of pattern work could be accomplished by means much easier, and, to most people, fairly satisfactory; while something more on a level with his own "Arras" tapestry would be a fitter subject for the nobler means of expression.

I think of all the various branches of Morris work, pattern design is the one which has had the most direct influence on the work of today; and it is also one of the branches which may be said to be most completely William Morris's own work. From the early days when, driven to accept this "substitute," as he called it, for hand-worked decoration, and finding it impossible to procure things which reached his own ideals, he commenced the work of pattern designing and manufacture, until almost the end, he was the sole author of nearly every pattern the firm placed upon the market. Neither did he leave us in any doubt as to what his ideals were. His utterances upon the various arts he practised, copious and always delightful, were never more so than when he was talking of patterns, and no excuse is needed for quoting again from them at some length—his aims can never be better set forth than in his own words.

Of wall-paper designing he says: "You may be as intricate and elaborate in your pattern as you please; nay, the more and the more mysteriously you interweave your sprays and stems the better for your purpose, as the whole thing has to be pasted flat on a wall and the cost of all this intricacy will that come out of your own brain and hand. For the rest, the fact that in this art we are so little helped by beautiful and varying material imposes on us and necessity of being especially thoughtful in our designs; every one of them must have a distinct idea in it; some beautiful piece of nature must have pressed itself on our notice so forcibly that we are quite full of it, and can, by submitting ourselves to the rules of art, express our pleasure to others, and give them some of the keen delight that we ourselves have felt."[7] In these latter words one seems to find the keynote of the ideality and "romanticism" to be seen in much pattern design today —qualities very lacking in work prior to Morris's. The former part of the above quotation, in common with the following: "Every one who has practised the designing of patterns knows the necessity for covering the ground equably and richly. This is really to a great extent the secret of obtaining the look of satisfying mystery aforesaid, and it is the very test of capacity in a designer,"[8]—may read some more strangely now, when the leading fashion of the hour, especially on walls, is for sparser and dainty decoration. But Morris worked prior to the general use of the many inventions which now go far to give "quality" to wallpapers; things change to; he worked for his own time, and above all was dominated by his own strong taste for luxuriant and rich decoration. There is a word for the New Art devotee though in Morris's day "L'Art Nouveau" had not risen to the dignity of that appellation: "So I will content myself with saying this on these qualities [invention and imagination], that though a designer may put all manner of strangeness and surprise into his patterns, he must not do so at the expense of beauty. . . . The fertile man, he of resource, has not to worry himself about invention. He need but think of beauty and simplicity of expression; his work will grow on and on, one thing leading to another, as it fairs with a beautiful tree."[9] These are words of gold, needed more today, perhaps, than when they were uttered. Again here is a lesson which I think we may say we of today have learned, and its value is almost as much as the difference between hope and despair in the art: "No pattern should be without some sort of meaning. True it is that the meaning may have come down to us traditionally, and not be our own invention; yet we must at heart understand it, or we can neither receive it, nor hand it down to our successors."[10] Morris evidently thought deeply upon the subject, and held pattern design in a high estimation, which the growing importance of the art during the last quarter of the century has justified.

Without in any way minimising the influence of some designers who were at work when Morris began, and others whose work has held honourable place side-by-side and contemporary with his, it may be allowed that the Morris influence was most largely responsible for bringing the wallpaper art into the position it now enjoys. But no doubt the scheme by which he was enabled to put and keep his designs on the market and always to the fore, without the confusion and want of continuity inevitable under the ordinary commercial conditions of the day, was an almost inestimably large cause of this influence, as, indeed it was of equal value also in other branches of pattern, printed and woven textiles, etc.

Cont./

In his own work in pattern design, in later years, Morris went back, as usual, to his favourite periods, selecting the best, whether it were Sicilian, Byzantine, Italian, or Persian, skipping always the Renaissance, with which he had no sympathy, and looking upon Japan as "outside the pale of evolution in art." In his earlier and more naturalistic work he appears to have fallen more into the humour of his own time and country; and, as some of us think, there were in this qualities, especially in the matters of drawing and the actual designing, which have had more influence on the work of this generation of designers than has his later work.

In wall-papers for instance, some of the earlier designs, such as the "Daisy," "Marigold," "Willow," "Vine," "Acanthus," and "Pimpernel" viewed in the searching light of his own poetical *dicta* of what a pattern should be, will be found to contain the qualities he demands with a degree of vitality which appears to be lacking in some of the later designs of the well-known type of the "Norwich," for instance, where the drawing seems, by contrast, most unsympathetic, the shapes appearing as if they had been cut out in tin.

A somewhat similar divergency is most noticeable in the designs for printed cotton fabrics, where the "Honeysuckle" (produced about 1873) and the "Wandle" (produced about 1884), two of the grandest of Morris's designs, may be taken as typifying two radically different styles of work. The perfect drawing of the "Honeysuckle," the nobility of the planning and the large objects, the wealth of naturalistic detail, yet with quite decorative treatment, have always appealed, and will still most strongly appeal, to designers, in contrast to the "Wandle," which, though incomparably rich in colour effect, and admirably designed for the method of printing adopted by Morris in later years, does not display the same vitality in motive or sympathetic handling in drawing. Possibly the affection we feel for the "Honeysuckle," the great forerunner of the "Cretonne" style, has something to do with our preference for it. The earlier style of work of which we take the "Honeysuckle" as a type, agrees, broadly speaking, with the period prior to the commencement of calico printing by the firm at Merton; the designs made in the later period, and specially for the ancient processes of printing which Morris revived and brought to such perfection on the banks of the Wandle, seem to bear more relation in character to the design he named after that historic stream.

This leads to a matter which may here be spoken of that whereas Morris does not appear to have introduced any new processes in wall-paper printing, he made, by his use of the simpler ancient dyes, one of the most remarkable departures in calico printing of the nineteenth century. Indigo work on cotton has always been, and is still, largely practised in this country, but I do not know of any other instance in which the whole range of colours is employed in the ancient method as it is to-day in Morris & Co.'s Merton Abbey works. There is no room here for a comparison of the artistic values and possibilities of what Morris, somewhat unfairly, termed "natural" and "chemical" dyes, and the subject must be dismissed with the bald assertion that it is unlikely the former will ever oust the latter in these days; the utmost that can be hoped for it is that the two methods may be employed contemporaneously in ways suited to each.

Morris's cotton prints are frequently alluded to as "chintzes", but, as we understand and to-day are accustomed to use it, such an appellation can hardly be said to be correct. In the modern sense of the term—meaning an open design, delicately spotted at intervals with groups (generally) of naturalistic flowers, not connected by the strong bands or involved lines, such as he was so fond of using, and unmixed with anything of the character of his favourite heavy scrolls or leaves, for instance, and most often displayed on a pure white ground—it cannot be said that Morris ever designed a chintz in his life. He saw decorative possibilities in cotton cloth and the printing processes. which he developed to the utmost, but more in the direction of the fully coloured and heavily decorative design which we were accustomed to associate with other and more costly materials and methods of production. In this way we may look upon Morris as the founder of that kind of design, in which so much fine decorative work has been produced during the last twenty years, and which has come to be generally known by the name of the cloth on which it is usually produced—"cretonne." The rapidity with which and the extent to which this branch of decorative art has flourished in that time has been one of the wonders of the industrial world of late years; but there are signs to-day of waning, and of revulsion, on the one hand, towards what is beginning to be considered a more legitimate employment of cotton printing, and, on the other, towards seeking such high decorative effects in more noble materials and methods. But the influence of Morris's work has banished entirely, from the upper strata, at all events, the scratchy, colourless, and nerveless things that too often formerly represented this industry (or is it more correct to say that it has made an "upper stratum" possible?), while in all branches of pattern he has given us a taste for pure and definite line, noble form, and rich and decorative colour effects.

The absorbing study of processes and ancient styles of work, which may have been a cause of the want of feeling in touch in the later calico printing and wallpaper work, to which I have ventured to allude above, was probably not a hindrance, but really helpful in the art of weaving. Here Morris's particular later methods of designing, his love of bold, blunt form, and other characteristics inherent in him and fostered by such study, found fitter expression, and one could point to many of the designs as being most exquisitely adapted to the material. In weaving he seems, as was perhaps natural, to have turned earlier to mediaeval work, upon which some of the best designs such as the "Peacock and Dragon," the "Bird and Vine," and the "Cross-twigs," are frankly based. He was most emphatic in enjoining honest workmanship in this craft, a precept much needed in these days of cheap and shoddy woven fabrics. It is gratifying to note, however, that several of the best known British firms of weavers, one of which wove some of the early Morris designs, are producing work which having the characteristics of the taste of to-day, is in strict accordance with the principles he taught in design and workmanship, and conspicuously opposed to the mass of shoddy work now coming (largely) from the Continent.

Turning to Morris's work in carpets, two distinct sections present themselves to us: those designed as repeating patterns. and for processes of manufacture largely practised in this country to-day, and representing, I think, mostly his earlier style of work; and the later hand-made "Hammersmith" pile carpets, with filling and border made in one piece, practically without repeat, and in the simpler and more ancient methods of the Eastern carpet weavers. Many of the former, simple and most charming arrangements of natural floral forms, perfectly adapted to the material and purpose, are still being sold by his firm, and some still rank in the trade as standards in their particular style. Notable among these are the "Tulip" Kidderminster and the "Lily" Wilton Pile, two patterns, both of very small repeat, the despair of legitimate imitators, and, I must say the prey of the straightforward copyist. The "Hammersmith" carpets are, not only in method of production, but also in design, frankly based on the ancient Persian, which Morris roundly declared the only period worthy of imitation. They read us a lesson in glowing colour and nobility of line and general plan, and Persian methods of colouring, though one could have wished for a selection of objects more in harmony with the aspirations of our own time and country.

In tiles, linoleums, and dress materials Morris did some work, but did not carry it far. In the former there are some very quaint and beautiful patterns still running, designed by himself and painted by his friends and others in the early days of the firm. The more successful appear to be the "powderings,"[11] notably the "Daisy"; in some of the larger scroll patterns his method of using the outline gives an effect not altogether pleasant. But this branch of art passed, for various reasons, into the hands of others more or less in association with him. Linoleum is almost a hopeless subject, and, many of us have considered, until late years, least objectionable when unadorned. Possibly this thought occurred to Morris, who worked in days before the introduction of a process which may lead to betterment. Of his dress patterns it is hard to speak, but I do not like to pass them over altogether, as we are giving with this paper one or two illustrations of very beautiful little designs intended for this purpose. Beautiful as they are, however, the wearers of dress patterns are, as a rule, very arbitrary in their judgments, and I fear would consider them more suitable for upholstery work.

Of embroidery Morris said: "It is not worth doing unless it is very copious or rich, or very delicate—or both." "There is no excuse for doing anything that is not strikingly beautiful." "It must be said that one of its aims should be the exhibition of beautiful material." While pressing for the utilisation of qualities peculiar to embroidery, as opposed to more mechanical arts, he drew the line at the picture, and did not encourage working on a frame, preferring work that could be done while held in the hand. It is difficult to understand how, holding the views he did of the preciousness of this art, he could have restricted his embroidery designs so much to repeating patterns, or have permitted their execution, even in small articles, on rough canvas, in loose open stitching. The result was sometimes scratchy, and, in consequence of repetition, somewhat mechanical in appearance. Perhaps the habit of drawing repeating patterns grows on one, if one gives way to it.

One or two designs for book covers—for hand-tooling and for machine—illustrated in Mr. Lewis Day's "William Morris and His Art,"[12] and executed, I believe, in very early days (Mr. Day dates one of them 1872), are obviously the direct forerunners of a style of book decoration which, in other hands, has been made the subject, at Arts and Crafts Exhibitions and elsewhere, of so much laudation. Book-cover decoration may very safely be described as one of the minor decorative arts, but it would appear as if here also Morris was responsible for the most notable departure of late years.

Morris's ornamental writing and the work of the Kelmscott Press perhaps do not, for various reasons, come within the scope of these remarks; both have, we know, come to an end. The beautiful borders used in the latter, to which he devoted some of the last hours he had to give to ornamental designing, and which are well-known masterpieces of decorative black-and-white, have become the model for much contemporary work in this branch. The future of the decorated book is a matter on which there is more than one opinion; but if the extreme care that he took in the selection and arrangement of the type bears fruit in more pleasantly set and readable pages, something will have been accomplished. He himself said, "I lay it down that a book quite unornamented can look absolutely and positively beautiful."[13]

Any one desirous of obtaining a proper idea of Morris's work in Decorative Art cannot do better than turn to Mr. Lewis Day's "William Morris and His Art," a masterpiece of lucid and picturesque writing, by a master in decorative design, which gives a critical survey of the subject in the smallest possible compass.

Notes

1 Society of Designers: The Society of Designers was founded in 1896, to safeguard the interests of professional designers of applied art, without holding exhibitions. The designer George Haité was the first president. The motto of the society, taken from

Voysey in 1896, was simply but shrewdly 'Head, Hand and Heart'. By 1899 the society had over 100 members. In c. 1908 the Society was renamed The Institute of Decorative Designers. The periodical *Artist and Journal of Home Culture* was its mouthpiece and included regular reports of their Proceedings.

2 *Art Workers' Quarterly*, 1, 1, 1902, p. 1.
3 *Bookman*, 31, 183, December 1906, p. 6.
4 W. Morris, "Textiles," *Arts and Crafts Essays* (London: Rivington, Percival, & Co.1893), p.23.
5 Stanmore Hall: The north London residence of William Knox D'Arcy from 1886 to 1917.
6 Morris's first secular commission carried out 1866–7 for the Tapestry Room and Armoury.
7 W. Morris *The Lesser Arts of Life* 1882.
8 W. Morris, *Hopes and Fears for Art* (London, Ellis & White, 1882).
9 W. Morris, *Hopes and Fears for Art* 1882.
10 W. Morris, *Hopes and Fears for Art* 1882.
11 powdering: The application of a pattern of small spots, figures, heraldic devices, etc., giving the appearance of having been sprinkled or scattered over a surface. Also refers to a decorative pattern of this kind.
12 L. F. Day, *The Art of William Morris* (London: Virtue, 1899).
13 W. Morris, *The Ideal Book* (London: Chiswick Press, 1899.